The Moral of the Story

D1545025

"Shelley called poets 'the unacknowledged legislators of the world.' Peter and Renata Singer have made novelists and playwrights (and poets!), its acknowledged ethicists. An intriguing collection."

RANDY COHEN, writer of "The Ethicist" for the *New York Times Magazine*

"This excellent, wide-ranging anthology reminds us that there is as much ethics in Tolstoy or Dostoyevsky as in Kant or Mill. Philosophy departments should leave around copies for students to dip into and be inspired by."

JONATHAN GLOVER, King's College London

"An essential and enriching anthology, selected with wisdom and care by Peter and Renata Singer . . . an invaluable light on the moral and ethical landscape."

CAROL ROCAMORA, New York University

About the Editors

Peter Singer is Ira W. DeCamp Professor of Bioethics at the University Center for Human Values, Princeton University. He is the author of *Animal Liberation* (1975), and is widely credited with triggering the modern animal rights movement. His other books include *Practical Ethics* (1979), *Rethinking Life and Death* (1995) and *One World* (2002). He is also the editor of *A Companion to Ethics* (Blackwell, 1991), *In Defense of Animals: The Second Wave* (Blackwell, 2005), and, with Helga Kuhse, of *A Companion to Bioethics* (Blackwell, 1999) and *Bioethics: An Anthology* (Blackwell, 1999). A collection of his best essays on ethics, *Unsanctifying Human Life*, edited by Helga Kuhse, was published by Blackwell in 2002.

Renata Singer has taught in Oxfordshire and New Jersey, developed anti-racist programs in Sydney and written about development programs in South Africa, El Salvador, and Ethiopia. Her first novel, *The Front of the Family*, was published in 2002. Among her non-fiction works are the books *True Stories from the Land of Divorce* (with Nelly Zola, 1995) and *Goodbye and Hello* (with Susie Orzech, 1985).

EDITED BY
PETER SINGER AND RENATA SINGER

THE MORAL
OF THE STORY

AN ANTHOLOGY OF ETHICS THROUGH LITERATURE

Blackwell
Publishing

Editorial material and organization © 2005 by Blackwell Publishing Ltd

BLACKWELL PUBLISHING
350 Main Street, Malden, MA 02148-5020, USA
9600 Garsington Road, Oxford OX4 2DQ, UK
550 Swanston Street, Carlton, Victoria 3053, Australia

The right of Peter Singer and Renata Singer to be identified as the Authors of the Editorial
Material in this Work has been asserted in accordance with the UK Copyright, Designs, and
Patents Act 1988.

First published 2005 by Blackwell Publishing Ltd

3   2005

Library of Congress Cataloging-in-Publication Data

The moral of the story : an anthology of ethics through literature / edited by Peter Singer and
Renata Singer.
          p.   cm.
    Includes bibliographical references and index.
    ISBN 1-4051-0583-6 (alk. paper)—ISBN 1-4051-0584-4 (pbk : alk. paper)
  1. Ethics—Literary collections. I. Singer, Peter, 1946– II. Singer, Renata. III. Title.

  PN6071.E74M67   2005
  808.8′0384—dc22

                                                                           2004016927

ISBN-13: 978-1-4051-0583-5 (alk. paper)—ISBN-13: 978-1-4051-0584-2 (pbk : alk. paper)

A catalogue record for this title is available from the British Library.

Set in 10½/12½ pt Weiss
by Graphicraft Ltd, Hong Kong.
Printed and bound in the United Kingdom
by TJ International, Padstow, Cornwall

The publisher's policy is to use permanent paper from mills that operate a sustainable forestry
policy, and which has been manufactured from pulp processed using acid-free and elementary
chlorine-free practices. Furthermore, the publisher ensures that the text paper and cover board
used have met acceptable environmental accreditation standards.

For further information on
Blackwell Publishing, visit our website:
www.blackwellpublishing.com

CONTENTS

PREFACE

She had quite forgotten the Duchess by this time, and was a little startled when she heard her voice close to her ear. "You're thinking about something, my dear, and that makes you forget to talk. I can't tell you just now what the moral of that is, but I shall remember it in a bit."

"Perhaps it hasn't one," Alice ventured to remark.

"Tut, tut, child!" said the Duchess. "Everything's got a moral, if only you can find it."

Lewis Carroll, *Alice in Wonderland*

Ethics, or moral philosophy, is the study of how we ought to live. It deals with our ultimate values, and with the principles or rules that should guide us when we make crucial decisions about how we are going to live and what we are going to do. It applies both to the fundamental choices that determine who we are, and to specific situations in which we must make choices that will be important for ourselves and for others. Among the wide range of questions that ethics helps us to answer are such questions as:

- What do we owe our families, our neighbors, and strangers in the wider world? Is it right to buy expensive toys for our children when elsewhere in the world parents cannot afford to get even basic medical care for their children?
- Should love be the sole basis for marriage, as we often assume in modern Western cultures? Is it wrong to have sex with someone whom we do not love, and to whom we do not want to be committed, simply because it brings mutual pleasure and the satisfaction of our desires?
- How do we decide on our profession, or our politics? And once we have made a decision, to what extent are we bound by the ethical standards internal to our chosen career, or to the organization of which we have become a part?
- Can our own interests clash with what we ought, ethically, to do? If so, how can we decide whether to follow self-interest or ethics?

In addition to trying to answer these practical ethical questions, philosophers also ask questions about the nature of ethics, that is, about what we are doing when we discuss issues in ethics. Some people think that ethics is always relative to culture, and there can be no objective ethics that is independent of a particular culture.

Others assert that ethical judgments can be true and false, and that reason, which is common to us all, can guide us in what we ought to do.

Philosophers like Plato, Aristotle, David Hume, Immanuel Kant, Jeremy Bentham, and John Stuart Mill have, over a period of two and a half millennia, set out their views on these questions. Long before the rise of systematic philosophical thought, however, people have been making up stories in order to convey what they think about how we ought to live. Inevitably, in telling stories, and in writing novels, plays, short stories, and poems, the authors and narrators raise moral questions and suggest possible ways of answering them. Thus ethics comes squarely within the field of literature, as well as within the field of philosophy. Each approach to ethics has its own strengths and weaknesses.

Philosophers analyze issues carefully and seek rigorous arguments for their conclusions. As a result the philosophical tradition is often helpful in eliminating confusions and misconceptions about ethics. A good philosopher states positions clearly, and readers know what they are being asked to accept, and why. The use of fictional examples is often part of this process. Plato used a story about a ring that made the wearer invisible in order to raise the question whether we only do what is right because we are fearful of being punished if we do not. The French philosopher Benjamin Constant imagined a situation in which someone is hiding in your house from someone else who wants to murder him. The would-be murderer comes to your door and asks if you have seen his intended victim. Constant thought that his example showed the absurdity of an absolute rule against lying, but Kant, the greatest philosopher of his day, was prepared to say that even in these circumstances, it would be wrong to lie. Nevertheless, for philosophers the example is merely a tool, like a piece of equipment for a scientist. As long as it does the job, they have no interest in embellishing it, for they are interested in abstract questions, not in the specifics. Philosophers seek theories that enable us to decide what is right and what is wrong, or they try to form a view about the possibility of reaching objectively true moral judgments. Hence philosophical examples in ethics usually lack depth, the characters in them are mere ciphers, and the context is absent or at best, briefly sketched. Sometimes we are asked to imagine things that are, in practical terms, impossible, or wildly implausible. For the purpose for which the philosopher wishes to use the example, this may not matter. A wholly hypothetical and implausible example can still be useful as a thought experiment, as long as its limitations are clearly understood.

Novels, short stories, plays, and poems shed different kinds of light on ethical questions. Some have thought that great literature should be edifying and provide models of good behavior. For moral examples, Plato drew on the very earliest literature in the Western tradition, Homer's *The Iliad* and *The Odyssey*. In the nineteenth century, the idea that literature should provide a kind of moral education for the masses was widely held. It then fell out of favor for a long time. In response to a question about whether his writing was intended to have a message for his readers, Ernest Hemingway is said to have retorted: "If I had a message, I'd send a telegram." Nevertheless, F. R. Leavis, perhaps the most influential British literary critic of the middle period of the twentieth century, asserted in his book *The Great Tradition* that works of literature are great only if they enhance our "awareness of the possibilities of life." and show concern with the "interests of life."[1] For Leavis, this meant concern with individuality and authenticity in personal relations, and opposition to whatever was incompatible with this. On these grounds he singled out, as truly great, only Jane Austen, George Eliot, Henry James, Joseph Conrad, and D. H. Lawrence. More recently, in *On Moral Fiction*, the novelist John Gardner defended the view that "true art is by its nature moral" and that great novels should address universal values.[2] Gardner was not saying that art should preach, but rather that it should be honest and truthful in its representation of the world. Iris Murdoch, a novelist who was also a philosopher, suggested that art provides a kind of "goodness by proxy" because it can "enlarge the sensibility of its consumer."[3] This view is in turn surprisingly close to that of Richard Rorty, perhaps the best-known philosophical defender of pragmatist and postmodernist ways of thinking, who has nevertheless said that fiction like that of Charles Dickens can be valuable because it "gives us the details about kinds of suffering being endured by people to whom we have previously not attended," while other writers like Henry James give us "the details about what sorts of cruelty we ourselves are capable of" and therefore make it possible for us to change.[4] Feminist literary critics – beginning with Kate Millett's explosive *Sexual Politics*, which blasted writers like Henry Miller and Norman Mailer for their views of women – have certainly not hesitated to evaluate literature in strongly ethical terms.[5]

It is surely true that the detailed and creative exploration of a situation that can emerge from a good novel can help us to understand more about ourselves, and how we ought to live. In contrast to the examples discussed in works of philosophy, discussions of ethical issues in fiction tend to be concrete, rather than abstract, and to give a rich context for the distinctive moral views or choices that are portrayed. Literature therefore often presents a more nuanced view of character and circumstances than is to be found in the works of philosophers. And of course, because most readers like to engage with characters and to read works that have plots, literary works usually reach a wider audience than works of philosophy.

This anthology is an attempt to draw on some of the best works of fiction, playwriting, and poetry to throw light on some of the perennial questions of ethics, but it is not, despite our title, an attempt to draw "morals" from stories, in the sense in which Aesop's fables allow us to draw a moral. On the question of whether great literature should have high moral values, we take no explicit stand, but we have tended to avoid works with an obvious or heavy-handed message, for they rarely make good reading. There are exceptions, however, and we have included some of them. Our aim, in a sentence, is to offer good reading that stimulates thought about issues in ethics. We have sought readings that lead to more reflection and thought, and not those that reinforce widely accepted ideas and leave readers feeling satisfied with the views they have held all along.

We assume no prior knowledge in our readers of ethics or moral philosophy, nor of literature. In the introduction to each section of the book, we indicate what we see as the main ethical issues raised by the selections it contains, and we link these to some of the more important philosophical discussions of these topics. Where a reading is not a self-contained short story or poem, it is preceded by a paragraph designed to enable the reader to know what has come before. At the end of the book you will find a section headed "Issues" in which, for each reading, we mention some specific ethical issues it raises. We do not, however, want to come between our readers and their enjoyment of the literary qualities of the selections. Inevitably, sometimes our discussion of the issues raised by a piece gives away the ending of the story, so we strongly suggest that you read each selection before turning to the back for our discussion of the issues the selection raises.

We have structured this book so that the readings cover a range of ethical issues within an overarching framework that starts from questions concerned with the nature of the individual self and works out from there, in a series of expanding circles. So our first selections are focused on formative life-choices that raise issues of one's own identity: about sexuality, about whether to accept the subordinate status society gives you because of your race, and about whether one is the kind of person who will live a lie in order to make life easier, or, perhaps, simply to continue to live at all. From where do we get our standards, and our way of life? Under what circumstances, if any, might we raise the question of whether our life is worth living, and thus consider what the French existentialist writer Albert Camus called "the only truly serious philosophical problem," namely, suicide?[6]

From the inward-looking choices that form our own identity and determine our way of existence, or non-existence, the first outward step takes us to our relationships with those closest to us, our parents, siblings, and our children, our lovers and spouses. What obligations do we have towards those close to us, and what do we do when those obligations come up against our own interests, against the law of the land, or against the needs of many others more distant from us? Does a fetus within a woman's body count as another being to whom she has an obligation? Or is she entitled to end the pregnancy, if it is inconvenient? Sometimes illness can lead to an even more difficult dilemma: whether the most loving thing to do might be to assist the person one loves to die. How should we choose when love conflicts with family interests, social standards, or sworn vows? (So many works of fiction revolve around that last question that we could easily have filled this entire volume with selections about it.)

Beyond the family lies the work we do, to earn our living or to follow our chosen profession. How do we retain our personal values when we work for others, who assign us to do things that we regard as meaningless, or wrong? Why does society consider some ways of earning a living in the marketplace to be "immoral" while others, equally unhealthy and demeaning, are not? What do we do when our employer wants us to act in ways that we think are contrary to our professional integrity, or when standing by a friend means betraying the values of our profession?

When we turn to the wider community, there are a host of different issues, only a few of which we have been able to cover in our selections. Race and sex often determine a person's standing in a community, and what he or she may or may not do. Sometimes it is clear how one ought to respond to such prejudices, and all that is required is sufficient courage. In other situations, it is less easy to determine the best course of action. Can we be under an obligation to risk our lives to save that of a stranger, within or outside our community? Or even to give up some of our comforts to prevent much greater hardship to someone we do not know? What attitude should we take to advances in science and technology that develop new forms of life, seek to increase our intelligence beyond the normal human range, or bring us closer to the ancient dream of immortality? If we enter politics, should we regard the usual moral rules as suspended, because we cannot gain power without compromising our principles, and without power we can accomplish nothing?

Some assume that ethics is always community-based and that there is no sense to the idea of ethical obligations that extend beyond a community. This is one possible implication of the social contract tradition in ethics: I can only have ethical obligations to those with whom I have an implicit contract, that I shall not harm them, and in return they will not harm me. Consistently with that view, at least when it is narrowly interpreted, ethics does not apply to international relations unless there is some kind of community between nations. Whether that can ever be sufficiently strong, in a world of sovereign nations, to generate ethical obligations is one question; but when relations have broken down to such an extent that two nations go to war, it does seem that there can be no community between them. Hence war has been seen as a realm in which ethics does not apply, as suggested by the saying "all's fair in love and war." Others, sometimes still drawing on the same social contract idea, have denied that we can have ethical obligations to any being or entity that is incapable of reciprocating. This would mean that ethics simply does not apply to questions about our treatment of nonhuman animals, or what we do to the environment. These views have a very limited amount of support in philosophical discussions of ethics. Writers of fiction have no difficulty in raising ethical issues when they discuss war, the treatment of animals, the environment, or even our duties to divine beings.

The selections that extend ethics beyond our own species take us to the end of the expanding circles of ethical questions, but not to the end of this volume. In the final section, we include readings that raise skeptical doubts about the nature of ethics. Are ethical standards relative to culture, so that we cannot judge an action as right or wrong except within a particular cultural context? Another fundamental question is why any individual has reason to do what is right, if it is not in her or his own interests. These are questions about ethics, but in this last section we have also placed readings that ask, in various ways, whether we should all take happiness – not just our own happiness, but the happiness of all those affected by our actions – as the ultimate goal of our strivings, individual and collective. This question leads us to the heart of what has been one of the central debates in philosophical ethics, engaging the minds of many of the great philosophers, and also of some of the greatest literary figures: whether we should judge right and wrong by conformity to absolute rules, like those that tell us not to violate the rights of a single innocent human being, even if that is the only way in which we can prevent the deaths of far more innocents.

We want our selections to offer an enjoyable experience, as well as a thought-provoking one. Although the book will, we trust, be useful for students taking courses both in ethics and in literature, we have designed the book for readers who, whether or not they are students in the formal sense, like reading good literature and have an interest in the issues with which this book deals. (And we find it hard to imagine anyone who reads at all and does not have an interest in those issues.) So in making our final selection there was an inevitable trade-off between literary quality and ethical relevance. Some of our favorite authors had to be left out because we could not find a passage of suitable length that raised an ethical question. Other selections were included because they were so superbly focused on an important ethical issue, even if their writing was not of the very highest standard. No doubt other editors would have made different choices. Feel free to send us outraged letters expressing amazement at our omission of your favorite author or short story. We may be able to include them in a future edition. You may email us at renatasinger@hotmail.com. If you prefer to send ordinary mail, the address is: Peter and Renata Singer, c/o University Center for Human Values, Princeton University, Princeton, NJ 08544, USA. Anyway, here are our current favorites.

NOTES

1 F. R. Leavis, *The Great Tradition*, London: Peregrine, 1962, pp. 10, 16 (first published 1948).
2 John Gardner, *On Moral Fiction*, New York: Basic Books, 1977, p. 19.
3 Iris Murdoch, *The Sovereignty of Good*, New York: Schocken Books, 1971, p. 87.
4 Richard Rorty, *Contingency, Irony, and Solidarity*, Cambridge: Cambridge University Press, 1989, p. xvi.
5 Kate Millett, *Sexual Politics*, New York: Ballantine, 1980; first published 1969.
6 Albert Camus, "The Myth of Sisyphus," in *The Myth of Sisyphus and Other Essays* (tr. Justin O'Brien), New York: Vintage, 1955.

PART ONE PERSONAL MORAL ISSUES

I

WHO AM I?

From the age at which we are capable of thinking for ourselves, we make choices that shape the kind of person we will become. Or perhaps we fail to choose, and allow ourselves to be pushed in the direction that our parents, our teachers, or our peers want us to go. Then for the rest of our lives we have to deal with the consequences. In some cases we follow a path laid down in adolescence and never again reflect on our direction. In others, perhaps prompted by an unexpected crisis, we pause and reconsider our life. The question "Who Am I?" is fundamentally an ethical question, one that raises deep issues about what it is to be moral, how we can develop the kind of self that makes ethical choices, and in accordance with what values we will choose to live.

The Stoic philosopher Epictetus, who lived in the second century of the Christian era, was a slave, but he insisted that his will was not enslaved. Our mind remains free, in his view, no matter what our external circumstances may be. Sixteen hundred years later the German philosopher Immanuel Kant drew on the Stoic tradition to argue that because we are able to reason, we are autonomous moral agents, capable of free choice and responsible for the choices we make. Even today, despite two centuries of development in the social sciences and the existence of the entirely new science of genetics, Kant could still argue that whatever these scientists may tell us about the factors influencing our decisions, in the moment of making a decision we are conscious of our freedom to choose as we see fit. In the twentieth century the French existentialist Jean-Paul Sartre thought that the rejection of the idea of God, and therefore of belief in a divine plan, means that we have no preordained essence. "You are free," he wrote, "therefore choose − that is to say, invent."[1] Another French thinker, Michel Foucault, followed this line of thinking: "From the idea that the self is not given to us, I think there is only one practical consequence: we have to create ourselves as a work of art."[2]

Against the abstract rationalism of Kant's view, and the free individualism of Sartre and Foucault, the contemporary philosopher Alasdair MacIntyre has insisted that "I am someone's son or daughter, someone else's cousin or uncle; I am a citizen of this or that city, a member of this or that guild or profession; I belong to this tribe, that clan, this nation." MacIntyre concludes that these aspects of my life "constitute the given of my life, my moral starting point."[3] MacIntyre is right, of course, to say that when we choose our identity, we do not start with a blank slate. Epictetus, Kant, and Sartre were also right to insist that we always have choices to make. The most we can do is try to become as aware of our starting point as we can, and to reflect critically on it. When we do so, the life we are living can be seen as an embodiment of our consciously chosen values, rather than as something based on values we have unquestioningly absorbed from others.

The most fundamental of these choices is whether to try to live an ethical life. Not everyone makes this choice consciously, but most of us face moments at which we must choose between our own interests, as we see them, and doing something that could be more difficult, and perhaps would involve some hardship or sacrifice, but that seems to be the right thing to do from some larger perspective than simply consideration of our own interests. In one of the earliest philosophical uses of a story to make an ethical point, Plato has Glaucon, one of the characters in his *Republic*, tell the story of Gyges, a shepherd who served the king of Lydia. He was looking after his flock when, during a storm, a chasm opened up in the ground. In it was a dead body of superhuman stature with a golden ring on its finger. The shepherd took the ring and put it on his own finger. Later, while talking with some other shepherds, he happened to turn the ring, and to his amazement discovered that when he turned the ring a certain way, the other shepherds could no longer see him. After discovering this he made his way to the king's palace, and used the ring to seduce the queen – although exactly how being invisible enabled him to do that we are not told. Then he plotted with the queen against the king, killed him, and became king in his place. Glaucon uses the story in order to argue that we only act justly because we are afraid of being punished if we do not. Anyone who had the ring of Gyges, Glaucon suggests, would throw off all ethical constraints and do whatever advanced their own interests.

The story of Gyges and his ring makes us think of Macbeth. In Shakespeare's play, Macbeth has no magic ring, but Duncan's visit to his castle provides him with a similar opportunity to kill the king and usurp the throne. In seizing that moment, Macbeth takes his stand on the ultimate question of whether to act ethically, and chooses what he knows to be wrong. That is one possible way of answering the question, though Shakespeare shows us, as the story unfolds, that even in terms of Macbeth's own interests, it is not a good one. In that respect Shakespeare is in the tradition of Plato, who, through the character of Socrates, rejects Glaucon's view, and argues that the wise person will always do what is just, and will have a better life by doing so.

Others have followed Plato in arguing that living an ethical life gives one the best chance of also living a happy life. They appeal to the "paradox of hedonism," that is, the idea that those who aim at maximizing their own happiness often end up living less happy lives than those who aim at some other goal, and find happiness in pursuing that goal. The life of Sherman McCoy in Tom Wolfe's *The Bonfire of the Vanities* could be offered as an illustration of the paradox of hedonism. But apparently many people do not find this a sufficiently convincing reason for being an ethical person. (If it were convincing, why would religions need to hold out the prospect of reward and punishment in an afterlife in order to try to persuade people to act ethically?)

In the eighteenth century, British philosophers like Shaftesbury, Butler, and, above all, David Hume urged that we all have feelings of benevolence and sympathy and it is these emotions that are the basis of morality. Reinforced by the influence of society, and our desire for a good reputation, and the benefits that this will bring, these emotions will motivate most of us to do what is right. But Hume, at least, admitted that there are limits to this form of motivation. If a person simply does not feel sympathy or benevolence, and is able to behave unjustly without being detected, there is little more that one can say to persuade him or her to live an ethical life.

Other philosophers have spurned the idea that ethics can be based on such changeable aspects of human existence as our emotions or the prospect of some kind of gain in happiness. Kant thought that unless we act from respect for the moral law as such, our actions have no moral worth. But in arguing that we can, and indeed ought to, act from respect for the moral law as such, and in rejecting not only self-interested motivation, but also impulses derived from emotions like benevolence and sympathy, Kant placed a heavy burden on reason. Given that we are not purely rational beings, but creatures with emotions and desires, how can reason alone, unaided by desire, move us to act? Kant gives no convincing answer to this question.

Towards the end of the nineteenth century the British neo-Hegelian philosopher F. H. Bradley said that virtue consists in doing good for its own sake, and that to recommend a life of virtue because of the pleasures it will bring is to "degrade and prostitute" virtue.[4] If this is true, we can have little to say to those who, like Macbeth, are in doubt about whether to do what they know to be right. All we can say is that they should do what is right for its own sake. What is really important, Bradley thought, is to ensure that people grow up in a society that gives them a station in life, and a set of duties to perform, and makes them a part of the larger ethical community. Then they will find their identity in that community, and will feel part of the larger whole. They will not ask why they should do what is right, any more than your arm asks why it should serve your body. They will do what is right because they feel themselves a part of an organic whole. But what if the society has no place for homosexuals, or offers only a humiliating station and degrading duties to women, or to those who belong to a racial minority? Bradley's organic society looks alarmingly close to a totalitarian form of nationalism, in which the individual's autonomy is subordinated to a larger whole. The twentieth century made us only too aware of the dangers that such societies pose.

Today's liberal societies are not as homogeneous as Bradley's imaginary organic society. Yet this does not necessarily mean that people freely choose their identity independently of the subtle coercion of culture. Without making any explicit choice, many people accept the values of a subculture and do not even ask how their subculture fits into the larger society in which they are living. The subculture may be that of 1980s Wall Street bond traders, as described in the extract from *The Bonfire of the Vanities*, or of 1970s teenage surfies on Sydney's beaches in Kathy Lette and Gabrielle Carey's *Puberty Blues*.

Neither Sherman McCoy, in *The Bonfire of the Vanities*, nor Deb, in *Puberty Blues*, shows any signs of having reflected on what is important in life. Instead, they accept the values of the group to which they belong, or aspire to belong. Of course, the teenage culture of *Puberty Blues* is one that people pass through, as they grow up, and it is easy to excuse young people for unquestioningly accepting the culture of their peers. We allow adolescents time to become their own person. The problem is more serious when people live their entire lives unreflectively, without ever having asked themselves what their goals are, and why they are doing what they do. Until you have asked yourself these fundamental questions, you have not chosen your life and have not decided who you are.

NOTES

1   Jean-Paul Sartre, "Existentialism is a Humanism," in Walter Kaufman (ed.), *Existentialism from Dostoyevsky to Sartre* (New York: New American Library, 1975), p. 356.
2   Michel Foucault, *Beyond Structuralism and Hermeneutics*, 2nd edn, ed. H. Dreyfus and P. Rabinow, Chicago: University of Chicago Press, 1983, p. 237.
3   Alasdair MacIntyre, *After Virtue*, Notre Dame, IN: University of Notre Dame Press, Notre Dame, 1984, p. 220.
4   F. H. Bradley, *Ethical Studies*, Oxford: Oxford University Press, 1962, p. 63.

1

RALPH ELLISON

Invisible Man

Invisible Man is a classic of modern African American life. It mixes comedy, irony, and burlesque, often in unexpected places. The story begins with this terrifying experience after the hero's graduation from high school.

It goes a long way back, some twenty years. All my life I had been looking for something, and everywhere I turned someone tried to tell me what it was. I accepted their answers too, though they were often in contradiction and even self-contradictory. I was naïve. I was looking for myself and asking everyone except myself questions which I, and only I, could answer. It took me a long time and much painful boomeranging of my expectations to achieve a realization everyone else appears to have been born with: That I am nobody but myself. But first I had to discover that I am an invisible man!

And yet I am no freak of nature, nor of history. I was in the cards, other things having been equal (or unequal) eighty-five years ago. I am not ashamed of my grandparents for having been slaves. I am only ashamed of myself for having at one time been ashamed. About eighty-five years ago they were told that they were free, united with others of our country in everything pertaining to the common good, and, in everything social, separate like the fingers of the hand. And they believed it. They exulted in it. They stayed in their place, worked hard, and brought up my father to do the same. But my grandfather is the one. He was an odd old guy, my grandfather, and I am told I take after him. It was he who caused the trouble. On his deathbed he called my father to him and said, "Son, after I'm gone I want you to keep up the good fight. I never told you, but our life is a war and I have been a traitor all my born days, a spy in the enemy's country ever since I give up my gun back in the Reconstruction. Live with your head in the lion's mouth. I want you to overcome 'em with yeses, undermine 'em with grins, agree 'em to death and destruction, let 'em swoller you till they vomit or bust wide

RALPH ELLISON, pp. 13–26 from *Invisible Man*. New York: Random House, 2002 (originally published 1947). © 1947. 1948, 1952 by Ralph Ellison; copyright renewed 1975, 1976, 1980 by Ralph Ellison. Used by permission of Random House, Inc.

open." They thought the old man had gone out of his mind. He had been the meekest of men. The younger children were rushed from the room, the shades drawn and the flame of the lamp turned so low that it sputtered on the wick like the old man's breathing. "Learn it to the younguns," he whispered fiercely; then he died.

But my folks were more alarmed over his last words than over his dying. It was as though he had not died at all, his words caused so much anxiety. I was warned emphatically to forget what he had said and, indeed, this is the first time it has been mentioned outside the family circle. It had a tremendous effect upon me, however. I could never be sure of what he meant. Grandfather had been a quiet old man who never made any trouble, yet on his deathbed he had called himself a traitor and a spy, and he had spoken of his meekness as a dangerous activity. It became a constant puzzle which lay unanswered in the back of my mind. And whenever things went well for me I remembered my grandfather and felt guilty and uncomfortable. It was as though I was carrying out his advice in spite of myself. And to make it worse, everyone loved me for it. I was praised by the most lily-white men of the town. I was considered an example of desirable conduct – just as my grandfather had been. And what puzzled me was that the old man had defined it as *treachery*. When I was praised for my conduct I felt a guilt that in some way I was doing something that was really against the wishes of the white folks, that if they had understood they would have desired me to act just the opposite, that I should have been sulky and mean, and that that really would have been what they wanted, even though they were fooled and thought they wanted me to act as I did. It made me afraid that some day they would look upon me as a traitor and I would be lost. Still I was more afraid to act any other way because they didn't like that at all. The old man's words were like a curse. On my graduation day I delivered an oration in which I showed that humility was the secret, indeed, the very essence of progress. (Not that I believed this – how could I, remembering my grandfather? – I only believed that it worked.) It was a great success. Everyone praised me and I was invited to give the speech at a gathering of the town's leading white citizens. It was a triumph for our whole community.

It was in the main ballroom of the leading hotel. When I got there I discovered that it was on the occasion of a smoker, and I was told that since I was to be there anyway I might as well take part in the battle royal to be fought by some of my schoolmates as part of the entertainment. The battle royal came first.

All of the town's big shots were there in their tuxedoes, wolfing down the buffet foods, drinking beer and whiskey and smoking black cigars. It was a large room with a high ceiling. Chairs were arranged in neat rows around three sides of a portable boxing ring. The fourth side was clear, revealing a gleaming space of polished floor. I had some misgivings over the battle royal, by the way. Not from a distaste for fighting, but because I didn't care too much for the other fellows who were to take part. They were tough guys who seemed to have no grandfather's curse worrying their minds. No one could mistake their toughness. And besides, I suspected that fighting a battle royal might detract from the dignity of my speech. In those pre-invisible days I visualized myself as a potential

Booker T. Washington. But the other fellows didn't care too much for me either, and there were nine of them. I felt superior to them in my way, and I didn't like the manner in which we were all crowded together into the servants' elevator. Nor did they like my being there. In fact, as the warmly lighted floors flashed past the elevator we had words over the fact that I, by taking part in the fight, had knocked one of their friends out of a night's work.

We were led out of the elevator through a rococo hall into an anteroom and told to get into our fighting togs. Each of us was issued a pair of boxing gloves and ushered out into the big mirrored hall, which we entered looking cautiously about us and whispering, lest we might accidentally be heard above the noise of the room. It was foggy with cigar smoke. And already the whiskey was taking effect. I was shocked to see some of the most important men of the town quite tipsy. They were all there – bankers, lawyers, judges, doctors, fire chiefs, teachers, merchants. Even one of the more fashionable pastors. Something we could not see was going on up front. A clarinet was vibrating sensuously and the men were standing up and moving eagerly forward. We were a small tight group, clustered together, our bare upper bodies touching and shining with anticipatory sweat; while up front the big shots were becoming increasingly excited over something we still could not see. Suddenly I heard the school superintendent, who had told me to come, yell, "Bring up the shines, gentlemen! Bring up the little shines!"

We were rushed up to the front of the ballroom, where it smelled even more strongly of tobacco and whiskey. Then we were pushed into place. I almost wet my pants. A sea of faces, some hostile, some amused, ringed around us, and in the center, facing us, stood a magnificent blonde – stark naked. There was dead silence. I felt a blast of cold air chill me. I tried to back away, but they were behind me and around me. Some of the boys stood with lowered heads, trembling. I felt a wave of irrational guilt and fear. My teeth chattered, my skin turned to goose flesh, my knees knocked. Yet I was strongly attracted and looked in spite of myself. Had the price of looking been blindness, I would have looked. The hair was yellow like that of a circus kewpie doll, the face heavily powdered and rouged, as though to form an abstract mask, the eyes hollow and smeared a cool blue, the color of a baboon's butt. I felt a desire to spit upon her as my eyes brushed slowly over her body. Her breasts were firm and round as the domes of East Indian temples, and I stood so close as to see the fine skin texture and beads of pearly perspiration glistening like dew around the pink and erected buds of her nipples. I wanted at one and the same time to run from the room, to sink through the floor, or go to her and cover her from my eyes and the eyes of the others with my body; to feel the soft thighs, to caress her and destroy her, to love her and murder her, to hide from her, and yet to stroke where below the small American flag tattooed upon her belly her thighs formed a capital V. I had a notion that of all in the room she saw only me with her impersonal eyes.

Booker T. Washington (1856–1915) – an influential African American educator who sought economic gains at the price of 'not rocking the boat' over disenfranchisement and segregation

shines – derogatory word for African Americans

And then she began to dance, a slow sensuous movement; the smoke of a hundred cigars clinging to her like the thinnest of veils. She seemed like a fair bird-girl girdled in veils calling to me from the angry surface of some gray and threatening sea. I was transported. Then I became aware of the clarinet playing and the big shots yelling at us. Some threatened us if we looked and others if we did not. On my right I saw one boy faint. And now a man grabbed a silver pitcher from a table and stepped close as he dashed ice water upon him and stood him up and forced two of us to support him as his head hung and moans issued from his thick bluish lips. Another boy began to plead to go home. He was the largest of the group, wearing dark red fighting trunks much too small to conceal the erection which projected from him as though in answer to the insinuating low-registered moaning of the clarinet. He tried to hide himself with his boxing gloves.

And all the while the blonde continued dancing, smiling faintly at the big shots who watched her with fascination, and faintly smiling at our fear. I noticed a certain merchant who followed her hungrily, his lips loose and drooling. He was a large man who wore diamond studs in a shirtfront which swelled with the ample paunch underneath, and each time the blonde swayed her undulating hips he ran his hand through the thin hair of his bald head and, with his arms upheld, his posture clumsy like that of an intoxicated panda, wound his belly in a slow and obscene grind. This creature was completely hypnotized. The music had quickened. As the dancer flung herself about with a detached expression on her face, the men began reaching out to touch her. I could see their beefy fingers sink into the soft flesh. Some of the others tried to stop them and she began to move around the floor in graceful circles, as they gave chase, slipping and sliding over the polished floor. It was mad. Chairs went crashing, drinks were spilt, as they ran laughing and howling after her. They caught her just as she reached a door, raised her from the floor, and tossed her as college boys are tossed at a hazing, and above her red, fixed-smiling lips I saw the terror and disgust in her eyes, almost like my own terror and that which I saw in some of the other boys. As I watched, they tossed her twice and her soft breasts seemed to flatten against the air and her legs flung wildly as she spun. Some of the more sober ones helped her to escape. And I started off the floor, heading for the anteroom with the rest of the boys.

Some were still crying and in hysteria. But as we tried to leave we were stopped and ordered to get into the ring. There was nothing to do but what we were told. All ten of us climbed under the ropes and allowed ourselves to be blindfolded with broad bands of white cloth. One of the men seemed to feel a bit sympathetic and tried to cheer us up as we stood with our backs against the ropes. Some of us tried to grin. "See that boy over there?" one of the men said. "I want you to run across at the bell and give it to him right in the belly. If you don't get him, I'm going to get you. I don't like his looks." Each of us was told the same. The blindfolds were put on. Yet even then I had been going over my speech. In my mind each word was as bright as flame. I felt the cloth pressed into place, and frowned so that it would be loosened when I relaxed.

But now I felt a sudden fit of blind terror. I was unused to darkness. It was as though I had suddenly found myself in a dark room filled with poisonous cottonmoths. I could hear the bleary voices yelling insistently for the battle royal to begin.

"Get going in there!"

"Let me at that big nigger!"

I strained to pick up the school superintendent's voice, as though to squeeze some security out of that slightly more familiar sound.

"Let me at those black sonsabitches!" someone yelled.

"No, Jackson, no!" another voice yelled. "Here, somebody, help me hold Jack."

"I want to get at that ginger-colored nigger. Tear him limb from limb," the first voice yelled.

I stood against the ropes trembling. For in those days I was what they called ginger-colored, and he sounded as though he might crunch me between his teeth like a crisp ginger cookie.

Quite a struggle was going on. Chairs were being kicked about and I could hear voices grunting as with a terrific effort. I wanted to see, to see more desperately than ever before. But the blindfold was tight as a thick skin-puckering scab and when I raised my gloved hands to push the layers of white aside a voice yelled, "Oh, no you don't, black bastard! Leave that alone!"

"Ring the bell before Jackson kills him a coon!" someone boomed in the sudden silence. And I heard the bell clang and the sound of the feet scuffling forward.

A glove smacked against my head. I pivoted, striking out stiffly as someone went past, and felt the jar ripple along the length of my arm to my shoulder. Then it seemed as though all nine of the boys had turned upon me at once. Blows pounded me from all sides while I struck out as best I could. So many blows landed upon me that I wondered if I were not the only blindfolded fighter in the ring, or if the man called Jackson hadn't succeeded in getting me after all.

Blindfolded, I could no longer control my motions. I had no dignity. I stumbled about like a baby or a drunken man. The smoke had become thicker and with each new blow it seemed to sear and further restrict my lungs. My saliva became like hot bitter glue. A glove connected with my head, filling my mouth with warm blood. It was everywhere. I could not tell if the moisture I felt upon my body was sweat or blood. A blow landed hard against the nape of my neck. I felt myself going over, my head hitting the floor. Streaks of blue light filled the black world behind the blindfold. I lay prone, pretending that I was knocked out, but felt myself seized by hands and yanked to my feet. "Get going, black boy! Mix it up!" My arms were like lead, my head smarting from blows. I managed to feel my way to the ropes and held on, trying to catch my breath. A glove landed in my mid-section and I went over again, feeling as though the smoke had become a knife jabbed into my guts. Pushed this way and that by the legs milling around me, I finally pulled erect and discovered that I could see the black, sweat-washed forms weaving in the smoky-blue atmosphere like drunken dancers weaving to the rapid drum-like thuds of blows.

Everyone fought hysterically. It was complete anarchy. Everybody fought everybody else. No group fought together for long. Two, three, four, fought one, then turned to fight each other, were themselves attacked. Blows landed below the belt and in the kidney, with the gloves open as well as closed, and with my eye partly opened now there was not so much terror. I moved carefully, avoiding blows, although not too many to attract attention, fighting from group to group. The boys groped about like blind, cautious crabs crouching to protect their mid-sections, their heads pulled in short against their shoulders, their arms stretched nervously before them, with their fists testing the smoke-filled air like the knobbed feelers of hyper-sensitive snails. In one corner I glimpsed a boy violently punching the air and heard him scream in pain as he smashed his hand against a ring post. For a second I saw him bent over holding his hand, then going down as a blow caught his unprotected head. I played one group against the other, slipping in and throwing a punch then stepping out of range while pushing the others into the melee to take the blows blindly aimed at me. The smoke was agonizing and there were no rounds, no bells at three minute intervals to relieve our exhaustion. The room spun round me, a swirl of lights, smoke, sweating bodies surrounded by tense white faces. I bled from both nose and mouth, the blood spattering upon my chest.

The men kept yelling, "Slug him, black boy! Knock his guts out!"

"Uppercut him! Kill him! Kill that big boy!"

Taking a fake fall, I saw a boy going down heavily beside me as though we were felled by a single blow, saw a sneaker-clad foot shoot into his groin as the two who had knocked him down stumbled upon him. I rolled out of range, feeling a twinge of nausea.

The harder we fought the more threatening the men became. And yet, I had begun to worry about my speech again. How would it go? Would they recognize my ability? What would they give me?

I was fighting automatically when suddenly I noticed that one after another of the boys was leaving the ring. I was surprised, filled with panic, as though I had been left alone with an unknown danger. Then I understood. The boys had arranged it among themselves. It was the custom for the two men left in the ring to slug it out for the winner's prize. I discovered this too late. When the bell sounded two men in tuxedoes leaped into the ring and removed the blindfold. I found myself facing Tatlock, the biggest of the gang. I felt sick at my stomach. Hardly had the bell stopped ringing in my ears than it clanged again and I saw him moving swiftly toward me. Thinking of nothing else to do I hit him smash on the nose. He kept coming, bringing the rank sharp violence of stale sweat. His face was a black blank of a face, only his eyes alive – with hate of me and aglow with a feverish terror from what had happened to us all. I became anxious. I wanted to deliver my speech and he came at me as though he meant to beat it out of me. I smashed him again and again, taking his blows as they came. Then on a sudden impulse I struck him lightly and as we clinched, I whispered, "Fake like I knocked you out, you can have the prize."

"I'll break your behind," he whispered hoarsely.

"For *them*?"

"For *me*, sonofabitch!"

They were yelling for us to break it up and Tatlock spun me half around with a blow, and as a joggled camera sweeps in a reeling scene, I saw the howling red faces crouching tense beneath the cloud of blue-gray smoke. For a moment the world wavered, unraveled, flowed, then my head cleared and Tatlock bounced before me. That fluttering shadow before my eyes was his jabbing left hand. Then falling forward, my head against his damp shoulder, I whispered,

"I'll make it five dollars more."

"Go to hell!"

But his muscles relaxed a trifle beneath my pressure and I breathed, "Seven?"

"Give it to your ma," he said, ripping me beneath the heart.

And while I still held him I butted him and moved away. I felt myself bombarded with punches. I fought back with hopeless desperation. I wanted to deliver my speech more than anything else in the world, because I felt that only these men could judge truly my ability, and now this stupid clown was ruining my chances. I began fighting carefully now, moving in to punch him and out again with my greater speed. A lucky blow to his chin and I had him going too – until I heard a loud voice yell, "I got my money on the big boy."

Hearing this, I almost dropped my guard. I was confused: Should I try to win against the voice out there? Would not this go against my speech, and was not this a moment for humility, for nonresistance? A blow to my head as I danced about sent my right eye popping like a jack-in-the-box and settled my dilemma. The room went red as I fell. It was a dream fall, my body languid and fastidious as to where to land, until the floor became impatient and smashed up to meet me. A moment later I came to. An hypnotic voice said FIVE emphatically. And I lay there, hazily watching a dark red spot of my own blood shaping itself into a butterfly, glistening and soaking into the soiled gray world of the canvas.

When the voice drawled TEN I was lifted up and dragged to a chair. I sat dazed. My eye pained and swelled with each throb of my pounding heart and I wondered if now I would be allowed to speak. I was wringing wet, my mouth still bleeding. We were grouped along the wall now. The other boys ignored me as they congratulated Tatlock and speculated as to how much they would be paid. One boy whimpered over his smashed hand. Looking up front, I saw attendants in white jackets rolling the portable ring away and placing a small square rug in the vacant space surrounded by chairs. Perhaps, I thought, I will stand on the rug to deliver my speech.

Then the M.C. called to us, "Come on up here boys and get your money."

We ran forward to where the men laughed and talked in their chairs, waiting. Everyone seemed friendly now.

"There it is on the rug," the man said. I saw the rug covered with coins of all dimensions and a few crumpled bills. But what excited me, scattered here and there, were the gold pieces.

"Boys, it's all yours," the man said. "You get all you grab."

"That's right, Sambo," a blond man said, winking at me confidentially.

I trembled with excitement, forgetting my pain. I would get the gold and the bills, I thought. I would use both hands. I would throw my body against the boys nearest me to block them from the gold.

"Get down around the rug now," the man commanded, "and don't anyone touch it until I give the signal."

"This ought to be good," I heard.

As told, we got around the square rug on our knees. Slowly the man raised his freckled hand as we followed it upward with our eyes.

I heard, "These niggers look like they're about to pray!"

Then, "Ready," the man said. "Go!"

I lunged for a yellow coin lying on the blue design of the carpet, touching it and sending a surprised shriek to join those rising around me. I tried frantically to remove my hand but could not let go. A hot, violent force tore through my body, shaking me like a wet rat. The rug was electrified. The hair bristled up on my head as I shook myself free. My muscles jumped, my nerves jangled, writhed. But I saw that this was not stopping the other boys. Laughing in fear and embarrassment, some were holding back and scooping up the coins knocked off by the painful contortions of the others. The men roared above us as we struggled.

"Pick it up, goddamnit, pick it up!" someone called like a bass-voiced parrot. "Go on, get it!"

I crawled rapidly around the floor, picking up the coins, trying to avoid the coppers and to get greenbacks and the gold. Ignoring the shock by laughing, as I brushed the coins off quickly, I discovered that I could contain the electricity – a contradiction, but it works. Then the men began to push us onto the rug. Laughing embarrassedly, we struggled out of their hands and kept after the coins. We were all wet and slippery and hard to hold. Suddenly I saw a boy lifted into the air, glistening with sweat like a circus seal, and dropped, his wet back landing flush upon the charged rug, heard him yell and saw him literally dance upon his back, his elbows beating a frenzied tattoo upon the floor, his muscles twitching like the flesh of a horse stung by many flies. When he finally rolled off, his face was gray and no one stopped him when he ran from the floor amid booming laughter.

"Get the money," the M.C. called. "That's good hard American cash!"

And we snatched and grabbed, snatched and grabbed. I was careful not to come too close to the rug now, and when I felt the hot whiskey breath descend upon me like a cloud of foul air I reached out and grabbed the leg of a chair. It was occupied and I held on desperately.

"Leggo, nigger! Leggo!"

The huge face wavered down to mine as he tried to push me free. But my body was slippery and he was too drunk. It was Mr. Colcord, who owned a chain of movie houses and "entertainment palaces." Each time he grabbed me I slipped out of his hands. It became a real struggle. I feared the rug more than I did the drunk, so I held on, surprising myself for a moment by trying to topple *him* upon the rug. It was such an enormous idea that I found myself actually carrying it out. I tried not to be obvious, yet when I grabbed his leg, trying to tumble him out of the chair, he raised up roaring with laughter, and, looking at me with soberness dead in the eye, kicked me viciously in the chest. The chair leg flew out of my hand and I felt myself going and rolled. It was as though I had rolled through a bed of hot coals. It seemed a whole century would pass before I would roll free, a century in which I was seared through the deepest levels of my body to the fearful breath within me and the breath seared and heated to the point of explosion. It'll all be over in a flash, I thought as I rolled clear. It'll all be over in a flash.

But not yet, the men on the other side were waiting, red faces swollen as though from apoplexy as they bent forward in their chairs. Seeing their fingers coming toward me I rolled away as a fumbled football rolls off the receiver's fingertips, back into the coals. That time I luckily sent the rug sliding out of place and heard the coins ringing against the floor and the boys scuffling to pick them up and the M.C. calling, "All right, boys, that's all. Go get dressed and get your money."

I was limp as a dish rag. My back felt as though it had been beaten with wires.

When we had dressed the M.C. came in and gave us each five dollars, except Tatlock, who got ten for being last in the ring. Then he told us to leave. I was not to get a chance to deliver my speech, I thought. I was going out into the dim alley in despair when I was stopped and told to go back. I returned to the ballroom, where the men were pushing back their chairs and gathering in groups to talk.

The M.C. knocked on a table for quiet. "Gentlemen," he said, "we almost forgot an important part of the program. A most serious part, gentlemen. This boy was brought here to deliver a speech which he made at his graduation yesterday . . ."

"Bravo!"

"I'm told that he is the smartest boy we've got out there in Greenwood. I'm told that he knows more big words than a pocket-sized dictionary."

Much applause and laughter.

"So now, gentlemen, I want you to give him your attention."

There was still laughter as I faced them, my mouth dry, my eye throbbing. I began slowly, but evidently my throat was tense, because they began shouting, "Louder! Louder!"

"We of the younger generation extol the wisdom of that great leader and educator," I shouted, "who first spoke these flaming words of wisdom: 'A ship lost at sea for many days suddenly sighted a friendly vessel. From the mast of the unfortunate vessel was seen a signal: "Water, water; we die of thirst!" The answer from the friendly vessel came back: "Cast down your bucket where you are." The captain of the distressed vessel, at last heeding the injunction, cast down his bucket, and it came up full of fresh sparkling water from the mouth of the Amazon River.' And like him I say, and in his words, 'To those of my race who depend upon bettering their condition in a foreign land, or who underestimate the importance of cultivating friendly relations with the Southern white man, who is his next-door neighbor, I would say: "Cast down your bucket where you are" – cast it down in making friends in every manly way of the people of all races by whom we are surrounded . . .'"

I spoke automatically and with such fervor that I did not realize that the men were still talking and laughing until my dry mouth, filling up with blood from the cut, almost strangled me. I coughed, wanting to stop and go to one of the tall brass, sand-filled spittoons to relieve myself, but a few of the men, especially the superintendent, were listening and I was afraid. So I gulped it down, blood, saliva and all, and continued. (What powers of endurance I had during those days! What enthusiasm! What a belief in the rightness of things!) I spoke even louder in spite of the pain. But still they talked and still they laughed, as though deaf with cotton in dirty ears. So I spoke with greater emotional emphasis. I closed my ears and swallowed blood until I was nauseated. The speech seemed a hundred times as long as before, but I could not leave out a single word. All had to be said, each memorized nuance considered, rendered. Nor was that all. Whenever I uttered a word of three or more syllables a group of voices would yell for me to repeat it. I used the phrase "social responsibility" and they yelled:

"What's that word you say, boy?"

"Social responsibility," I said.

"What?"

"Social . . ."

"Louder."

". . . responsibility."

"More!"

"Respon—"

"Repeat!"

"—sibility."

The room filled with the uproar of laughter until, no doubt, distracted by having to gulp down my blood, I made a mistake and yelled a phrase I had often seen denounced in newspaper editorials, heard debated in private.

"Social . . ."

"What?" they yelled.

". . . equality —"

The laughter hung smokelike in the sudden stillness. I opened my eyes, puzzled. Sounds of displeasure filled the room. The M.C. rushed forward. They shouted hostile phrases at me. But I did not understand.

A small dry mustached man in the front tow blared out, "Say that slowly, son!"

"What, sir?"

"What you just said!"

"Social responsibility, sir," I said.

"You weren't being smart, were you, boy?" he said, not unkindly.

"No, sir!"

"You sure that about 'equality' was a mistake?"

"Oh, yes, sir," I said. "I was swallowing blood."

"Well, you had better speak more slowly so we can understand. We mean to do right by you, but you've got to know your place at all times. All right, now, go on with your speech."

I was afraid. I wanted to leave but I wanted also to speak and I was afraid they'd snatch me down.

"Thank you, sir," I said, beginning where I had left off, and having them ignore me as before.

Yet when I finished there was a thunderous applause. I was surprised to see the superintendent come forth with a package wrapped in white tissue paper, and, gesturing for quiet, address the men.

"Gentlemen, you see that I did not overpraise this boy. He makes a good speech and some day he'll lead his people in the proper paths. And I don't have to tell you that that is important in these days and times. This is a good, smart boy, and so to encourage him in the right direction, in the name of the Board of Education I wish to present him a prize in the form of this . . ."

He paused, removing the tissue paper and revealing a gleaming calfskin brief case.

". . . in the form of this first-class article from Shad Whitmore's shop."

"Boy," he said, addressing me, "take this prize and keep it well. Consider it a badge of office. Prize it. Keep developing as you are and some day it will be filled with important papers that will help shape the destiny of your people."

I was so moved that I could hardly express my thanks. A rope of bloody saliva forming a shape like an undiscovered continent drooled upon the leather and I wiped it quickly away. I felt an importance that I had never dreamed.

"Open it and see what's inside," I was told.

My fingers a-tremble, I complied, smelling the fresh leather and finding an official-looking document inside. It was a scholarship to the state college for Negroes. My eyes filled with tears and I ran awkwardly off the floor.

I was overjoyed; I did not even mind when I discovered that the gold pieces I had scrambled for were brass pocket tokens advertising a certain make of automobile.

When I reached home everyone was excited. Next day the neighbors came to congratulate me. I even felt safe from grandfather, whose deathbed curse usually spoiled my triumphs. I stood beneath his photograph with my brief case in hand and smiled triumphantly into his stolid black peasant's face. It was a face that fascinated me. The eyes seemed to follow everywhere I went.

That night I dreamed I was at a circus with him and that he refused to laugh at the clowns no matter what they did. Then later he told me to open my brief case and read what was inside and I did, finding an official envelope stamped with the state seal; and inside the envelope I found another and another, endlessly, and I thought I would fall of weariness. "Them's years," he said. "Now open that one." And I did and in it I found an engraved document containing a short message in letters of gold. "Read it," my grandfather said. "Out loud!"

"To Whom It May Concern," I intoned. "Keep This Nigger-Boy Running."

I awoke with the old man's laughter ringing in my ears.

(It was a dream I was to remember and dream again for many years after. But at that time I had no insight into its meaning. First I had to attend college.)

2

KATHY LETTE AND GABRIELLE CAREY

Puberty Blues

Puberty Blues is a tragi-comic portrayal of teenage life in the surfside suburbs of Sydney, Australia, in the late 1970s. At 13, Sue and Deb, the narrator, are desperate to be cool and part of the in-crowd. But belonging involves abiding by a strict code of sexual behavior.

You had to "go out" with a guy for at least two weeks before you'd let him screw you. You had to time it perfectly. If you waited too long you were a tight-arsed prickteaser. If you let him too early, you were a slack-arsed moll. So, after a few weeks, he'd ask you for a root, and if you wanted to keep him, you'd do it.

I was thirteen.
　　I'd been out of primary school a year.
　　It was in the back of a panel van.
I hadn't even got my periods yet.
I didn't even know where my hole was.
Actually, I thought there was only one hole, for pissing and having sex.
I tried to find out about it at school that day. I couldn't ask Sue 'cause she knew as much as me. I asked Tracey and Cheryl and the gang. I hadn't learnt that girls don't talk about doing it.
"What am I s'posed to do?"
"Just lay back. He'll know what he's doin'."
He'd kissed me the first night. Titted-me-off the second night. And fingered me the next night. I bluffed it for a few days . . . "Oh, I'm on m' rags." But it was my duty on Friday night at the drive-in, to go all the way. I counted the hours to my initiation.
"Six . . . seven . . . eight hours to go . . . I'm packin' shit."

Kathy Lette and Gabrielle Carey, pp. 25–7, 40–1, and 55–7 from *Puberty Blues*. Melbourne, Australia: McPhee Gribble Publishers, 1979. Reprinted by permission of Pan Macmillan and Ed Victor Ltd.

---

root – the act of sexual intercourse

rags – period

"Look, you've used a Med, haven't you?" Tracey reassured me.

"No."

A flicker of concern crossed her face. "Oh, you'll be all right."

There were six of us in the panel van. I sat in the front, calmly smoking a cigarette, listening to the suppressed screams of agony as Sue lost her virginity to Danny in the back.

That's the way it goes for girls. Every car in the parking lot was doing it . . . rocking up and down to the panel van bop. Then it was my turn. I couldn't say no. Bruce had picked me out of all the other girls. Bruce was the top guy of the gang. Even better than Darren Peters. He was the eldest. He had a car, a job, money and the biggest prick.

He parted the purple curtains his mother had made for him, and pulled me over the seat. We undressed in silence, hauling off our jumpers and straight-legged Levis. I stretched out on the pink mattress. The windows began to fog.

He had a little tin in the back of the panel van, that everyone called the "Tool Kit" – full of frenchies. He used one with me.

After much fumbling . . . "Ah . . ." A groan of satisfaction, "Now I'm gettin' somewhere."

"That's my bum hole," I whispered, embarrassed.

I produced the jar of Vaseline he'd asked me to bring. Things got mighty slippery . . . but it still hurt. I thought I was going to pass out.

He grunted and pushed harder. I clutched on to his hips.

"Stop squeezin' m' hips." I pressed my feet up against the back of the seat. He groped around for my breast. It was so small he couldn't find it.

After a while he gave up. I didn't know whether it'd worked or not. I didn't know what it was supposed to feel like.

I don't remember what happened next. We were just putting on our clothes . . . strapping myself into a bra that was holding up air.

"I can't find my underpants." I fumbled around and put everything on inside out. We climbed into the front as Kim and Dave got in the back. "K'niver cigarette?" I asked.

And that was the initiation in the Greenhills gang. That's the way every girl in the gang lost her virginity. The boys had to be good surfers and the girls had to be good screws.

Well, at least I was doing something on Saturday nights.

[. . .]

Bruce was still trying to screw me. We both took off our clothes. I could see this great, hulking, looming thing in the darkness, with blonde hair and glasses. Then there was a hand on my breast. Knead. Knead. Knead. Not that I had much breast.

Med – tampon

jumpers – sweaters

frenchies – condoms

I had developed certain positions to make my boobs seem bigger. There was the lying-on-my-side-crunching-them-together-with-my-arms-position. There was the bending-over-letting-them-hang position . . . because when I lay down on my back, they seemed to disappear.

I didn't know how he got an erection. I didn't even know what an erection was. There was just this hard, mysterious thing zooming towards me as Bruce mounted and shoved it in. Well, he tried to shove it in. He tried and tried and tried to shove it in. For half an hour he tried.

"We need some Vaseline." He broke the painful silence.

I had to put all my clothes back on; orange hip-nipper underpants, little white shirt, zippered coat, shoes and socks. I smoothed down my hair, climbed over the Coolite and left the little room . . . alone.

Vaseline was an essential in surfie-life. It was used to soften eye-brows before plucking, rub into surfboard rashes, pull off your randy horse and various other things.

Everybody watched me as I crossed the room and went up the spiral staircase. I searched everywhere; in bathroom cupboards and dressing tables. Down I went again.

"Where's the Vaseline?" I whispered to Sue.

"In the bathroom drawer."

Now the whole gang knew why I was going backwards and forwards across the room like a ping-pong ball.

When I returned Bruce was waiting naked and patiently. I pulled the Vaseline out from my underpants, handed it to the Maestro and undressed in the darkness.

Things got gooey. He drowned me in petroleum jelly and coated himself. He mounted me and tried again. He tried and tried and tried to shove it in. It just wouldn't work. What a marvellous sensation! Being split up the middle!

"Stop 'angin' onoo me 'ips."

I let go and clutched the bedspread, digging in my fingernails. I waited in agony to pass out.

He gave up.

We dressed in silence, dismantled the surfboard security system and it was Tracey and Johnno's turn.

I've still got that rusty little jar of Vaseline, all these years later, full of eyebrow and pubic hair. A little something to remember my first love.

And that was our Saturday night. It never much varied. It was either a night in the back of the panel van at the drive-in, hanging someone's place when their parents were out or gate-crashing a party.

[. . .]

In the smothering darkness, the girls lay side by side.

"What's it like?" Kim asked.

Coolite – ice chest

"What's what like?"

"You know."

"What?"

"Screwing," she said.

"I don't know." Sue acted innocently.

"Yes you do, Danny told me."

"What!"

"It's all right. After all, I *am* his sister."

Susan blushed hotly in the darkness, and said nothing. Kim wasn't even her best friend.

"I can hardly breathe."

"Come on, tell me," Kim demanded. She was terrified.

"Sssshhh!"

They could hear the muffled voice of the attendant, "Four adults? Five dollars . . ."

Once inside the drive-in, Kim and Susan were allowed out from under the mattress. They were giggling and dishevelled.

"I thought I was going to die!" said Sue, tucking in her shirt. "I couldn't hardly breathe."

Kim was brushing her long, thick, brown hair. I was lucky. I was Bruce's girl and got to ride in the front the whole way.

The boys had arranged it beforehand. Susan and Danny got in the back first . . . that way they only missed out on the beginning of the movie. They were quick and never made a noise. Except sometimes you could hear Danny undoing his belt. Sue lay there, straining to get a glimpse of the movie over his pumping shoulder. They finished before the feature film, *Easy Rider*.

Then there was interval. The boys ate hot chips while the girls smoked cigarettes. Towards the end of the ads, Bruce pulled me over the seat and drew the curtain. It was easy enough taking all my clothes off, but I couldn't always find them again, so I usually left my shoes and socks on.

"Didja bring the Vaseline?"

I had the jar tucked up my sleeve. It was an awkward thing to carry around.

"What are you taking that for?" my mother would ask.

"Oh, I've got cracked lips."

Bruce applied it to me, then saddled his dick with a rubber frenchie from his "Tool Kit". After basting his utensil, it was a series of: "Ugh . . . Grunt. Push. Ouch! Ugh! Ugh!"

"Move back," Bruce complained. "I'm hittin' me 'ead."

Edging back, I tried to spread wider. I gritted my teeth and fixed my eyes on a poster on the panel van wall. "Things to do to-day," it said, with two stiff figures copulating in the traditional position.

It never worked, Vaseline or no Vaseline. It was physically impossible. I was under-developed and thirteen. Bruce was over-developed and seventeen. It seemed hours before he gave up. But it wasn't over yet. Bruce had to get his money's worth, after all he'd paid for me to get into the drive-in.

Next thing I knew I was being smothered by hair, thighs and a determined utensil. I choked, spluttered, sucked, gasped and gulped.

"Watch out for ya teef!" Bruce ordered.

Then it was a fumbling grope for underwear. Buttoning. Zipping. Hooking. Pulling on everything inside out. And at last, back to the film.

It was different for Kim and Dave. They liked each other. We all knew they were both virgins and after a few minutes it was quite clear . . . "Oww! Ooh no. It's hurting. Ouch!" Sob. But you have to keep going.

Danny and Sue and Bruce and I all sat in the front seat watching the film.

"K'niver drag?"

"Aw, righto."

"Move over Danny."

Sue and I glanced nervously at each other and now and then stole glimpses of Danny, Kim's brother. His face remained blank and impartial. The noises in the back grew more frantic as the love scene on the big, white screen climaxed.

A few days later, Bruce stopped ringing me up. This meant I was dropped. Sue confirmed it at school.

"Hey Deb . . . Bruce told me he doesn't want to go roun' wiv you anymore."

3

JAMES BALDWIN

Giovanni's Room

Published in 1956, *Giovanni's Room* is one of the first American novels to deal frankly with homosexuality. David, the narrator, is an African American living in Paris, where he is having a passionate affair with Giovanni, an Italian. Reflecting back, he explores the social pressures that affected the choices he made then.

I repent now – for all the good it does – one particular lie among the many lies I've told, told, lived, and believed. This is the lie which I told to Giovanni, but never succeeded in making him believe, that I had never slept with a boy before. I had. I had decided that I never would again. There is something fantastic in the spectacle I now present to myself of having run so far, so hard, across the ocean even, only to find myself brought up short once more before the bulldog in my own backyard – the yard, in the meantime, having grown smaller and the bulldog bigger.

I have not thought of that boy – Joey – for many years; but I see him quite clearly tonight. It was several years ago, I was still in my teens, he was about my age, give or take a year. He was a very nice boy, too, very quick and dark, and always laughing. For a while he was my best friend. Later, the idea that such a person *could* have been my best friend was proof of some horrifying taint in me. So I forgot him. But I see him very well tonight.

It was in the summer, there was no school. His parents had gone someplace for the weekend and I was spending the weekend at his house, which was near Coney Island, in Brooklyn. We lived in Brooklyn too, in those days, but in a better neighborhood than Joey's. I think we had been lying around the beach, swimming a little and watching the near-naked girls pass, whistling at them, and laughing. I am sure that if any of the girls we whistled at that day had shown any signs of responding the ocean would not have been deep enough to drown our shame and terror. But the girls, no doubt, had some intimation of this, possibly from the way

JAMES BALDWIN, extract from *Giovanni's Room*, pp. 223–6 in *James Baldwin: Early Novels and Stories* (Library of America edition), first published in 1956. © 1956 by James Baldwin. Used by permission of Doubleday, a division of Random House, Inc., and by arrangement with the James Baldwin Estate.

we whistled, and they ignored us. As the sun was setting we started up the boardwalk towards his house, with our wet bathing trunks on under our trousers.

And I think it began in the shower. I know that I felt something – as we were horsing around in that small, steamy room, stinging each other with wet towels – which I had not felt before, which mysteriously, and yet aimlessly, included him. I remember in myself a heavy reluctance to get dressed: I blamed it on the heat. But we did get dressed, sort of, and we ate cold things out of his icebox and drank a lot of beer. We must have gone to the movies. I can't think of any other reason for our going out and I remember walking down the dark, tropical Brooklyn streets with heat coming up from the pavements and banging from the walls of houses with enough force to kill a man, with all the world's grownups, it seemed, sitting shrill and dishevelled on the stoops and all the world's children on the sidewalks or in the gutters or hanging from fire-escapes, with my arm around Joey's shoulder. I was proud, I think, because his head came just below my ear. We were walking along and Joey was making dirty wisecracks and we were laughing. Odd to remember, for the first time in so long, how good I felt that night, how fond of Joey.

When we came back along those streets it was quiet; we were quiet too. We were very quiet in the apartment and sleepily got undressed in Joey's bedroom and went to bed. I fell asleep – for quite awhile, I think. But I woke up to find the light on and Joey examining the pillow with great, ferocious care.

"What's the matter?"

"I think a bedbug bit me."

"You slob. You got bedbugs?"

"I think one bit me."

"You ever have a bedbug bite you before?"

"No."

"Well, go back to sleep. You're dreaming."

He looked at me with his mouth open and his dark eyes very big. It was as though he had just discovered that I was an expert on bedbugs. I laughed and grabbed his head as I had done God knows how many times before, when I was playing with him or when he had annoyed me. But this time when I touched him something happened in him and in me which made this touch different from any touch either of us had ever known. And he did not resist, as he usually did, but lay where I had pulled him, against my chest. And I realized that my heart was beating in an awful way and that Joey was trembling against me and the light in the room was very bright and hot. I started to move and to make some kind of joke but Joey mumbled something and I put my head down to hear. Joey raised his head as I lowered mine and we kissed, as it were, by accident. Then, for the first time in my life, I was really aware of another person's body, of another person's smell. We had our arms around each other. It was like holding in my hand some rare, exhausted, nearly doomed bird which I had miraculously happened to find. I was very frightened, I am sure he was frightened too, and we shut our eyes. To remember it so clearly, so painfully tonight tells me that I have never for an instant truly forgotten it. I feel in myself now a faint, a dreadful stirring of what so overwhelmingly stirred in me then, great thirsty heat, and trembling, and tenderness so painful I thought my heart would burst. But out of this astounding, intolerable pain came joy, we gave each other joy that night. It seemed, then, that a lifetime would not be long enough for me to act with Joey the act of love.

But that lifetime was short, was bounded by that night – it ended in the morning. I awoke while Joey was still sleeping, curled like a baby on his side, toward me. He looked like a baby, his mouth half open, his cheek flushed, his curly hair darkening the pillow and half hiding his damp round forehead and his long eyelashes glinting slightly in the summer sun. We were both naked and the sheet we had used as a cover was tangled around our feet. Joey's body was brown, was sweaty, the most beautiful creation I had ever seen till then. I would have touched him to wake him up but something stopped me. I was suddenly afraid. Perhaps it was because he looked so innocent lying there, with such perfect trust; perhaps it was because he was so much smaller than me; my own body suddenly seemed gross and crushing and the desire which was rising in me seemed monstrous. But, above all, I was suddenly afraid. It was borne in on me: *But Joey is a boy*. I saw suddenly the power in his thighs, in his arms, and in his loosely curled fists. The power and the promise and the mystery of that body made me suddenly afraid. That body suddenly seemed the black opening of a cavern in which I would be tortured till madness came, in which I would lose my manhood. Precisely, I wanted to know that mystery and feel that power and have that promise fulfilled through me. The sweat on my back grew cold. I was ashamed. The very bed, in its sweet disorder, testified to vileness. I wondered what Joey's mother would say when she saw the sheets. Then I thought of my father, who had no one in the world but me, my mother having died when I was little. A cavern opened in my mind, black, full of rumor, suggestion, of half-heard, half-forgotten, half-understood stories, full of dirty words. I thought I saw my future in that cavern. I was afraid. I could have cried, cried for shame and terror, cried for not understanding how this could have happened to me, how this could have happened *in* me. And I made my decision. I got out of bed and took a shower and was dressed and had breakfast ready when Joey woke up.

I did not tell him my decision, that would have broken my will. I did not wait to have breakfast with him but only drank some coffee and made an excuse to go home. I knew the excuse did not fool Joey; but he did not know how to protest or insist; he did not know that this was all he needed to have done. Then I, who had seen him that summer nearly every day till then, no longer went to see him. He did not come to see me. I would have been very happy to see him if he had, but the manner of my leavetaking had begun a constriction which neither of us knew how to arrest. When I finally did see him, more or less by accident, near the end of the summer, I made up a long and totally untrue story about a girl I was going with and when school began again I picked up with a rougher, older crowd and was very nasty to Joey. And the sadder this made him, the nastier I became. He moved away at last, out of the neighborhood, away from our school, and I never saw him again.

4

TOM WOLFE

The Bonfire of the Vanities

This satire of 1980s money-mad New York City tells the story of Sherman McCoy, who has it all – a Park Avenue apartment, a job that brings wealth, power, and prestige, a beautiful wife, and an even more beautiful mistress. Driving through the Bronx one night in his Mercedes he hits a black man and doesn't stop. From this moment, McCoy's life spirals downward into chaos and turmoil. The first of the two extracts below comes before the accident, and the second takes place after the event that threatens to expel McCoy from his life of wealth and privilege.

At ten o'clock, Sherman, Rawlie, and five others convened in the conference room of Eugene Lopwitz's suite of offices to decide on Pierce & Pierce's strategy for the main event of the day in the bond markets, which was a U.S. Treasury auction of 10 billion bonds maturing in twenty years. It was a measure of the importance of the bond business to Pierce & Pierce that Lopwitz's offices opened right out into the bond trading room.

The conference room had no conference table. It looked like the lounge in the English hotel for the Yanks where they serve tea. It was full of small antique tables and cabinets. They were so old, brittle, and highly polished, you got the feeling that if you flicked one of them hard with your middle finger, it would shatter. At the same time, a wall of plate glass shoved a view of the Hudson River and the rotting piers of New Jersey into your face.

Sherman sat in a George II armchair. Rawlie sat next to him, in an old chair with a back shaped like a shield. In other antique or antiqued chairs, with Sheraton and Chippendale side tables beside them, were the head government trader, George Connor, who was two years younger than Sherman; his deputy, Vic Scaasi, who was only twenty-eight; the chief market analyst, Paul Feiffer; and Arnold Parch, the executive vice president, who was Lopwitz's first lieutenant.

Everyone in the room sat in a classic chair and stared at a small brown plastic speaker on top of a cabinet. The cabinet was a 220-year-old Adam bowfront, from

---

Tom Wolfe, pp. 67–72 and 343–8 from *The Bonfire of the Vanities*. New York: Bantam Books, 1988. © 1988 by Tom Wolfe. Reprinted by permission of Farrar, Straus and Giroux, LLC. First published by Farrar, Straus and Giroux in 1987.

the period when the brothers Adam liked to paint pictures and ornate borders on wooden furniture. On the center panel was an oval-shaped painting of a Greek maiden sitting in a dell or grotto in which lacy leaves receded fuzzily in deepening shades of green into a dusky teal sky. The thing had cost an astonishing amount of money. The plastic speaker was the size of a bedside clock radio. Everyone stared at it, waiting for the voice of Gene Lopwitz. Lopwitz was in London, where it was now 4:00 p.m. He would preside over this meeting by telephone.

An indistinct noise came out of the speaker. It might have been a voice and it might have been an airplane. Arnold Parch rose from his armchair and approached the Adam cabinet and looked at the plastic speaker and said, "Gene, can you hear me all right?"

He looked imploringly at the plastic speaker, without taking his eyes off it, as if in fact it *were* Gene Lopwitz, transformed, the way princes are transformed into frogs in fairy tales. For a moment the plastic frog said nothing. Then it spoke.

"Yeah, I can hear you, Arnie. There was a lotta cheering going on." Lopwitz's voice sounded as if it were coming from out of a storm drain, but you could hear it.

"Where are you, Gene?" asked Parch.

"I'm at a cricket match." Then less clearly: "What's the name a this place again?" He was evidently with some other people. "Tottenham Park, Arnie. I'm on a kind of a terrace."

"Who's playing?" Parch smiled, as if to show the plastic frog that this wasn't a serious question.

"Don't get technical on me, Arnie. A lot of very nice young gentlemen in cable-knit sweaters and white flannel pants, is the best I can tell you."

Appreciative laughter broke out in the room, and Sherman felt his own lips bending into the somehow obligatory smile. He glanced about the room. Everyone was smiling and chuckling at the brown plastic speaker except for Rawlie, who had his eyes rolled up in the Oh Brother mode.

Then Rawlie leaned over toward Sherman and said, in a noisy whisper: "Look at all these idiots grinning. They think the plastic box has eyes."

This didn't strike Sherman as very funny, since he himself had been grinning. He was also afraid that Lopwitz's loyal aide, Parch, would think he was Rawlie's confederate in making sport of the maximum leader.

"Well, everybody's here, Gene," Parch said to the box, "and so I'm gonna get George to fill you in on where we stand on the auction as of now."

Parch looked at George Connor and nodded and walked back to his chair, and Connor got up from his and walked over to the Adam cabinet and stared at the brown plastic box and said: "Gene? This is George."

"Yeah, hi, George," said the frog. "Go ahead."

"Here's the thing, Gene," said Connor, standing in front of the Adam commode, unable to take his eyes off the plastic box, "it feels pretty good. The old twenties are trading at 8 percent. The traders are telling us they'll come in on the new ones at 8.05, but we think they're playing games with us. We think we're gonna get action right down to 8. So here's what I figure. We'll scale in at 8.01, 8.02, 8.03, with the balance at 8.04. I'm ready to go 60 percent of the issue."

Which, translated, meant: he was proposing to buy $6 billion of the $10 billion in bonds offered in the auction, with the expectation of a profit of two thirty-seconds of a dollar – $6^{1}/_{4}$¢ – on every one hundred dollars put up. This was known as "two ticks."

Sherman couldn't resist another look at Rawlie. He had a small, unpleasant smile on his face, and his gaze seemed to pass several degrees to the right of the Adam commode, toward the Hoboken docks. Rawlie's presence was like a glass of ice water in the face. Sherman resented him all over again. He knew what was on his mind. Here was this outrageous arriviste, Lopwitz – Sherman knew Rawlie thought of him that way – trying to play the nob on the terrace of some British cricket club and at the same time conduct a meeting in New York to decide whether Pierce & Pierce was going to stake two billion, four billion, or six billion on a single government bond issue three hours from now. No doubt Lopwitz had his own audience on hand at the cricket club to watch this performance, as his great words bounced off a communications satellite somewhere up in the empyrean and hit Wall Street. Well, it wasn't hard to find something laughable in it, but Lopwitz was, in truth, a Master of the Universe. Lopwitz was about forty-five years old. Sherman wanted nothing less seven years down the line, when he was forty-five. To be astride the Atlantic . . . with billions at stake! Rawlie could snigger . . . and sink into his kneecaps . . . but to think what Lopwitz now had in his grasp, to think what he made each year, just from Pierce & Pierce, which was at least $25 million, to think of the kind of life he led – and what Sherman thought of first was Lopwitz's young wife, Snow White. That was what Rawlie called her. Hair as dark as ebony, lips as red as blood, skin as white as snow . . . She was Lopwitz's fourth wife, French, a countess, apparently, no more than twenty-five or twenty-six, with an accent like Catherine Deneuve doing a bath-oil commercial. She was something . . . Sherman had met her at a party at the Petersons'. She had put her hand on his forearm, just to make a point in conversation – but the way she kept the pressure on his arm and stared at him from about eight inches away! She was a young and frisky animal. Lopwitz had taken what he wanted. He had wanted a young and frisky animal with lips as red as blood and skin as white as snow, and that was what he had taken. What had ever happened to the other three Mrs. Eugene Lopwitzes was a question Sherman had never heard brought up. When you had reached Lopwitz's level, it didn't even matter.

"Yeah, well, that sounds all right, George," said the plastic frog. "What about Sherman? Are you there, Sherman?"

"Hi, Gene!" said Sherman, rising from the George II armchair. His own voice sounded very odd to him, now that he was talking to a plastic box, and he didn't dare even take a quick glance at Rawlie as he walked over to the Adam commode and took his stance and stared, rapt, at the machine on top.

"Gene, all my customers are talking 8.05. My gut feeling, though, is that they're on our side. The market has a good tone. I think we can bid ahead of the customer interest."

"Okay," said the voice in the box, "but just make sure you and George stay on top a the trading accounts. I don't wanna hear about Salomon or anybody horsing around with shorts."

Sherman found himself marveling at the frog's wisdom.

Some sort of throttled roar came over the speaker. Everybody stared at it.

Lopwitz's voice returned. "Somebody just hit the hell outta the ball," he said. "The ball's kinda dead, though. Well, you kinda hadda be there." It wasn't clear what he meant by that. "Well, look, George. Can you hear me, George?"

Connor hopped to it, rose from his chair, hustled over to the Adam commode. "I can hear you, Gene."

"I was just gonna say, if you feel like stepping up to the plate and taking a good whack at it today, go ahead. It sounds okay."

And that was that.

At forty-five seconds before the auction deadline of 1:00 p.m., George Connor, at a telephone in the middle of the bond trading room, read off his final scaled-in bids to a Pierce & Pierce functionary sitting at a telephone at the Federal Building, which was the physical site of the auction. The bids averaged $99.62643 per $100 worth of bonds. Within a few seconds after 1:00 p.m., Pierce & Pierce now owned, as planned, $6 billion worth of the twenty-year bond. The bond department had four hours in which to create a favorable market. Vic Scaasi led the charge on the bond trading desk, reselling the bonds mainly to the brokerage houses – by telephone. Sherman and Rawlie led the bond salesmen, reselling the bonds mainly to insurance companies and trust banks – by telephone. By 2:00 p.m., the roar in the bond trading room, fueled more by fear than greed, was unearthly. They all shouted and sweated and swore and devoured their electric doughnuts.

By 5:00 p.m. they had sold 40 percent – $2.4 billion – of the $6 billion at an average price of $99.75062 per $100 worth of bonds, for a profit of not two but four ticks! *Four ticks!* That was a profit of twelve and a half cents per one hundred dollars. *Four ticks!* To the eventual retail buyer of these bonds, whether an individual, a corporation or an institution, this spread was invisible. But – *four ticks!* To Pierce & Pierce it meant a profit of almost $3 million for an afternoon's work. And it wouldn't stop there. The market was holding firm and edging up. Within the next week they might easily make an additional $5 to $10 million on the 3.6 billion bonds remaining. *Four ticks!*

By five o'clock Sherman was soaring on adrenaline. He was part of the pulverizing might of Pierce & Pierce, Masters of the Universe. The audacity of it all was breathtaking. To risk $6 billion in one afternoon to make *two ticks* – six and a quarter cents per one hundred dollars – and then to make four ticks – *four ticks!* – the audacity! – the audacity! Was there any more exciting power on the face of the earth? Let Lopwitz watch all the cricket matches he wants to! Let him play the plastic frog! Master of the Universe – the audacity!

The audacity of it flowed through Sherman's limbs and lymph channels and loins. Pierce & Pierce was the power, and he was wired into the power, and the power hummed and surged in his very innards.

[. . .]

Sherman and Judy arrived at the Bavardages' building on Fifth Avenue in a black Buick sedan, with a white-haired driver, hired for the evening from Mayfair Town

Car, Inc. They lived only six blocks from the Bavardages, but walking was out of the question. For a start, there was Judy's dress. It was bare-shouldered but had short puffed sleeves the size of Chinese lampshades covering the upper arms. It had a fitted waist but was puffed up in the skirt to a shape that reminded Sherman of an aerial balloon. The invitation to dinner at the Bavardages' prescribed "informal" dress. But this season, as *tout le monde* knew, women dressed far more extravagantly for informal dinners in fashionable apartments than for formal dances in grand ballrooms. In any event, it was impossible for Judy to walk down the street in this dress. A five-mile-an-hour head wind would have stopped her cold.

But there was a yet more compelling reason for the hired car and driver. It would be perfectly *okay* for the two of them to arrive for dinner at a Good Building (the going term) on Fifth Avenue by taxi, and it would cost less than three dollars. But what would they do *after* the party? How could they walk *out* of the Bavardages' building and have all the world, *tout le monde*, see them standing out in the street, the McCoys, that game couple, their hands up in the air, bravely, desperately, pathetically trying to hail a taxi? The doormen would be no help, because they would be tied up ushering *tout le monde* to their limousines. So he had hired this car and this driver, this white-haired driver, who would drive them six blocks, wait three and a half or four hours, then drive them six blocks and depart. Including a 15 percent tip and the sales tax, the cost would be $197.20 or $246.50, depending on whether they were charged for four or five hours in all.

Hemorrhaging money! Did he even have a job left! Churning fear . . . Lopwitz . . . Surely, Lopwitz wouldn't *sack* him . . . because of three miserable days . . . *and $6 million, you ninny!* . . . Must start cutting back . . . tomorrow . . . Tonight, of course, it was imperative to have a car and driver.

To make matters worse, the driver couldn't pull up to the sidewalk near the entrance, because so many limousines were in the way. He had to double-park. Sherman and Judy had to thread their way between the limousines . . . Envy . . . envy . . . From the license plates Sherman could tell that these limousines were not hired. They were *owned* by those whose sleek hides were hauled here in them. A chauffeur, a good one willing to work long hours and late hours, cost $36,000 a year, minimum; garage space, maintenance, insurance, would cost another $14,000 at least; a total of $50,000, none of it deductible. *I make a million dollars a year — and yet I can't afford that!*

He reached the sidewalk. [. . .]

Now Sherman and Judy were under the canopy, only three or four steps behind [an] old man and [a] blonde, heading for the entrance. A doorman in a starched white dickie pushed it open. He wore white cotton gloves. The blonde entered first. The old man, who was not much taller than she was, looked sleepy and somber. His thinning gray hair was combed straight back. He had a big nose and heavy eyelids, like a movie Indian. *Wait a minute — I know him* . . . No, he had *seen* him somewhere . . . But where? . . . *Bango!* . . . In a picture, of course . . . It was Baron Hochswald, the German financier.

This was all Sherman needed, on this night of all nights . . . After the catastrophes of the past three days, in this perilous low point of his career on Wall

Street, to run into this man, whose success was so complete, so permanent, whose wealth was so vast and unassailable – to have to set eyes upon this immovably secure and ancient German –

Perhaps the baron merely *lived* in this building . . . Please, God, don't let him be going to the same dinner party –

In that very moment he heard the baron say to the doorman in a heavy European accent: "Bavardage." The doorman's white glove gestured toward the rear of the lobby.

Sherman despaired. He despaired of this evening and of this life. Why hadn't he gone to Knoxville six months ago? A little Georgian house, a leaf-blowing machine, a badminton net in the back yard for Campbell . . . But no! He had to tag along behind this walnut-eyed German, heading for the home of some overbearingly vulgar people named Bavardage, a glorified traveling salesman and his wife.

Sherman said to the doorman, "The Bavar*dages*', please." He hit the accented syllable hard, so that no one would think he had paid the slightest attention to the fact that the noble one, Baron Hochswald, had said the same thing. The baron, the blonde, Judy, and Sherman headed for the elevator. The elevator was paneled in old mahogany. It glowed. The grain was showy but rich and mellow. As he entered, Sherman overheard Baron Hochswald saying the name *Bavardage* to the operator. So Sherman repeated it, as before. "The Bavar*dages*'" – lest the baron himself get the impression that he, Sherman, was cognizant of his existence.

Now all four of them knew they were going to the same dinner party, and they had to make a decision. Did you do the decent, congenial, neighborly, and quite American thing – the sort of thing that would have been done without hesitation on an elevator in a similar building on Beacon Hill or Rittenhouse Square – or in a building in New York, for that matter, if the party were being given by someone of good blood and good bone, such as Rawlie or Pollard (in the present company, Pollard suddenly seemed quite okay, quite a commendable old Knickerbocker) – did you do the good-spirited thing and smile and introduce yourselves to one another . . . or did you do the vulgar snobbish thing and stand there and pretend you were unaware of your common destination and stare stiffly at the back of the elevator operator's neck while this mahogany cab rose up its shaft?

Sherman cut an exploratory glance at Hochswald and the blonde. Her dress was a black sheath that ended several inches above her knees and hugged her luscious thighs and the lubricious declivity of her lower abdomen and rose up to a ruff at the top that resembled flower petals. Christ, she was sexy! Her creamy white shoulders and the tops of her breasts swelled up as if she was dying to shed the sheath and run naked through the begonias . . . Her blond hair was swept back to reveal a pair of enormous ruby earrings . . . No more than twenty-five years old . . . A tasty morsel! A panting animal! . . . The old bastard had taken what he wanted, hadn't he! . . . Hochswald wore a black serge suit, a white shirt with a spread collar, and a black silk necktie with a large, almost rakish knot . . . all of it

---

Knickerbocker – a descendant of the Dutch families of New York fashioned *just so* . . . Sherman was glad Judy had pressured him into wearing the navy suit and navy tie . . . Nevertheless, the baron's ensemble seemed terribly smart by comparison.

Now he caught the old German flicking his eyes up and down Judy and himself. Their glances engaged for the briefest of instants. Then both stared once more at the piping on the back of the collar of the elevator operator.

So they ascended, an elevator operator and four social mutes, toward some upper floor. The answer was: You did the vulgar snobbish thing.

The elevator stopped, and the four mutes walked out into the Bavardages' elevator vestibule. It was lit by clusters of tiny silk lampshades on either side of a mirror with a gilded frame. There was an open doorway . . . a rich and rosy glow . . . the sound of a hive of excited voices . . .

They went through the doorway, into the apartment's entry gallery. Such voices! Such delight! Such laughter! Sherman faced catastrophe in his career, catastrophe in his marriage – and the police were circling – and yet the hive – the hive! – the hive! – the sonic waves of the hive made his very innards vibrate. Faces full of grinning, glistening, boiling teeth! How fabulous and fortunate we are, we few, to be in these upper rooms together with our radiant and incarnadine glows!

The entry gallery was smaller than Sherman's, but whereas his (decorated by his wife, the interior designer) was grand and solemn, this one was dazzling, effervescent. The walls were covered in a brilliant Chinese-red silk, and the silk was framed by narrow gilded moldings, and the moldings were framed by a broad burnt-umber upholsterer's webbing, and the webbing was framed by more gilded moldings, and the light of a row of brass sconces made the gilt gleam, and the glow of the gilt and the Chinese-red silk made all the grinning faces and lustrous gowns yet more glorious.

He surveyed the crowd and immediately sensed a pattern . . . *presque vu! presque vu!* almost seen! . . . and yet he couldn't have put it into words. That would have been beyond him. All the men and women in this hall were arranged in clusters, conversational bouquets, so to speak. There were no solitary figures, no strays. All faces were white. (Black faces might show up, occasionally, at fashionable charity dinners but not in fashionable private homes.) There were no men under thirty-five and precious few under forty. The women came in two varieties. First, there were women in their late thirties and in their forties and older (women "of a certain age"), all of them skin and bones (starved to near perfection). To compensate for the concupiscence missing from their juiceless ribs and atrophied backsides, they turned to the dress designers. This season no puffs, flounces, pleats, ruffles, bibs, bows, battings, scallops, laces, darts, or shirrs on the bias were too extreme. They were the social X rays, to use the phrase that had bubbled up into Sherman's own brain. Second, there were the so-called Lemon Tarts. These were women in their twenties or early thirties, mostly blondes (the Lemon in the Tarts), who were the second, third, and fourth wives or live-in girlfriends of men over forty or fifty or sixty (or seventy), the sort of women men refer to, quite without thinking, as *girls.* This season the Tart was able to flaunt the natural advantages of youth by showing her legs from well above the knee and emphasizing her round bottom (something no X ray had). What was entirely missing from *chez* Bavardage was that manner of woman who is neither very young nor very old, who has laid in a lining of subcutaneous fat, who glows with plumpness and a rosy face that speaks, without a word, of home and hearth and hot food ready at six and stories read aloud at night and conversations while seated on the edge of the bed, just before the Sandman comes. In short, no one ever invited . . . Mother.

5

GEORGE ELIOT

Middlemarch

In *Middlemarch* George Eliot portrays a whole community – tradespeople, middle classes, country gentry – in a rising provincial town, circa 1830. One of the characters, Nicholas Bulstrode, is now a respectable banker. But he made his fortune from a business that involved receiving stolen goods. Recently a former employee, Raffles, has discovered Bulstrode's whereabouts and has been blackmailing him. Raffles knows that Bulstrode's former business belonged to Will Ladislaw's grandfather. Ladislaw, an impecunious artist, is in love with the recently widowed Dorothea, who was married to his Uncle Casaubon. Ladislaw has been recruited by Dorothea's uncle, Mr Brooke, to work on a newspaper, the *Pioneer*, that is campaigning for political and social reform. In this scene Bulstrode seeks to make recompense to Will Ladislaw.

He had long poured out utterances of repentance. But to-day a repentance had come which was of a bitterer flavour, and a threatening Providence urged him to a kind of propitiation which was not simply a doctrinal transaction. The divine tribunal had changed its aspect for him; self-prostration was no longer enough, and he must bring restitution in his hand. It was really before his God that Bulstrode was about to attempt such restitution as seemed possible: a great dread had seized his susceptible frame, and the scorching approach of shame wrought in him a new spiritual need. Night and day, while the resurgent threatening past was making a conscience within him, he was thinking by what means he could recover peace and trust – by what sacrifice he could stay the rod. His belief in these moments of dread was, that if he spontaneously did something right, God would save him from the consequences of wrong-doing. For religion can only change when the emotions which fill it are changed; and the religion of personal fear remains nearly at the level of the savage.

He had seen Raffles actually going away on the Brassing coach, and this was a temporary relief; it removed the pressure of an immediate dread, but did not put an end to the spiritual conflict and the need to win protection. At last he came to a difficult resolve, and wrote a letter to Will Ladislaw, begging him to be at the Shrubs that evening for a private interview at nine o'clock. Will had felt no

---

George Eliot, from Book 7, Chapter LXI in *Middlemarch*, first published in 1872.

particular surprise at the request, and connected it with some new notions about the *Pioneer;* but when he was shown into Mr Bulstrode's private room, he was struck with the painfully worn look on the banker's face, and was going to say, "Are you ill?" when, checking himself in that abruptness, he only inquired after Mrs Bulstrode, and her satisfaction with the picture bought for her.

"Thank you, she is quite satisfied; she has gone out with her daughters this evening. I begged you to come, Mr Ladislaw, because I have a communication of a very private – indeed, I will say, of a sacredly confidential nature, which I desire to make to you. Nothing, I daresay, has been farther from your thoughts than that there had been important ties in the past which could connect your history with mine."

Will felt something like an electric shock. He was already in a state of keen sensitiveness and hardly allayed agitation on the subject of ties in the past, and his presentiments were not agreeable. It seemed like the fluctuations of a dream – as if the action begun by that loud bloated stranger were being carried on by this pale-eyed sickly-looking piece of respectability, whose subdued tone and glib formality of speech were at this moment almost as repulsive to him as their remembered contrast. He answered, with a marked change of colour –

"No, indeed, nothing."

"You see before you, Mr Ladislaw, a man who is deeply stricken. But for the urgency of conscience and the knowledge that I am before the bar of One who seeth not as man seeth, I should be under no compulsion to make the disclosure which has been my object in asking you to come here to-night. So far as human laws go, you have no claim on me whatever."

Will was even more uncomfortable than wondering. Mr Bulstrode had paused, leaning his head on his hand, and looking at the floor. But he now fixed his examining glance on Will and said –

"I am told that your mother's name was Sarah Dunkirk, and that she ran away from her friends to go on the stage. Also, that your father was at one time much emaciated by illness. May I ask if you can confirm these statements?"

"Yes, they are all true," said Will, struck with the order in which an inquiry had come, that might have been expected to be preliminary to the banker's hints. But Mr Bulstrode had to-night followed the order of his emotions; he entertained no doubt that the opportunity for restitution had come, and he had an over-powering impulse towards the penitential expression by which he was deprecating chastisement.

"Do you know any particulars of your mother's family?" he continued.

"No; she never liked to speak of them. She was a very generous, honourable woman," said Will, almost angrily.

"I do not wish to allege anything against her. Did she never mention her mother to you at all?"

"I have heard her say that she thought her mother did not know the reason of her running away. She said 'poor mother' in a pitying tone."

"That mother became my wife," said Bulstrode, and then paused a moment before he added, "you have a claim on me, Mr Ladislaw: as I said before, not a legal claim, but one which my conscience recognises. I was enriched by that marriage – a result which would probably not have taken place – certainly not to the same extent – if your grandmother could have discovered her daughter. That daughter, I gather is no longer living!"

"No," said Will, feeling suspicion and repugnance rising so strongly within him, that without quite knowing what he did, he took his hat from the floor and stood up. The impulse within him was to reject the disclosed connection.

"Pray be seated, Mr Ladislaw," said Bulstrode, anxiously. "Doubtless you are startled by the suddenness of this discovery. But I entreat your patience with one who is already bowed down by inward trial."

Will reseated himself, feeling some pity which was half contempt for this voluntary self-abasement of an elderly man.

"It is my wish, Mr Ladislaw, to make amends for the deprivation which befell your mother. I know that you are without fortune, and I wish to supply you adequately from a store which would have probably already been yours had your grandmother been certain of your mother's existence and been able to find her."

Mr Bulstrode paused. He felt that he was performing a striking piece of scrupulosity in the judgment of his auditor, and a penitential act in the eyes of God. He had no clue to the state of Will Ladislaw's mind, smarting as it was from the clear hint of Raffles, and with its natural quickness in construction stimulated by the expectation of discoveries which he would have been glad to conjure back into darkness. Will made no answer for several moments, till Mr Bulstrode, who at the end of his speech had cast his eyes on the floor, now raised them with an examining glance, which Will met fully, saying –

"I suppose you did know of my mother's existence, and knew where she might have been found."

Bulstrode shrank – there was a visible quivering in his face and hands. He was totally unprepared to have his advances met in this way, or to find himself urged into more revelation than he had beforehand set down as needful. But at that moment he dared not tell a lie, and he felt suddenly uncertain of his ground which he had trodden with some confidence before.

"I will not deny that you conjecture rightly," he answered, with a faltering in his tone. "And I wish to make atonement to you as the one still remaining who has suffered a loss through me. You enter, I trust, into my purpose, Mr Ladislaw, which has a reference to higher than merely human claims, and as I have already said, is entirely independent of any legal compulsion. I am ready to narrow my own resources and the prospects of my family by binding myself to allow you five hundred pounds yearly during my life, and to leave you a proportional capital at my death – nay, to do still more, if more should be definitely necessary to any laudable project on your part." Mr Bulstrode had gone on to particulars in the expectation that these would work strongly on Ladislaw, and merge other feelings in grateful acceptance.

But Will was looking as stubborn as possible, with his lip pouting and his fingers in his side-pockets. He was not in the least touched, and said firmly –

"Before I make any reply to your proposition, Mr Bulstrode, I must beg you to answer a question or two. Were you connected with the business by which that fortune you speak of was originally made?"

Mr Bulstrode's thought was, "Raffles has told him." How could he refuse to answer when he had volunteered what drew forth the question? He answered, "Yes."

"And was that business – or was it not – a thoroughly dishonourable one – nay, one that, if its nature had been made public, might have ranked those concerned in it with thieves and convicts?"

Will's tone had a cutting bitterness: he was moved to put his question as nakedly as he could.

Bulstrode reddened with irrepressible anger. He had been prepared for a scene of self-abasement, but his intense pride and his habit of supremacy overpowered penitence, and even dread, when this young man, whom he had meant to benefit, turned on him with the air of a judge.

"The business was established before I became acquainted with it, sir; nor is it for you to institute an inquiry of that kind," he answered, not raising his voice, but speaking with quick defiantness.

"Yes, it is," said Will, starting up again with his hat in his hand. "It is eminently mine to ask such questions, when I have to decide whether I will have transactions with you and accept your money. My unblemished honour is important to me. It is important to me to have no stain on my birth and connections. And now I find there is a stain which I can't help. My mother felt it, and tried to keep as clear of it as she could, and so will I. You shall keep your ill-gotten money. If I had any fortune of my own, I would willingly pay it to any one who could disprove what you have told me. What I have to thank you for is that you kept the money till now, when I can refuse it. It ought to lie with a man's self that he is a gentleman. Good-night, sir."

Bulstrode was going to speak, but Will with determined quickness was out of the room in an instant, and in another the hall-door had closed behind him. He was too strongly possessed with passionate rebellion against this inherited blot which had been thrust on his knowledge to reflect at present whether he had not been too hard on Bulstrode – too arrogantly merciless towards a man of sixty, who was making efforts at retrieval when time had rendered them in vain.

No third person listening could have thoroughly understood the impetuosity of Will's repulse or the bitterness of his words. No one but himself then knew how everything connected with the sentiment of his own dignity had an immediate bearing for him on his relation to Dorothea and to Mr Casaubon's treatment of him. And in the rush of impulses by which he flung back that offer of Bulstrode's, there was mingled the sense that it would have been impossible for him ever to tell Dorothea that he had accepted it.

As for Bulstrode – when Will was gone he suffered a violent reaction, and wept like a woman. It was the first time he had encountered an open expression of scorn from any man higher than Raffles; and with that scorn hurrying like venom through his system, there was no sensibility left to consolations. But the relief of weeping had to be checked. His wife and daughters soon came home from hearing the address of an Oriental missionary, and were full of regret that papa had not heard, in the first instance, the interesting things which they tried to repeat to him.

Perhaps, through all other hidden thoughts, the one that breathed most comfort, was that Will Ladislaw at least was not likely to publish what had taken place that evening.

6

ARTHUR MILLER

The Crucible

The Crucible is based on the Salem witchraft trials of 1692. The play hinges on the accusations of 17-year-old Abigail Williams and a group of teenage girls. Abigail, the niece of Reverend Parris, was a servant in the home of Elizabeth and John Proctor until Elizabeth dismissed her on discovering that Abigail was her husband's lover. The only way those accused can save themselves is to confess their evil doings with the Devil and name more people they claim to have seen with the Devil. Some towns-people see how they can benefit or get revenge by joining in the accusations. Anyone who challenges the girls' testimony is accused of working with the Devil. So begins a reign of terror.

Set in a Salem jail cell several months after the first accusations, this extract comes at the end of the play. The town is now in shambles because so many people are in jail. News arrives that Abigail has stolen money and left town. Reverend Hale, who was brought into town as an expert on witchcraft, realizes that the girls are lying, but it is too late to stop the course of events. Amid rumblings of unrest, Hale and Parris argue that a confession from Proctor will stabilize the situation. Danforth therefore agrees to allow Elizabeth Proctor, who will not be executed because she is pregnant, to plead with her husband.

Other characters appearing in this scene are: Herrick, the Marshall of Salem; Hathorne, the presiding judge at the witchcraft trials; Cheever, the clerk of courts at the witchcraft trials; and Rebecca Nurse, the much respected town midwife.

HALE: Goody Proctor, your husband is marked to hang this morning.

(*Pause.*)

ELIZABETH (*quietly*): I have heard it.
HALE: You know, do you not, that I have no connection with the court? (*She seems to doubt it.*) I come of my own, Goody Proctor. I would save your husband's life, for if he is taken I count myself his murderer. Do you understand me?

ARTHUR MILLER, extract from *The Crucible*, pp. 131–45 from the Viking Critical Library edition edited by Gerald Weales and published by Penguin Books. First published 1952. © 1952, 1953, 1954, renewed © 1980, 1981, 1982 by Arthur Miller. Used with permission of Viking Penguin, a division of Penguin Group (USA) Inc., and International Creative Management Inc.

ELIZABETH: What do you want of me?

HALE: Goody Proctor, I have gone this three month like our Lord into the wilderness. I have sought a Christian way, for damnation's doubled on a minister who counsels men to lie.

HATHORNE: It is no lie, you cannot speak of lies.

HALE: It is a lie! They are innocent!

DANFORTH: I'll hear no more of that!

HALE (*continuing to* ELIZABETH): Let you not mistake your duty as I mistook my own. I came into this village like a bridegroom to his beloved, bearing gifts of high religion; the very crowns of holy law I brought, and what I touched with my bright confidence, it died; and where I turned the eye of my great faith, blood flowed up. Beware, Goody Proctor – cleave to no faith when faith brings blood. It is mistaken law that leads you to sacrifice. Life, woman, life is God's most precious gift; no principle, however glorious, may justify the taking of it. I beg you, woman, prevail upon your husband to confess. Let him give his lie. Quail not before God's judgment in this, for it may well be God damns a liar less than he that throws his life away for pride. Will you plead with him? I cannot think he will listen to another.

ELIZABETH (*quietly*): I think that be the Devil's argument.

HALE (*with a climactic desperation*): Woman, before the laws of God we are as swine! We cannot read His will!

ELIZABETH: I cannot dispute with you, sir; I lack learning for it.

DANFORTH (*going to her*): Goody Proctor, you are not summoned here for disputation. Be there no wifely tenderness within you? He will die with the sunrise. Your husband. Do you understand it? (*She only looks at him.*) What say you? Will you contend with him? (*She is silent.*) Are you stone? I tell you true, woman, had I no other proof of your unnatural life, your dry eyes now would be sufficient evidence that you delivered up your soul to Hell! A very ape would weep at such calamity! Have the devil dried up any tear of pity in you? (*She is silent.*) Take her out. It profit nothing she should speak to him!

ELIZABETH (*quietly*): Let me speak with him, Excellency.

PARRIS (*with hope*): You'll strive with him? (*She hesitates.*)

DANFORTH: Will you plead for his confession or will you not?

ELIZABETH: I promise nothing. Let me speak with him.

(*A sound – the sibilance of dragging feet on stone. They turn. A pause.* HERRICK *enters with John* PROCTOR. *His wrists are chained. He is another man, bearded, filthy, his eyes misty as though webs had overgrown them. He halts inside the doorway, his eye caught by the sight of* ELIZABETH. *The emotion flowing between them prevents anyone from speaking for an instant. Now Hale, visibly affected, goes to* DANFORTH *and speaks quietly.*)

HALE: Pray, leave them, Excellency.

DANFORTH (*pressing* HALE *impatiently aside*): Mr Proctor, you have been notified, have you not? (PROCTOR *is silent, staring at* ELIZABETH.) I see light in the sky, Mister; let you counsel with your wife, and may God help you turn your back on Hell. (PROCTOR *is silent, staring at* ELIZABETH.)

HALE (*quietly*): Excellency, let –

(DANFORTH *brushes past* HALE *and walks out.* HALE *follows.* CHEEVER *stands and follows,* HATHORNE *behind.* HERRICK *goes.* PARRIS, *from a safe distance, offers:*)

PARRIS: If you desire a cup of cider, Mr Proctor, I am sure I – (PROCTOR *turns an icy stare at him, and he breaks off.* PARRIS *raises his palms toward* PROCTOR.) God lead you now. (PARRIS *goes out.*)

(*Alone.* PROCTOR *walks to her, halts. It is as though they stood in a spinning world. It is beyond sorrow, above it. He reaches out his hand as though toward an embodiment not quite real, and as he touches her, a strange soft sound, half laughter, half amazement, comes from his throat. He pats her hand. She covers his hand with hers. And then, weak, he sits. Then she sits, facing him.*)

PROCTOR: The child?
ELIZABETH: It grows.
PROCTOR: There is no word of the boys?
ELIZABETH: They're well. Rebecca's Samuel keeps them.
PROCTOR: You have not seen them?
ELIZABETH: I have not. (*She catches a weakening in herself and downs it.*)
PROCTOR: You are a – marvel, Elizabeth.
ELIZABETH: You – have been tortured?
PROCTOR: Aye. (*Pause. She will not let herself be drowned in the sea that threatens her.*) They come for my life now.
ELIZABETH: I know it.

(*Pause.*)

PROCTOR: None – have yet confessed?
ELIZABETH: There be many confessed.
PROCTOR: Who are they?
ELIZABETH: There be a hundred or more, they say. Goody Ballard is one; Isaiah Goodkind is one. There be many.
PROCTOR: Rebecca?
ELIZABETH: Not Rebecca. She is one foot in Heaven now; naught may hurt her more.
PROCTOR: And Giles?
ELIZABETH: You have not heard of it?
PROCTOR: I hear nothin', where I am kept.
ELIZABETH: Giles is dead.

(*He looks at her incredulously.*)

PROCTOR: When were he hanged?
ELIZABETH (*quietly, factually*): He were not hanged. He would not answer aye or nay to his indictment; for if he denied the charge they'd hang him surely, and

auction out his property. So he stand mute, and died Christian under the law. And so his sons will have his farm. It is the law, for he could not be condemned a wizard without he answer the indictment, aye or nay.

PROCTOR: Then how does he die?

ELIZABETH (*gently*): They press him, John.

PROCTOR: Press?

ELIZABETH: Great stones they lay upon his chest until he plead aye or nay. (*With a tender smile for the old man*): They say he give them but two words. "More weight," he says. And died.

PROCTOR (*numbed – a thread to weave into his agony*): "More weight."

ELIZABETH: Aye. It were a fearsome man, Giles Corey.

(*Pause.*)

PROCTOR (*with great force of will, but not quite looking at her*): I have been thinking I would confess to them, Elizabeth. (*She shows nothing.*) What say you? If I give them that?

ELIZABETH: I cannot judge you, John.

(*Pause.*)

PROCTOR (*simply – a pure question*): What would you have me do?

ELIZABETH: As you will, I would have it. (*Slight pause*): I want you living, John. That's sure.

PROCTOR (*pauses, then with a flailing of hope*): Giles' wife? Have she confessed?

ELIZABETH: She will not.

(*Pause.*)

PROCTOR: It is a pretense, Elizabeth.

ELIZABETH: What is?

PROCTOR: I cannot mount the gibbet like a saint. It is a fraud. I am not that man. (*She is silent.*) My honesty is broke, Elizabeth; I am no good man. Nothing's spoiled by giving them this lie that were not rotten long before.

ELIZABETH: And yet you've not confessed till now. That speak goodness in you.

PROCTOR: Spite only keeps me silent. It is hard to give a lie to dogs. (*Pause, for the first time he turns directly to her.*) I would have your forgiveness, Elizabeth.

ELIZABETH: It is not for me to give, John, I am –

PROCTOR: I'd have you see some honesty in it. Let them that never lied die now to keep their souls. It is pretense for me, a vanity that will not blind God nor keep my children out of the wind. (*Pause.*) What say you?

ELIZABETH (*upon a heaving sob that always threatens*): John, it come to naught that I should forgive you, if you'll not forgive yourself. (*Now he turns away a little, in great agony.*) It is not my soul, John, it is yours. (*He stands, as though in physical pain, slowly rising to his feet with a great immortal longing to find his answer. It is difficult to say, and she is on the verge of tears.*) Only be sure of this, for I know it now: Whatever you will do, it is a good man does it. (*He turns his doubting, searching gaze upon her.*) I have read my heart this three month, John. (*Pause.*) I have sins of my own to count. It needs a cold wife to prompt lechery.

PROCTOR (*in great pain*): Enough, enough –

ELIZABETH (*now pouring out her heart*): Better you should know me!

PROCTOR: I will not hear it! I know you!

ELIZABETH: You take my sins upon you, John –

PROCTOR (*in agony*): No, I take my own, my own!

ELIZABETH: John, I counted myself so plain, so poorly made, no honest love could come to me! Suspicion kissed you when I did; I never knew how I should say my love. It were a cold house I kept! (*In fright, she swerves, as* HATHORNE *enters.*)

HATHORNE: What say you, Proctor? The sun is soon up.

(PROCTOR, *his chest heaving, stares, turns to* ELIZABETH. *She comes to him as though to plead, her voice quaking.*)

ELIZABETH: Do what you will. But let none be your judge. There be no higher judge under Heaven than Proctor is! Forgive me, forgive me, John – I never knew such goodness in the world! (*She covers her face, weeping.*)

(PROCTOR *turns from her to* HATHORNE; *he is off the earth, his voice hollow.*)

PROCTOR: I want my life.

HATHORNE (*electrified, surprised*): You'll confess yourself?

PROCTOR: I will have my life.

HATHORNE (*with a mystical tone*): God be praised! It is a providence! (*He rushes out the door, and his voice is heard calling down the corridor*): He will confess! Proctor will confess!

PROCTOR (*with a cry, as he strides to the door*): Why do you cry it? (*In great pain he turns back to her.*) It is evil, is it not? It is evil.

ELIZABETH (*in terror, weeping*): I cannot judge you, John, I cannot!

PROCTOR: Then who will judge me? (*Suddenly clasping his hands*): God in Heaven, what is John Proctor, what is John Proctor? (*He moves as an animal, and a fury is riding in him, a tantalized search.*) I think it is honest, I think so; I am no saint. (*As though she had denied this he calls angrily at her*): Let Rebecca go like a saint; for me it is fraud!

(*Voices are heard in the hall, speaking together in suppressed excitement.*)

ELIZABETH: I am not your judge, I cannot be. (*As though giving him release*): Do as you will, do as you will!

PROCTOR: Would you give them such a lie? Say it. Would you ever give them this? (*She cannot answer.*) You would not; if tongs of fire were singeing you you would not! It is evil. Good, then – it is evil, and I do it!

(HATHORNE *enters with* DANFORTH, *and, with them,* CHEEVER, PARRIS, *and* HALE. *It is a businesslike, rapid entrance, as though the ice had been broken.*)

DANFORTH (*with great relief and gratitude*): Praise to God, man, praise to God; you shall be blessed in Heaven for this. (CHEEVER *has hurried to the bench with pen, ink, and paper.* PROCTOR *watches him.*) Now then, let us have it. Are you ready, Mr Cheever?

PROCTOR (*with a cold, cold horror at their efficiency*): Why must it be written?

DANFORTH: Why, for the good instruction of the village, Mister; this we shall post upon the church door! (*To* PARRIS, *urgently*): Where is the marshal?

PARRIS (*runs to the door and calls down the corridor*): Marshal! Hurry!

DANFORTH: Now, then, Mister, will you speak slowly, and directly to the point, for Mr Cheever's sake. (*He is on record now, and is really dictating to* CHEEVER, *who writes.*) Mr Proctor, have you seen the Devil in your life? (*Proctor's jaws lock.*) Come, man, there is light in the sky; the town waits at the scaffold; I would give out this news. Did you see the Devil?

PROCTOR: I did.

PARRIS: Praise God!

DANFORTH: And when he come to you, what were his demand? (PROCTOR *is silent.* DANFORTH *helps.*) Did he bid you to do his work upon the earth?

PROCTOR: He did.

DANFORTH: And you bound yourself to his service? (DANFORTH *turns, as* REBECCA NURSE *enters, with* HERRICK *helping to support her. She is barely able to walk.*) Come in, come in, woman!

REBECCA (*brightening as she sees* PROCTOR): Ah, John! You are well, then, eh?

(PROCTOR *turns his face to the wall.*)

DANFORTH: Courage, man, courage – let her witness your good example that she may come to God herself. Now hear it, Goody Nurse! Say on, Mr Proctor. Did you bind yourself to the Devil's service?

REBECCA (*astonished*): Why, John!

PROCTOR (*through his teeth, his face turned from* REBECCA): I did.

DANFORTH: Now, woman, you surely see it profit nothin' to keep this conspiracy any further. Will you confess yourself with him?

REBECCA: Oh, John – God send his mercy on you!

DANFORTH: I say, will you confess yourself, Goody Nurse?

REBECCA: Why, it is a lie, it is a lie; how may I damn myself? I cannot, I cannot.

DANFORTH: Mr Proctor. When the Devil came to you did you see Rebecca Nurse in his company? (PROCTOR *is silent.*) Come, man, take courage – did you ever see her with the Devil?

PROCTOR (*almost inaudibly*): No.

(DANFORTH, *now sensing trouble, glances at John and goes to the table, and picks up a sheet – the list of condemned.*)

DANFORTH: Did you ever see her sister, Mary Easty, with the Devil?

PROCTOR: No, I did not.

DANFORTH (*his eyes narrow on* PROCTOR): Did you ever see Martha Corey with the Devil?

PROCTOR: I did not.

DANFORTH (*realizing, slowly putting the sheet down*): Did you ever see anyone with the Devil?

PROCTOR: I did not.

DANFORTH: Proctor, you mistake me. I am not empowered to trade your life for a lie. You have most certainly seen some person with the Devil. (PROCTOR *is silent.*) Mr Proctor, a score of people have already testified they saw this woman with the Devil.

PROCTOR: Then it is proved. Why must I say it?

DANFORTH: Why "must" you say it! Why, you should rejoice to say it if your soul is truly purged of any love for Hell!

PROCTOR: They think to go like saints. I like not to spoil their names.

DANFORTH (*inquiring, incredulous*): Mr Proctor, do you think they go like saints?

PROCTOR (*evading*): This woman never thought she done the Devil's work.

DANFORTH: Look you, sir. I think you mistake your duty here. It matters nothing what she thought – she is convicted of the unnatural murder of children, and you for sending your spirit out upon Mary Warren. Your soul alone is the issue here, Mister, and you will prove its whiteness or you cannot live in a Christian country. Will you tell me now what persons conspired with you in the Devil's company? (PROCTOR *is silent.*) To your knowledge was Rebecca Nurse ever –

PROCTOR: I speak my own sins; I cannot judge another. (*Crying out, with hatred*): I have no tongue for it.

HALE (*quickly to* DANFORTH): Excellency, it is enough he confess himself. Let him sign it, let him sign it.

PARRIS (*feverishly*): It is a great service, sir. It is a weighty name; it will strike the village that Proctor confess. I beg you, let him sign it. The sun is up, Excellency!

DANFORTH (*considers; then with dissatisfaction*): Come, then, sign your testimony. (*To* Cheever): Give it to him. (*Cheever goes to* PROCTOR, *the confession and a pen in hand.* PROCTOR *does not look at it.*) Come, man, sign it.

PROCTOR (*after glancing at the confession*): You have all witnessed it – it is enough.

DANFORTH: You will not sign it?

PROCTOR: You have all witnessed it; what more is needed?

DANFORTH: Do you sport with me? You will sign your name or it is no confession, Mister! (*His breast heaving with agonized breathing,* PROCTOR *now lays the paper down and signs his name.*)

PARRIS: Praise be to the Lord!

(PROCTOR *has just finished signing when* DANFORTH *reaches for the paper. But* PROCTOR *snatches it up, and now a wild terror is rising in him, and a boundless anger.*)

DANFORTH (*perplexed, but politely extending his hand*): If you please, sir.

PROCTOR: No.

DANFORTH (*as though* PROCTOR *did not understand*): Mr Proctor, I must have –

PROCTOR: No, no. I have signed it. You have seen me. It is done! You have no need for this.

PARRIS: Proctor, the village must have proof that –

PROCTOR: Damn the village! I confess to God, and God has seen my name on this! It is enough!

DANFORTH: No, sir, it is –

PROCTOR: You came to save my soul, did you not? Here! I have confessed myself; it is enough!

DANFORTH: You have not con –

PROCTOR: I have confessed myself! Is there no good penitence but it be public? God does not need my name nailed upon the church! God sees my name; God knows how black my sins are! It is enough!

DANFORTH: Mr Proctor –

PROCTOR: You will not use me! I am no Sarah Good or Tituba, I am John Proctor! You will not use me! It is no part of salvation that you should use me!

DANFORTH: I do not wish to –

PROCTOR: I have three children – how may I teach them to walk like men in the world, and I sold my friends?

DANFORTH: You have not sold your friends –

PROCTOR: Beguile me not! I blacken all of them when this is nailed to the church the very day they hang for silence!

DANFORTH: Mr Proctor, I must have good and legal proof that you –

PROCTOR: You are the high court, your word is good enough! Tell them I confessed myself; say Proctor broke his knees and wept like a woman; say what you will, but my name cannot –

DANFORTH (*with suspicion*): It is the same, is it not? If I report it or you sign to it?

PROCTOR (*– he knows it is insane*): No, it is not the same! What others say and what I sign to is not the same!

DANFORTH: Why? Do you mean to deny this confession when you are free?

PROCTOR: I mean to deny nothing!

DANFORTH: Then explain to me, Mr Proctor, why you will not let –

PROCTOR (*with a cry of his whole soul*): Because it is my name! Because I cannot have another in my life! Because I lie and sign myself to lies! Because I am not worth the dust on the feet of them that hang! How may I live without my name? I have given you my soul; leave me my name!

DANFORTH (*pointing at the confession in* PROCTOR's *hand*): Is that document a lie? If it is a lie I will not accept it! What say you? I will not deal in lies, Mister! (PROCTOR *is motionless.*) You will give me your honest confession in my hand, or I cannot keep you from the rope. (PROCTOR *does not reply.*) Which way do you go, Mister?

(*His breast heaving, his eyes staring,* PROCTOR *tears the paper and crumples it, and he is weeping in fury, but erect.*)

DANFORTH: Marshal!

PARRIS (*hysterically, as though the tearing paper were his life*): Proctor, Proctor!

HALE: Man, you will hang! You cannot!

PROCTOR (*his eyes full of tears*): I can. And there's your first marvel, that I can. You have made your magic now, for now I do think I see some shred of goodness in John Proctor. Not enough to weave a banner with, but white enough to keep it from such dogs. (ELIZABETH, *in a burst of terror, rushes to him and weeps against his hand.*) Give them no tear! Tears pleasure them! Show honor now, show a stony heart and sink them with it! (*He has lifted her, and kisses her now with great passion.*)

REBECCA: Let you fear nothing! Another judgment waits us all!

DANFORTH: Hang them high over the town! Who weeps for these, weeps for corruption! (*He sweeps out past them.* HERRICK *starts to lead* REBECCA, *who almost collapses, but* PROCTOR *catches her, and she glances up at him apologetically.*)

REBECCA: I've had no breakfast.

HERRICK: Come, man.

(HERRICK *escorts them out,* HATHORNE *and* CHEEVER *behind them.* ELIZABETH *stands staring at the empty doorway.*)

PARRIS (*in deadly fear, to* ELIZABETH): Go to him, Goody Proctor! There is yet time!

(*From outside a drumroll strikes the air.* PARRIS *is startled.* ELIZABETH *jerks about toward the window.*)

PARRIS: Go to him! (*He rushes out the door, as though to hold back his fate.*) Proctor! Proctor!

(*Again, a short burst of drums.*)

HALE: Woman, plead with him! (*He starts to rush out the door, and then goes back to her.*) Woman! It is pride, it is vanity. (*She avoids his eyes, and moves to the window. He drops to his knees.*) Be his helper! – What profit him to bleed? Shall the dust praise him? Shall the worms declare his truth? Go to him, take his shame away!

ELIZABETH (*supporting herself against collapse, grips the bars of the window, and with a cry*): He have his goodness now. God forbid I take it from him!

(*The final drumroll crashes, then heightens violently.* HALE *weeps in frantic prayer, and the new sun is pouring in upon her face, and the drums rattle like bones in the morning air.*)

7

WILLIAM SHAKESPEARE

Macbeth

Probably composed in late 1606 or early 1607, *Macbeth* is the last of Shakespeare's four great tragedies, the others being *Hamlet, King Lear,* and *Othello. Macbeth* is one of Shakespeare's most popular plays and follows the fortunes of an ambitious Scottish lord.

After a victory on the battlefield brings Macbeth glory and honor, he meets three witches who foretell that he will become king. When his wife learns of this prophecy she encourages Macbeth to kill Duncan, the current king, on his forthcoming visit to the Macbeths' castle. This scene from the play takes place on the night of Duncan's arrival.

Macbeth's Castle

MACBETH: If it were done when 'tis done, then 'twere well
  It were done quickly. If the assassination
  Could trammel up the consequence, and catch,
  With his surcease, success; that but this blow
  Might be the be-all and the end-all here,
  But here, upon this bank and shoal of time, –
  We'd jump the life to come. But in these cases
  We still have judgment here; that we but teach
  Bloody instructions, which being taught, return
  To plague the inventor: this even-handed justice
  Commends the ingredients of our poison'd chalice
  To our own lips. He's here in double trust:
  First, as I am his kinsman and his subject,
  Strong both against the deed: then, as his host,
  Who should against his murderer shut the door,
  Not bear the knife myself. Besides, this Duncan
  Hath borne his faculties so meek, hath been

WILLIAM SHAKESPEARE, from Act I, Scene VII in *Macbeth,* first published in 1623.

So clear in his great office, that his virtues
Will plead like angels, trumpet-tongued, against
The deep damnation of his taking-off:
And pity, like a naked new-born babe,
Striding the blast, or heaven's cherubin, hors'd
Upon the sightless couriers of the air,
Shall blow the horrid deed in every eye,
That tears shall drown the wind. – I have no spur
To prick the sides of my intent, but only
Vaulting ambition, which o'erleaps itself,
And falls on the other.

(*Enter* LADY MACBETH.)

                              How now! what news?
LADY MACBETH: He has almost supp'd: why have you left the chamber?
MACBETH: Hath he ask'd for me?
LADY MACBETH: Know you not he has?
MACBETH: We will proceed no further in this business:
    He hath honour'd me of late; and I have bought
    Golden opinions from all sorts of people,
    Which would be worn now in their newest gloss,
    Not cast aside so soon.
LADY MACBETH: Was the hope drunk
    Wherein you dress'd yourself? Hath it slept since?
    And wakes it now, to look so green and pale
    At what it did so freely? From this time
    Such I account thy love. Art thou afeard
    To be the same in thine own act and valour
    As thou art in desire? Wouldst thou have that
    Which thou esteem'st the ornament of life,
    And live a coward in thine own esteem;
    Letting *I dare not* wait upon *I would*,
    Like the poor cat i' the adage?
MACBETH: Pr'ythee, peace:
    I dare do all that may become a man;
    Who dares do more is none.
LADY MACBETH: What beast was't, then,
    That made you break this enterprise to me?
    When you durst do it, then you were a man;
    And, to be more than what you were, you would
    Be so much more the man. Nor time nor place
    Did then adhere, and yet you would make both:
    They have made themselves, and that their fitness now
    Does unmake you. I have given suck, and know
    How tender 'tis to love the babe that milks me:

I would, while it was smiling in my face,
Have pluck'd my nipple from his boneless gums,
And dash'd the brains out, had I so sworn as you
Have done to this.
MACBETH: If we should fail?
LADY MACBETH: We fail!
But screw your courage to the sticking place,
And we'll not fail. When Duncan is asleep, –
Whereto the rather shall his day's hard journey
Soundly invite him, his two chamberlains
Will I with wine and wassail so convince
That memory, the warder of the brain,
Shall be a fume, and the receipt of reason
A limbeck only: when in swinish sleep
Their drenched natures lie as in a death,
What cannot you and I perform upon
The unguarded Duncan? what not put upon
His spongy officers; who shall bear the guilt
Of our great quell?
MACBETH: Bring forth men-children only;
For thy undaunted mettle should compose
Nothing but males. Will it not be receiv'd,
When we have mark'd with blood those sleepy two
Of his own chamber, and us'd their very daggers,
That they have done't?
LADY MACBETH: Who dares receive it other,
As we shall make our griefs and clamour roar
Upon his death?
MACBETH: I am settled, and bend up
Each corporal agent to this terrible feat.
Away, and mock the time with fairest show:
False face must hide what the false heart doth know.

II

DUTIES TO KIN

Every human society recognizes that people in certain relationships have special duties to each other. This is, in fact, one of the clearest counter-examples to the common belief that there are no universal ethical standards. The most widely accepted obligation is that of parents (or in societies where paternity is uncertain, mothers) to care for their children. In many cultures, obligations extend to wide circles of kin and are quite central to domestic and economic life. There is nothing surprising about this. Although culture undoubtedly shapes moral codes, it is always working within the framework of our evolved biological nature as social mammals. Since our children are not born capable of surviving on their own, mothers who do not look after their children are not likely to pass their genes on to future generations. So it is easy to understand how caring for one's children should become part of our nature. Hence the idea of a duty of mothers to their children is an ethical principle that reinforces a trait that lies deep in our nature. Of course, societies can have other arrangements, where children are cared for by their aunts, or adopted into unrelated families, but systems that go against the grain of biological relationships are rare.

For fathers, the biological imperative is not so clear. For a woman, each pregnancy and birth represents a considerable investment of her time and physical resources, and in earlier days, a significant risk to her health and life. The number of children she can bear is strictly limited, and she knows (or knew, in the days before embryo and egg donation were possible) that every child she bears is genetically her own. Men, on the other hand, are physically capable of fathering hundreds of children, if they have the reproductive opportunities to do so. While fathering a small number of children and maximizing the chances of survival of each of those children is one way in which their genes may survive into future generations, a man who fathers a much larger number of children may also leave many descendants, even if, without a father's care, a smaller proportion of them survive. When we add to this a degree of uncertainty about paternity, we can see why the duty of a father to care for his children may not be quite as universal as the corresponding duty of a mother.

Favoring kin other than our children may also have a biological basis. Someone once asked J. B. S. Haldane whether, as an evolutionary biologist, he could ever lay down his life for his brother. After a quick calculation he replied that he would lay down his life for two brothers or sisters, four nephews or nieces, or eight first cousins. That answer reflects the percentage of our genes that we share with our kin. My sisters and brothers will, on average, have 50 percent of my genes, since like me they have half of my mother's and half of my father's genes. I share 25 percent of my genes with my nieces and nephews, and 12.5 percent with my first cousins. Hence for Haldane to exchange his life for eight of his first cousins would not result in any loss of his genes from the population. The common estimate of the strength of our duties to our kin also loosely reflects these genetic facts, weakening as the percentage of shared genes declines. We think of the duty to a brother or sister as stronger than that to a cousin. Of course, we do not really base our actions on whether or not they will help our genes to survive in future generations. In that respect, caring for our kin may be like having sex. The evolutionary explanation of our sexual desire is that it leads to reproduction. It would be wrong to conclude from that correct explanation that when we want sex, we want to reproduce.

That grown-up children have duties to their parents is a common view, though not quite as widely held a view as its converse. Perhaps that is because there is no obvious evolutionary basis for children to make sacrifices for older parents, especially when the parents are past the age of reproduction and past the point at which they can confer some reciprocal benefit on the children. In some cultures children move far from home when they become adults or marry, and have little subsequent contact. (If today's children don't even pick up the phone to call their parents, no wonder that earlier generations did not trudge across the mountains to keep in touch.) Modern psychological theories stress the need for children, if they are to become autonomous adults, to separate from and become independent of the family. Yet despite all these factors, in many cultures children do have a strong sense of obligation to their parents. Since children owe their very existence to their parents, and usually much more besides, the idea that children have an obligation to respect their parents and to look after them in their old age is, presumably, an aspect of another virtually universally recognized obligation, that of gratitude.

Accepting an evolutionary explanation of our concern for our kin does not imply that this concern is right or good. Explanation is not justification, and we should not equate "natural" with "right." Some diseases are natural, but we employ all the technology of modern medicine to fight them off. War, racism, and male dominance may all be natural to our species, but that would not make them right. Indeed, we might even draw the opposite conclusion: if a near-universally moral principle is so widely held because it is part of our common evolutionary heritage, perhaps we should subject it to more critical scrutiny than we would if we thought its universality was a sign that it is a timeless truth of reason.

From an ethical perspective the obligations that arise from special relationships, whether of parents to children, or between other kin, are in need of justification. Ethics, it is widely thought, requires us to put aside selfishness and consider the larger whole. The Golden Rule tells us to treat others as we would like them to treat us. Many ethicists have said that, when judging ethically, we should take an impartial perspective, not giving preference to our own interests. Kant said that we should only act on maxims that we can accept as a universal law – which rules out special exceptions in our own favor. Utilitarians tell us to do what will have the best consequences for all those affected by our actions, not only for those who are related to us. How, then, can ethics require us to give preference to the interests of our children, or other kin?

Some philosophers and social reformers answer this question by denying that it is ethically proper to give preference to our kin. In a famous passage, the late eighteenth-century philosopher William Godwin said that if a building was on fire, and you had time to rescue only Archbishop Fénelon, a celebrated writer of the time, or his chambermaid, who happened to be your mother, you should rescue the archbishop, knowing that his works had brought consolation to many thousands. As Godwin puts it, "What magic is there in the pronoun 'my' to over-turn the decisions of everlasting truth? My wife or my mother may be a fool or a prostitute, malicious, lying or dishonest. If they be, of what consequence is it that they are mine?"[1]

Plato was among the first to criticize the family because of the conflict of loyalties it creates. In the *Republic* he suggested a form of communal marriage for the Guardians, who rule his ideal society. Thus they would be "all of one opinion about what is near and dear to them," and would work together for the common good.[2] More than two thousand years later, in the Israeli *kibbutzim*, or collective settlements, an attempt was made to put something like this into practice, not just for a special class of rulers, but for the entire community. Childen were reared collectively, and the formation of bonds between parents and their children was discouraged. But separating parents from their children proved hard on both, and on surviving *kibbutzim*, the rules have been relaxed. Today it is hard to find anyone who wants to completely abolish or repress partiality for kin.

Other ethicists contend that an impartial ethic is too demanding for beings who are moved so much more by our own interests and our own kin than by impartial good. They favor a morality that allows each moral agent to show a degree of partiality for his or her own interests and concerns. Among this group are feminist ethicists – although not all feminists writing in ethics take this view – who urge that ethics should be based on the emotional response of caring for another, rather than on more abstract or universal ethical principles. Others defend impartialism at the highest, most abstract level of our moral thinking, but claim that impartiality itself can provide reasons why we may accept special duties to our kin. Kantians, for example, point out that it is possible to sup-port as a universal law the view that "a parent has a special duty to further the interests of her or his child, in preference to the interests of the children of strangers." Utilitarians suggest that, since children do better when they grow up in a loving family, accepting a moral rule that recognizes the special duty of parents to care for their children will have better consequences than insisting that parents show no more concern for their own children than for any other child. But for any ethic that seeks to allow some degree of partiality, the question will always arise: what are the limits to partiality for one's kin? What are we required to do for our kin that we are not required to do for strangers? And when the needs, or dignity, or even the very lives of our kin are at stake, how far are we permitted to go in breaching laws or moral rules that it would otherwise be wrong to breach?

In compiling this section, we selected the best stories and extracts we could find on the theme of duties to kin. When we had made the final selection and begun writing this introduction, we noticed that all of the readings on the obligations of parents to children dealt with mothers, and none with fathers. Similarly both our extracts on the duties of siblings to each other are about sisters who are called upon to sacrifice for their brothers. It is only in the section on the duties of children to their parents that males appear as the protagonists, and though one son attempts, belatedly, to care for his father, the other takes a very different ethical stance. This imbalance in the behavior of men and women in respect of their duties to kin is reinforced by two other readings that come later in this volume but could quite easily have gone in this section – the extracts from *Iphigeneia at Aulis* and from Genesis. On noticing this, we could, of course, have searched for different selections to provide gender balance. But we thought it would be more useful to present the selections we have found, and allow readers to draw their own conclusions about the significance of the imbalance. We do, however, draw it to your attention, so that as you read the selections that follow, you may ask yourself whether the author would have taken the same attitude if the story had been about someone of the other sex.

NOTES

1 William Godwin, *An Enquiry Concerning Political Justice and its Influence on General Virtue and Happiness*, 1st edn, ed. and abridged by Raymond Preston, New York: Knopf, 1926; first published in 1793, pp. 41–2.
2 Plato, *Republic* V, 264.

THE DUTIES OF PARENTS TO THEIR CHILDREN

8

CHARLOTTE PERKINS GILMAN

The Unnatural Mother

"Don't tell me!" said old Mis' Briggs, with a forbidding shake of the head. "No mother that was a mother would desert her own child for anything on earth!"

"And leaving it a care on the town, too!" put in Susannah Jacobs." As if we hadn't enough to do to take care of our own!"

Miss Jacobs was a well-to-do old maid, owning a comfortable farm and homestead, and living alone with an impoverished cousin acting as general servant, companion, and protégée. Mis' Briggs, on the contrary, had had thirteen children, five of whom remained to bless her, so that what maternal feeling Miss Jacobs might lack, Mis' Briggs could certainly supply.

"I should think," piped little Martha Ann Simmons, the village dressmaker, "that she might 'a saved her young one first and then tried what she could do for the town."

Martha had been married, had lost her husband, and had one sickly boy to care for.

The youngest Briggs girl, still unmarried at thirty-six, and in her mother's eyes a most tender infant, now ventured to make a remark.

"You don't any of you seem to think what she did for all of us – if she hadn't left hers we should all have lost ours, sure."

"You ain't no call to judge, Maria 'Melia," her mother hastened to reply. "You've no children of your own, and you can't judge of a mother's duty. No mother ought to leave her child, whatever happens. The Lord gave it to her to take care of – he never gave her other people's. You needn't tell me!"

"She was an unnatural mother," repeated Miss Jacobs harshly, "as I said to begin with!"

"What is the story?" asked the City Boarder. The City Boarder was interested in stories from a business point of view, but they did not know that. "What did this woman do?" she asked.

CHARLOTTE PERKINS GILMAN, "The Unnatural Mother," pp. 281–5 from *The Forerunner*, a monthly journal on women's rights and related issues, edited (and mostly written) by Charlotte Perkins Gilman, which ran from November 1909 to December 1916. Currently available in Charlotte Perkins Gilman, *Herland, the Yellow Wall-Paper, and Selected Writings* (London: Penguin, 1999).

There was no difficulty in eliciting particulars. The difficulty was rather in discriminating amidst their profusion and contradictoriness. But when the City Boarder got it clear in her mind, it was somewhat as follows:

The name of the much-condemned heroine was Esther Greenwood, and she lived and died here in Toddsville.

Toddsville was a mill village. The Todds lived on a beautiful eminence overlooking the little town, as the castles of robber barons on the Rhine used to overlook their little towns. The mills and the mill hands' houses were built close along the bed of the river. They had to be pretty close, because the valley was a narrow one, and the bordering hills were too steep for travel, but the water power was fine. Above the village was the reservoir, filling the entire valley save for a narrow road beside it, a fair blue smiling lake, edged with lilies and blue flag, rich in pickerel and perch. This lake gave them fish, it gave them ice, it gave the power that ran the mills that gave the town its bread. Blue Lake was both useful and ornamental.

In this pretty and industrious village Esther had grown up, the somewhat neglected child of a heart-broken widower. He had lost a young wife, and three fair babies before her – this one was left him, and he said he meant that she should have all the chance there was.

"That was what ailed her in the first place!" they all eagerly explained to the City Boarder. "She never knew what 'twas to have a mother, and she grew up a regular tomboy! Why, she used to roam the country for miles around, in all weather like an Injun! And her father wouldn't take no advice!"

This topic lent itself to eager discussion. The recreant father, it appeared, was a doctor, not their accepted standby, the resident physician of the neighborhood, but an alien doctor, possessed of "views."

"You never heard such things as he advocated," Miss Jacobs explained. "He wouldn't give no medicines, hardly; said 'nature' did the curing – he couldn't."

"And he couldn't either – that was clear," Mrs Briggs agreed. "Look at his wife and children dying on his hands, as it were! 'Physician, heal thyself,' I say."

"But, Mother," Maria Amelia put in, "she was an invalid when he married her, they say; and those children died of polly – polly – what's that thing that nobody can help?"

"That may all be so," Miss Jacobs admitted, "but all the same, it's a doctor's business to give medicine. If 'nature' was all that was wanted, we needn't have any doctor at all!"

"I believe in medicine and plenty of it. I always gave my children a good clearance, spring and fall, whether anything ailed 'em or not, just to be on the safe side. And if there was anything the matter with 'em, they had plenty more. I never had anything to reproach myself with on that score," stated Mrs Briggs, firmly. Then as a sort of concession to the family graveyard, she added piously, "The Lord giveth and the Lord taketh away."

"You should have seen the way he dressed that child!" pursued Miss Jacobs. "It was a reproach to the town. Why, you couldn't tell at a distance whether it was a boy or a girl. And barefoot! He let that child go barefoot till she was so big we was actually mortified to see her."

It appeared that a wild, healthy childhood had made Esther very different in her early womanhood from the meek, well-behaved damsels of the little place. She was well enough liked by those who knew her at all, and the children of the place adored her, but the worthy matrons shook their heads and prophesied no good of a girl who was "queer."

She was described with rich detail in reminiscence, how she wore her hair short till she was fifteen – "just shingled like a boy's – it did seem a shame that girl had no mother to look after her – and her clo'se was almost a scandal, even when she did put on shoes and stockings. Just gingham – brown gingham – and *short!*"

"I think she was a real nice girl," said Maria Amelia. "I can remember her just as well! She was *so* nice to us children. She was five or six years older than I was, and most girls that age won't have anything to do with little ones. But she was kind and pleasant. She'd take us berrying and on all sorts of walks, and teach us new games and tell us things. I don't remember anyone that ever did us the good she did!"

Maria Amelia's thin chest heaved with emotion, and there were tears in her eyes; but her mother took her up somewhat sharply.

"That sounds well I must say – right before your own mother that's toiled and slaved for you! It's all very well for a young thing that's got nothing on earth to do to make herself agreeable to young ones. That poor blinded father of hers never taught her to do the work a girl should – naturally he couldn't."

"At least he might have married again and given her another mother," said Susannah Jacobs, with decision, with so much decision, in fact, that the City Boarder studied her expression for a moment and concluded that if this recreant father had not married again it was not for lack of opportunity.

Mrs Simmons cast an understanding glance upon Miss Jacobs, and nodded wisely.

"Yes, he ought to have done that, of course. A man's not fit to bring up children, anyhow. How can they? Mothers have the instinct – that is, all natural mothers have. But, dear me! There's some as don't seem to *be* mothers – even when they have a child!"

"You're quite right, Mis' Simmons," agreed the mother of thirteen. "It's a divine instinct, I say. I'm sorry for the child that lacks it. Now this Esther. We always knew she wan't like other girls – she never seemed to care for dress and company and things girls naturally do, but was always philandering over the hills with a parcel of young ones. There wan't a child in town but would run after her. She made more trouble 'n a little in families, the young ones quotin' what Aunt Esther said, and tellin' what Aunt Esther did to their own mothers, and she only a young girl. Why, she actually seemed to care more for them children than she did for beaux or anything – it wasn't natural!"

"But she did marry?" pursued the City Boarder.

"Marry! Yes, she married finally. We all thought she never would, but she did. After the things her father taught her, it did seem as if he'd ruined *all* her chances. It's simply terrible the way that girl was trained."

"Him being a doctor," put in Mrs Simmons, "made it different, I suppose."

"Doctor or no doctor," Miss Jacobs rigidly interposed, "it was a crying shame to have a young girl so instructed."

"Maria 'Melia," said her mother, "I want you should get me my smelling salts. They're up in the spare chamber, I believe. When your Aunt Marcia was here she had one of her spells – don't you remember? – and she asked for salts. Look in the top bureau drawer – they must be there."

Maria Amelia, thirty-six but unmarried, withdrew dutifully, and the other ladies drew closer to the City Boarder.

"It's the most shocking thing I ever heard of," murmured Mrs Briggs. "Do you know he – a father – actually taught his daughter how babies come!"

There was a breathless hush.

"He did," eagerly chimed in the little dressmaker. "All the particulars. It was perfectly awful!"

"He said," continued Mrs Briggs, "that he expected her to be a mother and that she ought to understand what was before her!"

"He was waited on by a committee of ladies from the church, married ladies, all older than he was," explained Miss Jacobs severely. "They told him it was creating a scandal in the town – and what do you think he said?"

There was another breathless silence.

Above, the steps of Maria Amelia were heard, approaching the stairs.

"It ain't there, Ma!"

"Well, you look in the highboy and in the top drawer; they're somewhere up there," her mother replied.

Then, in a sepulchral whisper:

"He told us – yes, ma'am, I was on that committee – he told us that until young women knew what was before them as mothers, they would not do their duty in choosing a father for their children! That was his expression – 'choosing a father'! A nice thing for a young girl to be thinking of – a father for her children!"

"Yes, and more than that," inserted Miss Jacobs, who, though not on the committee, seemed familiar with its workings. "He told them –" But Mrs Briggs waved her aside and continued swiftly –

"He taught that innocent girl about – the Bad Disease! Actually!"

"He did!" said the dressmaker. "It got out, too, all over town. There wasn't a man here would have married her after that."

Miss Jacobs insisted on taking up the tale. "I understand that he said it was 'to protect her'! Protect her, indeed! Against matrimony! As if any man alive would want to marry a young girl who knew all the evil of life! I was brought up differently, I assure you!"

"Young girls should be kept innocent!" Mrs Briggs solemnly proclaimed. "Why, when I was married I knew no more what was before me than a babe unborn, and my girls were all brought up so, too!"

Then, as Maria Amelia returned with the salts, she continued more loudly. "But she did marry after all. And a mighty queer husband she got, too. He was an artist or something, made pictures for the magazines and such as that, and they do say she met him first out in the hills. That's the first 'twas known of it here, anyhow – them two traipsing about all over; him with his painting things! They married and just settled down to live with her father, for she vowed she wouldn't leave him; and he said it didn't make no difference where he lived, he took his business with him."

"They seemed very happy together," said Maria Amelia.

"Happy! Well, they might have been, I suppose. It was a pretty queer family, I think." And her mother shook her head in retrospection. "They got on all right for a while; but the old man died, and those two – well, I don't call it house-keeping – the way they lived!"

"No," said Miss Jacobs. "They spent more time out-of-doors than they did in the house. She followed him around everywhere. And for open lovemaking –"

They all showed deep disapproval at this memory. All but the City Boarder and Maria Amelia.

"She had one child, a girl," continued Mrs Briggs, "and it was just shocking to see how she neglected that child from the beginnin'. She never seemed to have no maternal feelin' at all!"

"But I thought you said she was very fond of children," remonstrated the City Boarder.

"Oh, *children*, yes. She'd take up with any dirty-faced brat in town, even them Canucks. I've seen her again and again with a whole swarm of the mill hands' young ones round her, goin' on some picnic or other – 'open air school,' she used to call it – *such* notions as she had. But when it come to her own child! Why –" Here the speaker's voice sank to a horrified hush. "She never had no baby clo'se for it! Not a single sock!"

The City Boarder was interested. "Why, what did she do with the little thing?"

"The Lord knows!" answered old Mis' Briggs. "She never would let us hardly see it when 'twas little. 'Shamed too, I don't doubt. But that's strange feelin's for a mother. Why, I was so proud of my babies! And I kept 'em lookin' so pretty! I'd 'a sat up all night and sewed and washed, but I'd 'a had my children look well!" And the poor old eyes filled with tears as she thought of the eight little graves in the churchyard, which she never failed to keep looking pretty, even now. "She just let that young one roll round in the grass like a puppy with hardly nothin' on! Why, a squaw does better. She does keep 'em done up for a spell! That child was treated worse 'n an Injun! We all done what we could, of course. We felt it no more 'n right. But she was real hateful about it, and we had to let her be."

"The child died?" asked the City Boarder.

"Died! Dear no! That's it you saw going by; a great strappin' girl she is, too, and promisin' to grow up well, thanks to Mrs. Stone's taking her. Mrs. Stone always thought a heap of Esther. It's a mercy to the child that she lost her mother, I do believe! How she ever survived that kind of treatment beats all! Why, that woman never seemed to have the first spark of maternal feeling to the end! She seemed just as fond of the other young ones after she had her own as she was before, and that's against nature. The way it happened was this. You see, they lived up the valley nearer to the lake than the village. He was away, and was coming home that night, it seems, driving from Drayton along the lake road. And she set out to meet him. She must 'a walked up to the dam to look for him; and we think maybe she saw the team clear across the lake. Maybe she thought he could get to the house and save little Esther in time – that's the only explanation we ever could put on it. But this is what she did; and you can judge for yourselves if any mother in her senses *could* 'a done such a thing! You see 'twas the time of that awful disaster, you've read of it, likely, that destroyed three villages. Well, she got to the dam and seen that 'twas givin' way – she was always great for knowin' all such things. And she just turned and ran. Jake Elder was up on the hill after a stray cow, and he seen her go. He was too far off to imagine what ailed her, but he said he never saw a woman run so in his life.

"And, if you'll believe it, she run right by her own house – never stopped – never looked at it. Just run for the village. Of course, she may have lost her head with the fright, but that wasn't like her. No, I think she had made up her mind to leave that innocent baby to die! She just ran down here and give warnin', and, of course, we sent word down valley on horseback, and there was no lives lost in all three villages. She started to run back as soon as we was 'roused, but 'twas too late then.

"Jake saw it all, though he was too far off to do a thing. He said he couldn't stir a foot, it was so awful. He seen the wagon drivin' along as nice as you please till it got close to the dam, and then Greenwood seemed to see the danger and shipped up like mad. He was the father, you know. But he wasn't quite in time – the dam give way and the water went over him like a tidal wave. She was almost to the gate when it struck the house and her – and we never found her body nor his for days and days. They was washed clear down river.

"Their house was strong, and it stood a little high and had some big trees between it and the lake, too. It was moved off the place and brought up against the side of the stone church down yonder, but 'twant wholly in pieces. And that child was found swimmin' round in its bed, most drowned, but not quite. The wonder is, it didn't die of a cold, but it's here yet – must have a strong constitution. Their folks never did nothing for it – so we had to keep it here."

"Well, now, Mother," said Maria Amelia Briggs. "It does seem to me that she did her duty. You know yourself that if she hadn't give warnin' all three of the villages would 'a been cleaned out – a matter of fifteen hundred people. And if she'd stopped to lug that child, she couldn't have got here in time. Don't you believe she was thinkin' of those mill hands' children?"

"Maria 'Melia, I'm ashamed of you!" said old Mis' Briggs. "But you ain't married and ain't a mother. A mother's duty is to her own child! She neglected her own to look after other folks' – the Lord never gave her them other children to care for!"

"Yes," said Miss Jacobs, "and here's her child, a burden on the town! She was an unnatural mother!"

9

CHARLES DICKENS

Bleak House

Bleak House, like all Dickens' novels, was originally published in monthly installments. It concerns a drawn-out inheritance case in the High Court of Chancery. In this extract John Jarndyce sends his wards Ada Clare and Richard Carstone, and their companion, Esther Summerson, to stay at Mrs Jellyby's house. Mr Kenge is John Jarndyce's lawyer and Mr Guppy works for the lawyer.

We were to pass the night, Mr Kenge told us when we arrived in his room, at Mrs Jellyby's; and then he turned to me, and said he took it for granted I knew who Mrs Jellyby was?

"I really don't, sir," I returned. "Perhaps Mr Carstone – or Miss Clare –"

But no, they knew nothing whatever about Mrs Jellyby.

"In-deed! Mrs Jellyby," said Mr Kenge, standing with his back to the fire, and casting his eyes over the dusty hearth-rug as if it were Mrs Jellyby's biography, "is a lady of very remarkable strength of character, who devotes herself entirely to the public. She has devoted herself to an extensive variety of public subjects, at various times, and is at present (until something else attracts her) devoted to the subject of Africa; with a view to the general cultivation of the coffee berry – *and* the natives – and the happy settlement, on the banks of the African rivers, of our superabundant home population. Mr Jarndyce, who is desirous to aid in any work that is considered likely to be a good work, and who is much sought after by philanthropists, has, I believe, a very high opinion of Mrs Jellyby."

Mr Kenge, adjusting his cravat, then looked at us.

"And Mr Jellyby, sir?" suggested Richard.

"Ah! Mr Jellyby," said Mr Kenge, "is – a – I don't know that I can describe him to you better than by saying that he is the husband of Mrs Jellyby."

"A nonentity, sir?" said Richard with a droll look.

"I don't say that," returned Mr Kenge, gravely. "I can't say that, indeed, for I know nothing whatever *of* Mr Jellyby. I never, to my knowledge, had the pleasure of seeing Mr Jellyby. He may be a very superior man; but he is, so to speak,

---

CHARLES DICKENS, from Chapter 4 ("Telescopic Philanthropy") in *Bleak House*, first published in 1852–3.

merged – Merged – in the more shining qualities of his wife." Mr Kenge proceeded to tell us that as the road to Bleak House would have been very long, dark, and tedious, on such an evening, and as we had been travelling already, Mr Jarndyce had himself proposed this arrangement. A carriage would be at Mrs Jellyby's to convey us out of town, early in the forenoon of to-morrow. [. . .]

[W]e turned up under an archway, to our destination: a narrow street of high houses, like an oblong cistern to hold the fog. There was a confused little crowd of people, principally children, gathered about the house at which we stopped, which had a tarnished brass plate on the door, with the inscription, Jellyby.

"Don't be frightened!" said Mr Guppy, looking in at the coach-window. "One of the young Jellybys been and got his head through the area railings!"

"O poor child," said I, "let me out, if you please!"

"Pray be careful of yourself, miss. The young Jellybys are always up to something," said Mr Guppy.

I made my way to the poor child, who was one of the dirtiest little unfortunates I ever saw, and found him very hot and frightened, and crying loudly, fixed by the neck between two iron railings, while a milkman and a beadle, with the kindest intentions possible, were endeavouring to drag him back by the legs, under a general impression that his skull was compressible by those means. As I found (after pacifying him), that he was a little boy, with a naturally large head, I thought that, perhaps, where his head could go, his body could follow, and mentioned that the best mode of extrication might be to push him forward. This was so favorably received by the milkman and beadle, that he would immediately have been pushed into the area, if I had not held his pinafore, while Richard and Mr Guppy ran down through the kitchen, to catch him when he should be released. At last he was happily got down without any accident, and then he began to beat Mr Guppy with a hoop-stick in quite a frantic manner.

Nobody had appeared belonging to the house, except a person in pattens, who had been poking at the child from below with a broom; I don't know with what object, and I don't think she did. I therefore supposed that Mrs Jellyby was not at home; and was quite surprised when the person appeared in the passage without the pattens, and going up to the back room on the first floor, before Ada and me, announced us as, "Them two young ladies, Missis Jellyby!" We passed several more children on the way up, whom it was difficult to avoid treading on in the dark; and as we came into Mrs Jellyby's presence, one of the poor little things fell down stairs – down a whole flight (as it sounded to me), with a great noise.

Mrs Jellyby, whose face reflected none of the uneasiness which we could not help showing in our own faces, as the dear child's head recorded its passage with a bump on every stair – Richard afterwards said he counted seven, besides one for the landing – received us with perfect equanimity. She was a pretty, very diminutive, plump woman, of from forty to fifty, with handsome eyes, though they had a curious habit of seeming to look a long way off. As if – I am quoting Richard again – they could see nothing nearer than Africa!

---

pattens – wooden soled shoes, usually worn to keep feet out of mud

"I am very glad indeed," said Mrs Jellyby, in an agreeable voice, "to have the pleasure of receiving you. I have a great respect for Mr Jarndyce; and no one in whom he is interested can be an object of indifference to me."

We expressed our acknowledgments, and sat down behind the door where there was a lame invalid of a sofa. Mrs Jellyby had very good hair, but was too much occupied with her African duties to brush it. The shawl in which she had been loosely muffled, dropped on to her chair when she advanced to us; and as she turned to resume her seat, we could not help noticing that her dress didn't nearly meet up the back, and that the open space was railed across with a lattice-work of stay-lace – like a summer-house.

The room, which was strewn with papers and nearly filled by a great writing-table covered with similar litter, was, I must say, not only very untidy, but very dirty. We were obliged to take notice of that with our sense of sight, even while, with our sense of hearing, we followed the poor child who had tumbled down stairs: I think into the back kitchen, where somebody seemed to stifle him.

But what principally struck us was a jaded, and unhealthy-looking, though by no means plain girl, at the writing-table, who sat biting the feather of her pen, and staring at us. I suppose nobody ever was in such a state of ink. And, from her tumbled hair to her pretty feet, which were disfigured with frayed and broken satin slippers trodden down at heel, she really seemed to have no article of dress upon her, from a pin upwards, that was in its proper condition or its right place.

"You find me, my dears," said Mrs Jellyby, snuffing the two great office candles in tin candlesticks which made the room taste strongly of hot tallow (the fire had gone out, and there was nothing in the grate but ashes, a bundle of wood, and a poker), "you find me, my dears, as usual, very busy; but that you will excuse. The African project at present employs my whole time. It involves me in correspondence with public bodies, and with private individuals anxious for the welfare of their species all over the country. I am happy to say it is advancing. We hope by this time next year to have from a hundred and fifty to two hundred healthy families cultivating coffee and educating the natives of Borrioboola-Gha, on the left bank of the Niger."

As Ada said nothing, but looked at me, I said it must be very gratifying.

"It *is* gratifying," said Mrs Jellyby. "It involves the devotion of all my energies, such as they are; but that is nothing, so that it succeeds; and I am more confident of success every day. Do you know, Miss Summerson, I almost wonder that *you* never turned your thoughts to Africa?"

This application of the subject was really so unexpected to me, that I was quite at a loss how to receive it. I hinted that the climate –

"The finest climate in the world!" said Mrs Jellyby.

"Indeed, ma'am?"

"Certainly. With precaution," said Mrs Jellyby. "You may go into Holborn, without precaution, and be run over. You may go into Holborn, with precaution, and never be run over. Just so with Africa."

I said, "No doubt." – I meant as to Holborn.

"If you would like," said Mrs Jellyby, putting a number of papers towards us, "to look over some remarks on that head, and on the general subject (which have been extensively circulated), while I finish a letter I am now dictating – to my eldest daughter, who is my amanuensis –"

The girl at the table left off biting her pen, and made a return to our recognition, which was half bashful and half sulky.

"– I shall then have finished for the present," proceeded Mrs Jellyby, with a sweet smile; "though my work is never done. Where are you, Caddy?"

"'Presents her compliments to Mr Swallow, and begs –'" said Caddy.

"'– And begs,'" said Mrs Jellyby, dictating, "'to inform him, in reference to his letter of inquiry on the African project.' – No, Peepy! Not on any account!"

Peepy (so self-named) was the unfortunate child who had fallen down stairs, who now interrupted the correspondence by presenting himself, with a strip of plaister on his forehead, to exhibit his wounded knees, in which Ada and I did not know which to pity most – the bruises or the dirt. Mrs Jellyby merely added, with the serene composure with which she said everything, "Go along, you naughty Peepy!" and fixed her fine eyes on Africa again.

However, as she at once proceeded with her dictation, and as I interrupted nothing by doing it, I ventured quietly to stop poor Peepy as he was going out, and to take him up to nurse. He looked very much astonished at it, and at Ada's kissing him; but soon fell fast asleep in my arms, sobbing at longer and longer intervals, until he was quiet. I was so occupied with Peepy that I lost the letter in detail, though I derived such a general impression from it of the momentous importance of Africa, and the utter insignificance of all other places and things, that I felt quite ashamed to have thought so little about it.

"Six o'clock!" said Mrs Jellyby. "And our dinner hour is nominally (for we dine at all hours) five! Caddy, show Miss Clare and Miss Summerson their rooms. You will like to make some change, perhaps? You will excuse me, I know, being so much occupied. O, that very bad child! Pray put him down, Miss Summerson!"

I begged permission to retain him, truly saying that he was not at all troublesome; and carried him upstairs and laid him on my bed. Ada and I had two upper rooms, with a door of communication between. They were excessively bare and disorderly, and the curtain to my window was fastened up with a fork.

"You would like some hot water, wouldn't you?" said Miss Jellyby, looking round for a jug with a handle to it, but looking in vain.

"If it is not being troublesome," said we.

"O, it's not the trouble," returned Miss Jellyby; "the question is, if there *is* any."

The evening was so very cold, and the rooms had such a marshy smell, that I must confess it was a little miserable; and Ada was half crying. We soon laughed, however, and were busily unpacking, when Miss Jellyby came back to say, that she was sorry there was no hot water; but they couldn't find the kettle, and the boiler was out of order.

We begged her not to mention it, and made all the haste we could to get down to the fire again. But all the little children had come up to the landing outside, to look at the phenomenon of Peepy lying on my bed; and our attention was distracted by the constant apparition of noses and fingers, in situations of danger between the hinges of the doors. It was impossible to shut the door of either room; for my lock, with no knob to it, looked as if it wanted to be wound up; and though the handle of Ada's went round and round with the greatest smoothness, it was attended with no effect whatever on the door. Therefore I proposed to the children that they should come in and be very good at my table, and I would tell them the story of little Red Riding Hood while I dressed; which they did, and were as quiet as mice, including Peepy, who awoke opportunely before the appearance of the wolf.

When we went downstairs we found a mug, with "A Present from Tunbridge Wells" on it, lighted up in the staircase window with a floating wick; and a young woman, with a swelled face bound up in a flannel bandage, blowing the fire of the drawing-room (now connected by an open door with Mrs Jellyby's room), and choaking dreadfully. It smoked to that degree in short, that we all sat coughing and crying with the windows open for half an hour; during which Mrs Jellyby, with the same sweetness of temper, directed letters about Africa. Her being so employed was, I must say, a great relief to me; for Richard told us that he had washed his hands in a pie-dish, and that they had found the kettle on his dressing-table; and he made Ada laugh so, that they made me laugh in the most ridiculous manner.

Soon after seven o'clock we went down to dinner; carefully, by Mrs Jellyby's advice; for the stair-carpets, besides being very deficient in stair-wires, were so torn as to be absolute traps. We had a fine cod-fish, a piece of roast beef, a dish of cutlets, and a pudding; an excellent dinner, if it had had any cooking to speak of, but it was almost raw. The young woman with the flannel bandage waited, and dropped everything on the table wherever it happened to go, and never moved it again until she put it on the stairs. The person I had seen in pattens (who I suppose to have been the cook), frequently came and skirmished with her at the door, and there appeared to be ill-will between them.

All through dinner; which was long, in consequence of such accidents as the dish of potatoes being mislaid in the coal skuttle, and the handle of the corkscrew coming off, and striking the young woman in the chin; Mrs Jellyby preserved the evenness of her disposition. She told us a great deal that was interesting about Borrioboola-Gha and the natives; and received so many letters that Richard, who sat by her, saw four envelopes in the gravy at once. Some of the letters were proceedings of ladies' committees, or resolutions of ladies' meetings, which she read to us; others were applications from people excited in various ways about the cultivation of coffee, and natives; others required answers, and these she sent her eldest daughter from the table three or four times to write. She was full of business, and undoubtedly was, as she had told us, devoted to the cause.

I was a little curious to know who a mild bald gentleman in spectacles was, who dropped into a vacant chair (there was no top or bottom in particular) after the fish was taken away, and seemed passively to submit himself to Borrioboola-Gha, but not to be actively interested in that settlement. As he never spoke a word, he might have been a native, but for his complexion. It was not until we left the table, and he remained alone with Richard, that the possibility of his being Mr Jellyby ever entered my head. But he *was* Mr Jellyby; and a loquacious young man called Mr Quale, with large shining knobs for temples, and his hair all brushed to the back of his head, who came in the evening, and told Ada he was a philanthropist, also informed her that he called the matrimonial alliance of Mrs Jellyby with Mr Jellyby the union of mind and matter.

This young man, besides having a great deal to say for himself about Africa, and a project of his for teaching the coffee colonists to teach the natives to turn piano-forte legs and establish an export trade, delighted in drawing Mrs Jellyby out by saying, "I believe now, Mrs Jellyby, you have received as many as from one hundred and fifty to two hundred letters respecting Africa in a single day, have you not?" or, "If my memory does not deceive me, Mrs Jellyby, you once mentioned that you had sent off five thousand circulars from one post-office at one time?" – always repeating Mrs Jellyby's answer to us like an interpreter. During the whole evening, Mr Jellyby sat in a corner with his head against the wall, as if he were subject to low spirits. It seemed that he had several times opened his mouth when alone with Richard, after dinner, as if he had something on his mind; but had always shut it again, to Richard's extreme confusion, without saying anything.

Mrs Jellyby, sitting in quite a nest of waste paper, drank coffee all the evening, and dictated at intervals to her eldest daughter. She also held a discussion with Mr Quale; of which the subject seemed to be – if I understood it – the Brother-hood of Humanity; and gave utterance to some beautiful sentiments. I was not so attentive an auditor as I might have wished to be, however, for Peepy and the other children came flocking about Ada and me in a corner of the drawing-room to ask for another story: so we sat down among them, and told them in whispers Puss in Boots and I don't know what else, until Mrs Jellyby, accidentally remembering them, sent them to bed. As Peepy cried for me to take him to bed, I carried him upstairs; where the young woman with the flannel bandage charged into the midst of the little family like a dragoon, and overturned them into cribs.

After that, I occupied myself in making our room a little tidy, and in coaxing a very cross fire that had been lighted, to burn; which at last it did, quite brightly. On my return downstairs, I felt that Mrs Jellyby looked down upon me rather, for being so frivolous; and I was sorry for it; though at the same time I knew that I had no higher pretensions.

It was nearly midnight before we found an opportunity of going to bed; and even then we left Mrs Jellyby among her papers drinking coffee, and Miss Jellyby biting the feather of her pen.

"What a strange house!" said Ada, when we got upstairs. "How curious of my cousin Jarndyce to send us here!"

"My love," said I, "it quite confuses me. I want to understand it, and I can't understand it at all."

"What?" asked Ada, with her pretty smile.

"All this, my dear," said I. "It *must* be very good of Mrs Jellyby to take such pains about a scheme for the benefit of Natives – and yet – Peepy and the housekeeping!"

Ada laughed; and put her arm about my neck, as I stood looking at the fire; and told me I was a quiet, dear, good creature, and had won her heart. "You are so thoughtful, Esther," she said, "and yet so cheerful! and you do so much, so unpretendingly! You would make a home out of even this house."

10

JOSEPH KANON

The Good German

Reporter Jake Geismar, the hero of *The Good German*, has returned to Berlin in July 1945. In the first of these three extracts from the novel he is attending the trial of Renate Naumann, who worked for him as a "stringer" before the war.

Renate stood behind a cagelike railing of new plywood next to the bench, facing the room, as if her expression during the testimony would be recorded as a kind of evidence. Behind her stood two soldiers with machine guns, gazing stolidly at her back. Bernie said she had changed, but she was recognizably the same – thinner, with the hollowed-out look you saw everywhere in Berlin, but still Renate. Only her dark hair was different, cropped close and turned a premature, indeterminate pale. She was dressed in a loose gray prison shift, belted, her collarbones sticking out, and the face he remembered as pretty and animated seemed rearranged – beaten, perhaps, or somehow disfigured by her life. But there were the eyes, sharp and knowing, glancing defiantly around the crowd as if she were even now looking for news items. The same way, Jake thought, she must have hunted for Jews.

She spotted him instantly, raising her eyebrows in surprise, then dropping them in bewilderment. A friend sitting at the table of her accusers. Did she think he was there to testify against her? What would he have said? A girl with a quick smile who liked to take chances, bold enough to cadge a cigarette from a Nazi on a train platform. A sharp eye, trained for snatching prey in the street. How could she have done it? But that was always the question – how could any of them have done it? He wanted suddenly to signal some absurd reassurance. I remember who you were. Not a monster, not then. How can I judge? But who could? Three Russian soldiers on a makeshift platform, whose fleshy faces seemed to ask no questions at all.

They were only minutes into the trial before Jake realized they hadn't come to establish guilt, just the sentence. And was there any doubt? The Germans had kept

JOSEPH KANON, pp. 243–7, 255–8, and 330–8 from *The Good German*. New York: Henry Holt and Co., 2001. © 2001 by Joseph Kanon. Reprinted by permission of Henry Holt and Company, LLC and by permission of the author c/o Rogers, Coleridge & White Ltd, 20 Powis Mews, London, W11 1JN, UK.

records of her activity, more columns of numbers. As the prosecution read out its indictments, Jake watched her lower her head, as if she too were overwhelmed by the sweep of it, all the snatches, one by one, until finally there were enough to fill boxcars. So many. Had she known them all, or just guessed, smelling fear when it walked into one of her cafés? Each number a face-to-face moment, real to her, not anonymous like a pilot opening the bomb bay.

The method was as Bernie had described – the sighting, the hurried call, the nod of her head to make the arrest, her colleagues bundling people into cars as she walked away. Why hadn't she kept walking? Instead she'd gone back to the collection center, her room there its own kind of short leash, but still not a prison. Why not just keep walking away? Gunther had moved his wife fourteen times. But he had had papers and friends prepared to help. No U-boat could survive alone. Where, after all, would she have gone?

The Russian prosecutor then switched, oddly, to a detailed account of Renate's own capture, the manhunt that finally ran her to ground in a basement in Wedding. For a moment Jake thought the Soviets were simply congratulating themselves for the press, now busily taking notes. Then he noticed Bernie in a lawyer's huddle, heard Gunther mentioned by name as the hunter, and saw that it was something more – the old DA's ploy, establishing your witness, the good guy in the neat jacket and tie. He needn't have bothered. The story, with its breathless chase, seemed lost on the first judge, who shifted in his seat and lit a cigarette. The Russian next to him leaned over and whispered. The judge, annoyed, put it out and gazed at the window, where a standing fan was lazily moving the stuffy air. Apparently an unexpected western custom. Jake wondered how long it would take to call a recess.

He'd assumed from the buildup that Gunther would be the star witness. Who else was there? The records supplied the mechanics of the crime, but its victims were dead, no longer able to accuse. Gunther had actually seen her do it. And a DA always started with the police, to weight his case at the beginning. The first person called, however, was a Frau Gersh, a more theatrical choice, a frail woman who had to be helped to the witness chair on crutches. The prosecutor began, solicitously, with her feet.

"From frostbite. On the death march," she said, halting but matter-of-fact. "They made us leave the camp so the Russians wouldn't find out. We had to walk in the snow. If you fell, they shot you."

"But you were fortunate."

"No, I fell. They shot me. Here," she said, pointing to her hip. "They thought I was dead, so they left me. But I couldn't move. In the snow. So the feet."

She spoke simply, her voice low, so that chairs creaked as people strained forward to hear. Then she looked over at Renate.

"The camp where she sent me," she said, louder, spitting it out.

"I didn't know", Renate said, shaking her head. "I didn't know."

The judge glared at her, startled to hear her speak but unsure what to do about it. No one seemed to know what the rules were supposed to be, least of all the defense attorney, who could only silence her with a wave of his hand and nod at the judge, an uneasy apology.

"She did!" the woman said, forceful now. "She knew."

"Frau Gersh," the prosecutor said deliberately, as if the outburst hadn't happened, "do you recognize the prisoner?"

"Of course. The *greifer*."

"She was known to you personally?"

"No. But I know that face. She came for me, with the men."

"That was the first time you saw her?"

"No. She talked to me at the shoe repair. I should have known, but I didn't. Then, that same afternoon –"

"The shoe repair?" one of the judges said, confusing the past with the crutches now on display.

"One of her contacts," the prosecutor said. "People in hiding wore out their shoes – from all the walking, to keep moving. So Fräulein Naumann made friends with the shoe men. 'Who's been in today? Any strangers?' She found many this way. This particular shop –" He made a show of checking his notes. "In Schöneberg. Hauptstrasse. That's correct?"

"Yes, Hauptstrasse," Frau Gersh said.

Jake looked at Renate. Clever, if that's what you were after, collecting items from cobblers. All her news-gathering tricks, offered to murderers.

"So she talked to you there?"

"Yes, you know, the weather, the raids. Just to talk. I didn't like it – I had to be careful – so I left."

"And went home?"

"No, I had to be careful. I walked to Viktoria Park, then here and there. But when I got back, she was there. With the men. The others – good German people, helping me – were already gone. She sent them away too."

"I must point out," the defense lawyer said, "that at this time, 1944, it was against the law for German citizens to hide Jews. This was an illegal act."

The judge looked at him, amazed. "We are not interested in German law," he said finally. "Are you suggesting that Fräulein Naumann acted correctly?"

"I'm suggesting that she acted legally." He looked down. "At the time."

"Go on," the judge said to the prosecutor. "Finish it."

"You were taken away then. On what charge?"

"Charge? I was a Jew."

"How did Fräulein Naumann know this? You hadn't told her?"

Frau Gersh shrugged. "She said she could always tell. I have papers, I said. No, she told them, she's a Jew. And of course they listened to her. She worked for them."

The prosecutor turned to Renate. "Did you say this?"

"She was a Jew."

"You could tell. How?"

"The look she had."

"What kind of look was that?"

Renate lowered her eyes. "A Jewish look."

---

greifer – from verb meaning to grip or seize, i.e. one who seizes others

"May I ask the prisoner – such a skill – were you ever mistaken?"

Renate looked at him directly. "No, never. I always knew."

Jake sat back, feeling sick. Proud of it. His old friend.

"Continue, Frau Gersh. You were taken where?"

"The Jewish Old Age Home. Grosse Hamburger Strasse." A precise detail, coached.

"And what happened there?"

"We were held until they had enough to fill a truck. Then to the train. Then east," she said, her voice dropping.

"To the camp," the prosecutor finished.

"Yes, to the camp. To the gas. I was healthy, so I worked, The others –" She broke off, then looked again at Renate. "The others you sent were killed."

"I didn't send them. I didn't know," Renate said.

This time the judge held up his hand to silence her.

"You *saw*. You saw," the woman shouted.

"Frau Gersh," the prosecutor said, his calm voice a substitute for a gavel, "can you positively identify the prisoner as the woman who came to your house to arrest you?"

"Yes, positive."

Bernie leaned over in another huddle.

"And did you see her again?"

Jake glanced at the prosecutor, wondering where he was heading.

"Yes, from the truck. She was watching us from her window. When they took us away. Watching."

An echo of the story from Bernie. A shoe shop in Schöneberg, the American sector. So Bernie had found her, another gift to the Russians.

"The same woman. You're positive."

Now the woman was shaking, slipping out of control. "The same. The same." She started to rise from the chair, staring at Renate. "A Jew. Killing your own. You watched them take us away." The beginning of a sob, no longer in court. "Your own people. Animal! Eating your own, like an animal."

"No!" Renate shouted back.

The judge slapped the desk with his palm and said something in Russian, presumably calling a recess, but the prosecutor hurried up to the bench and began whispering. The judge nodded, slightly taken aback, then said formally to the room, "We will stop for fifteen minutes, but first the photographers will be allowed in. The prisoner will remain standing."

The next witness is former police officer Gunther Behn, who testifies that Renate betrayed his Jewish wife Marthe to the SS.

"Were you at the Café Heil? Did you report Marthe Behn? Did you identify her? Answer."

"Yes," Renate said.

"Not a stranger. A woman you knew," the prosecutor said, his voice rising.

"I had to." She looked down. "You don't understand. I needed one more that week. The quota. There were not so many left then. I needed one more."

Jake felt his stomach move. A number to fill the truck.

"To save yourself."

"Not for myself," she said, shaking her head. "Not for myself."

"Fräulein Naumann," the defense said, formal again. "Please tell the court who was also being held in custody in Grosse Hamburger Strasse."

"My mother."

"Under what conditions?"

"She was kept there so that I would come back in the evening, when my work was finished," she said, resigned now, aware that it wouldn't matter. But she had lifted her head and was looking at Jake, the way a public speaker pinpoints a face in an audience, talking only to him, a private explanation, the interview they probably would never have. "They knew I wouldn't leave her. We were taken together. First to work at Siemenstadt. Slaves. Then, when the deportations started, they told me they would keep her name off the list if I worked for them. So many every week. I couldn't send her east."

"So you sent other Jews," the prosecutor said.

"But then there were not so many left," she said, still to Jake.

"To – what did you call them? – labor camps."

"Yes, labor camps. But she was an old woman. I knew the conditions were hard. To survive that –"

"But that's not all you did, is it?" the prosecutor said, pressing now. "Your superior" – he glanced at a paper – "Hans Becker. We have testimony that you were intimate with him. Were you intimate with him?"

"Yes," she said, her eyes on Jake. "That too."

"And did he keep your mother off the list? For your good efforts?"

"At first. Then he sent her to Theresienstadt. He said it was easier there." She paused. "He ran out of names."

"Tell the court what happened to her there," the defense said.

"She died."

"But you continued your work after that," the prosecutor said. "You still came back every night, didn't you?"

"By then, where could I go? The Jews knew about me – I couldn't hide with them. There was no one."

"Except Hans Becker. You continued your relations with him."

"Yes."

"Even after he deported your mother."

"Yes."

"And you still say you were protecting her?"

"Does it matter to you what I say?" she said wearily.

"When it's the truth, yes."

"The truth? The truth is that he forced me. Over and over. He liked that. I kept my mother alive. I kept myself alive. I did what I had to do. I thought, there's nothing worse than this, but it will end, the Russians will come. Not much longer. Then you came and hunted me down like a dog. Becker's girlfriend, they called me. Girlfriend, when he did that to me. What is my crime? That I'm still alive?"

"Fräulein, that's not the crime here."

"No, the punishment," she said to Jake. "Still alive."

"Yes," Gunther said unexpectedly from the witness chair, but not looking anywhere, so that no one was sure what he meant.

The Russian prosecutor cleared his throat. "I'm sure we're all enlightened to hear that the Nazis are to blame for everything, fräulein. A pity, perhaps, that you did their work so well."

"I did what I had to do," she said, still staring, until finally Jake had to look away. What did she expect him to say? I forgive you?

"Are you finished with the witness?" the judge said, restless.

"One more question," the defense said. "Herr Behn, you're a large man. Strong. You did not struggle with the men in the café?"

"With Gestapo? No."

"No, you saved yourself." A pointed look at Renate. "Or, to be exact, your wife saved you. I believe that's what you said."

"Yes, she saved me. It was too late for her, once they knew."

"And after this you remained on the police force?"

"Yes."

"Enforcing the laws of the government that had arrested your wife."

"The racial laws were not our responsibility."

"I see. Some of the laws, then. Not all. But you made arrests?"

"Of criminals, yes."

"And they were sent where?"

"To prison."

"So late in the war? Most were sent to 'labor camps,' weren't they?"

Gunther said nothing.

"Tell us, how did you decide which laws to enforce for the National Socialists?"

"Decide? It wasn't for me to decide. I was a policeman. I had no choice."

"I see. So only Fräulein Naumann had this choice."

"I object," the prosecutor said. "This is nonsense. The situations were not at all similar. What is the defense trying to suggest?"

"That this testimony is compromised from start to finish. This is a personal grievance, not Soviet justice. You hold this woman accountable for the crimes of the Nazis? She had no choice. Listen to your own witness. No one had a choice."

The only possible defense left. Everyone was guilty; no one was guilty.

"She had a choice," Gunther said, his voice thick.

The defense nodded, pleased with himself, finally where he wanted to be.

"Did you?"

"Don't answer," the prosecutor said quickly.

But Gunther raised his head, unflinching — a moment he'd expected, even if Bernie hadn't, the other reckoning. Not to be put off, even by a bottle to blot himself out. He gazed straight ahead, eyes stone.

"Yes, I had a choice. And I worked for them too," he said, his voice as firm and steady as the hand on the razor. "Her murderers. Even after that."

The room, suddenly embarrassed, was silent. Not the answer any of them had wanted, a little death, pulled out of him like Liz's gasp. One cut.

He turned to Renate. "We all did," he said, his voice lower now. "But you – you could have looked away. Your friend. Just the once."

At this she did look away, facing the stenographers, so that her words were almost lost.

"I needed one more," she said, as if it answered everything. "One more."

After the trial Renate asks Jake to visit her in prison.

At the detention center near the Alex he was shown into a small room as plain as the makeshift court – a single table, two chairs, a picture of Stalin. The escort, with elaborate courtesy, offered coffee and then left him alone to wait. Nothing to look at but the ceiling fixture, a frosted glass bowl that might once have been lighted with gas, a Wilhelmine leftover. Renate was led in through the opposite door by two guards, who left her at the table and positioned themselves against the wall, still as sconces.

"Hello, Jake," she said, her smile so tentative that her face seemed not to move at all. The same pale gray smock and roughly cut hair.

"Renate."

"Give me a cigarette – they'll think you have permission," she said in English, sitting down.

"You want to do this in English?"

"Some, so they won't suspect anything. One of them speaks German. Thank you," she said, switching now to German as she took the light and inhaled. "My god, it's better than food. You never lose your taste for it. I'm not allowed to smoke, back there. Where is your notebook?"

"I don't need one," Jake said, confused. Suspect what?

"No, please, I want you to write things down. You have it?"

He pulled the pad out of his pocket, noticing for the first time that her hand was trembling, nervous under the sure voice. The cigarette shook a little as she lowered it to the ashtray.

He busied himself with his pen, at a loss. Ask her how it felt, Gunther said, but what could she possibly say? A hundred nods, watching people being bundled into cars.

"It's so difficult to look at me?"

Reluctantly he raised his head and met her eyes, still familiar under the jagged hair.

"I don't know how to talk to you," he said simply.

She nodded. "The worst person in the world. I know – that's what you see. Worse than anybody."

"I didn't say that."

"But you don't look, either. Worse than anybody. How could she do those things? That's the first question?"

"If you like."

"Do you know the answer? She didn't – somebody else did. In here." She tapped her chest. "Two people. One is the monster. The other is the same person you used to know. The same. Look at that one. Can you do that? Just for now. They don't even know she exists," she said, tilting her head slightly toward the guards. "But you do."

Jake said nothing, waiting.

"Write something, please. We don't have much time." Another jerky pull on the cigarette, anxious.

"Why did you ask to see me?"

"Because you know me. Not this other person. You remember those days?" She looked up from the ashtray. "You wanted to sleep with me once. Yes, don't deny it. And you know, I would have said yes. In those days, the Americans, they were all glamorous to us. Like people in the films. Everyone wanted to go there. I would have said yes. Isn't it funny, how things turn out."

Jake looked at her, appalled; her voice was wavering like her hand, edgy and intimate at the same time, the desperate energy of a crazy person.

He glanced down at the notebook, anchoring himself. "Is that what you want? To talk about old times?"

"Yes, a little," she said in English. "Please. It's important for them." Her eyes moved to the guards again, then fixed back on him, steady, not crazy. A girl getting away with something. "So," she said in her German voice, "what happened to everybody? Do you know?"

When he didn't answer, still disconcerted, she reached over to touch his hand. "Tell me."

"Hal went back to the States," he began, confused, watching her. "At least, he was on his way the last time I saw him." She nodded, encouraging him to go on. "Remember Hannelore? She's here, in Berlin. I saw her. Thinner. She kept his flat." The small talk of catching up. What did the guards make of it, standing under Stalin?

Renate nodded, taking another cigarette. "They were lovers."

"So she said. I never knew."

"Well, I was a better reporter."

"The best," he said, smiling a little, involuntarily drawn back with her. "Nothing escaped you." He stopped, embarrassed, in the room again.

"No. It's a talent," she said, looking away. "And you? What happened to you?"

"I write for magazines."

"No more radio. And your voice was so good."

"Renate, we need to –"

"And Lena?" she said, ignoring him. "She's alive?"

Jake nodded. "She's here. With me."

Her face softened. "I'm happy for you. So many years. She left the husband?"

"She will, when they find him. He's missing."

"When who finds him?"

"The Americans want him to work for them – a scientist. He's a valuable piece of property."

"Is he?" she said to herself, intrigued by this. "And always so quiet. How things turn out." She looked back at him. "So they're all still alive."

"Well, I haven't heard from Nanny Wendt."

"Nanny Wendt," she said, her voice distant, in a kind of reverie. "I used to think about all of you. From that time. You know, I was happy. I loved the work. You did that for me. No German would do that, not then. Even off the books. I wondered, sometimes, why you did. Not even Jewish. You could have been arrested."

"Maybe I was too dumb to know any better."

"When I saw you in the court –" She lowered her head, her voice trailing off. "Now he knows too, I thought. Now he'll only see her." She tapped the right side of her chest. "The *greifer.*"

"But you still asked to see me."

"There's no one else. You helped me once. You remember who I was."

Jake shifted in his chair, awkward. "Renate, I can't help you. I have nothing to do with the court."

"Oh that," she said, waving her cigarette. "No, not that. They'll hang me, I know it. I'm going to die," she said easily.

"They're not going to hang you."

"It's so different? They'll send me east. No one comes back from the east. Always the east. First the Nazis, now them. No one comes back. I used to see them go. I know."

"You said you didn't know."

"I knew," she said, pointing again, then to the other side. "She didn't. She didn't want to know. How else to do it? Every week, more faces. How could you do it if you knew? After a while she could do anything. No tears. A job. It's all true, what they said in there. The shoes, the Café Heil, all of it. And the work camps, she thought that. How else could she do it? That's what happened to her."

Jake looked up, nodding to her real side. "And what happened to her?"

"Yes," she said wearily, "you came for that. Go ahead, write." She sat up, darting her eyes sideways to the guards. "Where shall we start? After you left? The visa never came. Twenty-six marks. A birth certificate, four passport pictures, and twenty-six marks. That's all. Except somebody had to take you, and there were too many Jews already. Even with my English. I can still speak it. You see?" she said, switching. "Not a bad accent. Speak for a while – they'll think I'm showing off for you. So they'll be used to it."

"The accent's fine," Jake said, still confused but meeting her gaze, "but I'm not sure I understand everything you're saying."

"Any change of expression from them?" she said.

"No."

"So I stayed in Berlin," she said in German. "And of course things got worse. The stars. The special benches in the park. You know all that. Then the Jews had to work in factories. I was in Siemenstadt. My mother too, an old woman. She could barely stand at the end of the day. Still, we were alive. Then the roundups started. Our names were there. I knew what it would mean – how could she live? So we went underground."

"U-boats?"

"Yes, that's how I knew, you see. How it was, what they would do. All their tricks. The shoes – no one else thought of that. So clever, they told me. But I knew. I had the same problem, so I knew they would go there. And of course they did."

"But you didn't stay underground."

"No, they caught me."

"How?"

She smiled to herself, a grimace. "A *greifer*. A boy I used to know. He always liked me. I wouldn't go with him – a Jew. I never thought of myself as Jewish, you see. I was – what? German. To think of that now. An idiot. But there he was, in the café, and I knew he must be underground, too, by that time. I hadn't spoken to anyone in days. Do you know what that's like, not to talk? You get hungry for it, like food. And I knew he liked me and I thought maybe he would help me. Anyone who could help –"

"And did he?"

She shrugged. "To the Gestapo car. They took me in and beat me. Not so bad, not like some of the others, but enough. So I knew I wasn't German anymore. And the next time would be worse. They wanted to know where my mother was. I didn't tell them, but I knew I would the next time. And then he did help. He had friends there – friends, the devils he worked for. He said he could make a bargain for me. I could work with him and they'd keep us off the list, my mother too. If I went with him. After this? I said. And you know what he said to me? 'It's never too late to make a bargain in this life. Only in the next.'" She paused. "So I went with him. That was the bargain. He got me and I kept my life. The first time I was sent out, we went together. His pupil. But I was the one who spotted the woman that day. I knew the look, you see. And after the first time – well, what does it matter how many, it's just the first one, over and over."

"What happened to him?"

"He was deported. When he was with me, it was all right for him. We were a team. But then they split us up, and on his own he was not so successful. I was the one, I had the eye. He had nothing to bargain anymore. So." She squashed out the cigarette.

"But you did," Jake said, watching her.

"Well, I was better at it. And Becker liked me. I kept my looks. You see here?" She pointed to her left cheek, folded up near the edge of her eye. "Only this. When they beat me, my face was swollen, but it went down. Only this. And Becker liked that. It reminded him, maybe. I don't know of what." She looked away, finally distressed. "Oh my god, how can we talk this way? How can I describe what it was like? What difference does it make? Write anything you want. It can't be worse. You think I'm making excuses. It was David, it was Becker. Yes, and it was me. I thought I could do this, that we could talk, but when I talk about it – look at your face – you see *her*. The one who killed her own. That's what they want for the magazines."

"I'm just trying to understand it."

"Understand it? You want to understand what happened in Germany? How can you understand a nightmare? How could I do it? How could they do it? You wake up, you still can't explain it. You begin to think maybe it never happened at all. How could it? That's why they have to get rid of me. No evidence, no *greifer*, it never happened."

She was shaking her head and looking away, her eyes beginning to fill.

"Now look. I thought I was finished with that, no tears. Not like my mother. She cried enough for both. 'How can you do this?' Well, it was easy for her. I had to do the work, not her. Every time I looked at her, tears. You know when they stopped? When she got in the truck. Absolutely dry. I thought, she's relieved not to have to live this way anymore. To see me."

Jake took a handkerchief from his back pocket and handed it to her. "She didn't think that."

Renate blew her nose, still shaking her head. "No, she did. But what could I do? Oh, stop," she said to herself, wiping her face. "I didn't want to do this, not in front of you. I wanted you to see the old Renate, so you would help."

Jack put down the pen. "Renate," he said quietly, "you know it won't make any difference what I write. It's a Soviet court. It doesn't matter to them."

"No, not that. I need your help. Please." She reached for his hand again. "You're the last chance. It's finished for me. Then I saw you in the court and I thought, not yet, not yet, there's one more chance. He'll do it."

"Do what?"

"Oh, look at this," she said, wiping her eyes again. "I knew if I started –" She turned to the guards, and for an instant it occurred to Jake that she was playing, the tears part of some larger performance.

"Do what?" he said again.

"Please," she said to the guard, "would you bring me some water?"

The guard on the right, the German speaker, nodded, said something in Russian to the other, and left the room.

"Write this down," she said to Jake in English, her voice low, as if it were coming from the back of a sob. "Worterstrasse, in Prenzlauer, the third building down from the square. On the left, toward Schönhauserallee. An old Berliner building, the second courtyard. Frau Metzger."

"What is this, Renate?"

"Write it, please. There's not much time. You remember in court I told you I didn't do it for myself?"

"Yes, I know. Your mother."

"No." She looked at him, her eyes sharp and dry. "I have a child."

Jake's pen stopped. "A child?"

"Write it. Metzger. She doesn't know about me. She thinks I work in a factory. I pay her. But the money runs out this month. She won't keep him now."

"Renate –"

"Please. His name is Erich. A German name – he's a German child, you understand? I never had it done. You know, down there." She pointed to her groin, suddenly shy.

"Circumcised."

"Yes. He's a German child. No one knows. Only you. Not the magazines either, promise me? Only you."

"What do you want me to do?"

"Take him. Prenzlauer's in the east. She'll give him up to the Russians. You must take him – there's no one else. Jake, if you were ever fond of me at all –"

"Are you crazy?"

"Yes, crazy. Do you think after everything else I've done, I couldn't ask this? Do you have children?"

"No."

"Then you don't know. You can do anything for a child. Even this," she said, spreading her hand to the room, the *greifer*'s life. "Even this. Was I right to do it? Ask God, I don't know. But he's alive. I saved him, with their money. They gave me pocket money, you know, for the cafés, for –" She stopped. "Every pfennig was for him. I thought, you're paying to keep a Jew alive. At least one of us is going to live. That's why I had to stay alive, not for me. But now –"

"Renate, I can't take a child."

"Yes, please. Please. There's no one else. You were decent, always. Do this for him, if not the mother, what you think of her. Everything I did – one more day, one more day alive. How can I give up now? If you take him to America, they can hang me, at least I'll know I got him out. Safe. Out of this place." She grabbed his hand again. "He'd never know what his mother did. To live with that. He'd never know."

"Renate, how could I take a child to America?"

"The west, then, anywhere but here. You could find a place for him – I trust you, I know you'd make it all right, decent people. Not some Russian camp."

"What do I tell him?"

"That his mother died in the war. He's so young, he won't remember. Just some woman who used to come sometimes. You can tell him you used to know her when she was a girl, but she died in the war. She did," she said, looking down. "It's not a lie."

ii

THE DUTIES OF SISTERS AND BROTHERS

11

SOPHOCLES

Antigone

Antigone is the conclusion of Sophocles' Theban trilogy, which begins with *Oedipus the King*. Antigone and Ismene are the daughters of Oedipus. The play opens on the morning after a battle in Thebes between opposing armies, each led by one of Oedipus' sons, Eteocles and Polyneikes, both of whom were killed in the battle. Kreon, the uncle of Antigone and Ismene, is now ruling Thebes and determined to restore the rule of law. He has decreed that Eteocles is to be honored, and Polyneikes condemned as a traitor.

ANTIGONE: My own sister, dear sister, Ismene.
   Tell me this: are there any evils coming from Oedipus that
   Zeus does not fulfil through us – the two still living?
   Pain, ruin, shame
   all of these
   I see in your evils and mine.

   And now what is this proclamation the general has made to all of Thebes?
   Have you heard anything? Are you aware that evils appropriate for our enemies
   are to be endured by our loved ones?
ISMENE: I have no word, Antigone, concerning loved ones.
   Nothing sweet, nothing bitter, has come my way since we two were bereft of
   our two brothers – one day's double blow of a double death. And with the
   departure of the armies from Argos last night, I do not know whether to feel
   more fortunate or more distressed.
ANTIGONE: I know –
   And I've brought you outside the gates of the house so you alone can hear.
ISMENE: What is it? You're troubled – brooding over some story.
ANTIGONE: We have two brothers. Hasn't Kreon honoured one with a tomb and
   shamed the other?

SOPHOCLES, pp. 91–3 from *Antigone* in *The Thebans* (tr. Timberlake Wertenbaker). London: Faber & Faber, 1992. Reprinted by permission of Faber & Faber Ltd.

Eteocles, they say, has been buried, with due observance of justice and custom, under the ground, to be honoured among the dead.

As for Polyneikes, they say it is forbidden by decree to bury him, or mourn him, but he is to be left unwept, unburied, a sweet morsel for the birds as they look down – their treasure store of tasty meat.

That is the good Kreon's proclamation to you and to me – yes, to me – and he is coming here to make this clear to those who may still not know.

And this is no small matter.

Whoever does these things anyway will be stoned in front of the people of the city. That's how it is for you as well and you will soon show whether you are well born or the bad shoot of good stock.

ISMENE: If these things are so, my poor sister, what can I do? Not do?

ANTIGONE: Think if you will share in the work, the act.

ISMENE: Share in what? What do you mean?

ANTIGONE: Will you help this hand to lift the dead?

ISMENE: You are thinking of burying him – and this has been forbidden?

ANTIGONE: He is my own brother, and yours too, even if you do not wish it. I will not be known as the one who betrayed him.

ISMENE: Such purpose – and Kreon has forbidden it.

ANTIGONE: Not for him to keep me from my own.

ISMENE: *Oimoi.*

Think,

sister

how our father died –

hated, in shame

shunned

uncovering himself his own guilt and striking his two eyes with his own hands. And then the mother, wife, double name, mangling her life in that tangle of ropes.

And finally, our two brothers, in one day each miserably slaying the other, trapped in a shared fate wreaked by their own hands.

We are the two left behind. Alone. We too will die most miserably if we violate the decree and defy the power of the tyrant.

We must remember we are born women and are not meant to do battle against men.

And then that we are ruled by those who are the stronger and we must obey this and things even more painful.

And so I beg forgiveness of those below, I am compelled: I have to obey those in power.

There is no sense in the excessive gesture.

ANTIGONE: I won't urge you any more – no, even if you changed and wanted to do it – you would no longer be welcome.

Think as you will.

I will bury him.

And I will die well doing this.

I will lie with him I love, my friend, my kin – guilty, yes, but of a holy crime.
I believe I owe more of my time to pleasing the dead below than those here:
there, I shall lie for ever.

Think as you will, but you will be guilty of dishonouring the gods.

ISMENE: I am not doing them a dishonour.

I cannot act against the will of the city.

ANTIGONE: Such is your excuse.

I will go and raise a tomb for my beloved brother.

ISMENE: Hard-suffering, I fear for you.

ANTIGONE: Don't fear for me; straighten out your own destiny.

ISMENE: At least keep this plan to yourself. I will do the same.

ANTIGONE: Announce it. I will hate you more if you remain silent and you don't
proclaim this to everyone.

ISMENE: You have a hot spirit for chill acts.

ANTIGONE: I know I am giving satisfaction to those I owe it to.

ISMENE: If you have that power. But you want the impossible.

ANTIGONE: And so – when I have no more strength, I shall stop.

ISMENE: For a start, it is not proper to pursue the impossible.

ANTIGONE: If you keep saying these things, you will incur not only my own hatred
but that of the dead as well; you will be exposed as their enemy.

Let me suffer my own folly in this terrible deed. I would suffer more if I did not
come to a good death.

ISMENE: Go, if it seems right to you.

And know this: you go thoughtlessly, but rightly loved by your loved ones.

12

WILLIAM SHAKESPEARE

Measure for Measure

The Duke of Vienna is traveling and has transferred his powers and duties to Lord Angelo while he is out of town. Claudio is engaged to be married to his beloved, but the couple have been unable to restrain their passion until the wedding, and his fiancée is already pregnant. Angelo, known for his strict morality, has Claudio arrested and sentenced to death. Claudio's sister Isabella is in training to become a nun, but she leaves her convent to plead with Angelo for her brother's life. Angelo offers to spare her brother, but the offer is not unconditional. In this scene Isabella visits her brother in his prison to tell him of Angelo's offer.

CLAUDIO: Now, sister, what's the comfort?
ISABELLA: Why, as all comforts are; most good in deed:
 Lord Angelo, having affairs to heaven,
 Intends you for his swift embassador,
 Where you shall be an everlasting lieger.
 Therefore, your best appointment make with speed;
 To-morrow you set on.
CLAUDIO: Is there no remedy?
ISABELLA: None, but such remedy as, to save a head,
 To cleave a heart in twain.
CLAUDIO: But is there any?
ISABELLA: Yes, brother, you may live:
 There is a devilish mercy in the judge,
 If you'll implore it, that will free your life,
 But fetter you till death.
CLAUDIO: Perpetual durance?
ISABELLA: Ay, just perpetual durance; a restraint,
 Though all the world's vastidity you had,
 To a determin'd scope.
CLAUDIO: But in what nature?

WILLIAM SHAKESPEARE, from Act III, Scene I in *Measure for Measure*, first published in 1623.

ISABELLA: In such a one as, you consenting to't,
　　Would bark your honour from that trunk you bear,
　　And leave you naked.
CLAUDIO:　　　　　Let me know the point.
ISABELLA: O, I do fear thee, Claudio; and I quake,
　　Lest thou a feverous life shouldst entertain,
　　And six or seven winters more respect
　　Than a perpetual honour. Dar'st thou die?
　　The sense of death is most in apprehension;
　　And the poor beetle that we tread upon,
　　In corporal sufferance finds a pang as great
　　As when a giant dies.
CLAUDIO:　　　Why give you me this shame?
　　Think you I can a resolution fetch
　　From flowery tenderness? If I must die
　　I will encounter darkness as a bride,
　　And hug it in mine arms.
ISABELLA: There spake my brother; there my father's grave
　　Did utter forth a voice! Yes, thou must die:
　　Thou art too noble to conserve a life
　　In base appliances. This outward-sainted deputy, –
　　Whose settled visage and deliberate word
　　Nips youth i' the head, and follies doth emmew
　　As falcon doth the fowl, – is yet a devil;
　　His filth within being cast, he would appear
　　A pond as deep as hell.
CLAUDIO:　　　　　The princely Angelo?
ISABELLA: O, 'tis the cunning livery of hell,
　　The damned'st body to invest and cover
　　In princely guards! Dost thou think, Claudio,
　　If I would yield him my virginity
　　Thou mightst be freed?
CLAUDIO:　　　　O heavens! it cannot be.
ISABELLA: Yes, he would give it thee, from this rank offence
　　So to offend him still. This night's the time
　　That I should do what I abhor to name,
　　Or else thou diest to-morrow.
CLAUDIO:　　　　　Thou shalt not do't.
ISABELLA: O, were it but my life,
　　I'd throw it down for your deliverance
　　As frankly as a pin.
CLAUDIO:　　　Thanks, dear Isabel.
ISABELLA: Be ready, Claudio, for your death to-morrow.
CLAUDIO: Yes. – Has he affections in him
　　That thus can make him bite the law by the nose
　　When he would force it? Sure it is no sin;

Or of the deadly seven it is the least.

ISABELLA: Which is the least?

CLAUDIO: If it were damnable, he, being so wise,
  Why would he for the momentary trick
  Be perdurably fined? – O Isabel!

ISABELLA: What says my brother?

CLAUDIO: Death is a fearful thing.

ISABELLA: And shamed life a hateful.

CLAUDIO: Ay, but to die, and go we know not where;
  To lie in cold obstruction, and to rot;
  This sensible warm motion to become
  A kneaded clod; and the delighted spirit
  To bathe in fiery floods or to reside
  In thrilling regions of thick-ribbed ice;
  To be imprison'd in the viewless winds,
  And blown with restless violence round about
  The pendent world; or to be worse than worst
  Of those that lawless and incertain thoughts
  Imagine howling! – 'tis too horrible!
  The weariest and most loathed worldly life
  That age, ache, penury, and imprisonment
  Can lay on nature is a paradise
  To what we fear of death.

ISABELLA: Alas! alas!

CLAUDIO: Sweet sister, let me live:
  What sin you do to save a brother's life
  Nature dispenses with the deed so far
  That it becomes a virtue.

ISABELLA: O you beast!
  O faithless coward! O dishonest wretch!
  Wilt thou be made a man out of my vice?
  Is't not a kind of incest to take life
  From thine own sister's shame. What should I think?
  Heaven shield my mother play'd my father fair!
  For such a warped slip of wilderness
  Ne'er issued from his blood. Take my defiance:
  Die; perish! might but my bending down
  Reprieve thee from thy fate, it should proceed:
  I'll pray a thousand prayers for thy death, –
  No word to save thee.

CLAUDIO: Nay, hear me, Isabel.

ISABELLA: O fie, fie, fie!
  Thy sin's not accidental, but a trade:
  Mercy to thee would prove itself a bawd:
  'Tis best that thou diest quickly.   (*Going.*)

iii

THE DUTIES OF CHILDREN TO THEIR PARENTS

13

ZITKALA-ŠA

The Soft-Hearted Sioux

I

Beside the open fire I sat within our tepee. With my red blanket wrapped tightly about my crossed legs, I was thinking of the coming season, my sixteenth winter. On either side of the wigwam were my parents. My father was whistling a tune between his teeth while polishing with his bare hand a red stone pipe he had recently carved. Almost in front of me, beyond the center fire, my old grandmother sat near the entranceway.

She turned her face toward her right and addressed most of her words to my mother. Now and then she spoke to me, but never did she allow her eyes to rest upon her daughter's husband, my father. It was only upon rare occasions that my grandmother said anything to him. Thus his ears were open and ready to catch the smallest wish she might express. Sometimes when my grandmother had been saying things which pleased him, my father used to comment upon them. At other times, when he could not approve of what was spoken, he used to work or smoke silently.

On this night my old grandmother began her talk about me. Filling the bowl of her red stone pipe with dry willow bark, she looked across at me.

"My grandchild, you are tall and are no longer a little boy." Narrowing her old eyes, she asked, "My grandchild, when are you going to bring here a handsome young woman?" I stared into the fire rather than meet her gaze. Waiting for my answer, she stooped forward and through the long stem drew a flame into the red stone pipe.

I smiled while my eyes were still fixed upon the bright fire, but I said nothing in reply. Turning to my mother, she offered her the pipe. I glanced at my grandmother. The loose buckskin sleeve fell off at her elbow and showed a wrist covered with silver bracelets. Holding up the fingers of her left hand, she named off the desirable young women of our village.

"Which one, my grandchild, which one?" she questioned.

ZITKALA-ŠA, "The Soft-Hearted Sioux," pp. 505–8 from *Harper's* (March 1901). More recently reprinted in Karen L. Kilcup (ed.), *Native American Women's Writing c.1800–1924: An Anthology*. Oxford: Blackwell, 2000.

"Hoh!" I said, pulling at my blanket in confusion. "Not yet!" Here my mother passed the pipe over the fire to my father. Then she, too, began speaking of what I should do.

"My son, be always active. Do not dislike a long hunt. Learn to provide much buffalo meat and many buckskins before you bring home a wife." Presently my father gave the pipe to my grandmother, and he took his turn in the exhortations.

"Ho, my son, I have been counting in my heart the bravest warriors of our people. There is not one of them who won his title in his sixteenth winter. My son, it is a great thing for some brave of sixteen winters to do."

Not a word had I to give in answer. I knew well the fame of my warrior father. He had earned the right of speaking such words, though even he himself was a brave only at my age. Refusing to smoke my grandmother's pipe because my heart was too much stirred by their words, and sorely troubled with a fear lest I should disappoint them, I arose to go. Drawing my blanket over my shoulders, I said, as I stepped toward the entranceway: "I go to hobble my pony. It is now late in the night."

II

Nine winters' snows had buried deep that night when my old grandmother, together with my father and mother, designed my future with the glow of a camp fire upon it.

Yet I did not grow up the warrior, huntsman, and husband I was to have been. At the mission school I learned it was wrong to kill. Nine winters I hunted for the soft heart of Christ, and prayed for the huntsmen who chased the buffalo on the plains.

In the autumn of the tenth year I was sent back to my tribe to preach Christianity to them. With the white man's Bible in my hand, and the white man's tender heart in my breast, I returned to my own people.

Wearing a foreigner's dress, I walked, a stranger, into my father's village.

Asking my way, for I had not forgotten my native tongue, an old man led me toward the tepee where my father lay. From my old companion I learned that my father had been sick many moons. As we drew near the tepee, I heard the chanting of a medicine-man within it. At once I wished to enter in and drive from my home the sorcerer of the plains, but the old warrior checked me. "Ho, wait outside until the medicine-man leaves your father," he said. While talking he scanned me from head to feet. Then he retraced his steps toward the heart of the camping-ground.

My father's dwelling was on the outer limits of the round-faced village. With every heartthrob I grew more impatient to enter the wigwam.

While I turned the leaves of my Bible with nervous fingers, the medicine-man came forth from the dwelling and walked hurriedly away. His head and face were closely covered with the loose robe which draped his entire figure.

He was tall and large. His long strides I have never forgot. They seemed to me then the uncanny gait of eternal death. Quickly pocketing my Bible, I went into the tepee.

Upon a mat lay my father, with furrowed face and gray hair. His eyes and cheeks were sunken far into his head. His sallow skin lay thin upon his pinched nose and high cheekbones. Stooping over him, I took his fevered hand. "How, Ate?" I greeted him. A light flashed from his listless eyes and his dried lips parted. "My son!" he murmured, in a feeble voice. Then again the wave of joy and recognition receded. He closed his eyes, and his hand dropped from my open palm to the ground.

Looking about, I saw an old woman sitting with bowed head. Shaking hands with her, I recognized my mother. I sat down between my father and mother as I used to do, but I did not feel at home. The place where my old grandmother used to sit was now unoccupied. With my mother I bowed my head. Alike our throats were choked and tears were streaming from our eyes; but far apart in spirit our ideas and faiths separated us. My grief was for the soul unsaved; and I thought my mother wept to see a brave man's body broken by sickness.

Useless was my attempt to change the faith in the medicine-man to that abstract power named God. Then one day I became righteously mad with anger that the medicine-man should thus ensnare my father's soul. And when he came to chant his sacred songs I pointed toward the door and bade him go! The man's eyes glared upon me for an instant. Slowly gathering his robe about him, he turned his back upon the sick man and stepped out of our wigwam. "Ha, ha, ha! my son, I can not live without the medicine-man!" I heard my father cry when the sacred man was gone.

III

On a bright day, when the winged seeds of the prairie-grass were flying hither and thither, I walked solemnly toward the centre of the camping-ground. My heart beat hard and irregularly at my side. Tighter I grasped the sacred book I carried under my arm. Now was the beginning of life's work.

Though I knew it would be hard, I did not once feel that failure was to be my reward. As I stepped unevenly on the rolling ground, I thought of the warriors soon to wash off their war-paints and follow me.

At length I reached the place where the people had assembled to hear me preach. In a large circle men and women sat upon the dry red grass. Within the ring I stood, with the white man's Bible in my hand. I tried to tell them of the soft heart of Christ.

In silence the vast circle of bareheaded warriors sat under an afternoon sun. At last, wiping the wet from my brow, I took my place in the ring. The hush of the assembly filled me with great hope.

I was turning my thoughts upward to the sky in gratitude, when a stir called me to earth again.

A tall, strong man arose. His loose robe hung in folds over his right shoulder. A pair of snapping black eyes fastened themselves like the poisonous fangs of a serpent upon me. He was the medicine-man. A tremor played about my heart and a chill cooled the fire in my veins.

Scornfully he pointed a long forefinger in my direction and asked:

"What loyal son is he who, returning to his father's people, wears a foreigner's dress?" He paused a moment, and then continued: "The dress of that foreigner of whom a story says he bound a native of our land, and heaping dry sticks around him, kindled a fire at his feet!" Waving his hand toward me, he exclaimed, "Here is the traitor to his people!"

I was helpless. Before the eyes of the crowd the cunning magician turned my honest heart into a vile nest of treachery. Alas! the people frowned as they looked upon me.

"Listen!" he went on. "Which one of you who have eyed the young man can see through his bosom and warn the people of the nest of young snakes hatching there? Whose ear was so acute that he caught the hissing of snakes whenever the young man opened his mouth? This one has not only proven false to you, but even to the Great Spirit who made him. He is a fool! Why do you sit here giving ear to a foolish man who could not defend his people because he fears to kill, who could not bring venison to renew the life of his sick father? With his prayers, let him drive away the enemy! With his soft heart, let him keep off starvation! We shall go elsewhere to dwell upon an untainted ground."

With this he disbanded the people. When the sun lowered in the west and the winds were quiet, the village of cone-shaped tepees was gone. The medicine-man had won the hearts of the people.

Only my father's dwelling was left to mark the fighting-ground.

IV

From a long night at my father's bedside I came out to look upon the morning. The yellow sun hung equally between the snow-covered land and the cloudless blue sky. The light of the new day was cold. The strong breath of winter crusted the snow and fitted crystal shells over the rivers and lakes. As I stood in front of the tepee, thinking of the vast prairies which separated us from our tribe, and wondering if the high sky likewise separated the soft-hearted Son of God from us, the icy blast from the North blew through my hair and skull. My neglected hair had grown long and fell upon my neck.

My father had not risen from his bed since the day the medicine-man led the people away. Though I read from the Bible and prayed beside him upon my knees, my father would not listen. Yet I believed my prayers were not unheeded in heaven.

"Ha, ha, ha! my son," my father groaned upon the first snowfall. "My son, our food is gone. There is no one to bring me meat! My son, your soft heart has unfitted you for everything!" Then covering his face with the buffalo-robe, he said no more. Now while I stood out in that cold winter morning, I was starving. For two days I had not seen any food. But my own cold and hunger did not harass my soul as did the whining cry of the sick old man.

Stepping again into the tepee, I untied my snow-shoes, which were fastened to the tentpoles.

My poor mother, watching by the sick one, and faithfully heaping wood upon the centre fire, spoke to me:

"My son, do not fail again to bring your father meat, or he will starve to death."

"How, Ina," I answered, sorrowfully. From the tepee I started forth again to hunt food for my aged parents. All day I tracked the white level lands in vain. Nowhere, nowhere were there any other footprints but my own! In the evening of this third fast-day I came back without meat. Only a bundle of sticks for the fire I brought on my back. Dropping the wood outside, I lifted the door-flap and set one foot within the tepee.

There I grew dizzy and numb. My eyes swam in tears. Before me lay my old gray-haired father sobbing like a child. In his horny hands he clutched the buffalo-robe, and with his teeth he was gnawing off the edges. Chewing the dry stiff hair and buffalo-skin, my father's eyes sought my hands. Upon seeing them empty, he cried out:

"My son, your soft heart will let me starve before you bring me meat! Two hills eastward stand a herd of cattle. Yet you will see me die before you bring me food!"

Leaving my mother lying with covered head upon her mat, I rushed out into the night.

With a strange warmth in my heart and swiftness in my feet, I climbed over the first hill, and soon the second one. The moonlight upon the white country showed me a clear path to the white man's cattle. With my hand upon the knife in my belt, I leaned heavily against the fence while counting the herd.

Twenty in all I numbered. From among them I chose the best-fattened creature. Leaping over the fence, I plunged my knife into it.

My long knife was sharp, and my hands, no more fearful and slow, slashed off choice chunks of warm flesh. Bending under the meat I had taken for my starving father, I hurried across the prairie.

Toward home I fairly ran with the life-giving food I carried upon my back. Hardly had I climbed the second hill when I heard sounds coming after me. Faster and faster I ran with my load for my father, but the sounds were gaining upon me. I heard the clicking of snowshoes and the squeaking of the leather straps at my heels; yet I did not turn to see what pursued me, for I was intent upon reaching my father. Suddenly like thunder an angry voice shouted curses and threats into my ear! A rough hand wrenched my shoulder and took the meat from me! I stopped struggling to run. A deafening whir filled my head. The moon and stars began to move. Now the white prairie was sky, and the stars lay under my feet. Now again they were turning. At last the starry blue rose up into place. The noise in my ears was still. A great quiet filled the air. In my hand I found my long knife dripping with blood. At my feet a man's figure lay prone in blood-red snow. The horrible scene about me seemed a trick of my senses, for I could not understand it was real. Looking long upon the blood-stained snow, the load of meat for my starving father reached my recognition at last. Quickly I tossed it over my shoulder and started again homeward.

Tired and haunted I reached the door of the wigwam. Carrying the food before me, I entered with it into the tepee.

"Father, here is food!" I cried, as I dropped the meat near my mother. No answer came. Turning about, I beheld my gray-haired father dead! I saw by the unsteady firelight an old gray-haired skeleton lying rigid and stiff.

Out into the open I started, but the snow at my feet became bloody.

V

On the day after my father's death, having led my mother to the camp of the medicine-man, I gave myself up to those who were searching for the murderer of the paleface.

They bound me hand and foot. Here in this cell I was placed four days ago.

The shrieking winter winds have followed me hither. Rattling the bars, they howl unceasingly: "Your soft heart! your soft heart will see me die before you bring me food!" Hark! something is clanking the chain on the door. It is being opened. From the dark night without a black figure crosses the threshold. . . . It is the guard. He comes to warn me of my fate. He tells me that tomorrow I must die. In his stern face I laugh aloud. I do not fear death.

Yet I wonder who shall come to welcome me in the realm of strange sight. Will the loving Jesus grant me pardon and give my soul a soothing sleep? or will my warrior father greet me and receive me as his son? Will my spirit fly upward to a happy heaven? or shall I sink into the bottomless pit, an outcast from a God of infinite love?

Soon, soon I shall know, for now I see the east is growing red. My heart is strong. My face is calm. My eyes are dry and eager for new scenes. My hands hang quietly at my side. Serene and brave, my soul awaits the men to perch me on the gallows for another flight. I go.

14

AMBROSE BIERCE

A Horseman in the Sky

I

One sunny afternoon in the autumn of the year 1861 a soldier lay in a clump of laurel by the side of a road in western Virginia. He lay at full length upon his stomach, his feet resting upon the toes, his head upon the left forearm. His extended right hand loosely grasped his rifle. But for the somewhat methodical disposition of his limbs and a slight rhythmic movement of the cartridge-box at the back of his belt he might have been thought to be dead. He was asleep at his post of duty. But if detected he would be dead shortly afterward, death being the just and legal penalty of his crime.

The clump of laurel in which the criminal lay was in the angle of a road which after ascending southward a steep acclivity to that point turned sharply to the west, running along the summit for perhaps one hundred yards. There it turned southward again and went zigzagging downward through the forest. At the salient of that second angle was a large flat rock, jutting out northward, overlooking the deep valley from which the road ascended. The rock capped a high cliff; a stone dropped from its outer edge would have fallen sheer downward one thousand feet to the tops of the pines. The angle where the soldier lay was on another spur of the same cliff. Had he been awake he would have commanded a view, not only of the short arm of the road and the jutting rock, but of the entire profile of the cliff below it. It might well have made him giddy to look.

The country was wooded everywhere except at the bottom of the valley to the northward, where there was a small natural meadow, through which flowed a stream scarcely visible from the valley's rim. This open ground looked hardly larger than an ordinary door-yard, but was really several acres in extent. Its green was more vivid than that of the inclosing forest. Away beyond it rose a line of giant cliffs similar to those upon which we are supposed to stand in our survey of

---

AMBROSE BIERCE, "A Horseman in the Sky," first published in his *Tales of Soldiers and Civilians*. San Francisco: E. L. G. Steele, 1891. More recently reprinted in Ambrose Bierce, *Civil War Stories*. New York: Dover Publications, 1994.

---

acclivity – an upward slope

the savage scene, and through which the road had somehow made its climb to the summit. The configuration of the valley, indeed, was such that from this point of observation it seemed entirely shut in, and one could but have wondered how the road which found a way out of it had found a way into it, and whence came and whither went the waters of the stream that parted the meadow more than a thousand feet below.

No country is so wild and difficult but men will make it a theatre of war; concealed in the forest at the bottom of that military rat-trap, in which half a hundred men in possession of the exits might have starved an army to submission, lay five regiments of Federal infantry. They had marched all the previous day and night and were resting. At nightfall they would take to the road again, climb to the place where their unfaithful sentinel now slept, and descending the other slope of the ridge fall upon a camp of the enemy at about midnight. Their hope was to surprise it, for the road led to the rear of it. In case of failure, their position would be perilous in the extreme; and fail they surely would should accident or vigilance apprise the enemy of the movement.

II

The sleeping sentinel in the clump of laurel was a young Virginian named Carter Druse. He was the son of wealthy parents, an only child, and had known such ease and cultivation and high living as wealth and taste were able to command in the mountain country of western Virginia. His home was but a few miles from where he now lay. One morning he had risen from the breakfast-table and said, quietly but gravely: "Father, a Union regiment has arrived at Grafton. I am going to join it."

The father lifted his leonine head, looked at the son a moment in silence, and replied: "Well, go, sir, and whatever may occur do what you conceive to be your duty. Virginia, to which you are a traitor, must get on without you. Should we both live to the end of the war, we will speak further of the matter. Your mother, as the physician has informed you, is in a most critical condition; at the best she cannot be with us longer than a few weeks, but that time is precious. It would be better not to disturb her."

So Carter Druse, bowing reverently to his father, who returned the salute with a stately courtesy that masked a breaking heart, left the home of his childhood to go soldiering. By conscience and courage, by deeds of devotion and daring, he soon commended himself to his fellows and his officers; and it was to these qualities and to some knowledge of the country that he owed his selection for his present perilous duty at the extreme outpost. Nevertheless, fatigue had been stronger than resolution and he had fallen asleep. What good or bad angel came in a dream to rouse him from his state of crime, who shall say? Without a movement, without a sound, in the profound silence and the languor of the late afternoon, some invisible messenger of fate touched with unsealing finger the eyes of his consciousness — whispered into the ear of his spirit the mysterious awakening word which no human lips ever have spoken, no human memory ever has recalled. He quietly raised his forehead from his arm and looked between the masking stems of the laurels, instinctively closing his right hand about the stock of his rifle.

His first feeling was a keen artistic delight. On a colossal pedestal, the cliff – motionless at the extreme edge of the capping rock and sharply outlined against the sky – was an equestrian statue of impressive dignity. The figure of the man sat on the figure of the horse, straight and soldierly, but with the repose of a Grecian god carved in the marble which limits the suggestion of activity. The gray costume harmonized with its aerial background; the metal of accoutrement and caparison was softened and subdued by the shadow; the animal's skin had no points of high light. A carbine strikingly foreshortened lay across the pommel of the saddle, kept in place by the right hand grasping it at the "grip"; the left hand, holding the bridle rein, was invisible. In silhouette against the sky the profile of the horse was cut with the sharpness of a cameo; it looked across the heights of air to the confronting cliffs beyond. The face of the rider, turned slightly away, showed only an outline of temple and beard; he was looking downward to the bottom of the valley. Magnified by its lift against the sky and by the soldier's testifying sense of the formidableness of a near enemy the group appeared of heroic, almost colossal, size.

For an instant Druse had a strange, half-defined feeling that he had slept to the end of the war and was looking upon a noble work of art reared upon that eminence to commemorate the deeds of an heroic past of which he had been an inglorious part. The feeling was dispelled by a slight movement of the group: the horse, without moving its feet, had drawn its body slightly backward from the verge; the man remained immobile as before. Broad awake and keenly alive to the significance of the situation, Druse now brought the butt of his rifle against his cheek by cautiously pushing the barrel forward through the bushes, cocked the piece, and glancing through the sights covered a vital spot of the horseman's breast. A touch upon the trigger and all would have been well with Carter Druse. At that instant the horseman turned his head and looked in the direction of his concealed foeman – seemed to look into his very face, into his eyes, into his brave, compassionate heart.

Is it then so terrible to kill an enemy in war – an enemy who has surprised a secret vital to the safety of one's self and comrades – an enemy more formidable for his knowledge than all his army for its numbers? Carter Druse grew pale; he shook in every limb, turned faint, and saw the statuesque group before him as black figures, rising, falling, moving unsteadily in arcs of circles in a fiery sky. His hand fell away from his weapon, his head slowly dropped until his face rested on the leaves in which he lay. This courageous gentleman and hardy soldier was near swooning from intensity of emotion.

It was not for long; in another moment his face was raised from earth, his hands resumed their places on the rifle, his forefinger sought the trigger; mind, heart, and eyes were clear, conscience and reason sound. He could not hope to capture that enemy; to alarm him would but send him dashing to his camp with his fatal

---

caparison – an ornamental covering for a horse

news. The duty of the soldier was plain: the man must be shot dead from ambush
– without warning, without a moment's spiritual preparation, with never so much
as an unspoken prayer, he must be sent to his account. But no – there is a hope; he
may have discovered nothing – perhaps he is but admiring the sublimity of the
landscape. If permitted, he may turn and ride carelessly away in the direction
whence he came. Surely it will be possible to judge at the instant of his withdraw-
ing whether he knows. It may well be that his fixity of attention – Druse turned his
head and looked through the deeps of air downward, as from the surface to the
bottom of a translucent sea. He saw creeping across the green meadow a sinuous
line of figures of men and horses – some foolish commander was permitting the
soldiers of his escort to water their beasts in the open, in plain view from a dozen
summits!

Druse withdrew his eyes from the valley and fixed them again upon the group
of man and horse in the sky, and again it was through the sights of his rifle. But
this time his aim was at the horse. In his memory, as if they were a divine mandate,
rang the words of his father at their parting: "Whatever may occur, do what you
conceive to be your duty." He was calm now. His teeth were firmly but not rigidly
closed; his nerves were as tranquil as a sleeping babe's – not a tremor affected any
muscle of his body; his breathing, until suspended in the act of taking aim, was
regular and slow. Duty had conquered; the spirit had said to the body: "Peace, be
still." He fired.

III

An officer of the Federal force, who in a spirit of adventure or in quest of knowledge had left the hidden bivouac in the valley, and with aimless feet had made his
way to the lower edge of a small open space near the foot of the cliff, was
considering what he had to gain by pushing his exploration further. At a distance
of a quarter-mile before him, but apparently at a stone's throw, rose from its fringe
of pines the gigantic face of rock, towering to so great a height above him that it
made him giddy to look up to where its edge cut a sharp, rugged line against the
sky. It presented a clean, vertical profile against a background of blue sky to a
point half the way down, and of distant hills, hardly less blue, thence to the tops
of the trees at its base. Lifting his eyes to the dizzy altitude of its summit the
officer saw an astonishing sight – a man on horseback riding down into the valley
through the air!

Straight upright sat the rider, in military fashion, with a firm seat in the saddle,
a strong clutch upon the rein to hold his charger from too impetuous a plunge.
From his bare head his long hair streamed upward, waving like a plume. His hands
were concealed in the cloud of the horse's lifted mane. The animal's body was as
level as if every hoofstroke encountered the resistant earth. Its motions were those
of a wild gallop, but even as the officer looked they ceased, with all the legs
thrown sharply forward as in the act of alighting from a leap. But this was a flight!

Filled with amazement and terror by this apparition of a horseman in the sky
– half believing himself the chosen scribe of some new Apocalypse, the officer was

overcome by the intensity of his emotions; his legs failed him and he fell. Almost the same instant he heard a crashing sound in the trees – a sound that died without an echo – and all was still.

The officer rose to his feet, trembling. The familiar sensation of an abraded shin recalled his dazed faculties. Pulling himself together he ran rapidly obliquely away from the cliff to a point distant from its foot; thereabout he expected to find his man; and thereabout he naturally failed. In the fleeting instant of his vision his imagination had been so wrought upon by the apparent grace and ease and intention of the marvelous performance that it did not occur to him that the line of march of aerial cavalry is directly downward, and that he could find the objects of his search at the very foot of the cliff. A half-hour later he returned to camp.

This officer was a wise man; he knew better than to tell an incredible truth. He said nothing of what he had seen. But when the commander asked him if in his scout he had learned anything of advantage to the expedition he answered:

"Yes, sir; there is no road leading down into this valley from the southward."

The commander, knowing better, smiled.

IV

After firing his shot, Private Carter Druse reloaded his rifle and resumed his watch. Ten minutes had hardly passed when a Federal sergeant crept cautiously to him on hands and knees. Druse neither turned his head nor looked at him, but lay without motion or sign of recognition.

"Did you fire?" the sergeant whispered.

"Yes."

"At what?"

"A horse. It was standing on yonder rock – pretty far out. You see it is no longer there. It went over the cliff."

The man's face was white, but he showed no other sign of emotion. Having answered, he turned away his eyes and said no more. The sergeant did not understand.

"See here, Druse," he said, after a moment's silence, "it's no use making a mystery. I order you to report. Was there anybody on the horse?"

"Yes."

"Well?"

"My father."

The sergeant rose to his feet and walked away. "Good God!" he said.

15

ALICE MUNRO

The Peace of Utrecht

"The Peace of Utrecht" appeared in Alice Munro's first collection of short stories, *Dance of the Happy Shades*. Helen has come back to her home town of Jubilee for the first time since her mother's death.

The rhythm of life in Jubilee is primitively seasonal. Deaths occur in the winter; marriages are celebrated in the summer. There is good reason for this; the winters are long and full of hardship and the old and weak cannot always get through them. Last winter was a catastrophe, such as may be expected every ten or twelve years; you can see how the pavement in the streets is broken up, as if the town had survived a minor bombardment. A death is dealt with then in the middle of great difficulties; there comes time now in the summer to think about it, and talk. I find that people stop me in the street to talk about my mother. I have heard from them about her funeral, what flowers she had and what the weather was like on that day. And now that she is dead I no longer feel that when they say the words "your mother" they deal a knowing, cunning blow at my pride. I used to feel that; at those words. I felt my whole identity, that pretentious adolescent construction, come crumbling down.

Now I listen to them speak of her, so gently and ceremoniously, and I realize that she became one of the town's possessions and oddities, its brief legends. This she achieved in spite of us, for we tried, both crudely and artfully, to keep her at home, away from that sad notoriety; not for her sake, but for ours, who suffered such unnecessary humiliation at the sight of her eyes rolling back in her head in a temporary paralysis of the eye muscles, at the sound of her thickened voice, whose embarrassing pronouncements it was our job to interpret to outsiders. So bizarre was the disease she had in its effects that it made us feel like crying out in apology (though we stayed stiff and white) as if we were accompanying a particularly tasteless sideshow. All wasted, our pride; our purging its rage in wild caricatures we did for each other (no, not caricatures, for she was one herself;

ALICE MUNRO, from "The Peace of Utrecht," first published in *Dance of the Happy Shades: And Other Stories* (1968). Reproduced by the permission of McGraw-Hill Ryerson Ltd.

imitations). We should have let the town have her; it would have treated her better.

About Maddy and her ten-years' vigil they say very little; perhaps they want to spare my feelings, remembering that I was the one who went away and here are my two children to show for it, while Maddy is alone and has nothing but that discouraging house. But I don't think so; in Jubilee the feelings are not spared this way. And they ask me point-blank why I did not come home for the funeral; I am glad I have the excuse of the blizzard that halted air travel that week, for I do not know if I would have come anyway, after Maddy had written so vehemently urging me to stay away. I felt strongly that she had a right to be left alone with it, if she wanted to be, after all this time.

After all this time. Maddy was the one who stayed. First, she went away to college, then I went. You give me four years, I'll give you four years, she said. But I got married. She was not surprised; she was exasperated at me for my wretched useless feelings of guilt. She said that she had always meant to stay. She said that Mother no longer "bothered" her. "Our Gothic Mother," she said, "I play it out now, I let her be. I don't keep trying to make her *human* any more. You know." It would simplify things so much to say that Maddy was religious, that she felt the joys of self-sacrifice, the strong, mystical appeal of total rejection. But about Maddy who could say that? When we were in our teens, and our old aunts, Aunt Annie and Auntie Lou, spoke to us of some dutiful son or daughter who had given up everything for an ailing parent, Maddy would quote impiously the opinions of modern psychiatry. Yet she stayed. All I can think about that, all I have ever been able to think, to comfort me, is that she may have been able and may even have chosen to live without time and in perfect imaginary freedom as children do, the future untampered with, all choices always possible.

To change the subject, people ask me what it is like to be back in Jubilee. But I don't know, I am still waiting for something to tell me, to make me understand that I am back. The day I drove up from Toronto with my children in the back seat of the car I was very tired, on the last lap of a twenty-five-hundred-mile trip. I had to follow a complicated system of highways and sideroads, for there is no easy way to get to Jubilee from anywhere on earth. Then about two o'clock in the afternoon I saw ahead of me, so familiar and unexpected, the gaudy, peeling cupola of the town hall, which is no relation to any of the rest of the town's squarely-built, dingy grey-and-red-brick architecture. (Underneath it hangs a great bell, to be rung in the event of some mythical disaster.) I drove up the main street – a new service station, new stucco front on the Queen's Hotel – and turned into the quiet, decaying side streets where old maids live, and have birdbaths and blue delphiniums in their gardens. The big brick houses that I knew, with their wooden verandahs and gaping, dark-screened windows, seemed to me plausible but unreal. (Anyone to whom I have mentioned the dreaming sunken feeling of these streets wants to take me out to the north side of town where there is a new soft-drink bottling plant, some new ranch-style houses and a Tastee-Freez.) Then I parked my car in a little splash of shade in front of the house where I used to live. My little girl, whose name is Margaret, said neutrally yet with some disbelief, "Mother, is that your house?"

And I felt that my daughter's voice expressed a complex disappointment – to which, characteristically, she seemed resigned, or even resigned *in advance;* it contained the whole flatness and strangeness of the moment in which is revealed the source of legends, the unsatisfactory, apologetic and persistent reality. The red brick of which the house is built looked harsh and hot in the sun and was marked in two or three places by long grimacing cracks; the verandah, which always had the air of an insubstantial decoration, was visibly falling away. There was – there *is* – a little blind window of coloured glass beside the front door. I sat staring at it with a puzzled lack of emotional recognition. I sat and looked at the house and the window shades did not move, the door did not fly open, no one came out on the verandah; there was no one at home. This was as I had expected, since Maddy works now in the office of the town clerk, yet I was surprised to see the house take on such a closed, bare, impoverished look, merely by being left empty. And it was brought home to me, as I walked across the front yard to the steps, that after all these summers on the Coast I had forgotten the immense inland heat, which makes you feel as if you have to carry the whole burning sky on your head.

A sign pinned to the front door announced, in Maddy's rather sloppy and flamboyant hand: VISITORS WELCOME, CHILDREN FREE, RATES TO BE ARRANGED LATER (YOU'LL BE SORRY) WALK IN. On the hall table was a bouquet of pink phlox whose velvety scent filled the hot air of a closed house on a summer afternoon. "Upstairs!" I said to the children, and I took the hand of the little girl and her smaller brother, who had slept in the car and who rubbed against me, whimpering, as he walked. Then I paused, one foot on the bottom step, and turned to greet, matter-of-factly, the reflection of a thin, tanned, habitually watchful woman, recognizably a Young Mother, whose hair, pulled into a knot on top of her head, exposed a jawline no longer softly fleshed, a brown neck rising with a look of tension from the little sharp knobs of the collarbone – this in the hall mirror that had shown me, last time I looked, a commonplace pretty girl, with a face as smooth and insensitive as an apple, no matter what panic and disorder lay behind it.

But this was not what I had turned for; I realized that I must have been waiting for my mother to call, from her couch in the dining-room, where she lay with the blinds down in the summer heat, drinking cups of tea which she never finished, eating – she had dispensed altogether with mealtimes, like a sickly child – little bowls of preserved fruit and crumblings of cake. It seemed to me that I could not close the door behind me without hearing my mother's ruined voice call out to me, and feeling myself go heavy all over as I prepared to answer it. Calling, *Who's there?*

I led my children to the big bedroom at the back of the house, where Maddy and I used to sleep. It has thin, almost worn-out white curtains at the windows and a square of linoleum on the floor; there is a double bed, a washstand which Maddy and I used as a desk when we were in high school, and a cardboard wardrobe with little mirrors on the inside of the doors. As I talked to my children I was thinking – but carefully, not in a rush – of my mother's state of mind when she called out *Who's there?* I was allowing myself to hear – as if I had not dared before – the cry for help – undisguised, oh, shamefully undisguised and raw and supplicating – that sounded in her voice. A cry repeated so often, and, things being as they were, so uselessly, that Maddy and I recognized it only as one of those household sounds which must be dealt with, so that worse may not follow. *You go and deal with Mother,* we would say to each other, or *I'll be out in a minute, I have to deal with Mother.*

It might be that we had to perform some of the trivial and unpleasant services endlessly required, or that we had to supply five minutes' expediently cheerful conversation, so remorselessly casual that never for a moment was there a recognition of the real state of affairs, never a glint of pity to open the way for one of her long debilitating sieges of tears. But the pity denied, the tears might come anyway; so that we were defeated, we were forced – to stop that noise – into parodies of love. But we grew cunning, unfailing in cold solicitude; we took away from her our anger and impatience and disgust, took all emotion away from our dealings with her, as you might take away meat from a prisoner to weaken him, till he died.

We would tell her to read, to listen to music and enjoy the changes of season and be grateful that she did not have cancer. We added that she did not suffer any pain, and that is true – if imprisonment is not pain. While she demanded our love in every way she knew, without shame or sense, as a child will. And how could we have loved her, I say desperately to myself, the resources of love we had were not enough, the demand on us was too great. Nor would it have changed anything.

"Everything has been taken away from me," she would say. To strangers, to friends of ours whom we tried always unsuccessfully to keep separate from her, to old friends of hers who came guiltily infrequently to see her, she would speak like this, in the very slow and mournful voice that was not intelligible or quite human; we would have to interpret. Such theatricality humiliated us almost to death; yet now I think that without that egotism feeding stubbornly even on disaster she might have sunk rapidly into some dim vegetable life. She kept herself as much in the world as she could, not troubling about her welcome; restlessly she wandered through the house and into the streets of Jubilee. Oh, she was not resigned; she must have wept and struggled in that house of stone (as I can, but will not, imagine) until the very end.

But I find the picture is still not complete. Our Gothic Mother, with the cold appalling mask of the Shaking Palsy laid across her features, shuffling, weeping, devouring attention wherever she can get it, eyes dead and burning, fixed inward on herself; this is not all. For the disease is erratic and leisurely in its progress; some mornings (gradually growing fewer and fewer and farther apart) she wakes up better; she goes out to the yard and straightens up a plant in such a simple housewifely way; she says something calm and lucid to us; she listens attentively to the news. She has wakened out of a bad dream; she tries to make up for lost time, tidying the house, forcing her stiff trembling hands to work a little while at the sewing machine. She makes us one of her specialties, a banana cake or a lemon meringue pie. Occasionally since she died I have dreams of her (I never dreamt of her when she was alive) in which she is doing something like this, and I think, why did I exaggerate so to myself, see, she is all right, only that her hands are trembling –

At the end of these periods of calm a kind of ravaging energy would come over her; she would make conversation insistently and with less and less coherence; she would demand that we rouge her cheeks and fix her hair; sometimes she might even hire a dressmaker to come in and make clothes for her, working in the dining room where she could watch – spending her time again more and more on the couch. This was extravagant, unnecessary from any practical point of view (for why did she need these clothes, where did she wear them?) and nerve-racking, because the dressmaker did not understand what she wanted and sometimes neither did we. I remember after I went away receiving from Maddy several amusing, distracted, quietly overwrought letters describing these sessions with the dress-maker. I read them with sympathy but without being able to enter into the once-familiar atmosphere of frenzy and frustration which my mother's demands could produce. In the ordinary world it was not possible to re-create her. The picture of her face which I carried in my mind seemed too terrible, unreal. Similarly the complex strain of living with her, the feelings of hysteria which Maddy and I once dissipated in a great deal of brutal laughter, now began to seem partly imaginary; I felt the beginnings of a secret, guilty estrangement.

I stayed in the room with my children for a little while because it was a strange place, for them it was only another strange place to go to sleep. Looking at them in this room I felt that they were particularly fortunate and that their life was safe and easy, which may be what most parents think at one time or another. I looked in the wardrobe but there was nothing there, only a hat trimmed with flowers from the five-and-ten, which one of us must have made for some flossy Easter. When I opened the drawer of the washstand I saw that it was crammed full of pages from a loose-leaf notebook. I read: "The Peace of Utrecht, 1713, brought an end to the War of the Spanish Succession." It struck me that the handwriting was my own. Strange to think of it lying here for ten years – more; it looked as if I might have written it that day.

For some reason reading these words had a strong effect on me; I felt as if my old life was lying around me, waiting to be picked up again. Only then for a few moments in our old room did I have this feeling. The brown halls of the old High School (a building since torn down) were re-opened for me, and I remembered the Saturday nights in spring, after the snow had melted and all the country people crowded into town. I thought of us walking up and down the main street, arm in arm with two or three other girls, until it got dark, then going in to Al's to dance, under a string of little coloured lights. The windows in the dance hall were open; they let in the raw spring air with its smell of earth and the river; the hands of farm boys crumpled and stained our white blouses when we danced. And now an experience which seemed not at all memorable at the time (in fact Al's was a dismal place and the ritual of walking up and down the street to show ourselves off we thought crude and ridiculous, though we could not resist it) had been trans-formed into something curiously meaningful for me, and complete; it took in more than the girls dancing and the single street, it spread over the whole town, its rudimentary pattern of streets and its bare trees and muddy yards just free of the snow, over the dirt roads where the lights of cars appeared, jolting towards the town, under an immense pale wash of sky.

Also: we wore ballerina shoes, and full black taffeta skirts, and short coats of such colours as robin's egg blue, cerise red, lime green. Maddy wore a great funereal bow at the neck of her blouse and a wreath of artificial daisies in her hair. These were the fashions, or so we believed, of one of the years after the war. Maddy; her bright skeptical look; my sister.

I ask Maddy, "Do you ever remember what she was like before?"

"No," says Maddy. "No, I can't."

"I sometimes think I can," I say hesitantly. "Not very often." Cowardly tender nostalgia, trying to get back to a gentler truth.

"I think you would have to have been away," Maddy says, "You would have to have been away these last — quite a few — years to get those kind of memories."

It was then she said: No exorcising.

And the only other thing she said was, "She spent a lot of time sorting things. All kinds of things. Greeting cards. Buttons and yarn. Sorting and putting them into little piles. It would keep her quiet by the hour."

On her third visit to the home of her aunts, Aunt Annie asks Helen to come upstairs on her own.

"She was gone sooner than anybody would have expected," Aunt Annie said. I turned around surprised and she said, "Your mother." Then I wondered if the clothes had been the main thing after all; perhaps they were only to serve as the introduction to a conversation about my mother's death, which Aunt Annie might feel to be a necessary part of our visit. Auntie Lou would feel differently; she had an almost superstitious dislike of certain rituals of emotionalism; such a conversation could never take place with her about.

"Two months after she went into the hospital," Aunt Annie said. "She was gone in two months." I saw that she was crying distractedly, as old people do, with miserable scanty tears. She pulled a handkerchief out of her dress and rubbed at her face.

"Maddy told her it was nothing but a check-up," she said. "Maddy told her it would be about three weeks. Your mother went in there and she thought she was coming out in three weeks." She was whispering as if she was afraid of us being overheard. "Do you think she wanted to stay in there where nobody could make out what she was saying and they wouldn't let her out of her bed? She wanted to come home!"

"But she was too sick," I said.

"No, she wasn't, she was just the way she'd always been, just getting a little worse and a little worse as time went on. But after she went in there she felt she would die, everything kind of closed in around her, and she went down so fast."

"Maybe it would have happened anyway," I said. "Maybe it was just the time."

Aunt Annie paid no attention to me. "I went up to see her," she said. "She was so glad to see me because I could tell what she was saying. She said Aunt Annie, they won't keep me in here for good, will they? And I said to her, No. I said, No.

"And she said, Aunt Annie ask Maddy to take me home again or I'm going to die. She didn't want to die. Don't you ever think a person wants to die, just because it seems to everybody else they have got no reason to go on living. So I told Maddy. But she didn't say anything. She went to the hospital every day and saw your mother and she wouldn't take her home. Your mother told me Maddy said to her, I won't take you home."

"Mother didn't always tell the truth," I said. "Aunt Annie, you know that."

"Did you know your mother got out of the hospital?"

"No," I said. But strangely I felt no surprise, only a vague physical sense of terror, a longing not to be told – and beyond this a feeling that what I would be told I already knew, I had always known.

"Maddy, didn't she tell you?"

"No."

"Well she got *out*. She got out the side door where the ambulance comes in, it's the only door that isn't locked. It was at night when they haven't so many nurses to watch them. She got her dressing gown and her slippers on, the first time she ever got anything on herself in years, and she went out and there it was January, snowing, but she didn't go back in. She was away down the street when they caught her. After that they put the board across her bed."

The snow, the dressing gown and slippers, the board across the bed. It was a picture I was much inclined to resist. Yet I had no doubt that this was true, all this was true and exactly as it happened. It was what she would do; all her life as long as I had known her led up to that flight.

"Where was she going?" I said, but I knew there was no answer.

"I don't know. Maybe I shouldn't have told you. Oh, Helen, when they came after her she tried to run. She tried to *run*."

The flight that concerns everybody. Even behind my aunt's soft familiar face there is another, more primitive old woman, capable of panic in some place her faith has never touched.

She began folding the clothes up and putting them back in the box. "They nailed a board across her bed. I saw it. You can't blame the nurses. They can't watch everybody. They haven't the time.

"I said to Maddy after the funeral, Maddy, may it never happen like that to you. I couldn't help it, that's what I said." She sat down on the bed herself now, folding things and putting them back in the box, making an effort to bring her voice back to normal – and pretty soon succeeding, for having lived this long who would not be an old hand at grief and self-control?

"We thought it was hard," she said finally. "Lou and I thought it was hard."

Is this the last function of old women, beyond making rag rugs and giving us five-dollar bills – making sure the haunts we have contracted for are with us, not one gone without?

She was afraid of Maddy – through fear, had cast her out for good. I thought of what Maddy had said: nobody speaks the same language.

When I got home Maddy was out in the back kitchen making a salad. Rectangles of sunlight lay on the rough linoleum. She had taken off her high-heeled shoes and was standing there in her bare feet. The back kitchen is a large untidy pleasant room with a view, behind the stove and the drying dishtowels, of the sloping back yard, the CPR station and the golden, marshy river that almost encircles the town of Jubilee. My children who had felt a little repressed in the other house immediately began to play under the table.

"Where have you been?" Maddy said.

"Nowhere. Just to see the Aunts."

"Oh, how are they?"

"They're fine. They're indestructible."

"Are they? Yes I guess they are. I haven't been to see them for a while. I don't actually see that much of them any more."

"Don't you?" I said, and she knew then what they had told me.

"They were beginning to get on my nerves a bit, after the funeral. And Fred got me this job and everything and I've been so busy –" She looked at me, waiting for what I would say, smiling a little derisively, patiently.

"Don't be guilty, Maddy," I said softly. All this time the children were running in and out and shrieking at each other between our legs.

"I'm not guilty," she said. "Where did you get that? I'm not guilty." She went to turn on the radio, talking to me over her shoulder. "Fred's going to eat with us again since he's alone. I got some raspberries for dessert. Raspberries are almost over for this year. Do they look all right to you?"

"They look all right," I said. "Do you want me to finish this?"

"Fine," she said. "I'll go and get a bowl."

She went into the dining room and came back carrying a pink cut-glass bowl, for the raspberries.

"I couldn't go on," she said. "I wanted my life."

She was standing on the little step between the kitchen and the dining room and suddenly she lost her grip on the bowl, either because her hands had begun to shake or because she had not picked it up properly in the first place; it was quite a heavy and elaborate old bowl. It slipped out of her hands and she tried to catch it and it smashed on the floor.

Maddy began to laugh. "Oh, hell," she said. "Oh, hell, oh *Hel*-en," she said, using one of our old foolish ritual phrases of despair. "Look what I've done now. In my bare feet yet. Get me a broom."

"Take your life, Maddy. Take it."

"Yes I will," Maddy said. "Yes I will."

"Go away, don't stay here."

"Yes I will."

Then she bent down and began picking up the pieces of broken pink glass. My children stood back looking at her with awe and she was laughing and saying, "It's no loss to me. I've got a whole shelf full of glass bowls. I've got enough glass bowls to do me the rest of my life. Oh, don't stand there looking at me, go and get me a broom!" I went around the kitchen looking for a broom because I seemed to have forgotten where it was kept and she said, "But why can't I, Helen? *Why can't I?*"

III

LOVE, MARRIAGE, AND SEX

If love features in more novels, stories, plays, poems, and movies than any other topic, no area of human behavior looms larger in discussions of popular morality than sex. Traditionally, in the West, sex was supposed to take place only within marriage, conceived of as a life-long exclusive union with a person of the opposite sex. A good example of how strictly this rule was interpreted in nineteenth-century England can be found in the extract from Anthony Trollope's *Dr Wortle's School* in Section XIV. A person – or more specifically, a woman – who violated this rule was considered "fallen" and shunned by all "decent society."

There has been an extraordinary change in sexual morality over the past century. Nevertheless, at some point in their lives, most human beings still commit themselves to a close, and hopefully long-lasting, union with another person, and that commitment usually takes the form of marriage. Even when marriage laws in many countries make divorce relatively easy, the decision to marry – and whom to marry – will have more impact on our lives than most other decisions we make. Though such decisions fill the pages of many great novels, and an even larger number of trashy bestsellers, there has been relatively little serious discussion about the values underlying the choice of a mate. Yet as the readings in this section show, there are quite distinct views of what values are most important in such a choice.

The dominant model in modern urban societies is the romantic one: we fall in love and marry the person with whom we are in love. *Romeo and Juliet* presents this model in its extreme form, love at first sight. Often, although not necessarily, this goes along with the idea that there is only one true love for each of us – a wildly improbable thesis, and a totally depressing one, if we stop to think about it. For, among the hundreds of millions of people of the right sex and roughly the right age for us to fall in love with, how many do we actually get to meet? Perhaps a few hundred, or at the very most a few thousand. So the chances of meeting *the* one true love would be vanishingly small, and most of us would die without having ever met the one person with whom we could find happiness.

The narrator of Guy de Maupassant's story "The Model" takes a more worldly-wise view of romance, when he describes an artist falling in love with a pretty model "as a man always falls in love with any attractive woman whom he sees a lot of." The perceptive narrator points out what a curious phenomenon it is, that a man may know very well that when, in the past, he has fallen in love, his love has soon faded; and yet when he falls in love the next time, he is genuinely convinced that this time it is for ever. (Women, the story suggests, take a different view of marriage.) For a relationship to last, the narrator continues, mere passion is not enough, there must be "a deeper union of minds."

Guy de Maupassant's view – assuming that his narrator speaks for him – lies somewhere on the spectrum between Romeo and Juliet's marriage in the first flush of love, and a traditional arranged marriage. In many parts of the world it is still common for parents to select a partner for their daughter or son – with varying degrees of input from the daughter or son. In Jane Austen's *Pride and Prejudice*, Lady Catherine de Bourgh tells Elizabeth Bennet that Mr Darcy has a "tacit engagement" to marry her daughter, because they were "intended for each other" from infancy. Such arrangements no longer prevail among the English aristocracy, but they still survive in some countries, for example in parts of India. Perhaps that is why Lata Mehra, the young Indian woman who is the central figure in Vikram Seth's *A Suitable Boy*, does not assume that she should marry the man for whom she feels the strongest passion. Although she is able to choose her husband, she does so much more coolly than Juliet, and on the basis of very different values. It is not even de Maupassant's "deeper union of minds" that moves her, but something quite different again.

Is there any solid ground for believing that one way of choosing a partner is better than another? Arranged marriages – or even family pressure on the choice of partner, of the sort that Lady Catherine tries to exert on Elizabeth Bennet – are contrary to the modern Western tradition of individual autonomy. The Universal Declaration of Human Rights declares, in Article 16 (2), that "marriage shall be entered into only with the free and full consent of the intending spouses." No doubt spouses may consent to the choice their parents make for them, but family pressure often makes it doubtful that this consent is "free and full." In any case, the Universal Declaration of Human Rights is not the last word, ethically, and it is also worth asking whether the romantic idea of falling in love and marrying leads to happier, or more lasting, unions than the idea that if a suitable partner can be found, marriage should come first and love will follow. Yet since this is one of the aspects of human behavior least suitable for a large-scale randomized trial, it is very difficult to compare the outcomes of different ways of selecting a marriage partner. Studies of couples who have chosen their partners in different ways cannot avoid comparing people from very different cultures and family backgrounds.

Marriage is supposed to commit a couple to be together for the rest of their lives: in sickness and in health, for richer, for poorer, for better or for worse. The ideal marriage is an intimate union, physical, intellectual, and emotional, in which two become one. Yet there are many bad marriages, and even more, it seems, in literature than in real life. What do spouses owe each other if they find themselves trapped in a marriage with a person they do not love, and perhaps cannot even respect? In traditional Christian wedding services, the bride promises "to love, honor and obey" her husband, while he promises only to "love, cherish and protect" her. Perhaps that is why Casaubon, in George Eliot's *Middlemarch*, appears to believe that he has a right to ask Dorothea to obey his judgment, rather than use her own, and Dorothea, independent-minded as she is, feels the force of her obligation to her husband. Today, outside conservative religious circles, few people would think that a wife has an obligation to obey her husband, simply because she is a woman and her husband is a man. But even with equality between the sexes, there is still a question about what and how much spouses are obliged to do for each other.

As we have already seen, the ideal marriage is also an exclusive union – but in only one respect. A husband who objects to his wife becoming closely involved intellectually with a fellow-worker, perhaps a colleague with whom she is involved in a research project, is widely thought to be excessively jealous. The same would be true if his wife shared an emotional bond with another man, perhaps a love for the same kinds of music, or a passion for the same football team. Yet as soon as she has sex with another man – no matter how far apart she and that man may be intellectually or emotionally – the husband's jealousy immediately becomes appropriate and we think him justified in seeing the marriage as threatened, or even in ending it.

The origins of this focus on sexual fidelity no doubt lie in the male evolutionary imperative to ensure that he is the father of his wife's children, and in the female concern that the father of her children should assist and protect them during their vulnerable years, rather than investing his resources and energy elsewhere. One might expect that the availability of contraception and abortion would lead to a reduced focus on sexual fidelity in marriage. It is true that the discovery that one partner has been unfaithful is no longer automatically seen as the end of the marriage. "Open marriages" are not unknown, but they remain unusual, and the era of "free love" anticipated by eighteenth- and nineteenth-century radicals and revived by 1960s hippies has yet to take hold. Perhaps emotions like jealousy are too deeply based to be changed by a century or two of free thought and a few decades of effective contraception. But that creates a dilemma, for the impulse to adultery is as strong as ever, especially in an age in which the right to great sex seems, for many, to be an essential aspect of the right to the pursuit of happiness. No one, from fundamentalist preachers to presidents, seems immune to the adulterous impulse. Such behavior usually receives severe condemnation. Nevertheless, in a culture in which people fall in love and marry while the infatuation is still strong, many marriages will end when the bloom of passion wears off. If divorce is easy, the result may be "serial monogamy," with people having several partners over a lifetime, but only one at a time.

Like infidelity, prostitution continues to defy popular moral opinion, showing no sign of diminishing. It is said to be the world's oldest profession, and arguments about the ethics of it are probably just as old. The medieval Catholic scholar Thomas Aquinas thought that it was immoral, but should not be suppressed. He quotes Augustine as saying "If you do away with harlots, the world will be convulsed with lust." Prostitution is legal in many countries, including Britain, Australia, and Canada, and in some countries, for example in Germany, the Netherlands, New Zealand, as well as some Australian states, brothels are licensed and regulated by the state. In the United States, it is legal only in parts of Nevada. Nevertheless, the view that prostitution is immoral still generally holds sway even where it can be practiced openly.

Feminists are divided on the issue. In the 1970s, attacks on prostitution by conservative Christians received support from feminists who regarded it as the ultimate form of male exploitation of women. However, a few feminists see the issue differently. They acknowledge that it would no doubt be better if those who work in the sex industry had ways of earning a decent living that did not require them to be intimate with strangers. They also do not deny that prostitution can be hazardous and sex workers are liable to be exploited, especially when the trade is illegal. But as Mrs Warren argues, in Shaw's play that bears her name, factory work can also be hazardous and exploitative, and it usually involves longer hours for much lower pay. Making prostitution illegal is the real cause of exploitation in the sex industry, these feminists say, because then sex workers cannot call in the law against abusive clients, and so they become dependent on the services of a male pimp. A legal sex industry with sex workers organized to demand better conditions and a larger share of the profits would overcome many of the problems that otherwise exist in the industry. Under good conditions, prostitution can even be seen as a way in which otherwise relatively powerless young women can exploit men, making them pay for their desire for casual, anonymous sex.

The traditional view approves sexual acts with a long-term partner, but even then limits the kind of acts that are "normal," seeing others as "perversions." (Consider the attitudes that James Baldwin expresses in the extract from *Giovanni's Room* in the first section.) Homosexuality, like prostitution, is often seen as "immoral," even by people who do not think that the state should interfere with private sexual acts between consenting adults. But rather than carve out an area of immorality that is not the law's business, would it not be better to ask why we should think that any form of sexual behavior that consenting adults enjoy is immoral? Is enjoying sexual pleasure for its own sake "vice" because one does not wish to procreate, or perhaps because one does not love – or even wish to see again – the person with whom one is having sex? Or must harm be caused to someone for a sex act to be so condemned? Our responses to these questions relate to our understandings of sex. Can sex be viewed simply as an enjoyable physical act, like eating a slice of cake? Or does the intimacy of the physical connection mean that sex is necessarily more complex and thus fraught with consequences that are not merely physical?

One objection to the view that no sexual act that brings enjoyment to consenting adults is immoral is that this definition would also include incest, when both partners are consenting adults, and yet if there is any form of sexual behavior that is almost universally disapproved of, it is incest. Here inhibitions acquired in the process of evolution certainly play a role, for there seems to be some kind of incest taboo in chimpanzees too. But now that we have effective contraception, the problems of inbreeding need no longer play a role in our judgment of incest. Why then do we still disapprove of incest so strongly? Jonathan Haidt, a psychologist at the University of Virginia, has shed some light on this issue. He asked people to respond to the following story:

Julie and Mark are brother and sister. They are traveling together in France on summer vacation from college. One night they are staying alone in a cabin near the beach. They decide that it would be interesting and fun if they tried making love. At the very least it would be a new experience for each of them. Julie was already taking birth control pills, but Mark uses a condom too, just to be safe. They both enjoy making love but decide not to do it again. They keep that night as a special secret between them, which makes them feel even closer to each other. What do you think about that? Was it OK for them to make love?

Haidt reports that most people are quick to say that what Julie and Mark did was wrong. They then try to give reasons for their answer. They may mention the dangers of inbreeding, but then recall Julie and Mark used two forms of birth control. Or they may suggest that the siblings could be hurt, even though it is clear from the story that they were not. Eventually, many people say something like: "I don't know, I can't explain it, I just know it's wrong."[1] Evidently, the judgment these people reach is based not on the reasons they offer, but on an intuitive response, no doubt a legacy from a pre-contraceptive era, for they stick to their immediate, intuitive judgment, even after they have withdrawn the reasons they initially offered for it, and are unable to find better ones. But in reading some of the extracts that follow, it is worth bearing in mind that the fact that an intuition is ancient and universal does not prove it to be a sound basis for a moral judgment.

NOTE

1   J. Haidt, "The Emotional Dog and Its Rational Tail: A Social Intuitionist Approach to Moral Judgment," *Pyschological Review*, vol. 108, no. 4 (2000), pp. 814–34.

16

JANE AUSTEN

Pride and Prejudice

Pride and Prejudice opens with one of the most famous lines in English literature: "It is a truth universally acknowledged, that a single man in possession of a good fortune must be in want of a wife." Mr Darcy is a nobleman in possession of a good fortune, but his haughty arrogance initially repels Elizabeth Bennet, and she rebuffs his proposal of marriage. Subsequently she gets to know him better, and grows to love him, but with little hope that he will ever propose to her again.

When this chapter opens, Mr Darcy and his friend Mr Bingley have recently returned from London and Mr Bingley has become engaged to Elizabeth's older sister Jane. Elizabeth's best friend Charlotte is married to Mr Collins, a cousin of the Bennets and the rector of a church under the patronage of Mr Darcy's aunt, Lady Catherine de Bourgh.

One morning, about a week after Bingley's engagement with Jane had been formed, as he and the females of the family were sitting together in the dining-room, their attention was suddenly drawn to the window by the sound of a carriage; and they perceived a chaise and four driving up the lawn. It was too early in the morning for visitors, and besides, the equipage did not answer to that of any of their neighbours. The horses were post; and neither the carriage, nor the livery of the servant who preceded it, were familiar to them. As it was certain, however, that somebody was coming, Bingley instantly prevailed on Miss Bennet to avoid the confinement of such an intrusion, and walk away with him into the shrubbery. They both set off, and the conjectures of the remaining three continued, though with little satisfaction, till the door was thrown open, and their visitor entered. It was Lady Catherine de Bourgh.

They were of course all intending to be surprised; but their astonishment was beyond their expectation; and on the part of Mrs Bennet and Kitty, though she was perfectly unknown to them, even inferior to what Elizabeth felt.

She entered the room with an air more than usually ungracious, made no other reply to Elizabeth's salutation than a slight inclination of the head, and sat down without saying a word. Elizabeth had mentioned her name to her mother on her ladyship's entrance, though no request of introduction had been made.

JANE AUSTEN, from Chapter LVI in *Pride and Prejudice*, first published in 1813.

Mrs Bennet, all amazement, though flattered by having a guest of such high importance, received her with the utmost politeness. After sitting for a moment in silence, she said, very stiffly, to Elizabeth,

"I hope you are well, Miss Bennet. That lady, I suppose, is your mother?"

Elizabeth replied very concisely that she was.

"And *that*, I suppose, is one of your sisters?"

"Yes, madam," said Mrs Bennet, delighted to speak to a Lady Catherine. "She is my youngest girl but one; my youngest of all is lately married; and my eldest is somewhere about the grounds, walking with a young man, who, I believe, will soon become a part of the family."

"You have a very small park here," returned Lady Catherine, after a short silence.

"It is nothing in comparison of Rosings, my lady, I dare say; but I assure you, it is much larger than Sir William Lucas's."

"This must be a most inconvenient sitting-room for the evening in summer; the windows are full west."

Mrs Bennet assured her that they never sat there after dinner, and then added,

"May I take the liberty of asking your ladyship whether you left Mr and Mrs Collins well?"

"Yes, very well. I saw them the night before last."

Elizabeth now expected that she would produce a letter for her from Charlotte, as it seemed the only probable motive for her calling. But no letter appeared, and she was completely puzzled.

Mrs Bennet, with great civility, begged her ladyship to take some refreshment; but Lady Catherine very resolutely, and not very politely, declined eating anything; and then rising up, said to Elizabeth:

"Miss Bennet, there seemed to be a prettyish kind of a little wilderness on one side of your lawn. I should be glad to take a turn in it, if you will favour me with your company."

"Go, my dear," cried her mother, "and shew her ladyship about the different walks. I think she will be pleased with the hermitage."

Elizabeth obeyed, and running into her own room for her parasol, attended her noble guest down stairs. As they passed through the hall, Lady Catherine opened the doors into the dining-parlour and drawing-room, and pronouncing them, after a short survey, to be decent looking rooms, walked on.

Her carriage remained at the door, and Elizabeth saw that her waiting-woman was in it. They proceeded in silence along the gravel walk that led to the copse; Elizabeth was determined to make no effort for conversation with a woman, who was now more than usually insolent and disagreeable.

"How could I ever think her like her nephew?" said she, as she looked in her face.

As soon as they entered the copse, Lady Catherine began in the following manner:

"You can be at no loss, Miss Bennet, to understand the reason of my journey hither. Your own heart, your own conscience, must tell you why I come."

Elizabeth looked with unaffected astonishment.

"Indeed, you are mistaken, madam. I have not been at all able to account for the honour of seeing you here."

"Miss Bennet," replied her ladyship, in an angry tone, "you ought to know, that I am not to be trifled with. But however insincere *you* may choose to be, you shall not find *me* so. My character has ever been celebrated for its sincerity and frankness, and in a cause of such moment as this, I shall certainly not depart from it. A report of a most alarming nature reached me two days ago. I was told, that not only your sister was on the point of being most advantageously married, but that *you*, that Miss Elizabeth Bennet, would, in all likelihood, be soon afterwards united to my nephew, my own nephew, Mr Darcy. Though I *know* it must be a scandalous falsehood; though I would not injure him so much as to suppose the truth of it possible, I instantly resolved on setting off for this place, that I might make my sentiments known to you."

"If you believed it impossible to be true", said Elizabeth, colouring with astonishment and disdain, "I wonder you took the trouble of coming so far. What could your ladyship propose by it?"

"At once to insist upon having such a report universally contradicted."

"Your coming to Longbourn, to see me and my family," said Elizabeth coolly, "will be rather a confirmation of it; if, indeed, such a report is in existence."

"If! do you, then, pretend to be ignorant of it? Has it not been industriously circulated by yourselves? Do you not know that such a report is spread abroad?"

"I never heard that it was."

"And can you likewise declare, that there is no *foundation* for it?"

"I do not pretend to possess equal frankness with your ladyship. *You* may ask questions, which *I* shall not choose to answer."

"This is not to be borne. Miss Bennet, I insist on being satisfied. Has he, has my nephew, made you an offer of marriage?"

"Your ladyship has declared it to be impossible."

"It ought to be so; it must be so, while he retains the use of his reason. But *your* arts and allurements may, in a moment of infatuation, have made him forget what he owes to himself and to all his family. You may have drawn him in."

"If I have, I shall be the last person to confess it."

"Miss Bennet, do you know who I am? I have not been accustomed to such language as this. I am almost the nearest relation he has in the world, and am entitled to know all his dearest concerns."

"But you are not entitled to know *mine*; nor will such behaviour as this ever induce me to be explicit."

"Let me be rightly understood. This match, to which you have the presumption to aspire, can never take place. No, never. Mr Darcy is engaged to *my daughter*. Now, what have you to say?"

"Only this; that if he is so, you can have no reason to suppose he will make an offer to me."

Lady Catherine hesitated for a moment, and then replied,

"The engagement between them is of a peculiar kind. From their infancy, they have been intended for each other. It was the favourite wish of *his* mother, as well as of hers. While in their cradles, we planned the union: and now, at the moment when the wishes of both sisters would be accomplished, in their marriage, to be prevented by a young woman of inferior birth, of no importance in the world, and wholly unallied to the family! Do you pay no regard to the wishes of his friends? To his tacit engagement with Miss de Bourgh? Are you lost to every feeling of propriety and delicacy? have you not heard me say, that from his earliest hours he was destined for his cousin?"

"Yes, and I had heard it before. But what is that to me? if there is no other objection to my marrying your nephew, I shall certainly not be kept from it, by knowing that his mother and aunt wished him to marry Miss de Bourgh. You both did as much as you could, in planning the marriage. Its completion depended on others. If Mr Darcy is neither by honour nor inclination confined to his cousin, why is not he to make another choice? and if I am that choice, why may not I accept him?"

"Because honour, decorum, prudence, nay, interest, forbid it. Yes, Miss Bennet, interest; for do not expect to be noticed by his family or friends, if you wilfully act against the inclinations of all. You will be censured, slighted, and despised, by every one connected with him. Your alliance will be a disgrace; your name will never even be mentioned by any of us."

"These are heavy misfortunes," replied Elizabeth. "But the wife of Mr Darcy must have such extraordinary sources of happiness necessarily attached to her situation, that she could, upon the whole, have no cause to repine."

"Obstinate, headstrong girl! I am ashamed of you! Is this your gratitude for my attentions to you last spring? Is nothing due to me on that score?

"Let us sit down. You are to understand, Miss Bennet, that I came here with the determined resolution of carrying my purpose; nor will I be dissuaded from it. I have not been used to submit to any person's whims. I have not been in the habit of brooking disappointment."

"*That* will make your ladyship's situation at present more pitiable; but it will have no effect on *me*."

"I will not be interrupted! Hear me in silence. My daughter and my nephew are formed for each other. They are descended on the maternal side, from the same noble line; and, on the father's, from respectable, honourable, and ancient, though untitled families. Their fortune on both sides is splendid. They are destined for each other by the voice of every member of their respective houses; and what is to divide them? — the upstart pretensions of a young woman without family, connections, or fortune. Is this to be endured! But it must not, shall not be! If you were sensible of your own good, you would not wish to quit the sphere in which you have been brought up."

"In marrying your nephew, I should not consider myself as quitting that sphere. He is a gentleman; I am a gentleman's daughter: so far we are equal."

"True. You *are* a gentleman's daughter. But who was your mother? Who are your uncles and aunts? Do not imagine me ignorant of their condition."

"Whatever my connections may be," said Elizabeth, "if your nephew does not object to them, they can be nothing to *you*."

"Tell me once for all, are you engaged to him?"

Though Elizabeth would not, for the mere purpose of obliging Lady Catherine, have answered this question; she could not but say, after a moment's deliberation,

"I am not."

Lady Catherine seemed pleased.

"And will you promise me, never to enter into such an engagement?"

"I will make no promise of the kind."

"Miss Bennet, I am shocked and astonished. I expected to find a more reasonable young woman. But do not deceive yourself into a belief that I will ever recede. I shall not go away till you have given me the assurance I require."

"And I certainly *never* shall give it. I am not to be intimidated into any thing so wholly unreasonable. Your ladyship wants Mr Darcy to marry your daughter; but would my giving you the wished-for promise, make *their* marriage at all more probable? Supposing him to be attached to me, would *my* refusing to accept his hand make him wish to bestow it on his cousin? Allow me to say, Lady Catherine, that the arguments with which you have supported this extraordinary application, have been as frivolous as the application was ill judged. You have widely mistaken my character, if you think I can be worked on by such persuasions as these. How far your nephew might approve of your interference in *his* affairs, I cannot tell; but you have certainly no right to concern yourself in mine. – I must beg, therefore, to be importuned no farther on the subject."

"Not so hasty if you please. I have by no means done. To all the objections I have already urged, I have still another to add. I am no stranger to the particulars of your youngest sister's infamous elopement. I know it all; that the young man's marrying her was a patched-up business, at the expense of your father and uncle. And is *such* a girl to be my nephew's sister? Is *her* husband, is the son of his late father's steward, to be his brother? Heaven and earth! – of what are you thinking! Are the shades of Pemberley to be thus polluted?"

"You can *now* have nothing farther to say," she resentfully answered. "You have insulted me, in every possible method. I must beg to return to the house."

And she rose as she spoke. Lady Catherine rose also, and they turned back. Her ladyship was highly incensed.

"You have no regard, then, for the honour and credit of my nephew! Unfeeling, selfish girl! Do you not consider that a connection with you must disgrace him in the eyes of every body?"

"Lady Catherine, I have nothing further to say. You know my sentiments."

"You are then resolved to have him?"

"I have said no such thing. I am only resolved to act in that manner, which will, in my own opinion, constitute my happiness, without reference to *you*, or to any person so wholly unconnected with me."

"It is well. You refuse, then, to oblige me. You refuse to obey the claims of duty, honour, and gratitude. You are determined to ruin him in the opinion of all his friends, and make him the contempt of the world."

"Neither duty, nor honour, nor gratitude", replied Elizabeth, "have any possible claim on me, in the present instance. No principle of either would be violated by my marriage with Mr Darcy. And with regard to the resentment of his family, or the indignation of the world, if the former *were* excited by his marrying me, it would not give me one moment's concern – and the world in general would have too much sense to join in the scorn."

"And this is your real opinion! This is your final resolve! Very well. I shall now know how to act. Do not imagine, Miss Bennet, that your ambition will ever be gratified. I came to try you. I hoped to find you reasonable; but depend upon it I will carry my point."

In this manner Lady Catherine talked on, till they were at the door of the carriage, when turning hastily round, she added,

"I take no leave of you, Miss Bennet. I send no compliments to your mother. You deserve no such attention. I am most seriously displeased."

Elizabeth made no answer; and without attempting to persuade her ladyship to return into the house, walked quietly into it herself. She heard the carriage drive away as she proceeded up stairs. Her mother impatiently met her at the door of the dressing-room, to ask why Lady Catherine would not come in again and rest herself.

"She did not choose it," said her daughter; "she would go."

"She is a very fine-looking woman! and her calling here was prodigiously civil! for she only came, I suppose, to tell us the Collinses were well. She is on her road somewhere, I dare say, and so, passing through Meryton, thought she might as well call on you. I suppose she had nothing particular to say to you, Lizzy?"

Elizabeth was forced to give into a little falsehood here; for to acknowledge the substance of their conversation was impossible.

17

WILLIAM SHAKESPEARE

Romeo and Juliet

This early Shakespearean play has become a classic tale of young love. Set in Verona, it tells the story of two lovers whose families, the Montagues and the Capulets, are feuding. Romeo and Juliet meet for the first time at the Capulet ball, exchange a few words and one kiss. This scene takes place later on the same night.

Capulet's Orchard

(*Enter* ROMEO)

ROMEO: He jests at scars that never felt a wound.

(JULIET *appears above at a window*)

But, soft! what light through yonder window breaks?
It is the east, and Juliet is the sun.
Arise, fair sun, and kill the envious moon,
Who is already sick and pale with grief,
That thou her maid art far more fair than she:
Be not her maid, since she is envious;
Her vestal livery is but sick and green
And none but fools do wear it; cast it off.
It is my lady, O, it is my love!
O, that she knew she were!
She speaks yet she says nothing: what of that?
Her eye discourses; I will answer it.
I am too bold, 'tis not to me she speaks:
Two of the fairest stars in all the heaven,
Having some business, do entreat her eyes
To twinkle in their spheres till they return.

WILLIAM SHAKESPEARE, from Act II, Scene II in *Romeo and Juliet*, first published in 1597.

What if her eyes were there, they in her head?
The brightness of her cheek would shame those stars,
As daylight doth a lamp; her eyes in heaven
Would through the airy region stream so bright
That birds would sing and think it were not night.
See, how she leans her cheek upon her hand!
O, that I were a glove upon that hand,
That I might touch that cheek!
JULIET: Ay me!
ROMEO: She speaks:
O, speak again, bright angel! for thou art
As glorious to this night, being o'er my head
As is a winged messenger of heaven
Unto the white-upturned wondering eyes
Of mortals that fall back to gaze on him
When he bestrides the lazy-pacing clouds
And sails upon the bosom of the air.
JULIET: O Romeo, Romeo! wherefore art thou Romeo?
Deny thy father and refuse thy name;
Or, if thou wilt not, be but sworn my love,
And I'll no longer be a Capulet.
ROMEO: (*Aside*) Shall I hear more, or shall I speak at this?
JULIET: 'Tis but thy name that is my enemy;
Thou art thyself, though not a Montague.
What's Montague? it is nor hand, nor foot,
Nor arm, nor face, nor any other part
Belonging to a man. O, be some other name!
What's in a name? that which we call a rose
By any other name would smell as sweet;
So Romeo would, were he not Romeo call'd,
Retain that dear perfection which he owes
Without that title. Romeo, doff thy name,
And for that name which is no part of thee
Take all myself.
ROMEO: I take thee at thy word:
Call me but love, and I'll be new baptized;
Henceforth I never will be Romeo.
JULIET: What man art thou that thus bescreen'd in night
So stumblest on my counsel?
ROMEO: By a name
I know not how to tell thee who I am:
My name, dear saint, is hateful to myself,
Because it is an enemy to thee;
Had I it written, I would tear the word.
JULIET: My ears have not yet drunk a hundred words
Of that tongue's utterance, yet I know the sound:

Art thou not Romeo and a Montague?

ROMEO: Neither, fair saint, if either thee dislike.

JULIET: How camest thou hither, tell me, and wherefore?
  The orchard walls are high and hard to climb,
  And the place death, considering who thou art,
  If any of my kinsmen find thee here.

ROMEO: With love's light wings did I o'er-perch these walls;
  For stony limits cannot hold love out,
  And what love can do that dares love attempt;
  Therefore thy kinsmen are no let to me.

JULIET: If they do see thee, they will murder thee.

ROMEO: Alack, there lies more peril in thine eye
  Than twenty of their swords: look thou but sweet,
  And I am proof against their enmity.

JULIET: I would not for the world they saw thee here.

ROMEO: I have night's cloak to hide me from their sight;
  And but thou love me, let them find me here:
  My life were better ended by their hate,
  Than death prorogued, wanting of thy love.

JULIET: By whose direction found'st thou out this place?

ROMEO: By love, who first did prompt me to inquire;
  He lent me counsel and I lent him eyes.
  I am no pilot; yet, wert thou as far
  As that vast shore wash'd with the farthest sea,
  I would adventure for such merchandise.

JULIET: Thou know'st the mask of night is on my face,
  Else would a maiden blush bepaint my cheek
  For that which thou hast heard me speak to-night.
  Fain would I dwell on form, fain, fain deny
  What I have spoke: but farewell compliment!
  Dost thou love me? I know thou wilt say "Ay,"
  And I will take thy word: yet if thou swear'st,
  Thou mayst prove false; at lovers' perjuries
  They say, Jove laughs. O gentle Romeo,
  If thou dost love, pronounce it faithfully:
  Or if thou think'st I am too quickly won,
  I'll frown and be perverse and say thee nay,
  So thou wilt woo; but else, not for the world.
  In truth, fair Montague, I am too fond,
  And therefore thou mayst think my 'havior light:
  But trust me, gentleman, I'll prove more true
  Than those that have more cunning to be strange.
  I should have been more strange, I must confess,
  But that thou overheard'st, ere I was ware,
  My true love's passion: therefore pardon me,
  And not impute this yielding to light love,

Which the dark night hath so discovered.
ROMEO: Lady, by yonder blessed moon I swear
   That tips with silver all these fruit-tree tops –
JULIET: O, swear not by the moon, the inconstant moon,
   That monthly changes in her circled orb,
   Lest that thy love prove likewise variable.
ROMEO: What shall I swear by?
JULIET: Do not swear at all;
   Or, if thou wilt, swear by thy gracious self,
   Which is the god of my idolatry,
   And I'll believe thee.
ROMEO: If my heart's dear love –
JULIET: Well, do not swear: although I joy in thee,
   I have no joy of this contract to-night:
   It is too rash, too unadvised, too sudden;
   Too like the lightning, which doth cease to be
   Ere one can say 'It lightens.' Sweet, good night!
   This bud of love, by summer's ripening breath,
   May prove a beauteous flower when next we meet.
   Good night, good night! as sweet repose and rest
   Come to thy heart as that within my breast!
ROMEO: O, wilt thou leave me so unsatisfied?
JULIET: What satisfaction canst thou have to-night?
ROMEO: The exchange of thy love's faithful vow for mine.
JULIET: I gave thee mine before thou didst request it:
   And yet I would it were to give again.
ROMEO: Wouldst thou withdraw it? for what purpose, love?
JULIET: But to be frank, and give it thee again.
   And yet I wish but for the thing I have:
   My bounty is as boundless as the sea,
   My love as deep; the more I give to thee,
   The more I have, for both are infinite.

(NURSE *calls within*)

   I hear some noise within; dear love, adieu!
   Anon, good nurse! Sweet Montague, be true.
   Stay but a little, I will come again.

(*Exit, above*)

ROMEO: O blessed, blessed night! I am afeard.
   Being in night, all this is but a dream,
   Too flattering-sweet to be substantial.

(*Re-enter* JULIET, *above*)

JULIET: Three words, dear Romeo, and good night indeed.
   If that thy bent of love be honourable,
   Thy purpose marriage, send me word to-morrow,
   By one that I'll procure to come to thee,
   Where and what time thou wilt perform the rite;
   And all my fortunes at thy foot I'll lay
   And follow thee my lord throughout the world.
NURSE: (*Within*) Madam!
JULIET: I come, anon. – But if thou mean'st not well,
   I do beseech thee –
NURSE: (*Within*) Madam!
JULIET: By and by, I come: –
   To cease thy suit, and leave me to my grief:
   To-morrow will I send.
ROMEO: So thrive my soul –
JULIET: A thousand times good night!

(*Exit, above*)

18

VIKRAM SETH

A Suitable Boy

Vikram Seth's *A Suitable Boy* (1993) is set in India in the 1950s. Lata Mehra has been searching for a husband. She has three suitors to choose from: Kabir, the dashing Muslim cricketer; the sophisticated poet Amit; and Haresh, the self-made man.

On the front wall of Pran's house, the yellow jasmine had begun to bloom. Inside, Mrs Rupa Mehra muttered, "Plain, purl, plain, purl. Where's Lata?"

"She's gone out to buy a book," said Savita.

"Which book?"

"I don't think she knows yet. A novel, probably."

"She shouldn't be reading novels but studying for her exams."

This was, as it happened, what the bookseller was telling Lata at almost the same moment. Luckily for his business, students rarely took his advice.

He reached out for the book with one hand, and extracted wax from his ear with the other.

"I've studied enough, Balwantji," said Lata. "I'm tired of my studies. In fact, I'm tired of everything," she ended dramatically.

"You look just like Nargis when you say that," said Balwant.

"I am afraid I only have a five-rupee note."

"Don't worry," said Balwant. "Where is your friend Malatiji?" he continued. "I never see her these days."

"That's because she's not wasting her time buying novels," said Lata. "She's studying hard. I hardly see her myself."

Kabir entered the shop, looking quite cheerful. He noticed Lata and stopped.

The whole of their last meeting flashed before Lata's eyes – and, immediately afterwards, their first meeting in the bookstore. They looked at each other for a few seconds before Lata broke the silence with a hello.

"Hello," replied Kabir. "I see you're on your way out." Here was another meeting brought about by coincidence, and to be governed, no doubt, by awkwardness.

VIKRAM SETH, pp. 1285–99 (chapters 18.16–18.21) from *A Suitable Boy*. New York: HarperCollins, 1993. Copyright © 1993 by Vikram Seth. Reprinted by permission of HarperCollins Publishers, Inc.; Little, Brown and Company, Inc.; and Phoenix Books.

"Yes," said Lata. "I came in to buy a Wodehouse, but I've bought myself a Jane Austen instead."

"I'd like you to have a coffee with me at the Blue Danube." It was a statement more than a request.

"I have to get back," said Lata. "I told Savita I'd be back in an hour."

"Savita can wait. I was going to buy a book, but that too can wait."

"Which book?" asked Lata.

"What does it matter?" replied Kabir. "I don't know. I was just going to browse. Not in Poetry or Mathematics, though," he added.

"All right," said Lata recklessly.

"Good. The cake will be better, at least. Of course, I don't know what excuse you'll make if someone you know walks in."

"I don't care," said Lata.

"Good."

The Blue Danube was just a couple of hundred yards along Nabiganj. They sat down and placed their orders.

Neither spoke. Finally Lata said:

"Good news about the cricket."

"Excellent." India had just won the fifth Test Match against England in Madras by an innings and eight runs, and no one could quite believe it.

After a while the coffee came. Stirring it slowly, Kabir said: "Were you serious?"

"About what?"

"You are writing to this man?"

"Yes."

"How serious is it?"

"Ma wants me to marry him."

Kabir said nothing, but looked down at his right hand as it kept stirring the coffee.

"Aren't you going to say something?" she asked him.

He shrugged.

"Do you hate me?" asked Lata. "Don't you care whom I marry?"

"Don't be stupid." Kabir sounded disgusted with her. "And please stop those tears. They won't improve your coffee or my appetite." For again, though she was half unconscious of them, tears had slowly filled Lata's eyes and were falling down her cheeks one by one. She did not try to wipe them away, nor did she take her eyes off Kabir's face. She did not care what the waiters or anyone else thought. Or even he, for that matter.

He continued to stir his coffee with a troubled look.

"I know of two mixed marriages –" he began.

"Ours wouldn't work. No one else will let it work. And now I can't even trust myself."

"Then why are you sitting here with me?" he said.

"I don't know."

"And why are you crying?"

Lata said nothing.

"My handkerchief is dirty," said Kabir. "If you haven't brought a handkerchief, use that napkin."

Lata dabbed at her eyes.

"Come on, eat your cake, it'll do you good. I'm the one who's been rejected, and I'm not sobbing my poor little heart out."

She shook her head. "Now I must go," she said. "Thank you."

Kabir did not try to dissuade her.

"Don't leave your book behind," he said. "*Mansfield Park?* I haven't read that one. Tell me if it's any good."

Neither of them turned around to look at the other as Lata walked towards the door.

*

So unsettled was Lata by her meeting with Kabir – but when was she not unsettled by a meeting with him? she wondered – that she took a long walk near the banyan tree. She sat down on the great, twisted root, remembered their first kiss, read some poetry, fed the monkeys, and fell into a reverie.

Walks are my panacea, she thought, bitterly; and my substitute for any decisive action.

The next day, however, she took action of the most decisive kind.

Two letters arrived for Lata by the morning post. She sat on the verandah with its trellis of yellow jasmine and slit open both envelopes. Mrs Rupa Mehra was not at home when they arrived, or she would have recognized the handwriting on the envelopes and demanded to know what news they contained.

The contents of the first envelope consisted of eight lines and a heading, type-written and unsigned:

A MODEST PROPOSAL

As you've asked for black and white,
May I send these lines to you
In the tacit hope you might
Take my type at least as true.

Let this distance disappear
And our hearts approach from far
Till we come to be as near
As acrostically we are.

Lata began to laugh. The poem was a little trite, but it was skilful and entirely personalized, and it pleased her. She tried to recall exactly what she had said; had she really asked for black and white or merely told Amit that that was all she would believe? And how serious was this "modest" proposal? After thinking the matter over, she was inclined to believe it was serious; and, as a result, it pleased her somewhat less.

Would she have preferred it to be determinedly sombre and passionate – or not to have been written in the first place? Would a passionate proposal have been in

Amit's style at all – or at least in his style with her? Many of his poems were far from light in either sense of the word, but it seemed almost as if he hid that side of himself from her for fear that looking into that dark, pessimistic cynicism might trouble her too greatly and make her shy away.

And yet, what was it he had said about her own poem, the despairing one that she had hesitantly shown him? That he had liked it – but only, he had implied, as a poem. If he disapproved of gloom, what was he doing as a poet? Would he not – at least for his own sake – have been far better off in the practical profession of law? But perhaps he did not disapprove of gloom as such in himself or others, only on the fruitless dwelling on it – which, she had to admit, that poem of hers had been guilty of. Clearly, the unhappiness or unease of Amit's own strongest poems was typical not of his daily behaviour but of certain moments of intensity. Still, Lata felt that high hills rarely rise direct and isolated from the plains, and that there had to be some deeper organic connection between the poet of "The Fever Bird" and Amit Chatterji as she knew him than he himself encouraged herself or others to believe.

And what would it be like to be married to such a man? Lata got up and paced restlessly about the verandah. How could she consider him seriously – Meenakshi and Kuku's brother, her own friend and guide to Calcutta, the purveyor of pineapples, the castigator of Cuddles? He was just Amit – to convert him into a husband was absurd – the thought of it made Lata smile and shake her head. But again she sat down, and again she read the poem, and she looked out beyond the hedge to the campus, from where the sloped and slated roof of the examination hall was distantly visible. She realized that she had the poem by heart already – as she had his earlier acrostic, and "The Fever Bird", and other poems besides. Without any attempt on her part to learn them, they had become a part of herself.

*

The second letter was from Haresh.

> My dearest Lata,
>
> I hope everything is well with you and with the family. I have been so busy with work these last few weeks that I have come home exhausted, and not been in that state of mind in which you deserve to hear from me. But the Goodyear Welted line is going from strength to strength, and I have even persuaded the management to take on a new scheme of mine, by which entire uppers can be made outside and assembled for final manufacture here at Praha. Of course, that would be in other lines, such as brogues. All in all, I think I have already shown them that it was not a mistake to take me on, and that I am not merely someone imposed on them by Mr Khandelwal.
>
> I have some good news to convey. There is talk of promoting me to Group Foreman soon. If so, it will not come a moment too soon, as I find it difficult to keep down my expenses. I am a bit lavish by nature, and it will be good if someone helps me to curb it. If that is so, then it will certainly be true what they say, that two can live cheaper than one.

I have talked to Arun and Meenakshi a few times on the phone, although the line from Prahapore to Calcutta is not as clear as it could be. They have unfortunately been busy with various engagements, but they have promised to make time to come for dinner sometime in the near future.

My own family is well. My doubting Uncle Umesh has been impressed by my obtaining a job like this one so quickly. My foster-mother, who is really like a real mother to me, is also pleased. I remember when I went to England first, she said: "Son, people go to England to become doctors, engineers, barristers. Why do you need to go all the way to become a cobbler?" I could not help smiling at the time, and even now I smile when I think of it. I am happy, however, that I am not a burden on them, that I am standing on my own two feet, and that my work is useful in its own circle.

You will be glad to know that I have given up eating paan. I was warned by Kalpana that your family does not think it attractive, and, whatever I think about it, I have decided to be accommodating in this respect. I hope you are impressed by all these efforts of mine to Mehraize myself.

There is something I have not touched upon in either of my last two letters, and it is good of you not to have mentioned its absence. As you know, I was very upset about a word you used, which I realize in retrospect you did not intend as I took it. I wrote to Kalpana about it that same evening, because I felt the need to unburden myself. For some reason I was also uneasy in general. She ticked me off for my "thick-skinned sensitivity" (she had a way with words even in college) and told me I should apologize at once and not be truculent. Well, I did not feel sorry, so I did not write it. But now with the passing of the weeks I realize that I was in the wrong.

I am a practical man and I am proud of it – but sometimes I come across situations that I do not know how to handle despite my well-formed opinions, and I find that after all perhaps there is less reason to be proud than I thought. So please accept my apologies, Lata, and forgive me for ending New Year's Day in such an unpleasing manner.

I hope that when we get married – I am hoping that it is *when*, and not *if* – you will tell me, with that lovely quiet smile of yours, whenever I take things amiss that are not badly intended.

Baoji has been asking me about my marriage plans, but on that score I have not been able to reassure him as yet. As soon as you are sure in your mind that I would make you the right husband, please do tell me. I give thanks every day that I should have met you and that you and I should have got to know each other through words and meetings. The feelings I have for you increase every day, and, unlike my shoes, do not take Saturday and Sunday off. Needless to say, I have your framed photograph on my desk before me, and it brings to me tender thoughts of the original.

---

paan – betel leaf, widely grown in India, which is chewed for mouth-freshening and medicinal purposes

Apart from what one sometimes reads in the Calcutta papers, I have had a little news of the Kapoor family in the course of some business dealings with Kedarnath, and my deep sympathy goes to all of them. It must be a terrible time for everyone. He says that Veena and Bhaskar are most agitated, but he makes light of his own anxieties. I can also imagine how hard it is for Pran, with his brother's difficulties and the death of his mother coming side by side. It is good that Savita has her baby and her law studies to provide other thoughts, but it could not be easy to concentrate, especially on some subject as hard as law. I do not know what I can do to help in any way, but if there is anything I can do, please tell me. Some things – the latest law-books and so on – are available in Calcutta more easily than in Brahmpur, I think.

I hope you are studying somehow through all this. I am keeping my fingers crossed for you and am very confident, my Lata, that you will come out in flying colours.

My love to Ma, whom I often thank in my mind for bringing you to Kanpur, and to Pran and Savita and the baby. Please tell Kedarnath if you happen to meet him that I will be writing to him very shortly, probably within the week, depending on certain consultations at this end.

With all my love,
Your own,
Haresh

*

As Lata read, she smiled to herself from time to time. He had crossed out "Cawnpore" to write "Kanpur". When she came to the end she read it through once more. She was glad to hear about Umesh Uncle and his resolved doubts. She could imagine Haresh's father demanding a similar resolution to his own.

Over the months her world had begun to be populated by the various people Haresh continually mentioned. She even missed Simran; Haresh had probably left her out of this letter for fear of treading on her sensitivities. But Lata realized with a start that, however much she liked Haresh, she was not jealous of Simran.

And who were these people in reality? She thought of Haresh: generous, robust, optimistic, impatient, responsible. There he stood in Prahapore, as solid as a pair of Goodyear Welted shoes, twinkling his eyes affectionately at her from the pages of his letter and telling her as well as he could that he was lonely without her.

But Haresh stood alone: Umesh Uncle, Simran, his foster-father, all these figures whom she felt she knew, could turn out to be entirely different from what she had imagined. And his family of conservative Old Delhi khatris: how could she possibly behave with them as she behaved with Kuku or Dipankar or Mr Justice Chatterji? What would she talk about to the Czechs? But there was something adventurous in losing herself entirely in a world that she did not know with a man whom she

---

khatris – an Indian tribe, or caste, associated with trade and business

trusted and had begun to admire – and who cared for her so deeply and steadily. She thought of a paan-less Haresh, smiling his open smile; she sat him down at a table so that she could not see his co-respondent shoes; she ruffled his hair a bit, and – well, he was quite attractive! She liked him. Perhaps, given time and luck, she could even learn to love him.

*

A letter from Arun arrived in the afternoon post and helped clarify her thoughts:

> My dear Lata,
>
> You will not mind if I take an elder brother's prerogative to write to you on a matter of great importance to your future and to the future of the family. We are, as such things go, an exceptionally close family, and perhaps as a result of Daddy's death we have been forced even closer together. I, for example, would not have taken on the responsibilities that I have, had Daddy been alive. Varun would probably not have been staying with me, nor would I feel it incumbent on myself to advise him about finding a direction in life, something that left to himself he would, I am afraid, be disinclined to do. Nor would I have the sense that I am, in a manner of speaking, in loco parentis to you.
>
> I imagine you have already guessed the matter I am referring to. Suffice it to say that I have thought about it from every possible angle, and I find myself in disagreement with Ma's judgment on the subject. Hence this letter. Ma has too great a tendency to be swayed by sentiment, and she appears to have taken an irrationally strong liking to Haresh – as well as a strong antipathy – irrational or otherwise – to other people. I experienced something similar in her attitude to my own marriage, which, contrary to her expectations, has turned out to be a happy one based on mutual affection and trust. I believe that as a result I have gained a more objective sense of the choices facing you.
>
> Apart from your temporary infatuation with a certain person in Brahmpur, about which the less said the better, you do not have much experience of the tangled thickets of life, nor have you had the chance to develop criteria for judging the alternatives unguided. It is in this context that I am proffering my advice.
>
> I believe that Haresh has some excellent qualities. He is hardworking, he is in some sense self-made, and he has been educated at – or has at least obtained a degree from – one of the better colleges in India. He is, from all accounts, competent at the trade he has chosen. He has confidence, and he is unafraid to speak his mind. One must give the man his due. That said, however, let me make it clear that I believe that he would not make a suitable addition to our family, and for the following reasons:
>
> 1. Despite his having studied English at St Stephen's and having lived in England for two years, his use of the English language leaves a great deal to

be desired. This is no trivial point. Conversation between man and wife is the staple of a marriage based on true understanding. They must be able to communicate, to be, as they say, on the same wave-length. Haresh is simply not on the same wave-length as you – or any of us for that matter. This is not merely a question of his accent, which immediately betrays the fact that English is very far from being his first language; it is a question of his idiom and diction, of his very sense, sometimes, of what is being said. I am glad I was not present at home when that ludicrous fracas about the word "mean" took place but, as you know, Ma informed me (with many tears and in great detail) about what had occurred the moment Meenakshi and I returned home. If you take the view that Mother knows best, and become engaged to this man, you will continually face painful and absurd situations of this kind.

2. A second, not unrelated, point, is that Haresh does not, and can never aspire to, move in the same social circles as we do. A foreman is not a covenanted assistant, and Praha is simply not Bentsen Pryce. The smell of leather clings rather too closely to the name; the Czechs, who are his bosses, are technicians, sometimes barely literate in English, not graduates from the best universities in England. In a certain sense, by choosing a trade rather than a profession after his graduation from St Stephen's, Haresh has downgraded himself. I hope you do not mind my speaking frankly on a matter of such importance to your future happiness. Society matters, and society is exacting and cruel; you will find yourself excluded from certain circles simply by virtue of being Mrs Khanna.

Nor can Haresh's own background or demeanour counteract the Praha trademark. Unlike say, Meenakshi or Amit, whose father and grandfather have been High Court judges, his family are small people from Old Delhi, and are, to put it bluntly, entirely undistinguished. Certainly, it does him credit that he has brought himself to where he is; but, being a self-made man, he has a tendency to be rather pleased with himself – indeed, a little bumptious. I have noticed that this is often true of short people; he may well have an additional chip on his shoulder as a result of this. I know that Ma thinks of him as a rough diamond. All I can say is that the cut and polish of a stone matter. One does not wear a rough diamond – or one that is chipped – in a wedding ring.

Family, if I may put it plainly, will out. It shows in Haresh's manner of dress, in his liking for snuff and paan, in the fact that, despite his stint in England, he lacks the small social graces. I warned Ma about family background at the time of Savita's engagement to Pran, but she would not listen; and the result, socially speaking, has been the disgraceful connection, through us, of the family of a jailbird to the family of a judge. This is another reason why I feel it is my duty to speak to you before it is too late.

3. Your future family income will in all likelihood not permit you to send your children to the kind of school – for example, St George's or St Sophia's or Jheel or Mayo or Loreto or Doon – that our children – Meenakshi's and mine – will go to. Besides, even if you could afford it, Haresh may have

very different views from you about the upbringing of his children or the proportion of the family budget to be devoted to education. With respect to Savita's husband, since he is an academic, I have no concerns on this particular count. But with Haresh I do, and I have to put them to you. I wish the family to remain close, indeed, I feel responsible for the maintenance of this closeness; and differences in the upbringing of our children are bound to draw us apart in time, and to cause you a great deal of heartache besides.

I must ask you to treat this letter as a personal one; to think deeply about it, as befits its contents, but not to show it around the family. Ma would no doubt take it amiss, and, I suppose, so would Savita. As for the subject of this letter, I will only add that he has been pestering us with offers of hospitality; we have been cool to him, and have so far avoided going to Prahapore for another gargantuan lunch. He should, we believe, not presume to be considered part of the family unless he in fact becomes part of it. Needless to say, the choice is yours, and we would welcome your husband, whoever he happened to be, in our private capacity. But it is no use meaning well if you cannot also speak freely, and that is what I have done in this letter.

Rather than add news and small talk, which can wait for another occasion, I will simply end with my love and fondest hopes for your future happiness. Meenakshi, who agrees with me on all points, does the same.

Yours,
Arun Bhai

Lata read the letter through several times, the first time – owing mainly to Arun's wildly erratic handwriting – very slowly; and, as instructed, she pondered its contents deeply. Her first instinct was to have a heart-to-heart talk with Savita, or Malati, or her mother – or with each of them. Then she decided that it would make no difference and would, if anything, only serve to confuse her. This decision was hers to make.

She wrote to Haresh the same evening, accepting with gratitude – and, indeed, warmth – his often repeated offer of marriage.

*

"No!" cried Malati, staring at Lata. "No! I refuse to believe it. Have you posted the letter yet?"

"Yes," said Lata.

They were sitting in the shadow of the Fort on the Pul Mela sands, looking out over the warm, grey Ganga, which was glinting in the sunlight.

"You are mad – absolutely mad. How could you do it?"

"Don't be like my mother – 'O my poor Lata, O my poor Lata!'"

"Was that her reaction? I thought she was keen on Haresh," said Malati. "Trust you to do just what Mummy says. But I won't have it, Lata, you can't ruin your life like this."

"I'm not ruining my life," said Lata heatedly. "And yes, that might well be her reaction. She's taken against Haresh for some reason. And Arun's been against him from the beginning. But no, Mummy didn't say. In fact, Mummy doesn't even know. You're the first person I'm telling, and you shouldn't be trying to make me feel miserable."

"I should. I should. I hope you feel really miserable," said Malati, her eyes flashing green fire. "Then perhaps you'll see some sense and undo what you've done. You love Kabir, and you must marry him."

"There's no must about it. Go and marry him yourself," said Lata, her cheeks red. "No – don't! Don't! I'll never forgive you. Please don't talk about Kabir, Malu, please."

"You're going to regret it bitterly," said Malati. "I'm telling you that."

"Well, that's my look-out," said Lata, struggling to control herself.

"Why didn't you ask me before you decided?" demanded Malati. "Whom did you consult? Or did you just make up your silly mind by yourself?"

"I consulted my monkeys," said Lata calmly.

Malati had the strong urge to slap Lata for making stupid jokes at such a time.

"And a book of poetry," added Lata.

"Poetry!" said Malati with contempt. "Poetry has been your complete undoing. You have too good a brain to waste on English literature. No, perhaps you don't, after all."

"You were the first person to tell me to give him up," said Lata. "You told me. Or have you forgotten all that?"

"I changed my mind," said Malati. "You know I did. I was wrong, terribly wrong. Look at the danger caused to the world by that sort of attitude –"

"Why do you think I'm giving him up?" asked Lata, turning towards her friend.

"Because he's Muslim."

Lata didn't answer for a while. Then she said:

"It's not that. It's not just that. There isn't any single reason."

Malati gave a disgusted snort at this pathetic prevarication.

Lata sighed. "Malati, I can't describe it – my feelings with him are so confused. I'm not myself when I'm with him. I ask myself who is this – this jealous, obsessed woman who can't get a man out of her head – why should I make myself suffer like this? I know that it'll always be like this if I'm with him."

"Oh, Lata – don't be blind –" exclaimed Malati. "It shows how passionately you love him –"

"I don't want to," cried Lata, "I don't want to. If that's what passion means, I don't want it. Look at what passion has done to the family. Maan's broken, his mother's dead, his father's in despair. When I thought that Kabir was seeing someone else, what I remember feeling was enough to make me hate passion. Passionately and forever."

"It's my fault," said Malati bitterly, shaking her head from side to side. "I wish to God I'd never written that letter to Calcutta. And you're going to wish the same."

"It isn't, Malati. And I'm not. Thank God you did."

Malati looked at Lata with sick unhappiness. "You just don't realize what you're throwing away, Lata. You're choosing the wrong man. Stay unmarried for a while.

Take your time to make up your mind again. Or simply remain unmarried – it's not so tragic."

Lata was silent. On the side that Malati could not see, she let a handful of sand pass through her fingers.

"What about that other chap?" said Malati – "that poet, Amit? How has he put himself out of the running?"

Lata smiled at the thought of Amit. "Well, he wouldn't be my undoing, as you put it, but I don't see myself as his wife at all. We're too alike. His moods veer and oscillate as wildly as mine. Can you imagine the life of our poor children? And if his mind's on a book I don't know if he'll have any time for me. Sensitive people are usually very insensitive – I should know. As a matter of fact, he's just proposed to me."

Malati looked shocked and angry.

"You never tell me anything!"

"Everything happened all of a sudden yesterday," said Lata, fishing Amit's acrostic out of the pocket of her kameez. "I brought this along, since you usually like to see the documents in the case."

Malati read it in silence, then said: "I'd marry anyone who wrote me this."

"Well, he's still available," laughed Lata. "And I won't veto that marriage." She put her arm around Malati's shoulder before continuing: "For me, marrying Amit would be madness. Quite apart from everything else, I get more than enough of my brother Arun. To live five minutes away from him would be the ultimate lunacy!"

"You could live somewhere else."

"Oh no –" said Lata, picturing Amit in his room overlooking the laburnum in bloom. "He's a poet and a novelist. He wants things laid on for him. Meals, hot water, a running household, a dog, a lawn, a Muse. And why not? After all, he did write 'The Fever Bird'! But he won't be able to write if he has to fend for himself away from his family. Anyway, you seem to be happy with anyone but Haresh. Why? Why are you so dead-set against him?"

"Because I see nothing, nothing, nothing at all in common between you two," said Malati. "And it's completely obvious you don't love him. Have you thought this thing through, Lata, or are you just making up your mind in a sort of trance? Like that nun business that Ma keeps talking about. Think. Do you like the idea of sharing your possessions with this man? Of making love with him? Does he attract you? Can you cope with the things that irritate you about him – Cawnpore and paan and all that? Please, please, Lata, don't be stupid. Use your brains. What about this Simran woman – doesn't that bother you? And what do you want to do with yourself after your marriage – or are you just content to be a housewife in a walled compound full of Czechs?"

"Do you think I haven't thought about any of this?" said Lata, removing her arm, annoyed once more. "Or that I haven't tried to visualize what life will be like with him? It'll be interesting, I think. Haresh is practical, he's forceful, he isn't cynical. He gets things done and he helps people without making a fuss about it. He's helped Kedarnath and Veena a great deal."

"So what? . . . Will he let you teach?"

"Yes, he will."

"Have you asked him?" pressed Malati.

"No. That's not the best idea," said Lata. "But I'm sure of it, I think I know him well enough by now. He hates to see anyone's talent wasted. He encourages them. And he's really concerned about people – about me, about Maan, about Savita and her studies, about Bhaskar –"

"– who, incidentally, is alive today only because of Kabir," Malati could not resist interposing.

"I don't deny it." Lata sighed deeply, and looked at the warm sands all around.

For a while neither said anything. Then Malati spoke.

"But what has he done, Lata?" she said quietly. "What has he done that is wrong – that he should be treated like this? He loves you and he never deserved to be doubted. Is it fair? Just think, is it fair?"

"I don't know," said Lata slowly, looking over towards the far shore. "No, it isn't, I suppose. But life isn't always a question of justice, is it? What is that line? – 'Use every man after his desert, and who should 'scape whipping?' But it's true the other way around as well. Use every man after his desert and you'll become a complete emotional bankrupt."

"That's a really mean-spirited view of the world," said Malati.

"Don't call me mean," cried Lata passionately.

Malati looked at her in astonishment.

Lata shivered. "All I meant was, Malati, that when I'm with Kabir, or even away from him but thinking about him, I become utterly useless for anything. I feel I'm out of control – like a boat heading for the rocks – and I don't want to become a wreck."

"So you're going to instruct yourself not to think of him?"

"If I can," said Lata, almost to herself.

"What did you say? Speak up," demanded Malati, wanting to shake her into seeing sense.

"If I can," said Lata.

"How can you deceive yourself like this?"

Lata was silent.

"Malu, I'm not going to quarrel with you," she said after a while. "I care for you as much as I care for any of these men, and I always will. But I'm not going to undo what I've done. I do love Haresh, and I –"

"What?" cried Malati, looking at Lata as if she were an imbecile.

"I do."

"You're full of surprises today," said Malati, very angry now.

"And, well, you're full of incredulities. But I do. Or I think I do. Thank God it isn't what I feel for Kabir."

"I don't believe you. You're just making that up."

"You must. He's grown on me, he really has. I don't find him unattractive. And there's something else – I won't feel I'll be making a fool of myself with him – with regard to, well, with regard to sex."

Malati stared at her. What a crazy thing to say.

"And with Kabir you will?"

"With Kabir – I just don't know –"

Malati said nothing. She shook her head slowly, not looking at Lata, half lost in her own thoughts.

Lata said: "Do you know those lines of Clough that go: 'There are two different kinds, I believe, of human attraction'?"

Again Malati said nothing but merely shook her head.

"Well, they go something like this:

> There are two different kinds, I believe, of human attraction.
> One that merely excites, unsettles, and makes you uneasy;
> The other that –

Well, I can't remember exactly, but he talks about a calmer, less frantic love, which helps you to grow where you were already growing, 'to live where as yet I had languished' – I just read it yesterday, it isn't in my head yet, but it said everything that I couldn't express on my own. Do you understand what I mean? . . . Malati?"

"All I understand," said Malati, "is that you can't live on other people's words. You're throwing away the golden casket and the silver one, and you seem to think that you'll be as lucky with the bronze casket as your English literature tells you you'll be. Well, I hope you will, I really hope you will. But you won't be. You won't."

"You'll grow to like him too, Malu."

Malati didn't answer.

"You haven't even met him," continued Lata with a smile. "And I remember at first you refused to like Pran."

"I hope you're right." Malati sounded weary. Her heart was sick for both Lata and Kabir.

"It's more like Nala and Damyanti than Portia and Bassanio," said Lata, trying to cheer her up. "Haresh's feet touch the ground, and he has dust and sweat and a shadow. The other two are a bit too God-like and ethereal to be any good for me."

"So you're at ease," said Malati, searching her friend's face. "You're at ease with yourself. And you know exactly what you're going to do. Well, tell me, out of curiosity, before you write him off, are you at least going to drop a line to Kabir?"

Lata's lips began to tremble.

"I'm not at ease – I'm not –" she cried. "It's not easy – Malu, how can you think it is? I hardly know who I am or what I'm doing – I can't study or even think these days – everything is pressing in on me. I can't bear it when I'm with him, and I can't bear not to see him. How do I know what I may or may not do? I only hope I have the courage to stick to my decision."

19

GUY DE MAUPASSANT

The Model

The little crescent-shaped town of Étretat, with its white cliffs, white shingle and blue sea, was dozing peacefully in the brilliant July sunshine. At the tips of the crescent two arches of rock jutted out into the calm water, the smaller to the north like a dwarf foot, the larger to the south like a giant leg; and beyond it the Needle, tapering upwards from a broad base almost to the height of the cliff, towered skywards.

On the beach along the water's edge a crowd of people were sitting about watching the bathers. The Casino terrace, where another crowd was sitting or strolling along, looked like a flower-bed, with the brightly coloured ladies' dresses and their red and blue silk-embroidered sunshades.

On the promenade at the far end of the terrace there were others enjoying its restful atmosphere, sauntering up and down, far from the chatter of the well-dressed throng.

A young man, Jean Summer, well known as a painter of distinction, was walking beside an invalid chair, in which his young wife was sitting, looking thoroughly miserable. A man-servant was pushing the bath-chair slowly, and the crippled lady was gazing sadly at the brightness of the sky, the cheerful sunlight and the light-hearted crowd.

They neither spoke nor looked at each other.

"Let's stop a minute," said the lady.

They stopped, and the painter sat down on a camp-stool, which the man-servant handed him.

The people passing behind the motionless silent couple looked pityingly at them. Their romance had become a local legend; he had married her, it was said, in spite of her infirmity, touched by her love.

Not far off two young men were sitting on a winch, talking and gazing vacantly out to sea.

"No, it's not true; I know Jean Summer quite well."

"Then why did he ever marry her? She was an invalid at the time, wasn't she?"

GUY DE MAUPASSANT, "The Model," pp. 96–103 from *Boule de Suif and Other Stories* (tr. H. N. P. Sloman). London: Penguin Books, 1946. Copyright in this translation by H. N. P. Sloman 1946.

"Yes, she was. He married her . . . well, he married her, as a man always does marry, because he was a fool."

"But there must have been some other reason."

"Other reason, my dear man? – there is no other reason. A man is a fool because he is a fool. Besides, as you know, painters specialize in absurd marriages. They nearly always marry a model, who has been somebody else's mistress before – damaged goods in every sense of the word. Why do they do it? Nobody knows. One would have thought that constant association with the type of imbecile we call a model must have sickened them for ever of this kind of female. But not a bit of it. They make them pose, and then they marry them. You ought to read Alphonse Daudet's little book, *Artists' Wives* – a gem of a book, so true to life and so cruel.

"In the case of the couple over there, the accident happened in an unusual way, that was rather tragic. The girl staged a comedy, or rather a melodrama. In fact, she risked everything on a single throw. Was she sincere? Was she in love with Jean? One can never tell in these cases. Who can say how much the element of cruelty and how much that of sincerity ever enters into women's actions? They are always sincere at the moment, but their feelings are always changing. They are passionate, criminal, devoted, heroic or mean, at the bidding of fleeting emotions, of which they are quite unconscious. They are always telling lies, involuntarily, thoughtlessly, automatically; and with all this, and in spite of all this, they have an absolute honesty of emotion and sentiment; they show this by decisions which are violent, unexpected, incomprehensible, irrational, which defeat all our reasoning, our habits of caution and all our selfish calculations. Owing to the unexpectedness and suddenness of their determinations they always remain indecipherable riddles to us men. We are always asking ourselves: Are they sincere, or are they acting a part?

"My dear fellow, they are sincere and insincere at one and the same time, because it is part of their nature to be both to the highest degree and yet to be neither.

"Think of the means the best of them adopt to attain their ends from us. These means are at once complicated and simple. So complicated that we never guess them in advance, and yet so simple that, after falling into the trap, we can't help being surprised at ourselves and saying: 'Well, did she really fool me as easily as that?'

"And they always get their own way, old man, especially when they want to get married.

"But, anyway, this is Summer's story.

"The girl was a model, of course; she used to pose for him. She was pretty and, even more, she was smart, and she had a divine figure according to all accounts. He fell in love with her, as a man always falls in love with any attractive woman whom he sees a lot of. He imagined he really loved her. It is a curious phenomenon. As soon as a man wants a woman, he is genuinely convinced that he will never be able to do without her for the rest of his natural life. He is fully aware that the same thing has happened to him before and that, when desire is satisfied, disgust ensues; he knows that, in order to spend one's whole life with another human being, it is not the transient passion of the primitive animal that is needed, but a kinship of soul, temperament and feeling. He must be able to distinguish, in the midst of the attraction he feels, whether it is the result of purely physical factors, a kind of intoxication of the senses, or of the deeper union of minds.

"Anyhow, he convinced himself that he did love her; he vowed eternal fidelity a hundred times over and never looked at any other woman.

"She was genuinely attractive, for she had that gift of superficial smartness which comes so easily to many Paris girls. She babbled and chattered and said foolish things that seemed witty by the amusing way she said them. She was never at a loss for a graceful pose, well calculated to please a painter's eye. Whenever she raised her arm or bent down or got into a carriage or shook hands, her every movement was perfectly timed and just right.

"For three months Jean didn't realise that at bottom she was just like all other models.

"They rented a small house at Andressy for the summer.

"I was there one evening, when the first doubts began to force themselves into my friend's consciousness.

"It was a gorgeous night, and we decided to take a stroll along the river. The moonlight was dancing on the shimmering water, its reflexions broken up into golden spangles by the eddies and currents of the broad, sluggish stream.

"We were walking along the bank, slightly intoxicated by the vague feeling of happiness that often comes over one on a perfect evening like this. We felt as though we could perform superhuman feats and fall in love with the fictitious creations of our own poetical imagination; we were oddly aware of the stirring of strange emotions, longings and aspirations. We were silent, thrilled by the calm exhilarating freshness of this perfect night, and the cool moonlight seemed to go right through us, penetrating the body and drowning the soul in a scented bath of contentment. Suddenly Joséphine – that's her name – uttered a cry:

"'Oh! did you see that big fish jump over there?'

"He answered without looking or taking in her words:

"'Yes, darling.'

"She lost her temper:

"'No, you didn't; your back was turned.'

"He smiled:

"'Yes, you're quite right; it's such a lovely night that I'm not thinking of anything at all.'

"She said no more; but a minute later she felt the need to talk and asked:

"'Are you going to Paris to-morrow?'

"He declared:

"'I don't know.'

"She got annoyed again:

"'I suppose you think it's amusing to go for a walk and never say a word. People who aren't half-wits talk.'

"He made no answer. Then, realizing, with a woman's perverse intuition, that it would exasperate him, she began singing that irritating song that has been dinned into our ears, insulting our intelligence, for the last two years:

'I was gazing at the sky.'

"He murmured:

"'Do be quiet!'

"She retorted angrily:

"'Why should I be quiet?'

"He replied:

"'You're spoiling the evening for us.'

"Then occurred the inevitable scene, the hateful silly scene, with unpremeditated reproaches and tactless recriminations, and then tears; they ran through the whole gamut. At last they went home; he had let her run on without interruption, mesmerized by the beauty of the night and overwhelmed by the storm of her senseless reproaches.

"Three months later he was struggling desperately in the grip of the unbreakable, invisible bonds that such an association weaves round us. She used her emotional hold over him to dominate him and make his whole life a misery. They quarrelled from morning to night, abused each other and fought.

"Finally he made up his mind to end it all and break away. He sold all his canvases, borrowed money from his friends, raised twenty thousand francs – he had not made his name then – and left them on the chimney-piece with a farewell letter.

"He sought refuge in my house.

"About three o'clock that afternoon there was a ring at the bell; I went and opened the door. A woman faced me, pushed me aside and forced her way into my studio; it was Joséphine.

"He got up as she entered the room.

"She threw the letter with the bank-notes at his feet with a gesture of no little dignity and said curtly:

"'There's your money; I don't want it.'

"She was trembling and very pale, in a state when she might do anything. As for him, I saw him turn pale too, pale with anger and exasperation, which might easily lead to violence.

"He asked:

"'What do you want?'

"She replied:

"'I don't want to be treated like a harlot. You wanted me and you had your will. I asked nothing from you; now you can't cast me off.'

"He stamped his foot:

"'No, this is too much. If you think you're going to . . .'

"I had seized his arm:

"'Don't say anything more, Jean; leave it to me.'

"I went up to her and gently, gradually, I talked reason to her, using all the stock arguments that one can employ in such a case. She listened to me motionless, staring in front of her, silent and obstinate.

"At last, having said everything I could and seeing no hope of a happy ending to the scene, I thought of a last argument. I declared:

"'He still loves you, my dear; but his family want him to marry; you see what I mean.'

"She started:

"'Ah! I see now . . .' And, turning to him, she went on: 'You're going . . . you're going to marry?'

"He answered bluntly:

"'Yes.'

"She took a step forward:

"'If you marry, I shall kill myself . . . you understand that.'

"He shrugged his shoulders:

"'Very well – kill yourself.'

"'You say . . . you say . . . say that again.'

"He repeated:

"'Well, kill yourself, if you want to.'

"She went on, alarmingly pale:

"'Don't think I don't mean it; I'll throw myself out of the window.'

"He began to laugh, went to the window, opened it and, like a man bowing a guest out of a room, said politely:

"'This way – after you!'

"She stared at him for a moment with the light of madness in her eyes; then, taking a run as if she were going to jump over a hedge in a field, she dashed past both of us and, clearing the balcony railing, disappeared from sight.

"I shall never forget the effect of that open window on me, when I saw the falling body pass across it; it suddenly looked as wide as the sky and as empty as space. I instinctively shrank back, afraid to look down, as if I should fall out myself.

"Jean stood motionless in a daze.

"The poor girl was carried in with both legs broken; she would never walk again. Her lover, mad with remorse, and perhaps, too, feeling that he owed it to her, took her back and married her.

"Well, that's the story, old man."

It was getting dark. The girl, feeling chilly, wanted to go home, and the servant began to push the bath-chair towards the village. The painter walked by his wife's side; they had not said a word to each other for an hour.

20

GEORGE ELIOT

Middlemarch

When Dorothea Brooke married the dry, scholarly Casaubon, she was awed by the life of scholarship, and intended to become his helpmate. Now she has come to see that his grand project of finding the "key to all mythology" is barren, a sterile piece of research that will bear no fruit. But, since his recent attack and the advice of Dr Lydgate to cut down his workload, Casaubon is increasingly relying on Dorothea as a research assistant.

After dinner, at the hour when she usually began to read aloud, Mr Casaubon proposed that they should go into the library, where, he said, he had ordered a fire and lights. He seemed to have revived and to be thinking intently.

In the library Dorothea observed that he had newly arranged a row of his note-books on a table, and now he took up and put into her hand a well-known volume, which was a table of contents to all the others.

"You will oblige me, my dear," he said, seating himself, "if instead of other reading this evening, you will go through this aloud, pencil in hand, and at each point where I say 'mark,' will make a cross with your pencil. This is the first step in a sifting process which I have long had in view, and as we go on I shall be able to indicate to you certain principles of selection whereby you will, I trust, have an intelligent participation in my purpose."

This proposal was only one more sign added to many since his memorable interview with Lydgate, that Mr Casaubon's original reluctance to let Dorothea work with him had given place to the contrary disposition, namely, to demand much interest and labour from her.

After she had read and marked for two hours, he said, "We will take the volume up-stairs – and the pencil, if you please – and in case of reading in the night, we can pursue this task. It is not wearisome to you, I trust, Dorothea?"

"I prefer always reading what you like best to hear," said Dorothea, who told the simple truth; for what she dreaded was to exert herself in reading or anything else which left him as joyless as ever.

GEORGE ELIOT, from Book V, Chapter XLVIII in *Middlemarch*, first published in 1872.

It was a proof of the force with which certain characteristics in Dorothea impressed those around her, that her husband, with all his jealousy and suspicion, had gathered implicit trust in the integrity of her promises, and her power of devoting herself to her idea of the right and best. Of late he had begun to feel that these qualities were a peculiar possession for himself, and he wanted to engross them.

The reading in the night did come. Dorothea in her young weariness had slept soon and fast: she was awakened by a sense of light, which seemed to her at first like a sudden vision of sunset after she had climbed a steep hill: she opened her eyes and saw her husband wrapped in his warm gown seating himself in the arm-chair near the fire-place where the embers were still glowing. He had lit two candles, expecting that Dorothea would awake, but not liking to rouse her by more direct means.

"Are you ill, Edward?" she said, rising immediately.

"I felt some uneasiness in a reclining posture. I will sit here for a time." She threw wood on the fire, wrapped herself up, and said, "You would like me to read to you?"

"You would oblige me greatly by doing so, Dorothea," said Mr Casaubon, with a shade more meekness than usual in his polite manner. "I am wakeful: my mind is remarkably lucid."

"I fear that the excitement may be too great for you," said Dorothea, remembering Lydgate's cautions.

"No, I am not conscious of undue excitement. Thought is easy." Dorothea dared not insist, and she read for an hour or more on the same plan as she had done in the evening, but getting over the pages with more quickness. Mr Casaubon's mind was more alert, and he seemed to anticipate what was coming after a very slight verbal indication, saying, "That will do – mark that" – or "Pass on to the next head – I omit the second excursus on Crete." Dorothea was amazed to think of the bird-like speed with which his mind was surveying the ground where it had been creeping for years. At last he said –

"Close the book now, my dear. We will resume our work to-morrow. I have deferred it too long, and would gladly see it completed. But you observe that the principle on which my selection is made, is to give adequate, and not dis-proportionate illustration to each of the theses enumerated in my introduction, as at present sketched. You have perceived that distinctly, Dorothea?"

"Yes," said Dorothea, rather tremulously. She felt sick at heart.

"And now I think that I can take some repose," said Mr Casaubon. He lay down again and begged her to put out the lights. When she had lain down too, and there was a darkness only broken by a dull glow on the hearth, he said –

"Before I sleep, I have a request to make, Dorothea."

"What is it?" said Dorothea, with a dread in her mind.

"It is that you will let me know, deliberately, whether, in case of my death, you will carry out my wishes: whether you will avoid doing what I should deprecate, and apply yourself to do what I should desire."

Dorothea was not taken by surprise: many incidents had been leading her to the conjecture of some intention on her husband's part which might make a new yoke for her. She did not answer immediately.

"You refuse?" said Mr Casaubon, with more edge in his tone.

"No, I do not yet refuse," said Dorothea, in a clear voice, the need of freedom asserting itself within her; "but it is too solemn – I think it is not right – to make a promise when I am ignorant what it will bind me to. Whatever affection prompted I would do without promising."

"But you would use your own judgment: I ask you to obey mine; you refuse."

"No, dear, no!" said Dorothea, beseechingly, crushed by opposing fears. "But may I wait and reflect a little while? I desire with my whole soul to do what will comfort you; but I cannot give any pledge suddenly – still less a pledge to do I know not what."

"You cannot then confide in the nature of my wishes?"

"Grant me till to-morrow," said Dorothea, beseechingly.

"Till to-morrow then," said Mr Casaubon.

Soon she could hear that he was sleeping, but there was no more sleep for her. While she constrained herself to lie still lest she should disturb him, her mind was carrying on a conflict in which imagination ranged its forces first on one side and then on the other. She had no presentiment that the power which her husband wished to establish over her future action had relation to anything else than his work. But it was clear enough to her that he would expect her to devote herself to sifting those mixed heaps of material, which were to be the doubtful illustration of principles still more doubtful. The poor child had become altogether unbelieving as to the trustworthiness of that "Key" which had made the ambition and the labour of her husband's life. It was not wonderful that, in spite of her small instruction, her judgment in this matter was truer than his: for she looked with unbiassed comparison and healthy sense at probabilities on which he had risked all his egoism. And now she pictured to herself the days, and months, and years which she must spend in sorting what might be called shattered mummies, and fragments of a tradition which was itself a mosaic wrought from crushed ruins – sorting them as food for a theory which was already withered in the birth like an elfin child. Doubtless a vigorous error vigorously pursued has kept the embryos of truth a-breathing: the quest of gold being at the same time a questioning of substances, the body of chemistry is prepared for its soul, and Lavoisier is born. But Mr Casaubon's theory of the elements which made the seed of all tradition was not likely to bruise itself unawares against discoveries: it floated among flexible conjectures no more solid than those etymologies which seemed strong because of likeness in sound, until it was shown that likeness in sound made them impossible: it was a method of interpretation which was not tested by the necessity of forming anything which had sharper collisions than an elaborate notion of Gog and Magog: it was as free from interruption as a plan for threading the stars together. And Dorothea had so often had to check her weariness and impatience over this questionable riddle-guessing, as it revealed itself to her instead of the fellowship in high knowledge which was to make life worthier! She could understand well enough now why her husband had come to cling to her, as possibly the only hope left that his labours would ever take a shape in which they could be given to the world. At first it had seemed that he wished to keep even her aloof from any close knowledge of what he was doing;

but gradually the terrible stringency of human need – the prospect of a too speedy death –

And here Dorothea's pity turned from her own future to her husband's past – nay, to his present hard struggle with a lot which had grown out of that past: the lonely labour, the ambition breathing hardly under the pressure of self-distrust; the goal receding, and the heavier limbs; and knew at last the sword visibly trembling above him! And had she not wished to marry him that she might help him in his life's labour? – But she had thought the work was to be something greater, which she could serve in devoutly for its own sake. Was it right, even to soothe his grief – would it be possible, even if she promised – to work as in a treadmill fruitlessly?

And yet, could she deny him? Could she say, "I refuse to content this pining hunger?" It would be refusing to do for him dead, what she was almost sure to do for him living. If he lived, as Lydgate had said he might, for fifteen years or more, her life would certainly be spent in helping him and obeying him.

Still, there was a deep difference between that devotion to the living, and that indefinite promise of devotion to the dead. While he lived, he could claim nothing that she would not still be free to remonstrate against, and even to refuse. But – the thought passed through her mind more than once, though she could not believe in it – might he not mean to demand something more from her than she had been able to imagine, since he wanted her pledge to carry out his wishes without telling her exactly what they were? No; his heart was bound up in his work only: that was the end for which his failing life was to be eked out by hers.

And now, if she were to say, "No! if you die, I will put no finger to your work" – it seemed as if she would be crushing that bruised heart.

For four hours Dorothea lay in this conflict, till she felt ill and bewildered, unable to resolve, praying mutely. Helpless as a child which has sobbed and sought too long, she fell into a late morning sleep, and when she waked Mr Casaubon was already up. Tantripp told her that he had read prayers, breakfasted, and was in the library.

"I never saw you look so pale, madam," said Tantripp, a solid-figured woman who had been with the sisters at Lausanne.

"Was I ever high-coloured, Tantripp?" said Dorothea, smiling faintly.

"Well, not to say high-coloured, but with a bloom like a Chiny rose. But always smelling those leather books, what can be expected? Do rest a little this morning, madam. Let me say you are ill and not able to go into that close library."

"Oh no, no! let me make haste," said Dorothea. "Mr Casaubon wants me particularly."

When she went down she felt sure that she should promise to fulfil his wishes; but that would be later in the day – not yet.

As Dorothea entered the library, Mr Casaubon turned round from the table where he had been placing some books, and said –

"I was waiting for your appearance, my dear. I had hoped to set to work at once this morning, but I find myself under some indisposition, probably from too much excitement yesterday. I am going now to take a turn in the shrubbery, since the air is milder."

"I am glad to hear that," said Dorothea. "Your mind, I feared, was too active last night."

"I would fain have it set at rest on the point I last spoke of, Dorothea. You can now, I hope, give me an answer."

"May I come out to you in the garden presently?" said Dorothea, winning a little breathing space in that way.

"I shall be in the Yew-Tree Walk for the next half-hour," said Mr Casaubon, and then he left her.

Dorothea, feeling very weary, rang and asked Tantripp to bring her some wraps. She had been sitting still for a few minutes, but not in any renewal of the former conflict: she simply felt that she was going to say "Yes" to her own doom: she was too weak, too full of dread at the thought of inflicting a keen-edged blow on her husband, to do anything but submit completely. She sat still and let Tantripp put on her bonnet and shawl, a passivity which was unusual with her, for she liked to wait on herself.

"God bless you, madam!" said Tantripp, with an irrepressible movement of love towards the beautiful, gentle creature for whom she felt unable to do anything more, now that she had finished tying the bonnet.

This was too much for Dorothea's highly-strung feeling, and she burst into tears, sobbing against Tantripp's arm. But soon she checked herself, dried her eyes, and went out at the glass door into the shrubbery.

"I wish every book in that library was built into a caticom for your master," said Tantripp to Pratt, the butler, finding him in the breakfast-room. She had been at Rome, and visited the antiquities, as we know; and she always declined to call Mr Casaubon anything but "your master," when speaking to the other servants.

Pratt laughed. He liked his master very well, but he liked Tantripp better.

When Dorothea was out on the gravel walks, she lingered among the nearer clumps of trees, hesitating, as she had done once before, though from a different cause. Then she had feared lest her effort at fellowship should be unwelcome; now she dreaded going to the spot where she foresaw that she must bind herself to a fellowship from which she shrank. Neither law nor the world's opinion compelled her to this — only her husband's nature and her own compassion, only the ideal and not the real yoke of marriage. She saw clearly enough the whole situation, yet she was fettered: she could not smite the stricken soul that entreated hers. If that were weakness, Dorothea was weak. But the half-hour was passing, and she must not delay longer. When she entered the Yew-Tree Walk she could not see her husband; but the walk had bends, and she went, expecting to catch sight of his figure wrapped in a blue cloak, which, with a warm velvet cap, was his outer garment on chill days for the garden. It occurred to her that he might be resting in the summer-house, towards which the path diverged a little. Turning the angle, she could see him seated on the bench, close to a stone table. His arms were resting on the table, and his brow was bowed down on them, the blue cloak being dragged forward and screening his face on each side.

"He exhausted himself last night," Dorothea said to herself, thinking at first that he was asleep, and that the summer-house was too damp a place to rest in. But then she remembered that of late she had seen him take that attitude when she was reading to him, as if he found it easier than any other; and that he would sometimes speak, as well as listen, with his face down in that way. She went into the summer-house and said, "I am come, Edward; I am ready."

He took no notice, and she thought that he must be fast asleep. She laid her hand on his shoulder, and repeated, "I am ready!" Still he was motionless; and with a sudden confused fear, she leaned down to him, took off his velvet cap, and leaned her cheek close to his head, crying in a distressed tone,

"Wake, dear, wake! Listen to me. I am come to answer."

But Dorothea never gave her answer.

Later in the day, Lydgate was seated by her bedside, and she was talking deliriously, thinking aloud, and recalling what had gone through her mind the night before. She knew him, and called him by his name, but appeared to think it right that she should explain everything to him; and again, and again, begged him to explain everything to her husband.

"Tell him I shall go to him soon: I am ready to promise. Only, thinking about it was so dreadful – it has made me ill. Not very ill. I shall soon be better. Go and tell him."

But the silence in her husband's ear was never more to be broken.

21

LEO TOLSTOY

Anna Karenina

Unhappy in her loveless marriage, Anna falls madly in love with the dashing bachelor Count Alexei Vronsky. In their high society circles of Moscow and St. Petersburg it is acceptable to conduct a discreet affair. But Anna has something to tell Vronsky that will make discretion impossible.

The beauty of her whole figure, her head, her neck, her hands, struck Vronsky every time as something new and unexpected. He stood still, gazing at her in ecstasy. But, directly he would have made a step to come nearer to her, she was aware of his presence, pushed away the watering pot, and turned her flushed face towards him.

"What's the matter? You are ill?" he said to her in French, going up to her. He would have run to her, but remembering that there might be spectators, he looked round towards the balcony door, and reddened a little, as he always reddened, feeling that he had to be afraid and be on his guard.

"No, I'm quite well," she said, getting up and pressing his outstretched hand tightly. "I did not expect . . . thee."

"Mercy! what cold hands!" he said.

"You startled me," she said. "I'm alone, and expecting Seryozha; he's out for a walk; they'll come in from this side."

But, in spite of her efforts to be calm, her lips were quivering.

"Forgive me for coming, but I couldn't pass the day without seeing you," he went on, speaking French, as he always did to avoid using the stiff Russian plural form, so impossibly frigid between them, and the dangerously intimate singular.

"Forgive you? I'm so glad!"

"But you're ill or worried," he went on, not letting go her hands and bending over her. "What were you thinking of?"

"Always the same thing," she said, with a smile.

She spoke the truth. If ever at any moment she had been asked what she was thinking of, she could have answered truly: of the same thing, of her happiness

Leo Tolstoy, from Part II, Chapters XXII and XXIII in *Anna Karenina* (tr. Constance Garnett), first published in 1876.

and her unhappiness. She was thinking, just when he came upon her, of this: why
was it, she wondered, that to others, to Betsy (she knew of her secret connection
with Tushkevitch) it was all easy, while to her it was such torture? Today this
thought gained special poignancy from certain other considerations. She asked
him about the races. He answered her questions, and, seeing that she was agitated,
trying to calm her, he began telling her in the simplest tone the details of his
preparations for the races.

"Tell him or not tell him?" she thought, looking into his quiet, affectionate eyes.
"He is so happy, so absorbed in his races that he won't understand as he ought, he
won't understand all the gravity of this fact to us."

"But you haven't told me what you were thinking of when I came in," he said,
interrupting his narrative; "please tell me!"

She did not answer, and, bending her head a little, she looked inquiringly
at him from under her brows, her eyes shining under their long lashes. Her
hand shook as it played with a leaf she had picked. He saw it, and his face
expressed that utter subjection, that slavish devotion, which had done so much to
win her.

"I see something has happened. Do you suppose I can be at peace, knowing you
have a trouble I am not sharing? Tell me, for God's sake," he repeated imploringly.

"Yes, I shan't be able to forgive him if he does not realize all the gravity of it.
Better not tell; why put him to the proof?" she thought, still staring at him in the
same way, and feeling the hand that held the leaf was trembling more and more.

"For God's sake!" he repeated, taking her hand.

"Shall I tell you?"

"Yes, yes, yes . . ."

"I'm with child," she said, softly and deliberately. The leaf in her hand shook
more violently, but she did not take her eyes off him, watching how he would take
it. He turned white, would have said something, but stopped; he dropped her
hand, and his head sank on his breast. "Yes, he realizes all the gravity of it," she
thought, and gratefully she pressed his hand.

But she was mistaken in thinking he realized the gravity of the fact as she, a
woman, realized it. On hearing it, he felt come upon him with tenfold intensity
that strange feeling of loathing of someone. But at the same time, he felt that the
turning-point he had been longing for had come now; that it was impossible to go
on concealing things from her husband, and it was inevitable in one way or
another that they should soon put an end to their unnatural position. But, besides
that, her emotion physically affected him in the same way. He looked at her with
a look of submissive tenderness, kissed her hand, got up, and, in silence, paced up
and down the terrace.

"Yes," he said, going up to her resolutely. "Neither you nor I have looked on our
relations as a passing amusement, and now our fate is sealed. It is absolutely
necessary to put an end" – he looked round as he spoke – "to the deception in
which we are living."

"Put an end? How put an end, Alexey?" she said softly.

She was calmer now, and her face lighted up with a tender smile.

"Leave your husband and make our life one."

"It is one as it is," she answered, scarcely audibly.

"Yes, but altogether, altogether."

"But how, Alexey, tell me how?" she said in melancholy mockery at the hopelessness of her own position. "Is there any way out of such a position? Am I not the wife of my husband?"

"There is a way out of every position. We must take our line," he said. "Anything's better than the position in which you're living. Of course, I see how you torture yourself over everything – the world and your son and your husband."

"Oh, not over my husband," she said, with a quiet smile. "I don't know him, I don't think of him. He doesn't exist."

"You're not speaking sincerely. I know you. You worry about him too."

"Oh, he doesn't even know," she said, and suddenly a hot flush came over her face; her cheeks, her brow, her neck crimsoned, and tears of shame came into her eyes. "But we won't talk of him."

*

Vronsky had several times already, though not so resolutely as now, tried to bring her to consider their position, and every time he had been confronted by the same superficiality and triviality with which she met his appeal now. It was as though there were something in this which she could not or would not face, as though directly she began to speak of this, she, the real Anna, retreated somehow into herself, and another strange and unaccountable woman came out, whom he did not love, and whom he feared, and who was in opposition to him. But to-day he was resolved to have it out.

"Whether he knows or not," said Vronsky, in his usual quiet and resolute tone, "that's nothing to do with us. We cannot . . . you cannot stay like this, especially now."

"What's to be done, according to you?" she asked with the same frivolous irony. She who had so feared he would take her condition too lightly was now vexed with him for deducing from it the necessity of taking some step.

"Tell him everything, and leave him."

"Very well, let us suppose I do that," she said. "Do you know what the result of that would be? I can tell you it all beforehand," and a wicked light gleamed in her eyes, that had been so soft a minute before. "'Eh, you love another man, and have entered into criminal intrigues with him?'" (Mimicking her husband, she threw an emphasis on the word "criminal," as Alexey Alexandrovitch did.) "'I warned you of the results in the religious, the civil, and the domestic relation. You have not listened to me. Now I cannot let you disgrace my name, –'" "and my son," she had meant to say, but about her son she could not jest, – "'disgrace my name, and' – and more in the same style," she added. "In general terms, he'll say in his official manner, and with all distinctness and precision, that he cannot let me go, but will take all measures in his power to prevent scandal. And he will calmly and punctually act in accordance with his words. That's what will happen. He's not a man, but a machine, and a spiteful machine when he's angry," she added, recalling Alexey Alexandrovitch as she spoke, with all the peculiarities of his figure and manner of speaking, and reckoning against him every defect she could find in him, softening nothing for the great wrong she herself was doing him.

"But, Anna," said Vronsky, in a soft and persuasive voice, trying to soothe her, "we absolutely must, anyway, tell him, and then be guided by the line he takes."

"What, run away?"

"And why not run away? I don't see how we can keep on like this. And not for my sake – I see that you suffer."

"Yes, run away, and become your mistress," she said angrily.

"Anna," he said, with reproachful tenderness.

"Yes," she went on, "become your mistress, and complete the ruin of . . ."

Again she would have said "my son," but she could not utter that word.

Vronsky could not understand how she, with her strong and truthful nature, could endure this state of deceit, and not long to get out of it. But he did not suspect that the chief cause of it was the word – *son*, which she could not bring herself to pronounce. When she thought of her son, and his future attitude to his mother, who had abandoned his father, she felt such terror at what she had done, that she could not face it; but, like a woman, could only try to comfort herself with lying assurances that everything would remain as it always had been, and that it was possible to forget the fearful question of how it would be with her son.

"I beg you, I entreat you," she said suddenly, taking his hand, and speaking in quite a different tone, sincere and tender, "never speak to me of that!"

"But, Anna . . ."

"Never. Leave it to me. I know all the baseness, all the horror of my position; but it's not so easy to arrange as you think. And leave it to me, and do what I say. Never speak to me of it. Do you promise me? . . . No, no, promise! . . ."

"I promise everything, but I can't be at peace, especially after what you have told me. I can't be at peace, when you can't be at peace. . . ."

"I?" she repeated. "Yes, I am worried sometimes; but that will pass, if you will never talk about this. When you talk about it – it's only then it worries me."

"I don't understand," he said.

"I know," she interrupted him, "how hard it is for your truthful nature to lie, and I grieve for you. I often think that you have ruined your whole life for me."

"I was just thinking the very same thing," he said; "how could you sacrifice everything for my sake? I can't forgive myself that you're unhappy."

"I unhappy?" she said, coming closer to him, and looking at him with an ecstatic smile of love. "I am like a hungry man who has been given food. He may be cold, and dressed in rags, and ashamed, but he is not unhappy. I unhappy? No, this is my unhappiness. . . ."

She could hear the sound of her son's voice coming towards them, and glancing swiftly round the terrace, she got up impulsively. Her eyes glowed with the fire he knew so well; with a rapid movement she raised her lovely hands, covered with rings, took his head, looked a long look into his face, and, putting up her face with smiling, parted lips, swiftly kissed his mouth and both eyes, and pushed him away. She would have gone, but he held her back.

"When?" he murmured in a whisper, gazing in ecstasy at her.

"To-night, at one o'clock," she whispered, and, with a heavy sigh, she walked with her light, swift step to meet her son.

22

GEORGE BERNARD SHAW

Mrs Warren's Profession

Mrs Warren's Profession was published in 1894 but banned from being performed in England for eight years. It still shocks with its challenge to our moral assumptions and conventions.

Vivie Warren has just graduated with great distinction from Newnham College, Cambridge. Having spent her whole life at school in England, she hardly knows her mother, who lived in Brussels and Vienna and came to see her for only a few days a year. This scene opens as Vivie discovers – to her shock – that her mother's income comes from running brothels.

MRS WARREN: Listen to her talking! Do you think I was brought up like you? able to pick and choose my own way of life? Do you think I did what I did because I liked it, or thought it right, or wouldnt rather have gone to college and been a lady if I'd had the chance?

VIVIE: Everybody has some choice, mother. The poorest girl alive may not be able to choose between being Queen of England or Principal of Newnham; but she can choose between ragpicking and flowerselling, according to her taste. People are always blaming their circumstances for what they are. I dont believe in circumstances. The people who get on in this world are the people who get up and look for the circumstances they want, and, if they cant find them, make them.

MRS WARREN: Oh, it's easy to talk, very easy, isnt it? Here! would you like to know what my circumstances were?

VIVIE: Yes: you had better tell me. Wont you sit down?

MRS WARREN: Oh, I'll sit down: dont you be afraid. (*She plants her chair farther forward with brazen energy, and sits down.* VIVIE *is impressed in spite of herself*). D'you know what your gran'mother was?

VIVIE: No.

MRS WARREN: No, you dont. I do. She called herself a widow and had a fried-fish shop down by the Mint, and kept herself and four daughters out of it. Two of us

---

GEORGE BERNARD SHAW, pp. 192–9 from *Mrs Warren's Profession*. London: Constable and Company, 1919. Reprinted by permission of The Society of Authors, on behalf of the Bernard Shaw Estate.

were sisters: that was me and Liz; and we were both good-looking and well made. I suppose our father was a well-fed man: mother pretended he was a gentleman; but I dont know. The other two were only half sisters: undersized, ugly, starved looking, hard working, honest poor creatures: Liz and I would have half-murdered them if mother hadnt half-murdered us to keep our hands off them. They were the respectable ones. Well, what did they get by their respectability? I'll tell you. One of them worked in a whitelead factory twelve hours a day for nine shillings a week until she died of lead poisoning. She only expected to get her hands a little paralyzed; but she died. The other was always held up to us as a model because she married a Government laborer in the Deptford victualling yard, and kept his room and the three children neat and tidy on eighteen shillings a week – until he took to drink. That was worth being respectable for, wasnt it?

VIVIE (*now thoughtfully attentive*): Did you and your sister think so?

MRS WARREN: Liz didnt, I can tell you: she had more spirit. We both went to a church school – that was part of the ladylike airs we gave ourselves to be superior to the children that knew nothing and went nowhere – and we stayed there until Liz went out one night and never came back. I know the school-mistress thought I'd soon follow her example; for the clergyman was always warning me that Lizzie'd end by jumping off Waterloo Bridge. Poor fool: that was all he knew about it! But I was more afraid of the whitelead factory than I was of the river; and so would you have been in my place. That clergyman got me a situation as scullery maid in a temperance restaurant where they sent out for anything you liked. Then I was waitress; and then I went to the bar at Waterloo station: fourteen hours a day serving drinks and washing glasses for four shillings a week and my board. That was considered a great promotion for me. Well, one cold, wretched night, when I was so tired I could hardly keep myself awake, who should come up for a half of Scotch but Lizzie, in a long fur cloak, elegant and comfortable, with a lot of sovereigns in her purse.

Vivie (*grimly*): My aunt Lizzie!

MRS WARREN: Yes; and a very good aunt to have, too. She's living down at Winchester now, close to the cathedral, one of the most respectable ladies there. Chaperones girls at the county ball, if you please. No river for Liz, thank you! You remind me of Liz a little: she was a first-rate business woman – saved money from the beginning – never let herself look too like what she was – never lost her head or threw away a chance. When she saw I'd grown up good-looking she said to me across the bar "What are you doing there, you little fool? wearing out your health and your appearance for other people's profit!" Liz was saving money then to take a house for herself in Brussels; and she thought we two could save faster than one. So she lent me some money and gave me a start; and I saved steadily and first paid her back, and then went into business with her as her partner. Why shouldnt I have done it? The house in Brussels was real high class: a much better place for a woman to be in than the factory where Anne Jane got poisoned. None of our girls were ever treated as I was treated in the scullery of that temperance place, or at the Waterloo bar, or at home. Would you have had me stay in them and become a worn out old drudge before I was forty?

VIVIE (*intensely interested by this time*): No; but why did you choose that business? Saving money and good management will succeed in any business.

MRS WARREN: Yes, saving money. But where can a woman get the money to save in any other business? Could you save out of four shillings a week and keep yourself dressed as well? Not you. Of course, if youre a plain woman and cant earn anything more; or if you have a turn for music, or the stage, or newspaper-writing: thats different. But neither Liz nor I had any turn for such things: all we had was our appearance and our turn for pleasing men. Do you think we were such fools as to let other people trade in our good looks by employing us as shopgirls, or bar-maids, or waitresses, when we could trade in them ourselves and get all the profits instead of starvation wages? Not likely.

VIVIE: You were certainly quite justified – from the business point of view.

MRS WARREN: Yes; or any other point of view. What is any respectable girl brought up to do but to catch some rich man's fancy and get the benefit of his money by marrying him? – as if a marriage ceremony could make any difference in the right or wrong of the thing! Oh, the hypocrisy of the world makes me sick! Liz and I had to work and save and calculate just like other people; elseways we should be as poor as any good-for-nothing drunken waster of a woman that thinks her luck will last for ever. (*With great energy*) I despise such people: theyve no character; and if theres a thing I hate in a woman, its want of character.

VIVIE: Come now, mother: frankly! Isnt it part of what you call character in a woman that she should greatly dislike such a way of making money?

MRS WARREN: Why, of course. Everybody dislikes having to work and make money; but they have to do it all the same. I'm sure Ive often pitied a poor girl, tired out and in low spirits, having to try to please some man that she doesnt care two straws for – some half-drunken fool that thinks he's making himself agreeable when he's teasing and worrying and disgusting a woman so that hardly any money could pay her for putting up with it. But she has to bear with disagreeables and take the rough with the smooth, just like a nurse in a hospital or anyone else. It's not work that any woman would do for pleasure, goodness knows; though to hear the pious people talk you would suppose it was a bed of roses.

VIVIE: Still, you consider it worth while. It pays.

MRS WARREN: Of course it's worth while to a poor girl, if she can resist temptation and is good-looking and well conducted and sensible. It's far better than any other employment open to her. I always thought that oughtnt to be. It cant be right, Vivie, that there shouldnt be better opportunities for women. I stick to that: it's wrong. But it's so, right or wrong; and a girl must make the best of it. But of course it's not worth while for a lady. If you took to it youd be a fool; but I should have been a fool if I'd taken to anything else.

VIVIE (*more and more deeply moved*): Mother: suppose we were both as poor as you were in those wretched old days, are you quite sure that you wouldnt advise me to try the Waterloo bar, or marry a laborer, or even go into the factory?

MRS WARREN (*indignantly*): Of course not. What sort of mother do you take me for! How could you keep your self-respect in such starvation and slavery? And whats a woman worth? whats life worth? without self-respect! Why am I independent and able to give my daughter a first-rate education, when other women that had just as good opportunities are in the gutter? Because I always knew how to respect myself and control myself. Why is Liz looked up to in a cathedral town? The same reason. Where would we be now if we'd minded the clergyman's foolishness? Scrubbing floors for one and sixpence a day and nothing to look forward to but the workhouse infirmary. Dont you be led astray by people who dont know the world, my girl. The only way for a woman to provide for herself decently is for her to be good to some man that can afford to be good to her. If she's in his own station of life, let her make him marry her; but if she's far beneath him she cant expect it: why should she? it wouldnt be for her own happiness. Ask any lady in London society that has daughters; and she'll tell you the same, except that I tell you straight and she'll tell you crooked. Thats all the difference.

VIVIE (*fascinated, gazing at her*): My dear mother: you are a wonderful woman: you are stronger than all England. And are you really and truly not one wee bit doubtful – or – or – ashamed?

MRS WARREN: Well, of course, dearie, it's only good manners to be ashamed of it: it's expected from a woman. Women have to pretend to feel a great deal that they dont feel. Liz used to be angry with me for plumping out the truth about it. She used to say that when every woman could learn enough from what was going on in the world before her eyes, there was no need to talk about it to her. But then Liz was such a perfect lady! She had the true instinct of it; while I was always a bit of a vulgarian. I used to be so pleased when you sent me your photos to see that you were growing up like Liz: youve just her ladylike, deter-mined way. But I cant stand saying one thing when everyone knows I mean another. Whats the use in such hypocrisy? If people arrange the world that way for women, theres no good pretending that it's arranged the other way. No: I never was a bit ashamed really. I consider I had a right to be proud of how we managed everything so respectably, and never had a word against us, and how the girls were so well taken care of. Some of them did very well: one of them married an ambassador. But of course now I darent talk about such things: whatever would they think of us! (*She yawns*). Oh dear! I do believe I'm getting sleepy after all. (*She stretches herself lazily, thoroughly relieved by her explosion, and placidly ready for her night's rest*).

VIVIE: I believe it is I who will not be able to sleep now. (*She goes to the dresser and lights the candle. Then she extinguishes the lamp, darkening the room a good deal*). Better let in some fresh air before locking up. (*She opens the cottage door, and finds that it is broad moonlight*). What a beautiful night! Look! (*She draws aside the curtains of the window. The landscape is seen bathed in the radiance of the harvest moon rising over Blackdown*).

MRS WARREN (*with a perfunctory glance at the scene*): Yes, dear; but take care you dont catch your death of cold from the night air.

VIVIE (*contemptuously*): Nonsense.

MRS WARREN (*querulously*): Oh yes: everything I say is nonsense, according to you.

VIVIE (*turning to her quickly*): No: really that is not so, mother. You have got com-pletely the better of me tonight, though I intended it to be the other way. Let us be good friends now.

MRS WARREN (*shaking her head a little ruefully*): So it has been the other way. But I suppose I must give in to it. I always got the worst of it from Liz; and now I suppose it'll be the same with you.

VIVIE: Well, never mind. Come: goodnight, dear old mother. (*She takes her mother in her arms*).

MRS WARREN (*fondly*): I brought you up well, didnt I, dearie?

VIVIE: You did.

MRS WARREN: And youll be good to your poor old mother for it, wont you?

VIVIE: I will, dear. (*Kissing her*) Goodnight.

MRS WARREN (*with unction*): Blessings on my own dearie darling! a mother's blessing!

(*She embraces her daughter protectingly, instinctively looking upward for divine sanction.*)

23

JOHN CLELAND

Memoirs of a Woman of Pleasure

John Cleland's *Memoirs of a Woman of Pleasure* (1749) is written as letters addressed from Fanny Hill to another woman.

Young Fanny Hill is an orphan left friendless in London. She falls in love and lives with Charles. But Charles is tricked by his father into sailing to the South Seas. On hearing this news, Fanny falls ill. She slowly recovers, only to be threatened by her landlady with imprisonment for her unpaid rent. The landlady introduces Fanny to "a very honourable gentleman" who will advise her on how to overcome her financial difficulties.

The gentleman, on his entering the room, made me a very civil bow, which I had scarce strength, or presence of mind enough to return a curtsy to; when the landlady, taking upon her to do all the honours of the first interview (for I had never, that I remember'd, seen the gentleman before), sets a chair for him, and another for herself. All this while not a word on either side; a stupid stare was all the face I could put on this strange visit.

The tea was made, and the landlady, unwilling, I suppose, to lose any time, observing my silence and shyness before this entire stranger: "Come, Miss Fanny," says she, in a coarse familiar style, and tone of authority, "hold up your head, child, and do not let sorrow spoil that pretty face of yours. What! sorrows are only for a time; come, be free, here is a worthy gentleman who has heard of your misfortunes and is willing to serve you; you must be better acquainted with him; do not you now stand upon your punctilio's, and this and that, but make your market while you may."

At this so delicate and eloquent harangue, the gentleman, who saw I look'd frighted and amaz'd, and indeed, incapable of answering, took her up for breaking things in so abrupt a manner, as rather to shock than incline me to an acceptance of the good he intended me; then, addressing himself to me, told me he was perfectly acquainted with my whole story and every circumstance of my distress,

---

Jᴏʜɴ Cʟᴇʟᴀɴᴅ, from *Memoirs of a Woman of Pleasure*. New York: G. P. Putnam's Sons, 1963 (originally published 1747).

which he own'd was a cruel plunge for one of my youth and beauty to fall into; that he had long taken a liking to my person, for which he appeal'd to Mrs Jones, there present, but finding me so absolutely engag'd to another, he had lost all hopes of succeeding till he had heard the sudden reverse of fortune that had happen'd to me, on which he had given particular orders to my landlady to see that I should want for nothing; and that, had he not been forc'd abroad to The Hague, on affairs he could not refuse himself to, he would himself have attended me during my sickness; that on his return, which was but the day before, he had, on learning my recovery, desir'd my landlady's good offices to introduce him to me, and was as angry, at least, as I was shock'd, at the manner in which she had conducted herself towards obtaining him that happiness; but, that to shew me how much he disown'd her procedure, and how far he was from taking any ungenerous advantage of my situation, and from exacting any security for my gratitude, he would before my face, that instant, discharge my debt entirely to my landlady and give me her receipt in full; after which I should be at liberty either to reject or grant his suit, as he was much above putting any force upon my inclinations.

Whilst he was exposing his sentiments to me, I ventur'd just to look up to him, and observed his figure, which was that of a very sightly gentleman, well made, about forty, drest in a suit of plain cloaths, with a large diamond ring on one of his fingers, the lustre of which play'd in my eyes as he wav'd his hand in talking, and rais'd my notions of his importance. In short, he might pass for what is commonly call'd a comely black man, with an air of distinction natural to his birth and condition.

To all his speeches, however, I answer'd only in tears that flow'd plentifully to my relief, and choking up my voice, excus'd me from speaking, very luckily, for I should not have known what to say.

The sight, however, mov'd him, as he afterwards told me, irresistibly, and by way of giving me some reason to be less powerfully afflicted, he drew out his purse, and calling for pen and ink, which the landlady was prepar'd for, paid her every farthing of her demand, independent of a liberal gratification which was to follow unknown to me; and taking a receipt in full, very tenderly forc'd me to secure it, by guiding my hand, which he had thrust it into, so as to make me passively put it into my pocket.

Still I continued in a state of stupidity, or melancholy despair, as my spirits could not yet recover from the violent shocks they had receiv'd; and the accommodating landlady had actually left the room, and me alone with this strange gentleman, before I observ'd it, and then I observ'd it without alarm, for I was now lifeless and indifferent to everything.

The gentleman, however, no novice in affairs of this sort, drew near me; and under the pretence of comforting me, first with his handkerchief dried my tears as they ran down my cheeks: presently he ventur'd to kiss me: on my part, neither resistance nor compliance. I sat stock-still; and now looking on myself as bought by the payment that had been transacted before me, I did not care what became of my wretched body: and wanting life, spirits, or courage to oppose the least struggle, even that of the modesty of my sex, I suffer'd, tamely, whatever the gentleman pleased; who proceeding insensibly from freedom to freedom, insinuated his hand between my handkerchief and bosom, which he handled at discretion: finding thus no repulse, and that every thing favour'd, beyond expectation, the completion of his desires, he took me in his arms, and bore me, without life or motion, to the bed, on which laying me gently down, and having me at what advantage he pleas'd, I did not so much as know what he was about, till recovering from a trance of lifeless insensibility, I found him buried in me, whilst I lay passive and innocent of the least sensation of pleasure: a death-cold corpse could scarce have less life or sense in it. As soon as he had thus pacified a passion which had too little respected the condition I was in, he got off, and after recomposing the disorder of my cloaths, employ'd himself with the utmost tenderness to calm the transports of remorse and madness at myself with which I was seized, too late, I confess, for having suffer'd on that bed the embraces of an utter stranger. I tore my hair, wrung my hands, and beat my breast like a mad-woman. But when my new master, for in that light I then view'd him, applied himself to appease me, as my whole rage was levell'd at myself, no part of which I thought myself permitted to aim at him, I begged of him, with more submission than anger, to leave me alone that I might, at least, enjoy my affliction in quiet. This he positively refused, for fear, as he pretended, I should do myself a mischief.

Violent passions seldom last long, and those of women least of any. A dead still calm succeeded this storm, which ended in a profuse shower of tears.

Had any one, but a few instants before, told me that I should have ever known any man but Charles, I would have spit in his face; or had I been offer'd infinitely a greater sum of money than that I saw paid for me, I had spurn'd the proposal in cold blood. But our virtues and our vices depend too much on our circumstances; unexpectedly beset as I was, betray'd by a mind weakened by a long severe affliction, and stunn'd with the terrors of a jail, my defeat will appear the more excusable, since I certainly was not present at, or a party in any sense, to it. However, as the first enjoyment is decisive, and he was now over the bar, I thought I had no longer a right to refuse the caresses of one that had got that advantage over me, no matter how obtain'd; conforming myself then to this maxim, I consider'd myself as so much in his power that I endur'd his kisses and embraces without affecting struggles or anger; not that they, as yet, gave me any pleasure, or prevail'd over the aversion of my soul to give myself up to any sensation of that sort; what I suffer'd, I suffer'd out of a kind of gratitude, and as a matter of course after what had pass'd.

24

DANIEL DEFOE

Moll Flanders

Written as if it's an autobiography, Daniel Defoe's *Moll Flanders* was very popular when published in 1722.

In this extract from the novel, Betty (Moll Flanders) has remarried and travels with her husband from England to his estates in Virginia. There she meets his mother, originally a transported convict. As Betty pieces together this woman's story, she makes a terrible discovery.

We arrived in York River in Virginia, and coming to our plantation, we were received with all the tenderness and affection, by my husband's mother, that could be expressed.

We lived here together, my mother-in-law, at my entreaty, continuing in the house, for she was too kind a mother to be parted with; my husband likewise continued the same as at first, and I thought myself the happiest creature alive, when an odd and surprising event put an end to all that felicity in a moment, and rendered my condition the most uncomfortable in the world.

My mother was a mighty cheerful, good-humoured old woman – I may call her so, for her son was above thirty; I say she was very pleasant, good company, and used to entertain me, in particular, with abundance of stories to divert me, as well of the country we were in as of the people.

Among the rest, she often told me how the greatest part of the inhabitants of the colony came thither in very indifferent circumstances from England; that, generally speaking, they were of two sorts; either, first, such as were brought over by masters of ships to be sold as servants; or, secondly, such as are transported after having been found guilty of crimes punishable with death. [. . .]

She was going on with that part of the story, when her own part in it interrupted her, and with a great deal of good-humoured confidence she told me she was one of the second sort of inhabitants herself; that she came away openly, having ventured too far in a particular case, so that she was become a criminal. "And here's the mark of it, child," says she; and showed me a very fine white arm and hand, but branded in the inside of the hand, as in such cases it must be.

DANIEL DEFOE, from Chapter XVII in *Moll Flanders*, first published in 1722.

This story was very moving to me, but my mother, smiling, said, "You need not think such a thing strange, daughter, for some of the best men in this country are burnt in the hand, and they are not ashamed to own it. There's Major————," says she, "he was an eminent pick-pocket; there's Justice Ba————r, was a shop-lifter, and both of them were burnt in the hand; and I could name you several such as they are."

We had frequent discourses of this kind, and abundance of instances she gave me of the like. After some time, as she was telling some stories of one that was transported but a few weeks ago, I began in an intimate kind of way to ask her to tell me something of her own story, which she did with the utmost plainness and sincerity; how she had fallen into very ill company in London in her young days. [. . .]

[S]he went on with her own story so long, and in so particular a manner, that I began to be very uneasy; but coming to one particular that required telling her name, I thought I should have sunk down in the place. She perceived I was out of order, and asked me if I was not well, and what ailed me? I told her I was so affected with the melancholy story she had told, that it had overcome me, and I begged of her to talk no more of it. "Why, my dear," says she very kindly, "what need these things trouble you? These passages were long before your time, and they give me no trouble at all now; nay, I look back on them with a particular satisfaction, as they have been a means to bring me to this place." Then she went on to tell me how she fell into a good family, where, behaving herself well, and her mistress dying, her master married her, by whom she had my husband and his sister, and that by her diligence and good management after her husband's death, she had improved the plantations to such a degree as they then were, so that most of the estate was of her getting, not her husband's, for she had been a widow upwards of sixteen years.

I heard this part of the story with very little attention, because I wanted much to retire and give vent to my passions; and let any one judge what must be the anguish of my mind, when I came to reflect that this was certainly no more or less than my own mother, and I had now had two children and was big with another by my own brother, and lay with him still every night.

I was now the most unhappy of all women in the world. Oh! had the story never been told me, all had been well; it had been no crime to have lain with my husband if I had known nothing of it.

I had now such a load on my mind that it kept me perpetually waking; to reveal it I could not find would be to any purpose, and yet to conceal it would be next to impossible; nay, I did not doubt but I should talk in my sleep, and tell my husband of it whether I would or no. If I discovered it, the least thing I could expect was to lose my husband, for he was too nice and too honest a man to have continued my husband after he had known I had been his sister; so that I was perplexed to the last degree.

I leave it to any man to judge what difficulties presented to my view. I was away from my native country, at a distance prodigious, and the return to me unpassable. I lived very well, but in a circumstance insufferable in itself. If I had discovered myself to my mother, it might be difficult to convince her of the particulars, and I had no way to prove them. On the other hand, if she had questioned or doubted me, I had been undone, for the bare suggestion would have immediately separated me from my husband, without gaining my mother or him; so that between the surprise on one hand, and the uncertainty on the other, I had been sure to be undone.

In the meantime, as I was but too sure of the fact, I lived therefore in open avowed incest and whoredom, and all under the appearance of an honest wife; and though I was not much touched with the crime of it, yet the action had something in it shocking to nature, and made my husband, as he thought himself, even nauseous to me.

However, upon the most sedate consideration, I resolved that it was absolutely necessary to conceal it all, and not make the least discovery of it either to mother or husband; and thus I lived with the greatest pressure imaginable for three years more. [. . .]

Then I told her my own story, and my name, and assured her, by such other tokens as she could not deny, that I was no other, nor more or less, than her own child, her daughter, born of her body in Newgate; the same that had saved her from the gallows by being in her belly, and that she left in such-and-such hands when she was transported.

It is impossible to express the astonishment she was in; she was not inclined to believe the story or to remember the particulars, for she immediately foresaw the confusion that must follow in the family upon it. But everything concurred so exactly with the stories she had told me of herself, and which, if she had not told me, she would perhaps have been content to have denied, that she had stopped her own mouth, and she had nothing to do but take me about the neck and kiss me, and cry most vehemently over me without speaking one word for a long time together. At last she broke out: "Unhappy child!" says she. "What miserable chance could bring thee hither? and in the arms of my son, too! Dreadful girl!" says she, "Why, we are all undone! Married to thy own brother! Three children, and two alive, all of the same flesh and blood! My son and my daughter lying together as husband and wife! All confusion and distraction! Miserable family! What will become of us? What is to be said? What is to be done?" And thus she run on for a great while; nor had I any power to speak, or if I had, did I know what to say, for every word wounded me to the soul. With this kind of amazement we parted for the first time, though my mother was more surprised than I was because it was more news to her than to me. However, she promised again that she would say nothing of it to her son till we had talked of it again.

It was not long, you may be sure, before we had a second conference upon the same subject, when, as if she had been willing to forget the story she had told me of herself, or to suppose that I had forgot some of the particulars, she began to tell them with alterations and omissions. But I refreshed her memory in many things which I supposed she had forgot, and then came in so opportunely with the whole history that it was impossible for her to go from it; and then she fell into her rhapsodies again, and exclamations at the severity of her misfortunes. When these things were a little over with her, we fell into a close debate about what should be first done before we gave an account of the matter to my husband. But to what purpose could be all our consultations? We could neither of us see our way through it nor how it could be safe to open such a scene to him. It was impossible to make any judgment, or give any guess at what temper he would receive it in, or what measures he would take upon it. And if he should have so little government of himself as to make it public, we easily foresaw that it would be the ruin of the whole family. And if at last he should take the advantage the law would give him, he might put me away with disdain and leave me to sue for the little portion that I had, and perhaps waste it all in the suit, and then be a beggar. And thus I should see him perhaps in the arms of another wife in a few months, and be myself the most miserable creature alive.

My mother was as sensible of this as I; and upon the whole, we knew not what to do. After some time we came to more sober resolutions, but then it was with this misfortune too, that my mother's opinion and mine were quite different from one another and, indeed, inconsistent with one another. For my mother's opinion was that I should bury the whole thing entirely, and continue to live with him as my husband till some other event should make the discovery of it more convenient; and that in the meantime she would endeavour to reconcile us together again, and restore our mutual comfort and family peace; that we might lie as we used to do together, and so let the whole matter remain a secret as close as death. "For, child," says she, "we are both undone if it comes out."

To encourage me to this, she promised to make me easy in my circumstances and to leave me what she could at her death, secured for me separately from my husband, so that if it should come out afterwards, I should be able to stand on my own feet and procure justice too from him.

This proposal did not agree with my judgment, though it was very fair and kind in my mother; but my thoughts run quite another way. [. . .]

In this directly opposite opinion to one another my mother and I continued a long time, and it was impossible to reconcile our judgments. Many disputes we had about it, but we could never either of us yield our own or bring over the other.

I insisted on my aversion to lying with my own brother, and she insisted upon its being impossible to bring him to consent to my going to England. And in this uncertainty we continued, not differing so as to quarrel, or anything like it, but so as not to be able to resolve what we should do to make up that terrible breach.

At last I resolved on a desperate course and told my mother my resolution, viz., that, in short, I would tell him of it myself. My mother was frighted to the last degree at the very thoughts of it; but I bid her be easy, told her I would do it gradually and softly and with all the art and good humour I was mistress of, and time it also as well as I could, taking him in good humour too. I told her I did not question but if I could be hypocrite enough to feign more affection to him than I really had, I should succeed in all my design, and we might part by consent and with a good agreement, for I might love him well enough for a brother, though I could not for a husband.

All this while he lay at my mother to find out, if possible, what was the meaning of that dreadful expression of mine, as he called it, which I mentioned before

– namely, that I was not his lawful wife, nor my children his legal children. My mother put him off, told him she could bring me to no explanations but found there was something that disturbed me very much, and she hoped she should get it out of me in time, and in the meantime recommended to him earnestly to use me more tenderly, and win me with his usual good carriage; told him of his terrifying and affrighting me with his threats of sending me to a madhouse and the like, and advised him not to make a woman desperate on any account whatever.

He promised her to soften his behaviour, and bid her assure me that he loved me as well as ever, and that he had no such design as that of sending me to a madhouse, whatever he might say in his passion; also he desired my mother to use the same persuasions to me too, and we might live together as we used to do.

I found the effects of this treaty presently. My husband's conduct was immediately altered, and he was quite another man to me. Nothing could be kinder and more obliging than he was to me upon all occasions; and I could do no less than make some return to it, which I did as well as I could, but it was but in an awkward manner at best, for nothing was more frightful to me than his caresses, and the apprehensions of being with child again by him was ready to throw me into fits. And this made me see that there was an absolute necessity of breaking the case to him without any more delay, which, however, I did with all the caution and reserve imaginable.

He had continued his altered carriage to me near a month, and we began to live a new kind of life with one another; and could I have satisfied myself to have gone on with it, I believe it might have continued as long as we had continued alive together. One evening, as we were sitting and talking together under a little awning which served as an arbour at the entrance into the garden, he was in a very pleasant, agreeable humour and said abundance of kind things to me relating to the pleasure of our present good agreement, and the disorders of our past breach, and what a satisfaction it was to him that we had room to hope we should never have any more of it.

I fetched a deep sigh, and told him there was nobody in the world could be more delighted than I was in the good agreement we had always kept up, or more afflicted with the breach of it; but I was sorry to tell him that there was an unhappy circumstance in our case, which lay too close to my heart and which I knew not how to break to him, that rendered my part of it very miserable, and took from me all the comfort of the rest.

He importuned me to tell him what it was. I told him I could not tell how to do it; that while it was concealed from him, I alone was unhappy, but if he knew it also, we should be both so; and that therefore to keep him in the dark about it was the kindest thing that I could do, and it was on that account alone that I kept a secret from him, the very keeping of which I thought would first or last be my destruction.

It is impossible to express his surprise at this relation, and the double importunity which he used with me to discover it to him. He told me I could not be called kind to him, nay, I could not be faithful to him if I concealed it from him. I told him I thought so too, and yet I could not do it. He went back to what I had said before to him, and told me he hoped it did not relate to what I said in my passion, and that he had resolved to forget all that as the effect of a rash, provoked spirit. I told him I wished I could forget it all too, but that it was not to be done; the impression was too deep, and it was impossible.

He then told me he was resolved not to differ with me in anything, and that therefore he would importune me no more about it, resolving to acquiesce in whatever I did or said; only begged I would then agree that whatever it was, it should no more interrupt our quiet and our mutual kindness.

This was the most provoking thing he could have said to me, for I really wanted his farther importunities that I might be prevailed with to bring out that which indeed was like death to me to conceal; so I answered him plainly that I could not say I was glad not to be importuned, though I could not tell how to comply. "But come, my dear," said I, "what conditions will you make with me upon the opening this affair to you?"

"Any conditions in the world," said he, "that you can in reason desire of me." "Well," said I, "come, give it me under your hand that if you do not find I am in any fault, or that I am willingly concerned in the causes of the misfortune that is to follow, you will not blame me, use me the worse, do me any injury, or make me be the sufferer for that which is not my fault."

"That," says he, "is the most reasonable demand in the world not to blame you for that which is not your fault. Give me a pen and ink," says he. So I ran in and fetched pen, ink, and paper, and he wrote the condition down in the very words I had proposed it, and signed it with his name. "Well," says he, "what is next, my dear?" "Why," says I, "the next is that you will not blame me for not discovering the secret to you before I knew it." "Very just again," says he; "with all my heart." So he wrote down that also, and signed it.

"Well, my dear," says I, "then I have but one condition more to make with you, and that is that as there is nobody concerned in it but you and I, you shall not discover it to any person in the world, except your own mother; and that in all the measures you shall take upon the discovery, as I am equally concerned in it with you, though as innocent as yourself, you shall do nothing in a passion, nothing to my prejudice or to your mother's prejudice without my knowledge and consent."

This a little amazed him, and he wrote down the words distinctly but read them over and over before he signed them, hesitating at them several times and repeating them: "My mother's prejudice! and your prejudice! What mysterious thing can this be?" However, at last he signed it.

"Well," says I, "my dear, I'll ask you no more under your hand; but as you are to hear the most unexpected and surprising thing that perhaps ever befell any family in the world, I beg you to promise me you will receive it with composure and a presence of mind suitable to a man of sense."

"I'll do my utmost," says he, "upon condition you will keep me no longer in suspense, for you terrify me with all these preliminaries."

"Well then," says I, "it is this: As I told you before in a heat that I was not your lawful wife and that our children were not legal children, so I must let you know now in calmness and in kindness, but with affliction enough, that I am your own sister, and you my own brother, and that we are both the children of our mother now alive and in the house, who is convinced of the truth of it in a manner not to be denied or contradicted."

I saw him turn pale and look wild. And I said: "Now remember your promise, and receive it with presence of mind; for who could have said more to prepare you for it than I have done?" However, I called a servant, and got him a little glass of rum (which is the usual dram of the country), for he was just fainting away.

When he was a little recovered, I said to him: "This story, you may be sure, requires a long explanation, and therefore have patience and compose your mind to hear it out, and I'll make it as short as I can." And with this, I told him what I thought was needful of the fact, and particularly how my mother came to discover it to me, as above. "And now, my dear," says I, "you will see reason for my capitulations, and that I neither have been the cause of this matter, nor could be so, and that I could know nothing of it before now."

"I am fully satisfied of that," says he, "but 'tis a dreadful surprise to me; however, I know a remedy for it all, and a remedy that shall put an end to your difficulties without your going to England." "That would be strange," said I, "as all the rest." "No, no," says he, "I'll make it easy; there's nobody in the way of it all but myself." He looked a little disordered when he said this, but I did not apprehend anything from it at that time, believing, as it used to be said, that they who do those things never talk of them, or that they who talk of such things never do them.

But things were not come to their height with him, and I observed he became pensive and melancholy; and in a word, as I thought, a little distempered in his head. I endeavoured to talk him into temper and into a kind of scheme for our government in the affair, and sometimes he would be well, and talk with some courage about it. But the weight of it lay too heavy upon his thoughts and went so far that he made two attempts upon himself, and in one of them had actually strangled himself, and had not his mother come into the room in the very moment, he had died; but with the help of a negro servant she cut him down and recovered him.

Things were now come to a lamentable height. My pity for him now began to revive that affection which at first I really had for him, and I endeavoured sincerely, by all the kind carriage I could, to make up the breach; but in short, it had gotten too great a head: it preyed upon his spirits, and it threw him into a lingering consumption, though it happened not to be mortal. In this distress I did not know what to do, as his life was apparently declining, and I might perhaps have married again there, very much to my advantage had it been my business to have stayed in the country. But my mind was restless too; I hankered after coming to England, and nothing would satisfy me without it.

In short, by an unwearied importunity, my husband, who was apparently decaying, as I observed, was at last prevailed with; and so my fate pushing me on, the way was made clear for me, and my mother concurring, I obtained a very good cargo for my coming to England.

When I parted with my brother (for such I am now to call him), we agreed that after I arrived he should pretend to have an account that I was dead in England, and so might marry again when he would. He promised, and engaged to me to correspond with me as a sister, and to assist and support me as long as I lived; and that if he died before me, he would leave sufficient to his mother to take care of me still, in the name of a sister, and he was in some respects just to this; but it was so oddly managed that I felt the disappointments very sensibly afterwards, as you shall hear in its time.

IV

ABORTION, EUTHANASIA, AND SUICIDE

Abortion

The traditional ethic of the sanctity of human life is under challenge. Abortion, which was illegal almost everywhere until the 1960s, is now legal under at least some circumstances in most countries. For the characters in Maeve Binchy's story "Shepherd's Bush," abortion is not as deeply troubling as opponents of abortion might expect. In this, the characters are representative of millions of women who have abortions without undergoing a great deal of anguish. That fact does not, of course, show that it is a morally justified procedure. On the contrary, especially in the United States, abortion remains a hotly contested issue.

The debate over abortion is often seen as one between those who are "pro-life" and those who are "pro-choice," but neither label really characterizes the position accurately. Those who are "pro-life" generally have nothing against killing animals to eat them, even when we have an ample range of vegetarian sources of food. So they are in favor of protecting innocent human life, not life in general. On the other side, it is difficult to sustain a "pro-choice" position without also taking a view on the moral status of the fetus. If the fetus is a living human being, with the same right to life as any other human being, then it would need to be argued that a woman's right to control her body should override the fetus's right to life. If abortion is to be justifiable even when the pregnancy does not threaten the life or health of the pregnant woman, the fetus must have either no right to life, or a right to life that is more easily overridden than that of more mature human being.

If we were to put the case against abortion as a formal argument, it would go something like this:

1 It is always wrong to kill an innocent human being.
2 Abortion kills a fetus.
3 A fetus is an innocent human being.
Therefore
4 Abortion is always wrong.

Most supporters of abortion attack the third premise, denying that the fetus counts as an innocent human being. But the fetus is certainly human, in the sense that it is a member of the species *Homo sapiens*, and it is alive – we can know what it is for a fetus to die in the womb – and obviously innocent, even if only in the trivial sense that it has no capacity to do anything wrong. So it does look as if abortion is the killing of an innocent human being.

Advocates of abortion, in our view, need to shift the focus of the argument from discussion of the third premise, whether the fetus is a living human being, to the first premise – whether it is always wrong to kill an innocent human being. Perhaps it takes more than mere membership of the species *Homo sapiens* to have a right to life. A fetus may be human, but it cannot think, has no awareness of itself, and until at least twenty weeks of gestation cannot even feel pain. So why should it have a greater right to life than nonhuman animals who are capable of feeling pain? Is it because of its potential? But potential is not enough to give rise to a right, until the potential is realized. We do not value an acorn as much as an ancient oak, or give the Prince of Wales the rights of the King of England. If a woman does not want to have a child, she is free to abstain from sexual intercourse, or to use contraception to prevent the child being conceived. If the child is nevertheless conceived, but not yet a conscious, let alone self-aware, being, why should she not be equally free to end its life before it is born? Each of these courses of action prevents the existence of an unwanted future human being and – if the abortion is carried out early in pregnancy – each does it without inflicting suffering on anyone. Seen from that perspective, abortion is a justifiable procedure even when it is not necessary to protect the life or health of the pregnant woman.

Withdrawing Life-Support

The movement to legalize abortion avoided directly confronting the traditional ethic of the sanctity of human life, because its advocates persuaded the wider public that the fetus inside the womb is not an independent human being with the same right to life as other human beings. But challenges to the traditional ethic have come from other directions too. Not long ago, it was widely accepted that physicians have a duty to save life whenever it is possible to do so. A few physicians took a more flexible approach, making their own judgments about when it was good to save a life, and when a patient should be allowed to die. But, in general, the assumption that physicians are there to save life outweighed other considerations to such an extent that even patients capable of expressing a view on whether they wished to go on living were not asked for their opinions. As the power of modern medical technology to prolong life grew, however, this assumption increasingly came into question. Patients with no prospect of recovery, in pain and distress, were being kept alive long past the point at which, a decade or two earlier, they would have died. During the 1960s and 1970s, patients or, where the patients could not express their views, the families of patients began to demand more of a say in how they were treated. Patient advocacy organizations and philosophers, theologians, and physicians working in the newly developing field of bioethics supported the growing movement for patients' rights.

Today, most bioethicists would agree that a competent patient has the right to refuse further medical treatment, and in many countries the law now recognizes this right. The situation is more difficult if the patient who wishes to die is not on any form of life-support, and therefore needs active assistance, such as an overdose of a barbiturate. Voluntary euthanasia is now legal in the Netherlands and Belgium, and physician-assisted suicide (in which the physician may prescribe, but not administer, a lethal dose of a drug to a terminally ill patient) is permitted in Switzerland and the American state of Oregon. Elsewhere, it is against the law, although that does not mean that it does not happen. Some bioethicists support a principle known as "double effect," which allows physicians to give large doses of morphine, knowing that the dose they are giving will bring about the patient's death. On this view it is what the physician intends, not what he or she foresees will happen, that makes the difference between murder and good medical care. (As we shall see when we look at the ethics of war, the same distinction can be used in other circumstances.) Whether or not we think the distinction between intention and foresight really is so critical to the morality of our actions, it is undeniable that intentions are difficult to prove, and that physicians may intend to end the life of a patient, but know that if they were ever questioned by the authorities, they could say that the doses were necessary to relieve pain. The case would be most unlikely to go to court or, if it did, to result in a conviction.

Perhaps the most difficult cases are those involving Alzheimer's disease and other forms of dementia. As more people live beyond 80, such cases have become increasingly common. Because dementia usually progresses slowly, it is often difficult to say when a patient's quality of life has declined to the point at which he or she would no longer wish to remain alive. As we see in Kate Jennings' *Moral Hazard*, although some patients provide clear "living wills" expressing their wishes about such situations, not all jurisdictions recognize the validity of such documents, and even when they are recognized, they can be used only as a basis for the withdrawal of treatment, never for active euthanasia. Many people with dementia live for years without requiring medical treatment. Sometimes the spouse or children of a person with dementia are driven to desperate measures to end the suffering of the person they love, and these cases do end up in the courts, occasionally leading to long prison sentences. There must be a better way to resolve these heart-breaking situations.

Suicide

Hamlet's belief that suicide is against God's law was supported by the seventeenth-century philosopher John Locke, who thought it God's role to decide when human beings should live or die. The suicide is therefore like a soldier who deserts his station before his commander orders him relieved of his duty. This view obviously has no appeal to those who do not believe in God. Suicide was also seen as a crime against the king, because it deprived him of a subject, and the more subjects a king had, the richer and more powerful he was liable to be. But we no longer see citizens as the property of their sovereign. Kant thought that suicide is a violation of a duty to oneself, and based that duty on a claim that it contradicts a will to live that is part of nature. But Kant's argument seems to rely on the idea that what is natural is also good, and when we understand our nature in Darwinian terms, we can see that there is no moral purpose behind nature, or in the desires that it has given us. As we saw in Section I, we must choose what to make of our lives.

Laws against suicide have now been repealed in many countries, perhaps because people believe that private acts that do not harm others are not the law's business, or perhaps because of the absurdity of trying to deter a would-be suicide by the threat of punishment. Nevertheless, suicide is usually seen as a tragedy that society should try to prevent. That view is no doubt right for people in whom the motives for suicide are likely to pass. The love-sick teenager who thinks his life is over because his true love has rejected him needs to be encouraged to take a less gloomy view of his future. But what of those who, though not terminally ill, calmly and rationally decide that they do not wish to live any longer? If they have no dependents, are they doing anything wrong? Or does the tragedy lie not in the suicide itself so much as in the fact that society could find no way to give such people enough reason to live?

25

MAEVE BINCHY

Shepherd's Bush

May is unmarried, pregnant, and living in Ireland, where abortion is not legal. To terminate her pregnancy, she comes to London, where she stays with her friend Celia.

Tuesday morning. Celia was gone. Dr Harris's address was neatly written on the pad by the phone with instructions how to get there. Also Celia's phone number at work, and a message that May never believed she would hear from Celia. "Good luck."

He was small, and Jewish, and worried and kind. His examination was painless and unembarrassing. He confirmed what she knew already. He wrote down dates, and asked general questions about her health. May wondered whether he had a family, there were no pictures of wife or children in the surgery. But then there were none in Andy's office, either. Perhaps his wife was called Rebecca and she too worried because her husband worked so hard, they might have two children, a boy who was a gifted musician, and a girl who wanted to get married to a Christian. Maybe they all walked along these leafy roads on Saturdays to synagogue and Rebecca cooked all those things like gefilte fish and bagels.

With a start, May told herself to stop dreaming about him. It was a habit she had got into recently, fancying lives for everyone she met, however briefly. She usually gave them happy lives with a bit of problem-to-be-solved thrown in. She wondered what a psychiatrist would make of that. As she was coming back to real life, Dr Harris was saying that if he was going to refer her for a termination he must know why she could not have the baby. He pointed out that she was healthy, and strong, and young. She should have no difficulty with pregnancy or birth. Were there emotional reasons? Yes, it would kill her parents, she wouldn't be able to look after the baby, she didn't want to look after one on her own either, it wouldn't be fair on her or the baby.

"And the father?" Dr Harris asked.

Maeve Binchy, "Shepherd's Bush," from *London Transports*. London: Hutchinson, 1978. Now published by Century and reprinted by permission of the Random House Group Ltd.

"Is my boss, is heavily married, already has four babies of his own. It would break up his marriage which he doesn't want to do . . . yet. No, the father wouldn't want me to have it either."

"Has he said that?" asked Dr Harris as if he already knew the answer.

"I haven't told him, I can't tell him, I won't tell him," said May.

Dr Harris sighed. He asked a few more questions; he made a telephone call; he wrote out an address. It was a posh address near Harley Street.

"This is Mr White. A well-known surgeon. These are his consulting-rooms, I have made an appointment for you at 2.30 this afternoon. I understand from your friend Miss . . ." He searched his mind and his desk for Celia's name and then gave up. "I understand anyway that you are not living here, and don't want to try and pretend that you are, so that you want the termination done privately. That's just as well, because it would be difficult to get it done on the National Health. There are many cases that would have to come before you."

"Oh I have the money," said May, patting her handbag. She felt nervous but relieved at the same time. Almost exhilarated. It was working, the whole thing was actually moving. God bless Celia.

"It will be around £180 to £200, and in cash, you know that?"

"Yes, it's all here, but why should a well-known surgeon have to be paid in cash, Dr Harris? You know it makes it look a bit illegal and sort of underhand, doesn't it?"

Dr Harris smiled a tired smile. "You asked me why he has to be paid in cash. Because he says so. Why he says so, I don't know. Maybe it's because some of his clients don't feel too like paying him after the event. It's not like plastic surgery or a broken leg, where they can see the results. In a termination you see no results. Maybe people don't pay so easily then. Maybe also Mr White doesn't have a warm relationship with his Income Tax people. I don't know."

"Do I owe you anything?" May asked, putting on her coat.

"No, my dear, nothing." He smiled and showed her to the door.

"It feels wrong. I'm used to paying a doctor at home or they send bills," she said.

"Send me a picture postcard of your nice country sometime," he said. "When my wife was alive she and I spent several happy holidays there before all this business started." He waved a hand to take in the course of Anglo-Irish politics and difficulties over the last ten years.

May blinked a bit hard and thanked him. She took a taxi which was passing his door and went to Oxford Street. She wanted to see what was in the shops because she was going to pretend that she had spent £200 on clothes and then they had all been lost or stolen. She hadn't yet worked out the details of this deception, which seemed unimportant compared to all the rest that had to be gone through. But she would need to know what was in the shops so that she could say what she was meant to have bought.

Imagining that she had this kind of money to spend, she examined jackets, skirts, sweaters, and the loveliest boots she had ever seen. If only she didn't have to throw this money away, she could have these things. It was her savings over ten months, she put by £30 a month with difficulty. Would Andy have liked her in the boots? She didn't know. He never said much about the way she looked. He saw her mostly in uniform when she could steal time to go to the flat he had for himself in the hotel. On the evenings when he was meant to be working late, and she was in fact cooking for him, she usually wore a dressing-gown, a long velvet one. Perhaps she might have bought a dressing-gown. She examined some, beautiful Indian silks, and a Japanese satin one in pink covered with little black butterflies. Yes, she would tell him she had bought that, he would like the sound of it, and be sorry it had been stolen.

She had a cup of coffee in one of the big shops and watched the other shoppers resting between bouts of buying. She wondered, did any of them look at her, and if so, would they know in a million years that her shopping money would remain in her purse until it was handed over to a Mr White so that he could abort Andy's baby? Why did she use words like that, why did she say things to hurt herself, she must have a very deep-seated sense of guilt. Perhaps, she thought to herself with a bit of humour, she should save another couple of hundred pounds and come over for a few sessions with a Harley Street shrink. That should set her right.

It wasn't a long walk to Mr White's rooms, it wasn't a pleasant welcome. A kind of girl that May had before only seen in the pages of fashion magazines, bored, disdainful, elegant, reluctantly admitted her.

"Oh yes, Dr Harris's patient," she said, as if May should have come in some tradesman's entrance. She felt furious, and inferior, and sat with her hands in small tight balls, and her eyes unseeing in the waiting-room.

Mr White looked like a caricature of a diplomat. He had elegant grey hair, elegant manicured hands. He moved very gracefully, he talked in practised, concerned clichés, he knew how to put people at their ease, and despite herself, and while still disliking him, May felt safe.

Another examination, another confirmation, more checking of dates. Good, good, she had come in plenty of time, sensible girl. No reasons she would like to discuss about whether this was the right course of action? No? Oh well, grown-up lady, must make up her own mind. Absolutely certain then? Fine, fine. A look at a big leather-bound book on his desk, a look at a small notebook. Leather-bound for the tax people, small notebook for himself, thought May viciously. Splendid, splendid. Tomorrow morning then, not a problem in the world, once she was sure, then he knew this was the best, and wisest thing. Very sad the people who dithered.

May could never imagine this man having dithered in his life. She was asked to see Vanessa on the way out. She knew that the girl would be called something like Vanessa.

Vanessa yawned and took £194 from her. She seemed to have difficulty in finding the six pounds in change. May wondered wildly whether this was meant to be a tip. If so, she would wait for a year until Vanessa found the change. With the notes came a discreet printed card advertising a nursing home on the other side of London.

"Before nine, fasting, just the usual overnight things," said Vanessa helpfully.

"Tomorrow morning?" checked May.

"Well yes, naturally. You'll be out at eight the following morning. They'll arrange everything like taxis. They have super food," she added as an afterthought.

"They'd need to have for this money," said May spiritedly.

"You're not just paying for the food," said Vanessa wisely.

It was still raining. She rang Celia from a public phonebox. Everything was organized, she told her. Would Celia like to come and have a meal somewhere, and maybe they could go on to a theatre?

Celia was sorry, she had to work late, and she had already bought liver and bacon for supper. Could she meet May at home around nine? There was a great quiz show on telly, it would be a shame to miss it.

May went to a hairdresser and spent four times what she would have spent at home on a hair-do.

She went to a cinema and saw a film which looked as if it were going to be about a lot of sophisticated witty French people on a yacht and turned out to be about a sophisticated witty French girl who fell in love with the deck-hand on the yacht and when she purposely got pregnant, in order that he would marry her, he laughed at her and the witty sophisticated girl threw herself overboard. Great choice that, May said glumly, as she dived into the underground to go back to the smell of liver frying.

Celia asked little about the arrangements for the morning, only practical things like the address so that she could work out how long it would take to get there.

"Would you like me to come and see you?" she asked. "I expect when it's all over, all finished you know, they'd let you have visitors. I could come after work."

She emphasized the word "could" very slightly. May immediately felt mutinous. She would love Celia to come, but not if it was going to be a duty, something she felt she had to do, against her principles, her inclinations.

"No, don't do that," she said in a falsely bright voice. "They have telly in the rooms apparently, and anyway, it's not as if I were going to be there for more than twenty-four hours."

Celia looked relieved. She worked out taxi times and locations and turned on the quiz show.

In the half light May looked at her. She was unbending, Celia was. She would survive everything, even the fact that Martin would never marry her. Christ, the whole thing was a mess. Why did people start life with such hopes, and as early as their mid-twenties become beaten and accepting of things. Was the rest of life going to be like this?

She didn't sleep so well, and it was a relief when Celia shouted that it was seven o'clock.

Wednesday. An ordinary Wednesday for the taxi-driver, who shouted some kind of amiable conversation at her. She missed most of it, because of the noise of the engine, and didn't bother to answer him half the time except with a grunt.

The place had creeper on the walls. It was a big house, with a small garden, and an attractive brass handle on the door. The nurse who opened it was Irish. She checked May's name on a list. Thank God it was O'Connor, there were a million O'Connors. Suppose she had had an unusual name, she'd have been found out immediately.

The bedroom was big and bright. Two beds, flowery covers, nice furniture. A magazine rack, a bookshelf. A television, a bathroom.

The Irish nurse offered her a hanger from the wardrobe for her coat as if this was a pleasant family hotel of great class and comfort. May felt frightened for the first time. She longed to sit down on one of the beds and cry, and for the nurse to put her arm around her and give her a cigarette and say that it would be all right. She hated being so alone.

The nurse was distant.

"The other lady will be in shortly. Her name is Miss Adams. She just went downstairs to say goodbye to her friend. If there's anything you'd like, please ring."

She was gone, and May paced the room like a captured animal. Was she to undress? It was ridiculous to go to bed. You only went to bed in the day-time if you were ill. She was well, perfectly well.

Miss Adams burst in the door. She was a chubby, pretty girl about twenty-three. She was Australian, and her name was Hell, short for Helen.

"Come on, bedtime," she said, and they both put on their nightdresses and got into beds facing each other. May had never felt so silly in her whole life.

"Are you sure we're meant to do this?" she asked.

"Positive," Helen announced. "I was here last year. They'll be in with the screens for modesty, the examination, and the pre-med. They go mad if you're not in bed. Of course that stupid Paddy of a nurse didn't tell you, they expect you to be inspired."

Hell was right. In five minutes, the nurse and Mr White came in. A younger nurse carried a screen. Hell was examined first, then May for blood pressure and temperature, and that kind of thing. Mr White was charming. He called her Miss O'Connor, as if he had known her all his life.

He patted her shoulder and told her she didn't have anything to worry about. The Irish nurse gave her an unsmiling injection which was going to make her drowsy. It didn't immediately.

Hell was doing her nails.

"You were really here last year?" asked May in disbelief.

"Yeah, there's nothing to it. I'll be back at work tomorrow."

"Why didn't you take the Pill?" May asked.

"Why didn't you?" countered Hell.

"Well, I did for a bit, but I thought it was making me fat, and I then anyway, you know, I thought I'd escaped for so long before I started the Pill that it would be all right. I was wrong."

"I know." Hell was sympathetic. "I can't take it. I've got varicose veins already and I don't really understand all those things they give you in the Family Planning clinics, jellies, and rubber things, and diaphragms. It's worse than working out income tax. Anyway, you never have time to set up a scene like that before going to bed with someone, do you? It's like preparing for a battle."

May laughed.

"It's going to be fine, love," said Hell. "Look, I know, I've been here before. Some of my friends have had it done four or five times. I promise you, it's only the people who don't know who worry. This afternoon you'll wonder what you were thinking about to look so white. Now if it had been terrible, would I be here again?"

"But your varicose veins?" said May, feeling a little sleepy.

"Go to sleep, kid," said Hell. "We'll have a chat when it's all over."

Then she was getting onto a trolley, half-asleep, and going down corridors with lovely prints on the walls to a room with a lot of light, and transferring onto another table. She felt as if she could sleep for ever and she hadn't even had the anaesthetic yet. Mr White stood there in a coat brighter than his name. Someone was dressing him up the way they do in films.

She thought about Andy. "I love you," she said suddenly.

"Of course you do," said Mr White, coming over and patting her kindly without a trace of embarrassment.

Then she was being moved again, she thought they hadn't got her right on the operating table, but it wasn't that, it was back into her own bed and more sleep.

There was a tinkle of china. Hell called over from the window.

"Come on, they've brought us some nice soup. Broth they call it."

May blinked.

"Come on, May. I was done after you and I'm wide awake. Now didn't I tell you there was nothing to it?"

May sat up. No pain, no tearing feeling in her insides. No sickness. "Are you sure they did me?" she asked.

They both laughed.

They had what the nursing-home called a light lunch. Then they got a menu so that they could choose dinner.

"There are some things that England does really well, and this is one of them," Hell said approvingly, trying to decide between the delights that were offered. "They even give us a small carafe of wine. If you want more you have to pay for it. But they kind of disapprove of us getting pissed."

Hell's friend Charlie was coming in at six when he finished work. Would May be having a friend too, she wondered? No. Celia wouldn't come.

"I don't mean Celia," said Hell. "I mean the bloke."

"He doesn't know, he's in Dublin, and he's married," said May.

"Well, Charlie's married, but he bloody knows, and he'd know if he were on the moon."

"It's different."

"No, it's not different. It's the same for everyone, there are rules, you're a fool to break them. Didn't he pay for it either, this guy?"

"No. I told you he doesn't know."

"Aren't you noble," said Hell scornfully. "Aren't you a real Lady Galahad. Just visiting London for a day or two, darling, just going to see a few friends, see you soon. Love you darling. Is that it?"

"We don't go in for so many darlings as that in Dublin," said May.

"You don't go in for much common sense either. What will you gain, what will he gain, what will anyone gain? You come home penniless, a bit lonely. He doesn't know what the hell you've been doing, he isn't extra-sensitive and loving and grateful because he doesn't have anything to be grateful about as far as he's concerned."

"I couldn't tell him. I couldn't. I couldn't ask him for £200 and say what it was for. That wasn't in the bargain, that was never part of the deal."

May was almost tearful, mainly from jealousy she thought. She couldn't bear Hell's Charlie to come in, while her Andy was going home to his wife because there would be nobody to cook him something exciting and go to bed with him in his little manager's flat.

"When you go back, tell him. That's my advice," said Hell. "Tell him you didn't want to worry him, you did it all on your own because the responsibility was yours since you didn't take the Pill. That's unless you think he'd have wanted it?"

"No, he wouldn't have wanted it."

"Well then, that's what you do. Don't ask him for the money straight out, just let him know you're broke. He'll react some way then. It's silly not to tell them at all. My sister did that with her bloke back in Melbourne. She never told him at all, and she got upset because he didn't know the sacrifice she had made, and every time she bought a drink or paid for a cinema ticket she got resentful of him. All for no reason, because he didn't bloody know."

"I might," said May, but she knew she wouldn't. [. . .]

May didn't think Hell had got it right about telling Andy all about the abortion. Andy might be against that kind of thing. He was very moral in his own way, was Andy.

26

BRIAN CLARK

Whose Life is it Anyway?

Ken Harrison is in hospital several months after a near fatal car accident that has left him permanently paralyzed from the neck down. He has asked his doctor to stop treating him.

(MRS GILLIAN BOYLE *enters. She is thirty-five, attractive, and very professional in her manner. She is a medical social worker*)

MRS BOYLE: Good morning.

KEN: Morning.

MRS BOYLE: Mr Harrison?

KEN (*Cheerfully*): It used to be.

MRS BOYLE: My name is Mrs Boyle.

KEN: And you've come to cheer me up.

MRS BOYLE: I wouldn't put it like that.

KEN: How would you put it?

MRS BOYLE: I've come to see if I can help.

KEN: Good. You can.

MRS BOYLE: How?

KEN: Go and convince Dr Frankenstein that he has successfully made his monster and he can now let it go.

MRS BOYLE: Dr Emerson is a first-rate physician. My goodness, they have improved this room.

KEN: Have they?

MRS BOYLE: It used to be really dismal. All dark green and cream. It's surprising what pastel colors will do, isn't it? Really cheerful.

KEN: Yes; perhaps they should try painting me. I'd hate to be the thing that ruins the decor.

MRS BOYLE: What on earth makes you say that? You don't ruin anything.

BRIAN CLARK, pp. 50–60, 79–83, and 130–44 from *Whose Life is it Anyway?* New York: Dodd, Mead & Company, 1978. Reprinted by permission of Judy Daish Associates Ltd.

KEN: I'm sorry. That was a bit . . . whining. Well, don't let me stop you.

MRS BOYLE: Doing what?

KEN: What you came for, I suppose. What do you do? Conjuring tricks? Funny stories? Or a belly dance? If I have any choice, I'd prefer the belly dance.

MRS BOYLE: I'm afraid I've left my bikini at home.

KEN: Who said anything about a bikini?

MRS BOYLE: Dr Emerson tells me that you don't want any more treatment.

KEN: Good.

MRS BOYLE: Why good?

KEN: I didn't think he'd heard what I'd said.

MRS BOYLE: Why not?

KEN: He didn't take any notice.

MRS BOYLE: Well as you can see, he did.

KEN: He sent you?

MRS BOYLE: Yes.

KEN: And you are my new treatment; get in.

MRS BOYLE: Why don't you want any more treatment?

KEN: I'd rather not go on living like this.

MRS BOYLE: Why not?

KEN: Isn't it obvious?

MRS BOYLE: Not to me. I've seen many patients like you.

KEN: And they all want to live?

MRS BOYLE: Usually.

KEN: Why?

MRS BOYLE: They find a new way of life.

KEN: How?

MRS BOYLE: You'll be surprised how many things you will be able to do with training and a little patience.

KEN: Such as?

MRS BOYLE: We can't be sure yet. But I should think that you will be able to operate reading machines and perhaps an adapted typewriter.

KEN: Reading and writing. What about arithmetic?

MRS BOYLE (*Smiling*): I dare say we could fit you up with a comptometer if you really wanted one.

KEN: Mrs Boyle, even educationalists have realized that the three r's do not make a full life.

MRS BOYLE: What did you do before the accident?

KEN: I taught in an art school. I was a sculptor.

MRS BOYLE: I see.

KEN: Difficult, isn't it? How about an electrically operated hammer and chisel? No, well. Or a cybernetic lump of clay?

MRS BOYLE: I wouldn't laugh if I were you. It's amazing what can be done. Our scientists are wonderful.

KEN: They are. But it's not good enough you see, Mrs Boyle. I really have absolutely no desire at all to be the object of scientific virtuosity. I have thought things over very carefully. I do have plenty of time for thinking and I have decided that I do not want to go on living with so much effort for so little result.

MRS BOYLE: Yes, well, we shall have to see about that.

KEN: What is there to see?

MRS BOYLE: We can't just stop treatment, just like that.

KEN: Why not?

MRS BOYLE: It's the job of the hospital to save life, not to lose it.

KEN: The hospital's done all it can, but it wasn't enough. It wasn't the hospital's fault; the original injury was too big.

MRS BOYLE: We have to make the best of the situation.

KEN: No. "We" don't have to do anything. I have to do what is to be done and that is to cash in the chips.

MRS BOYLE: It's not unusual, you know, for people injured as you have been, to suffer with this depression for a considerable time before they begin to see that a life is possible.

KEN: How long?

MRS BOYLE: It varies.

KEN: Don't hedge.

MRS BOYLE: It could be a year or so.

KEN: And it could last for the rest of my life.

MRS BOYLE: That would be most unlikely.

KEN: I'm sorry, but I cannot settle for that.

MRS BOYLE: Try not to dwell on it. I'll see what I can do to get you started on some occupational therapy. Perhaps we could make a start on the reading machines.

KEN: Do you have many books for those machines?

MRS BOYLE: Quite a few.

KEN: Can I make a request for the first one?

MRS BOYLE: If you like.

KEN: "How to be a sculptor with no hands."

MRS BOYLE: I'll be back tomorrow with the machine.

KEN: It's marvelous, you know.

MRS BOYLE: What is?

KEN: All you people have the same technique. When I say something really awkward you just pretend I haven't said anything at all. You're all the bloody same . . . Well there's another outburst. That should be your cue to comment on the light-shade or the color of the walls.

MRS BOYLE: I'm sorry if I have upset you.

KEN: Of course you have upset me. You and the doctors with your appalling so-called professionalism, which is nothing more than a series of verbal tricks to prevent you relating to your patients as human beings.

MRS BOYLE: You must understand; we have to remain relatively detached in order to help . . .

KEN: That's all right with me. Detach yourself. Tear yourself off on the dotted line that divides the woman from the social worker and post yourself off to another patient.

MRS BOYLE: You're very upset. . . .

KEN: Christ Almighty, you're doing it again. Listen to yourself, woman. I say something offensive about you and you turn your professional cheek. If you were human, if you were treating me as human, you'd tell me to bugger off. Can't you see that this is why I've decided that life isn't worth living? I am not human and I'm even more convinced of that by your visit than I was before, so how does that grab you? The very exercise of your so-called professionalism makes me want to die.

MRS BOYLE: I'm . . . Please . . .

KEN: Go . . . For God's sake get out . . . Go on . . . Get out . . . Go out.

(*She goes into* SISTER'*s room.* SISTER *hears* KEN'*s shouts*)

SISTER: What's the matter, Mrs Boyle?

MRS BOYLE: It's Mr Harrison . . . He seems very upset.

KEN (*Shouting*): . . . I am upset.

Harrison has asked to see a lawyer, pretending that he is interested in seeking compensation for his accident. When the lawyer, Mr Hill, arrives, however, he asks him to assist him in getting a discharge from the hospital so that he can die.

DR EMERSON: Mr Hill? Sister just rang through.

HILL: Dr Emerson?

(*They shake hands*)

DR EMERSON: You've been seeing Mr Harrison?

HILL: Yes.

DR EMERSON: Tragic case . . . I hope you'll be able to get enough money for him to ease his mind.

HILL: Dr Emerson. It's not about that I wanted to see you. I thought I was coming about that, but Mr Harrison wishes to retain me to represent him on quite another matter.

DR EMERSON: Oh?

HILL: Yes, he wants to be discharged.

DR EMERSON: That's impossible.

HILL: Why?

DR EMERSON: To put it bluntly, he would die if we did that.

HILL: He knows that. It's what he wants.

DR EMERSON: And you are asking me to kill my patient?

HILL: I am representing Mr Harrison's wishes to you and asking for your reaction.

DR EMERSON: Well, you've had it. It's impossible. Now if that's really all you came about . . .

HILL: Dr Emerson, you can, of course, dismiss me like that if you choose to, but I would hardly think it serves anyone's interests, least of all Mr Harrison's.

DR EMERSON: I am trying to save Mr Harrison's life. There is no need to remind me of my duty to my patient, Mr Hill.

HILL: Or mine to my client, Dr Emerson.

DR EMERSON: . . . Are you telling me that you have accepted the job of coming to me to urge a course of action that will lose your client his life?

HILL: I hadn't accepted it . . . no . . . I told Mr Harrison I would talk to you first. Now I have and I begin to see why he thought it necessary to be represented.

DR EMERSON: All right . . . Let's start again. Now tell me what you want to know.

HILL: Mr Harrison wishes to be discharged from hospital. Will you please make the necessary arrangements?

DR EMERSON: No.

HILL: May I ask why not?

DR EMERSON: Because Mr Harrison is incapable of living outside the hospital and it is my duty as a doctor to preserve life.

HILL: I take it that Mr Harrison is a voluntary patient here.

DR EMERSON: Of course.

HILL: Then I fail to see the legal basis for your refusal.

DR EMERSON: Can't you understand that Mr Harrison is suffering from depression? He is incapable of making a rational decision about his life and death.

HILL: Are you maintaining that Mr Harrison is mentally unbalanced?

DR EMERSON: Yes.

HILL: Would you have any objection to my bringing in a psychiatrist for a second opinion?

DR EMERSON: Of course not, but why not ask the consultant psychiatrist here? I'm sure he will be able to convince you.

HILL: Has he examined Mr Harrison?

DR EMERSON: No, but that can be quickly arranged.

HILL: That's very kind of you Dr Emerson, but I'm sure you'll understand if I ask for my own – whose opinion you are not sure of *before* he examines the patient.

DR EMERSON: Good afternoon, Mr Hill.

HILL: Good afternoon.

(MR HILL *takes up his briefcase and leaves*)

A judge has been brought in to rule on the dispute between Harrison and his doctor. Mr Eden represents the hospital, and Mr Kershaw represents Harrison.

JUDGE: I have decided in consultation with Mr Kershaw and Mr Hill that we shall proceed thus. I will hear a statement from Dr Michael Emerson as to why he believes Mr Harrison is legally detained, and then a statement from Dr Richard Barr, who will support the application. We have decided not to subject Mr Harrison to examination and cross-examination.

KEN: But I . . .

JUDGE (*Sharply*): Just a moment, Mr Harrison. If, as appears likely, there remains genuine doubt as to the main issue, I shall question Mr Harrison myself. Dr Scott, I wonder if you would ask Dr Emerson to come in.

DR SCOTT: Yes, my Lord.

(*She goes out*)

Would you come in now, sir?

(SISTER *and* DR EMERSON *come into* KEN's *room*)

JUDGE: Dr Emerson, I would like you to take the oath.

(*The* JUDGE *hands* DR EMERSON *a card with the oath written on it*)

DR EMERSON: I swear the evidence that I give shall be the truth, the whole truth and nothing but the truth.

JUDGE: Stand over there, please.

(*The* JUDGE *nods to* MR EDEN)

EDEN: You are Dr Michael Emerson?

DR EMERSON: I am.

EDEN: And what is your position here?

DR EMERSON: I am a consultant physician and in charge of the intensive care unit.

EDEN: Dr Emerson, would you please give a brief account of your treatment of this patient.

DR EMERSON (*Referring to notes*): Mr Harrison was admitted here on the afternoon of October 9th, as an emergency following a road accident. He was suffering from a fractured left tibia and right tibia and fibia, a fractured pelvis, four fractured ribs, one of which had punctured the lung, and a dislocated fourth vertebra, which had ruptured the spinal cord. He was extensively bruised and had minor lacerations. He was deeply unconscious and remained so for thirty hours. As a result of treatment all the broken bones and ruptured tissue have healed with the exception of a severed spinal cord and this, together with a mental trauma, is now all that remains of the initial injury.

EDEN: Precisely, Doctor. Let us deal with those last two points. The spinal cord. Will there be any further improvement in that?

DR EMERSON: In the present state of medical knowledge, I would think not.

EDEN: And the mental trauma you spoke of?

DR EMERSON: It's impossible to injure the body to the extent that Mr Harrison did and not affect the mind. It is common in these cases that depression and the tendency to make wrong decisions goes on for months, even years.

EDEN: And in your view Mr Harrison is suffering from such a depression?

DR EMERSON: Yes.

EDEN: Thank you, Doctor.

JUDGE: Mr Kershaw?

KERSHAW: Doctor. Is there any objective way you could demonstrate this trauma? Are there, for example, the results of any tests, or any measurements you can take to show it to us?

DR EMERSON: No.

KERSHAW: Then how do you distinguish between a medical syndrome and a sane, even justified, depression?

DR EMERSON: By using my thirty years' experience as a physician, dealing with both types.

KERSHAW: No more questions, my Lord.

JUDGE: Mr Eden, do you wish to re-examine?

EDEN: No, my Lord.

JUDGE: Thank you, Doctor. Would you ask Dr Barr if he would step in please?

(DR EMERSON *goes out*)

DR EMERSON: It's you now, Barr.

(SISTER *brings* DR BARR *into* KEN's *room*)

SISTER: Dr Barr.

JUDGE: Dr Barr, will you take the oath please.

(*He does so*)

Mr Kershaw.

KERSHAW: You are Dr Richard Barr?

DR BARR: I am.

KERSHAW: And what position do you hold?

DR BARR: I am a consultant psychiatrist at Norwood Park Hospital.

KERSHAW: That is primarily a mental hospital is it not?

DR BARR: It is.

KERSHAW: Then you must see a large number of patients suffering from depressive illness.

DR BARR: I do, yes.

KERSHAW: You have examined Mr Harrison?

DR BARR: I have, yes.

KERSHAW: Would you say that he was suffering from such an illness?

DR BARR: No, I would not.

KERSHAW: Are you quite sure, Doctor?

DR BARR: Yes, I am.

KERSHAW: The court has heard evidence that Mr Harrison is depressed. Would you dispute that?

DR BARR: No, but depression is not necessarily an illness. I would say that Mr Harrison's depression is reactive rather than endogenous. That is to say, he is reacting in a perfectly rational way to a very bad situation.

KERSHAW: Thank you, Dr Barr.

JUDGE: Mr Eden?

EDEN: Dr Barr. Are there any objective results that you could produce to prove Mr Harrison is capable?

DR BARR: There are clinical symptoms of endogenous depression, of course, disturbed sleep patterns, loss of appetite, lassitude, but, even if they were present, they would be masked by the physical condition.

EDEN: So how can you be sure this *is* in fact just a reactive depression?

DR BARR: Just by experience, that's all, and by discovering when I talk to him that he has a remarkably incisive mind and is perfectly capable of understanding his position and of deciding what to do about it.

EDEN: One last thing, Doctor, do you think Mr Harrison has made the right decision?

KERSHAW (*Quickly*): Is that really relevant, my Lord? After all . . .

JUDGE: Not really . . .

DR BARR: I should like to answer it though.

JUDGE: Very well.

DR BARR: No, I thought he made the wrong decision.

(*To* KEN): Sorry.

EDEN: No more questions, my Lord.

JUDGE: Do you wish to re-examine, Mr Kershaw?

KERSHAW: No, thank you, my Lord.

JUDGE: That will be all, Dr Barr.

(DR BARR *goes out. The* JUDGE *stands*)

JUDGE: Do you feel like answering some questions?

KEN: Of course.

JUDGE: Thank you.

KEN: You are too kind.

JUDGE: Not at all.

KEN: I mean it. I'd prefer it if you were a hanging judge.

JUDGE: There aren't any any more.

KEN: Society is now much more sensitive and humane?

JUDGE: You could put it that way.

KEN: I'll settle for that.

JUDGE: I would like you to take the oath. Dr Scott, his right hand, please.

(KEN *takes the oath*)

The consultant physician here has given evidence that you are not capable of making a rational decision.

KEN: He's wrong.

JUDGE: When then do you think he came to that opinion?

KEN: He's a good doctor and won't let a patient die if he can help it.

JUDGE: He found that you were suffering from acute depression.

KEN: Is that surprising? I am almost totally paralyzed. I'd be insane if I *weren't* depressed.

JUDGE: But there is a difference between being unhappy and being depressed in the medical sense.

KEN: I would have thought that my psychiatrist answered that point.

JUDGE: But, surely, wishing to die must be strong evidence that the depression has moved beyond a mere unhappiness into a medical realm?

KEN: I don't wish to die.

JUDGE: Then what is this case all about?

KEN: Nor do I wish to live at any price. Of course I want to live, but as far as I am concerned I'm dead already. I merely require the doctors to recognize the fact. I cannot accept this condition constitutes life in any real sense at all.

JUDGE: Certainly, you're alive legally.

KEN: I think I could challenge even that.

JUDGE: How?

KEN: Any reasonable definition of life must include the idea of its being self-supporting. I seem to remember something in the papers – when all the heart transplant controversy was on – about it being all right to take someone's heart if they require constant attention from respirators and so on to keep them alive.

JUDGE: There also has to be absolutely no brain activity at all. Yours is certainly working.

KEN: It is and sanely.

JUDGE: That is the question to be decided.

KEN: My Lord, I am not asking anyone to kill me. I am only asking to be discharged from this hospital.

JUDGE: It comes to the same thing.

KEN: Then that proves my point; not just the fact that I will spend the rest of my life in hospital, but that whilst I am here, everything is geared just to keeping my brain active, with no real possibility of it ever being able to direct anything. As far as I can see, that is an act of deliberate cruelty.

JUDGE: Surely, it would be more cruel if society let people die, when it could, with some effort, keep them alive.

KEN: No, not *more* cruel, *just* as cruel.

JUDGE: Then why should the hospital let you die – if it is just as cruel?

KEN: The cruelty doesn't reside in saving someone or allowing them to die. It resides in the fact that the choice is removed from the man concerned.

JUDGE: But a man who is very desperately depressed is not capable of making a reasonable choice.

KEN: As you said, my Lord, that is the question to be decided.

JUDGE: All right. You tell me why it is a reasonable choice that you decided to die.

KEN: It is a question of dignity. Look at me here. I can do nothing, not even the basic primitive functions. I cannot even urinate, I have a permanent catheter attached to me. Every few days my bowels are washed out. Every few hours two nurses have to turn me over or I would rot away from bedsores. Only my brain functions unimpaired but even that is futile because I can't act on any conclusions it comes to. This hearing proves that. Will you please listen.

JUDGE: I am listening.

KEN: I choose to acknowledge the fact that I am in fact dead and I find the hospital's persistent effort to maintain this shadow of life an indignity and it's inhumane.

JUDGE: But wouldn't you agree that many people with appalling physical handicaps have overcome them and lived essentially creative, dignified lives?

KEN: Yes, I would, but the dignity starts with their choice. If I choose to live, it would be appalling if society killed me. If I choose to die, it is equally appalling if society keeps me alive.

JUDGE: I cannot accept that it is undignified for society to devote resources to keeping someone alive. Surely it enhances that society.

KEN: It is not undignified if the man wants to stay alive, but I must restate that the dignity starts with his choice. Without it, it is degrading because technology has taken over from human will. My Lord, if I cannot be a man, I do not wish to be a medical achievement. I'm fine . . . I am fine.

JUDGE: It's all right. I have no more questions.

(*The* JUDGE *stands up and walks to the window. He thinks a moment*)

JUDGE: This is a most unusual case. Before I make a judgment I want to state that I believe all the parties have acted in good faith. I propose to consider this for a moment. The law on this is fairly clear. A deliberate decision to embark on a course of action that will lead inevitably to death is not *ipso facto* evidence of insanity. If it were, society would have to reward many men with a dishonorable burial rather than a posthumous medal for gallantry. On the other hand, we do have to bear in mind that Mr Harrison has suffered massive physical injuries and it is possible that his mind is affected. Any judge in his career will have met men who are without doubt insane in the meaning of the Act and yet appear in the witness box to be rational. We must, in this case, be most careful not to allow Mr Harrison's obvious wit and intelligence to blind us to the fact that he could be suffering from a depressive illness . . . and so we have to face the disturbing fact of the divided evidence . . . and bear in mind that, however much we may sympathize with Mr Harrison in his cogently argued case to be allowed to die, the law instructs us to ignore it if it is the product of a disturbed or clinically depressed mind . . . However, I am satisfied that Mr Harrison is a brave and cool man who is in complete control of his mental faculties and I shall therefore make an order for him to be set free.

(*A pause. The* JUDGE *walks over to* KEN)

Well, you got your hanging judge!

KEN: I think not, my Lord. Thank you.

(*The* JUDGE *nods and smiles*)

27

KATE JENNINGS

Moral Hazard

Bailey is twenty-five years older than Cath, his wife, and he has Alzheimer's. As his condition deteriorates, she faces difficult decisions.

W̶e had gone through the nightly routine.

First, a Stouffer's frozen dinner, the extent of my cooking abilities. In the good years, Bailey always cooked for us. For him, food was a ceremony; even if he were eating by himself, he set the table as if for a special event. But cloves had wound up in the pepper grinder, plastic wrapping left on meat, a kitchen towel placed on a burner. He gave it up voluntarily, as he was giving up everything, redrawing his boundaries in order to preserve his dignity, but keeping an illusion of activity.

Then we watched the evening news, which included a segment on the newest hope for people with Alzheimer's. These segments ran, cruelly, at least once a week. They still do. Current advice to prevent Alzheimer's: Eat leafy green vegetables. At that time, though, they mostly involved the results of a study of Canadian nuns. The better educated the nun, the more she exercised her brain, a researcher had concluded, the less likely she would be to develop Alzheimer's. This was the opposite view of New York's home healthcare workers, with whom I chatted in the elevator of our apartment building. Jamaican and Filipino women with reserves of compassion, they believed that Alzheimer's was the result of overworking the brain, no doubt because the people they cared for had the money to hire them, entailing education, careers.

That night, the segment was about the development of genetically engineered, memory-impaired mice. It was billed as a major breakthrough. I always watched these segments with hope pricking in me – hope that turned to blasphemous fury when "the latest best new hope for Alzheimer's sufferers" turned out to be insulting generalizations derived from small and unrepresentative populations, or scientific

KATE JENNINGS, pp. 42–6, 143–50, and 158–62 from *Moral Hazard*. London: Fourth Estate, 2002. Copyright © Kate Jennings, 2002. Reprinted by permission of HarperCollins Publishers Ltd and Pan Macmillan Australia.

breakthroughs that would yield real results in twenty years' time. "Fucking nuns," I'd say, out of Bailey's earshot. That night: "Fucking mice."

Next, coaxing him out of his clothes and under the shower. Once a fastidious man, vain about his appearance, he would come to bed fully dressed and unwashed if I let him. The business of bathing was too complex for him, the feel of water alien on his skin.

The refusal to wear a diaper, now a necessity at night. "That's for children!" he protested. I tried humor, prancing around with the diaper on my head, pretending to be Queen Victoria. Finally, he was tucked in. Another day over without major mishap, another night ahead of us.

Our cat climbed onto the bed and stretched out on Bailey's stomach. Their noses almost touching, Bailey said to the cat, his tone triumphant, "Eva Truilly, Zora Diamond, Lulu Lawes!" These names were talismans: his boyhood school-teachers. Prompted by the results of the nun study, Bailey had convinced himself that if he could remember their names, he would not succumb to Alzheimer's. I'd catch him at odd moments reciting this litany under his breath. "You know, I couldn't remember them this morning," he'd confided earlier. "They were gone. But just now they returned. They were sitting on top of my brain, fluffing their feathers."

The segment on the evening news spurred me to talk with Bailey about what was happening to him. I'd try this now and again, to see how aware he was. And I probably nursed a hope that he would become my partner again, rather than my charge, able to aid and comfort me as I him. Come back from wherever you're going, be whole again, adult and wise, understand how hard this is for me, too.

There was another reason: Bailey's mother had been an outspoken member of the Hemlock Society. And she'd carried out her belief, taking her life rather than enter a nursing home. Before Alzheimer's, Bailey often talked about her courage and his own commitment to "dignity in death." The catch-22 with Alzheimer's was that he needed to make his "exit" not in the extremity of the disease, but early, while he still had the ability to carry out his wish. While he still had some life left to enjoy.

Bailey's reaction was to turn to the wall. "Talk to me, Bailey," I said. "You always said you didn't want to live if you could no longer work. When you couldn't look after yourself." *Oh God.* I hope I was gentle.

"I am working. I am looking after myself." Muffled crying. "You will take care of it when the right time comes. You and the doctor."

"We can't, my darling."

"You will! You must!"

I tried to explain. But he wasn't listening. He had drifted back to Eva Truilly, Zora Diamond, and Lulu Lawes.

That night, Bailey woke again and again. The first time, he fell and became wedged between furniture. The second time, he stuffed his diaper down the toilet. The third time, having disposed of the diaper, he left a trail of urine on the floor. I slept through this last accident, to be shaken awake by Bailey. Stuttering badly, tears flowing in anguish, he pointed at the urine. I quieted him, cleaned up. Back in bed, he told me how disappointed he was with his life. This sense of failure was growing larger by the day. He carried it with him, shouldering it like a sack of coals.

When a bed becomes available in a nursing home, Cath takes Bailey there against his expressed wishes and objections. After he is confined to a wheelchair she hires Gwen as his personal aide.

Bailey was hemorrhaging. The night nurse stuttered this news into the phone, apparently, unnerved, by the amount of blood. I pulled on clothes and arrived at the home just as they were bringing Bailey out to an ambulance. He was glassy-eyed, clammy, swooning; the medics were jovial. It was two in the morning, crisp and cold. His time to die.

The ER at St——is disorderly, crowded, ungentle; any New Yorker will tell you that. Walls, ceiling, floor tiles – they are impregnated with fear.

"He's in the final stages of Alzheimer's," I told the triage team. "He's DNR. Make him comfortable, please, but nothing else." The words came out clumsily. I was surprised to hear them. Let this person, who is dearest to me, who is my family, die.

They paid me no heed. I might as well have been invisible. They consulted his medical records, which had come with him from the home. A plump bag of blood appeared and was attached to an I.V. pole.

"What are you doing? Why are you transfusing him?"

They were deaf. I asked for the doctor in charge. He had a damp, limp hand-shake. He didn't bother to hide his impatience.

"I beg of you, return him to the nursing home."

"He will die," said the doctor, "if we do that."

I changed my tack. "Palliative care. Don't you have palliative care?"

"No need for that." Stern.

"We have living wills. Healthcare proxies. No extreme measures."

The doctor turned away, flicking me from his consciousness as if I were lint.

Bailey kept on hemorrhaging. The transfusions continued apace. His skin became translucent: cold, colder, coldest. Around seven in the morning, he stirred. He opened his eyes and smiled shyly. "Cath," he said, "the party's over."

I searched his face, shocked by his lucidity. Did he know what was happening? A few minutes passed in silence, and then he gestured at the other patients on gurneys – firemen suffering from smoke inhalation, an electrocuted electrician, a construction worker with a crushed leg, an asthma sufferer – and said, with utmost seriousness, "Do *all* these people have invitations?"

Bailey was admitted to a ward in the hospital. Interns gathered around his bed, white-coated ghouls strung with stethoscopes. "What year is it?" "Who is the president?" Solicitous at first, then, when he didn't respond, loud.

"He's not deaf. He has Alzheimer's." Fluttering at the edge of the group.

"Who are you? His daughter?"

"His wife."

Raised eyebrows. The interrogation continued. "Where are you?"

"In a hotel on Madison Avenue," said Bailey.

"No! You're in a *hospital*." Loud *and* impatient.

Bailey pulled back into his pillow, terrified.

"He needs his medication," I told them, "or you won't be able to control him."

"The elderly are overmedicated." Accusing.

Within an hour, Bailey had pulled out all his tubes and drips, spraying the room with blood. The nurses berated him, cleaned up, reinserted everything, only to have him pull them out again. He heaved himself out of the bed and fell to the floor, where he lay, beached. They strapped him to the bed.

The next morning, to prevent bed sores, he was removed from his bed and placed in a restraining device called a Johnny chair. Gwen, who came when she could, was sitting with him. I greeted him in my usual way, my cheek against his concave, stubbly one. No answer. He didn't recognize me. From time to time, he had forgotten my name but never who I was: his protector. Gwen looked stricken for me.

That day, all he wanted was to get free of the chair. The angle of it, the confinement, hurt him. He banged and pushed at the chair's railing, snorting with frustration. When that didn't work, he began to examine its construction with fierce absorption, to no avail.

The care in the hospital was minimal and grudging. It became even less so when the hospital aides learned I had Gwen. I arrived one morning to find his bed a swamp, his body smeared with excrement. Beyond rage, only wanting him clean, I went to find a nurse. They sat with the interns at computer terminals, tap-tapping. Irrationally, I felt what was happening was my fault. I found a basin and towels. Gwen arrived and together we cleaned him. He was oblivious to our ministrations. An animal determination to survive gleamed in the back of his lusterless eyes. Pinpricks of life surrounded by dullness.

Tests were conducted and botched. The cause of the hemorrhaging was never found, and Bailey was returned to the nursing home, where flu was raging. He caught it, developed a lung infection, and, for the second time in a month, hung on the edge of life. He was dosed with quantities of antibiotics, again without my permission, and recovered. Pneumonia used to be called the old people's friend. Not any longer.

It was customary at the nursing home to line up residents far gone in their diseases near the nursing station, where they could be watched with the least trouble. They sat strapped into wheelchairs, lolling, slumped, empty-eyed, indifferent to their surroundings, some silent, some gibbering, occupying a slope of hell. Bailey joined the line for the first time, sitting upright and stiff, but as vacant as the rest. His last wits had been shocked out of him. He had forgotten to remember. Finally, reduced to a nub. Seeing him in the line, I gave up.

[. . .]

Reconstructing those last months, I suspect – I know! – I was not in my right mind. All the same, my mind – my wrong mind? – was made up. Scar on my soul be damned. He'd asked me to take care of it when the time came. Now I would. Mrs Death. Not an assisted suicide, though. A mercy killing. Merciful for him. And merciful for me. I was on a life raft, Bailey was in the water, going down but holding my hand with an iron grip, pulling me after him.

I arranged that in the event of another emergency he be taken to a hospital that might be more respectful of our wishes. Then I obtained the pills for an overdose from a doctor who was part of a guerrilla network willing to help in these situations; many have trodden this path before me. To reveal more would be to incriminate others. Accessories to manslaughter, if not murder, according to the laws of New York State.

I *can* tell you that the doctor's office was one of those thousands of windowless shoeboxes that the medical profession inhabit on the ground floors of apartment buildings on the Upper East Side. Pin-tidy. An arrangement of silk flowers. A huge computer, which she consulted occasionally. She'd done her homework on Bailey, on me.

After we ran through Bailey's medical history and recent experiences, we discussed ethics. I'd read Peter Singer, Ronald Dworkin, and Sherwin Nuland early in Bailey's illness, consulted books with titles like *The Moral Challenge of Alzheimer Disease*. I knew about slippery slopes and the argument that what healthy people want in the last stages of life might not be the same when they get there. That is, if Bailey had a mind, he might tell me he had changed it.

She asked me if I had fully considered the risk I was running. Truth be known, I was past questions of risk or morality, boxed in, as animal in my instincts as Bailey. All I knew was that living wills and healthcare proxies could be blithely ignored, that common sense concerning the final stages of disease is often absent. All I knew was that it was time. Stand in judgment if you like. If you must.

The doctor handed over the pills in a small turquoise box. A Tiffany box. Put her arm around my shoulder as she walked me to the door that let out into the street.

[...]

An afterthought. It was almost an afterthought. If thinking is what I was doing; I was about to go to bed, mentally checking off the things I had needed to do to be prepared for the next day. Clothes ironed, shoes polished. And then I remembered: One more task.

I had already bought the drink. Nantucket Nectars. Orange mango. I decanted the pills from the Tiffany box into a breakfast bowl and ground them with the back of a teaspoon. I eased the powder into the drink, shook the bottle. What didn't dissolve was disguised by the sediment in the bottom.

The day passed as any in the office. Around six, I closed down my computer and caught a taxi to the home, up the FDR Drive, along the river, by the bridges. Swooping, soaring.

I chose that night because it was his bath day. He would smell sweet, the odors of incontinence, folded flesh, rotting teeth and gut disguised by lotions, powder, soap. To bathe him, Gwen and another aide lifted him into a high plastic chair and wheeled him to the shower room. In the early days, they giggled, flirted, teased, but no longer. When I arrived, he was already in bed, his face turned up, unapprehending. I kissed him, nuzzled his hair, and then went over to nip dead leaves and spent blossoms from the geranium plants on the windowsill. More alert now, he followed my movements not with the incuriosity that had encased him these last months but approval. Or so I thought.

The time for last words, for ceremony, had passed years ago, so I got on with what I had come to do. I supported his head while he sucked at the straw. He always did have a sweet tooth.

I drew up a chair by the bed, took his hand, and read him Elizabeth Bishop's "*Invitation to Miss Marianne Moore.*" This wasn't planned; the trip along the FDR Drive had reminded me of it:

> *From Brooklyn, over the Brooklyn Bridge, on this fine morning,*
> *please come flying*
> *In a cloud of fiery pale chemicals,*
> *please come flying,*
> *to the rapid rolling of thousands of small blue drums*
> *descending out of the mackerel sky*
> *over the glittering grandstand of harbor-water,*
> *please come flying . . .*

Pure joy on his face. I swear. Pure trust. Within minutes, he was asleep. Unconscious. Out of the here into the nowhere. I don't remember what I then said or did, how long I sat with him. I probably kissed him, told him how much I loved him. *This is how much I love you.* Maybe I didn't. Maybe I just walked out of the room. Goodnight to the staff on duty, down the elevator into the street. The air tasted bitter, of walnuts gone black in the shell.

The phone rang as I walked through the front door to my apartment. "Your husband is not responding. You must come." Cold, suspicious.

The medics were in his room, easing him onto a stretcher, ready to take him to the hospital I had specified. Outside were two fresh-faced policemen, caps bigger than their heads, bulky with nightsticks, walkie-talkies, guns.

"He's in the last stages of Alzheimer's," I said, looking them in the eye. And they left.

He was three nights and two days dying – ample time to observe my handiwork. The skin on his face stretched tight, turned opalescent. His breathing, noisy at first, quieted. When he was moved, his eyelids shot open like a doll's. No tubes, no drips, no monitors, propped on pillows, a cotton blanket pulled neatly under his arms. The occupant of the other bed in the room, a frail man covered in liver spots, was hooked up to all manner of machines, his family keeping an anguished vigil. Each to our own.

The first two nights, I climbed up on the bed and slept next to him, cradling him. I woke the first morning to find Gwen standing over us, horrified. Later, I asked her why, and she said she was afraid he might die in the night and I would wake to cold flesh. On the final night, his body closing down, blackening, I sat next to him, his hand in mine, sleeping fitfully. *I'm here.*

When he died in the morning, it was without even a sigh. He simply ceased to breathe.

A call was placed to the funeral parlor where I had made arrangements two years earlier, as the Medicaid law required. A no-frills cremation, as he wished, the ashes delivered to me when it was done. At the time, I asked if I could stay with the body, see it to the flames, complete the journey. But I was finally too tired. In the mortician's little van he could go the last leg alone. I went home to blistering loneliness.

28

WILLIAM SHAKESPEARE

Hamlet

Written in 1601 or 1602, Shakespeare's tragedy concerns a young man trying to decide on the moral course of action. Very early in the play Prince Hamlet, distressed by his father's death and his mother Queen Gertrude's hasty marriage to the new King, Claudius, begs:

> That this too too solid flesh would melt
> Thaw and resolve itself into a dew!
> Or that the Everlasting had not fix'd
> His canon 'gainst self-slaughter!

By the time he asks the existential question: 'to be or not to be?', Hamlet has proof that his uncle Claudius is guilty of fratricide.

HAMLET: To be, or not to be, – that is the question: –
Whether 'tis nobler in the mind to suffer
The slings and arrows of outrageous fortune,
Or to take arms against a sea of troubles,
And by opposing end them? – To die, – to sleep, –
No more; and by a sleep to say we end
The heart-ache and the thousand natural shocks
That flesh is heir to, – 'tis a consummation
Devoutly to be wish'd. To die, – to sleep; –
To sleep! perchance to dream: – ay, there's the rub;
For in that sleep of death what dreams may come,
When we have shuffled off this mortal coil,
Must give us pause: there's the respect
That makes calamity of so long life;
For who would bear the whips and scorns of time,
The oppressor's wrong, the proud man's contumely,
The pangs of despis'd love, the law's delay,

WILLIAM SHAKESPEARE, from Act III, Scene I in *Hamlet, Prince of Denmark,* first published in 1623.

The insolence of office, and the spurns
That patient merit of the unworthy takes,
When he himself might his quietus make
With a bare bodkin? who would fardels bear,
To grunt and sweat under a weary life,
But that the dread of something after death, —
The undiscover'd country, from whose bourn
No traveller returns, — puzzles the will,
And makes us rather bear those ills we have
Than fly to others that we know not of?
Thus conscience does make cowards of us all;
And thus the native hue of resolution
Is sicklied o'er with the pale cast of thought;
And enterprises of great pith and moment,
With this regard, their currents turn awry,
And lose the name of action.

29

ARNA BONTEMPS

A Summer Tragedy

Old Jeff Patton, the black share farmer, fumbled with his bow tie. His fingers trembled and the high, stiff collar pinched his throat. A fellow loses his hand for such vanities after thirty or forty years of simple life. Once a year, or maybe twice if there's a wedding among his kinfolks, he may spruce up; but generally fancy clothes do nothing but adorn the wall of the big room and feed the moths. That had been Jeff Patton's experience. He had not worn his stiff-bosomed shirt more than a dozen times in all his married life. His swallow-tailed coat lay on the bed beside him, freshly brushed and pressed, but it was as full of holes as the overalls in which he worked on weekdays. The moths had used it badly. Jeff twisted his mouth into a hideous toothless grimace as he contended with the obstinate bow. He stamped his good foot and decided to give up the struggle.

"Jennie," he called.

"What's that, Jeff?" His wife's shrunken voice came out of the adjoining room like an echo. It was hardly bigger than a whisper.

"I reckon you'll have to he'p me wid this heah bow tie, baby," he said meekly. "Dog if I can hitch it up."

Her answer was not strong enough to reach him, but presently the old woman came to the door, feeling her way with a stick. She had a wasted, dead-leaf appearance. Her body, as scrawny and gnarled as a string bean, seemed less than nothing in the ocean of frayed and faded petticoats that surrounded her. These hung an inch or two above the tops of her heavy unlaced shoes and showed little grotesque piles where the stockings had fallen down from her negligible legs.

"You oughta could do a heap mo' wid a thing like that'n me – beingst as you got yo' good sight."

"Looks like I oughta could," he admitted. "But my fingers is gone democrat on me. I get all mixed up in the looking glass an' can't tell wicha way to twist the devilish thing."

ARNA BONTEMPS, "A Summer Tragedy," pp. 54–63 from John Henrik Clarke (ed.), *Black American Short Stories: A Century of the Best*. New York: Hill & Wang, 2000. The anthology first published 1966 by Hill & Wang as *American Negro Short Stories*; "A Summer Tragedy" originally published 1933. Reprinted with permission of the Arna Bontemps African American Museum and Cultural Arts Center, 1327 Third Street, Alexandria, Louisiana 71301, USA.

Jennie sat on the side of the bed, and old Jeff Patton got down on one knee while she tied the bow knot. It was a slow and painful ordeal for each of them in this position. Jeff's bones cracked, his knee ached, and it was only after a half dozen attempts that Jennie worked a semblance of a bow into the tie.

"I got to dress maself now," the old woman whispered. "These is ma old shoes an' stockings, and I ain't so much as unwrapped ma dress."

"Well, don't worry 'bout me no mo', baby," Jeff said. "That 'bout finishes me. All I gotta do now is slip on that old coat 'n ves' an' I'll be fixed to leave."

Jennie disappeared again through the dim passage into the shed room. Being blind was no handicap to her in that black hole. Jeff heard the cane placed against the wall beside the door and knew that his wife was on easy ground. He put on his coat, took a battered top hat from the bed post, and hobbled to the front door. He was ready to travel. As soon as Jennie could get on her Sunday shoes and her old black silk dress, they would start.

Outside the tiny log house, the day was warm and mellow with sunshine. A host of wasps were humming with busy excitement in the trunk of a dead sycamore. Gray squirrels were searching through the grass for hickory nuts, and blue jays were in the trees, hopping from branch to branch. Pine woods stretched away to the left like a black sea. Among them were scattered scores of log houses like Jeff's, houses of black share farmers. Cows and pigs wandered freely among the trees. There was no danger of loss. Each farmer knew his own stock and knew his neighbor's as well as he knew his neighbor's children.

Down the slope to the right were the cultivated acres on which the colored folks worked. They extended to the river, more than two miles away, and they were today green with the unmade cotton crop. A tiny thread of a road, which passed directly in front of Jeff's place, ran through these green fields like a pencil mark.

Jeff, standing outside the door, with his absurd hat in his left hand, surveyed the wide scene tenderly. He had been forty-five years on these acres. He loved them with the unexplained affection that others have for the countries to which they belong.

The sun was hot on his head, his collar still pinched his throat, and the Sunday clothes were intolerably hot. Jeff transferred the hat to his right hand and began fanning with it. Suddenly the whisper that was Jennie's voice came out of the shed room.

"You can bring the car round front whilst you's waitin'," it said feebly. There was a tired pause; then it added, "I'll soon be fixed to go."

"A'right, baby," Jeff answered. "I'll get it in a minute."

But he didn't move. A thought struck him that made his mouth fall open. The mention of the car brought to his mind, with new intensity, the trip he and Jennie were about to take. Fear came into his eyes; excitement took his breath. Lord, Jesus!

"Jeff. . . . O Jeff," the old woman's whisper called.

He awakened with a jolt. "Hunh, baby?"

"What you doin'?"

"Nuthin. Jes studyin'. I jes been turnin' things round 'n round in ma mind."

"You could be gettin' the car," she said.

"Oh yes, right away, baby."

He started round to the shed, limping heavily on his bad leg. There were three frizzly chickens in the yard. All his other chickens had been killed or stolen recently. But the frizzly chickens had been saved somehow. That was fortunate indeed, for these curious creatures had a way of devouring "poison" from the yard and in that way protecting against conjure and black luck and spells. But even the frizzly chickens seemed now to be in a stupor. Jeff thought they had some ailment; he expected all three of them to die shortly.

The shed in which the old T-model Ford stood was only a grass roof held up by four corner poles. It had been built by tremulous hands at a time when the little rattletrap car had been regarded as a peculiar treasure. And, miraculously, despite wind and downpour, it still stood.

Jeff adjusted the crank and put his weight upon it. The engine came to life with a sputter and bang that rattled the old car from radiator to tail light. Jeff hopped into the seat and put his foot on the accelerator. The sputtering and banging increased. The rattling became more violent. That was good. It was good banging, good sputtering and rattling, and it meant that the aged car was still in running condition. She could be depended on for this trip.

Again Jeff's thought halted as if paralyzed. The suggestion of the trip fell into the machinery of his mind like a wrench. He felt dazed and weak. He swung the car out into the yard, made a half turn, and drove around to the front door. When he took his hands off the wheel, he noticed that he was trembling violently. He cut off the motor and climbed to the ground to wait for Jennie.

A few minutes later she was at the window, her voice rattling against the pane like a broken shutter.

"I'm ready, Jeff."

He did not answer, but limped into the house and took her by the arm. He led her slowly through the big room, down the step, and across the yard.

"You reckon I'd oughta lock the do'?" he asked softly.

They stopped and Jennie weighed the question. Finally she shook her head.

"Ne' mind the do'," she said. "I don't see no cause to lock up things."

"You right," Jeff agreed. "No cause to lock up."

Jeff opened the door and helped his wife into the car. A quick shudder passed over him. Jesus! Again he trembled.

"How come you shaking so?" Jennie whispered.

"I don't know," he said.

"You mus' be scairt, Jeff."

"No, baby, I ain't scairt."

He slammed the door after her and went around to crank up again. The motor started easily. Jeff wished that it had not been so responsive. He would have liked a few more minutes in which to turn things around in his head. As it was, with Jennie chiding him about being afraid, he had to keep going. He swung the car into the little pencil-mark road and started off toward the river, driving very slowly, very cautiously.

Chugging across the green countryside, the small battered Ford seemed tiny indeed. Jeff felt a familiar excitement, a thrill, as they came down the first slope to the immense levels on which the cotton was growing. He could not help reflecting that the crops were good. He knew what that meant, too; he had made forty-five of them with his own hands. It was true that he had worn out nearly a dozen mules, but that was the fault of old man Stevenson, the owner of the land. Major Stevenson had the odd notion that one mule was all a share farmer needed to work a thirty-acre plot. It was an expensive notion, the way it killed mules from overwork, but the old man held to it. Jeff thought it killed a good many share farmers as well as mules, but he had no sympathy for them. He had always been strong, and he had been taught to have no patience with weakness in men. Women or children might be tolerated if they were puny, but a weak man was a curse. Of course, his own children —

Jeff's thought halted there. He and Jennie never mentioned their dead children any more. And naturally, he did not wish to dwell upon them in his mind. Before he knew it, some remark would slip out of his mouth and that would make Jennie feel blue. Perhaps she would cry. A woman like Jennie could not easily throw off the grief that comes from losing five grown children within two years. Even Jeff was still staggered by the blow. His memory had not been much good recently. He frequently talked to himself. And, although he had kept it a secret, he knew that his courage had left him. He was terrified by the least unfamiliar sound at night. He was reluctant to venture far from home in the daytime. And that habit of trembling when he felt fearful was now far beyond his control. Sometimes he became afraid and trembled without knowing what had frightened him. The feeling would just come over him like a chill.

The car rattled slowly over the dusty road. Jennie sat erect and silent with a little absurd hat pinned to her hair. Her useless eyes seemed very large, very white in their deep sockets. Suddenly Jeff heard her voice, and he inclined his head to catch the words.

"Is we passed Delia Moore's house yet?" she asked.

"Not yet," he said.

"You must be drivin' mighty slow, Jeff."

"We just as well take our time, baby."

There was a pause. A little puff of steam was coming out of the radiator of the car. Heat wavered above the hood. Delia Moore's house was nearly half a mile away. After a moment Jennie spoke again.

"You ain't really scairt, is you, Jeff?"

"Nah, baby, I ain't scairt."

"You know how we agreed — we gotta keep on goin'."

Jewels of perspiration appeared on Jeff's forehead. His eyes rounded, blinked, became fixed on the road.

"I don't know," he said with a shiver, "I reckon it's the only thing to do."

"Hm."

A flock of guinea fowls, pecking in the road, were scattered by the passing car. Some of them took to their wings; others hid under bushes. A blue jay, swaying on a leafy twig, was annoying a roadside squirrel. Jeff held an even speed till he came near Delia's place. Then he slowed down noticeably.

Delia's house was really no house at all, but an abandoned store building converted into a dwelling. It sat near a crossroads, beneath a single black cedar tree.

There Delia, a cattish old creature of Jennie's age, lived alone. She had been there more years than anybody could remember, and long ago had won the disfavor of such women as Jennie. For in her young days Delia had been gayer, yellower, and saucier than seemed proper in those parts. Her ways with menfolks had been dark and suspicious. And the fact that she had had as many husbands as children did not help her reputation.

"Yonder's old Delia," Jeff said as they passed.

"What she doin'?"

"Jes sittin' in the do'," he said.

"She see us?"

"Hm," Jeff said. "Musta did."

That relieved Jennie. It strengthened her to know that her old enemy had seen her pass in her best clothes. That would give the old she-devil something to chew her gums and fret about, Jennie thought. Wouldn't she have a fit if she didn't find out? Old evil Delia! This would be just the thing for her. It would pay her back for being so evil. It would also pay her, Jennie thought, for the way she used to grin at Jeff – long ago, when her teeth were good.

The road became smooth and red, and Jeff could tell by the smell of the air that they were nearing the river. He could see the rise where the road turned and ran along parallel to the stream. The car chugged on monotonously. After a long silent spell, Jennie leaned against Jeff and spoke.

"How many bale o' cotton you think we got standin'?" she said.

Jeff wrinkled his forehead as he calculated.

"'Bout twenty-five, I reckon."

"How many you make las' year?"

"Twenty-eight," he said. "How come you ask that?"

"I's jes thinkin'," Jennie said quietly.

"It don't make a speck o' difference though," Jeff reflected. "If we get much or if we get little, we still gonna be in debt to old man Stevenson when he gets through counting up agin us. It's took us a long time to learn that."

Jennie was not listening to these words. She had fallen into a trance-like meditation. Her lips twitched. She chewed her gums and rubbed her gnarled hands nervously. Suddenly, she leaned forward, buried her face in the nervous hands, and burst into tears. She cried aloud in a dry, cracked voice that suggested the rattle of fodder on dead stalks. She cried aloud like a child, for she had never learned to suppress a genuine sob. Her slight old frame shook heavily and seemed hardly able to sustain such violent grief.

"What's the matter, baby?" Jeff asked awkwardly. "Why you cryin' like all that?"

"I's jes thinkin'," she said.

"So you the one what's scairt now, hunh?"

"I ain't scairt, Jeff. I's jes thinkin' 'bout leavin' eve'thing like this – eve'thing we been used to. It's right sad-like."

Jeff did not answer, and presently Jennie buried her face again and cried.

The sun was almost overhead. It beat down furiously on the dusty wagon-path road, on the parched roadside grass and the tiny battered car. Jeff's hands, gripping the wheel, became wet with perspiration; his forehead sparkled. Jeff's lips parted.

His mouth shaped a hideous grimace. His face suggested the face of a man being burned. But the torture passed and his expression softened again.

"You mustn't cry, baby," he said to his wife. "We gotta be strong. We can't break down."

Jennie waited a few seconds, then said, "You reckon we oughta do it, Jeff? You reckon we oughta go 'head an' do it, really?"

Jeff's voice choked; his eyes blurred. He was terrified to hear Jennie say the thing that had been in his mind all morning. She had egged him on when he had wanted more than anything in the world to wait, to reconsider, to think things over a little longer. Now she was getting cold feet. Actually, there was no need of thinking the question through again. It would only end in making the same painful decision once more. Jeff knew that. There was no need of fooling around longer.

"We jes as well to do like we planned," he said. "They ain't nothin' else for us now – it's the bes' thing."

Jeff thought of the handicaps, the near impossibility, of making another crop with his leg bothering him more and more each week. Then there was always the chance that he would have another stroke, like the one that had made him lame. Another one might kill him. The least it could do would be to leave him helpless. Jeff gasped – Lord, Jesus! He could not bear to think of being helpless, like a baby, on Jennie's hands. Frail, blind Jennie.

The little pounding motor of the car worked harder and harder. The puff of steam from the cracked radiator became larger. Jeff realized that they were climbing a little rise. A moment later the road turned abruptly, and he looked down upon the face of the river.

"Jeff."

"Hunh?"

"Is that the water I hear?"

"Hm. Tha's it."

"Well, which way you goin' now?"

"Down this-a way," he said. "The road runs 'long 'side o' the water a lil piece."

She waited a while calmly. Then she said, "Drive faster."

"A'right, baby," Jeff said.

The water roared in the bed of the river. It was fifty or sixty feet below the level of the road. Between the road and the water there was a long smooth slope, sharply inclined. The slope was dry, the clay hardened by prolonged summer heat. The water below, roaring in a narrow channel, was noisy and wild.

"Jeff."

"Hunh?"

"How far you goin'?"

"Jes a lil piece down the road."

"You ain't scairt, is you, Jeff?"

"Nah, baby," he said trembling. "I ain't scairt."

"Remember how we planned it, Jeff. We gotta do it like we said. Brave-like."

"Hm."

Jeff's brain darkened. Things suddenly seemed unreal, like figures in a dream. Thoughts swam in his mind foolishly, hysterically, like little blind fish in a pool within a dense cave. They rushed again. Jeff soon became dizzy. He shuddered violently and turned to his wife.

"Jennie, I can't do it. I can't." His voice broke pitifully.

She did not appear to be listening. All the grief had gone from her face. She sat erect, her unseeing eyes wide open, strained and frightful. Her glossy black skin had become dull. She seemed as thin, as sharp and bony, as a starved bird. Now, having suffered and endured the sadness of tearing herself away from beloved things, she showed no anguish. She was absorbed with her own thoughts, and she didn't even hear Jeff's voice shouting in her ear.

Jeff said nothing more. For an instant there was light in his cavernous brain. The great chamber was, for less than a second, peopled by characters he knew and loved. They were simple, healthy creatures, and they behaved in a manner that he could understand. They had quality. But since he had already taken leave of them long ago, the remembrance did not break his heart again. Young Jeff Patton was among them, the Jeff Patton of fifty years ago who went down to New Orleans with a crowd of country boys to the Mardi Gras doings. The gay young crowd, boys with candy-striped shirts and rouged brown girls in noisy silks, was like a picture in his head. Yet it did not make him sad. On that very trip Slim Burns had killed Joe Beasley – the crowd had been broken up. Since then Jeff Patton's world had been the Greenbriar Plantation. If there had been other Mardi Gras carnivals, he had not heard of them. Since then there had been no time; the years had fallen on him like waves. Now he was old, worn out. Another paralytic stroke (like the one he had already suffered) would put him on his back for keeps. In that condition, with a frail blind woman to look after him, he would be worse off than if he were dead.

Suddenly Jeff's hands became steady. He actually felt brave. He slowed down the motor of the car and carefully pulled off the road. Below, the water of the stream boomed, a soft thunder in the deep channel. Jeff ran the car onto the clay slope, pointed it directly toward the stream, and put his foot heavily on the accelerator. The little car leaped furiously down the steep incline toward the water. The movement was nearly as swift and direct as a fall. The two old black folks, sitting quietly side by side, showed no excitement. In another instant the car hit the water and dropped immediately out of sight.

A little later it lodged in the mud of a shallow place. One wheel of the crushed and upturned little Ford became visible above the rushing water.

PART TWO   THE COMMUNITY AND BEYOND

V

WORK

Between maturity and retirement, if we are fortunate enough to have a job, we spend a large part of our waking hours at work. The workplace is the site of many moral decisions, ranging from whether to take pens home for our personal use, to our response to pressure from the boss to sign a set of corporate accounts we know to be dubious. Courses in business ethics have multiplied over the past decade, but major corporate scandals seem to be keeping pace with them. Sometimes there are outright breaches of the law, as became evident in the collapse of Enron and WorldCom, but other scandals are more about ethics than the law. In 2003, Richard Grasso, chairman of the New York Stock Exchange, was forced to resign when it became known that he had negotiated a $140 million pay and retirement package. It was felt to be improper that the person in charge of regulating the Stock Exchange should be so richly rewarded. And it's not just at the top, or in multi-million dollar enterprises, that moral dilemmas are faced by employees. A 1998 survey of American workers found that 56 percent of workers felt some pressure to act unethically or illegally on the job. Almost half of all workers reported that, due to pressure, they had engaged in one or more unethical and/or illegal actions during the last year.[1]

In the wake of the Enron scandal, President George W. Bush said that "America's greatest economic need is higher ethical standards."[2] However, the continuing prevalence of unethical conduct in the workplace, despite such rhetoric, suggests that the combination of ethics and economics is not a harmonious one. That is reflected in the fact that while few question the existence and significance of medical ethics, the term "business ethics" is often said, and not entirely in jest, to be an oxymoron. This may have something to do with the differing nature of business and a profession like medicine.

At the beginning of Western civilization, among the ancient Greeks, there was considerable suspicion about money making. Aristotle thought that it was natural to want to acquire the things that one needs, and even to store up for needs that could be anticipated, but for the wise person, money was always only a means to an end. To seek to accumulate money for its own sake was to mistake the means for the end. By this standard, there are plenty of foolish billionaires in the world today. Christianity, for its first fifteen hundred years, took an even stronger line against wealth. Jesus had said that it was easier for a camel to pass through the eye of a needle than for a rich man to go to heaven. Early Christians took this teaching to heart, and debated such questions as "Can a merchant be pleasing to God?" They generally answered in the negative. Usury – which was defined not as charging excessive interest, but simply as charging any interest at all on a loan – was one of the most damnable sins, and avarice, or greed, was always top of the medieval table of vices. Medieval artists delighted in portraying the way in which the greedy would suffer in hell, often with devils crushing them under bags of gold.

All this changed during the Protestant Reformation, for the Reformers needed the support of the rising middle classes. John Calvin, the stern reformist leader of Geneva, swept aside the traditional prohibitions on usury, and, for the first time, treated earthly wealth not as something that makes it difficult to go to heaven, but rather as a sign that one belongs to "the elect" – those predestined to be saved. That made it possible for the middle class to grow in prestige and status, but it was not until the nineteenth-century industrial revolution that capitalism really began to transform the working life of the majority of the population, creating the conditions described in Elizabeth Gaskell's novel *North and South*. Although nineteenth-century capitalism led to twelve-hour days for workers, some of them children, in dangerous and unhealthy conditions, the factory owners fought to keep labor unions out of their factories, and argued against state regulation of working hours or occupational health and safety. In support of their case, they championed "Social Darwinism." This misappropriation of Darwin's theory of evolution purported to show that, as John D. Rockefeller, Jr argued,

> The growth of a large business is merely a survival of the fittest. . . . The American Beauty rose can be produced in the splendor and fragrance which bring cheer to its beholder only by sacrificing the early buds which grow around it. This is not an evil tendency in business. It is merely the working out of a law of nature and a law of God.[3]

Curiously, Karl Marx, one of capitalism's greatest critics, would have agreed with Rockefeller to the extent that he did not see any role for ethics in softening the impact of capitalism on the lives of the working class. Although he vividly described the way in which the factories of nineteenth-century England overworked and maimed their workers while paying them a bare subsistence wage, Marx ridiculed reformers who tried to make capitalism more just. In capitalist terms, he thought, the wages paid to laborers were set by the laws of supply and demand, and that was, in capitalist terms, a "just wage." Morality is, in his view, determined by the economic mode of production, and under a capitalist system, one must expect capitalist morality to prevail. A better society could only come into existence, he thought, as the result of a revolution that abolished the capitalist mode of production.

The conditions described in *North and South* are no longer the rule in the developed world, but they have not disappeared. Globalization has led corporations to establish factories in developing countries, where wages are low, unions are illegal or easily bought off, and state regulation is virtually non-existent. Even in the United States, illegal immigrants often work in appalling conditions.

Is there an alternative view to those of Social Darwinists and Marxists, one that makes it possible for ethics to be taken seriously in a free market system? Some corporate leaders appear to be taking seriously the idea that they have a responsibility not only to maximize profits for their shareholders, but also to be concerned for the interests of all their "stakeholders" – all those who have a stake in the corporation – including workers, customers, and the communities in which they operate. But in the competitive world of business, ethics can only thrive if it brings economic advantage. That is not impossible. Workers will respond with greater loyalty to a corporation that treats them as more than cogs in the machine, and communities will be more supportive of enterprises that show concern for their welfare. But perhaps the most important prerequisite for more ethical business is educated customers who are prepared to switch their purchases away from corporations that they see as behaving unethically.

Though these large questions are of global significance, the ethical issues most workers face are more specific. They work to earn money to be able to live, and few are fortunate enough to have work they both enjoy and know to be worthwhile. So simply doing the job one has been employed to do often involves an ethical compromise. Artists and writers who would like to create something significant may end up designing ads and writing copy for deodorants and antacid tablets. When does work become so contrary to one's ethical principles, or so degrading, that one ought to refuse to do it, no matter what the consequences may be? And if that moment does arrive, is the right course of action simply to leave, or should one try to subvert the project on which one is working?

In some of the readings in this section the protagonists face conflicts between the ethics of their vocations – as documentary film maker, doctor, or scientist – and their other obligations – to their employer, local community, family, or friend. The central theme of Henrik Ibsen's play *An Enemy of the People* is the ethical dilemma that we now call "whistleblowing." In 2002 *Time* magazine named three women whistleblowers "Persons of the Year." But loyalty is generally regarded as a virtue, and that includes loyalty to one's employer, or to one's fellow-workers. Whistleblowers usually finish up pariahs rather than heroes. By going public about their concerns, they harm their career prospects and put their livelihoods and personal relationships at risk. The problem therefore is to decide when loyalty and legitimate self-interest are outweighed by other ethical concerns. If an employee learns that the factory in which she works is poisoning villagers downstream by pouring toxic wastes into a river, some action is clearly ethically required. If taking her concerns to the management is ineffective, she may have go to the media with the information. But when the wrongdoing is not life-threatening, ethical decisions become more difficult. If you work for a corporation that makes a product reputed to stop men going bald, and you discover that the study on which this reputation was based is flawed, do you have an obligation to ensure that your corporation's customers know this? Not all decisions in business are black and white.

NOTES

1 "Reducing the Risk of Unethical Business Practices," *Circuit*, December 1998, available at *http://sensor.northgrum.com/ethics/Circuit/Reducing.htm*
2 "Remarks by the President on Corporate Responsibility," New York, July 9, 2002, available at *http://www.whitehouse.gov/news/releases/2002/07/print/20020709-4.html*
3 Richard Huber, *The American Idea of Success*, New York: McGraw-Hill, 1971, p. 66.

30

ELIZABETH GASKELL

North and South

Published in 1854, *North and South* depicts the era of industrialization in which workers were struggling for better working conditions. Margaret Hale is transplanted from
the "civilized" south of England and enters a grim new world in industrial Milton-
Northern. Through her friendship with some of the workers, Margaret comes to
sympathize with their plight.

In this first extract, Mr Thornton, a factory owner who wishes to become better
educated, is conversing with his tutor, Mr Hale, and Mr Hale's daughter Margaret,
about rumors of a strike.

"Yes; the fools will have a strike. Let them. It suits us well enough. But we
gave them a chance. They think trade is flourishing as it was last year. We
see the storm on the horizon and draw in our sails. But because we don't
explain our reasons, they won't believe we're acting reasonably. We must give
them line and letter for the way we choose to spend or save our money [. . .] But
we Milton masters have today sent in our decision. We won't advance a penny.
We tell them we may have to lower wages; but can't afford to raise. So here we
stand, waiting for their next attack."

"And what will that be?" asked Mr Hale.

"I conjecture, a simultaneous strike. You will see Milton without smoke in a few
days, I imagine, Miss Hale."

"But why," asked she, "could you not explain what good reason you have for
expecting a bad trade? I don't know whether I use the right words, but you will
understand what I mean."

"Do you give your servants reasons for your expenditure, or your economy in
the use of your own money? We, the owners of capital, have a right to choose
what we will do with it."

"A human right," said Margaret, very low.

"I beg your pardon, I did not hear what you said."

ELIZABETH GASKELL, pp. 110–13 (Chapter XV), 214–16 (Chapter XXVIII), and 334–6 (Chapter XLII)
from *North and South*, first published in 1854.

"I would rather not repeat it," said she; "it related to a feeling which I do not think you would share."

"Won't you try me?" pleaded he; his thoughts suddenly bent upon learning what she had said. She was displeased with his pertinacity, but did not choose to affix too much importance to her words.

"I said you had a human right. I meant that there seemed no reason but religious ones, why you should not do what you like with your own."

"I know we differ in our religious opinions; but don't you give me credit for having some, though not the same as yours?"

He was speaking in a subdued voice, as if to her alone. She did not wish to be so exclusively addressed. She replied out in her usual tone:

"I do not think that I have any occasion to consider your special religious opinions in the affair. All I meant to say is, that there is no human law to prevent the employers from utterly wasting or throwing away all their money, if they choose; but that there are passages in the Bible which would rather imply – to me at least – that they neglected their duty as stewards if they did so. However, I know so little about strikes, and rate of wages, and capital, and labour, that I had better not talk to a political economist like you."

"Nay, the more reason," said he eagerly. "I shall only be too glad to explain to you all that may seem anomalous or mysterious to a stranger; especially at a time like this, when our doings are sure to be canvassed by every scribbler who can hold a pen."

"Thank you," she answered, coldly. "Of course, I shall apply to my father in the first instance for any information he can give me, if I get puzzled with living here amongst this strange society."

"You think it strange. Why?"

"I don't know – I suppose because, on the very face of it, I see two classes dependent on each other in every possible way, yet each evidently regarding the interests of the other as opposed to their own; I never lived in a place before where there were two sets of people always running each other down."

"Who have you heard running the masters down? I don't ask who you have heard abusing the men; for I see you persist in misunderstanding what I said the other day. But who have you heard abusing the masters?"

Margaret reddened; then smiled as she said,

"I am not fond of being catechised. I refuse to answer your question. Besides, it has nothing to do with the fact. You must take my word for it, that I have heard some people, or, it may be, only someone of the work-people speak as though it were the interest of the employers to keep them from acquiring money – that it would make them too independent if they had a sum in the savings' bank."

"I dare say it was that man Higgins who told you all this," said Mrs Hale. Mr Thornton did not appear to hear what Margaret evidently did not wish him to know. But he caught it, nevertheless.

"I heard, moreover, that it was considered to the advantage of the masters to have ignorant workmen – not hedge-lawyers, as Captain Lennox used to call those men in his company who questioned and would know the reason for every order."

This latter part of her sentence she addressed rather to her father than to Mr Thornton. Who is Captain Lennox? asked Mr Thornton of himself, with a strange kind of displeasure that prevented him for the moment from replying to her! Her father took up the conversation.

"You never were fond of schools, Margaret, or you would have seen and known before this, how much is being done for education in Milton."

"No!" said she, with sudden meekness. "I know I do not care enough about schools. But the knowledge and the ignorance of which I was speaking, did not relate to reading and writing, – the teaching or information one can give to a child. I am sure, that what was meant was ignorance of the wisdom that shall guide men and women. I hardly know what that is. But he – that is, my informant – spoke as if the masters would like their hands to be merely tall, large children – living in the present moment – with a blind unreasoning kind of obedience."

"In short, Miss Hale, it is very evident that your informant found a pretty ready listener to all the slander he chose to utter against the masters," said Mr Thornton, in an offended tone.

Margaret did not reply. She was displeased at the personal character Mr Thornton affixed to what she had said.

Mr Hale spoke next:

"I must confess that, although I have not become so intimately acquainted with any workmen as Margaret has, I am very much struck by the antagonism between the employer and the employed, on the very surface of things. I even gather this impression from what you yourself have from time to time said."

Mr Thornton paused awhile before he spoke. Margaret had just left the room, and he was vexed at the state of feeling between himself and her. However, the little annoyance, by making him cooler and more thoughtful, gave a greater dignity to what he said:

"My theory is, that my interests are identical with those of my workpeople, and vice versa. Miss Hale, I know, does not like to hear men called 'hands', so I won't use that word, though it comes most readily to my lips as the technical term, whose origin, whatever it was, dates before my time. On some future day – in some millennium – in Utopia, this unity may be brought into practice – just as I can fancy a republic the most perfect form of government."

"We will read Plato's *Republic* as soon as we have finished Homer."

"Well, in the Platonic year, it may fall out that we are all – men, women, and children – fit for a republic: but give me a constitutional monarchy in our present state of morals and intelligence. In our infancy we require a wise despotism to govern us. Indeed, long past infancy, children and young people are the happiest under the unfailing laws of a discreet, firm authority. I agree with Miss Hale so far as to consider our people in the condition of children, while I deny that we, the masters, have anything to do with the making or keeping them so. I maintain that despotism is the best kind of government for them; so that in the hours in which I come in contact with them I must necessarily be an autocrat. I will use my best discretion – from no humbug or philanthropic feeling, of which we have had rather too much in the North – to make wise laws and come to just decisions in the conduct of my business – laws and decisions which work for my own good in the first instance – for theirs in the second; but I will neither be forced to give my reasons, nor flinch from what I have once declared to be my resolution. Let them turn out! I shall suffer as well as they: but at the end they will find I have not bated nor altered one jot."

The strike goes ahead but, after a long struggle, Thornton's prophecy is proven correct. The workers get nothing for their hardship. Margaret and her father are here discussing this outcome with Higgins, one of the strike leaders. (Margaret was close to his daughter, who recently died of a disease caused by the lack of ventilation in the factory in which she worked.) Higgins blames the failure of the strike on a riot incited, against strict union orders, by a union member called Boucher.

"How came he into the Union?" asked Margaret innocently. "You don't seem to have much respect for him; nor gained much good from having him in." Higgins's brow clouded. He was silent for a minute or two. Then he said, shortly enough:

"It's not for me to speak o' th' Union. What they does, they does. Them that is of a trade mun hang together; and if they're not willing to take their chance along wi' th' rest, th' Union has ways and means."

Mr Hale saw that Higgins was vexed at the turn the conversation had taken, and was silent. Not so Margaret, though she saw Higgins's feeling as clearly as he did. By instinct she felt, that if he could but be brought to express himself in plain words, something clear would be gained on which to argue for the right and the just.

"And what are the Union's ways and means?"

He looked up at her, as if on the point of dogged resistance to her wish for information. But her calm face, fixed on his, patient and trustful, compelled him to answer.

"Well! If a man doesn't belong to th' Union, them as works next looms has orders not to speak to him – if he's sorry or ill it's a' the same; he's out o' bounds; he's none o' us; he comes among us, he works among us, but he's none o' us. I' some places them's fined who speaks to him. Yo' try that, miss; try living a year or two among them as looks away if yo' look at 'em, try working within two yards o' crowds o' men, who, yo' know, have a grinding grudge at yo' in their hearts – to whom if yo' say yo'r glad, not an eye brightens, nor a lip moves, – to whom, if your heart's heavy, yo' can never say naught, because they'll ne'er take notice on your sighs or sad looks (and a man's no man who'll groan out loud 'bout folk asking him what's the matter?) – just yo' try that, miss – ten hours for three hundred days, and yo'll know a bit what th' Union is."

"Why!" said Margaret, "what tyranny this is! Nay, Higgins, I don't care one straw for your anger. I know you can't be angry with me if you would, and I must tell you the truth: that I never read, in all the history I have read, of a more slow, lingering torture than this. And you belong to the Union! And you talk of the tyranny of the masters!"

"Nay," said Higgins, "yo' may say what yo' like! The dead stand between yo' and every angry word o' mine. D'ye think I forget who's lying *there*, and how hoo loved yo'? And it's the masters as has made us sin, if th' Union is a sin. Not this generation maybe, but their fathers. Their fathers ground our fathers to the very dust; ground us to powder! Parson! I reckon, I've heerd my mother read out a text, 'The fathers have eaten sour grapes and th' children's teeth are set on edge.' It's so wi' them. In those days of sore oppression th' Unions began; it were a necessity. It's a necessity now, according to me. It's a withstanding of injustice, past, present, or to come. It may be like war; along wi' it come crimes; but I think it were a greater crime to let it alone. Our only chance is binding men together in one common interest; and if some are cowards and some are fools, they mun come along and join the great march, whose only strength is in numbers."

"Oh!" said Mr Hale, sighing, "your Union in itself would be beautiful, glorious, – it would be Christianity itself – if it were but for an end which affected the good of all, instead of that of merely one class as opposed to another."

"I reckon it's time for me to be going, sir," said Higgins, as the clock struck ten.

Time passes, and Margaret continues to urge Mr Thornton to reduce the antagonism between owners and workers. The conversation that follows is between Mr Thornton and Margaret's godfather, Mr Bell, a native of Milton who now teaches at Oxford University. Bell asks the initial question.

"What is that heap of brick and mortar we came against in the yard? Any repairs wanted?"

"No, none, thank you."

"Are you building on your own account? If you are, I'm very much obliged to you."

"I'm building a dining-room – for the men I mean – the hands."

"I thought you were hard to please, if this room wasn't good enough to satisfy you, a bachelor."

"I've got acquainted with a strange kind of chap, and I put one or two children in whom he is interested to school. So, as I happened to be passing near his house one day, I just went there about some trifling payment to be made; and I saw such a miserable black frizzle of a dinner – a greasy cinder of meat, as first set me a-thinking. But it was not till provisions grew so high this winter that I bethought me how, by buying things wholesale, and cooking a good quantity of provisions together, much money might be saved, and much comfort gained. So I spoke to my friend – or my enemy – the man I told you of – and he found fault with every detail of my plan; and in consequence I laid it aside, both as impracticable, and also because if I forced it into operation I should be interfering with the independence of my men; when, suddenly, this Higgins came to me and graciously signified his approval of a scheme so nearly the same as mine, that I might fairly have claimed it; and, moreover, the approval of several of his fellow-workmen, to whom he had spoken. I was a little 'riled', I confess, by his manner, and thought of throwing the whole thing overboard to sink or swim. But, it seemed childish to relinquish a plan which I had once thought wise and well-laid, just because I myself did not receive all the honour and consequence due to the originator. So I coolly took the part assigned to me, which is something like that of steward to a club. I buy in the provisions wholesale, and provide a fitting matron or cook."

"I hope you give satisfaction in your new capacity. Are you a good judge of potatoes and onions? But I suppose Mrs Thornton assists you in your marketing."

"Not a bit," replied Mr Thornton. "She disapproves of the whole plan, and now we never mention it to each other. But I manage pretty well, getting in great stocks from Liverpool, and being served in butcher's meat by our own family butcher. I can assure you, the hot dinners the matron turns out are by no means to be despised."

"Do you taste each dish as it goes in, in virtue of your office? I hope you have a white wand."

"I was very scrupulous at first, in confining myself to the mere purchasing part, and even in that I rather obeyed the men's orders, conveyed through the house-keeper, than went by my own judgement. At one time the beef was too large, at another the mutton was not fat enough. I think they saw how careful I was to leave them free, and not to intrude my own ideas upon them; so, one day, two or three of the men – my friend Higgins among them – asked me if I would not come in and take a snack. It was a very busy day, but I saw that the men would be hurt if, after making the advance, I didn't meet them halfway, so I went in, and I never made a better dinner in my life. I told them (my next neighbours I mean, for I'm no speech-maker) how much I'd enjoyed it: and for some time, whenever that especial dinner recurred in their dietary, I was sure to be met by these men, with a 'Master, there's hot-pot for dinner today, win yo' come?' If they had not asked me, I would no more have intruded on them than I'd have gone to the mess at the barracks without invitation."

"I should think you were rather a restraint on your hosts' conversation. They can't abuse the masters while you're there. I suspect they take it out on non-hot-pot days."

"Well! hitherto we've steered clear of all vexed questions. But if any of the old disputes came up again, I would certainly speak out my mind hot-pot day. But you are hardly acquainted with our Darkshire fellows, for all you're a Darkshire man yourself. They have such a sense of humour, and such a racy mode of expression! I am getting really to know some of them now, and they talk pretty freely before me."

"Nothing like the act of eating for equalising men. Dying is nothing to it. The philosopher dies sententiously – the pharisee ostentatiously – the simple-hearted humbly – the poor idiot blindly, as the sparrow falls to the ground; the philo-sopher and idiot, publican and pharisee, all eat after the same fashion – given an equally good digestion. There's theory for theory for you!"

"Indeed I have no theory; I hate theories."

"I beg your pardon. To show my penitence, will you accept a ten-pound note towards your marketing, and give the poor fellows a feast?"

"Thank you; but I'd rather not. They pay me rent for the oven and cooking-places at the back of the mill: and will have to pay more for the new dining-room. I don't want it to fall into a charity. I don't want donations. Once let in the principle, and I should have people going and talking, and spoiling the simplicity of the whole thing."

"People will talk about any new plan. You can't help that."

"My enemies, if I have any, may make a philanthropic fuss about this dinner-scheme; but you are a friend, and I expect you will pay my experiment the respect of silence. It is but a new broom at present, and sweeps clean enough. But by and by we shall meet with plenty of stumbling-blocks, no doubt."

31

EDWIN SEAVER

The Company

Originally entitled "The Jew," this story was first published in *The New Republic* in January 1928 and anthologized in *The Best Stories of 1928* and the *Yearbook of the American Short Story*. In 1930 it came out as part of the Seaver's novel *The Company*. This novel is composed of vignettes about the hopes and disappointments of the people who work for the Universal Illuminating Company.

After Aarons left the office we all felt much better. Not that Aarons was a bad sort. On the contrary we all liked him quite a lot even though he was a Jew. Yet somehow we felt relieved when one day, out of a clear sky, Aarons rose from his desk and slamming a drawer shut with such a bang we all jumped in our chairs, said:

— I'm through.

Then he took his hat and coat and without saying goodbye to anybody closed the door behind him.

We were all so surprised nobody even thought of asking Aarons where he was going. We simply sat there staring at each other. It was so still in the office you could hear the clock on Mr Mold's desk ticking away patiently.

Suddenly we all began talking and laughing at once. We actually became hilarious and laughed at each other's remarks as if everything that was said was unbearably funny.

— The crazy Jew, Mr Mold said, his mouth still open in amazement, now what do you suppose has bitten him?

— Oh lord, gasped Miss Childe, throwing up her hands and leaning back in her chair so that her skirts came up way over her knees, that's the richest yet.

As for Mr Nash, he was beside himself. Taking a handful of papers from his wastebasket he hurled them into the air and cried:

— Hurrah for Aarons! There's one Jew less in the Company.

It was as if a load had suddenly dropped from our shoulders. The very atmosphere of the office seemed lighter now and when we returned to our typewriters

EDWIN SEAVER, pp. 145–52 from *The Company*. London: Macmillan, 1930.

we all felt unusually elated. Nothing so remarkable had happened in the office for years.

When you come right down to it I guess we didn't like Aarons so much after all. He was a strange yid; we could never make him out.

I suppose Aarons was what you might call a Red. I mean he was a born trouble-maker. Before he came to the office we all got along together fine. As members of the editorial bureau we felt that we were important factors in the Company. After all it was we who presented the Company to the public; it was we who wrote the bosses' speeches for them. In our way we were, as the vice president-commercial relations once said to us in conference, artists.

As soon as Aarons came all that went by the board. What I mean is he made us all feel kind of foolish and before we knew what had happened we were all playing up to him. It wasn't any one thing in particular that he did. I guess it was just the fact that he was among us upset the whole morale of the office. We began to make fun of our work. We would read aloud to each other the most serious parts of a speech or an article we were preparing just to get a laugh.

— How's that for the bunk? we would say, winking to one another or sticking our tongue in our cheek and pulling a sly face.

Now I ask you, is that right? It seems to me a fellow owes something to the Company that's hiring him. Deuce take it, if we don't like our jobs we know what we can do. A man's got to feel some respect for himself and his work. Aarons robbed us of our selfrespect. Every day we took our jobs more and more as a joke. We made out to each other we were getting real reckless and didn't give a hang for anything or anybody but underneath it all I think we were beginning to get scared of ourselves.

You see, it was affecting our work. We no longer could turn out copy the way we used to. It became harder and harder to write inspirationally the way the boss wanted us to and we would sit for hours before our machines tearing up sheet after sheet of paper and cursing ourselves and our jobs. But the more fun Aarons made of his work the better copy he turned out. You had to hand it to him.

— When you're a harlot you have to know how, eh boys? he would say, banging away at his machine and talking all the time. And he would grin down his long nose as if we were the big joke.

Now what kind of way is that for a fellow to talk about his work, especially with ladies in the office. That's the trouble with these Jews; they never know when to stop. It used to make me sick to see Miss Childe shining up to Aarons and trying to appear clever just to get him to say something nice about her copy.

But the climax came one day when the boss called us into conference. What do you suppose he said? He said we were all letting up on our jobs except Aarons and that Aarons was the only one that was worth anything to him.

— You could all take a lesson from Aarons, the boss said. When he writes he puts his whole heart into it. He convinces you in whatever he does because he's convinced before he puts down a word on paper. I want to see more of his conviction in your work hereafter.

And there was Aarons sitting there all the time as cool as you please. It's a wonder we didn't choke on the boss' words. Believe me we felt pretty cheap, I can tell you.

After we got back to our desks Aarons didn't say anything for some time. He sat there holding his head in his hands as if he had a headache. He had never been so quiet before.

— There's no fool like an old fool, eh Mr Aarons, Miss Childe said sort of laughing, but you could see she was bursting with envy for what the boss had said to him.

Aarons didn't even answer her. He lifted his head and speaking in a voice we had never heard before, almost as if he were begging Mr Mold to listen to him, he said:

— Mold you've got a wife and child, you'll understand me. Suppose you couldn't get a job, suppose no matter how hard you tried you couldn't fit in anywhere would you let your wife walk the streets for you?

Mr Mold was so surprised he actually turned pale.

— Why what do you mean? he stammered.

— Don't get angry please, Aarons went on in that strange pleading voice that was so new to us. Look at it in another way. Suppose you didn't want another job, you just couldn't stick it any longer, see, and you knew you could never be satisfied with another job, would you let your wife and child go shift for themselves sooner than go on humiliating yourself?

Mr Mold stared at Aarons and then a broad grin broke over his face.

— Say what are you up to now Aarons? he said, and we all laughed with relief to think Aarons was only joking again.

But Aarons didn't laugh at all. He merely shrugged his shoulders and suddenly he looked extraordinarily sad as if he were going to cry. Then he got up, went over to the washstand in the corner of the office and began washing his hands.

Mr Nash rapped his forehead with his knuckles and nodded to us as much as to say: I told you so.

And the next thing we knew Aarons had quit.

32

RUTH L. OZEKI

My Year of Meats

Jane Takagi-Little, an American Japanese, is making a series for Japanese television called *My American Wife!*, with Suzuki, a cameraman sent from Japan. The series is sponsored by BEEF-EX, a lobby group for the beef industry. Each episode is based on a different "typically American" family and a meal they prepare.

I 'll never forget the look of astonishment that lit up Suzuki's moonlike face the first time he walked into a Wal-Mart. To a Japanese person, Wal-Mart is awesome, the capitalist equivalent of the wide-open spaces and endless horizons of the American geographical frontier. All this for the taking! Your breast expands with greed and need and wonder. I followed Suzuki around the store as he pored over a dozen brands of car caddies, fingered garden hoses, and lingered on the edge of Lingerie, watching farmwives choose brassieres. He loved the fact that you could buy real firearms, not just air guns, over the counter at Wal-Mart, but that was where I drew the line.

I was learning. *This* was the heart and soul of *My American Wife!*: re-creating for Japanese housewives this spectacle of raw American abundance. So we put Suzuki in a shopping cart, Betacam on his shoulder, and wheeled him up and down the endless aisles of superstores, filming *goods* to induce in our Japanese wives a state of *want* (as in both senses, "lack" and "desire"), because *want is good*. We panned the shelves, stacked floor to ceiling, tracked women as they filled their carts with Styrofoam trays of freezer steaks, each of which, from a Japanese housewife's perspective, would feed her entire family for several days. "Stocking up" is what our robust Americans called it, laughing nervously, because profligate abundance automatically evokes its opposite, the unspoken specter of dearth.

Locating our subjects felt like a confidence game, really. I'd inveigle a nice woman with her civic duty to promote American meat abroad and thereby help rectify the trade imbalance with Japan. Overwhelmed with a sense of the importance of the task, she'd open up her life to us. We'd spend two or three days with her, picking through the quotidian minutiae of her existence, then we'd roll out of town and on to the next one. We tried to be considerate, but you have to remember that *My American Wife!* was a *series*. You are doing a wife or two a week. While you are shooting them, they are your entire world and you live in the warm, beating heart of their domestic narratives, but as soon as you drive away from the house, away from the family all fond and waving, then it is over. Their lives are sealed in your box of tapes, locked away in the van, and you send these off with the director to edit back in Tokyo, and that's it. Easy. Done.

That was the idea, anyway. Sometimes, though, it doesn't happen exactly that way.

[. . .]

"His name is Joichi Ueno," I explained to my ex-flight attendant PA. "That's pronounced 'Wayno.' He likes to be called John."

The flight attendant groaned. I shrugged. Actually, I was the one who had given him the nickname, during the initial planning meetings for the show. Kato told me he was so proud of it that he insisted on using it all the time, even to his colleagues in Japan.

"Listen," I continued sternly. "Don't give him attitude. This is the big man, the Chief Beef. I'm giving you a major responsibility here. I want you to pick him up at the airport and fall in love with him, and more importantly, I want him to fall in love with you. Got it? Your job is to take care of him, keep him out of the way. You are uniquely suited to this assignment. The two of you have similar tastes."

As the representative of the ad agency in charge of marketing the meats, Ueno was my de facto boss. He was a real hands-on kind of guy and he always showed up for the commercial shoots. Each episode of *My American Wife!* carried four attractive commercial spots for BEEF-EX. The strategy was "to develop a powerful synergy between the commercials and the documentary vehicles, in order to stimulate consumer purchase motivation." In other words, the commercials were to bleed into the documentaries, and documentaries were to function as commercials.

We had bigger crews for the commercials. I didn't coordinate them, since I am a documentarian, but I was asked to help out, in order to reinforce the synergy.

[. . .]

The two faxes that I was interested in were pinned to my bulletin board. One was from my mole at the Japanese Network and the other was from John Ueno. I read the mole's fax first.

---

7 July

Dear miss Takagi,

Congratulations on your program of Indiana's Bukowsky family that earned highest ratings for the time slot in this season, penetrating more than 10,000,000 households, perhaps! Our Network producer is quite satisfy and say please to continue good work on authentic American family that only you can choose. But I warn you please to beware of agency rep Mr J. Ueno who is exceedingly anger or so I have heard.

Sincerely,

Tashiro

p.s. if you like to know why is J. Ueno exceedingly anger it is because of your show causing all of the lams to sell out of butcher stores in Tokyo on Saturday afternoon, which became so famous story as to be highlight on national evening news! Maybe this is very funny for you but not good for American sponsor and especially Mr J. Ueno!

The second fax read:

---

10 July

Dear Ms Jane Takagi,

This is to inform you of your grave flaw in last program of *My American Wife!*, which is the Mrs Bukowsky program, and that is the LAMB. You must never put LAMB into the program of *My American Wife!* ever because LAMB come mostly from Australia, which is not good for program sponsor of BEEF-EX since it is unAmerican. Do you understand? I must say very severely to you even though this is a needless to say thing. TV program depend on sponsor. It is business. Please do not do again. I hope you will understand my meaning.

Sincerely,

Joichi Ueno

"It's your gig, primarily. You can handle it as you like. But I'd watch it if I were you. . . ."

Kenji had a habit of sneaking up behind you on his soft Italian soles. I knew he had read the faxes and posted them on the board. He watched my reaction, then added:

"Kato called."

Kato was a man of vision who could see beyond the narrow promotional concerns of sponsors and could imagine programming that was truly unique yet served the needs of the market.

"What did he say?"

"'Congratulations. Don't do it again.' He told me to keep an eye on you."

Kenji's position was complex, I knew, as the despised and lowly courtier, exiled from the capital of Tokyo to the island of Manhattan, USA. On one hand I think he genuinely liked me and wanted to support me. On the other, he wanted me to fall on my face so he could take over directing and get to go to exotic parts of America, where he could take photographs with his antique Leica and eventually get himself noticed and recalled to the capital. And maybe find a wife. I understood his ambivalence and was accordingly a bit wary.

"Great, so now you spy for the enemy." [. . .]

"BEEF-EX is paying your rent," Kenji continued. "And mine too. So don't get all *auteur* on me, Takagi. It's just too boring."

"Screw you, Kenji," I said as he walked out the door. I mean, I was happy about the ratings. It wasn't an Emmy, and eight o'clock on Saturday morning wasn't the greatest slot in the world, but still I wanted to celebrate a little or at least have someone to commiserate with. I was annoyed that everyone was getting so bent about some dumb lamb chops, when obviously it was the *story* that counted.

[. . .]

When I got back to my apartment, I reread Ueno's fax. Of course he had never mentioned the ratings. That was fine with me. But the reprimand pissed me off, as did his attempt to curtail my freedom as a documentarian. I understood that he had to answer to his superiors at the agency, and ultimately to his American clients, and that my programming was undermining his credibility with BEEF-EX. But I chose to ignore this understanding, as I would ignore the new censorship he imposed. I couldn't help it. "Beef is Best." Hah. He was base. His wanton capitalist mandate had nothing to do with my vocation.

[. . .]

FAXES

Dear Miss Takagi,

I regret to inform you that your program of vegetarian lesbians is unacceptable to Mr J. Ueno who insist that you must resign from director of *My American Wife!* ever again. Your program will not be aired and our company must suffer grave humiliation of admitting failure to provide fresh program to Network and must air old rerun program in the slot.

Sincerely yours,

Mariko Nakano

(for Mr J. Ueno)

cc. Mr S. Kato

Takagi,

How stupid to think of putting lesbians on Saturday morning family television! This is not late night TV, you know! You have acted like selfish American, not thinking of your company, which will be disgrace if this show cannot air. Mr Ueno is trying to stop show but I have sent it to network and hope that they will say OK to airing.

If show will not be allowed, you must be fired, I am afraid. I cannot save you. I will inform you of final decision, but I suggest you to write the letter of apology to Mr J. Ueno nevertheless. I trusted you. Now I am sadly disappointed. S. Kato

----

[. . .]

MORE FAXES

Dear Takagi,

Well, you are very lucky this time. I just got a call from your mole, Tashiro, at the Network, and the show passed and aired. The network producer wasn't even aware of the storm that was brewing, and he said he found it "humane and moving," however the word on the street is that what really appealed to him was the novelty and shock value of putting lesbians on Saturday morning. Anyway, Kato is still very annoyed with you and he says that if you want your job, you are to write that letter of apology to Ueno and obey whatever conditions he places on program content in the future. Obey being the operant word, here.

Got it?

Cheers,

Kenji

Dear Mr Ueno,

Please accept my most humble apologies for making yet another program that violated the mandate of BEEF-EX while receiving, yet again, some of the highest ratings of the season.

Please allow me to continue directing *My American Wife!* Although my programs have been full of mistakes, I really think I am getting the hang of it now. With your patience and your wise guidance, I am confident that I will be able to make programs that will convince every housewife in Japan to buy BEEF-EX for her family's next dinner.

Sincerely yours,

Jane Takagi-Little

Dear Miss Takagi,

Please be advised that Mr J. Ueno has receive your humble apologies and reluctantly agree to give one more chance to you providing that you make next programs only about normal people and regarding the appropriate topic of meats.

Please tell what is next program idea as soon as possible, since from now on you must tell every details about your program before shooting. You may not make a program before you get approval from him first.

He additionally say that you should feel shame for teaching unwholesome ways to young Japanese people.

Sincerely yours,

M. Nakano

(for Mr J. Ueno)

cc. Mr S. Kato

Dear Mr Ueno:

Thank you so much for this chance to redeem myself. From now on I will only make wholesome programs about beef and normal people. Accordingly, I would like to propose a certain Mrs Payne from Peerless, Montana, who has written a cookbook called "Best O'Beef" that includes the following:

BEEF FUDGE

2 cups white sugar	1/2 cup ground roast beef
1 cup brown sugar	3 tablespoons butter
1/2 cup white corn syrup	2 oz. unsweetened chocolate
1/2 cup milk	1/2 cup chopped walnuts
1 teaspoon vanilla	

Cook all ingredients together without stirring in a heavy pot to 238° F. Remove from stove and cool to room temperature. Add vanilla and walnuts. Beat until thick. Pour into greased baking dish, chill, and cut as for fudge.

Doesn't this sound delicious?

Sincerely,

J. Takagi-Little

[. . .]

FAX

TO: "J." Ueno
FROM: Jane Takagi-Little
DATE: September 6
RE: Documentary Ethics

Dear Mr Ueno:

There are a couple of things that have come to light in my researches that I think you should know about. I have inadvertently discovered an unsavory side to the meat industry. I am talking about the use of drugs and hormones in meat production, which are being blamed for rising rates of cancer, sterility, impotence, reproductive disorders, as well as a host of other illnesses and harmful side effects. These drugs are routinely given to the cattle that end up as steak on the plates of the Japanese television viewing audience. I am concerned about the ethics of representing either the Blatsziks or the Dunns in a wholesome manner, knowing what I now know about the health hazards of meat production.

I am sending you a summary of all of my research. Since there is so much technical language, I've asked Kenji to translate it into Japanese. Please advise how to proceed.
Sincerely,

J. Takagi-Little

P.S. On a more personal note, while there is still no proven link to meat, did you know that now the average man produces less morphologically sound sperm than an average hamster?

FAX

September 6
Dear Dyann and Lara:

Thank you for your articles. They were very helpful in planning my next show. To answer your question, yes, the commercials for the program sponsor go into the black spaces in the tape. The copy I sent you, without commercials or titles, is called a "white mother." This time I am enclosing the "on-air" copy with the commercials included. Before you watch it there is something you should know – and I'm afraid it's going to make you angry. The program sponsor for *My American Wife!* is an organization called the Beef Export and Trade Syndicate, or BEEF-EX. I neglected to tell you this before the shoot, probably sensing that you wouldn't go along with it, and after the shoot was over it was too late. I didn't have time to reshoot, and your program was so *good*. I felt it could deliver a truly affirming message about sexuality and race and the many faces of motherhood to Japanese women. I know these aren't adequate excuses, nor do they tell the entire story, but there is nothing I can say that would be sufficient to exonerate myself. All I can do is apologize and ask you to forgive me and promise to make it up to you somehow.

Sincerely,

Jane

FAX

TO: J. Takagi-Little
FROM: J. Ueno
DATE: September 7
RE: Beef Safety

Dear Takagi-Little:

Please do not be concerned with these matters that are none of your business and which you know nothing about, and that is the wholesomeness of BEEF-EX. They have one good committee called the Meat Affirmation Task Force who assures me of high quality of all meats. So do not waste your time. This is not hobby. If you cannot be professional television director and make wholesome program of *My American Wife!* I have asked Mr Kato to send some another director instead.

Sincerely,

J. Ueno

33

HENRIK IBSEN

An Enemy of the People

An Enemy of the People, first performed in 1883, takes up one of Ibsen's central themes: the duty of the individual pitted against the conventions of society. Dr Thomas Stockmann, a medical officer, is charged with inspecting the public baths on which the prosperity of his native town depends. He finds that the water is contaminated, and people who pay to come to the baths for a cure are contracting typhus from it. He has reported the problem to his brother Peter, the Mayor of the town.

MRS STOCKMANN: That was a ring at the bell.

DR STOCKMANN: It must be he, then. (*A knock is heard at the door.*) Come in!

PETER STOCKMANN (*comes in from the hall*): Good morning.

DR STOCKMANN: Glad to see you, Peter!

MRS STOCKMANN: Good morning, Peter. How are you?

PETER STOCKMANN: So so, thank you. (*To* DR STOCKMANN.) I received from you yesterday, after office hours, a report dealing with the condition of the water at the Baths.

DR STOCKMANN: Yes. Have you read it?

PETER STOCKMANN: Yes, I have.

DR STOCKMANN: And what have you to say to it?

PETER STOCKMANN (*with a sidelong glance*): Hm! —

MRS STOCKMANN: Come along, Petra. (*She and* PETRA *go into the room on the left.*)

PETER STOCKMANN (*after a pause*): Was it necessary to make all these investigations behind my back?

DR STOCKMANN: Yes, because until I was absolutely certain about it —

PETER STOCKMANN: Then you mean that you are absolutely certain now?

DR STOCKMANN: Surely you are convinced of that.

PETER STOCKMANN: Is it your intention to bring this document before the Baths Committee as a sort of official communication?

DR STOCKMANN: Certainly. Something must be done in the matter — and that quickly.

HENRIK IBSEN, pp. 174–85, from *An Enemy of the People* (tr. R. Farquharson Sharp). London: J. M. Dent, 1961. First published 1911.

PETER STOCKMANN: As usual, you employ violent expressions in your report. You
say, amongst other things, that what we offer visitors in our Baths is a permanent supply of poison.

DR STOCKMANN: Well, can you describe it any other way, Peter? Just think – water
that is poisonous, whether you drink it or bathe in it! And this we offer to the
poor sick folk who come to us trustfully and pay us at an exorbitant rate to be
made well again!

PETER STOCKMANN: And your reasoning leads you to this conclusion, that we must
build a sewer to draw off the alleged impurities from Mölledal and must relay
the water-conduits.

DR STOCKMANN: Yes. Do you see any other way out of it? I don't.

PETER STOCKMANN: I made a pretext this morning to go and see the town engineer,
and, as if only half seriously, broached the subject of these proposals as a thing
we might perhaps have to take under consideration some time later on.

DR STOCKMANN: Some time later on!

PETER STOCKMANN: He smiled at what he considered to be my extravagance,
naturally. Have you taken the trouble to consider what your proposed alterations would cost? According to the information I obtained, the expenses would
probably mount up to fifteen or twenty thousand pounds.

DR STOCKMANN: Would it cost so much?

PETER STOCKMANN: Yes; and the worst part of it would be that the work would take
at least two years.

DR STOCKMANN: Two years? Two whole years?

PETER STOCKMANN: At least. And what are we to do with the Baths in the meantime?
Close them? Indeed we should be obliged to. And do you suppose any one
would come near the place after it had got about that the water was dangerous?

DR STOCKMANN: Yes but, Peter, that is what it is.

PETER STOCKMANN: And all this at this juncture – just as the Baths are beginning
to be known. There are other towns in the neighbourhood with qualification
to attract visitors for bathing purposes. Don't you suppose they would immediately strain every nerve to divert the entire stream of strangers to themselves?
Unquestionably they would; and then where should we be? We should probably have to abandon the whole thing, which has cost us so much money – and
then you would have ruined your native town.

DR STOCKMANN: I – should have ruined –!

PETER STOCKMANN: It is simply and solely through the Baths that the town has
before it any future worth mentioning. You know that just as well as I.

DR STOCKMANN: But what do you think ought to be done, then?

PETER STOCKMANN: Your report has not convinced me that the condition of the
water at the Baths is as bad as you represent it to be.

DR STOCKMANN: I tell you it is even worse! – or at all events it will be in summer,
when the warm weather comes.

PETER STOCKMANN: As I said, I believe you exaggerate the matter considerably. A
capable physician ought to know what measures to take – he ought to be
capable of preventing injurious influences or of remedying them if they become
obviously persistent.

DR STOCKMANN: Well? What more?

PETER STOCKMANN: The water supply for the Baths is now an established fact, and in consequence must be treated as such. But probably the Committee, at its discretion, will not be disinclined to consider the question of how far it might be possible to introduce certain improvements consistently with a reasonable expenditure.

DR STOCKMANN: And do you suppose that I will have anything to do with such a piece of trickery as that?

PETER STOCKMANN: Trickery!!

DR STOCKMANN: Yes, it would be a trick – a fraud, a lie, a downright crime towards the public, towards the whole community!

PETER STOCKMANN: I have not, as I remarked before, been able to convince myself that there is actually any imminent danger.

DR STOCKMANN: You have! It is impossible that you should not be convinced. I know I have represented the facts absolutely truthfully and fairly. And you know it very well, Peter, only you won't acknowledge it. It was owing to your action that both the Baths and the water-conduits were built where they are; and that is what you won't acknowledge – that damnable blunder of yours. Pooh! – do you suppose I don't see through you?

PETER STOCKMANN: And even if that were true? If I perhaps guard my reputation somewhat anxiously, it is in the interests of the town. Without moral authority I am powerless to direct public affairs as seems, to my judgment, to be best for the common good. And on that account – and for various other reasons too – it appears to me to be a matter of importance that your report should not be delivered to the Committee. In the interests of the public, you must withhold it. Then, later on, I will raise the question and we will do our best, privately; but nothing of this unfortunate affair – not a single word of it – must come to the ears of the public.

DR STOCKMANN: I am afraid you will not be able to prevent that now, my dear Peter.

PETER STOCKMANN: It must and shall be prevented.

DR STOCKMANN: It is no use, I tell you. There are too many people that know about it.

PETER STOCKMANN: That know about it? Who? Surely you don't mean those fellows on the "People's Messenger"?

DR STOCKMANN: Yes, they know. The liberal-minded independent press is going to see that you do your duty.

PETER STOCKMANN (*after a short pause*): You are an extraordinarily independent man, Thomas. Have you given no thought to the consequences this may have for yourself?

DR STOCKMANN: Consequences? – for me?

PETER STOCKMANN: For you and yours, yes.

DR STOCKMANN: What the deuce do you mean?

PETER STOCKMANN: I believe I have always behaved in a brotherly way to you – have always been ready to oblige or to help you?

DR STOCKMANN: Yes, you have, and I am grateful to you for it.

PETER STOCKMANN: There is no need. Indeed, to some extent I was forced to do so
– for my own sake. I always hoped that, if I helped to improve your financial
position, I should be able to keep some check on you.

DR STOCKMANN: What!! Then it was only for your own sake –!

PETER STOCKMANN: Up to a certain point, yes. It is painful for a man in an official
position to have his nearest relative compromising himself time after time.

DR STOCKMANN: And do you consider that I do that?

PETER STOCKMANN: Yes, unfortunately, you do, without even being aware of it. You
have a restless, pugnacious, rebellious disposition. And then there is that disastrous propensity of yours to want to write about every sort of possible and
impossible thing. The moment an idea comes into your head, you must needs
go and write a newspaper article or a whole pamphlet about it.

DR STOCKMANN: Well, but is it not the duty of a citizen to let the public share in
any new ideas he may have?

PETER STOCKMANN: Oh, the public doesn't require any new ideas. The public is best
served by the good, old-established ideas it already has.

DR STOCKMANN: And that is your honest opinion?

PETER STOCKMANN: Yes, and for once I must talk frankly to you. Hitherto I have
tried to avoid doing so, because I know how irritable you are; but now I must
tell you the truth, Thomas. You have no conception what an amount of harm
you do yourself by your impetuosity. You complain of the authorities, you even
complain of the government – you are always pulling them to pieces; you insist
that you have been neglected and persecuted. But what else can such a cantankerous man as you expect?

DR STOCKMANN: What next! Cantankerous, am I?

PETER STOCKMANN: Yes, Thomas, you are an extremely cantankerous man to work
with – I know that to my cost. You disregard everything that you ought to have
consideration for. You seem completely to forget that it is me you have to thank
for your appointment here as medical officer to the Baths –

DR STOCKMANN: I was entitled to it as a matter of course! – I and nobody else! I
was the first person to see that the town could be made into a flourishing
watering-place, and I was the only one who saw it at that time. I had to fight
single-handed in support of the idea for many years; and I wrote and wrote –

PETER STOCKMANN: Undoubtedly. But things were not ripe for the scheme then –
though, of course, you could not judge of that in your out-of-the-way corner up
north. But as soon as the opportune moment came I – and the others – took the
matter into our hands –

DR STOCKMANN: Yes, and made this mess of all my beautiful plan. It is pretty
obvious now what clever fellows you were!

PETER STOCKMANN: To my mind the whole thing only seems to mean that you are
seeking another outlet for your combativeness. You want to pick a quarrel with
your superiors – an old habit of yours. You cannot put up with any authority
over you. You look askance at anyone who occupies a superior official position;
you regard him as a personal enemy, and then any stick is good enough to beat
him with. But now I have called your attention to the fact that the town's
interests are at stake – and, incidentally, my own too. And therefore I must tell

you, Thomas, that you will find me inexorable with regard to what I am about
to require you to do.

DR STOCKMANN: And what is that?

PETER STOCKMANN: As you have been so indiscreet as to speak of this delicate
matter to outsiders, despite the fact that you ought to have treated it as entirely
official and confidential, it is obviously impossible to hush it up now. All sorts of
rumours will get about directly, and everybody who has a grudge against us will
take care to embellish these rumours. So it will be necessary for you to refute
them publicly.

DR STOCKMANN: I! How? I don't understand.

PETER STOCKMANN: What we shall expect is that, after making further investigations, you will come to the conclusion that the matter is not by any means
as dangerous or as critical as you imagined in the first instance.

DR STOCKMANN: Oho! – so that is what you expect!

PETER STOCKMANN: And, what is more, we shall expect you to make public profession of your confidence in the Committee and in their readiness to consider fully
and conscientiously what steps may be necessary to remedy any possible defects.

DR STOCKMANN: But you will never be able to do that by patching and tinkering at
it – never! Take my word for it, Peter; I mean what I say, as deliberately and
emphatically as possible.

PETER STOCKMANN: As an officer under the Committee, you have no right to any
individual opinion.

DR STOCKMANN (*amazed*): No right?

PETER STOCKMANN: In your official capacity, no. As a private person, it is quite
another matter. But as a subordinate member of the staff of the Baths, you have
no right to express any opinion which runs contrary to that of your superiors.

DR STOCKMANN: This is too much! I, a doctor, a man of science, have no right
to –!

PETER STOCKMANN: The matter in hand is not simply a scientific one. It is a complicated matter, and has its economic as well as its technical side.

DR STOCKMANN: I don't care what it is! I intend to be free to express my opinion on
any subject under the sun.

PETER STOCKMANN: As you please – but not on any subject concerning the Baths.
That we forbid.

DR STOCKMANN (*shouting*): You forbid –! You! A pack of –

PETER STOCKMANN: *I* forbid it – I, your chief; and if I forbid it, you have to obey.

DR STOCKMANN (*controlling himself*): Peter – if you were not my brother –

PETRA: (*throwing open the door*): Father, you shan't stand this!

MRS STOCKMANN (*coming in after her*): Petra, Petra!

PETER STOCKMANN: Oh, so you have been eavesdropping.

MRS STOCKMANN: You were talking so loud, we couldn't help –

PETRA: Yes, I was listening.

PETER STOCKMANN: Well, after all, I am very glad –

DR STOCKMANN (*going up to him*): You were saying something about forbidding and
obeying?

PETER STOCKMANN: You obliged me to take that tone with you.

DR STOCKMANN: And so I am to give myself the lie, publicly?

PETER STOCKMANN: We consider it absolutely necessary that you should make some such public statement as I have asked for.

DR STOCKMANN: And if I do not – obey?

PETER STOCKMANN: Then we shall publish a statement ourselves to reassure the public.

DR STOCKMANN: Very well; but in that case I shall use my pen against you. I stick to what I have said; I will show that I am right and that you are wrong. And what will you do then?

PETER STOCKMANN: Then I shall not be able to prevent your being dismissed.

DR STOCKMANN: What –?

PETRA: Father – dismissed!

MRS STOCKMANN: Dismissed!

PETER STOCKMANN: Dismissed from the staff of the Baths. I shall be obliged to propose that you shall immediately be given notice, and shall not be allowed any further participation in the Baths' affairs.

DR STOCKMANN: You would dare to do that!

PETER STOCKMANN: It is you that are playing the daring game.

PETRA: Uncle, that is a shameful way to treat a man like father!

MRS STOCKMANN: Do hold your tongue, Petra!

PETER STOCKMANN (*looking at* PETRA): Oh, so we volunteer our opinions already, do we? Of course. (*To Mrs* STOCKMANN.) Katherine, I imagine you are the most sensible person in this house. Use any influence you may have over your husband, and make him see what this will entail for his family as well as –

DR STOCKMANN: My family is my own concern and nobody else's!

PETER STOCKMANN: – for his own family, as I was saying, as well as for the town he lives in.

DR STOCKMANN: It is I who have the real good of the town at heart! I want to lay bare the defects that sooner or later must come to the light of day. I will show whether I love my native town.

PETER STOCKMANN: You, who in your blind obstinacy want to cut off the most important source of the town's welfare?

DR STOCKMANN: The source is poisoned, man! Are you mad? We are making our living by retailing filth and corruption! The whole of our flourishing municipal life derives its sustenance from a lie!

PETER STOCKMANN: All imagination – or something even worse. The man who can throw out such offensive insinuations about his native town must be an enemy to our community.

DR STOCKMANN (*going up to him*): Do you dare to –!

MRS STOCKMANN (*throwing herself between them*): Thomas!

PETRA (*catching her father by the arm*): Don't lose your temper, father!

PETER STOCKMANN: I will not expose myself to violence. Now you have had a warning; so reflect on what you owe to yourself and your family. Good-bye. (*Goes out.*)

DR STOCKMANN (*walking up and down*): Am I to put up with such treatment as this? In my own house, Katherine! What do you think of that!

MRS STOCKMANN: Indeed it is both shameful and absurd, Thomas –

PETRA: If only I could give uncle a piece of my mind –

DR STOCKMANN: It is my own fault. I ought to have flown out at him long ago! – shown my teeth! – bitten! To hear him call me an enemy to our community! Me! I shall not take that lying down, upon my soul!

MRS STOCKMANN: But, dear Thomas, your brother has power on his side –

DR STOCKMANN: Yes, but I have right on mine, I tell you.

MRS STOCKMANN: Oh yes, right – right. What is the use of having right on your side if you have not got might?

PETRA: Oh, mother! – how can you say such a thing!

DR STOCKMANN: Do you imagine that in a free country it is no use having right on your side? You are absurd, Katherine. Besides, haven't I got the liberal-minded, independent press to lead the way, and the compact majority behind me? That is might enough, I should think!

MRS STOCKMANN: But, good heavens, Thomas, you don't mean to –?

DR STOCKMANN: Don't mean to what?

MRS STOCKMANN: To set yourself up in opposition to your brother.

DR STOCKMANN: In God's name, what else do you suppose I should do but take my stand on right and truth?

PETRA: Yes, I was just going to say that.

MRS STOCKMANN: But it won't do you any earthly good. If they won't do it, they won't.

DR STOCKMANN: Oho, Katherine! Just give me time, and you will see how I will carry the war into their camp.

MRS STOCKMANN: Yes, you carry the war into their camp, and you get your dismissal – that is what you will do.

DR STOCKMANN: In any case I shall have done my duty towards the public – towards the community. I, who am called its enemy!

MRS STOCKMANN: But towards your family, Thomas? Towards your own home! Do you think that is doing your duty towards those you have to provide for?

PETRA: Ah, don't think always first of us, mother.

MRS STOCKMANN: Oh, it is easy for you to talk; you are able to shift for yourself, if need be. But remember the boys, Thomas; and think a little too of yourself, and of me –

DR STOCKMANN: I think you are out of your senses, Katherine! If I were to be such a miserable coward as to go on my knees to Peter and his damned crew, do you suppose I should ever know an hour's peace of mind all my life afterwards?

MRS STOCKMANN: I don't know anything about that; but God preserve us from the peace of mind we shall have, all the same, if you go on defying him! You will find yourself again without the means of subsistence, with no income to count upon. I should think we had had enough of that in the old days. Remember that, Thomas; think what that means.

DR STOCKMANN (*collecting himself with a struggle and clenching his fists*): And this is what this slavery can bring upon a free, honourable man! Isn't it horrible, Katherine?

MRS STOCKMANN: Yes, it is sinful to treat you so, it is perfectly true. But, good heavens, one has to put up with so much injustice in this world. – There are the boys, Thomas! Look at them! What is to become of them? Oh, no, no, you can never have the heart –. (EJLIF *and* MORTEN *have come in while she was speaking, with their school books in their hands.*)

DR STOCKMANN: The boys –! (*Recovers himself suddenly.*) No, even if the whole world goes to pieces, I will never bow my neck to this yoke! (*Goes towards his room.*)

MRS STOCKMANN (*following him*): Thomas – what are you going to do!

DR STOCKMANN (*at his door*): I mean to have the right to look my sons in the face when they are grown men. (*Goes into his room.*)

MRS STOCKMANN (*bursting into tears*): God help us all!

PETRA: Father is splendid! He will not give in.

34

C. P. SNOW

The Search

Arthur Miles, the narrator of *The Search*, has a life-long commitment to the ideals of scientific inquiry. In this, the last chapter of the novel, he has left science for broader political-educational work. Audrey, who was Arthur's girlfriend before his marriage to Ruth, is now the wife of Charles Sheriff, a scientist and friend from Arthur's student days.

I

Several times in the early summer I wrote to Sheriff, asking him how the work was progressing. His replies were cheerful, but I was worried that he gave me no details. When, in answer to some specific questions, I received a postcard: "Going splendidly. No time to write," I became suspicious. I persuaded Ruth to send a letter to Audrey so that I could add a line. In Audrey's reply she said: "Tell Arthur everything is all right. I talked to Hensman yesterday. Charles's present work was suggested by Arthur, and he has decided Constantine's idea was too speculative."

Ruth looked interested.

"I thought Sheriff might be spoiling all our plans," I said. "But I was being unfair."

Satisfied, I went back to my own work. I was getting busier and busier; and in June I had a minor success, which was very sweet. I found increasingly that I was enjoying the days, however busy I became. Once or twice I felt a little guilty that I had not been to Southampton to keep Sheriff going, but I had my hands full of work. Altogether I was out of touch with scientific news. I saw Constantine only once; it must have been from him I heard that a subsidiary Chair at Leeds would be vacant in the autumn. I remember thinking idly that if it had been a year or two later Sheriff might have got it.

It was a wet and dismal summer in England, and Ruth and I went abroad in July. My study was transported en bloc to a villa outside Portofino, where I worked on a terrace which hung over the sea. The first morning I felt again that lift of the heart, that sense of exhilarating peace, as I saw the sun gleaming on the water.

Ruth smiled: "Ah, darling, you should have spent your school holidays at Menton."

"And you should have lived in my town," I retorted.

The weeks went by. I was finishing a book; Ruth was busy getting together a conference of modern educators for the autumn. We had neither of us ever felt better. Our only social act was to walk into the village at night, talk bad Italian to the people outside the little inn, and dance under the plane trees.

One morning after the maid had thrown open the shutters of our bedroom, and I was blinking in the brilliant light, Ruth gave me a letter. "Whose handwriting is it?" she asked.

I stared at some queer unformed characters.

"Constantine's," I said. "I wonder why —"

"This is a splendid piece of work of Sheriff's," he wrote, "on that idea of mine about his sterols. He has put in for the job at Leeds. Austin and I are supporting him strongly. It's worth £800 and would give him time for research, which he ought to have. . . ."

I was puzzled, a little by Constantine's concern for Sheriff's income, much more by the way I had been deceived. Why had Audrey reassured me? Why had I been told nothing? How had the problem come out? I still could not understand. It was a triumph, a real and independent triumph; he would deserve this job and ought to get it; Audrey's troubles should be over, and Sheriff comfortable for life. And, more than anything else, I was extremely angry. I told Ruth.

"He's got there, anyway," she said. "And quicker. He ought to have told you, of course. I can't think why he didn't," she smiled. "Still, he's an engaging creature."

"It's sheer buffoonery," I said, more disturbed than I should have been, pricked in my own pride — and also vaguely uneasy. I was curiously upset, too much on edge to work. I went down to the village and sent a cable to Sheriff, saying I had had a letter from Constantine. Irritably I waited for a reply. There was no telegram, a letter would take two days. Two days passed, three, four, five. I spent my time watching for the post. Ruth became infected by my anxiety.

"You're letting this get on your nerves," she said.

"Of course I am," I said. "And it looks as though I'm right."

At the end of the week, a letter came for me, addressed in Audrey's handwriting. I was too much concerned to explain to Ruth. Audrey wrote:

"I've been trying to persuade Charles to write, but he won't. I only found your telegram by accident. He keeps saying he does not want to write to you until he has been appointed to the Leeds job. He'll have justified himself then, he says. He doesn't know I'm sending this; but I'm too ashamed not to answer you. As you know, I don't make excuses often, but I don't think he's himself now. This work must have been a strain and he's very moody and irritable.

"Isn't it splendid, though? I never thought he'd do anything as good on his own. I'm sorry I misled you over that; but it wasn't my fault. He had told Hensman that this idea was yours, so as to put me off if I enquired, I fancy. Charles doesn't leave these little personal things to chance, I ought to have known. He keeps saying that you'd have been hurt, because he wasn't doing your problem; and that his only justification for doing the other was to make a success of it.

"What a success, though. It's more in your line than his. Constantine came down last week to talk science. He's a darling. One night we all got a little drunk to celebrate, and Constantine held my hand absent-mindedly for a long time, and made a very eloquent speech to say that he didn't often come to a party in order to talk to his hostess. You would have got some sardonic amusement in watching Charles being absurdly jealous on the one hand, and not wanting to annoy Constantine for the sake of his career on the other. The career won. Some day I must meet Constantine again.

"I'm sending you one of Charles's reprints, which have just arrived. You won't let him know that I've written. . . ."

Quickly I read the reprint. He had sent the news of his discovery as a letter to the *Journal of Chemical Physics* in America; as I was reading, this struck me as strange, for although the American journals are very rapid, an Englishman ordinarily sends exciting work to *Nature*. I read it through twice. It was neat, crisp and logical; the facts marched to one solution; it was an important solution, and Constantine had foreseen it.

I had a flash of pleasure. After all, Sheriff had become a good scientist; I ought to expect oddities in his behaviour: this was first-rate work, and he had more than justified himself.

Then I read it again. It converged, as I had told Sheriff, on an old abandoned research of mine. I began to have stirrings of memory. I went into the room where Ruth had arranged my books. There, in one forlorn corner, were the notebooks of results. In a little while I found the one I wanted. I took it out into the sunshine, mentioned to Ruth that there were one or two side-lines from Sheriff's work that might be interesting, and went by myself to the end of the terrace.

There I compared Sheriff's results and my own. There should have been a stage where they agreed; they were wildly different. It happened to be the stage where I had given up just because the results fell into no sort of order. If Sheriff had found the same results at that stage, as he should, he too could have progressed no further. There was no solution there, not yet, nor perhaps for many years. Sheriff's results, however, were not the same; they had simplified themselves down to just those facts which led to a solution of spectacular clarity.

It was a mistake. I knew my facts were right; my assistant and I had been over them many times, hoping they would sift themselves out. It was a convenient mistake. Without it Sheriff would have wasted months of work. I thought for a moment. I pictured again the way these experiments were done: Sheriff in his room watching the movement of a thread of mercury in a pressure gauge, scrutinising a grey film with black spots against a background of light, seeing an illuminated circle swing across a scale. He must have done all these. It would be impossible to make the same mistake by accident. It was a deliberate mistake. When I said it to myself, I had no doubts at all. It was a deliberate mistake. He had committed the major scientific crime (I could still hear Hulme's voice trickling gently, firmly on).

Sheriff had given some false facts, suppressed some true ones. When I realised it, I was not particularly surprised. I could imagine his quick, ingenious, harassed mind thinking it over. For various reasons, he had chosen this problem; it would not take so much work, it would be more exciting, it might secure his niche straight away (for the Leeds job must have been in his mind quite early). To him, it looked as certain as mine. But I must not know, half because he was a little ashamed, half because I might interfere. So Hensman, who was not collaborating on this work, and Audrey, must, for safety's sake, also be deceived. All this he would do quite cheerfully. The problem began well. He felt he had a success of his own: Leeds was as good as his.

Then he came to that stage where every result seemed to contradict the last, where there was no clear road ahead, where there seemed no road ahead at all. There he must have hesitated. On the one hand he had lost months, there would be no position for years, he would have to come to me and confess; on the other his mind flitted round the chance of a fraud.

There was a risk, but he might secure all the success still. I scarcely think the ethics of scientific deceit troubled him; but the risk must have done. For if he were found out, he was ruined. He might keep on as a minor lecturer, but there would be nothing ahead.

What was the risk? The chance that anyone would do these experiments again for some time was very small. Given a few months he would have gained his position; and he could not be deposed from that even if there were whispers. Also, once in a Chair, how plausibly he could explain it away! He would do that more gracefully than anyone. There was myself, but he did not know how much I had done on the problem; he did not know that I had damning results. And, for fear of what I might know, he had actually taken all precautions against my hearing the news until the Leeds position was secured. After that, I supposed, he would have come up humorously, apologetically, and told me it was one of his little pranks.

There was only one mistake, I thought. He could not have foreseen that Constantine might let me know. That was too remote a chance. But he certainly ought to have told Audrey the whole story. She would have kept it secret and lied to me, angrily, protectively. As it was, probably a little jealous of her opinion of me, he had tried to keep his success in her eyes. He must have resented her disillusioned love: and he chose this time to put the illusion back. Successfully, so far as Audrey went, for she had been utterly deceived, so much deceived that unknowingly she had given me the whole story.

At lunch I told Ruth I was worried by one or two points in the letter. Afterwards I sat out on the terrace, considering what I should do. It was straightforward. Here was a published scientific communication; I knew it contained a mistake in fact; the motives behind it were irrelevant. In my hands I had the material to correct that mistake; unless I did so, and at once, I was an accessory after the fact.

I should have to write a letter to the journal in which it appeared, I thought. It would be a little less conspicuous than in *Nature*. I began to draft it through the hot afternoon. It was a long time since I had composed a scientific article; I found it strangely difficult to handle the clumsy conventional heavy prose. I wrote that some time ago I had worked on a problem similar to that described by Sheriff.

Some of the experiments were common to the two problems; my results for those experiments did not agree with Sheriff's. I had not published mine because as yet they were without any interpretation; if one substituted them for Sheriff's in his paper, the solution he gave was obviously untenable. The letter was quite short, and I made it carefully neutral in tone.

I typed it out after tea. When I read it through, I felt suddenly chilled.

II

Knowing all it meant for Sheriff and Audrey (sometimes one of them occurred in my thoughts, sometimes the other), I was doing this. Why? I asked myself. Was there anything more than scientific conscience? Was I hurrying to take my revenge at last for the time when Sheriff broke up my life by taking Audrey from me? Was there some undercurrent of resentment, long hidden, that was forcing itself through this best of all excuses?

I did not know. There was too much of my life entwined in this act: love, and friendship, and my own forsaken career, that – I knew for certain, now – I had tried to build again in Sheriff's, in case I should be drawn again to science and also as a sort of an amend. From this medley I was feeling anger, sorrow, and, beyond doubt, a harsh gladness as I wrote my letter. How they arose I could not tell; but, I thought, this is the mood in which most self-righteous acts are done. I could soften it by thinking what would I do if I had seen Sheriff's letter and not known the man; that is the way in which self-righteous acts are made more righteous still. In fact, I thought, if it had been by a stranger, I should not have studied the letter carefully enough to find the flaw. But, as it was by a friend, I was able to ruin him and be gratified.

I was quiet at tea-time, and told Ruth that I was still undecided about some details of Sheriff's work. Soon I left her, and walked down to the shore.

I shall not send the letter, I was thinking. Let him win his gamble. Let him cheat his way to the respectable success he wants. He will delight in it, and become a figure in the scientific world; and give broadcast talks and views on immortality; all of which he will love. And Audrey will be there, amused but rather proud. Oh, let him have it.

For me, if I do not send the letter, what then? There was only one answer; I was breaking irrevocably from science. This was the end, for me. Ever since I left professionally, I had been keeping a retreat open in my mind; supervising Sheriff had meant to myself that I could go back at any time. If I did not write I should be depriving myself of the loophole. I should have proved, once for all, how little science mattered to me.

There were no ways between. I could have held my hand until he was elected, and then threatened that either he must correct the mistake, or I would; but that was a compromise in action and not in mind. No, he should have his triumph to the full. Audrey should not know, she had seen so many disillusions, I would spare her this. Ruth should not know, though it would be hard when she saw in Sheriff's success what I might have done.

I stayed by the shore for a long time, in my hands the letter I should never send. The sun was setting, and suddenly, in the diffusely glowing sky, I saw the evening star, just as I had that night I walked with my father as a child. It was twenty years and more ago, I thought, that night when my scientific passion first broke hot upon me; and, through curiosity, satisfaction, ecstasy, strenuous work, a career, disaster, recovery, partial severance, I had come to this. The passion was over now. I lit a match and put it to the corner of the letter; the flame was steady in the still air, golden and smoky edged. The passion was over. I had repudiated it, and I should never feel it again.

And so after the years of struggle the personal things had won, I thought. Perhaps they were always bound to win. With one of memory's materialisations, I recalled the time my father and I had finished making our telescope; and how, to allay his disappointment, I had pretended to see wonders which were not there. Perhaps that was my first denial of science, right at the birth of my enthusiasm; and whether I had known much of myself or little now, I should still have saved Sheriff by the same instinctive drive. Ah well! I had acted at last; and now I was alone, having set myself apart from the final collective faith.

With a nostalgia for the past, I gazed at the evening star again. Whatever one has done, whatever one has lived through, has its claim on the heart from which it will never be cast off. The failures and successes, the scheming and comradeship, the hopes and aspirations, I never should forget. Yet I was free of a cloud that for so long had come between me and the future; I was liberated from all the faiths and superstitions, and at last there was only the honesty I should try to keep with myself. There was an exhilaration in the bleakness, a cold exhilaration as though after long waiting one had thrown open the window of a heated room and breathed the cold air outside. I was eager for the life that lay ahead.

I ceased to look at the starts shining over the sea. With a deep content, I walked towards the house, whose lights were streaming through the tranquil twilight.

VI

WHAT DO WE OWE TO OUR COUNTRY, COMPATRIOTS, AND STRANGERS?

The medieval scholar Thomas Aquinas held that "whatever a man has in superabundance is owed, of natural right, to the poor for their sustenance."[1] In the world today there are many people who "have in superabundance." After satisfying all their needs – for food, shelter, warmth, clothing, health care, and education, for themselves and their children, and some provision for those needs to be met in the future as well – they have money left over for items that are not, by any stretch of the imagination, needs. Aquinas could never have envisaged the kind of wealth many people have today – think only of central heating and air-conditioning, of exotic fresh fruits from both temperate and tropical lands delivered to your door, of being able to visit all the wonders of the world. People who have money to spare for good restaurants, concerts, vacation travel, books, CDs, or clothing that they buy because they want to keep up with the fashion, rather than because they need it to keep warm, are, by medieval standards, immensely rich.

If the rich are far richer than anyone in the thirteenth century could have imagined, however, the essential ingredients of poverty are the same. As in earlier times, the poor are those who do not have sufficient means to meet even the most basic of these needs, for example for food, shelter, and clothing. Today we would add that they also lack the resources to obtain even minimal health care, or to provide education for their children. There are today more than a billion people, living on no more than the purchasing power equivalent of $US1 per day. These are the people who are "absolutely poor." They are poor not only relative to others with whom they may compare themselves; but by a timeless standard related to the most basic human needs.

What attitude should the rich have towards the poor? What, if anything, are they obliged to do? The gospel story in which Jesus tells the parable of the good Samaritan is set in the context of an accepted moral rule that we should love our neighbors as we love ourselves, and help them when they are in need. But then the question arises, "who is my neighbor?" In response, Jesus relates how a man who was robbed, wounded, and left half-dead was helped not by members of his own Jewish community, but by a Samaritan.[2] The parable urges an extension of our obligations beyond our own community. But how far do we go? Do we have obligations to all human beings in need, irrespective of how far they are from us, either literally, in geographical terms, or metaphorically, in terms of ties of affinity and community? If we do, how much do those obligations require us to sacrifice for the benefit of others? And do our obligations diminish with distance?

The extent of our obligations to strangers is bound up with a related but distinct issue. Although there have been communities that considered it laudable to go outside the territory controlled by the community and kill any stranger one met there, today we generally accept that we have a duty not to harm strangers. That duty is universal: it is as bad to go halfway around the world to commit murder as it is to go across town to do it. But the obligation to aid someone in need seems to be more sensitive to distance. To enjoy a life of luxury knowing that your neighbor's child goes to bed hungry at night seems wrong; but it does not seem equally wrong to enjoy your luxuries while children in Sierra Leone die for want of food or basic health care.

Here we have one difference between the issues raised by Geraldine Brooks in *The Year of Wonders* and by Nick Hornby in *How to be Good*. The former is about not harming strangers, and the latter about helping them. But the difference between not harming and not helping here intersects with the question of how great a sacrifice we are required to make for strangers. If the only way to save your own life is to risk bringing a fatal disease to countless innocent strangers, are you justified in saving yourself? That was the question that faced the villagers of Eyam in *The Year of Wonders*. For David Carr's affluent family in *How to be Good*, their lives are not at stake. The issue is how much inconvenience and discomfort they ought to undergo in order to help a stranger in need.

In his book *Living High and Letting Die*,[3] the American philosopher Peter Unger presents an ingenious series of imaginary examples designed to show that the obligation to help those in need goes much further than we ordinarily think. Here's our paraphrase of one of these examples:

Bob is close to retirement. He has invested most of his savings in a very rare and valuable old car, a Bugatti, which he has not been able to insure. The Bugatti is his pride and joy. In addition to the pleasure he gets from driving and caring for his car, Bob knows that its rising market value means that he will always be able to sell it and live comfortably after retirement. One day when Bob is out for a drive, he parks the Bugatti near the end of a disused railway siding and goes for a walk up the track. As he does so, he sees that a runaway train, with no-one aboard, is running down the railway track. Looking further down the track he sees the small figure of a child playing in a tunnel and very likely to be killed by the runaway train. He can't stop the train and the child is too far away to warn of the danger, but he can throw a switch that will divert the train down the siding where his Bugatti is parked. Then nobody will be killed – but since the barrier at the end of the siding is in disrepair, the train will destroy his Bugatti. Thinking of his joy in owning the car, and the financial security it represents, Bob decides not to throw the switch. The child is killed, but for many years to come Bob enjoys owning his Bugatti and the financial security it represents.

Bob's conduct, most of us will immediately respond, was gravely wrong. Unger agrees. But then he reminds us that we too have opportunities to save the lives of children. We can give to organizations working to improve the lives of the world's poorest people. Unger estimates that a donation of $200 to an organization like

UNICEF or Oxfam International is probably enough to save the life of a child, even allowing for the cost of raising money, administrative expenses, and the cost of delivering aid where it is most needed. If this, or even something just roughly like it, is true, then our attitudes to Bob are at odds with our own behavior and that of other perfectly ordinary rich people who do not give significant amounts of their income to help those who are absolutely poor. Consider again Bob and his Bugatti. Is it possible to think that it was very wrong of Bob not to throw the switch that would have diverted the train and saved the child's life, but not wrong for rich people to fail to send very substantial amounts of money to help the poor?

If our obligations are as far-reaching as Unger suggests, we still have a problem in motivating people to act on them. The philosopher David Hume, ever the realist about human nature, observed that the breaking of a mirror at home concerns us more than the burning down of an entire house, if the house is sufficiently far away. He thought that we care for other human beings only when they are in some relationship to us, or have personal qualities that we admire. "Love of mankind," in general, he thought, was not an emotion that human beings have.[4] That view can serve as the background to the extracts in this section from *How to be Good*, and to Joyce Carol Oates' short story, "The Undesirable Table."

In addition to having obligations to individuals in need, it is popularly believed that we have a specific obligation to our country. We are asked to put aside our private concerns and think of the national interest. In wartime, young people are asked to risk their lives to serve their country – and some do it willingly, without coercion. It is easy to see why every nation would want to encourage patriotism. Perhaps we need to have a sense of belonging to a community, and patriotism makes us feel that we belong. In Euripides' play *Iphigeneia at Aulis*, Agamemnon represents this sense of belonging and its corresponding moral obligation, saying "It is *Greece* that compels me." E. M. Forster took the opposite standpoint when he wrote: "If I had to choose between betraying my country and betraying my friend, I hope I should have the guts to betray my country."[5] Given the devastation caused by "patriotic" wars, it is easy to sympathize with Forster. Some opponents of patriotism, however, would seek to replace it, not with narrower, more personal loyalties, but with a broader impartial concern for all of the world's peoples. Do I have a greater obligation to assist a fellow-citizen than I do to come to the aid of others who are beyond the borders of my country? If so, on what is that obligation based? Could our primary loyalty really be to humanity as a whole, rather than to my fellow-Americans, -French, -British, -Australians, or whatever else I may happen to be? Is it possible that the nation-state will eventually be replaced by a truly global community, and if that were to happen, would it be a good thing?

NOTES

1   Thomas Aquinas, *Summa Theologica*, II-II, Q 66 A 7, cited from A. P. d'Entreves (ed.), *Aquinas, Selected Political Writings* (tr. J. G. Dawson), Oxford: Blackwell, 1948, p. 171.
2   Luke 10:27–37.

3   Peter Unger, *Living High and Letting Die*, New York: Oxford University Press, 1996.

4   Both passages are from *A Treatise of Human Nature*, the first from Book II, Part 3, Sec. vii, and the second from Book III, Part 2, Sec. i.

5   E. M. Forster, "What I Believe," quoted from S. P. Rosenbaum (ed.), *A Bloomsbury Group Reader*, Oxford: Blackwell, 1993, p. 167.

35

EURIPIDES

Iphigeneia at Aulis

Paris has run off to Troy with Helen, the beautiful wife of Menelaos. The Greeks have assembled a fleet to sail to Troy to avenge this crime, but the fleet lies becalmed at Aulis. The goddess Artemis will provide wind only if Agamemnon, brother of Menelaos and leader of the Greek forces, sacrifices his daughter Iphigeneia.

Clytemnestra has brought Iphigeneia to Aulis, thinking her daughter is to be married to the warrior Achilles. As this scene opens, she has just discovered her husband's true purpose.

(IPHIGENEIA *enters from the left door, carrying* ORESTES. *With her free hand she covers her face with her robe.* CLYTEMNESTRA *too keeps her face turned from* AGAMEMNON.)

Here she is, obedient to your command.
For the rest,
I will answer for us both.
AGAMEMNON: Why are you crying, child? Aren't you still happy
to see me? Why are you holding your robe
in front of your eyes,
with your face turned to the ground?
CLYTEMNESTRA: I cannot think where
to start my bitter story,
for its beginning is grief,
its middle is grief,
its end
is grief.
AGAMEMNON: What is it? Why are all three of you
afraid to look at me?
CLYTEMNESTRA: My husband,
find the honesty of a man
and answer me with it.

EURIPIDES, pp. 73–9 and 85–6 from *Iphigeneia at Aulis* (tr. W. S. Merwin and George E. Dimock, Jr). New York: Oxford University Press, 1978. Copyright © 1992 by W. S. Merwin and George E. Dimock, Jr. Used by permission of Oxford University Press, Inc.

AGAMEMNON: There is no need for you to speak that way.
  Ask me your question.
CLYTEMNESTRA: Do you intend to kill your daughter?
AGAMEMNON: What a horrible thing to ask! What a vile suspicion!
CLYTEMNESTRA: Simply answer the question.
AGAMEMNON: Any reasonable question I would answer.
CLYTEMNESTRA: This question. This is the only one I care about.
AGAMEMNON: Oh immovable law of heaven! Oh my
  anguish, my relentless fate!
CLYTEMNESTRA: Yours? Mine. Hers. No relenting for any of us.
AGAMEMNON: How have you been wronged?
CLYTEMNESTRA: How can you ask? What a question
  for a man of sense!
AGAMEMNON (*to himself*): I am lost. Someone has betrayed me.
CLYTEMNESTRA: I know the whole story. I have found out
  what you mean to do to me.
  Your silence itself is a confession.
  So is your sighing. No need to waste words.
AGAMEMNON: Then I will say nothing. What good would it do
  to lie, and add shamelessness to my troubles?
CLYTEMNESTRA: Listen to me, then. I will use plain words, and not
  talk in riddles. In the first place
  you took me by force, you married me
  against my will.
  You killed the husband I had, Tantalos.
  You ripped from my breast
  my baby, still
  living, you smashed it on the ground.
  Then when my brothers, the sons
  of Zeus, on their shining horses,
  bore down on you bringing war,
  you came on your knees to my old father
  Tyndareos, and he saved you.
  So you got me for your wife, again.
  I came to love you. Admit
  that as your wife I have deserved no reproach.
  My demands in love have been modest. I have done
  what I could to increase your house
  so that you would be glad to come home, and you went out
  proud and at peace. It is not often
  that a man acquires a good wife.
  There is no end of the other kind. And I bore you
  this son, and three daughters, and now
  you have the cruelty
  to take one of these from me.
  And if anyone asks you

why you intend to kill her, what will you say?
Shall I answer for you? So that Menelaos
can have Helen back. Strange
bargain: you'll pay your child's life
as the price of a worthless woman.
We'll buy back our own harm
with what is most dear to us.
Now I want you to think of this. You'll sail
to the war, and I'll be left in the house.
You may be gone for years. There I'll be.
And with what heart, do you imagine, I will pass
my days in those halls, finding
all her places empty,
her girl's room empty of her forever, and
finding myself alone
with nothing but my tears and the endless
grieving at her fate: "My child,
it was your own father who killed you.
No one else. That was his hand,
no one else's. That was his reward for love.
And after that, he will come home again."
Then almost any occasion
would serve, for my other children and me
to give you the welcome you will have earned.
In the name of the gods, don't force me to turn
against you. Don't wrong me yourself.
As you kill our child what prayers will you be saying?
What blessing can you ask
as you have cut her throat? A bad voyage home,
since your setting out was the consequence of a crime?
And in justice, could I give you my blessing?
We would have to think the gods had no minds,
to pray for murderers.
And when you come back to Argos
will you kiss your children? It will be forbidden
by the gods. And which of the children
will dare even to look at you? They will be afraid
that you will kiss them only to kill them.
Did any of that ever cross your mind? Or do you
think of nothing but waving scepters
and leading armies? Would it not have been fair
to say to the Achaians, "Men of Argos,
you want to sail to Troy. Draw lots. Let us see
whose daughter will die." That way would have had
its justice. There is none
in your offering up your daughter

as a victim for the army. Or let Menelaos,
to whom it matters most, after all, cut his own
daughter's throat: Hermione's, for the sake
of her mother. But it is my own child
who is to be torn from me, when I have been
faithful to you,
while she who dishonored her husband's bed will find
her daughter safe at home, in Sparta,
and be happy. Now answer me,
tell me if one thing I've said is not true.
But if there is justice and truth
in what I say, do not kill your daughter and mine.
Turn back, be wise.
CHORUS: Do as she asks, Agamemnon.
It is good when people help each other,
to save children. Who can deny that?

(IPHIGENEIA *hands* ORESTES *to her mother, then kneels and clasps* AGAMEMNON'S *knees.*)

IPHIGENEIA: If I had the tongue of Orpheus, Father, whose song
could charm stones so that they followed after him,
if my words could persuade
whoever I wished to whatever I wished, I would use
all my arts now. But all that I know how to do
at this moment is cry. I offer you my tears.
I press against your knees
like a suppliant's torn branch, my body
which my mother bore you. Do not send me
into death before my time. It is sweet to see
the light. Do not make me look
at what is under the earth.
I was the first who called you father, the first
you called your child,
the first to climb on your knees, and we
held each other, we loved each other. You said,
"Will I see you living in your husband's house,
enjoying the happiness that is my daughter's right?"
And I answered, touching your beard, as I do now –
but now as the gesture
of a suppliant –, "And what will I do for you
then, Father? When you are old
will you come to live with me,
and let me nurse your age, in return
for what you have done for me?"
I remember what we said, but you have forgotten.

And now you want to kill me. Oh, in the name
of Pelops, of your father
Atreus, of my mother, suffering here
again as at my birth, do not let it happen.
What have I to do with Paris
and Helen,
and what they have done?
Why should Paris' coming to Argos mean that I
must die? Look at me. In my eyes. Kiss me,
so that at least I may remember that
when I am dying,
if you will not listen to what I say.

(AGAMEMNON *and* IPHIGENEIA *kiss*.) [. . .]

AGAMEMNON: I know when pity is due, and when it is not.
I love my children. Only the mad do not.
Wife, it is terrible to me
to bring myself to do this,
and terrible if I do not.
For I am forced to do it. (*to* IPHIGENEIA) Look: how many ships,
the war fleet, assembled here, the proud men of Greece
and their bronze battle-gear, and they
cannot sail to the towers
of Ilion, and seize
the famous citadel, Troy,
according to Kalchas the prophet, unless I
sacrifice you.
Some strange Aphrodite has crazed
the whole Greek army with a passion to sail at once
to the barbarians' own country
and end this piracy of Greek marriage.
If I disobey the goddess, if I ignore
the oracle, then the army will sail to Argos,
they will kill you and me, and your sisters
who are still at home. I have not become
Menelaos' creature. I am not guided by him.
It is *Greece* that compels me
to sacrifice you, whatever I wish.
We are in stronger hands than our own.
Greece must be free
if you and I can make her so. Being Greeks,
we must not be subject to barbarians,
we must not let them carry off our wives.

[. . .]

IPHIGENEIA: Mother, both of you, listen to me.
   I see now that you are wrong
   to be angry with your husband.
   It is hard to hold out against the inevitable. [. . .]
   Now mother, listen to the conclusion
   that I have reached. I have made up my mind to die.
   I want to come to it
   with glory, I want to have thrown off
   all weak and base thoughts. Mother,
   look at it with my eyes,
   and see how right I am.
   All the people, all the strength of Greece
   have turned to me. All those ships,
   whether they sail, whether Troy falls,
   depend on me. I will be the one
   to protect our women, in the future,
   if ever the barbarians dare to come near.
   When they have paid for the ruin
   of Helen, whom Paris carried away,
   they will never again be so bold as to ravish
   well-born wives out of Greece.
   All these good things I can win by dying.
   Because of me, Greece
   will be free, and my name will be blessed there.
   I must not cling to life too dearly.
   You brought me into the world for the sake
   of everyone in my country,
   and not just for your own.
   Thousands of men have slung shield on shoulder, thousands
   have taken hold of the oars
   when they saw their country wronged.
   And each of them will strike and, if need be, die
   for Greece. And shall my one life
   stand in the way of it all?
   What justice would there be in that? What answer
   could I make to those who are ready to die? [. . .]
   And if Artemis
   demands the offering of my body,
   I am a mortal: who am I
   to oppose the goddess? It is not to be
   considered. I give my life to Greece.
   Take me, kill me,
   and bring down Troy. That will be my monument
   for ages to come. That will be my wedding,
   my children, the meaning of my life.
   Mother, it is the Greeks

who must rule the barbarians,
not the barbarians the Greeks.
They are born to be slaves; we
to be free.
CHORUS: Young woman, what you have said is noble.
It is the role of destiny, in this,
and the role of the goddess,
that are sick.

36

GERALDINE BROOKS

Year of Wonders

Narrated by 18-year-old servant Anna Frith, *Year Of Wonders* tells of a village of lead miners and hill farmers during an outbreak of the plague. The story is based on events that took place in a real village, Eyam in Derbyshire, in 1665.

When the Plague hits London, the British monarchy has only recently been restored after the Civil War. Anna, a young widow with two small boys, is working for Colonel Bradford's family at the Hall. The Bradfords are the highest ranking family in the village. Anna is serving at a dinner at which Michael Mompellion, the local Minister, and his wife are among the guests. Mompellion is a member of the Church of England, which once again has become the established church after the restoration of the monarchy in 1660. Among the guests is a visiting Londoner whose news makes Anna fearful that George Viccars, the tailor who lodged with her before his sudden and recent death, may have brought the Plague to the village.

The Thunder of His Voice

At the Hall, I had learned to keep my mind on my duties and let the talk, which was mostly trivial, wash over me like the twittering of birds in a distant thicket. At that large table, little of the conversation was general. Most people exchanged empty pleasantries with those seated next to them, and the result was a low buzz of mingled voices, broken occasionally by Miss Bradford's affected, mirthless laugh. When I left the room with the meat platters, that was the state of things. But by the time I returned, carrying desserts, all the candles had been lit against the gathering dark and only the young Londoner next to Mrs Mompellion was speaking. He was a style of gentleman we did not much see in our small village, his periwig so large and elaborate that his rather pinched, white-powdered face seemed lost beneath its mass of tumbling curls. He wore a patch on his right cheek. I expect that whichever of the Bradfords' servants attended his toilet had been unfamiliar with how to affix such fashionable spots, for it flapped

GERALDINE BROOKS, "The Thunder of His Voice," "Venom in the Blood," and "Wide Green Prison," pp. 59–63 and 101–13 from *Year of Wonders*. London: Fourth Estate, 2001. Copyright © 2001 by Geraldine Brooks. Used by permission of Viking Penguin, a division of Penguin Group (USA) Inc. and HarperCollins Publishers Ltd.

distractingly as the young man chewed his food. I had thought him rather absurd on first glimpse, but now he looked grave, and as he spoke, his hands fluttered from lace cuffs like white moths, throwing long shadows across the table. The faces turned towards him were pale and alarmed.

"You have never seen anything like it on the roads. Innumerable men on horseback, wagons, and carts bulging with baggage. I tell you, everyone capable of leaving the city is doing so or plans to do it. The poor meantimes are pitching up tents out on Hampstead Heath. One walks, if one must walk, in the very centre of the roadway to avoid the contagion seeping from dwellings. Those who must move through the poorer parishes cover their faces in herb-stuffed masks contrived like the beaks of great birds. People go through the streets like drunkards, weaving from this side to that so as to avoid passing too close to any other pedestrian. And yet one cannot take a hackney, for the last person inside may have breathed contagion." He dropped his voice then and looked all around, seeming to enjoy the attention his words were garnering. "They say you can hear the screams of the dying, locked up all alone in the houses marked with the red crosses. The Great Orbs are all on the move, I tell you: there is talk that the king plans to remove his court to Oxford. For myself, I saw no reason to tarry. The city is emptying so fast that there is little worthwhile society to be had. One rarely sees a wigg'd gallant or a powdered lady, for wealth and connection are no shield against Plague."

The word dropped like an anvil among the tinkling silverware. The bright room dimmed for me as if someone had snuffed every candle all at once. I clutched the platter I carried so that I would not drop it and stood stock-still until I was sure of my balance. I gathered myself and tried to steady my breath. I had seen enough people carried off by illness in my life. There are many fevers that can kill a man other than the Plague. And George Viccars hadn't been near London in more than a year. So how could he have been touched by the city's pestilence?

Colonel Bradford cleared his throat. "Come now, Robert! Do not alarm the ladies. The next thing they will be shunning your company for fear of infection!"

"Do not joke, sir, for on the turnpike north of London, I encountered an angry mob, brandishing hoes and pitchforks, denying entry to their village inn to any who were travelling from London. It was a low place, in any wise, nowhere I would have sought shelter even on the filthiest of nights, so I rode onwards unmolested. But before long, to be a Londoner will not be a credential worth owning to. It will be surprising how many of us will invent rusticated histories for ourselves, mind me well. You'll soon learn that my chief abode these last years was Wetwang, not Westminster."

There was a little stir at this, for the town the young man was mocking was a good deal bigger than the one in which he was presently being entertained. "Well, good thing you got out, eh?" said the colonel, to cover the lapse. "Clean air up here, no putrid fevers."

Down the table, I noticed the Mompellions exchanging meaning looks. Trying to still my shaking hands, I set down the dessert I carried and stepped back into the shadows against the wall. "It's hard to believe," the young man continued, "but some few are staying in town who have the easy means to go. Lord Radisson – I believe you are acquainted with his lordship – has been bruiting it about that he feels it his duty to stay and 'set an example.' Example of what? A wretched death, I warrant."

"Think of what you are saying," Mr Mompellion interrupted. His voice – rich, loud, grave – cut off the Bradfords' airy laughter. Colonel Bradford turned to him with a raised eyebrow, as if to censure rudeness. Mrs Bradford tried to turn her titter to a cough. Mr Mompellion continued, "If all who have the means run each time this disease appears, then the seeds of the Plague will go with them and be sown far and wide throughout the land until the clean places are infected and the contagion is magnified a thousandfold. If God saw fit to send this scourge, I believe it would be His will that one face it where one was, with courage, and thus contain its evil."

"Oh?" said the colonel superciliously. "And if God sends a lion to rip your flesh, will you stand steadfastly then, too? I think not. I think you will run from the danger, as any sensible man would."

"Your analogy is excellent, sir," said Mr Mompellion; his voice had the commanding timbre that he used in the pulpit. "Let us explore it. For I will certainly stand and face the lion if, by running, I would cause the beast to follow me, and thus draw him closer to the dwelling places of innocents who demand my protection."

At the mention of innocents, Jamie's little face flashed before me. What if the young Londoner were correct? Jamie had lived in George Viccars's pocket. All that day before the illness first rose in him, Jamie had been climbing on his back, prancing by his side.

The young man broke into the silence that greeted Mr Mompellion's speech. "Well, sir, very bravely stated. But I must tell you that those who know this disease best – and that would be the physicians and the barber-surgeons – have been the fleetest of foot in leaving town. One cannot get cupped for a cough or bled for the gout, no matter if you have a sovereign to give in fee. Which leads me to conclude that the physicians have written us a clear prescription, and that is this: the best physick against the Plague is to run far away from it. And I, for one, intend to follow that prescription religiously."

"You say 'religiously,' but I think your choice of word is poor," said Mr Mompellion. "For if one speaks 'religiously,' then one must recall that God has the power to keep you safe in peril, or to bring peril to overtake you, no matter how far or fast you run."

"Indeed, sir. And many who believed that now are rotting corpses passing through the streets in cartloads, on their way to the great pits." Miss Bradford raised a hand to her brow, ostentatiously feigning a faintness that her avid eyes belied. The young man turned to her, reading her desire for morbid detail, and continued, "I have had it from one whose man had need to go there in fruitless search of a kinsman. He reported that the corpses are tipped in, afforded no more respect than one would give a dead dog. A layer of bodies, a few spades of soil, and then more bodies tumbled in atop. They lie there so, just like yonder dessert." He pointed at the layered cake, which I had set down upon the table. I saw the Mompellions wince, but the young man smirked at his own wit and then turned pointedly towards the rector.

"And do you know who were the fastest to follow the physicians out of the city, sir? Why, it were the Anglican ministers, just such as yourself. There's many a London pulpit being filled by a nonconformist on account of it."

Michael Mompellion looked down then and studied his hands. "If what you say is true, sir, then I am indeed sorry for it. I will say that if it be the case, then my brothers in faith are the lesser men." He sighed then and looked at his wife. "Perhaps they might believe that God now is preaching to the city, and what needs add their small utterance to the thunder of His voice?"

The Plague has come to the village, apparently in some cloth that had been sent to the tailor, and several villagers have died from it. On Sunday, all those who are still alive and well have gathered, as usual, in the church to hear Mr Mompellion preach. Mr Thomas Stanley, the dissenting Pastor of the town in Oliver Cromwell's reign, had to resign as he could not accept the tenets of the Church of England. Normally Stanley would not attend church, but this week Mompellion has asked him to come.

Venom in the Blood

M r Mompellion climbed the pulpit steps, and instead of the frown that had creased his brow all week, his face that morning looked serene. And so he launched into the sermon that sealed our fates, and yet he was more than halfway into it before anyone in the church realized where he was leading us.

"'Greater love no man hath than this, that he lay down his life for a friend.'" He said the familiar words and then dropped his head, letting the fragment of text hover in a silence so lengthy that I worried he had forgot what next he purposed to say. But when he looked up, his face was alight and wreathed in such a smile that the church felt suddenly warmer. His words flowed then, cadenced as a poem. He spoke with passion about God's love and the sufferings His son had endured for our sake, and he held every single one of us in his gaze, making us feel the power of that love and reminding us of how it had fallen, in our time, upon each of us. He intoxicated us with his words, lifting and carrying us away into a strange ecstasy, taking each of us to that place where we kept our sweetest memories.

And then, finally, he approached his point. Were we not bound to return this love to our fellow humans? Even to lay down our own lives, if that was what God asked of us? He had not, until then, mentioned the Plague, and I realized with a surprise that for the half hour he'd been speaking, I had not thought of it, who had thought of nothing else in many weeks.

"Dear brothers and sisters," he said then, his voice bathing us in affection, "we know that God sometimes has spoken to His people in a terrible voice, by visiting dread things upon them. And of these things, Plague – this venom in the blood – is one of the most terrible. Who would not fear it? Its boils and its blains and its great carbuncles. Grim Death, the King of Terrors, that marches at its heels.

"Yet God in His infinite and unknowable wisdom has singled us out, alone amongst all the villages in our shire, to receive this Plague. It is a trial for us, I am sure of it. Because of His great love for us, He is giving us here an opportunity that

He offers to very few upon this Earth. Here, we poor souls of this village may emulate Our Blessed Lord. Who amongst us would not seize such a chance? Dear friends, I believe we must accept this gift. It is a casket of gold! Let us plunge in our hands to the elbows and carry away these riches!"

He dropped his voice then, as if to let us in on a great secret. "There are some who would say that God sends us this thing not in love, but in rage. They will say Plague is here because we have earned it in our sinning. For is not the first Plague in all of human history the one that God sent to smite Egypt? Did not Pharaoh disobey God, and was his mighty kingdom not laid waste for it? And in the dark of night, when our firstborn is snatched from us" – here, he paused, his gaze moving across the many pews between us until his eyes, bright and glistening, looked straight into mine – "at such a time, it is easier to believe in God's vengeance than His mercy.

"But I do not think God sends us this Plague in anger. I do not think we here in this village are Pharaoh in His eyes. Oh, yes, surely we have sinned in our lives, each one of us, and many times. Do we not find Satan like a lapwing crying before us with enticement and vainglory, to draw our mind far away from the God of our salvation? Friends, all of us, in our time, have listened to the false music of those cries. There is none here who has not followed them – and fallen. None whose mind has not been tossed with corrupt fancies.

"But I think our God does not send this Plague as a punishment for our sins. No!" His eyes travelled across the congregation, searching our the miners and their families, and addressing himself to them, particularly. "Like the ore that must be melted all to liquid to find the pure metal, so must we be rendered in the fiery furnace of this disease. And as the smith tends his furnace, all through the night if need be, to secure the valuable ore within, so is God here, near to us, nearer perhaps than He has ever come, or ever will come, in all our lives." Five pews in front of me, I saw the white head of Alun Houghton, Barmester to our miners, coming slowly erect on his massive shoulders as the rector's words penetrated his understanding. The rector seized the moment and stretched out his hand towards him. "Therefore, let us not flinch, let us not fail! Let us choose *not* the dull lustre of our base state when God would have us shine!"

"Amen!" Houghton's gravelly voice rumbled. A scattering of "Amens" followed from the other miners.

The rector turned his eyes then to where the Hancocks, the Merrills, the Highfields, and the other farming families sat. "My friends, the plough that now runs deep in your furrows did not always do so. You know that many backs broke to wrest that soil from clutching root and stubborn stump; you know that hands bled, dragging forth the rocks that sit arrayed now as the fences that mark out worked land from wilderness. Good yield does not come without suffering, it does not come without struggle, and toil, and, yes, loss. Each one of you has cried for the crop blighted by drought or pest. Cried, as you did what you knew you must, and ploughed each plant under, so that the soil could be renewed in the hope of the better season coming. Cry now, my friends, but hope, also! For a better season will follow this time of Plague, if only we trust in God to perform His wonders!"

He looked down then and wiped his hand across his brow. The church was utterly still. We were all of us entirely concentrated on the pulpit and the tall man who stood there, his head bent as if gathering the strength to go on.

"Friends," he said at last, "some of us have the means to flee. Some of us have relatives nearby who would gladly shelter us. Others have connections upon whom we could prevail. Some few of us have means to go far from here – anywhere we choose."

My concentration broke as the Bradfords shifted in the foremost pew. "But how would we repay the kindness of those who received us, if we carried the seeds of the Plague to them? What burden would we bear if, because of us, hundreds die who might have lived? No! Let us accept this Cross. Let us carry it in God's Holy Name!" The rector's voice had been gaining in power till it rang like a bell. But now he dropped back into a tone of intimacy, like a lover addressing his beloved. "Dear friends, here we are, and here we *must* stay. Let the boundaries of this village become our whole world. Let none enter and none leave while this Plague lasts."

He turned then to the material particulars of his scheme for our voluntary besiegement, to which it seemed he had already given much thought. He said he had written to the earl at Chatsworth House not so many miles distant, setting out his proposal and asking aid. The earl had undertaken that if we sealed ourselves off he would provision us all from his own purse with our basic needs in food, fuel, and medicines. These would be left at the Boundary Stone at the southeastern edge of the village, to be collected only when the carters who had carried them were well clear. Those who wished to purchase other items would leave payment either in a shallow, spring-fed well to the north of Wright's Wood, where the flow of the water would carry away any Plague seeds, or in holes gouged into the Boundary Stone that would be kept filled with vinegar, which was said to kill contagion.

"Beloved, remember the words of the Prophet Isaiah: 'In returning and rest you shall be saved; in quietness and trust shall be your strength.'" He paused and repeated the phrase: "In quietness and trust," letting the words sink to a whisper, and from the whisper into silence. "In quietness and trust . . . Is that not how we should all wish to be?" Yes, we nodded, of course it was. But then, his voice came back, ringing into the very silence he had created. "But the Israelites did *not* trust, they were *not* quiet. Isaiah tells us this. He says: "And you would not, but you said: No! We will speed upon horses . . . we will ride upon swift steeds . . . A thousand shall flee at the threat of one, at the threat of five you shall flee, till you are left like a flag staff on the top of a mountain, like a signal on a hill." Well, my beloved, I say we shall not flee like the faithless Israelites! No, not at the threat of five, or of ten, or even of a score of deaths. For loneliness awaits those who flee. Loneliness – like a flag staff on a mountain. Loneliness and shunning. The shunning that has ever been the leper's lot. Loneliness, shunning, and fear. Fear will be your only faithful companion, and it will be with you day and night.

"Beloved, I hear you in your hearts, saying that we already fear. We fear this disease and the death it brings. But you will not leave this fear behind you. It will travel with you wheresoever you fly. And on your way, it will gather to itself a host of greater fears. For if you sicken in a stranger's house, they may turn you out, they may abandon you, they may lock you up to die in dreadful solitude. You will thirst, and none shall quench you. You will cry out, and your cries will fade into empty air. For in that stranger's house, all you will receive is blame. For surely they will blame you, for bringing this thing to them. And they will blame you justly! And they will heap their hatred upon you, in the hour when your greatest need is love!"

The voice eased now, and soothed: "Stay here, in the place that you know, and in the place where you are known. Stay here, upon that piece of Earth whose golden grain and gleaming ore has ever nourished you. Stay here, and here we will be for one another. Stay here, and the Lord's love will be here for us. Stay here, my dearest friends. And I promise you this: while I am spared no one in this village will face their death alone."

He advised us then to reflect and pray and said that shortly he would ask us for our decision. He came down from the pulpit and went amongst us with Elinor beside him, radiant and kindly, speaking quietly to any who would have words with him. Some families stayed in their pews, their heads bent in prayerful reflection. Others rose and wandered restlessly, forming into clusters here and there, seeking advice from friends and loved ones. It was only then that I noticed that Thomas Stanley had entered the church and taken a place in the very last pew. Now, he came forward, speaking softly to all those who had been, or secretly still were, of a precisian leaning and who perhaps had difficulty in trusting Mr Mompellion. Quietly, the old man was making clear his full support of the younger.

Sometimes, from amidst the hushed hum of discussion, a voice rose excitedly, and I saw to my shame that my father and Aphra were among a small group whose gestures and head-shakes indicated that they did not agree with the rector's scheme. Mr Mompellion moved towards these unconvinced, and before long, Mr Stanley joined them. My father and his wife had drawn a little away, and I came near to them to try to overhear what it was they were saying to each other.

"Think of our bread, husband! If we take to the road, who will feed us? Like as not, we will starve there. Here, he says we will have it surely."

"Aye, 'he says.' Well, *I* say that you cannot eat 'he says.' Fine words make piss-poor fodder. Oh, aye, I'm sure he and his lady wife will get their bread from his friend the earl, but when have the likes of them ever given a ha'penny for the likes of us?"

"Husband, where are your wits? It's nowt love of us will keep them to their word, but love of their own fine skins. It's a surety that the earl wants his estate kept free from Plague, and how better to do that than give us cause to bide here? A few penneth-worth of bread each day would look like a good bargain to him, I'll be bound." She was a shrewd woman, my stepmother, in spite of all her superstitious fancies.

She saw me then and seemed about to beckon me over to help her plead her case. But I wanted no part of responsibility for any person's decision other than my own, and I turned my face away.

When the Mompellions came to where I stood, Elinor Mompellion held out both her hands and took mine tenderly as the rector spoke to me. "And you,

Anna?" he said. The intensity of his gaze was such that I had to look away from him. "Tell us you will stay with us, for without you, Mrs Mompellion and I would be ill set. Indeed, I do not know what we would do without you." There was no turmoil within me, for I had made my decision. Still, I could not command my voice to give him a reply. When I nodded, Elinor Mompellion embraced me and held me to her for a long moment. The rector moved on, whispering quietly to Mary Hadfield, who was weeping and wringing her hands most piteously. By the time he mounted the steps again and faced us, he and Mr Stanley between them had shored up every doubter. All of us in the church that day gave their oath to God that we would stay, and not flee, whatever might befall us.

All of us, that is, except the Bradfords. They had slipped out of the church unnoticed and were already at the Hall, packing for their flight to Oxfordshire.

Wide Green Prison

I left the church that morning borne aloft by a strange bliss. It seemed we all partook of it: the faces that had been so gaunt and careworn now seemed warm and alive, and we smiled as we caught one another's eyes, aware of the common grace our decision had brought upon us. And so I was not prepared for the harried look of Maggie Cantwell, pacing by my gate. Maggie was the Bradfords' cook, and as a consequence of her employment had not been in church that morning. She still had on the large white pinafore she wore in the kitchen of Bradford Hall, and her big ruddy face was puce with exertion. A bundle of belongings lay in the snow at her feet.

"Anna, they have turned me off! Eighteen years, and ordered out on a second's notice!" Maggie had family in Bakewell, but whether she would go to them, or if they would receive her, I did not know. Still, I wondered that she had come to me for shelter, for my house and the Hadfields' and the Sydells' were notorious now as the Plague cottages. I motioned her to come inside, but she shook her head. "Thank you, Anna, and I mean no disrespect. But I am afraid to venture into your cottage, and I know you will understand me. I have come to ask your help to gather my few poor possessions from the Hall, for the Bradfords mean to leave this hour, and they have told us all that after their departure the Hall will be locked and guarded and none of us may enter in it. Only think, it has been our home, too, for all these years, and now they put us out without a roof or a way to earn our bread!" She had been nervously wringing a corner of her pinafore in her fleshy hands, and now she raised it to her cheek to catch her tears.

"Come, Maggie, we don't have time for this now," I said. "Your goods will be safe here. I will fetch a handcart and we will go directly for the rest of your things." And so we set off, Maggie, who was above forty years old and very stout from the enjoyment of her own fine cooking, labouring for breath as we toiled through the snowdrifts back up the hill to the Hall.

"Think of it, Anna," she panted. "There I was, basting the joint for the Sunday dinner, when they all storm in from church, early like, and I'm thinking, Ooh, there'll be what for if the meal's not on the table when the colonel looks for it, and

I'm rushing meself and worrying at Brand, me pantry boy, when in comes the colonel hisself, who, I don't have to tell *you*, I'm sure, never set foot in the kitchen until this very day, and it's turned off, we all are, just like that, and no thank you or how'll ye do, just put the food on the table and clear out."

While still far from the Hall, it was possible to perceive the uproar underway there. This was no stealthy retreat. The Hall hummed like a struck hive. Horses stamped in the drive as maids and footmen staggered in and out, bent under the weight of boxes. We entered through the kitchen and could hear the scurrying feet above us, punctuated by the high, imperious voices of the Bradford ladies giving their commands. Not particularly wanting to be noticed by the Bradfords, I crept behind Maggie up the narrow backstairs to the attic she shared with the maidservants. The little room had a steeply sloping roof and a high, square window through which the cold snowlight poured. There were three cots crammed in the tiny space, and by one of them crouched a pale, wide-eyed girl named Jenny, who was breathing hard, trying to tie her spare smock and few small possessions into a bundle and fumbling the knot in her hurry.

"Lordy, Cook, she says we are to be out of here this hour, yet she gives us no time to tend to our own going. I'm off my feet fetching and carting her things, and no sooner have I packed a sash than she says, no, take it out, this one rather. They are taking none of us, not even Mrs Bradford's maid, Jane, who you know has been with her since a girl. Jane cried and begged her, but she just shook her head and said no, that she and all of us have been too much about the village and might already have Plague in us, so they just mean to leave us here to die, and in the streets, for none of us has a place to go to!"

"No one is going to die, and certainly not in the streets," I said as calmly as I could. Maggie had a small oak coffer wedged tight beneath her bed, but her girth was such that she couldn't bend down low enough to get it. I dragged at it while she folded the quilt her sister had made for her. Such, with the small sack of clothing she'd left on my step, was the sum of her life's goods. With a little care, we managed to work the coffer down the narrow stairs, she taking most of the weight while I steered from above as best I could. In the kitchen, she paused, as I thought, for breath. But then I saw that her eyes were filling again. She ran her big red hands over the scored and scorched deal table. "My life, this is," she said. "I know every mark on this and how it came there. I know the heft of every blessed knife in here. And now I'm to turn me back and walk away with nothing." Her head drooped and a tear hung suspended on her fleshy cheek for a moment, then splashed onto the table.

Just then, there was a commotion from the courtyard. I glanced out the kitchen door in time to see Michael Mompellion pulling up Anteros in a scatter of stones. He was off the horse and upon the steps before the startled groom had gathered up his dropped reins. He did not wait to be announced.

"Colonel Bradford!" His voice in the entrance hall was so loud that all the clatter quieted at once. The dust sheets were already upon the large furnishings in the Hall. I crept behind the bulk of a shrouded settle, and from the cover of a fold of sheet I could see the colonel appear at the door to his library. He had a volume he'd evidently been considering for packing in one hand and a letter in the other.

Miss Bradford and her mother appeared at the top of the stairs, hesitating there, as if unsure of the etiquette of this encounter.

"Rector Mompellion?" said the colonel. He kept his voice low, in deliberate contrast to the rector's, and affected a quizzical tone. "You should not have troubled yourself to ride here to fare us well, so hard and in such haste. I had planned to make my adieus to you and your fair wife in this letter."

He extended his hand with the letter. Mompellion took it absently but didn't look at it. "I do not want your good-byes. I am here to urge you to reconsider your departure. Your family is first here. The villagers look to you. If you quail, how may I ask them to be brave?"

"I do *not* quail!" the colonel replied coldly. "I am merely doing what any man of means and sense must do: safeguarding what is mine."

Mompellion took a step towards him, his broad hands outstretched. "But think of those you are putting at risk . . ."

The colonel stepped back, keeping his distance from the rector. His voice became a slow, soft drawl, as if to mock the urgency of the rector's. "I believe, sir, that we have had this conversation, here in this very Hall, albeit then in a hypothetical context. Well, now the hypothesis is proven, and I mean to do as I said I would. I said then, and I say now, that my life and the lives of my family are of more consequence to me than some possible risk to strangers."

The rector was not to be gainsaid. He moved towards the colonel and clutched him by the arm. "Well, if the plight of strangers cannot move you, think of the good you might yet do here, among the villagers that know you and look to you. There will be much to be managed in this time of peril. Your courage has long been celebrated. Why not add a new chapter? You have led men to war. You have the skills to command all of us through this crisis. I do not have such skills. Furthermore, I am a newcomer to this place; I do not know these people as you and your family know them, who have been here for many generations. I could learn much from your counsel as to how best go on as events unfold here. And while I am pledged to do my utmost to bring these people comfort, from you and your wife, and from Miss Bradford, the smallest gesture would mean so much more."

On the landing, Elizabeth Bradford stifled a snort. Her father glanced up at her, his eyes sharing her amusement. "How flattering!" he exclaimed with a sneer. "Really, you do us too much honour. Dear sir, I did not raise my daughter to have her play wet nurse to a rabble. And if I desired to succour the afflicted I would have joined you in Holy Orders."

Mompellion dropped the colonel's arm as if he had just become aware that he had picked up something foul. "One does not have to be a priest to be a man!" he cried.

37

IAN MCEWAN

Enduring Love

Enduring Love, published in 1997, is narrated by science writer Joe Rose. In this opening chapter of the novel Rose is reunited, after six weeks apart, with his wife, the
Keats scholar Clarissa Mellon. They have been on a country walk and are beginning
their picnic when Joe responds to a cry for help.

The beginning is simple to mark. We were in sunlight under a turkey oak,
partly protected from a strong, gusty wind. I was kneeling on the grass
with a corkscrew in my hand, and Clarissa was passing me the bottle – a
1987 Daumas Gassac. This was the moment, this was the pinprick on the time
map: I was stretching out my hand, and as the cool neck and the black foil
touched my palm, we heard a man's shout. We turned to look across the field and
saw the danger. Next thing, I was running towards it. The transformation was
absolute: I don't recall dropping the corkscrew, or getting to my feet, or making a
decision, or hearing the caution Clarissa called after me. What idiocy, to be racing
into this story and its labyrinths, sprinting away from our happiness among the
fresh spring grasses by the oak. There was the shout again, and a child's cry,
enfeebled by the wind that roared in the tall trees along the hedgerows. I ran
faster. And there, suddenly, from different points around the field, four other men
were converging on the scene, running like me.

I see us from three hundred feet up, through the eyes of the buzzard we had
watched earlier, soaring, circling and dipping in the tumult of currents: five men
running silently towards the centre of a hundred-acre field. I approached from the
south-east, with the wind at my back. About two hundred yards to my left two
men ran side by side. They were farm labourers who had been repairing the fence
along the field's southern edge where it skirts the road. The same distance beyond
them was the motorist, John Logan, whose car was banked on the grass verge with
its door, or doors, wide open. Knowing what I know now, it's odd to evoke the

IAN MCEWAN, pp. 1–3 and 7–16 from *Enduring Love*. London: Vintage, 1998. First published by Jonathan
Cape, 1997. Copyright © 1997 by Ian McEwan. Used by permission of Doubleday, a division of
Random House, Inc.; Random House Group Ltd; and Alfred A. Knopf Canada.

figure of Jed Parry directly ahead of me, emerging from a line of beeches on the far side of the field a quarter of a mile away, running into the wind. To the buzzard Parry and I were tiny forms, our white shirts brilliant against the green, rushing towards each other like lovers, innocent of the grief this entanglement would bring. The encounter that would unhinge us was minutes away, its enormity disguised from us not only by the barrier of time but by the colossus in the centre of the field that drew us in with the power of a terrible ratio that set fabulous magnitude against the puny human distress at its base.

What was Clarissa doing? She said she walked quickly towards the centre of the field. I don't know how she resisted the urge to run. By the time it happened – the event I am about to describe, the fall – she had almost caught us up and was well placed as an observer, unencumbered by participation, by the ropes and the shouting, and by our fatal lack of co-operation. What I describe is shaped by what Clarissa saw too, by what we told each other in the time of obsessive re-examination that followed: the aftermath, an appropriate term for what happened in a field waiting for its early summer mowing. The aftermath, the second crop, the growth promoted by that first cut in May.

I'm holding back, delaying the information. I'm lingering in the prior moment because it was a time when other outcomes were still possible; the convergence of six figures in a flat green space has a comforting geometry from the buzzard's perspective, the knowable, limited plane of the snooker table. The initial conditions, the force and the direction of the force, define all the consequent pathways, all the angles of collision and return, and the glow of the overhead light bathes the field, the baize and all its moving bodies, in reassuring clarity. I think that while we were still converging, before we made contact, we were in a state of mathematical grace. I linger on our dispositions, the relative distances and the compass point – because as far as these occurrences were concerned, this was the last time I understood anything clearly at all.

What were we running towards? I don't think any of us would ever know fully. But superficially the answer was, a balloon. Not the nominal space that encloses a cartoon character's speech or thought, or, by analogy, the kind that's driven by mere hot air. It was an enormous balloon filled with helium, that elemental gas forged from hydrogen in the nuclear furnace of the stars, first step along the way in the generation of multiplicity and variety of matter in the universe, including our selves and all our thoughts.

We were running towards a catastrophe, which itself was a kind of furnace in whose heat identities and fates would buckle into new shapes. At the base of the balloon was a basket in which there was a boy, and by the basket, clinging to a rope, was a man in need of help.

[. . .]

We stopped to watch the buzzard as we were approaching Maidensgrove. The balloon may have re-crossed our path while we were in the woods that cover the valleys around the nature reserve. By the early afternoon we were on the Ridgeway Path, walking north along the line of the escarpment, Then we struck out along one of those broad fingers of land that project westwards from the Chilterns into the rich farmland below. Across the Vale of Oxford we could make out the outlines of the Cotswold Hills and beyond them, perhaps, the Brecon Beacons rising in a faint blue mass. Our plan had been to picnic right out on the end where the view was best, but the wind was too strong by now. We went back across the field and sheltered among the oaks along the northern side. And it was because of these trees that we did not see the balloon's descent. Later I wondered why it had not been blown miles away. Later still I discovered that the wind at five hundred feet was not the same that day as the wind at ground level.

The Keats conversation faded as we unpacked our lunch. Clarissa pulled the bottle from the bag and held it by its base as she offered it to me. As I have said, the neck touched my palm as we heard the shout. It was a baritone, on a rising note of fear. It marked the beginning and, of course, an end. At that moment a chapter, no, a whole stage of my life closed. Had I known, and had there been a spare second or two, I might have allowed myself a little nostalgia. We were seven years into a childless marriage of love. Clarissa Mellon was also in love with another man, but with his two hundredth birthday coming up he was little trouble. In fact he helped in the combative exchanges which were part of our equilibrium, our way of talking about work. We lived in an art deco apartment block in north London with a below average share of worries – a money shortage for a year or so, an unsubstantiated cancer scare, the divorces and illnesses of friends, Clarissa's irritation with my occasional and manic bouts of dissatisfaction with my kind of work – but there was nothing that threatened our free and intimate existence.

What we saw when we stood from our picnic was this: a huge grey balloon, the size of a house, the shape of a tear drop, had come down in the field. The pilot must have been half way out of the passenger basket as it touched the ground. His leg had become entangled in a rope that was attached to an anchor. Now, as the wind gusted, and pushed and lifted the balloon towards the escarpment, he was being half dragged, half carried across the field. In the basket was a child, a boy of about ten. In a sudden lull, the man was on his feet, clutching at the basket, or at the boy. Then there was another gust, and the pilot was on his back, bumping over the rough ground, trying to dig his feet in for purchase, or lunging for the anchor behind him in order to secure it in the earth. Even if he had been able, he would not have dared disentangle himself from the anchor rope. He needed his weight to keep the balloon on the ground, and the wind could have snatched the rope from his hands.

As I ran I heard him shouting at the boy, urging him to leap clear of the basket. But the boy was tossed from one side to another as the balloon lurched across the field. He regained his balance and got a leg over the edge of the basket. The balloon rose and fell, thumping into a hummock, and the boy dropped backwards out of sight. Then he was up again, arms stretched out towards the man and shouting something in return – words or inarticulate fear, I couldn't tell.

I must have been a hundred yards away when the situation came under control. The wind had dropped, the man was on his feet, bending over the anchor as he drove it into the ground. He had unlooped the rope from his leg. For some reason, complacency, exhaustion or simply because he was doing what he was told, the boy remained where he was. The towering balloon wavered and tilted and tugged, but the beast was tamed. I slowed my pace, though I did not stop. As the man straightened, he saw us – or at least the farm workers and me – and he waved us on. He still needed help, but I was glad to slow to a brisk walk. The farm labourers were also walking now. One of them was coughing loudly. But the man with the car, John Logan, knew something we didn't and kept on running. As for Jed Parry, my view of him was blocked by the balloon that lay between us.

The wind renewed its rage in the treetops just before I felt its force on my back. Then it struck the balloon which ceased its innocent comical wagging and was suddenly stilled. Its only motion was a shimmer of strain that rippled out across its ridged surface as the contained energy accumulated. It broke free, the anchor flew up in a spray of dirt, and balloon and basket rose ten feet in the air. The boy was thrown back, out of sight. The pilot had the rope in his hands and was lifted two feet clear off the ground. If Logan had not reached him and taken hold of one of the many dangling lines the balloon would have carried the boy away. Instead, both men were now being pulled across the field, and the farm workers and I were running again.

I got there before them. When I took a rope the basket was above head height. The boy inside it was screaming. Despite the wind, I caught the smell of urine. Jed Parry was on a rope seconds after me, and the two farm workers, Joseph Lacey and Toby Greene, caught hold just after him. Greene was having a coughing fit, but he kept his grip. The pilot was shouting instructions at us, but too frantically, and no one was listening. He had been struggling too long, and now he was exhausted and emotionally out of control. With five of us on the lines the balloon was secured. We simply had to keep steady on our feet and pull hand over hand to bring the basket down, and this, despite whatever the pilot was shouting, was what we began to do.

By this time we were standing on the escarpment. The ground dropped away sharply at a gradient of about twenty-five per cent, and then levelled out into a gentle slope towards the bottom. In winter this is a favourite tobogganing spot for local kids. We were all talking at once. Two of us, myself and the motorist, wanted to walk the balloon away from the edge. Someone thought the priority was to get the boy out. Someone else was calling for the balloon to be pulled down so that we could anchor it firmly. I saw no contradiction, for we could be pulling the balloon down as we moved back into the field. But the second opinion was prevailing. The pilot had a fourth idea, but no one knew or cared what it was.

I should make something clear. There may have been a vague communality of purpose, but we were never a team. There was no chance, no time. Coincidences of time and place, a predisposition to help had brought us together under the balloon. No one was in charge – or everyone was, and we were in a shouting match. The pilot, red-faced, bawling and sweating, we ignored. Incompetence came off him like heat. But we were beginning to bawl our own instructions too. I know that if I had been uncontested leader the tragedy would not have happened. Later I heard some of the others say the same thing about themselves. But there was not time, no opportunity for force of character to show. Any leader, any firm plan would have been preferable to none. No human society, from the

hunter-gatherer to the post-industrial, has come to the attention of anthropologists that did not have its leaders and the led; and no emergency was ever dealt
with effectively by democratic process.

It was not so difficult to bring the passenger basket down low enough for us to
see inside. We had a new problem. The boy was curled up on the floor. His arms
covered his face and he was gripping his hair tightly. "What's his name?" we said
to the red-faced man.

"Harry."

"Harry!" we shouted. "Come on Harry. Harry! Take my hand, Harry. Get out of
there Harry!"

But Harry curled up tighter. He flinched each time we said his name. Our words
were like stones thrown down at his body. He was in paralysis of will, a state
known as learned helplessness, often noted in laboratory animals subjected to
unusual stress; all impulses to problem-solving disappear, all instinct for survival
drains away. We pulled the basket down to the ground and managed to keep it
there, and we were just leaning in to try and lift the boy out when the pilot
shouldered us aside and attempted to climb in. He said later that he told us what
he was trying to do. We heard nothing but our own shouting and swearing. What
he was doing seemed ridiculous, but his intentions, it turned out, were completely
sensible. He wanted to deflate the balloon by pulling a cord that was tangled in
the basket.

"Yer great pillock!" Lacey shouted. "Help us reach the lad out."

I heard what was coming two seconds before it reached us. It was as though an
express train were traversing the treetops, hurtling towards us. An airy, whining,
whooshing sound grew to full volume in half a second. At the inquest the Met
office figures for wind speeds that day were part of the evidence, and there were
some gusts, it was said, of seventy miles an hour. This must have been one, but
before I let it reach us, let me freeze the frame – there's a security in stillness – to
describe our circle.

To my right the ground dropped away. Immediately to my left was John Logan,
a family doctor from Oxford, forty-two years old, married to a historian, with two
children. He was not the youngest of our group, but he was the fittest. He played
tennis to county level, and belonged to a mountaineering club. He had done a
stint with a mountain rescue team in the Western Highlands. Logan was a mild,
reticent man apparently, otherwise he might have been able to force himself use-
fully on us as a leader. To his left was Joseph Lacey, sixty-three, farm labourer, odd
job man, captain of his local bowls team. He lived with his wife in Watlington, a
small town at the foot of the escarpment. On his left was his mate, Toby Greene,
fifty-eight, also a farm labourer, unmarried, living with his mother at Russell's
Water. Both men worked for the Stonor estate. Greene was the one with the
smoker's cough. Next around the circle, trying to get into the basket, was the
pilot, James Gadd, fifty-five, an executive in a small advertising company, who
lived in Reading with his wife and one of their grown-up children who was
mentally handicapped. At the inquest Gadd was found to have breached half a
dozen basic safety procedures which the coroner listed tonelessly. Gadd's balloon-
ing licence was withdrawn. The boy in the basket was Harry Gadd, his grandson,

ten years old, from Camberwell, London. Facing me, with the ground sloping away to his left, was Jed Parry. He was twenty-eight, unemployed, living on an inheritance in Hampstead.

This was the crew. As far as we were concerned, the pilot had abdicated his authority. We were breathless, excited, determined on our separate plans, while the boy was beyond participating in his own survival. He lay in a heap, blocking out the world with his forearms. Lacey, Greene and I were attempting to fish him out, and now Gadd was climbing over the top of us. Logan and Parry were calling out their own suggestions. Gadd had placed one foot by his grandson's head, and Greene was cussing him when it happened. A mighty fist socked the balloon in two rapid blows, one-two, the second more vicious than the first. And the first was vicious. It jerked Gadd right out of the basket on to the ground, and it lifted the balloon five feet or so, straight into the air. Gadd's considerable weight was removed from the equation. The rope ran through my grip, scorching my palms, but I managed to keep hold, with two feet of line spare. The others kept hold too. The basket was right above our heads now, and we stood with arms upraised like Sunday bell ringers. Into our amazed silence, before the shouting could resume, the second punch came and knocked the balloon up and westwards. Suddenly we were treading the air with all our weight in the grip of our fists.

Those one or two ungrounded seconds occupy as much space in memory as might a long journey up an uncharted river. My first impulse was to hang on in order to keep the balloon weighted down. The child was incapable, and was about to be borne away. Two miles to the west were high-voltage power lines. A child alone and needing help. It was my duty to hang on, and I thought we would all do the same.

Almost simultaneous with the desire to stay on the rope and save the boy, barely a neuronal pulse later, came other thoughts in which fear and instant calculations of logarithmic complexity were fused. We were rising, and the ground was dropping away as the balloon was pushed westwards. I knew I had to get my legs and feet locked round the rope. But the end of the line barely reached below my waist and my grip was slipping. My legs flailed in the empty air. Every fraction of a second that passed increased the drop, and the point must come when to let go would be impossible or fatal. And compared to me Harry was safe curled up in the basket. The balloon might well come down safely at the bottom of the hill. And perhaps my impulse to hang on was nothing more than a continuation of what I had been attempting moments before, simply a failure to adjust quickly.

And again, less than one adrenally incensed heartbeat later, another variable was added to the equation: someone let go, and the balloon and its hangers-on lurched upwards another several feet.

I didn't know, nor have I ever discovered, who let go first. I'm not prepared to accept that it was me. But everyone claims not to have been first. What is certain is that if we had not broken ranks, our collective weight would have brought the balloon to earth a quarter of the way down the slope a few seconds later as the gust subsided. But as I've said, there was no team, there was no plan, no agreement to be broken. No failure. So can we accept that it was right, every man for himself? Were we all happy afterwards that this was a reasonable course? We never had that comfort, for there was a deeper covenant, ancient and automatic, written in our nature. Co-operation – the basis of our earliest hunting successes, the force behind our evolving capacity for language, the glue of our social cohesion. Our misery in the aftermath was proof that we knew we had failed ourselves. But letting go was in our nature too. Selfishness is also written on our hearts. This is our mammalian conflict – what to give to the others, and what to keep for yourself. Treading that line, keeping the others in check, and being kept in check by them, is what we call morality. Hanging a few feet above the Chilterns escarpment, our crew enacted morality's ancient, irresolvable dilemma: us, or me.

Someone said *me*, and then there was nothing to be gained by saying *us*. Mostly, we are good when it makes sense. A good society is one that makes sense of being good. Suddenly, hanging there below the basket, we were a bad society, we were disintegrating. Suddenly the sensible choice was to look out for yourself. The child was not my child, and I was not going to die for it. The moment I glimpsed a body fall away – but whose? – and I felt the balloon lurch upwards, the matter was settled; altruism had no place. Being good made no sense. I let go and fell, I reckon, about twelve feet. I landed heavily on my side and got away with a bruised thigh. Around me – before or after, I'm not so sure – bodies were thumping to the ground. Jed Parry was unhurt. Toby Greene broke his ankle. Joseph Lacey, the oldest, who had done his National Service with a paratroop regiment, did no more than wind himself.

By the time I got to my feet the balloon was fifty yards away, and one man was still dangling by his rope. In John Logan, husband, father, doctor and mountain rescue worker, the flame of altruism must have burned a little stronger. It didn't need much. When four of us let go, the balloon, with six hundred pounds shed, must have surged upwards. A delay of one second would have been enough to close his options. When I stood up and saw him, he was a hundred feet up, and rising, just where the ground itself was falling. He wasn't struggling, he wasn't kicking or trying to claw his way up. He hung perfectly still along the line of the rope, all his energies concentrated in his weakening grip. He was already a tiny figure, almost black against the sky. There was no sight of the boy. The balloon and its basket lifted away and westwards, and the smaller Logan became, the more terrible it was, so terrible it was funny, it was a stunt, a joke, a cartoon, and a frightened laugh heaved out of my chest. For this was preposterous, the kind of thing that happened to Bugs Bunny, or Tom, or Jerry, and for an instant, I thought it wasn't true, and that only I could see right through the joke, and that my utter disbelief would set reality straight and see Dr Logan safely to the ground.

I don't know whether the others were standing, or sprawling. Toby Greene was probably doubled up over his ankle. But I do remember the silence into which I laughed. No exclamations, no shouted instructions as before. Mute helplessness. He was two hundred yards away now, and perhaps three hundred feet above the ground. Our silence was a kind of acceptance, a death warrant. Or it was horrified shame, because the wind had dropped, and barely stirred against our backs. He had been on the rope so long that I began to think he might stay there until the balloon drifted down, or the boy came to his senses and found the valve that released the gas, or until some beam, or god, or some other impossible cartoon thing came and gathered him up. Even as I had that hope we saw him slip down right to the end of the rope. And still he hung there. For two seconds, three, four. And then he let go. Even then, there was a fraction of time when he barely fell, and I still thought there was a chance that a freak physical law, a furious thermal, some phenomenon no more astonishing than the one we were witnessing would intervene and bear him up. We watched him drop. You could see the acceleration. No forgiveness, no special dispensation for flesh, or bravery, or kindness. Only ruthless gravity. And from somewhere, perhaps from him, perhaps from some indifferent crow, a thin squawk cut through the stilled air. He fell as he had hung, a stiff little black stick. I've never seen such a terrible thing as that falling man.

38

NICK HORNBY

How to be Good

Katie Carr is a doctor living in an affluent London suburb with her two children and her cynical newspaper columnist husband David. Suddenly everything changes. Under the influence of a healer named GoodNews, David becomes a born-again do-gooder. In the extracts below David and GoodNews set in train their project for homeless youth.

They're serious; I realize that straight away. Plans are already sufficiently advanced that they have drawn up a list of the houses in the street, with as much information about the inhabitants therein as David possesses. Neither of them take any notice of me as I walk into the kitchen, so I stand behind David and listen and read over his shoulder. The list looks like this:

1. Not known.
3. Not known.
5. Not known.
7. Old lady. (Old man also? No difference, if sharing bed)
9. Not known
11. Richard, Mary, Daniel, Chloe
13. Nice Asian family. (4?)
15. Not known
17. Not known
19. Wendy and Ed
21. Martina
23. Hugh
25. Simon and Richard
27. Not-nice Asian family (6? + Alsatian)
29. Ros and Max
31. Annie and Pete + 2

NICK HORNBY, pp. 111–16 and 142–51 from *How to be Good*. London: Penguin, 2001. First published by Viking 2000. Copyright © 2001 by Nick Hornby. Used by permission of Riverhead Books, an imprint of Penguin Group (USA) and Penguin Books Ltd.

33. Roger and Mel + 3
35. For sale

And the same for the other side of the street. For a moment, I am distracted by
the obvious pattern of our acquaintance – we know who lives next to us, and
opposite us, but we know almost nothing of the people who live sixty or seventy
yards away – until the sheer lunacy of the conversation draws me back into the
room.

"By my reckoning there are at least forty spare bedrooms in this street,"
David is saying. "Isn't that incredible? Forty spare bedrooms, and thousands of
people out there without a bed? I'd never even thought of it in that way before.
I mean, when I see empty houses it pisses me off, but empty houses aren't
really the issue, are they? If there are forty spare bedrooms in this street, then
our postcode alone should be able to take care of most of the homeless kids out
there."

"We should be aiming at filling, say, ten of them," says GoodNews. "I'd be
happy with ten."

"Really?" David looks a little disappointed, as if persuading only ten of his
neighbours to house someone they didn't know was the sort of terrible compromise he wasn't prepared to make. This, then, is what we have come to: the spiritual
healer who can't get along with dishwashers is now the hard-nosed realist in my
house, and my husband is the wide-eyed optimist. "Wouldn't ten mean, I don't
know, that we'd lost the argument? 'Cos it's pretty unanswerable, surely, if we
pitch it right."

"Some people just won't get it," says GoodNews.

"Some people might need the spare rooms for other things," I say.

"Like what?" David asks, slightly aggressively. He used to use exactly these
tones when he wanted to challenge me in the old days – about why I wanted to
teach the kids about other forms of religion, say (he didn't want them to know
about any), or why I wanted to go and hear Maya Angelou read ("What, you're a
black feminist now?"). I had forgotten how wearing these tones were.

"You used to work in one of ours, for example."

"OK, so five out of the forty are used as offices."

"And what about if people have their parents to stay?"

"God, you're literal-minded."

"What's literal-minded about saying that people have parents?"

"It's not that. It's the spirit. You have none."

"Thank you."

"None of these things are real problems. You're just being negative."

"You have no idea about these people's lives. You don't even know their names."
I gesture at the paper in front of them. "But you're happy to tell me what's a real
problem for them and what isn't. What gives you the right?"

"What gives them the right to own half-empty houses when there are all these
people out there in cardboard boxes?"

"What gives them the right? Their bloody mortgages, that's what gives them the
right. These are their homes, David. And it's not like they're enormous homes,

either. Why don't you pick on Bill Gates? Or Tom Cruise? How many spare bedrooms have they got?"

"If they lived around the corner, I would pick on them. But they don't. And we don't need them, because there's plenty of room for everyone right here. You're just frightened of the embarrassment."

"That's not true." But it is, of course, completely true. I am terrified of the embarrassment, of which there will be lorryloads. I can hear the diesel engines rumbling towards us even as we speak. "How do you plan to go about this, anyway?"

"I don't know. Door-to-door."

"What about a party?" says GoodNews brightly. "We'll have a party here, and you can speak to everyone, and . . . and it'll be great."

"Brilliant," says David, with the air of someone who knows he's in the presence of genius.

"Brilliant," I say, with the air of someone who wants to put her head in the oven. But that sort of air doesn't interest them in the slightest.

OK: so they're wrong, clearly. And also completely mad. It's just that I can't quite work out why. What is the difference between offering spare bedrooms to evacuees in 1940 and offering spare bedrooms to the homeless in 2000? You might point out that the evacuees were in mortal danger; David and GoodNews would point out that the street kids have a lower life expectancy than the rest of us. You might argue that in 1940 the nation was united in its desire to look after its own; they would say that it is precisely this spirit we need now, for similar reasons. You could laugh at them, and say they were pious and sanctimonious, holy fools, moral blackmailers, zealots; they would tell you that they don't care what you think of them, that there is a greater good at stake. And do we have a moral right to keep a spare bedroom as a junk room, or a music room, or for overnight guests who never come, when it is February and freezing and wet and there are people on the pavements? Why isn't a standing order with Shelter enough? And what if my husband, or GoodNews, or both of them, turned out to be Jesus, or Gandhi, or Bob Geldof? What if the country had been crying out for this kind of energy, and they revolutionized the way we thought about private property, and homelessness was never again a problem in London, or Britain, or the Western World? What about my embarrassment then?

I no longer have the answers to any of these questions. All I know is that I don't want this party, and I don't want to put my neighbours through this, and I wish David and GoodNews were interested in starting up an Internet company so that they could make millions of pounds to spend on Page Three girls and swimming pools and cocaine and designer suits. People would understand that. That wouldn't upset the neighbours.

David and GoodNews tell the kids about the party the next morning at breakfast. Molly is curious; Tom sits at the table playing on his Gameboy and eating his cereal in between lives, apparently uninterested. I sit between the two of them while the men lean side-by-side with their backs to the work surface, answering questions. It is impossible not to notice how the dynamic in this household has changed, how my place now is with the children. And I don't mean that in the maternal sense, either; rather, I am reminded of going to large family parties when I was fourteen or fifteen, when there was always confusion as to whether I should sit with my younger cousins or with my aunts and uncles at mealtimes.

"Are we going to get a homeless person to stay, too?" Molly asks.

"Of course," says David.

"Haven't we got ours already?" I say, with meaningful looks at all the relevant parties.

"So who else will get one?"

"Anyone who wants one," says David, and his reply makes me snort with laughter. *Anyone who wants one* . . . It's Christmas, and this year everyone wants a homeless person, just as a couple of years ago everyone wanted a Buzz Lightyear. But at the homeless shop they never go out of stock.

"Would you like to tell us what's so funny, Katie?"

That's what he says, I swear. And he even sounds like a teacher: stern, vaguely distracted, following a script that was written a hundred years ago.

"That's not the line," I say. I suddenly feel that, as I am the oldest child, it is incumbent on me to be the naughtiest. 'The line is, 'Would you like to share the joke with the whole class?'"

"What are you talking about?"

"I get it," says Tom. "Don't you get it, Dad? You're the teacher and Mum's being naughty."

"Don't be silly."

"It's true," says Tom. "That's what you sound like."

"Well, I'm very sorry. I don't mean to. Anyway. Is everybody happy about this?"

"I've got a question." Sitting at the table with the kids, and being told off like a kid, has liberated me; my disenfranchisement has empowered me.

"Yes, Katie."

"What happens if a homeless person moves into a neighbour's house and cleans them out?" It takes a child to say the unsayable.

"What do you mean?"

"I mean . . . well, that. What if we assist in moving a thief into our neighbour's house? Someone who's broke and desperate with a drug habit?"

"You're stereotyping the homeless, Katie. I'm really not sure that's the right way to go."

"I appreciate what I'm doing, David. It's just, you know . . . The stereotype of a football fan is someone who gets drunk and breaks bottles over people's heads. And I know it's a stereotype, and I know lots of people who go to Arsenal who aren't like that. Just . . . There might actually be one or two who are. And I'm not sure I'd like to tell Ros and Max that they have to live with them."

"I just don't think this conversation is very helpful."

"Have you even thought about it?"

"Of course not."

"Right. Are you going to think about it?"

"No."

"Why not?"

"Because I want to change the way people think. And I can't change the way people think if I think like everybody else, can I? I want to believe the best of everybody. Otherwise what's the point?"

There are many, many answers to that last rhetorical question, but I can't bring myself to utter any of them. I shake my head, and get up from the table, and go to work, so that I can become an adult again.

[. . .]

The room fills up. Richard from *The Bill* arrives, and I forbid Molly to talk to him. The Asian family from next-door-but-one arrives, and GoodNews attempts to engage them in a debate about Eastern mysticism. I am chatted up by the seedy-looking builder from number 17 whose wife is in bed with flu. My brother Mark turns up, looking baffled. David must have invited him, because I didn't. I have no idea whether Mark is supposed to be a recipient or a donor of the expected largesse: he's right on the dividing line.

"What's going on?" he asks me.

"I don't know," I say.

"Who are these people?"

"I don't know."

He wanders off.

Remarkably, the party has started to resemble a party: people are laughing, talking, drinking, and the doorbell keeps ringing, and before long there is no more space in the living room, and people have spilled over into the kitchen. After a couple of glasses of wine, I even begin to feel a little sentimental. You know – here we all are, black, white, gay, straight, a microcosm of swinging, multicultural, multisexual London, eating cheese straws and talking about traffic schemes and mortgages, and getting on and isn't this great? And then David stands on a chair and bangs a saucepan with a wooden spoon, and I am woken from my little reverie.

"Good evening, everyone," says David.

"Good evening," shouts Mike, the seedy-looking builder, who, as luck would have it, is A Character.

"When our invitation dropped through your letterbox, you probably thought to yourself, 'What's the catch? Why is this guy who I don't know from Adam inviting us to a party?'"

"I'm only here for the beer," shouts Mike.

"Well, it is Double Diamond," shouts somebody else.

"No it isn't," Mike shouts back. The two shouters are convulsed for what seems like several minutes.

"I'd love to tell you that there isn't a catch, but there is. A big catch. Because tonight I'm going to ask you to change people's lives, and maybe change your own life, too."

"Backs to the wall!" shouts Mike. You don't have to be a psychoanalyst to worry about someone who thinks that changing one's own life probably has something to do with homosexuality.

"How many of you have got a spare bedroom?" David asks.

"Yes, thank you," Mike shouts. "It's where I sleep when the missus won't have me in with her."

"So that's one," says David. "Any more?"

Most people choose to examine either their wine glasses or their feet.

"Don't be shy," David says. "I'm not going to ask you to do anything you don't want to do. All I know is that this street is full of three-storey houses, and there must be quite a few empty rooms somewhere, because you haven't all got two-point-four children."

"What about if you live in a flat?" asks a young guy in a leather jacket.

"Is it a one-bedroom flat?"

"Yes."

"Well, you haven't got a spare bedroom."

"Can I go home, then?"

"You can go home any time you want. This is a party, not a detention centre."

"Could have fooled me," shouts Mike. His partner in comedy, the man who made the Double Diamond witticism, has come to stand by him, and offers him his hand for a high-five.

"I'm sorry to hear you're not enjoying yourself." For a moment I think I catch a glimpse of the old David, visible like old paint through the new undercoat: there's a sarcasm in there that only I would be able to hear. The old taste for verbal confrontation is peeking out, too, because he doesn't say anything else: he's waiting for Mike's follow-up, his next crack, and Mike hasn't got one, because in the end he's merely a bit of a twit, someone who would shout out daft things at any sort of gathering with alcohol, be it a wedding or a christening or a save-the-world party such as this, and he wants to push things so far but no further, and now David is calling his bluff.

"Aren't you having a very nice time?"

"No, you're all right," says Mike, deflated.

"Because *Eastenders* probably starts in a minute." And that gets a laugh – not a huge one, but bigger than anything Mike has managed so far.

"I don't watch *Eastenders*," says Mike. "I don't watch any soaps, actually." This gets the biggest laugh so far, but they're laughing at him, at the banality of the riposte, and the laughter clearly stings him a little bit.

"So you're staying?"

"I'll finish my drink, anyway."

"Glad to hear it."

Another chuckle, and now they're on his side. David has put down a heckler, and I feel obscurely, perhaps nostalgically proud. Now I come to think of it, heckler downputting would have been the perfect job for the old David. He had just the right combination of belligerence and quickwittedness. He'd have made a terrible stand-up, because he mumbles quite a lot, and loses the thread, in an unamusing, bumbling way, and anyway the objects of his derision were always obscure and complicated (theatre curtains, small tubs of ice-cream, etc.). But maybe if he'd teamed up with a comedian, he could have been brought on at crucial moments, like an anaesthetist. Maybe that was his calling. (And is that the nicest thing I can find to say about his talent? That it is perfectly suited to quelling verbal insurrection at alcoholic gatherings? This is hardly the mark of a polymath. Hardly the mark of someone lovable, either.)

He pauses, to let the mood change.

"Now, where was I? Oh yeah. Spare bedrooms. See, I don't know about you, but I turn on the TV, or I pick up a paper, and something terrible's happening in Kosovo or Uganda or Ethiopia, and sometimes I call a number and I give a tenner, and it changes nothing. The terrible thing continues to happen. And I feel guilty and powerless, and I continue to feel guilty and powerless when I go out later, to the pictures or for a curry or to the pub . . ."

The pub! The pub! Which "pub" would that be, David? The "local"? The Patronizing Bastard?

". . . And maybe I'm feeling guilty and powerless enough to keep it going, this feeling of wanting to do something, and there's this kid sitting by the cashpoint with a blanket and a dog, and I give him fifty pence, and that changes nothing either, because next time I go to the cashpoint he's still sitting there, and my fifty pence has done nothing. Well, of course it's done nothing, because it's fifty pence, and if I give him ten fifty pences, well, that'll do nothing either, because that's five quid. And I hate him sitting there. I think we all do. If you think about it for ten seconds, you can sort of guess just how horrible it would be, sleeping in the cold, begging for change, getting rained on, people coming up and abusing you . . ."

I look around. He's doing OK, apart from the pub bit. People are listening, and one or two are nodding, but you couldn't say that the light of conversion was shining in their eyes. He needs to pull something out of the bag, before he loses them.

Luckily, someone does it for him.

"I don't believe this," says Mike. "They're all arseholes, these people."

"Which people?"

"These bloody homeless people. And they're loaded, half of them. Loads of money."

"Ah," says David. "Loads of money. Which is why they sit on the pavement begging?"

"That's how they get it, isn't it? And then they blow it on drugs. I've been looking for bricklayers for six months, and have I heard from any of that lot? Course I haven't. They don't want to work."

There are a couple of snorts, one or two tuts, a great deal of head-shaking and exchanged glances followed by raised eyebrows. Mike is surrounded by gay actors, Health Service professionals, teachers, psychoanalysts, people whose hearts bleed right through their Gap T-shirts, and even if, in the middle of the night, they catch themselves thinking that the homeless only have themselves to blame and they all take drugs and have bank balances bigger than ours, they would never ever say so out loud, during waking hours, and especially not at a party. Mike has misjudged his audience, and in doing so, he changes the dynamic in the room. Two minutes ago, David was talking to a lot of bemused faces; no one here wished him any ill, but neither were they willing to pledge a substantial part of their house to his cause. Now, it's different. Whose side are they on? Are they going to line up with the forces of right-wing darkness, i.e., Mike? Or are they on the side of the (slightly eccentric, possibly misguided, but angelic nonetheless) angels? Hurrah for angels! the psychoanalysts cry. Down with the right-wing forces of darkness! shout the gay actors. Not that there's any actual shouting, of course. They're too restrained for that. But Mike certainly has a little more floor space than he did. People have shuffled away from him, as if he were about to launch into some fancy dance routine.

"If that's how you feel, then you wouldn't be interested in what I've got to say."

"No. I'm not. But I'm still finishing my drink."

"You're welcome to finish your drink. But could I ask you to keep your views to yourself? I'm not sure whether anyone here is very interested in them."

"That's 'cos they're a lot of stuck-up ponces."

Mike's floor space expands a little further. He could do a breakdancing routine now without landing on anyone's head. Even the other half of his comedy duo has moved away from him. Mike has called David the thing that most people in this room fear being called; after all, we want to fit in, become part of the neighbourhood. We want Mike to be one of us, and we want Mike to want us to be his neighbours. It is true that he probably paid a few hundred pounds for his house back in the late sixties, when nobody like us wanted to live here, and some of us paid a quarter of a million pounds for our houses a couple of years ago. (Not David and I, though! We paid a hundred thousand for our house ten years ago!) But does that make us ponces? After all, Mike's house is worth a quarter of a million, too, now. But of course that's not the point. The point is that we are the sort of people who can afford to pay a quarter of a million for a house (or rather, we are the sort of people to whom banks will lend a quarter of a million for a house); which makes us the sort of people who give money to beggars (and no wonder, if we are mad enough to pay a quarter of a million for a house); and then there's the pub at the end of the road, which once upon a time Mike might have drunk in, but which has now changed hands and clientele and serves Spanish sausages on a bed of something-or-other for ten pounds, and isn't really a pub at all, and let's face it, the ponces are responsible for that, as well as for other things, like the corner shop becoming an organic delicatessen . . . Golly, do we have a lot to answer for.

So Mike's exit (he bangs down his drink on the mantelpiece and storms out) is both a blessing and a defeat, because even though we all feel guilty about the homeless, we also feel guilty that we have failed to accommodate Mike, that he no longer feels a part of his own neighbourhood, and maybe this double guilt helps David, too, because there is now so much collective guilt in the room that the ponces are just dying to compensate somehow. They want to do something gritty and difficult just to prove that they are not ponces, that they are good, thoughtful people who are unafraid of difficulty. If David wanted people to give up their homes at this precise second, a couple of them might do so; a bedroom – pah! Nothing!

And David detects this mood, and storms through the rest of his speech, while GoodNews stands beside him with a self-satisfied beam on his face. Do these people want to be like Mike? Do they want to do something better than anything they have ever done in their lives? Because David doesn't care what we're doing now: however caring our job is, however much we give to charity, nothing is going to make as much difference to individuals as this. Six months without the use of a spare bedroom could literally save a life, because with a home and a permanent address and somewhere to shave and shower, then these kids can apply for jobs, and then they can earn, and with a wage comes self-respect, and the ability to build a life without this kind of intervention . . .

"I'm forty-one years old," says David, "and I have spent half my life regretting that I missed the sixties. I read about the energy, and I imagine what the music would have sounded like when you hadn't heard it a thousand times before, and when it actually meant something, and I've always been sad that the world is different now. I got a bit excited about Live Aid, but then you realize that these problems . . . They're too big now. They're never going to go away. We can't change the world, but we can change our street, and maybe if we can change our street, then other people will want to change theirs. We have hand-picked ten kids who are living rough and who need some help. They're good kids. They're not winos or junkies or thieves or lunatics; they're people whose lives have gone badly wrong through no fault of their own. Maybe their stepfather has thrown them out, maybe someone died on them and they couldn't cope . . . But we can vouch for them. If I can find ten spare bedrooms for these kids I'd feel that it was the greatest thing I'd ever done."

"Are you having one?" someone asks.

"Of course," says David. "How could I ask you to do this if I wasn't prepared to?"

"Can I ask where we'll be putting him or her?" This from the lady at the back, who already supports two children, a spiritual guru and a husband who has lost the will to work.

"We'll sort it out when everyone's gone," says David. "Does anyone want to talk more about this?"

Four people put their hands up.

"Four's no good to me. I need more."

One more hand, then nothing.

"OK. Half now, half later."

Weirdly, the whole room breaks into a spontaneous round of applause, and I feel as though I might cry the sort of tears that come at the end of soppy films.

GoodNews and David take the Famous Five into his study (a study that, presumably, is about to be converted into a bedroom) while the rest of us watch. It's like that bit in a church wedding where the bride and groom and a few others shuffle off round the corner to sign the register, and the congregation beam at them, without knowing quite what else to do. (Is there singing at that point? Maybe. Maybe we should sing now – *You've Got a Friend*, or *You'll Never Walk Alone*, something where the secular just starts to rub against the spiritual.)

Famous Five – the wholesome group of children with their dog who were always having intrepid adventures in a series written by Enid Blyton, the prolific children's author

For the record, the five volunteers are:

1. Simon and Richard, the gay couple at number 25.

2. Jude and Robert, a couple in their late thirties, who someone once told me were unable to have kids, and were trying to adopt, without much success. They're at number 6.

(So, for those of you who have a need to understand why anyone should wish to do what these people are doing, a theme begins to emerge . . .)

3. Ros and Max, diagonally opposite us at number 29. Don't know anything about them, because they've recently moved into the street, apart from 1) they have a daughter of Molly's age and 2) just before David turned, he said he'd seen Ros on the bus reading his column and laughing, so perhaps her willingness to offer up a bedroom is some kind of penance.

4. Wendy and Ed, an older couple at number 19. They've always stopped to talk when we've been out with the kids; I don't know much about them either, other than that they are both enormous and their children no longer live with them.

5. (Terrifying, this one) Martina, an old (properly old, seventy plus), frail Eastern European lady who lives on her own at number 21. Her grasp of English has always struck me as being remarkably weak for someone who has lived here for forty years, so heaven knows what she thinks she's volunteered for; we'll probably be given a large cake tomorrow, and she'll be baffled and horrified when someone with dreadlocks knocks on her door in a week's time.

A woman I've never seen before in my life comes up to me. "You must be very proud of him," she says. I smile politely, and say nothing.

We don't get to bed until after midnight, but David's much too hyper to sleep.
"Is five any good, do you think?"
"It's amazing," I tell him, and I mean it, because I had anticipated nobody, nothing, a dismal and humiliating failure and the end of the story.
"Really?"
"Did you honestly think you could get ten people to volunteer?"
"I didn't know. All I can say is that when I was going through it in my head, I couldn't think of any arguments against it."
That's it. That's the whole David/GoodNews thing, right there: "I couldn't think of any arguments against it." My problem exactly. I want to destroy David's whole save-the-world-and-love-everyone campaign, but I want to do it using his logic and philosophy and language, not the language of some moaning, spoiled, smug, couldn't-care-less, survival-of-the-fittest tabloid newspaper columnist. And of course

it's not possible, because David's fluent in his language, and I'm a beginner. It's as if I'm trying to argue with Plato in Greek.

"What arguments are there?" he says. "I mean, these people are . . ."

"I know, I know. You don't have to argue with me. But that's not the point, is it?"

"Isn't it?"

"There are never any arguments against anything you want to do. People are hungry, give them food if you've got it. Kids have nothing to play with, give them toys if you've got too many. I can never think of anything to say to you. But that doesn't mean I agree with you."

"But it has to."

"That isn't how the world works."

"Why not? OK, I know why not. Because people are selfish and scared and . . . and brainwashed into thinking that they have no alternatives. But they have. They have."

And what am I supposed to say now? That people have a right to be selfish if they want to? That they don't have any alternatives? And what's the Greek for "Please shut up and leave me alone"?

39

JOYCE CAROL OATES

The Undesirable Table

With mumbled apologies, the maître d' seated us at an undesirable table in our favorite restaurant Le Coq d'Or. The men in our party protested. But there was nothing to be done. It was a Saturday night in the holiday season, the more desirable tables had been booked weeks in advance. Our reservation had been made practically at the last minute, what could we expect? Even though we were – are – frequent patrons of Le Coq d'Or, and had imagined ourselves on special terms with the management.

As we took our seats, reluctantly, at the undesirable table, in a front bay window of the dining room, one of our party remarked, bemused, yet serious, that perhaps the maître d' had expected a twenty-dollar bill to be slipped surreptitiously to him. Was *that* it?

Seated at the undesirable table, in a front bay window of the dining room of Le Coq d'Or, we discussed this possibility in lowered, incensed voices. We are highly verbal people and much of dispute in our lives is resolved, if not satisfied, by speech. The more cynical among our party believed that yes, this might be so; though, in the past, and we'd dined in this restaurant innumerable times, the maître d' had not behaved like an extortionist. The more optimistic among our party believed that, no, that wasn't it, at all; surely not; our reservation had been made late, just the day before, the holiday season was frenzied this year, it *was* a Saturday night. And so why not enjoy ourselves? As we'd come out to do?

Even if it was something of a disappointment, and a rude surprise in a way, to be seated at an undesirable table in Le Coq d'Or.

And so, seated at the undesirable table, in a front bay window of the dining room of Le Coq d'Or, with an unwanted view of the street outside, we gave our drink orders to the waiter; we smiled gamely, and took up our hefty Le Coq d'Or menus (parchment-bound, gilt-printed, gold-tasseled, with elegantly scripted French, and English translations below) and perused the familiar categories of appetizers, first courses, entrees, desserts, wines. We chattered to one another discussing the

Joyce Carol Oates, "The Undesirable Table," pp. 213–18 from Joyce Carol Oates, *Will You Always Love Me? and Other Stories*. Princeton, NJ: E. P. Dutton, 1996. Copyright © 1996 by the Ontario Review, Inc. Reprinted by permission of Joyce Carol Oates.

dishes we might order, recalling previous meals at Le Coq d'Or, previous evenings
in one another's company that had been both intellectually stimulating and emotionally rewarding, evenings that had had *meaning* of a kind, precious to consider.
For food consumed in the presence of dear friends is not mere food but sustenance;
a sustenance of the soul. A formal meal, with excellent wines, in a restaurant of the
quality of Le Coq d'Or, in the right company, is a celebration. Yes?

So it was, we smiled gamely. We chattered happily. We were not to be cheated
of our evening's pleasure – for most of us, a well-deserved reward for the rigors of
the previous week – by the accident of being seated at an undesirable table. We
gave our orders to the waiter, who was all courtesy and attentiveness. We handed
back our hefty menus. When our drinks arrived, we lifted them to drink with
pleasure and relief. We were almost successfully ignoring two facts: that the
undesirable table in the bay window of the dining room was even more undesirable than the most pessimistic of us had anticipated; and that those of us unfortunate enough to be seated facing the bay window were particularly afflicted. Yet
such was our courtesy with one another, even after years of friendship, and so
awkward was the situation, that no one, not even those facing the bay window and
the street, chose to speak of it. For to *name* a problem is *to invest it with too much
significance*.

We, who are so highly verbal, whose lives, it might be said, are ingeniously
amassed cities of words, understand the danger as few others do. Ah, yes!

There followed then, with much animation, a discussion of wines – in which
several of our company, male, participated with great gusto and expertise, while
others listened with varying degrees of attentiveness and indulgence. Which
wines, of the many wines of Le Coq d'Or's excellent list, were to be ordered? –
considering that the party was to dine variously on seafood, fish, poultry, and
meat. Our conversations about wine are always lengthy and passionate, and touched
with a heartfelt urgency; even pedantry; yet there is an undercurrent of bemused
self-consciousness, too – for the wine connoisseurs are well aware of the absurdity
of their almost mystical fanaticism even as they unapologetically indulge in it.
After all, if there is a simple, direct, unalloyed ecstasy to be taken by the mouth,
savored by the tongue like a liquid communion wafer, how can it be denied to
those with the means to purchase it? – and by whom?

So, the usual spirited talk of wine among our party. And some argument. Where
there is passion there *is* argument. Not that the wine connoisseurs dominated
completely, despite their loud voices. Conversation became more general, there
were parenthetical asides, the usual warm queries of health? recent trips? family?
work? gossip of mutual acquaintances, colleagues? If there was a distracting scene
outside the window, on the street (which was in fact an avenue, broad, windy,
littered, eerily lit by streetlamps whose light seemed to withhold, not give, illum-
ination) or even on the sidewalk a few yards away from those of our company
with our backs stolidly to the window *we knew nothing of it: saw nothing*.

At last, our appetizers were brought to us. And the first of the wines. The
ceremonial uncorking, the tasting – exquisite!

Red caviar, and arugula salads. Giant shrimp delicately marinated. Pâté maison.
Escargots. Coquilles St Jacques. Consommé à la Barigoule. Steak tartare. And of

course the thick crusty brown bread that is a specialty of Le Coq d'Or. As we talked now of politics. Foreign, national, state, local. We talked of religion – is there any *demonstrable difference* between the actions of "believers" and "nonbelievers"? We asked after our friends' children in the hope and expectation that they would ask after ours.

(One of our party, her gaze drawn repeatedly to something outside the window, which, facing it as she was, at this undesirable table in the dining room of Le Coq d'Or, seemed to possess a morbid attraction for her, suddenly laid her fork down. Shut her eyes. As conversation swirled around her. But she said nothing, and nothing was said to her, and after a pause of some seconds she opened her eyes and, gazing now resolutely at her plate, picked up her fork and resumed eating.)

(Another of our party weakened. Laid his fork down too, pressed the back of his hand against his forehead. Again, conversation continued. Our eyes were firmly fixed on one another. And after a minute or so he, too, revived, with steely resolution lifting his wineglass to his mouth and draining it in a single swallow.)

Boeuf Stroganoff. Pompano à la Meunière. Bouillabaisse. Sweetbreads à la York. Chateaubriand. Blanquette of veal, coq au vin, sole Lyonnaise, and an elegantly grilled terrapin with black mushrooms. And julienne vegetables, lightly sauteed in olive oil. And another generous basket of crusty brown bread. And another bottle of wine, this time a Bordeaux.

One of our party, a woman with widened moist eyes, said, Oh! – what are they doing – ? staring out the window in an attitude of disbelieving horror. But adding quickly, a hot blush mottling her face, No really – *don't look.*

No one of us having looked, nor even heard. In any case.

(Yes, certainly it crossed the minds of those gentlemen of our party with their backs to the offending scene to offer to exchange seats with the women facing it. Yet we hesitated. And finally, as if by mutual consent, said nothing. For to *name* a problem, in particular an upsetting and demoralizing problem over which none of us has any control, is *to invest it with too much significance.*)

How popular Le Coq d'Or is! – a region, an atmosphere, an exquisite state of the soul rather than merely a *restaurant.* In such surroundings, amid the glitter of flashing cutlery, expensive glassware, and crystal chandeliers, animal gluttony is so tamed as to appear a kind of asceticism.

At Le Coq d'Or, a perfectly orchestrated meal – which, we were determined, ours would be, even at an undesirable table – is rarely a matter of less than two hours.

Casting our eyes resolutely *not* in the direction of the window, the avenue, the luckless creatures outside. But, rather, with some envy at parties seated at desirable tables. Impossible not to feel resentment, bitterness, rancor. Even as we smiled, smiled. Even as the maître d' hovered guiltily near, inquiring after the quality of our food and drink and service, which we assured him, with impeccable politeness, and a measure of coolness, was excellent as always. Yet: *Why are these other patrons favored with desirable tables, while we, equally deserving, possibly more deserving, are not?*

Perennial questions of philosophy. The mystery of good, evil. God, devil. More wine? – a final bottle uncorked. Through the plate glass bay window an occasional unwelcome, unheard stridency of sound. Keening wails, or sirens? No, mere vibrations. All sound *is* vibrations, devoid of meaning. Coffee, liqueurs. Desserts so delicious they must be shared: Sorbet à la Bruxelles, profiteroles au chocolate, meringue glacé, zabaglione frappé, strawberries flambé. And those luscious Swiss mints. It was observed that the rose-tinted wax candles in the center of the table had burned low, their flames had begun to flicker. A romance of candlelight. The circular table, draped in a fine oyster-white linen cloth – the rose-patterned cushioned chairs – were floating in a pool of darkness. Staring intensely at one another, friends, dear friends, the fever of our love for one another, our desperate faith in one another, transfixed by one another's faces. For there lies *meaning*. Yes?

You expected me to weaken. To surrender to an instinctive narrative momentum. In which the *not-named* is suddenly, and therefore irrevocably, *named*. Following the conventions of narration, I might have proceeded then to Events B, C, D, the horror of disclosure increasing in rhythm with the courses of our elaborate meal. By the climax – the emptying of the very last bottle of wine, the paying of the check, our rising to leave – a revelation would have occurred. *We would never be the same again after our experience at the undesirable table.* You expected that.

But that was not my way, because it did not happen that way. There was no *naming*, thus no *narrative*.

The check was paid, we rose to leave. One of us, fumbling for her hand bag, dropped it and it fell onto a chair and from the chair to the floor spilling some of its contents with a startled little cry.

We walked through the dining room of Le Coq d'Or without a backward glance at the undesirable table.

(Let the maître d', who wished us happy holidays with a forced smile, worry that we'll never return to his damned restaurant. Let him worry he's insulted us, and we'll spread the word to others. Our revenge!)

Fortunately, there is a high-rise parking structure directly accessible from Le Coq d'Or so that patrons are spared walking along the windswept, littered avenue, and the possible danger of this walk. We'd parked our cars there, on Level A, and in the cooler air felt a sudden giddy sense of release, like children freed from confinement. We were talking loudly, we were laughing. We shook hands warmly saying goodnight, we hugged one another, we kissed. Old friends, dear friends. Now the ordeal of the undesirable table was behind us it was possible to forget it. In fact, we were rapidly forgetting it. We would retain instead the far more meaningful memory of another superb shared meal at Le Coq d'Or, another memorable evening in one another's company. Of course we'll be back – many times.

For Le Coq d'Or is, quite simply, the finest restaurant available to us. It might be said we have no choice.

VII

ETHICS AND POLITICS

When members of the public are asked whom they trust most, politicians are usually ranked alongside used car salespeople, below lawyers, and far below teachers and physicians. There is a widespread view that in politics lip-service is paid to values like honesty, loyalty, and concern for others, but, that in reality, it is one of the most unethical areas of human endeavor. Is this because politics attracts people who are particularly untrustworthy? Or is it something to do with the nature of the politics itself that leads to actions that are perceived as breaches of trust? The answer could, of course, be that it is a combination of the two. Since politicians are ultimately responsible for disposing of very large sums of public money, politics provides tempting opportunities for personal enrichment by corrupt means. But that is not an ethical problem specific to politics, for it arises in business and other areas of life as well. The more interesting specifically political ethical issues are those to do with power: the ethical costs of obtaining it, and the ethical dilemmas in using it.

The life of politics, especially in the modern era, is personally demanding, involving long hours and little time for a private family life. Therefore many of those ambitious of high public office will at some stage have to ask themselves whether their career is worth the sacrifice of other things that are important to them. Some have chosen to give up any hope of a normal family life; others have made compromises that were difficult both for family and for their career; and a very few have abandoned their careers or lowered their objectives in order to live a more normal life. Politics is not, of course, the only demanding career that forces people to make these difficult choices, but it is unique in terms of the influence that successful political leaders can have on the future of their country, and perhaps even the world. Since ambitious politicians are generally able to persuade themselves that they need to be in office to make sure that the government does the right thing, or that they have something unique to offer the nation, there is often a stronger ethical pull in favor of making a success of a political career than there is in business or industry. These questions are posed by Anthony Trollope in his series of political novels: do those in politics owe more to their electors, or to their political party, or to the nation, than to their own family?

The quintessentially political ethical problem, however, is the Machiavellian one. Machiavelli's most sensational work, *The Prince*, was based on the author's observations of successful and unsuccessful rulers of the many states of Renaissance Italy. Written as a guide to rulers, advising them on what they must do to achieve their aims and secure their power, the book's significance for ethics lies precisely in the fact that Machiavelli's advice ignores the usual ethical rules: "It is necessary for a prince, who wishes to maintain himself, to learn how not to be good, and to use this knowledge and not use it, according to the necessities of the case."[1] To obtain and maintain power, Machiavelli suggested, it is necessary for a ruler to lie, to make promises and then break them, and, when the occasion requires it, ruthlessly to suppress opposition. Precisely how to interpret *The Prince* is a controversial issue among scholars, for some see it not as offering serious advice, but as satirizing the conduct of the princely rulers of Machiavelli's time. Whatever Machiavelli's intention may have been, the book ensured that his name became synonymous with political cynicism and deviousness. To condemn Machiavelli in this manner is, however, too simple a response, for his work forces us to confront the difference between the lofty ethical systems of philosophers and religious leaders and the practical realities of political life.

One way of putting the Machiavellian question is to ask when the end justifies the means. One response, traced back to the apostle Paul and defended by Kant, is that we may never do evil to achieve good – the end does not justify the means. But in politics strict adherence to this principle can be a guarantee of ineffectiveness. Suppose that one's opponents are prepared to use dirty tricks, smearing your reputation in order to gain power. If their tactics succeed and they win the election, they will cut social welfare payments to the poor in order to reduce the taxes of their wealthy allies, and cut back environmental regulations, causing irreversible harm to fragile wilderness areas. There is even the possibility, let us suppose, that they will take the country into unnecessary wars, causing great destruction and loss of life. Is it not justifiable to use the same tactics on them, in order to prevent these disastrous consequences? Contemporary politics is full of such dilemmas, and they are illustrated in the extract from Joe Klein's *Primary Colors*, which presents a fictionalized version of the problems faced by the supporters of Bill Clinton in his first campaign for the presidency.

In the real world, the line between honest and dishonest political practices, between dirty tricks and legitimate politics, is not as sharp as that example suggests. In modern politics "spin" – the ability to present an event in a manner favorable to your own political interests – has become an art form. The masters of spin do not tell outright lies, but they also do not present events in a neutral or objective manner. At what point does spin become dishonesty?

Machiavelli noted than even an autocratic prince needs to cultivate support among powerful sections of society if he is not to be overthrown. Today we reject dictatorship as inherently unethical, for it denies the citizens a say in how they are governed. It seems to be true that, as the British historian Lord Acton noted, "power tends to corrupt and absolute power corrupts absolutely."[2] Nevertheless, reading the extracts in this section – which deal with the political life of nineteenth-century Britain and late twentieth-century America – we can see that some aspects of political life change less than we might imagine. To succeed in politics a candidate needs money or patronage – a political party, a powerful person, a large interest group, wealthy backers – to fight an election. Are the successful candidates then beholden to the people and interests who supported them? If so, to what extent? And what if – as with Trollope's Phineas Finn – this obligation conflicts with obligations to the broader constituency of voters, or with the dictates of their conscience?

Modern democracies seek to place limits on the power of any individual, or even of a political party, but accepting the discipline of a political party leads to its own special ethical problems. To be a member of a party is to accept that there is an obligation to support the collective decisions reached by the party even if one does not personally agree with all of them. Therefore, although defenders of a highly principled approach to ethics tend to see a willingness to compromise as inherently unethical, in reality to reject compromise is to reject modern politics itself. The ethical issue then becomes not whether to compromise at all, but when to compromise. As a member of the government in the lead-up to an election, I may have to keep quiet about government policies with which I disagree, for disunity will harm our chances of re-election, and, on the whole, our policies are better than those of the opposition. As an opponent of the death penalty, I may have to do some bargaining in order to secure the passage of a bill that would abolish it. Perhaps the bill will fail unless an exception is made for those already serving a life sentence who are convicted of the murder of a prison warder. Even though I still think it is wrong to execute people even under those circumstances, it may be right to vote for a bill that will abolish 99 percent of all executions, rather than stick to my convictions and see the bill defeated. This kind of compromise is sometimes seen as a victory of "expediency" over "principle," but that does not mean it is unethical. If something worthwhile is gained that could not be gained in any other way, it may be the right thing to do.

NOTES

1 Niccolò Machiavelli, *The Prince* (tr. Luigi Ricci), New York: The Modern Library, 1950, Ch. 15, p. 56.
2 Letter to Bishop Mendell Creighton, 3 April 1887.

40

ANTHONY TROLLOPE

Can Your Forgive Her?

In this, the first of Trollope's Palliser novels, Plantagenet Palliser, the heir to a duke-dom, and a rising young politician, has recently married Lady Glencora. Mr Bott is Palliser's assistant in political matters. In this scene, Lady Glencora pursues a matter that her husband had raised the previous night.

"Plantagenet," she said, "you told me last night, as I was going to bed, that you had something to say about Lady Monk's party."

He put down the newspaper slowly, and turned towards her. "Yes, my dear. After what happened, I believe that I must say something."

"If you think anything, pray say it," said Glencora.

"It is not always easy for a man to show what he thinks by what he says," he replied. "My fear is that you should suppose me to think more than I do. And it was for that reason that I determined to sleep on it before I spoke to you."

"If anybody is angry with me I'd much rather they should have it out with me while their anger is hot. I hate cold anger."

"But I am not angry."

"That's what husbands always say when they're going to scold."

"But I am not going to scold. I am only going to advise you."

"I'd sooner be scolded. Advice is to anger just what cold anger is to hot."

"But my dear Glencora, surely if I find it necessary to speak –"

"I don't want to stop you, Plantagenet. Pray, go on. Only it will be so nice to have it over."

He was now more than ever averse to the task before him. Husbands, when they give their wives a talking, should do it out of hand, uttering their words hard, sharp, and quick – and should then go. There are some works that won't bear a preface, and this work of marital fault-finding is one of them. Mr Palliser was already beginning to find out the truth of this. "Glencora," he said, "I wish you to be serious with me."

ANTHONY TROLLOPE, from Chapters LVIII and LIX in *Can You Forgive Her?*, first published in 1864–5.

"I am very serious," she replied, as she settled herself in her chair with an air of mockery, while her eyes and mouth were bright and eloquent with a spirit which her husband did not love to see. Poor girl! There was seriousness enough in store for her before she would be able to leave the room.

"You ought to be serious. Do you know why Mrs Marsham came here from Lady Monk's last night?"

"Of course I do. She came to tell you that I was waltzing with Burgo Fitzgerald. You might as well ask me whether I knew why Mr Bott was standing at all the doors, glaring at me."

"I don't know anything about Mr Bott."

"I know something about him though," she said, again moving herself in her chair.

"I am speaking now of Mrs Marsham."

"You should speak of them both together as they hunt in couples."

"Glencora, will you listen to me, or will you not? If you say that you will not, I shall know what to do."

"I don't think you would, Plantagenet." And she nodded her little head at him, as she spoke. "I'm sure I don't know what you would do. But I will listen to you. Only, as I said before, it will be very nice when it's over."

"Mrs Marsham came here, not simply to tell me that you were waltzing with Mr Fitzgerald – and I wish that when you mention his name you would call him Mr Fitzgerald."

"So I do."

"You generally prefix his Christian name, which it would be much better that you should omit."

"I will try," she said, very gently; "but it's hard to drop an old habit. Before you married me you knew that I had learned to call him Burgo."

"Let me go on," said Mr Palliser.

"Oh, certainly."

"It was not simply to tell me that you were waltzing that Mrs Marsham came here."

"And it was not simply to see me waltzing that Mr Bott stood in the doorways, for he followed me about, and came down after me to the supper-room."

"Glencora, will you oblige me by not speaking of Mr Bott?"

"I wish you would oblige me by not speaking of Mrs Marsham." Mr Palliser rose quickly from his chair with a gesture of anger, stood upright for half a minute, and then sat down again. "I beg your pardon, Plantagenet," she said, "I think I know what you want, and I'll hold my tongue till you bid me speak."

"Mrs Marsham came here because she saw that everyone in the room was regarding you with wonder." Lady Glencora twisted herself about in her chair, but she said nothing. "She saw that you were not only dancing with Mr Fitzgerald, but that you were dancing with him – what shall I say?"

"Upon my word I can't tell you."

"Recklessly."

"Oh! recklessly, was I? What was I reckless of?"

"Reckless of what people might say; reckless of what I might feel about it; reckless of your own position."

"Am I to speak now?"

"Perhaps you had better let me go on. I think she was right to come to me."

"That's of course. What's the good of having spies, if they don't run and tell as soon as they see anything, especially anything – reckless?"

"Glencora, you are determined to make me angry. I am angry now – very angry. I have employed no spies. When rumours have reached me, not from spies, as you choose to call them, but through your dearest friends and mine –"

"What do you mean by rumours from my dearest friends?"

"Never mind. Let me go on."

"No; not when you say my dear friends have spread rumours about me. Tell me who they are. I have no dear friends. Do you mean Alice Vavasor?"

"It does not signify. But when I was warned that you had better not go to any house in which you could meet that man, I would not listen to it. I said that you were my wife, and that as such I could trust you anywhere, everywhere, with any person. Others might distrust you, but I would not do so. When I wished you to go to Monkshade, were there to be any spies there? When I left you last night at Lady Monk's, do you believe in your heart that I trusted to Mrs Marsham's eyes rather than to your own truth? Do you think that I have lived in fear of Mr Fitzgerald?"

"No, Plantagenet; I do not think so."

"Do you believe that I have commissioned Mr Bott to watch your conduct? Answer me, Glencora."

She paused a moment, thinking what actually was her true belief on that subject. "He does watch me, certainly," she said.

"That does not answer my question. Do you believe that I have commissioned him to do so?"

"No; I do not."

"Then it is ignoble in you to talk to me of spies. I have employed no spies. If it were ever to come to that, that I thought spies necessary, it would be all over with me."

There was something of feeling in his voice as he said this – something that almost approached to passion which touched his wife's heart. Whether or not spies would be of any avail, she knew that she had in truth done that of which he had declared that he had never suspected. She had listened to words of love from her former lover. She had received, and now carried about with her a letter from this man, in which he asked her to elope with him. She had by no means resolved that she would not do this thing. She had been false to her husband; and as her husband spoke of his confidence in her, her own spirit rebelled against the deceit which she herself was practising.

"I know that I have never made you happy," she said. "I know that I never can make you happy."

He looked at her, struck by her altered tone, and saw that her whole manner and demeanour were changed. "I do not understand what you mean," he said. "I have never complained. You have not made me unhappy." He was one of those men to whom this was enough. If his wife caused him no uneasiness, what more was he to expect from her? No doubt she might have done much more for him.

She might have given him an heir. But he was a just man, and knew that the blank he had drawn was his misfortune, and not her fault.

But now her heart was loosed and she spoke out, at first slowly, but after a while with all the quickness of strong passion. "No, Plantagenet; I shall never make you happy. You have never loved me, nor I you. We have never loved each other for a single moment. I have been wrong to talk to you about spies; I was wrong to go to Lady Monk's; I have been wrong in everything that I have done; but never so wrong as when I let them persuade me to be your wife!"

"Glencora!"

"Let me speak now, Plantagenet. It is better that I should tell you everything; and I will. I will tell you everything – everything! I do love Burgo Fitzgerald. I do! I do! I do! How can I help loving him? Have I not loved him from the first – before I had seen you? Did you not know that it was so? I do love Burgo Fitzgerald, and when I went to Lady Monk's last night, I had almost made up my mind that I must tell him so, and that I must go away with him and hide myself. But when he came to speak to me –"

"He has asked you to go with him, then?" said the husband, in whose bosom the poison was beginning to take effect, thereby showing that he was neither above nor below humanity.

Glencora was immediately reminded that though she might, if she pleased, tell her own secrets, she ought not, in accordance with her ideas of honour, tell those of her lover. "What need is there of asking, do you think, when people have loved each other as we have done?"

"You wanted to go with him, then?"

"Would it not have been the best for you? Plantagenet, I do not love you – not as women love their husbands when they do love them. But, before God, my first wish is to free you from the misfortune that I have brought on you." As she made this attestation she started up from her chair, and coming close to him, took him by the coat. He was startled, and stepped back a pace, but did not speak; and then stood looking at her as she went on.

"What matters it whether I drown myself, or throw myself away by going with such a one as him, so that you might marry again, and have a child? I'd die – I'd die willingly. How I wish I could die! Plantagenet, I would kill myself if I dared."

He was a tall man and she was short of stature, so that he stood over her and looked upon her, and now she was looking up into his face with all her eyes. "I would," she said. "I would – I would! What is there left for me that I should wish to live?"

Softly, slowly, very gradually, as though he were afraid of what he was doing, he put his arm round her waist. "You are wrong in one thing," he said. "I do love you."

She shook her head, touching his breast with her hair as she did so.

"I do love you," he repeated. "If you mean that I am not apt at telling you so, it is true, I know. My mind is running on other things."

"Yes," she said; "your mind is running on other things."

"But I do love you. If you cannot love me, it is a great misfortune to us both. But we need not therefore be disgraced. As for that other thing of which you spoke – of our having, as yet, no child" – and in saying this he pressed her somewhat closer with his arm – "you allow yourself to think too much of it – much more of it than I do. I have made no complaints on that head, even within my own breast."

"I know what your thoughts are, Plantagenet."

"Believe me that you wrong my thoughts. Of course I have been anxious, and have, perhaps, shown my anxiety by the struggle I have made to hide it. I have never told you what is false, Glencora."

"No; you are not false!"

"I would rather have you for my wife, childless – if you will try to love me – than any other woman, though another might give me an heir. Will you try to love me?"

She was silent. At this moment, after the confession that she had made, she could not bring herself to say that she would even try. Had she said so, she would have seemed to have accepted his forgiveness too easily.

"I think, dear," he said, still holding her by her waist, "that we had better leave England for a while. I will give up politics for this season. Should you like to go to Switzerland for the summer, or perhaps to some of the German baths, and then on to Italy when the weather is cold enough?" Still she was silent. "Perhaps your friend, Miss Vavasor, would go with us?"

He was killing her by his goodness. She could not speak to him yet; but now, as he mentioned Alice's name, she gently put up her hand and rested it on the back of his.

At that moment there came a knock at the door – a sharp knock, which was quickly repeated.

"Come in," said Mr Palliser, dropping his arm from his wife's waist, and standing away from her a few yards.

*

It was the butler who had knocked – showing that the knock was of more importance than it would have been had it been struck by the knuckles of the footman in livery. "If you please, sir, the Duke of St Bungay is here."

"The Duke of St Bungay!" said Mr Palliser, becoming rather red as he heard the announcement.

"Yes, sir, His Grace is in the library. He bade me tell you that he particularly wanted to see you; so I told him that you were with my lady."

"Quite right; tell His Grace that I will be with him in two minutes." Then the butler retired, and Mr Palliser was again alone with his wife.

"I must go now, my dear," he said; "and perhaps I shall not see you again till the evening."

"Don't let me put you out in any way," she answered.

"Oh no – you won't put me out. You will be dressing, I suppose, about nine."

"I did not mean as to that," she answered. "You must not think more of Italy. He has come to tell you that you are wanted in the Cabinet."

Again he turned very red. "It may be so," he answered, "but though I am wanted, I need not go. But I must not keep the Duke waiting. Goodbye." And he turned to the door.

She followed him and took hold of him as he went, so that he was forced to turn to her once again. She managed to get hold of both his hands, and pressed them closely, looking up into his face with her eyes laden with tears. He smiled at her gently, returned the pressure of the hands, and then left her – without kissing her. It was not that he was minded not to kiss her. He would have kissed her willingly enough had he thought that the occasion required it. "He says that he loves me," said Lady Glencora to herself, "but he does not know what love means."

But she was quite aware that he had behaved to her with genuine, true nobility. As soon as she was alone and certain of her solitude, she took out that letter from her pocket, and tearing it into very small fragments, without reading it, threw the pieces on the fire. As she did so, her mind seemed to be fixed, at any rate, to one thing – that she would think no more of Burgo Fitzgerald as her future master. I think, however, that she had arrived at so much certainty as this, at that moment in which she had been parting with Burgo Fitzgerald, in Lady Monk's dining-room. She had had courage enough – or shall we rather say sin enough – to think of going with him – to tell herself that she would do so; to put herself in the way of doing it; nay, she had had enough of both to enable her to tell her husband that she had resolved that it would be good for her to do so. But she was neither bold enough nor wicked enough to do the thing. As she had said of her own idea of destroying herself – she did not dare to take the plunge. Therefore, knowing now that it was so, she tore up the letter that she had carried so long, and burnt it in the fire.

She had in truth told him everything, believing that in doing so she was delivering her own death-warrant as regarded her future position in his house. She had done this, not hoping thereby for any escape; not with any purpose as regarded herself, but simply because deceit had been grievous to her, and had become unendurable as soon as his words and manner had in them any feeling of kindness. But her confession had no sooner been made than her fault had been forgiven. She had told him that she did not love him. She had told him, even, that she had thought of leaving him. She had justified by her own words any treatment of his, however harsh, which he might choose to practise. But the result had been – the immediate result – that he had been more tender to her than she had ever remembered him to be before. She knew that he had conquered her. However cold and heartless his home might be to her, it must be her home now. There could be no further thought of leaving him. She had gone out into the tilt-yard and had tilted with him, and he had been the victor.

Mr Palliser himself had not time for much thought before he found himself closeted with the Duke; but as he crossed the hall and went up the stairs, a thought or two did pass quickly across his mind. She had confessed to him, and he had forgiven her. He did not feel quite sure that he had been right, but he did feel quite sure that the thing had been done. He recognised it for a fact that, as regarded the past, no more was to be said. There were to be no reproaches, and there must be some tacit abandoning of Mrs Marsham's close attendance. As to Mr Bott – he had begun to hate Mr Bott, and had felt cruelly ungrateful, when that gentleman endeavoured to whisper a word into his ear as he passed through the doorway into Lady Monk's dining-room. And he had offered to go abroad – to go abroad and leave his politics, and his ambition, and his coming honours. He had persisted in his offer, even after his wife had suggested to him that the Duke of St Bungay was now in the house with the object of offering him that very thing for which he had so longed! As he thought of this his heart became heavy within him. Such chances – so he told himself – do not come twice in a man's way. When returning from a twelvemonth's residence abroad he would be nobody in politics. He would have lost everything for which he had been working all his life. But he was a man of his word, and as he opened the library door he was resolute – he thought that he could be resolute in adhering to his promise.

"Duke," he said, "I'm afraid I have kept you waiting." And the two political allies shook each other by the hand.

The Duke was in a glow of delight. There had been no waiting. He was only too glad to find his friend at home. He had been prepared to wait, even if Mr Palliser had been out. "And I suppose you guess why I'm come?" said the Duke.

"I would rather be told than have to guess," said Mr Palliser, smiling for a moment. But the smile quickly passed off his face as he remembered his pledge to his wife.

"He has resigned at last. What was said in the Lords last night made it necessary that he should do so, or that Lord Brock should declare himself able to support him through thick and thin. Of course, I can tell you everything now. He must have gone, or I must have done so. You know that I don't like him in the Cabinet. I admire his character and his genius, but I think him the most dangerous man in England as a statesman. He has high principles – the very highest; but they are so high as to be out of sight to ordinary eyes. They are too exalted to be of any use for everyday purposes. He is honest as the sun, I'm sure; but it's just like the sun's honesty – of a kind which we men below can't quite understand or appreciate. He has no instinct in politics, but reaches his conclusions by philosophical deduction. Now, in politics, I would a deal sooner trust to instinct than to calculation. I think he may probably know how England ought to be governed three centuries hence better than any man living, but of the proper way to govern it now, I think he knows less. Brock half likes him and half fears him. He likes the support of his eloquence, and he likes the power of the man; but he fears his restless activity, and thoroughly dislikes his philosophy. At any rate, he has left us, and I am here to ask you to take his place."

The Duke, as he concluded his speech, was quite contented, and almost jovial. He was thoroughly satisfied with the new political arrangement which he was proposing. He regarded Mr Palliser as a steady, practical man of business, luckily young, and therefore with a deal of work in him, belonging to the race from which English ministers ought, in his opinion, to be taken, and as being, in some respects, his own pupil. He had been the first to declare aloud that Plantagenet Palliser was the coming Chancellor of the Exchequer; and it had been long known, though no such declaration had been made aloud, that the Duke did not sit comfortably in the same Cabinet with the gentleman who had now resigned. Everything had now gone as the Duke wished; and he was prepared to celebrate some little ovation with his young friend before he left the house in Park Lane.

"And who goes out with him?" asked Mr Palliser, putting off the evil moment of his own decision; but before the Duke could answer him, he had reminded himself that under his present circumstances he had no right to ask such a question. His own decision could not rest upon that point. "But it does not matter," he said; "I am afraid I must decline the offer you bring me."

"Decline it!" said the Duke, who could not have been more surprised had his friend talked of declining heaven.

"I fear I must." The Duke had now risen from his chair, and was standing, with both his hands upon the table. All his contentment, all his joviality, had vanished. His fine round face had become almost ludicrously long; his eyes and mouth were struggling to convey reproach, and the reproach was almost drowned in vexation. Ever since Parliament had met he had been whispering Mr Palliser's name into the Prime Minister's ear, and now — But he could not, and would not, believe it. "Nonsense, Palliser," he said. "You must have got some false notion into your head. There can be no possible reason why you should not join us. Finespun himself will support us, at any rate for a time." Mr Finespun was the gentleman whose retirement from the ministry the Duke of St Bungay had now announced.

"It is nothing of that kind," said Mr Palliser, who perhaps felt himself quite equal to the duties proposed to him, even though Mr Finespun should not support him. "It is nothing of that kind — it is no fear of that sort that hinders me."

"Then, for mercy's sake, what is it? My dear Palliser, I looked upon you as being as sure in this matter as myself; and I had a right to do so. You certainly intended to join us a month ago, if the opportunity offered. You certainly did."

"It is true, Duke. I must ask you to listen to me now, and I must tell you what I would not willingly tell to any man." As Mr Palliser said this a look of agony came over his face. There are men who can talk easily of all their most inmost matters, but he was not such a man. It went sorely against the grain with him to speak of the sorrow of his home, even to such a friend as the Duke; but it was essentially necessary to him that he should justify himself.

"Upon my word," said the Duke, "I can't understand that there should be any reason strong enough to make you throw your party over."

"I have promised to take my wife abroad."

"Is that it?" said the Duke, looking at him with surprise, but at the same time with something of returning joviality in his face. "Nobody thinks of going abroad at this time of the year. Of course, you can get away for a time when Parliament breaks up."

"But I have promised to go at once."

"Then, considering your position, you have made a promise which it behoves you to break. I am sure Lady Glencora will see it in that light."

"You do not quite understand me, and I am afraid I must trouble you to listen to matters which, under other circumstances, it would be impertinent in me to obtrude upon you." A certain stiffness of demeanour, and measured propriety of voice, much at variance with his former manner, came upon him as he said this.

"Of course, Palliser, I don't want to interfere for a moment."

"If you will allow me, Duke. My wife has told me that, this morning, which makes me feel that absence from England is requisite for her present comfort. I was with her when you came, and had just promised her that she should go."

"But, Palliser, think of it. If this were a small matter, I would not press you; but a man in your position has public duties. He owes his services to his country. He has no right to go back, if it be possible that he should so do."

"When a man has given his word, it cannot be right that he should go back from that."

"Of course not. But a man may be absolved from a promise. Lady Glencora –"

"My wife would, of course, absolve me. It is not that. Her happiness demands it, and it is partly my fault that it is so. I cannot explain to you more fully why it is that I must give up the great object for which I have striven with all my strength."

"Oh, no!" said the Duke. "If you are sure that it is imperative –"

"It is imperative."

"I could give you twenty-four hours, you know." Mr Palliser did not answer at once, and the Duke thought that he saw some sign of hesitation. "I suppose it would not be possible that I should speak to Lady Glencora?"

"It could be of no avail, Duke. She would only declare, at the first word, that she would remain in London; but it would not be the less my duty on that account to take her abroad."

"Well; I can't say. Of course, I can't say. Such an opportunity may not come twice in a man's life. And at your age too! You are throwing away from you the finest political position that the world can offer to the ambition of any man. No one at your time of life has had such a chance within my memory. That a man under thirty should be thought fit to be Chancellor of the Exchequer, and should refuse it – because he wants to take his wife abroad! Palliser, if she were dying, you should remain under such an emergency as this. She might go, but you should remain."

Mr Palliser remained silent for a moment or two in his chair; he then rose and walked towards the window, as he spoke. "There are things worse than death," he said, when his back was turned. His voice was very low, and there was a tear in his eye as he spoke them; the words were indeed whispered, but the Duke heard them, and felt that he could not press him any more on the subject of his wife.

"And must this be final?" said the Duke.

"I think it must. But your visit here has come so quickly on my resolution to go abroad – which, in truth, was only made ten minutes before your name was brought to me – that I believe I ought to ask for a portion of those twenty-four hours which you have offered me. A small portion will be enough. Will you see me, if I come to you this evening, say at eight? If the House is up in the Lords I will go to you in St James's Square."

"We shall be sitting after eight, I think."

"Then I will see you there. And, Duke, I must ask you to think of me in this matter as a friend should think, and not as though we were bound together only by party feeling."

"I will – I will."

"I have told you what I shall never whisper to anyone else."

"I think you know that you are safe with me."

"I am sure of it. And, Duke, I can tell you that the sacrifice to me will be almost more than I can bear. This thing that you have offered me today is the only thing that I have ever coveted. I have thought of it and worked for it, have hoped and despaired, have for moments been vain enough to think that it was within my strength, and have been wretched for weeks together because I have told myself that it was utterly beyond me."

"As to that, neither Brock nor I, nor any of us, have any doubt. Finespun himself says that you are the man."

"I am much obliged to them. But I say all this simply that you may understand how imperative is the duty which, as I think, requires me to refuse the offer."

"But you haven't refused as yet," said the Duke. "I shall wait at the House for you, whether they are sitting or not. And endeavour to join us. Do the best you can. I will say nothing as to that duty of which you speak; but if it can be made compatible with your public service, pray – pray let it be done. Remember how much such a one as you owes to his country." Then the Duke went, and Mr Palliser was alone.

41

ANONYMOUS (JOE KLEIN)

Primary Colors

Jack Stanton, the womanizing Governor of a Southern state campaigning for the Democratic nomination for the Presidency, bears a remarkable resemblance to Bill Clinton. Stanton even has a smart lawyer wife, Susan. The story is told from the perspective of Henry Burton, an idealistic African American on Stanton's staff.

Stanton has disastrously lost the New York Primary to Fred Picker, a one-time Governor of Florida. Libby Holden has known the Stantons since they worked together on George McGovern's ill-fated Presidential campaign in 1972. A subplot involves Jack's possible culpability in the pregnancy of the teenage daughter of his favorite barbecue chef.

We were trounced in New York, two to one. It was definitive, crushing, a paralytic wipeout. Picker thanked New York on behalf of Martha Harris, and announced he was going home for a few days, to rest and "think about what's important, what's best for our country." We went home, too. Our campaign seemed over. Stanton didn't withdraw from the race immediately, but he returned to Mammoth Falls and the prosaic rituals of home-state governance. There was no travel schedule. There were no staff meetings. People began to leave.

I stayed. I called Daisy several times and left messages, but there was no answer. I ran along my old three-mile route, down the river and back again. I read *Middlemarch*. I went each day to the headquarters and cleared files; a few stray muffins remained, a few older women – local volunteers – continued to answer the phones when they rang, which wasn't often. I didn't dare ask the governor or Susan about what came next; for two days after New York, I didn't speak to them at all. We just needed a break from each other, I guess. There was no real rush. The primary schedule thinned out at that point; it would be three weeks before the next big one – Pennsylvania – if we remained in business that long. I tried to think about what I was going to do with my life, but couldn't.

I was staring off into space, not even pretending to be busy, when Libby walked into the office that Thursday. And that was the first thing I noticed: she walked, she didn't barge or boom. "Hey, kid," she said, scarily subdued, holding her out-back hat against her chest with both hands. "I got the tests. You're a part of this. You want to come up with me and tell the gov?"

It was a perfect spring day. We walked up the hill to the capitol, which was girded by a lush apron of coral, fuchsia and white azaleas. (Jack and Susan Stanton would preside over the Mammoth Azalea Festival that weekend; I remembered Donny O'Brien's line about going back to ribbon cuttings and highway contracts – I'm sure Stanton did, too.) There was a quietly efficient, back-to-normal air in the governor's office; phones were ringing, which distinguished it from the mausoleum our campaign headquarters had become.

Annie Marie ushered us in. Stanton sat behind his desk. I realized I had never seen him there before. In fact, it had been months since I'd been *in* that office – New Year's Eve, the day I met Daisy. She was the last person I'd seen sitting there. She'd been smoking a cigarette, flipping through Leon's New Hampshire cross-tabs. She pushed her glasses up on her forehead. She looked at me –

"Well, Jack, you're in the clear," Libby said dully. This was all dreamlike and *very* strange. "You're not the father." He stared at his hands and exhaled. "Hell," Libby said, reviving a bit. "Uncle Charlie's not even the father."

Stanton glanced at her sharply. "Does Willie know?" he asked.

"Doc Wilkinson will call them," Libby said.

"We should call them, too," Stanton said. "He's gonna be feeling awful, thinking he brought this thing down. Hell, we should all go over there for dinner tonight."

He swiveled, stared out the window, down the hill toward the few scraggly, undistinguished modern skyscrapers downtown. "Henry," he said, turning back, "any press calls on this, there's no comment. And Sunday evening, we'll pull everyone together at the Mansion, figure out where we take this thing from here – okay?"

The meeting was over. Sort of. Libby wasn't getting up from her chair. Actually, she seemed to be trying to get up but was unable to put the full force of her will behind it. I had never seen her indecisive before.

"Libby?" Stanton asked. "What on earth is the matter with you?"

"Well . . ."

"Libby?"

"Oh shit," she sighed. "You know, I've been kind of . . . interested in the Picker thing," she said softly, almost mumbling. "So I made some calls – one of them to Judy Lipinsky, an old *friend* of mine, used to be a scorp – police reporter and a good one, a very tough chick. She's got an advertising sheet in Fort Lauderdale now. And she made some calls. And she, ah, found this state senator who claims that Picker . . . well, that Picker gave him some money to vote for this project – a development, south of Naples."

"When he was governor?" Stanton asked.

"Uh-huh," Libby said. "The vote was state matching money for the county to build a connecting road, and also the approval of a federal water and sewer grant.

---

scorp – short for scorpion, the term used for journalists because of their potentially deadly sting

And the thing is, the project – Tidewater Estates – was being developed by Sunshine Brothers, which is a subsidiary of Sunshine Savings and Loan, which is owned by Edgardo Reyes Cardinale. And Edgardo Reyes Cardinale is the brother of Antonia Reyes Cardinale, who is –"

"Picker's former wife," Stanton said and whistled. "Jeez. Who else knows about this? What else do we know? Who's the senator? Will he talk?"

Libby just sat there. She didn't say anything.

"Libby, what the fuck is the matter with you?"

"I've been trying to decide . . ." she said, her voice trailing off.

"Decide what?"

"Whether I want to DO THIS for you, you *stupid SHIT*," she said, Libby once more. "I bust dust. I protect you. I don't do oppo . . ."

"Libby, what the fuck is the difference?"

"All the difference in the world," she said. "All the *moral* difference in the world. I'm not too interested in tearing Freddy Picker down."

"And if he's bent?" Stanton said. "If he's a crook?"

"It'll out," she said.

"Yeah, but when?" Stanton said. "Say he wins the nomination – and *then* it comes out. If it's there the Republicans'll find it, that's for sure. They may already have it. Libby, we should at least know what they know. We should at least know what's there. Think of it as dust-busting for the Democratic Party, for all of us."

"Don't *patronize* me, Jack. We've known each other too fucking long. . . . He *cleaned your clock*."

"But you'll do it," Stanton said.

"Oh, fuck you."

"I knew you would. Henry, how would *you* like a nice Florida vacation?" he asked. "Nothin's happening around here till Sunday. And" – he was smiling now, playing with us – "you guys worked *so well* together on the phony tapes."

If the handshake is the threshold act of politics, what can one say of oppo? It is the primal impulse, the headwaters of all tactics and strategy, the oldest and most dishonorable exercise linked to the Will to Power. The Greeks did oppo; they learned it from the gods. Cassius did oppo. Even our sainted FDR used the Internal Revenue Service to scope out his opponents. It is a foundation of the trade, the darkest tool, the inevitable destination; it is where the story always ends. It can be done elegantly or not – mostly not, in the late twentieth century. It can be done reluctantly or with relish, but it will always be done.

And we would do it for Jack Stanton, Libby and I. We would do it as a ceremonial act, a genuflection to the origins of our craft, and as a release – our final service to the Stantons. We would do it almost ironically, standing at a distance from ourselves, curious about where we were going, how far we'd be willing to go. Without Libby, I wouldn't have gone – it was clear that her impulse was the same as mine, that she was propelled by the desire for symmetry, the need to tie up all the loose ends, to see it through.

"We are in *limbo* now, Henri – in every sense of the word," she said as Jennifer Rogers drove us to the airport in Libby's red Jeep Cherokee. She was sitting up front, her left hand massaging Jenny's neck. I sat in the back. "We are . . . *outside the mainstream*. We are . . . *in purgatory*. We are . . . *lost*. We are . . . *testing our limits*. You remember the stupid song, 'Limbo Rock'? You remember the words? 'How *loooooowwwwww* can you *gooooooooo*? That's us, Henri. We are moral submariners. We dive down into the shit, hoping for a shit-balm, hoping for a cure."

"Libby, let me ask you," I said. "How did you know Jack wasn't the father of that child?"

"He was the father of the mother's ignorance," Libby said, deep into cryptic limbo mode.

"In English, Libby?"

"He gave in to the fundies on sex education," Libby said. "He wouldn't fight that fight. So the girl didn't know her vagina from the mailbox. Her folks sure as hell didn't tell her much. I had to run a goddamn sex seminar for the poor kid. She actually thought the first guy who got to you after menstruation planted the seed. In this case, the happy farmer turned out to be the *second* guy who got to her that particular month – Jarone Dixon, who sat next to her in sixth period, social studies. HOO-HAH! Seventh period was a study hall. Jarone Dixon and Loretta McCollister studied biology in a broom closet two days after she ovulated. Jarone, I can assure you, will make an entirely incompetent father."

"And the first guy who got to her that month was Jack Stanton?" I asked.

"We'll never know for sure, will we?" Libby said. "But your suspicion is as good as mine."

Libby and Henry travel to Florida looking for dirt that will discredit Fred Picker. Following a story about payoffs and corruption in building contracts they learn about Picker's cocaine use and meet the HIV-infected ex-prisoner who was Picker's lover.

"OOOOOOOO-EEEEEEE," Libby said, as we headed for the airport. "You just knew it was gonna be GOOD! You just knew it was gonna be IRRESISTIBLE. And this has EVERYfuckingTHING: SEX! DRUGS! CORRUPTION! And NONE of it – *none of it*, Henry, my man – NONE OF IT is clear-cut venality It's all kind of . . . *human* and lovely and luscious. It's weakness, not evil. I LOVE THIS GAME."

"What are you *talking* about?" I asked.

"When doing a social experiment," Libby said, going into a high-pitched Julia Child impersonation, "you do not want to stir *gently*. You WANT TO ROIL THE FUCKER. You want conditions right, you want it to be really tempting, y'know? You want it luscious. THIS is *dripping* with lusciosity."

"But I don't –"

"Understand? Ohhhhh, Henry! Of course you understand. We've been on the same fucking page from the start – if you hadn't been, I'da told you to stuff it, stay home, be a lackey. So don't play dumb with me. THIS IS A TEST. Of us and

---

Julia Child – famous television chef and co-author of *Mastering the Art of French Cooking* (1961)

them. Actually, of us and them and us again. We just passed the entrance exam. We got the dirt. We're fucking unbelievable – you know that? We're so good we're . . . *lucky.*"

"Libby, what are you *talking* about?" I asked, but I kind of knew. "What are we gonna do with this shit?"

"It ain't US! It ain't what *we're* gonna do. It ain't about US!" She slammed the horn on "us." "It is now about THEM! We are going to do what we do: we bust dust and tell all. The question is, what are Jack and Susan going to DO with it? Inquiring MINDS want to know! I mean, little buddy, isn't that *really* what we're both *after* here? I mean, after twenty fucking years, I get to see what THEY're about – not just hypothesize, not just HOPE. This is it. Graduation day. They graduate or I do. Tell the truth, Henry," she said, and dived to an intense whisper, staring at me with wild blue eyes, instead of at the road, "isn't this what you're really after, too?"

"Drive, Libby, goddammit!" I said.

"Well, isn't it?"

"I guess," I said, but I knew. "What if they react the wrong way? What if they flunk the test?"

"Then it's OUR turn at bat again," she said. "Hoo-HAH! Then we get to see what *we're* made of, and we gotta hope it ain't green cheese."

"Libby," I said. "I know this is hard, but I've seen you do it before. Could you please possibly get fucking *sane* for a minute and tell me what you're getting me into?"

"NO!" She said and swerved the car onto the shoulder, slamming the brakes, stopping with a lurch.

"Jesus!" I said.

"Henry," she said, staring at me – perfectly calm, perfectly sane. (I had done it.) "Do you remember the rules we set the day we vamped on that scumfucker Randy Culligan? Do you remember how we're sitting outside his law office and I told you I was about to do something crazy? And you could be in or out, but ask no questions?"

I nodded.

"Well, sweetie," she said, taking my chin in her hand, "we're back there now. Faith or nothing. You on?"

"You're not gonna shoot the Stantons, are you?"

"Not quite," she said.

"No violence of any kind."

"Don't *chivvy* me, Henry," she said. "You on or no?"

I nodded yes, my chin still in her hand. And she kissed me on the cheek.

The Sunday morning papers had Freddie Picker being endorsed by the governor of Pennsylvania and most of the state's congressional delegation. I read it as a civilian might, without a twinge. There had been days, *months,* when I could soar or dive on the hint of a nuance in a one-paragraph item buried in *The Washington Post;* that had been my life. But the campaign was over for me now. I called Daisy that morning and got her machine again. "Daisy, *please,*" I said. "I fucked up. But does one fuckup mean that I'm cast into the outer darkness for all eternity? I miss you."

Libby called later that morning. "We meet at five at the Mansion, just before the other meeting, which is – you're never fucking going to BELIEVE this – a dinner meeting. And Fat Willie is CATERING! I guess Jack figures, if he's goin' out, might as well go out with a full belly."

"Did he ask you anything?"

"Does a woodpecker have a long, sharp nose?"

"And?"

"Oh ye of little faith."

"Well, what did you say?"

"He said, 'Any luck?' I said, 'Depends on what you mean by luck.' He said, 'Did you find anything?' I said, 'Depends on what you mean by anything.' He said, 'C'mon Libby, don't fuck with me.' I said, 'I don't fuck, I make love. You aren't gonna risk another moment of passion now, Jack, after all the shit your wiener's gotten you into, are you?' . . . So, the question is: He call *you* yet?"

"No," I said.

"He will."

He did, about ten minutes after I got off with Libby.

"So how was Florida?" He asked.

"Humid," I said.

"Oh come *on*, Henry. Not you too?"

I didn't say anything.

"I need to know if there's any hope," he said.

I carefully considered what I said next. "It depends," I said, "what you mean by hope."

"Henry, goddammit, who are you working for?"

"Governor, I'm working *with* Libby," I said. "We figured it would be best if we made our report together. See you at five."

I spent the next few hours taking inventory of my apartment, trying to figure how much there would be to pack, how long it would take to leave. Then I went for a run and, afterward, sat on a bench next to the river, which had swollen with the spring, leaving the grassy banks soggy. Of all the things I had seen and done and experienced in Mammoth Falls, I would remember the river most vividly. It was the closest I'd ever come to a natural thing. I lived next to it, ran alongside it, sat by it, slowly learned its moods – and there were times that I could put myself in a half-trance, and imagine its swift current emptying my mind, carrying my worries off downstream. I never really stopped to consider the transcendental power of the river – I'm not very mystical, I guess – but I do find myself sitting in that spot, in my mind, from time to time, especially when I'm looking to get calm.

Howard and Lucille were with the Stantons in the study when I arrived – which was a matter of some concern. Howard telegraphed one of his furtive little ironic smiles; Lucille glared. Susan stood, gave me a kiss on the cheek and said, "What, you didn't us bring back any jelly?" She turned to Jack and asked, "Hey, did I ever tell you about this? Whenever my folks came back from Florida, they brought a package – three glass globes, globules – of jelly. One was orange, another orange-pineapple, another cher –"

"OUT!" It was Libby, pointing a finger – casually and from above, like God in the Sistine Chapel – at Lucille. "YOU ARE OUTTA-HERE, you slimetudinous sack of snail wuzzle. AND YOU TOO – YOU *ESPECIALLY* TOO," she said, whirling on Howard. "Life is too *fucking* SHORT to even have to *think* about your sorry ass. OUT!"

Neither moved. Howard looked to Jack; Lucille, Susan. "Ohhh-KAYYYYY," Libby said and turned toward the door.

"No, wait," Susan said, nodding toward Lucille, who began moving toward the door – then stopped, put her hands on her hips and said to Libby, "You are one *sick* puppy."

"HAWHAWHAWHAWHAWHAWHAW," Libby said, throwing her head back and not laughing. "Out . . . OUT, out . . . OUT," she said, barking like a dog. Then, to Howard, "You too, teenie-weenie. Time to BOOK. You're leavin' on that midnight train to JAWWW-JAH! Out . . . OUT, out . . . OUT! I've had twenty fucking years too much of *you*."

"Can *I* stay?" Susan asked, as Howard left, closing the study door behind him.

"Always." Libby smiled. "Sweetheart."

"Is all this really necessary?" Jack asked.

"NO!" Libby said, then added with a sudden Scottish burr. "But it's what happens when you send a LUNATIC to do a *mannnn's* work. So *here*, Governor – feast your eyes," she said, tossing Stanton, who was sitting in his usual wing chair, a manila legal file with a metal clasp at the top. "You too, m'lady." She handed a file to Susan, who was curled, barefoot, down the other end of the green couch from me.

Then Libby handed me a copy, accompanied by a small sigh and a clear-eyed, here-goes-nothing glance. As we read, she paced the edge of the room, next to the windows, hands clasped behind her back, head down, riffling the gauzy linen curtains as she passed.

The file was untitled. The first page said "Executive Summary." It had a row of bullets, setting off capitalized names: ORESTES FIGUEROA, EDGARDO REYES, REGINALD DUBOISE, LORENZO DELGADO – and a precise one-sentence summary of their "testimony." This was followed by more elaborate accounts of our interviews with the four, accounts that seemed entirely accurate – unhedged, unbiased – to me.

Jack Stanton whistled and looked up. Libby said, "Henry, does this square with your memory of our investigation?"

"Yes, absolutely."

"Remarkable," Stanton said, shaking his head. "How on earth did he ever think he could get *away* with this?"

"Well, he *was* running against YOU," Libby said.

Stanton ignored that. "What do we do with this?" he asked.

"The *Times*?" Susan said. "Or maybe *The Wall Street Journal* – more authoritative, in a way."

Libby glanced at me. They hadn't even hesitated. Not an instant of doubt.

"Through an intermediary," Susan said. "Someone not associated with the campaign."

"I don't *think* so," Libby said.

"What do you mean?" Stanton said, twisting around back toward a corner of the room behind the wing chair, where Libby leaned against a grandfather clock, positioning herself for his discomfort.

"I don't think there's anything of *use* here," she said.

"C'mon, Libby, you gotta be kidding," Stanton said. "At the very least, the Republicans already know about the Sunshine business, and the rest is eminently gettable, soon as people start looking for it."

"Mebbe," said Libby, sliding down to the floor, knees up, palms on her knees, next to the grandfather clock. Stanton couldn't see her at all now. He had to get up and turn around, a knee on the wing chair. "But it doesn't meet *my* standards," she said.

"What on earth do you mean, Olivia?" Susan asked sardonically.

"I mean, *madame*, two things," Libby said, popping up, pacing again. "First of all, this is mostly bullshit. It's horseflop and innuendo. The Sunshine business *looks* bad, but I don't think Freddy had all that much to do with it. As for the rest, well, Reggie Duboise ain't gonna talk, God bless him. And Renzo," she said, stopping, staring directly at Susan, "you wouldn't . . . *dare*."

She moved around the couch, directly behind me, put her hands on my shoulders. "Besides, legal eagles – point two is dispositive: Henry and I don't think the use of this material is proper. We have a moral objection. And *I* have a historical beef."

Stanton glanced at me; I gave him nothing back, the same cold void I'd once given Fat Willie on his behalf. "Awww c'mon, Libby," he said. "If you weren't gonna use it, why'd you go look for it?"

"He could've been a real shit," she said, resuming her pacing. "I didn't think he would be, and he isn't, but he *could* have been. But Jackie, my dearest – you are *off the fucking point*. The point is: WE DONT DO THIS SORT OF THING! Oh, I *will* be relentless busting dust and guarding your ass – I'd've even blown Randy Culligan's weenie off for you. Well, *maybe* I would have. But this is something else again. This is hurting someone else. This SUCKS. You want to know exactly why this sucks? Because YOU TOLD ME SO. You remember when, Jackie? Let me refresh your memory," and she dived into her leather satchel and produced three copies of an eight-by-ten black-and-white photo, which she handed to Jack, Susan and me.

It was remarkable. Jack and Susan both looked pretty much the same, but younger, fresher. They were dressed in turn-of-the-seventies clothes. Jack's hair was long and curly; he was wearing a ruffled Edwardian shirt with a laced draw-string top, sort of like Errol Flynn, and bell-bottoms. Susan's hair was long, straight and brown; she was wearing a bikini top and very short cut-off jeans. Both Stantons were wearing sandals. The real revelation, though, was Libby – who stood in the middle, an arm around Jack and Susan, towering over both, smiling with proud, parental satisfaction.

My first thought was, Why did Libby seem so tall? Then I realized: she was wearing heels. She was, in fact, very conventionally dressed and about a hundred pounds thinner. She had big hair (not yet gray) and was wearing a satiny sheath, and looked like a Kilgore Junior College Rangerette, or maybe one of Lyndon Johnson's daughters.

"Henry, weren't they just *gorgeous?*" She sighed.

"Yeah," I said, "but look at you."

"You little *shit*," she said. "I TOLD you I used to have a waist."

"Libby," Jack began.

"Oh hush UP," she said. "Don't ruin it. You remember when this was?" She looked at Stanton. "You *don't*, do you."

"The Miami headquarters in '72," Susan said.

"Well, of course," Libby said. "Henry, this was taken just after the convention. I'll never forget that convention – I was already running Florida, and Gary Hart finds me in a trailer, on the phone, whipping my delegation. And he has – *these* guys. 'O,' he said – he called me 'O' – 'I brought some reinforcements.' And it was like, wow. They were golden, y'know? A different life form. I mean, it was just clear as day as soon as they settled in. They were geniuses at this shit. We had a crappy old subtropical piece of shit office in downtown Miami – and the Stantons were . . . Well, this picture was taken the day they reported to work. God, they almost turned it into a real campaign. Jack was out, talking to groups – all these old Jews and New Dealers, none of whom wanted to support George McGovern and the Forces of Drugged Fucking Anarchy. But Jack could recite FDR's first inaugural by heart, bring a tear to their eye. And then he'd say, 'The Democratic Party has given you a good life. Would you be here – would you be able to afford living here – without Social Security? Are you willing to gamble your future, your children's future, on the people who fought against Social Security and Medicare and the GI Bill and every other thing that has made your lives a little better?'"

"Probably swung six or eight dozen votes," Stanton said.

"And Susan – Map Woman!" Libby said. "She laid out the state, had every precinct organized, had the office running like a fucking harvesting combine. 'Course the Stantons brought along some seaweed and shit in their wake, Howard and Lucille – the Progressive Labor Party's Fun Couple of 1971 – but, with the Stantons, the deal has always been: You take the bad with the spectacular."

"Libby, for Chrissake," Susan said. "What are you doing? What's the point?"

"The point is – EAGLETON," Libby said. "You remember, Jack? I must have known you – what, two days then? We hear about the electroshock, and it's weird: That was the first time I actually considered the possibility that we might lose to that fuckbrain Nixon. Before that, I was *absolutely convinced* we would win. I mean, who would ever vote for Tricky? No one *I* knew, 'cept the idiots I escaped from back in Partridge, Texas. Can you imagine, Henry? We were so *fucking* YOUNG. And this one, this one" – she nodded over toward Stanton – "he takes me out, we go to this

---

Thomas Eagleton – George McGovern's Vice-Presidential running mate until the media revealed that he had had electro-shock therapy and been hospitalized for "nervous exhaustion"

little open-air Cuban joint, and I've got my head in my hands. Life has *ended*. And THEY did it – the CIA. It had to be the CIA. I couldn't believe that Tom Eagleton would really be a nutcase. They had to have dragged him off and drugged him and made him crazy. It couldn't have been that McGovern was just – a COMPLETE FUCKING AMATEUR. No, *they* did dirty tricks. And I said to Jack, 'We gotta get the capability.' You remember, Jack? 'We gotta be able to do that, too.' And you said, 'No. Our job is to END all that. Our job is to make it clean. Because if it's clean, we win – because our ideas are better.' You remember that, Jack?"

Libby had tears in her eyes now.

"It was a long time ago," Stanton said gently.

"Libby, you said it yourself," Susan said coolly. "We were young. We didn't know how the world worked. Now we know. We know that if we don't move on this Picker situation, two things will happen. The first is, we're dead. Everything we've worked for since Miami twenty years ago dies. And fast. It will die tomorrow. The second thing that happens is, someday – someday soon – when the bloom is off the romance, when they've gotten sick of Freddy Picker's quiet, righteous act, when they want to pull his *wings* off, some enterprising journalist will stumble onto this. And if he doesn't, the Republicans will lead him to it, on *their* timetable, next fall. It'll be another Eagleton – only it'll be *our* fault this time, for letting it happen. Your fault Libby".

This was, I thought, a pretty strong argument. Libby didn't. "Honey," she said, "you may be right, but it just ain't who we're supposed to be."

"Maybe," Stanton said, "we could leak part of it, the Sunshine stuff – we *know* the Republicans have that."

"Oh Christ, Jack," Susan said, angry that he was softening. "You don't think they're gonna have the rest soon enough? You don't think Eddie Reyes is gonna do a *whooops* with someone else – you don't think he's gonna spill it all? I mean" – she riffled through Libby's file – "Libby, he *did* call Picker a *maricón* cokehead, didn't he?"

Libby and I exchanged a glance: yes, he had. We'd just dismissed it as another stray expletive at the time.

"So, you'd even give up the Renzo angle?" Libby asked. "What fucking *difference* does *orientation* make?"

"It'll mean something to the *National Flash*," Susan said.

"Ohhh, Susie," Libby moaned. "*You*, of all people."

Libby caught my surprise. "Oh come *on*, Henry – *you*, of all people. Remember what Eddie Reyes said: you should always assume everyone did everything back then. And, Henry, surely *you* are *familiar* with Mrs Stanton's need for physical solace in times of spousal despair."

Now it was Jack Stanton's turn to be shocked. He shot a furious look at Libby, who smiled; then at Susan, who was blushing; then at me, too stunned to blush. We had all betrayed him – and he, of course, us. Evidently, everyone *still* did everything.

"Children, children," Libby said, shaking her head, surveying the room. "Ain't we got fun."

"This has gone far enough," Stanton said. "We have to decide."

"What's to decide?" Susan asked.

"Keee-RECT," Libby said. "There is NOTHING to decide. A decision has been made, by me and Henri. This dies here."

"I don't think so," Susan said.

"I'm sorry, sweetheart," Libby said, "but it does. And here's why." She dived down into her satchel again and pulled out another manila file, which looked very much like the first. "I won't distribute this one. . . . I didn't want to make copies," she said – nervously, I thought. "But I'll tell you what it is, and Jackie here can vouch for its accuracy. Silence, Governor, will signify assent."

Susan glanced at Jack – a what's-*this?* look. "I guess life is still simple in the small towns of America," Libby began, quietly. "A doctor's office isn't very hard to get into after hours. And, Susan, when you told me I was on the McCollister case, and when I heard that Jack had had his blood taken, I figured I had no choice but to investigate the matter fully."

Stanton paled; his right hand came up, he didn't know what to do with it, so he put it flat on top of his head. "Doc Hastings kept very detailed notes about your case over the years," Libby said. "I guess he had . . . a rooting interest. I mean, he was a *full-service* family practitioner, wasn't he? OH! I never thought to ask: Does Susan know?" Stanton nodded yes. "Well, then, it's only Henry – and he knows everything else, so why not this?" She turned to me. "Doc Hastings is Governor Stanton's natural father. Momma used that Kansas City nonsense as a cover, and it worked real good, since Will Stanton never came back from Iwo to say otherwise. Momma told Jack about it – when? Doc's records say that you and he had your heart-to-heart after you graduated college. And being thoughtful folks, Jack and Momma kept it quiet – out of respect for Doc's wife and his two *other* boys. And also out of respect for Momma's reputation." Stanton stared at his lap. Susan stared at me. I stared into space. This was . . . Dogpatch.

Libby read my mind. "Yeah, Henry: this is who we are, Jackie and me. Piney-woods pigpokers – right, Jack? Rule Number One: If it moves, shoot it. . . . Or fuck it, 'specially if it's *family!* It's a wonder Momma wasn't Doc Hastings' *cousin.*"

"Libby!" Susan said. "You're out of control."

"Yeah, yeahyeah, "she agreed, taking a deep breath, calming herself. "I'm sorry. Where was I?" She moved forward and squatted directly in front of Stanton's wing chair. "So, Doc Hastings did have a rooting interest, didn't he? And root he did. Lord, Jackie! The machinations he went through to keep you out of the draft! But the part *I* like best is the most recent stuff: having Uncle Charlie take that blood test for you. I mean, would you actually have gone through with it – letting *Uncle Charlie* take the fall as the daddy? You think that would have been CREDIBLE? What kind of shit is that?"

Stanton moved his right hand from the top of his head to his brow, shading his eyes. He was *embarrassed.* I'd never seen him like this before. He was always so unabashed, so aggressively *in* the world, dominating every conversation, every room, even when he was just listening. But Libby had punctured that. She was in control here; the governor was in full retreat. He appeared to squirrel down deeper into his chair, trapped – with Libby in hot pursuit, down on her knees in front of him, peering up, trying to make eye contact. "What kind of shit *is* that, Jack?" she chided him gently, but with an edge of impatience. "Oh, excuse me – I forgot: it's the *same old* shit. There's always been a Doc Hastings or a Senator LaMott Dawson – or Uncle Charlie, or Susan – ready to fix your tickets whenever you fucked up. You have *never* paid the bill. Never. And no one ever calls you on it. Because you're so completely *fucking* SPECIAL. Everyone was always so PROUD of you. And me too. Me the worst."

She pushed him back, deeper into the chair, his knees jutting out. She leaned forward, rested her arms on top of his knees, rested her head on top of her arms. She perched at the edge of his lap, staring up at him, torturing him. "It just makes it a whole lot easier for me," she sighed. "I mean, it's totally depressing – What have I been *doing* this for, my whole pathetic fucking life?" She seemed to wait for him to say something. "Well," she said softly. "A situation like this does clear the *sinuses* now, doesn't it?"

And Stanton finally looked up, looked at her – pleading silently, but Libby wasn't buying. "So, here's the deal," she said. "You move on Picker, I move on you."

"You wouldn't," said Susan, whose eyes were red.

"Try me," Libby said, turning toward her, breaking off her pursuit of Jack Stanton.

"You would end his political career?" Susan asked.

"I bust dust," Libby said, getting to her feet now, moving toward her satchel, getting ready to leave. "My job is to prevent people from hurting you – including you. To my mind, you would hurt yourselves grievously if you acted to destroy Freddy Picker, who – I think we all agree – is a flawed but decent man." She hesitated, wiped her eyes – once, then again – but the tears were flowing now. "And so, yes," Libby concluded, "I *will* destroy this village in order to save it."

And she dashed out of that room, faster than it seemed possible for a big woman to move.

42

ANTHONY TROLLOPE

Phineas Finn

Phineas Finn is the second of Trollope's Palliser series of political novels. Many of the parliamentary characters are based on real-life politicians of the period.

Phineas Finn, an impoverished young Irish barrister, has recently been re-elected to Parliament, for the borough, or electoral district, of Loughton. There has been immense popular demand for parliamentary reform, both in extending the right to vote, and in redistributing electoral districts to make them more equal in numbers of voters. Loughton is one of the "pocket boroughs" where a small number of people invariably elect the member selected for them by the local Lord, who is usually also their landlord and patron.

It will be necessary that we should go back in our story for a very short period in order that the reader may be told that Phineas Finn was duly re-elected at Loughton after his appointment at the Treasury Board. There was some little trouble at Loughton, and something more of expense than he had before encountered. Mr Quintus Slide absolutely came down, and was proposed by Mr Vellum for the borough. Mr Vellum being a gentleman learned in the law, and hostile to the interests of the noble owner of Saulsby, was able to raise a little trouble against our hero. Mr Slide was proposed by Mr Vellum, and seconded by Mr Vellum's clerk – though, as it afterwards appeared, Mr Vellum's clerk was not in truth an elector – and went to the poll like a man. He received three votes, and at twelve o'clock withdrew. This in itself could hardly have afforded compensation for the expense which Mr Slide or his backers must have encountered – but he had an opportunity of making a speech, every word of which was reported in the *People's Banner;* and if the speech was made in the language given in the report, Mr Slide was really possessed of some oratorical power. Most of those who read the speech in the columns of the *People's Banner* were probably not aware how favourable an opportunity of retouching his sentences in type had been given to Mr Slide by the fact of his connection with the newspaper. The speech had been very severe upon our hero; and though the speaker had been so hooted and pelted at Loughton as to have been altogether inaudible – so maltreated that in point of fact he had not

---

ANTHONY TROLLOPE, from Chapter XLVII in *Phineas Finn*, first published in 1867–8.

been able to speak above a tenth part of his speech at all – nevertheless the speech did give Phineas a certain amount of pain. Why Phineas should have read it who can tell? But who is there that abstains from reading that which is printed in abuse of himself?

In the speech as it was printed Mr Slide declared that he had no thought of being returned for the borough. He knew too well how the borough was managed, what slaves the electors were – how they groaned under a tyranny from which hitherto they had been unable to release themselves. Of course the Earl's nominee, his lackey, as the honourable gentleman might be called, would be returned. The Earl could order them to return whichever of his lackeys he pleased. – There is something peculiarly pleasing to the democratic ear in the word lackey! Anyone serving a big man, whatever the service may be, is the big man's lackey in the *People's Banner*. – The speech throughout was very bitter. Mr Phineas Finn, who had previously served in Parliament as the lackey of an Irish earl, and had been turned off by him, had now fallen into the service of the English earl, and was the lackey chosen for the present occasion. But he, Quintus Slide, who boasted himself to be a man of the people – he could tell them that the days of their thraldom were coming to an end, and that their enfranchisement was near at hand. That friend of the people, Mr Turnbull, had a clause in his breeches pocket which he would either force down the unwilling throat of Mr Mildmay, or else drive the imbecile Premier from office by carrying it in his teeth. Loughton, as Loughton, must be destroyed, but it should be born again in a better birth as a part of a real electoral district, sending a real member, chosen by a real constituency, to a real Parliament. In those days – and they would come soon – Mr Quintus Slide rather thought that Mr Phineas Finn would be found "nowhere", and he rather thought also that when he showed himself again, as he certainly should do, in the midst of that democratic electoral district as the popular candidate for the honour of representing it in Parliament, that democratic electoral district would accord to him a reception very different from that which he was now receiving from the Earl's lackeys in the parliamentary village of Loughton. A prettier bit of fiction than these sentences as composing a part of any speech delivered, or proposed to be delivered, at Loughton, Phineas thought he had never seen. And when he read at the close of the speech that though the Earl's hired bullies did their worst, the remarks of Mr Slide were received by the people with reiterated cheering, he threw himself back in his chair at the Treasury and roared. The poor fellow had been three minutes on his legs, had received three rotten eggs, and one dead dog, and had retired. But not the half of the speech as printed in the *People's Banner* has been quoted. The sins of Phineas, who in spite of his inability to open his mouth in public had been made a Treasury hack by the aristocratic influence – "by aristocratic influence not confined to the male sex" – were described at great length, and in such language that Phineas for a while was fool enough to think that it would be his duty to belabour Mr Slide with a horsewhip. This notion, however, did not endure long with him, and when Mr Monk told him that things of that kind came as a matter of course, he was comforted.

But he found it much more difficult to obtain comfort when he weighed the arguments brought forward against the abominations of such a borough as that for which he sat, and reflected that if Mr Turnbull brought forward his clause, he, Phineas Finn, would be bound to vote against the clause, knowing the clause to be right, because he was a servant of the Government. The arguments, even though they appeared in the *People's Banner,* were true arguments; and he had on one occasion admitted their truth to his friend Lady Laura – in the presence of that great Cabinet Minister, her husband. "What business has such a man as that down there? Is there a single creature who wants him?" Lady Laura had said. "I don't suppose anybody does want Mr Quintus Slide," Phineas had replied; "but I am disposed to think the electors should choose the man they do want, and that at present they have no choice left to them." "They are quite satisfied," said Lady Laura, angrily. "Then, Lady Laura," continued Phineas, "that alone should be sufficient to prove that their privilege of returning a member to Parliament is too much for them. We can't defend it." "It is defended by tradition," said Mr Kennedy. "And by its great utility," said Lady Laura, bowing to the young member who was present, and forgetting that very useless old gentleman, her cousin, who had sat for the borough for many years. "In this country it doesn't do to go too fast," said Mr Kennedy. "And then the mixture of vulgarity, falsehood, and pretence!" said Lady Laura, shuddering as her mind recurred to the fact that Mr Quintus Slide had contaminated Loughton by his presence. "I am told that they hardly let him leave the place alive."

Whatever Mr Kennedy and Lady Laura might think about Loughton and the general question of small boroughs, it was found by the Government, to their great cost, that Mr Turnbull's clause was a reality. After two months of hard work, all questions of franchise had been settled, rating and renting, new and newfangled, fancy franchises and those which no one fancied, franchises for boroughs and franchises for counties, franchises single, dual, three-cornered, and four-sided – by various clauses to which the Committee of the whole House had agreed after some score of divisions – the matter of the franchise had been settled. No doubt there was the House of Lords, and there might yet be shipwreck. But it was generally believed that the Lords would hardly look at the bill – that they would not even venture on an amendment. The Lords would only be too happy to let the matter be settled by the Commons themselves. But then, after the franchise, came redistribution. How sick of the subject were all members of the Government, no one could tell who did not see their weary faces. The whole House was sick, having been whipped into various lobbies, night after night, during the heat of the summer, for weeks past. Redistribution! Why should there be any redistribution? They had got, or would get, a beautiful franchise. Could they not see what that would do for them? Why redistribute anything? But, alas, it was too late to go back to so blessed an idea as that! Redistribution they must have. But there should be as little redistribution as possible. Men were sick of it all, and would not be exigeant. Something should be done for overgrown counties – something for new towns which had prospered in brick and mortar. It would be easy to crush up a peccant borough or two – a borough that had been discovered in its sin. And a few boroughs now blessed with two members might consent to be blessed only with one. Fifteen small clauses might settle the redistribution – in spite of Mr Turnbull – if only Mr Daubeny would be good-natured.

Neither the weather, which was very hot, nor the tedium of the session, which had been very great, nor the anxiety of Ministers, which was very pressing, had any effect in impairing the energy of Mr Turnbull. He was as instant, as oratorical, as hostile, as indignant about redistribution as he had been about the franchise. He had been sure then, and he was sure now, that Ministers desired to burke the question, to deceive the people, to produce a bill that should be no bill. He brought out his clause – and made Loughton his instance. "Would the honourable gentleman who sat lowest on the Treasury bench – who at this moment was in sweet confidential intercourse with the right honourable gentleman now President of the Board of Trade, who had once been a friend of the people – would the young Lord of the Treasury get up in his place and tell them that no peer of Parliament had at present a voice in sending a member to their House of Commons – that no peer would have a voice if this bill, as proposed by the Government, were passed in its present useless, ineffectual, conservative, and most dishonest form?"

Phineas, who replied to this, and who told Mr Turnbull that he himself could not answer for any peers – but that he thought it probable that most peers would, by their opinions, somewhat influence the opinions of some electors – was thought to have got out of his difficulty very well. But there was the clause of Mr Turnbull to be dealt with – a clause directly disfranchising seven single-winged boroughs, of which Loughton was of course one – a clause to which the Government must either submit or object. Submission would be certain defeat in one way, and objection would be as certain defeat in another – if the gentlemen on the other side were not disposed to assist the ministers. It was said that the Cabinet was divided. Mr Gresham and Mr Monk were for letting the seven boroughs go. Mr Mildmay could not bring himself to obey Mr Turnbull, and Mr Palliser supported him. When Mr Mildmay was told that Mr Daubeny would certainly go into the same lobby with Mr Turnbull respecting the seven boroughs, he was reported to have said that in that case Mr Daubeny must be prepared with a Government. Mr Daubeny made a beautiful speech about the seven boroughs – the seven sins, and seven stars, and seven churches, and seven lamps. He would make no party question of this. Gentlemen who usually acted with him would vote as their own sense of right or wrong directed them – from which expression of a special sanction it was considered that these gentlemen were not accustomed to exercise the privilege now accorded to them. But in regarding the question as one of right and wrong, and in looking at what he believed to be both the wish of the country and its interests, he, Mr Daubeny – he, himself, being simply a humble member of that House – must support the clause of the honourable gentleman. Almost all those to whom had been surrendered the privilege of using their own judgment for that occasion only, used it discreetly – as their chief had used it himself – and Mr Turnbull carried his clause by a majority of fifteen. It was then 3 a.m., and Mr Gresham, rising after the division, said that his right honourable friend the First Lord of the Treasury was too tired to return to the House, and had requested him to state that the Government would declare their purpose at 6 p.m. on the following evening.

Phineas, though he had made his little speech in answer to Mr Turnbull with good-humoured flippancy, had recorded his vote in favour of the seven boroughs with a sore heart. Much as he disliked Mr Turnbull, he knew that Mr Turnbull was right in this. He had spoken to Mr Monk on the subject, as it were asking Mr Monk's permission to throw up his office, and vote against Mr Mildmay. But Mr Monk was angry with him, telling him that his conscience was of that restless, uneasy sort which is neither useful nor manly. "We all know," said Mr Monk, "and none better than Mr Mildmay, that we cannot justify such a borough as Loughton by the theory of our parliamentary representation – any more than we can justify the fact that Huntingdonshire should return as many members as the East Riding. There must be compromises, and you should trust to others who have studied the matter more thoroughly than you, to say how far the compromise should go at the present moment."

"It is the influence of the peer, not the paucity of the electors," said Phineas.

"And has no peer any influence in a county? Would you disfranchise Westmoreland? Believe me, Finn, if you want to be useful, you must submit yourself in such matters to those with whom you act."

Phineas had no answer to make, but he was not happy in his mind. And he was the less happy, perhaps, because he was very sure that Mr Mildmay would be beaten. Mr Low in these days harassed him sorely. Mr Low was very keen against such boroughs as Loughton, declaring that Mr Daubeny was quite right to join his standard to that of Mr Turnbull on such an issue. Mr Low was the reformer now, and Phineas found himself obliged to fight a losing battle on behalf of an acknowledged abuse. He never went near Bunce; but, unfortunately for him, Bunce caught him once in the street and showed him no mercy. "Slide was a little 'eavy on you in the *Banner* the other day – eh, Mr Finn? – too 'eavy, as I told him."

"Mr Slide can be just as heavy as he pleases, Bunce."

"That's in course. The press is free, thank God – as yet. But it wasn't any good rattling away at the Earl's little borough when it's sure to go. Of course it'll go, Mr Finn."

"I think it will."

"The whole seven on 'em. The 'ouse couldn't but do it. They tell me it's all Mr Mildmay's own work, sticking out for keeping on 'em. He's very old, and so we'll forgive him. But he must go, Mr Finn."

"We shall know all about that soon, Bunce."

"If you don't get another seat, Mr Finn, I suppose we shall see you back at the Inn. I hope we may. It's better than being member for Loughton, Mr Finn – you may be sure of that." And then Mr Bunce passed on.

Mr Turnbull carried his clause, and Loughton was doomed. Loughton and the other six deadly sins were anathematised, exorcised, and finally got rid of out of the world by the voices of the gentlemen who had been proclaiming the beauty of such pleasant vices all their lives, and who in their hearts hated all changes that tended towards popular representation. But not the less was Mr Mildmay beaten; and, in accordance with the promise made by his first lieutenant immediately after the vote was taken, the Prime Minister came forward on the next evening and made his statement. He had already put his resignation into the hands of Her Majesty, and Her Majesty had graciously accepted it. He was very old, and felt that the time had come in which it behoved him to retire into that leisure which he thought he had, perhaps, earned. He had hoped to carry this bill as the last act of his political life; but he was too old, too stiff, as he said, in his prejudices, to bend further than he had bent already, and he must leave the completion of the matter in other hands. Her Majesty had sent for Mr Gresham, and Mr Gresham had already seen Her Majesty. Mr Gresham and his other colleagues, though they dissented from the clause which had been carried by the united efforts of gentlemen opposite to him, and of gentlemen below him on his own side of the House, were younger men than he, and would, for the country's sake – and for the sake of Her Majesty – endeavour to carry the bill through. There would then, of course, be a dissolution, and the future Government would, no doubt, depend on the choice of the country. From all which it was understood that Mr Gresham was to go on with the bill to a conclusion, whatever might be the divisions carried against him, and that a new Secretary of State for Foreign Affairs must be chosen. Phineas understood, also, that he had lost his seat at Loughton. For the borough of Loughton there would never again be an election. "If I had been Mr Mildmay, I would have thrown the bill up altogether," Lord Brentford said afterwards; "but of course it was not for me to interfere."

The session was protracted for two months after that – beyond the time at which grouse should have been shot – and by the 23rd of August became the law of the land. "I shall never get over it," said Mr Ratler to Mr Finn, seated one terribly hot evening on a bench behind the Cabinet Ministers – "never. I don't suppose such a session for work was ever known before. Think what it is to have to keep men together in August, with the thermometer at 81 degrees, and the river stinking like – like the very mischief." Mr Ratler, however, did not die.

On the last day of the session Laurence Fitzgibbon resigned. Rumours reached the ears of Phineas as to the cause of this, but no certain cause was told him. It was said that Lord Cantrip had insisted upon it, Laurence having by mischance been called upon for some official statement during an unfortunate period of absence. There was, however, a mystery about it – but the mystery was not half so wonderful as the triumph to Phineas, when Mr Gresham offered him the place.

"But I shall have no seat," said Phineas.

"We shall none of us have seats tomorrow," said Mr Gresham.

"But I shall be at a loss to find a place to stand for."

"The election will not come on till November, and you must look about you. Both Mr Monk and Lord Brentford seem to think you will be in the House."

And so the bill was carried, and the session was ended.

VIII

RACISM AND SEXISM

T he first article of the Universal Declaration of Human Rights begins: "All human beings are born free and equal in dignity and rights." The second article goes on to say that everyone is entitled to the rights and freedoms set out in the declaration, "without distinction of any kind, such as race, colour, sex, language, religion, political or other opinion, national or social origin, property, birth or other status." Despite this, however, forms of prejudice and discrimination that violate these principles continue to be pervasive features of human life, as they have been throughout history.

The ancient Egyptians, Greeks, and Romans all had slaves, as did the Hebrews, Aztecs, Maya, Persians, Assyrians, Babylonians, Sumerians, Indians, Chinese, Americans, and Russians. Slaves were not always of a difference race – indeed, the concept of race is a relatively modern one – but the institution was often based on national or ethnic origin. Greeks, for example, enslaved "barbarians," a term that covered a wide range of non-Greek nations. Romans made slaves of those they captured in wars with border tribes. In Russia, serfdom was a social category that became hereditary in the seventeenth century, and was not ended until 1861. But whereas the liberated serfs could merge into the Russian population, slaves in the United States were of African descent and so could more easily be separated out from the majority white population and subjected to continuing racial discrimination.

The domination of one group by another that characterizes slavery has some parallels with the domination of women by men. Indeed, in the United States, this parallel was widely observed as those involved in the movement for women's suffrage were nearly always also abolitionists on the slavery question. Moreover, the term "sexism" was first used in the 1960s by feminists working in the civil rights movement to highlight the commonalities in the subordination of African Americans and women.

Historically, patriarchal societies appear to have been universal: although worship of a paramount goddess seems to have been widespread, the Amazons were mythical and there is no reliable evidence for the existence of other matriarchal societies. Patriarchy has also historically been part of Christianity, Judaism, Islam, Hinduism, and Confucianism. In the Judeo-Christian tradition, Eve served as the prime example of women's inferiority and tendency to lead men astray.

Later, scientific justifications of patriarchy became prominent. It was argued that nature decrees women's subordinate role and that patriarchy was a necessary outcome of evolution. Frederick Engels saw patriarchy as developing once men accumulated property: they then had to "own" women to ensure that their property passed to their legitimate heirs.

Although Mary Wollstonecraft had argued for women's rights in the late eighteenth century, the first widespread movements for equality began in Britain and the United States in the second half of the nineteenth century. It was not until the twentieth century, however, that women gained the vote and other legal rights. (Indeed, it was 1971 before Switzerland introduced women's suffrage, and only in November 1990 did the Swiss federal court force the last canton to grant women the vote.)

Racist, ethnic, sexist, or religious prejudice is to be found in its most explicit form not only in the readings in this section, but also in the readings from *Invisible Man* and *Puberty Blues* in Section I, *The Good German* in Section II, and *Huckleberry Finn* and "This Way for the Gas, Ladies and Gentleman" in Section XIII. One or more of these prejudices is also present, if less violently, in the readings from "The Soft-Hearted Sioux" in Section II, *Middlemarch* and *A Suitable Boy* in Section III, *The Company* in Section V, and *The Remains of the Day* in Section XIV.

The task of philosophy is to probe beneath the surface of widely accepted views to test the foundations on which they rest. Therefore philosophers have inquired into the basis of the assertion that all human beings are equal in dignity and rights, and have asked why racial and sexual discrimination are wrong. For it is immediately clear that human beings are not equal in the sense of being the same. Take any characteristic that we might value, whether it is intelligence, physical strength or agility, compassion, artistic creativity, sense of justice, sociability, or anything else, and we will find that people differ in each of these dimensions. Nor is it always true that those who are deficient in one respect always make up for it in another. If we nevertheless assert that all human beings have equal rights, this is evidently not a description of some state of affairs that holds in nature, but rather a moral principle, a prescription about how our fellow-humans ought to be treated.

It is common for people to make the mistake of assuming that this moral principle of equality must rest on some kind of factual equality. Those who make this mistake assume that to avoid racism, we must insist that there are no significant differences between the races. Some even deny that the concept of race is a coherent one. But while it is true that there is a great deal of genetic variation within, say, those we regard as "African" or "European" or "Asian," it is still true that there are genes that occur with greater frequency among Africans than they do among Europeans or Asians, and vice versa – if that were not the case, we would be unable to identify the race of an infant adopted into a family of different race. Similarly, knowing the race of a population is a useful indicator of the number of members of that population who will be affected by certain genetic diseases, like sickle-cell anemia and Tay–Sachs disease. Given this, there is no inherent improbability in the idea that some abilities may also vary with race. A glance at recent finalists in Olympic sprinting finals, for instance, would suggest that West African descent confers an advantage in races of that type. Obviously, this does not mean that every person of West African descent can run 100 meters faster than every person of European descent. We are talking here of averages, and the claim that people of West African descent have, on average, greater sprinting ability than people of European descent is perfectly compatible with the existence of Europeans who are better sprinters than 99.9 percent of West Africans. Since the process of Olympic selection and competition selects for the peak level of ability in a population, if Africans are just very slightly better than Europeans on average, there will still be many more West Africans with the ability necessary to compete at that level than there are Europeans.

Claims about racial differences in intelligence are both more controversial and more difficult to measure, both because "intelligence" is a less clear concept than "speed over 100 meters" and because cultural disadvantages that have an impact on test scores are much harder to exclude. It is also true that people may have racist motivations for making claims about the inferiority of a racial minority. Nevertheless, whether there are, on average, differences in intelligence between different races, and whether these differences have, in part, a genetic basis, is a scientific question, not a moral one. Perhaps one day it will be possible to answer it in an objective manner. But whatever the answer turns out to be, we can know now that it will not justify denying equal rights to members of any race. The moral principle of equality will remain justifiable on any plausible view of the facts of racial difference. One reason for this is that what differences there are, if any, will be apparent when we take averages across races or populations. At an individual level, there will be – as with sprinting – greater differences within each race than between races. Therefore it will remain wrong to treat individuals simply as members of a given race, rather than in accordance with their individual abilities. There is also a more fundamental reason why the moral principle of equality is not affected by factual differences between races of the kind we have been discussing. But before looking at that, we should consider the separate case of differences between males and females.

Both sexism and racism involve unjust discrimination, whether in attitudes, behaviors, or institutions, and inequalities of power and privilege. But there are differences too. That there are biologically distinct sexes is undeniable. (The existence of a small number of hermaphrodites, transsexuals, and other "queer" sexual identities cannot obscure the fact that most people, straight or gay, are biologically male or female. We couldn't even talk of heterosexuals and homosexuals unless we were clear about who is male and who is female.) Another important difference between racism and sexism is that men and women live together intimately, often in close and loving relationships. Every man had a mother, most have a wife or wives, and many have daughters. Women therefore are not likely to be as uniformly despised by the dominant sex as a racial minority can be despised by the dominant race. Nevertheless, the culture of patriarchy has supported men in their desire to possess women and make them subordinate. (Just as racist ideologies support the subordination of "inferior" peoples.) Like Nora in *A Doll's House*, a woman may, if she is married to a wealthy man, live in comfort and be pampered in many ways, yet she can still be an inferior, expected to look up to her husband and obey him. If women are strong-minded and outspoken in a patriarchal society, then they must expect the fate of Katharina in *The Taming of the Shrew*. In the real world, even today, this "taming" can be much more brutal than that suffered by Katharina.

Just as there has been a debate about whether there are genetic differences in the abilities of different races, so too some early feminists sought to show that all differences between men and women, other than the obvious anatomical ones, are the result of culture and conditioning. Boys are given toy guns to play with, and girls are given dolls, hence boys grow up aggressive and girls nurturing. But today's feminists are less likely to deny the influence of biology on the psychology of men and women. They urge, rather, that male-dominated societies tend to favor male ways of thinking and living, to the disadvantage of women, and often of society as a whole.

We still need to ask why we should consider all humans as having equal rights, rather than allowing these rights to vary in accordance with the characteristics of individual human beings. We can say that it is because all humans have equal inherent worth or dignity, but that merely puts off the difficulty, for we then need to ask why this is so. The most plausible answer is that all human beings have certain interests that do not vary in accordance with their race, color, sex, or other characteristics mentioned above. (To be strictly accurate, we should say "almost all," but in the present context we can put aside the rare cases of humans born with such severe brain damage that they will never even be conscious.) Humans benefit from adequate food and shelter, from protection from violent attack and physical suffering, from having an occupation, seeing their children grow up, and participating in the process by which they are governed. They have an important interest in self-respect, which is violated if they are forced to suffer indignities and are treated as a member of an inferior class.

In combating the idea that some humans are naturally inferior to others, and therefore lacking in some basic rights, literature and philosophy have played complementary roles. It was not always so. Aristotle notoriously defended the system of slavery that prevailed in ancient Greece, writing in his *Politics*: "It is thus clear that, just as some are by nature free, so others are by nature slaves, and for these latter the condition of slavery is both beneficial and just."[1] Many Catholic theologians also accepted slavery in the Spanish, Portuguese, and French colonies, while some of their Protestant counterparts supported it in the colonies that became the United States (though the Quakers were a conspicuous early exception). It was the Enlightenment philosophers of the eighteenth century like Rousseau and Voltaire who decisively rejected this way of thinking, and whose writings led to the great egalitarian declarations of human rights that formed the basis for later efforts to end slavery and racial discrimination. But in the United States, where slavery survived despite its evident inconsistency with the opening words of the Declaration of Independence, a work of fiction – Harriet Beecher Stowe's *Uncle Tom's Cabin* – probably did more to influence American popular opinion against slavery than any work by an American philosopher. It did so by displaying the extent of the violation of vital human interests that slavery necessarily causes. Later works like Ralph Ellison's *Invisible Man* (Section I) did something similar for the racist system that prevailed in the American South during the first half of the twentieth century.

The political writings of Mary Wollstonecraft and John Stuart Mill had an influence on the cause of women's rights. But so too did Henrik Ibsen's *A Doll's House*, which played to packed houses all over Europe and the United States. Charlotte Gilman Perkins, Rebecca West, Olive Schreiner, Virginia Woolf, and many others wrote novels that challenged and changed female stereotypes and changed the lives of women for the better. Nevertheless, despite the cumulative efforts of those writing in opposition to racism and sexism, slavery still exists in some parts of the world. Racial discrimination remains a potent force in many countries, including the United States (where researchers have shown that applicants for housing with distinctively African American names are still more likely to be refused than applicants with identical information who appear to be white) and in some countries, women still do not have the same rights as men.

NOTE

1   Aristotle, *The Politics*, Chapter V (1255a).

43

HARRIET BEECHER STOWE

Uncle Tom's Cabin

Uncle Tom's Cabin is a passionate indictment of slavery that changed history. Although labeled as racist and patronizing by some of today's critics, the novel made nineteenth-century whites see slaves as real people. Tom, "a man of humanity," is the first black hero in American fiction. At a time when many whites claimed slavery had "good effects" on blacks, *Uncle Tom's Cabin* depicts the cruel reality of black Kentucky families broken up and "sold down the river."

In this opening chapter of the novel Mr Shelby is negotiating the sale of his faithful servant Tom to cover his debts to Mr Haley.

Late in the afternoon of a chilly day in February, two gentlemen were sitting alone over their wine, in a well-furnished dining parlor, in the town of P———, in Kentucky. There were no servants present, and the gentlemen, with chairs closely approaching, seemed to be discussing some subject with great earnestness.

For convenience sake, we have said, hitherto, two *gentlemen*. One of the parties, however, when critically examined, did not seem, strictly speaking, to come under the species. He was a short, thick-set man, with coarse, commonplace features, and that swaggering air of pretension which marks a low man who is trying to elbow his way upward in the world. He was much over-dressed, in a gaudy vest of many colors, a blue neckerchief, bedropped gayly with yellow spots, and arranged with a flaunting tie, quite in keeping with the general air of the man. His hands, large and coarse, were plentifully bedecked with rings; and he wore a heavy gold watch-chain, with a bundle of seals of portentous size, and a great variety of colors, attached to it, – which, in the ardor of conversation, he was in the habit of flourishing and jingling with evident satisfaction. His conversation was in free and easy defiance of Murray's Grammar, and was garnished at convenient intervals with various profane expressions, which not even the desire to be graphic in our account shall induce us to transcribe.

HARRIET BEECHER STOWE, from Volume I, Chapter I in *Uncle Tom's Cabin*, first published in 1852.

His companion, Mr Shelby, had the appearance of a gentleman; and the arrangements of the house, and the general air of the housekeeping, indicated easy, and even opulent circumstances. As we before stated, the two were in the midst of an earnest conversation.

"That is the way I should arrange the matter," said Mr Shelby.

"I can't make trade that way – I positively can't, Mr Shelby," said the other, holding up a glass of wine between his eye and the light.

"Why, the fact is, Haley, Tom is an uncommon fellow; he is certainly worth that sum anywhere, – steady, honest, capable, manages my whole farm like a clock."

"You mean honest, as niggers go," said Haley, helping himself to a glass of brandy.

"No; I mean, really, Tom is a good, steady, sensible, pious fellow. He got religion at a camp-meeting, four years ago; and I believe he really *did* get it. I've trusted him, since then, with everything I have, – money, house, horses, – and let him come and go round the country; and I always found him true and square in everything."

"Some folks don't believe there is pious niggers, Shelby," said Haley, with a candid flourish of his hand, "but I *do*. I had a fellow, now, in this yer last lot I took to Orleans – 't was as good as a meetin, now, really, to hear that critter pray; and he was quite gentle and quiet like. He fetched me a good sum, too, for I bought him cheap of a man that was 'bliged to sell out; so I realized six hundred on him. Yes, I consider religion a valeyable thing in a nigger, when it's the genuine article, and no mistake."

"Well, Tom's got the real article, if ever a fellow had," rejoined the other. "Why, last fall, I let him go to Cincinnati alone, to do business for me, and bring home five hundred dollars. 'Tom,' says I to him, 'I trust you, because I think you're a Christian – I know you wouldn't cheat.' Tom comes back, sure enough; I knew he would. Some low fellows, they say, said to him – 'Tom, why don't you make tracks for Canada?' 'Ah, master trusted me, and I couldn't,' – they told me about it. I am sorry to part with Tom, I must say. You ought to let him cover the whole balance of the debt; and you would, Haley, if you had any conscience."

"Well, I've got just as much conscience as any man in business can afford to keep, – just a little, you know, to swear by, as 't were," said the trader, jocularly; "and, then, I'm ready to do anything in reason to 'blige friends; but this yer, you see, is a leetle too hard on a fellow – a leetle too hard." The trader sighed contemplatively, and poured out some more brandy.

"Well, then, Haley, how will you trade?" said Mr Shelby, after an uneasy interval of silence.

"Well, haven't you a boy or gal that you could throw in with Tom?"

"Hum! – none that I could well spare; to tell the truth, it's only hard necessity makes me willing to sell at all. I don't like parting with any of my hands, that's a fact."

Here the door opened, and a small quadroon boy, between four and five years of age, entered the room. There was something in his appearance remarkably

---

quadroon – a person of one-quarter African descent

beautiful and engaging. His black hair, fine as floss silk, hung in glossy curls about his round, dimpled face, while a pair of large dark eyes, full of fire and softness, looked out from beneath the rich, long lashes, as he peered curiously into the apartment. A gay robe of scarlet and yellow plaid, carefully made and neatly fitted, set off to advantage the dark and rich style of his beauty; and a certain comic air of assurance, blended with bashfulness, showed that he had been not unused to being petted and noticed by his master.

"Hulloa, Jim Crow!" said Mr Shelby, whistling, and snapping a bunch of raisins towards him, "pick that up, now!"

The child scampered, with all his little strength, after the prize, while his master laughed.

"Come here, Jim Crow," said he. The child came up, and the master patted the curly head, and chucked him under the chin.

"Now, Jim, show this gentleman how you can dance and sing." The boy commenced one of those wild, grotesque songs common among the negroes, in a rich, clear voice, accompanying his singing with many comic evolutions of the hands, feet, and whole body, all in perfect time to the music.

"Bravo!" said Haley, throwing him a quarter of an orange.

"Now, Jim, walk like old Uncle Cudjoe, when he has the rheumatism," said his master.

Instantly the flexible limbs of the child assumed the appearance of deformity and distortion, as, with his back humped up, and his master's stick in his hand, he hobbled about the room, his childish face drawn into a doleful pucker, and spitting from right to left, in imitation of an old man.

Both gentlemen laughed uproariously.

"Now, Jim," said his master, "show us how old Elder Robbins leads the psalm." The boy drew his chubby face down to a formidable length, and commenced toning a psalm tune through his nose, with imperturbable gravity.

"Hurrah! bravo! what a young 'un!" said Haley; "that chap's a case, I'll promise. Tell you what," said he, suddenly clapping his hand on Mr Shelby's shoulder, "fling in that chap, and I'll settle the business – I will. Come, now, if that ain't doing the thing up about the rightest!"

At this moment, the door was pushed gently open, and a young quadroon woman, apparently about twenty-five, entered the room.

There needed only a glance from the child to her, to identify her as its mother. There was the same rich, full, dark eye, with its long lashes; the same ripples of silky black hair. The brown of her complexion gave way on the cheek to a perceptible flush, which deepened as she saw the gaze of the strange man fixed upon her in bold and undisguised admiration. Her dress was of the neatest possible fit, and set off to advantage her finely moulded shape; – a delicately formed hand and a trim foot and ankle were items of appearance that did not escape the quick eye of the trader, well used to run up at a glance the points of a fine female article.

"Jim Crow" – a derogatory term for a black person; after the abolition of slavery, used to refer to the system of discrimination against blacks that operated in the South

"Well, Eliza?" said her master, as she stopped and looked hesitatingly at him.

"I was looking for Harry, please, sir;" and the boy bounded toward her, showing his spoils, which he had gathered in the skirt of his robe.

"Well, take him away, then," said Mr Shelby; and hastily she withdrew, carrying the child on her arm.

"By Jupiter," said the trader, turning to him in admiration, "there's an article, now! You might make your fortune on that ar gal in Orleans, any day. I've seen over a thousand, in my day, paid down for gals not a bit handsomer."

"I don't want to make my fortune on her," said Mr Shelby, dryly; and, seeking to turn the conversation, he uncorked a bottle of fresh wine, and asked his companion's opinion of it.

"Capital, sir, – first chop!" said the trader; then turning, and slapping his hand familiarly on Shelby's shoulder, he added –

"Come, how will you trade about the gal? – what shall I say for her – what'll you take?"

"Mr Haley, she is not to be sold," said Shelby. "My wife would not part with her for her weight in gold."

"Ay, ay! women always say such things, cause they ha'nt no sort of calculation. Just show 'em how many watches, feathers, and trinkets, one's weight in gold would buy, and that alters the case, *I* reckon."

"I tell you, Haley, this must not be spoken of; I say no, and I mean no," said Shelby, decidedly.

"Well, you'll let me have the boy, though," said the trader; "you must own I've come down pretty handsomely for him."

"What on earth can you want with the child?" said Shelby.

"Why, I've got a friend that's going into this yer branch of the business – wants to buy up handsome boys to raise for the market. Fancy articles entirely – sell for waiters, and so on, to rich 'uns, that can pay for handsome 'uns. It sets off one of yer great places – a real handsome boy to open door, wait, and tend. They fetch a good sum; and this little devil is such a comical, musical concern, he's just the article."

"I would rather not sell him," said Mr Shelby, thoughtfully; "the fact is, sir, I'm a humane man, and I hate to take the boy from his mother, sir."

"O, you do? – La! yes – something of that ar natur. I understand, perfectly. It is mighty onpleasant getting on with women, sometimes. I al'ays hates these yer screachin', screamin' times. They are *mighty* onpleasant; but, as I manages business, I generally avoids 'em, sir. Now, what if you get the girl off for a day, or a week, or so; then the thing's done quietly, – all over before she comes home. Your wife might get her some ear-rings, or a new gown, or some such truck, to make up with her."

"I'm afraid not."

"Lor bless ye, yes! These critters an't like white folks, you know; they gets over things, only manage right. Now, they say," said Haley, assuming a candid and confidential air, "that this kind o' trade is hardening to the feelings; but I never found it so. Fact is, I never could do things up the way some fellers manage the business. I've seen 'em as would pull a woman's child out of her arms, and set him up to sell, and she screechin' like mad all the time; – very bad policy – damages the article – makes 'em quite unfit for service sometimes. I knew a real handsome gal once, in Orleans, as was entirely ruined by this sort o' handling. The fellow that was trading for her didn't want her baby; and she was one of your real high sort, when her blood was up. I tell you, she squeezed up her child in her arms, and talked, and went on real awful. It kinder makes my blood run cold to think on't; and when they carried off the child, and locked her up, she jest went ravin' mad, and died in a week. Clear waste, sir, of a thousand dollars, just for want of management, – there's where 't is. It's always best to do the humane thing, sir; that's been *my* experience." And the trader leaned back in his chair, and folded his arm, with an air of virtuous decision, apparently considering himself a second Wilberforce.

The subject appeared to interest the gentleman deeply; for while Mr Shelby was thoughtfully peeling an orange, Haley broke out afresh, with becoming diffidence, but as if actually driven by the force of truth to say a few words more.

"It don't look well, now, for a feller to be praisin' himself; but I say it jest because it's the truth. I believe I'm reckoned to bring in about the finest droves of niggers that is brought in, – at least, I've been told so; if I have once, I reckon I have a hundred times, – all in good case, – fat and likely, and I lose as few as any man in the business. And I lays it all to my management, sir; and humanity, sir, I may say, is the great pillar of *my* management."

Mr Shelby did not know what to say, and so he said, "Indeed!"

"Now, I've been laughed at for my notions, sir, and I've been talked to. They an't pop'lar, and they an't common; but I stuck to 'em, sir; I've stuck to 'em, and realized well on 'em; yes, sir, they have paid their passage, I may say," and the trader laughed at his joke.

There was something so piquant and original in these elucidations of humanity, that Mr Shelby could not help laughing in company. Perhaps you laugh too, dear reader; but you know humanity comes out in a variety of strange forms now-a-days, and there is no end to the odd things that humane people will say and do.

Mr Shelby's laugh encouraged the trader to proceed.

"It's strange now, but I never could beat this into people's heads. Now, there was Tom Loker, my old partner, down in Natchez; he was a clever fellow, Tom was, only the very devil with niggers, – on principle 't was, you see, for a better hearted feller never broke bread; 't was his *system*, sir. I used to talk to Tom. 'Why, Tom,' I used to say, 'when your gals takes on and cry, what's the use o' crackin on 'em over the head, and knockin' on 'em round? It's ridiculous,' says I, 'and don't do no sort o' good. Why, I don't see no harm in their cryin',' says I; 'it's natur,' says I, 'and if natur can't blow off one way, it will another. Besides, Tom,' says I, 'it jest spiles your gals; they get sickly, and down in the mouth; and sometimes they gets ugly, – particular yellow gals do, – and it's the devil and all gettin' on 'em broke in. Now,' says I, 'why can't you kinder coax 'em up, and speak 'em fair? Depend on it, Tom, a little humanity, thrown in along, goes a heap further than all your jawin' and crackin'; and it pays better,' says I, 'depend on 't.' But Tom couldn't get the

---

William Wilberforce – British anti-slavery campaigner who led the movement that abolished the slave trade in 1807

hang on 't; and he spiled so many for me, that I had to break off with him, though he was a good-hearted fellow, and as fair a business hand as is goin'."

"And do you find your ways of managing do the business better than Tom's?" said Mr Shelby.

"Why, yes, sir, I may say so. You see, when I any ways can, I takes a leetle care about the onpleasant parts like selling young uns and that, – get the gals out of the way – out of sight, out of mind, you know, – and when it's clean done, and can't be helped, they naturally gets used to it. 'Tan't, you know, as if it was white folks, that's brought up in the way of 'spectin' to keep their children and wives, and all that. Niggers, you know, that's fetched up properly, ha'n't no kind of 'spectations of no kind; so all these things comes easier."

"I'm afraid mine are not properly brought up, then," said Mr Shelby.

"S'pose not; you Kentucky folks spile your niggers. You mean well by 'em, but 'tan't no real kindness, arter all. Now, a nigger, you see, what's got to be hacked and tumbled round the world, and sold to Tom, and Dick, and the Lord knows who, 'tan't no kindness to be givin' on him notions and expectations, and bringin' on him up too well, for the rough and tumble comes all the harder on him arter. Now, I venture to say, your niggers would be quite chop-fallen in a place where some of your plantation niggers would be singing and whooping like all possessed. Every man, you know, Mr Shelby, naturally thinks well of his own ways; and I think I treat niggers just about as well as it's ever worth while to treat 'em."

"It's a happy thing to be satisfied," said Mr Shelby, with a slight shrug, and some perceptible feelings of a disagreeable nature.

"Well," said Haley, after they had both silently picked their nuts for a season, "what do you say?"

"I'll think the matter over, and talk with my wife," said Mr Shelby. "Meantime, Haley, if you want the matter carried on in the quiet way you speak of, you'd best not let your business in this neighborhood be known. It will get out among my boys, and it will not be a particularly quiet business getting away any of my fellows, if they know it, I'll promise you."

"O! certainly, by all means, mum! of course. But I'll tell you, I'm in a devil of a hurry, and shall want to know, as soon as possible, what I may depend on," said he, rising and putting on his overcoat.

"Well, call up this evening, between six and seven, and you shall have my answer," said Mr Shelby, and the trader bowed himself out of the apartment.

"I'd like to have been able to kick the fellow down the steps," said he to himself, as he saw the door fairly closed, "with his impudent assurance; but he knows how much he has me at advantage. If anybody had ever said to me that I should sell Tom down south to one of those rascally traders, I should have said, 'Is thy servant a dog, that he should do this thing?' And now it must come, for aught I see. And Eliza's child, too! I know that I shall have some fuss with wife about that; and, for that matter, about Tom, too. So much for being in debt, – heigho! The fellow sees his advantage, and means to push it."

Perhaps the mildest form of the system of slavery is to be seen in the State of Kentucky. The general prevalence of agricultural pursuits of a quiet and gradual nature, not requiring those periodic seasons of hurry and pressure that are called for in the business of more southern districts, makes the task of the negro a more healthful and reasonable one; while the master, content with a more gradual style of acquisition, has not those temptations to hard-heartedness which always over-come frail human nature when the prospect of sudden and rapid gain is weighed in the balance, with no heavier counterpoise than the interests of the helpless and unprotected.

Whoever visits some estates there, and witnesses the good-humored indulgence of some masters and mistresses, and the affectionate loyalty of some slaves, might be tempted to dream the oft-fabled poetic legend of a patriarchal institution, and all that; but over and above the scene there broods a portentous shadow — the shadow of *law*. So long as the law considers all these human beings, with beating hearts and living affections, only as so many *things* belonging to a master, — so long as the failure, or misfortune, or imprudence, or death of the kindest owner, may cause them any day to exchange a life of kind protection and indulgence for one of hopeless misery and toil, — so long it is impossible to make anything beautiful or desirable in the best regulated administration of slavery.

Mr Shelby was a fair average kind of man, good-natured and kindly, and dis-posed to easy indulgence of those around him, and there had never been a lack of anything which might contribute to the physical comfort of the negroes on his estate. He had, however, speculated largely and quite loosely; had involved him-self deeply, and his notes to a large amount had come into the hands of Haley; and this small piece of information is the key to the preceding conversation.

Now, it had so happened that, in approaching the door, Eliza had caught enough of the conversation to know that a trader was making offers to her master for somebody.

She would gladly have stopped at the door to listen, as she came out; but her mistress just then calling, she was obliged to hasten away.

Still she thought she heard the trader make an offer for her boy; — could she be mistaken? Her heart swelled and throbbed, and she involuntarily strained him so tight that the little fellow looked up into her face in astonishment.

"Eliza, girl, what ails you to-day?" said her mistress, when Eliza had upset the wash-pitcher, knocked down the work-stand, and finally was abstractedly offering her mistress a long night-gown in place of the silk dress she had ordered her to bring from the wardrobe.

Eliza started. "O, missis!" she said, raising her eyes; then, bursting into tears, she sat down in a chair, and began sobbing.

"Why, Eliza, child! what ails you?" said her mistress.

"O! missis, missis," said Eliza, "there's been a trader talking with master in the parlor! I heard him."

"Well, silly child, suppose there has."

"O, missis, *do* you suppose mas'r would sell my Harry?" And the poor creature threw herself into a chair, and sobbed convulsively.

"Sell him! No, you foolish girl! You know your master never deals with those southern traders, and never means to sell any of his servants, as long as they behave well. Why, you silly child, who do you think would want to buy your Harry? Do you think all the world are set on him as you are, you goosie? Come, cheer up, and hook my dress. There now, put my back hair up in that pretty braid you learnt the other day, and don't go listening at doors any more."

"Well, but, missis, *you* never would give your consent – to – to –"

"Nonsense, child! to be sure, I shouldn't. What do you talk so for? I would as soon have one of my own children sold. But really, Eliza, you are getting altogether too proud of that little fellow. A man can't put his nose into the door, but you think he must be coming to buy him."

Reassured by her mistress' confident tone, Eliza proceeded nimbly and adroitly with her toilet, laughing at her own fears, as she proceeded.

Mrs Shelby was a woman of a high class, both intellectually and morally. To that natural magnanimity and generosity of mind which one often marks as characteristic of the women of Kentucky, she added high moral and religious sensibility and principle, carried out with great energy and ability into practical results. Her husband, who made no professions to any particular religious character, nevertheless reverenced and respected the consistency of hers, and stood, perhaps, a little in awe of her opinion. Certain it was that he gave her unlimited scope in all her benevolent efforts for the comfort, instruction, and improvement of her servants, though he never took any decided part in them himself. In fact, if not exactly a believer in the doctrine of the efficiency of the extra good works of saints, he really seemed somehow or other to fancy that his wife had piety and benevolence enough for two – to indulge a shadowy expectation of getting into heaven through her superabundance of qualities to which he made no particular pretension.

The heaviest load on his mind, after his conversation with the trader, lay in the foreseen necessity of breaking to his wife the arrangement contemplated, – meeting the importunities and opposition which he knew he should have reason to encounter.

Mrs Shelby, being entirely ignorant of her husband's embarrassments, and knowing only the general kindliness of his temper, had been quite sincere in the entire incredulity with which she had met Eliza's suspicions. In fact, she dismissed the matter from her mind, without a second thought; and being occupied in preparations for an evening visit, it passed out of her thoughts entirely.

44

LERONE BENNETT, JR

The Convert

The story takes place around 1954, when the US Supreme Court overturned the allegedly "separate but equal" system of segregation that had resulted in systematic discrimination against African Americans in public schools. Courts held that other forms of segregation, for example in public transport across state lines, were also unconstitutional.

A man don't know what he'll do, a man don't know what he is till he gets his back pressed up against a wall. Now you take Aaron Lott: there ain't no other way to explain the crazy thing he did. He was going alone fine, preaching the gospel, saving souls, and getting along with the white folks; and then, all of a sudden, he felt wood pressing against his back. The funny thing was that nobody knew he was hurting till he preached that Red Sea sermon where he got mixed up and seemed to think Mississippi was Egypt. As chairman of the deacons board, I felt it was my duty to reason with him. I appreciated his position and told him so, but I didn't think it was right for him to push us all in a hole. The old fool – he just laughed.

"Brother Booker," he said, "the Lord – He'll take care of me."

I knew then that that man was heading for trouble. And the very next thing he did confirmed it. The white folks called the old fool downtown to bear witness that the colored folks were happy. And you know what he did: he got down there amongst all them big white folks and he said: "Things ain't gonna change here overnight, but they gonna change. It's inevitable. The Lord wants it."

Well sir, you could have bought them white folks for a penny. Aaron Lott, pastor of the Rock of Zion Baptist Church, a man white folks had said was wise and sound and sensible, had come close – too close – to saying that the Supreme Court was coming to Melina, Mississippi. The surprising thing was that the white folks didn't do nothing. There was a lot of mumbling and whispering but nothing

---

bad happened till the terrible morning when Aaron came a-knocking at the door of my funeral home. Now things had been tightening up – you could feel it in the air – and I didn't want no part of no crazy scheme and I told him so right off. He walked on past me and sat down on the couch. He had on his preaching clothes, a shiny blue suit, a fresh starched white shirt, a black tie, and his Sunday black shoes. I remember thinking at the time that Aaron was too black to be wearing all them dark clothes. The thought tickled me and I started to smile but then I noticed something about him that didn't seem quite right. I ran my eyes over him closely. He was kinda middle-sized and he had a big clean-shaven head, a big nose, and thin lips. I stood there looking at him for a long time but I couldn't figure out what it was till I looked at his eyes: they were burning bright, like light bulbs do just before they go out. And yet he looked contented, like his mind was resting somewheres else.

"I wanna talk with you, Booker," he said, glancing sideways at my wife. "If you don't mind, Sister Brown –"

Sarah got up and went into the living quarters. Aaron didn't say nothing for a long time; he just sat there looking out the window. Then he spoke so soft I had to strain my ears to hear.

"I'm leaving for the Baptist convention," he said. He pulled out his gold watch and looked at it. "Train leaves in 'bout two hours."

"I know *that*, Aaron."

"Yeah, but what I wanted to tell you was that I ain't going Jim Crow. I'm going first class, Booker, right through the white waiting room. That's the law."

A cold shiver ran through me.

"Aaron," I said, "don't you go talking crazy now."

The old fool laughed, a great big body-shaking laugh. He started talking 'bout God and Jesus and all that stuff. Now, I'm a God-fearing man myself, but I holds that God helps those who help themselves. I told him so.

"You can't mix God up with these white folks," I said. "When you start to messing around with segregation, they'll burn you up and the Bible, too."

He looked at me like I was Satan.

"I sweated over this thing," he said. "I prayed. I got down on my knees and I asked God not to give me this cup. But He said I was the one. I heard Him, Booker, right here – he tapped his chest – in my heart."

The old fool's been having visions, I thought. I sat down and tried to figure out a way to hold him, but he got up, without saying a word, and started for the door.

"Wait!" I shouted. "I'll get my coat."

"I don't need you," he said. "I just came by to tell you so you could tell the board in case something happened."

"You wait," I shouted, and ran out of the room to get my coat.

We got in his beat-up old Ford and went by the parsonage to get his suitcase. Rachel – that was his wife – and Jonah were sitting in the living room, wringing

---

"Jim Crow" – the system of discrimination that operated against blacks in the South after the abolition of slavery (see also the extract from *Uncle Tom's Cabin* above, p. 330); specifically in this case, separate seating arrangements for blacks traveling by train

their hands. Aaron got his bag, shook Jonah's hand, and said, "Take care of your Mamma, boy." Jonah nodded. Aaron hugged Rachel and pecked at her cheek. Rachel broke down. She threwed her arms around his neck and carried on something awful. Aaron shoved her away.

"Don't go making no fuss over it, woman. I ain't gonna be gone forever. Can't a man go to a church meeting 'thout women screaming and crying."

He tried to make light of it, but you could see he was touched by the way his lips trembled. He held his hand out to me, but I wouldn't take it. I told him off good, told him it was a sin and a shame for a man of God to be carrying on like he was, worrying his wife and everything.

"I'm coming with you," I said. "Somebody's gotta see that you don't make a fool of yourself."

He shrugged, picked up his suitcase, and started for the door. Then he stopped and turned around and looked at his wife and his boy and from the way he looked I knew that there was still a chance. He looked at the one and then at the other. For a moment there, I thought he was going to cry, but he turned, quick-like, and walked out of the door.

I ran after him and tried to talk some sense in his head. But he shook me off, turned the corner, and went on up Adams Street. I caught up with him and we walked in silence, crossing the street in front of the First Baptist Church for whites, going on around the Confederate monument where, once, they hung a boy for fooling around with white women.

"Put it off, Aaron," I begged. "Sleep on it."

He didn't say nothing.

"What you need is a vacation. I'll get the board to approve, full pay and everything."

He smiled and shifted the suitcase over to his left hand. Big drops of sweat were running down his face and spotting up his shirt. His eyes were awful, all lit up and burning.

"Aaron, Aaron, can't you hear me?"

We passed the feed store, Bill Williams' grocery store, and the movie house.

"A man's gotta think about his family, Aaron. A man ain't free. Didn't you say that once, didn't you?"

He shaded his eyes with his hand and looked into the sun. He put the suitcase on the ground and checked his watch.

"Why don't you think about Jonah?" I asked. "Answer that. Why don't you think about your own son?"

"I am," he said. "That's exactly what I'm doing, thinking about Jonah. Matter of fact, he started *me* to thinking. I ain't never mentioned it before, but the boy's been worrying me. One day we was downtown here and he asked me something that hurt. 'Daddy,' he said, 'how come you ain't a man?' I got mad, I did, and told him: 'I am a man.' He said that wasn't what he meant. 'I mean,' he said, 'how come you ain't a man where white folks concerned.' I couldn't answer him, Booker. I'll never forget it till the day I die. I couldn't answer my own son, and I been preaching forty years."

"He don't know nothing 'bout it," I said. "He's hot-headed, like my boy. He'll find out when he grows up."

"I hopes not," Aaron said, shaking his head. "I hopes not."

Some white folks passed and we shut up till they were out of hearing. Aaron, who was acting real strange, looked up in the sky and moved his lips. He came back to himself, after a little bit, and he said: "This thing of being a man, Booker, is a big thing. The Supreme Court can't make you a man. The NAACP can't do it. God Almighty can do a lot, but even He can't do it. Ain't nobody can do it but you."

He said that like he was preaching and when he got through he was all filled up with emotion and he seemed kind of ashamed – he was a man who didn't like emotion outside the church. He looked at his watch, picked up his bag, and said, "Well, let's git it over with."

We turned into Elm and the first thing I saw at the end of the Street was the train station. It was an old red building, flat like a slab. A group of white men were fooling around in front of the door. I couldn't make them out from that distance, but I could tell they weren't the kind of white folks to be fooling around with.

We walked on, passing the dry goods store, the barber shop, and the new building that was going up. Across the street from that was the sheriff's office. I looked in the window and saw Bull Sampson sitting at his desk, his feet propped up on a chair, a fat brown cigar sticking out of his mouth. A ball about the size of a sweet potato started burning in my stomach.

"Please Aaron," I said. "Please. You can't get away with it. I know how you feel. Sometimes I feel the same way myself, but I wouldn't risk my neck to do nothing for these niggers. They won't appreciate it; they'll laugh at you."

We were almost to the station and I could make out the faces of the men sitting on the benches. One of them must have been telling a joke. He finished and the group broke out laughing.

I whispered to Aaron: "I'm through with it. I wash my hands of the whole mess."

I don't know whether he heard me or not. He turned to the right without saying a word and went on in the front door. The string-beany man who told the joke was so shocked that his cigarette fell out of his mouth.

"Y'all see that," he said. "Why, I'll –"

"Shut up," another man said. "Go git Bull."

I kept walking, fast, turned at the corner, and ran around to the colored waiting room. When I got in there, I looked through the ticket window and saw Aaron standing in front of the clerk. Aaron stood there for a minute or more, but the clerk didn't see him. And that took some not seeing. In that room, Aaron Lott stood out like a pig in a chicken coop.

There were, I'd say, about ten or fifteen people in there, but didn't none of them move. They just sat there, with their eyes glued on Aaron's back. Aaron cleared his throat. The clerk didn't look up; he got real busy with some papers. Aaron cleared his throat again and opened his mouth to speak. The screen door of the waiting room opened and clattered shut.

It got real quiet in that room, hospital quiet. It got so quiet I could hear my own heart beating. Now Aaron knew who opened that door, but he didn't bat an eyelid. He turned around real slow and faced High Sheriff Sampson, the baddest man in South Mississippi.

NAACP – National Association for the Advancement of Colored People

Mr Sampson stood there with his legs wide open, like the men you see on television. His beefy face was blood-red and his gray eyes were rattlesnake hard. He was mad; no doubt about it. I had never seen him so mad.

"Preacher," he said, "you done gone crazy?" He was talking low-like and mean.

"Nosir," Aaron said. "Nosir, Mr Sampson."

"What you think you doing?"

"Going to St Louis, Mr Sampson."

"You must done lost yo' mind, boy."

Mr Sampson started walking towards Aaron with his hand on his gun. Twenty or thirty men pushed through the front door and fanned out over the room. Mr Sampson stopped about two paces from Aaron and looked him up and down. That look had paralyzed hundreds of niggers; but it didn't faze Aaron none – he stood his ground.

"I'm gonna give you a chance, preacher. Git on over to the nigger side and git quick."

"I ain't bothering nobody, Mr Sampson."

Somebody in the crowd yelled: "Don't reason wit' the nigger, Bull. Hit 'em."

Mr Sampson walked up to Aaron and grabbed him in the collar and throwed him up against the ticket counter. He pulled out his gun.

"Did you hear me, deacon. I said, 'Git.'"

"I'm going to St Louis, Mr Sampson. That's cross state lines. The court done said –"

Aaron didn't have a chance. The blow came from nowhere. Laying there on the floor with blood spurting from his mouth, Aaron looked up at Mr Sampson and he did another crazy thing: he grinned. Bull Sampson jumped up in the air and came down on Aaron with all his two hundred pounds. It made a crunchy sound. He jumped again and the mob, maddened by the blood and heat, moved in to help him. They fell on Aaron like mad dogs. They beat him with chairs; they beat him with sticks; they beat him with guns.

Till this day, I don't know what come over me. The first thing I know I was running and then I was standing in the middle of the white waiting room. Mr Sampson was the first to see me. He backed off, cocked his pistol, and said: "Booker, boy, you come one mo' step and I'll kill you. What's a matter with you niggers today? All y'all gone crazy?"

"Please don't kill him," I begged. "You ain't got no call to treat him like that."

"So you saw it all, did you? Well, then, Booker you musta saw the nigger preacher reach for my gun?"

"He didn't do that, Mr Sampson," I said. "He didn't –"

Mr Sampson put a big hairy hand on my tie and pulled me to him.

"Booker," he said sweetly. "You saw the nigger preacher reach for my gun, didn't you?"

I didn't open my mouth – I couldn't I was so scared – but I guess my eyes answered for me. Whatever Mr Sampson saw there musta convinced him 'cause he throwed me on the floor besides Aaron.

"Git this nigger out of here," he said, "and be quick about it."

Dropping to my knees, I put my hand on Aaron's chest; I didn't feel nothing. I felt his wrist; I didn't feel nothing. I got up and looked at them white folks with tears in my eyes. I looked at the women, sitting crying on the benches. I looked at the men. I looked at Mr Sampson. I said, "He was a good man."

Mr Sampson said, "Move the nigger."

A big sigh came out of me and I wrung my hands.

Mr Sampson said, "Move the nigger."

He grabbed my tie and twisted it, but I didn't feel nothing. My eyes were glued to his hands; there was blood under the fingernails, and the fingers – they looked like fat little red sausages. I screamed and Mr Sampson flung me down on the floor.

He said, "*Move the nigger.*"

I picked Aaron up and fixed his body over my shoulder and carried him outside. I sent for one of my boys and we dressed him up and put him away real nice-like and Rachel and the boy came and they cried and carried on and yet, somehow, they seemed prouder of Aaron than ever before. And the colored folks – they seemed proud, too. Crazy niggers. Didn't they know? Couldn't they see? It hadn't done no good. In fact, things got worse. The Northern newspapers started kicking up a stink and Mr Rivers, the solicitor, announced they were going to hold a hearing. All of a sudden, Booker Taliaferro Brown became the biggest man in that town. My phone rang day and night: I got threats, I got promises, and I was offered bribes. Everywhere I turned somebody was waiting to ask me: "Whatcha gonna do? Whatcha gonna say?" To tell the truth, I didn't know myself. One day I would decide one thing and the next day I would decide another.

It was Mr Rivers and Mr Sampson who called my attention to that. They came to my office one day and called me a shifty, no-good nigger. They said they expected me to stand by "my statement" in the train station that I saw Aaron reach for the gun. I hadn't said no such thing, but Mr Sampson said I said it and he said he had witnesses who heard me say it. "And if you say anything else," he said, "I can't be responsible for your health. Now you know" – he put that bloody hand on my shoulder and he smiled his sweet death smile – "you *know* I wouldn't threaten you, but the boys" – he shook his head – "the boys are real worked up over this one."

It was long about then that I began to hate Aaron Lott. I'm ashamed to admit it now, but it's true: I hated him. He had lived his life; he had made his choice. Why should he live my life, too, and make me choose? It wasn't fair; it wasn't right; it wasn't Christian. What made me so mad was the fact that nothing I said would help Aaron. He was dead and it wouldn't help one whit for me to say that he didn't reach for that gun. I tried to explain that to Rachel when she came to my office, moaning and crying, the night before the hearing.

"Listen to me, woman," I said. "Listen. Aaron was a good man. He lived a good life. He did a lot of good things, but he's *dead, dead, dead!* Nothing I say will bring him back. Bull Sampson's got ten niggers who are going to swear on a stack of Bibles that they saw Aaron reach for that gun. It won't do me or you or Aaron no good for me to swear otherwise."

What did I say that for? That woman liked to had a fit. She got down on her knees and she begged me to go with Aaron.

"Go wit' him," she cried. "'Booker. *Booker!* If you's a man, if you's a father, if you's a friend, go wit' Aaron."

That woman tore my heart up. I ain't never heard nobody beg like that.

"Tell the truth, Booker," she said. "That's all I'm asking. Tell the truth."

"Truth!" I said. "Hah! That's all you niggers talk about: truth. What do you know about truth? Truth is eating good and sleeping good. Truth is living, Rachel. Be loyal to the living."

Rachel backed off from me. You would have thought that I had cursed her or something. She didn't say nothing; she just stood there pressed against the door. She stood there saying nothing for so long that my nerves snapped.

"Say something," I shouted. "Say something – anything!"

She shook her head, slowly at first, and then her head started moving like it wasn't attached to her body. It went back and forth, back and forth, back and forth. I started towards her, but she jerked open the door and ran out into the night, screaming.

That did it. I ran across the room to the filing cabinet, opened the bottom drawer, and took out a dusty bottle of Scotch. I started drinking, but the more I drank the soberer I got. I guess I fell asleep 'cause I dreamed I buried Rachel and that everything went along fine until she jumped out of the casket and started screaming. I came awake with a start and knocked over the bottle. I reached for a rag and my hand stopped in mid-air.

"Of course," I said out loud and slammed my fist down on the Scotch-soaked papers.

I didn't see nothing.

Why didn't I think of it before?

I didn't see nothing.

Jumping up, I walked to and fro in the office. Would it work? I rehearsed it in my mind. All I could see was Aaron's back. I don't know whether he reached for the gun or not. All I know is that *for some reason* the men beat him to death.

Rehearsing the thing in my mind, I felt a great weight slip off my shoulders. I did a little jig in the middle of the floor and went upstairs to my bed, whistling. Sarah turned over and looked me up and down.

"What you happy about?"

"Can't a man be happy?" I asked.

She sniffed the air, said, "Oh," turned over, and mumbled something in her pillow. It came to me then for the first time that she was 'bout the only person in town who hadn't asked me what I was going to do. I thought about it for a little while, shrugged, and fell into bed with all my clothes on.

When I woke up the next morning, I had a terrible headache and my tongue was a piece of sandpaper. For a long while, I couldn't figure out what I was doing laying there with all my clothes on. Then it came to me: this was the big day. I put on my black silk suit, the one I wore for big funerals, and went downstairs to breakfast. I walked into the dining room without looking and bumped into Russell, the last person in the world I wanted to see. He was my only child, but he didn't act like it. He was always finding fault. He didn't like the way I talked to Negroes; he didn't like the way I talked to white folks. He didn't like this; he didn't like that.

And to top it off, the young whippersnapper wanted to be an artist. Undertaking wasn't good enough for him. He wanted to paint pictures.

I sat down and grunted.

"Good morning, Papa." He said it like he meant it. He wants something, I thought, looking him over closely, noticing that his right eye was swollen.

"You been fighting again, boy?"

"Yes, Papa."

"You younguns. Education – that's what it is. Education! It's ruining you."

He didn't say nothing. He just sat there, looking down when I looked up and looking up when I looked down. This went on through the grits and the eggs and the second cup of coffee.

"Whatcha looking at?" I asked.

"Nothing, Papa."

"Whatcha thinking?"

"Nothing, Papa."

"You lying, boy. It's written all over your face."

He didn't say nothing.

I dismissed him with a wave of my hand, picked up the paper, and turned to the sports page.

"What are you going to do, Papa?"

The question caught me unawares. I know now that I was expecting it, that I wanted him to ask it; but he put it so bluntly that I was flabbergasted. I pretended I didn't understand.

"Do 'bout what, boy? Speak up!"

"About the trial, Papa."

I didn't say nothing for a long time. There wasn't much, in fact, I could say; so I got mad.

"Questions, questions, questions," I shouted. "That's all I get in this house – questions. You never have a civil word for your pa. I go out of here and work my tail off and you keep yourself shut up in that room of yours looking at them fool books and now soon as your old man gets his back against the wall you join the pack. I expected better than that of you, boy. A son ought to back his pa."

That hurt him. He picked up the coffee pot and poured himself another cup of coffee and his hand trembled. He took a sip and watched me over the rim.

"They say you are going to chicken out, Papa."

"Chicken out? What that mean?"

"They're betting you'll 'Tom.'"

I leaned back in the chair and took a sip of coffee.

"So they're betting, huh?" The idea appealed to me. "Crazy niggers – they'd bet on a funeral."

I saw pain on his face. He sighed and said: "I bet, too, Papa."

The cup fell out of my hand and broke, spilling black water over the tablecloth. "You did what?"

"I bet you wouldn't 'Tom.'"

"You little fool." I fell out laughing and then I stopped suddenly and looked at him closely. "How much you bet?"

"One hundred dollars."

I stood up.

"You're lying," I said. "Where'd you get that kind of money?"

"From Mamma."

"Sarah!" I shouted. "Sarah! You get in here. What kind of house you running, sneaking behind my back, giving this boy money to gamble with?"

Sarah leaned against the door jamb. She was in her hot iron mood. There was no expression on her face. And her eyes were hard.

"I gave it to him, Booker," she said. "They called you an Uncle Tom. He got in a fight about it. He wanted to bet on you, Booker. *He* believes in you."

Suddenly I felt old and used up. I pulled a chair to me and sat down.

"Please," I said, waving my hand. "Please. Go away. Leave me alone. Please."

I sat there for maybe ten or fifteen minutes, thinking, praying. The phone rang. It was Mr Withers, the president of the bank. I had put in for a loan and it had been turned down, but Mr Withers said there'd been a mistake. "New fellow, you know," he said, clucking his tongue. He said he knew that it was my lifelong dream to build a modern funeral home and to buy a Cadillac hearse. He said he sympathized with that dream, supported it, thought the town needed it, and thought I deserved it. "The loan will go through," he said. "Drop by and see me this morning after the hearing."

When I put that phone down, it was wet with sweat. I couldn't turn that new funeral home down and Mr Withers knew it. My father had raised me on that dream and before he died he made me swear on a Bible that I would make it good. And here it was on a platter, just for a word, a word that wouldn't hurt nobody.

I put on my hat and hurried to the courthouse. When they called my name, I walked in with my head held high. The courtroom was packed. The white folks had all the seats and the colored folks were standing in the rear. Whoever arranged the seating had set aside the first two rows for white men. They were sitting almost on top of each other, looking mean and uncomfortable in their best white shirts.

I walked up to the bench and swore on the Bible and took a seat. Mr Rivers gave me a little smile and waited for me to get myself set.

"State your name," he said.

"'Booker Taliaferro Brown." I took a quick look at the first two rows and recognized at least ten of the men who killed Aaron.

"And your age?"

"Fifty-seven."

"You're an undertaker?"

"Yessir."

"You been living in this town all your life?"

"Yessir."

"You like it here, don't you, Booker?"

Was this a threat? I looked Mr Rivers in the face for the first time. He smiled. I told the truth. I said, "Yessir."

"Now, calling your attention to the day of May 17th, did anything unusual happen on that day?"

The question threw me. I shook my head. Then it dawned on me. He was talking about –

"Yessir," I said. "That's the day Aaron got –" Something in Mr Rivers' face warned me and I pulled up – "that's the day of the trouble at the train station."

Mr Rivers smiled. He looked like a trainer who'd just put a monkey through a new trick. You could feel the confidence and the contempt oozing out of him. I looked at his prissy little mustache and his smiling lips and I got mad. Lifting my head a little bit, I looked him full in the eyes; I held the eyes for a moment and I tried to tell the man behind the eyes that I was a man like him and that he didn't have no right to be using me and laughing about it. But he didn't get the message. The bastard – he chuckled softly, turned his back to me, and faced the audience.

"I believe you were with the preacher that day."

The water was getting deep. I scroonched down in my seat, closed the lids of my eyes, and looked dense.

"Yessir, Mr Rivers," I drawled. "Ah was, Ah was."

"Now, Booker –" he turned around – "I believe you tried to keep the nigger preacher from getting out of line."

I hesitated. It wasn't a fair question. Finally, I said: "Yessir."

"You begged him not to go in the white side?"

"Yessir."

"And when that failed, you went over to *your* side – the *colored* side – and looked through the window?"

"Yessir."

He put his hand in his coat pocket and studied my face.

"You saw *everything*, didn't you?"

"Just about." A muscle on the inside of my thigh started tingling.

Mr Rivers shuffled some papers he had in his hand. He seemed to be thinking real hard. I pushed myself against the back of the chair. Mr Rivers moved close, quick, and stabbed his finger into my chest.

"Booker, did you see the nigger preacher reach for Mr Sampson's gun?"

He backed away, smiling. I looked away from him and I felt my heart trying to tear out of my skin. I looked out over the courtroom. It was still; wasn't even a fly moving. I looked at the white folks in front and the colored folks in back and I turned the question over in my mind. While I was doing that, waiting, taking my time, I noticed, out of the corner of my eye, that the smile on Mr Rivers' face was dying away. Suddenly, I had a terrible itch to know what that smile would turn into.

I said, "Nosir."

Mr Rivers stumbled backwards like he had been shot. Old Judge Sloan took off his glasses and pushed his head out over the bench. The whole courtroom seemed to be leaning in to me and I saw Aaron's widow leaning back with her eyes closed and it seemed to me at that distance that her lips were moving in prayer.

Mr Rivers was the first to recover. He put his smile back on and he acted like my answer was in the script.

"You mean," he said, "that you didn't see it. It happened so quickly that you missed it?"

I looked at the bait and I ain't gonna lie: I was tempted. He knew as well as I did what I meant, but he was gambling on my weakness. I had thrown away my funeral home, my hearse, everything I owned, and he was standing there like a magician, pulling them out of a hat, one at a time, dangling them, saying: "Looka here, looka here, don't they look pretty?" I was on top of a house and he was betting that if he gave me a ladder I would come down. He was wrong, but you can't fault him for trying. He hadn't never met no nigger who would go all the way. I looked him in the eye and went the last mile.

"Aaron didn't reach for that gun," I said. "Them people, they just fell on –"

"Hold it," he shouted. "I want to remind you that there are laws in this state against perjury. You can go to jail for five years for what you just said. Now I know you've been conferring with those NAACP fellows, but I want to remind you of the statements you made to Sheriff Sampson and me. Judge –" he dismissed me with a wave of his hand – "Judge, this *man* –" he caught himself and it was my turn to smile – "this *boy* is lying. Ten niggers have testified that they saw the preacher reach for the gun. Twenty white people saw it. You've heard their testimony. I want to withdraw this witness and I want to reserve the right to file perjury charges against him."

Judge Sloan nodded. He pushed his bottom lip over his top one.

"You can step down," he said. "I want to warn you that perjury is a very grave offense. You –"

"Judge, I didn't –"

"Nigger!" He banged his gavel. "Don't you interrupt me. Now git out of here."

Two guards pushed me outside and waved away the reporters. Billy Giles, Mr Sampson's assistant, came out and told me Mr Sampson wanted me out of town before sundown. "And he says you'd better get out before the Northern reporters leave. He won't be responsible for your safety after that."

I nodded and went on down the stairs and started out the door.

"Booker!"

Rachel and a whole line of Negroes were running down the stairs. I stepped outside and waited for them. Rachel ran up and throwed her arms around me. "It don't take but one, Booker," she said. "It don't take but one." Somebody else said: "They whitewashed it, they whitewashed it, but you spoiled it for 'em."

Russell came out then and stood over to the side while the others crowded around to shake my hands. Then the others sensed that he was waiting and they made a little aisle. He walked up to me kind of slow-like and he said, "Thank you, sir." That was the first time in his whole seventeen years that that boy had said "sir" to me. I cleared my throat and when I opened my eyes Sarah was standing beside me. She didn't say nothing; she just put her hand in mine and stood there. It was long about then, I guess, when I realized that I wasn't seeing so good. They say I cried, but I don't believe a word of it. It was such a hot day and the sun was shining so bright that the sweat rolling down my face blinded me. I wiped the sweat out of my eyes and some more people came up and said a lot of foolish things about me showing the white folks and following in Aaron's footsteps. I wasn't doing no such fool thing. Ol' Man Rivers just put the thing to me in a way it hadn't been put before – man to man. It was simple, really. Any man would have done it.

45

WILLIAM SHAKESPEARE

The Taming of the Shrew

The Taming of the Shrew is one of Shakespeare's early comedies. The main plot concerns Baptista Minola, who will not allow the marriage of his beautiful and amiable younger daughter Bianca until her older sister Katharina is wed. Bianca's suitors cast about for someone to marry Katharina, who is "shrewish and froward beyond all measure," a "wild-cat . . . famous for her scolding tongue." Petruchio has just arrived in Padua and is prepared to marry Katharina for her dowry of twenty thousand crowns and half her father's lands after his death. In this scene Petruchio greets Katharina, whom he is meeting for the first time.

Good-morrow, Kate; for that's your name, I hear.
KATHARINA: Well have you heard, but something hard of hearing:
    They call me Katharine that do talk of me.
PETRUCHIO: You lie, in faith; for you are call'd plain Kate,
    And bonny Kate, and sometimes Kate the curst;
    But, Kate, the prettiest Kate in Christendom,
    Kate of Kate-Hall, my super-dainty Kate,
    For dainties are all cates; and therefore, Kate,
    Take this of me, Kate of my consolation; –
    Hearing thy mildness prais'd in every town,
    Thy virtues spoke of, and thy beauty sounded, –
    Yet not so deeply as to thee belongs, –
    Myself am mov'd to woo thee for my wife.
KATHARINA: Mov'd! in good time: let him that mov'd you hither
    Remove you hence: [. . .]
PETRUCHIO: Come, come, you wasp; i' faith, you are too angry.
KATHARINA: If I be waspish, best beware my sting.
PETRUCHIO: My remedy is then, to pluck it out.
KATHARINA: Ay, if the fool could find it where it lies.
PETRUCHIO: Who knows not where a wasp doth wear his sting?
    In his tail.

WILLIAM SHAKESPEARE, from Act II, Scene I and Act V, Scene II in *The Taming of the Shrew*.

KATHARINA: In his tongue.
PETRUCHIO: Whose tongue?
KATHARINA: Yours, if you talk of tails; and so farewell.
PETRUCHIO: What, with my tongue in your tail? nay, come again,
Good Kate; I am a gentleman.
KATHARINA: That I'll try.

(*Striking him.*)

PETRUCHIO: I swear I'll cuff you, if you strike again.
KATHARINA: So may you lose your arms:
   If you strike me, you are no gentleman;
   And if no gentleman, why then no arms.
PETRUCHIO: A herald, Kate? O, put me in thy books!
KATHARINA: What is your crest? a coxcomb?
PETRUCHIO: A combless cock, so Kate will be my hen.
KATHARINA: No cock of mine; you crow too like a craven.
PETRUCHIO: Nay, come, Kate, come; you must not look so sour.
KATHARINA: It is my fashion, when I see a crab.
PETRUCHIO: Why, here's no crab; and therefore look not sour.
KATHARINA: There is, there is.
PETRUCHIO: Then show it me.
KATHARINA: Had I a glass I would.
PETRUCHIO: What, you mean my face?
KATHARINA: Well aim'd of such a young one.
PETRUCHIO: Now, by Saint George, I am too young for you.
KATHARINA: Yet you are wither'd.
PETRUCHIO: 'Tis with cares.
KATHARINA: I care not.
PETRUCHIO: Nay, hear you, Kate: in sooth, you 'scape not so.
KATHARINA: I chafe you, if I tarry; let me go.
PETRUCHIO: No, not a whit: I find you passing gentle.
   'Twas told me you were rough, and coy, and sullen,
   And now I find report a very liar;
   For thou art pleasant, gamesome, passing courteous;
   But slow in speech, yet sweet as spring-time flowers:
   Thou canst not frown, thou canst not look askance,
   Nor bite the lip, as angry wenches will;
   Nor hast thou pleasure to be cross in talk;
   But thou with mildness entertain'st thy wooers
   With gentle conference, soft and affable. [. . .]
KATHARINA: Where did you study all this goodly speech?
PETRUCHIO: It is extempore, from my mother-wit.
KATHARINA: A witty mother! witless else her son.
PETRUCHIO: Am I not wise?
KATHARINA: Yes, keep you warm.

PETRUCHIO: Marry, so I mean, sweet Katharine, in thy bed:
    And therefore, setting all this chat aside,
    Thus in plain terms: – Your father hath consented
    That you shall be my wife; your dowry 'greed on;
    And, will you, nill you, I will marry you.
    Now, Kate, I am a husband for your turn;
    For, by this light, whereby I see thy beauty, –
    Thy beauty that doth make me like thee well –
    Thou must be married to no man but me;
    For I am he am born to tame you, Kate;
    And bring you from a wild Kate to a Kate
    Conformable, as other household Kates.
    Here comes your father; never make denial;
    I must and will have Katharine to my wife.

(Re-enter BAPTISTA, GREMIO, *and* TRANIO.*)*

BAPTISTA: Now, Signior Petruchio, how speed you with my daughter?
PETRUCHIO: How but well, sir? how but well?
    It were impossible I should speed amiss.
BAPTISTA: Why, how now, daughter Katharine! in your dumps?
KATHARINA: Call you me daughter? now, I promise you
    You have show'd a tender fatherly regard
    To wish me wed to one half lunatic;
    A mad-cap ruffian and a swearing Jack,
    That thinks with oaths to face the matter out.
PETRUCHIO: Father, 'tis thus: – yourself and all the world,
    That talked of her, hath talk'd amiss of her;
    If she be curst, it is for policy;
    For she's not froward, but modest as the dove,
    She is not hot, but temperate as the morn;
    For patience she will prove a second Grissel,
    And Roman Lucrece for her chastity:
    And to conclude, we have 'greed so well together,
    That upon Sunday is the wedding-day.
KATHARINA: I'll see thee hang'd on Sunday first.
GREMIO: Hark, Petruchio; she says she'll see thee hang'd first.
TRANIO: Is this your speeding? nay, then, good-night our part!
PETRUCHIO: Be patient, gentlemen; I choose her for myself;
    If she and I be pleas'd, what's that to you?
    'Tis bargain'd 'twixt us twain, being alone,
    That she shall still be curst in company.
    I tell you, 'tis incredible to believe
    How much she loves me: O, the kindest Kate! –
    She hung about my neck, and kiss on kiss
    She vied so fast, protesting oath on oath,

That in a twink she won me to her love.
O, you are novices! 'tis a world to see,
How tame when men and women are alone,
A meacock wretch can make the curstest shrew. –
Give me thy hand, Kate: I will unto Venice,
To buy apparel 'gainst the wedding-day. –
Provide the feast, father, and bid the guests;
I will be sure my Katharine shall be fine.
BAPTISTA: I know not what to say: but give me your hands;
God send you joy, Petruchio! 'tis a match.
GREMIO, TRANIO: Amen, say we; we will be witnesses.
PETRUCHIO: Father, and wife, and gentlemen, adieu;
I will to Venice; Sunday comes apace: –
We will have rings, and things, and fine array;
And, kiss me, Kate, we will be married o' Sunday.

At their wedding Petruchio humiliates Katharina by appearing at the very last moment wearing ridiculous clothes. Immediately afterwards he forces Katharina to leave for his country house, saying that she is now his property and he may do with her as he pleases. At his house Petruchio "kills her with kindness" by pretending that he cannot allow her to eat his inferior food or sleep in his poorly made bed. Exhausted and hungry, Katharina is tamed.

   This final scene of the play takes place back in Padua, with all the characters gathered to celebrate Bianca's wedding. Petruchio bets 100 crowns that his wife is the most obedient of all. He wins the bet – only Katharina comes on being summoned by her husband. He then sends her to get the less obedient wives.

PETRUCHIO: Katharine, I charge thee, tell these headstrong women
What duty they do owe their lords and husbands.
WIDOW: Come, come, you're mocking: we will have no telling.
PETRUCHIO: Come on, I say; and first begin with her.
WIDOW: She shall not.
PETRUCHIO: I say she shall; – and first begin with her.
KATHARINA: Fie, fie! unknit that threat'ning unkind brow;
And dart not scornful glances from those eyes,
To wound thy lord, thy king, thy governor:
It blots thy beauty, as frosts do bite the meads;
Confounds thy fame, as whirlwinds shake fair buds;
And in no sense is meet or amiable.
A woman mov'd is like a fountain troubled –
Muddy, ill-seeming, thick, bereft of beauty;
And while it is so, none so dry or thirsty
Will deign to sip or touch one drop of it.
Thy husband is thy lord, thy life, thy keeper,
Thy head, thy sovereign; one that cares for thee

And for thy maintenance; commits his body
To painful labour both by sea and land,
To watch the night in storms, the day in cold,
Whilst thou liest warm at home, secure and safe;
And craves no other tribute at thy hands
But love, fair looks, and true obedience, –
Too little payment for so great a debt!
Such duty as the subject owes the prince,
Even such a woman oweth to her husband;
And when she is froward, peevish, sullen, sour,
And not obedient to his honest will,
What is she but a foul contending rebel,
And graceless traitor to her loving lord? –
I am asham'd that women are so simple
To offer war where they should kneel for peace,
Or seek for rule, supremacy, and sway,
When they are bound to serve, love, and obey.
Why are our bodies soft and weak, and smooth,
Unapt to toil and trouble in the world,
But that our soft conditions and our hearts
Should well agree with our external parts?
Come, come, you froward and unable worms!
My mind hath been as big as one of yours,
My heart as great; my reason, haply, more,
To bandy word for word and frown for frown:
But now I see our lances are but straws;
Our strength as weak, our weakness past compare, –
That seeming to be most, which we indeed least are
Then vail your stomachs, for it is no boot,
And place your hands below your husband's foot:
In token of which duty, if he please,
My hand is ready, may it do him ease.
PETRUCHIO: Why, there's a wench! – Come on, and kiss me, Kate.

46

HENRIK IBSEN

A Doll's House

The Doll's House caused a sensation when it was first produced in 1879 because of its depiction of the rapid unraveling of a marriage when a wife rebels against its confines. The action takes place over three days at Christmas. Several years previously, when Torvald Helmer was suffering from overwork, his wife Nora was told that unless he took time off and went to Italy with his family, his life would be in danger. To obtain the money for the trip, and avoid further burdening her husband with financial worries, Nora secretly borrowed money from Krogstad, a money-lender. But Krogstad demanded that Nora obtain her father's signature on the bond. Since her father was also ill, Nora forged her father's signature. Krogstad discovers the forgery and attempts to blackmail Nora. Now he has sent Torvald a letter telling him what Nora has done. Thorvald, a lawyer who is very severe on any kind of impropriety, has received the letter, but not yet opened it. In desperation at what will happen when he does read it, Nora is considering ending her life. Meanwhile Krogstad has met an old love, who is also a friend of Nora's, and regrets sending the letter.

This scene comes at the end of the play.

HELMER (*kissing her on the forehead*): Good night, my little singing-bird. Sleep well, Nora. Now I will read my letters through. (*He takes his letters and goes into his room, shutting the door after him.*)

NORA (*gropes distractedly about, seizes* HELMER's *domino, throws it round her, while she says in quick, hoarse, spasmodic whispers*): Never to see him again. Never! Never! (*Puts her shawl over her head.*) Never to see my children again either – never again. Never! Never! – oh! the icy, black water – the bottomless depths – If only it were over! He has got it now – now he is reading it. Good-bye, Torvald and my children! (*She is about to rush out through the hall, when* HELMER *opens his door hurriedly and stands with an open letter in his hand.*)

HELMER: Nora!

NORA: Oh! –

HELMER: What is this? Do you know what is in this letter?

HENRIK IBSEN, pp. 62–72 from *A Doll's House* (tr. R. Farquharson Sharp and Eleanor Marx-Aveling). London: Dent, 1985 (first published in 1911).

NORA: Yes, I know. Let me go! Let me get out!

HELMER (*holding her back*): Where are you going?

NORA (*trying to get free*): You shan't save me, Torvald!

HELMER (*reeling*): True? Is this true, that I read here? Horrible! No, no – it's impossible that it can be true.

NORA: It is true. I have loved you above everything else in the world.

HELMER: Oh, don't let us have any silly excuses.

NORA (*taking a step towards him*): Torvald – !

HELMER: Miserable creature – what have you done?

NORA: Let me go. You shall not suffer for my sake. You shall not take it upon yourself.

HELMER: No tragedy airs, please. (*Locks the hall door.*) Here you shall stay and give me an explanation. Do you understand what you have done? Answer me! Do you understand what you have done?

NORA (*looks steadily at him and says with a growing look of coldness in her face*): Yes, now I am beginning to understand thoroughly.

HELMER (*walking about the room*): What a horrible awakening! All these eight years – she who was my pride and joy – a hypocrite, a liar – worse, worse – a criminal! The unutterable ugliness of it all! – What disgraceful behaviour! (NORA *is silent and looks steadily at him. He stops in front of her.*) I ought to have suspected that something of the sort would happen. I ought to have foreseen it. All your father's want of principle – be silent! – all your father's want of principle has come out in you. No religion, no morality, no sense of duty – How I am punished for having winked at what he did! I did it for your sake, and this is how you repay me.

NORA: Yes, that's just it.

HELMER: Now you have destroyed all my happiness. You have ruined all my future. It is horrible to think of! I am in the power of an unscrupulous man; he can do what he likes with me, ask anything he likes of me, give me any orders he pleases – I dare not refuse. And I must sink to such miserable depths because of a thoughtless woman!

NORA: When I am out of the way, you will be free.

HELMER: No fine speeches, please. Your father had always plenty of those ready, too. What good would it be to me if you were out of the way, as you say? Not the slightest. He can make the affair known everywhere; and if he does, I may be falsely suspected of having been a party to your criminal action. Very likely people will think I was behind it all – that it was I who prompted you! And I have to thank you for all this – you whom I have cherished during the whole of our married life. Do you understand now what it is you have done for me?

NORA (*coldly and quietly*): Yes.

HELMER: It is so incredible that I can't take it in. But we must come to some understanding. Take off that shawl. Take it off, I tell you. I must try and appease him some way or another. The matter must be hushed up at any cost. And as for you and me, it must appear as if everything between us were just as before – but naturally only in the eyes of the world. You will still remain in my house, that

is a matter of course. But I shall not allow you to bring up the children; I dare
not trust them to you. To think that I should have to say this to one whom I
have loved so dearly, and whom I still – No, that is all over. From this moment
happiness is not the question; all that concerns us is to save the remains, the
fragments, the appearance –

(*A ring is heard at the front-door bell.*)

HELMER (*with a start*): What is that? So late! Can the worst – ? Can he – ? Hide
yourself, Nora. Say you are ill.

(NORA *stands motionless.* HELMER *goes and unlocks the hall door.*)

MAID (*half-dressed, comes to the door*): A letter for the mistress.
HELMER: Give it to me. (*Takes the letter, and shuts the door.*) Yes, it is from him. You
shall not have it; I will read it myself.
NORA: Yes, read it.
HELMER (*standing by the lamp*): I scarcely have the courage to do it. It may mean ruin
for both of us. No, I must know. (*Tears open the letter, runs his eye over a few lines, looks
at a paper enclosed, and gives a shout of joy.*) Nora! (*She looks at him questioningly.*) Nora!
– No, I must read it once again – Yes, it is true! I am saved! Nora, I am saved!
NORA: And I?
HELMER: You too, of course; we are both saved, both you and I. Look, he sends you
your bond back. He says he regrets and repents – that a happy change in his life
– never mind what he says! We are saved, Nora! No one can do anything to
you. Oh, Nora, Nora! – no, first I must destroy these hateful things. Let me see
– (*Takes a look at the bond.*) No, no, I won't look at it. The whole thing shall be
nothing but a bad dream to me. (*Tears up the bond and both letters, throws them all into
the stove, and watches them burn.*) There – now it doesn't exist any longer. He says
that since Christmas Eve you – These must have been three dreadful days for
you, Nora.
NORA: I have fought a hard fight these three days.
HELMER: And suffered agonies, and seen no way out but – No, we won't call any of
the horrors to mind. We will only shout with joy, and keep saying, "It's all over!
It's all over!" Listen to me, Nora. You don't seem to realize that it is all over.
What is this? – such a cold, set face! My poor little Nora, I quite understand;
you don't feel as if you could believe that I have forgiven you. But it is true,
Nora, I swear it; I have forgiven you everything. I know that what you did, you
did out of love for me.
NORA: That is true.
HELMER: You have loved me as a wife ought to love her husband. Only you had
not sufficient knowledge to judge of the means you used. But do you suppose
you are any the less dear to me, because you don't understand how to act
on your own responsibility? No, no; just lean on me; I will advise you and direct
you. I shouldn't be a man if this womanly helplessness did not actually give you
a double attractiveness in my eyes. You mustn't think any more about the hard

things I said in my first moment of consternation, when I thought everything was going to overwhelm me. I have forgiven you, Nora; I swear to you I have forgiven you.

NORA: Thank you for your forgiveness. (*She goes out through the door to the right.*)

HELMER: No, don't go – (*Looks in.*) What are you doing in there?

NORA (*from within*): Taking off my fancy dress.

HELMER (*standing at the open door*): Yes, do. Try and calm yourself, and make your mind easy again, my frightened little singing-bird. Relax, and feel secure; I have broad wings to shelter you under. (*Walks up and down by the door.*) How warm and cosy our home is, Nora. Here is shelter for you; here I will protect you like a hunted dove that I have saved from a hawk's claws; I will bring peace to your poor beating heart. It will come, little by little, Nora, believe me. To-morrow morning you will look upon it all quite differently; soon everything will be just as it was before. Very soon you won't need me to assure you that I have forgiven you; you will yourself feel the certainty that I have done so. Do you imagine I should ever think of such a thing as repudiating you, or even reproaching you? You have no idea what a true man's heart is like, Nora. There is something so indescribably sweet and satisfying, to a man, in the knowledge that he has forgiven his wife – forgiven her freely, and with all his heart. It seems as if that had made her, as it were, doubly his own; he has given her a new life, so to speak; and she has in a way become both wife and child to him. So you shall be for me after this, my little scared, helpless darling. Have no anxiety about anything, Nora; just be frank and open with me, and I will serve as will and conscience both to you – What is this? Not gone to bed? Have you changed your things?

NORA (*in everyday dress*): Yes, Torvald, I have changed my things now.

HELMER: But what for? – as late as this.

NORA: I shan't sleep to-night.

HELMER: But, my dear Nora –

NORA (*looking at her watch*): It is not so very late. Sit down here, Torvald. You and I have a lot to say to one another. (*She sits down at one side of the table.*)

HELMER: Nora – what is this? – this cold, set face?

NORA: Sit down. It will take some time; I have a lot to talk over with you.

HELMER (*sits down at the opposite side of the table*): You alarm me, Nora! – and I don't understand you.

NORA: No, that is just it. You don't understand me, and I have never understood you either – before to-night. No, you mustn't interrupt me. You must simply listen to what I say. Torvald, this is a settling of accounts.

HELMER: What do you mean by that?

NORA (*after a short silence*): Isn't there one thing that strikes you as strange in our sitting here like this?

HELMER: What is that?

NORA: We have been married now eight years. Doesn't it occur to you that this is the first time we two, you and I, husband and wife, have had a serious conversation?

HELMER: What do you mean by serious?

NORA: In all these eight years – longer than that – from the very beginning of our acquaintance, we have never exchanged a word on any serious subject.

HELMER: Was it likely that I would be continually and for ever telling you about worries that you could not help me to bear?

NORA: I am not speaking about business matters. I say that we have never sat down in earnest together to try and get at the bottom of anything.

HELMER: But, dearest Nora, would it have been any good to you?

NORA: That is just it; you have never understood me. I have been greatly wronged, Torvald – first by father and then by you.

HELMER: What! By us two – by us two, who have loved you better than anyone else in the world?

NORA (*shaking her head*): You have never loved me. You have only thought it pleasant to be in love with me.

HELMER: Nora, what do I hear you saying?

NORA: It is perfectly true, Torvald. When I was at home with father, he told me his opinion about everything, and so I had the same opinions; and if I differed from him I concealed the fact, because he would not have liked it. He called me his doll-child, and he played with me just as I used to play with my dolls. And when I came to live with you –

HELMER: What sort of an expression is that to use about our marriage?

NORA (*undisturbed*): I mean that I was simply transferred from father's hands into yours. You arranged everything according to your own taste, and so I got the same tastes as you – or else I pretended to, I am really not quite sure which – I think sometimes the one and sometimes the other. When I look back on it, it seems to me as if I had been living here like a poor woman – just from hand to mouth. I have existed merely to perform tricks for you, Torvald. But you wanted it like that. You and father have committed a great sin against me. It is your fault that I have made nothing of my life.

HELMER: How unreasonable and how ungrateful you are, Nora! Haven't you been happy here?

NORA: No, I have never been happy. I thought I was, but it has never really been so.

HELMER: Not – not happy!

NORA: No, only merry. And you have always been so kind to me. But our home has been nothing but a playroom. I have been your doll-wife, just as at home I was father's doll-child; and here the children have been my dolls. I thought it great fun when you played with me, just as they thought it great fun when I played with them. That is what our marriage has been, Torvald.

HELMER: There is some truth in what you say – exaggerated and strained as your view of it is. But in future it will be different. Playtime is over, and lesson-time will begin.

NORA: Whose lessons? Mine, or the children's?

HELMER: Both yours and the children's, my darling Nora.

NORA: I'm afraid, Torvald, you are not the man to educate me into being a proper wife for you.

HELMER: And you can say that!

NORA: And I – how am I fitted to bring up the children?

HELMER: Nora!

NORA: Didn't you say so yourself a little while ago – that you dare not trust me to bring them up?

HELMER: In a moment of anger! Why do you take any notice of that?

NORA: Actually, you were perfectly right. I am not fit for the task. There is another task I must undertake first. I must try and educate myself – you are not the man to help me in that. I must do that for myself. And that is why I am going to leave you now.

HELMER (*springing up*): What are you saying?

NORA: I must stand quite alone, if I am to understand myself and everything about me. It is for that reason that I cannot remain with you any longer.

HELMER: Nora, Nora!

NORA: I am going away from here now, at once. I am sure Christine will take me in for the night –

HELMER: You are out of your mind! I won't allow it! I forbid you!

NORA: It is no use forbidding me anything any longer. I will take with me only what belongs to me. I will take nothing from you, either now or later.

HELMER: What sort of madness is this!

NORA: To-morrow I shall go home – I mean, to my old home. It will be easiest for me to find something to do there.

HELMER: You blind, foolish woman!

NORA: I must try and get some sense, Torvald.

HELMER: To desert your home, your husband, and your children! And you don't consider what people will say!

NORA: I cannot consider that at all. I only know that it is necessary for me.

HELMER: It's shocking. This is how you would neglect your most sacred duties.

NORA: What do you consider my most sacred duties?

HELMER: Do I need to tell you that? Are they not your duties to your husband and your children?

NORA: I have other duties just as sacred.

HELMER: Indeed you have not. What duties could those be?

NORA: Duties to myself.

HELMER: Before all else, you are a wife and a mother.

NORA: I don't believe that any longer. I believe that before all else I am a reasonable human being, just as you are – or, at all events, that I must try and become one. I know quite well, Torvald, that most people would think you right, and that views of that kind are to be found in books; but I can no longer content myself with what most people say, or with what is found in books. I must think over things for myself and get to understand them.

HELMER: Can you not understand your place in your own home? Have you not a reliable guide in such matters as that? – have you no religion?

NORA: I am afraid, Torvald, I do not exactly know what religion is.

HELMER: What are you saying?

NORA: I know nothing but what the clergyman said, when I went to be confirmed. He told us that religion was this, and that, and the other. When I am away from all this, and am alone, I will look into that matter too. I will see if what the clergyman said is true, or at all events if it is true for me.

HELMER: This is unheard of in a girl of your age! But if religion cannot lead you aright, let me try and awaken your conscience. I suppose you have some moral sense? Or – answer me – am I to think you have none?

NORA: I assure you, Torvald, that is not an easy question to answer. I really don't know. The thing perplexes me altogether. I only know that you and I look at it in quite a different light. I am learning, too, that the law is quite another thing from what I supposed; but I find it impossible to convince myself that the law is right. According to it a woman has no right to spare her old dying father, or to save her husband's life. I can't believe that.

HELMER: You talk like a child. You don't understand the conditions of the world in which you live.

NORA: No, I don't. But now I am going to try. I am going to see if I can make out who is right, the world or I.

HELMER: You are ill, Nora; you are delirious; I almost think you are out of your mind.

NORA: I have never felt my mind so clear and certain as to-night.

HELMER: And is it with a clear and certain mind that you forsake your husband and your children?

NORA: Yes, it is.

HELMER: Then there is only one possible explanation.

NORA: What is that?

HELMER: You do not love me any more.

NORA: No, that is just it.

HELMER: Nora! – and you can say that?

NORA: It gives me great pain, Torvald, because you have always been so kind to me, but I cannot help it. I don't love you any more.

HELMER (*regaining his composure*): Is that a clear and certain conviction too?

NORA: Yes, absolutely clear and certain. That is the reason why I will not stay here any longer.

HELMER: And can you tell me what I have done to forfeit your love?

NORA: Yes, indeed I can. It was to-night, when the wonderful thing did not happen; then I saw you were not the man I had thought you.

HELMER: Explain yourself better. I don't understand you.

NORA: I have waited so patiently for eight years; for, goodness knows, I knew very well that wonderful things don't happen every day. Then this horrible misfortune came upon me; and then I felt quite certain that the wonderful thing was going to happen at last. When Krogstad's letter was lying out there, never for a moment did I imagine that you would consent to accept this man's conditions. I was so absolutely certain that you would say to him: Publish the thing to the whole world. And when that was done –

HELMER: Yes, what then? – when I had exposed my wife to shame and disgrace?

NORA: When that was done, I was so absolutely certain, you would come forward and take everything upon yourself, and say: I am the guilty one.

HELMER: Nora – !

NORA: You mean that I would never have accepted such a sacrifice on your part? No, of course not. But what would my assurances have been worth against yours? That was the wonderful thing which I hoped for and feared; and it was to prevent that, that I wanted to kill myself.

HELMER: I would gladly work night and day for you, Nora – bear sorrow and want for your sake. But no man would sacrifice his honour for the one he loves.

NORA: It is a thing hundreds of thousands of women have done.

HELMER: Oh, you think and talk like a thoughtless child.

NORA: Maybe. But you neither think nor talk like the man I could bind myself to. As soon as your fear was over – and it was not fear for what threatened me, but for what might happen to you – when the whole thing was past, as far as you were concerned it was exactly as if nothing at all had happened. Exactly as before, I was your little skylark, your doll, which you would in future treat with doubly gentle care, because it was so brittle and fragile. (*Getting up.*) Torvald – it was then it dawned upon me that for eight years I had been living here with a strange man, and had borne him three children – Oh, I can't bear to think of it! I could tear myself into little bits!

HELMER (*sadly*): I see, I see. An abyss has opened between us – there is no denying it. But, Nora, would it not be possible to fill it up?

NORA: As I am now, I am no wife for you.

HELMER: I have it in me to become a different man.

NORA: Perhaps – if your doll is taken away from you.

HELMER: But to part! – to part from you! No, no, Nora, I can't understand that idea.

NORA (*going out to the right*): That makes it all the more certain that it must be done. (*She comes back with her cloak and hat and a small bag which she puts on a chair by the table.*)

HELMER: Nora, Nora, not now! Wait till to-morrow.

NORA (*putting on her cloak*): I cannot spend the night in a strange man's room.

HELMER: But can't we live here like brother and sister – ?

NORA (*putting on her hat*): You know very well that wouldn't last long. (*Puts the shawl round her.*) Good-bye, Torvald. I won't see the little ones. I know they are in better hands than mine. As I am now, I can be of no use to them.

HELMER: But some day, Nora – some day?

NORA: How can I tell? I have no idea what is going to become of me.

HELMER: But you are my wife, whatever becomes of you.

NORA: Listen, Torvald. I have heard that when a wife deserts her husband's house, as I am doing now, he is legally freed from all obligations towards her. In any case I set you free from all your obligations. You are not to feel yourself bound in the slightest way, any more than I shall. There must be perfect freedom on both sides. See, here is your ring back. Give me mine.

HELMER: That too?

NORA: That too.

HELMER: Here it is.

NORA: That's right. Now it is all over. I have put the keys here. The maids know all about everything in the house – better than I do. To-morrow, after I have left her, Christine will come here and pack up my own things that I brought with me from home. I will have them sent after me.

HELMER: All over! All over! – Nora, will you never think of me again?

NORA: I know I shall often think of you and the children and this house.

HELMER: May I write to you, Nora?

NORA: No – never. You must not do that.

HELMER: But at least let me send you –

NORA: Nothing – nothing –

HELMER: Let me help you if you are in want.

NORA: No. I can receive nothing from a stranger.

HELMER: Nora – can I never be anything more than a stranger to you?

NORA (*taking her bag*): Ah, Torvald, the most wonderful thing of all would have to happen.

HELMER: Tell me what that would be!

NORA: Both you and I would have to be so changed that – Oh, Torvald, I don't believe any longer in wonderful things happening.

HELMER: But I will believe in it. Tell me! So changed that – ?

NORA: That our life together would be a real marriage. Good-bye. (*She goes out through the hall.*)

HELMER (*sinks down on a chair at the door and buries his face in his hands*): Nora! Nora! (*Looks round, and rises.*) Empty. She is gone. (*A hope flashes across his mind.*) The most wonderful thing of all – ?

(*The sound of a door shutting is heard from below.*)

IX

WAR

There is an extensive literature about war. Some authors glorify it, showing how war leads to immortal feats of courage and daring, and heroic self-sacrifice. Tennyson's pean to the Light Brigade is one example. Other authors write with the conviction that war is often senseless slaughter that brings out the cruelest tendencies in human nature. Wilfrid Owen's poems about the First World War are an example. In *War and Peace*, Tolstsoy allows both views of war to be expressed, and so, to some extent, does Shakespeare in *Henry V*. The ethical questions about war begin with the issue of whether it is ever right to go to war at all. Jesus famously said: "Do not resist one who is evil. But if anyone strikes you on the right cheek, turn to him the other also."[1] The early Christians took this seriously, and were pacifists. Contemporary pacifists, whether Christian or not, maintain that modern warfare is so destructive that we are never justified in going to war. During the Cold War, when there was a risk that any conflict would lead to all-out nuclear war between the United States and the Soviet Union, such a position seemed plausible. But with the receding of the nuclear threat, the pacifist view has become less prominent. Indeed, genocide and human rights atrocities in countries like Rwanda and Bosnia, combined with the greater mobility of armed forces, have led to new arguments for going to war in order to defend human rights. These arguments appeal to many of those who, in an earlier era, might have been sympathetic to pacifism.

The Christian view of war changed when Constantine, the Roman Emperor, converted. It was clearly impossible for a pacifist doctrine to become the official religion of the Roman Empire, which had always maintained itself by the superiority of its armed forces. Christian thinkers like Augustine began to develop the doctrine of the "just war" – that is, a set of rules outlining when it was just for a state to go to war, and when the citizens of that state could, without wrongdoing, fight in the army of that state. The first principle is that the cause must be just – for example, defense against aggression, or an attempt to stop atrocities being committed. In addition, the values at stake must be sufficiently important to over-ride the presumption against killing, and the likely costs of going to war, in terms of loss of life and destruction, must be outweighed by the good expected to be achieved. Finally, war should be a last resort, and force used only after less destructive alternatives have been exhausted.

It is not easy to say when these conditions have been satisfied. Prince Andrey, in *War and Peace*, believes that Russia is justified in defending itself against Napoleon's invasion. Given the importance we still place on national sovereignty, most people would probably agree, even today. But Napoleon's rule in other European countries he conquered – Spain, Italy, Austria, and Prussia – was usually more enlightened than that of the despots he replaced. Had he conquered, the liberation of Russia's serfs would probably have come half a century earlier than it did. So the immense suffering that resistance to Napoleon involved may not have been justified. The Second World War is a better candidate for a just war. It was fought to stop Hitler's aggression against Poland, which in turn followed aggression against Czechoslovakia, and would no doubt have been followed by further aggressive acts if it had been allowed to pass unchallenged. The triumph of Nazi rule would have been a disaster for all the conquered nations. The First World War, triggered by Austria-Hungary's attack on Serbia after the terrorist assassination of the Crown Prince and his wife in Sarajevo, is much less clear-cut. (It is, at least, difficult to condemn Austria-Hungary for its ultimatum to Serbia without also condemning the United States for its demands on Afghanistan following the terrorist attacks of September 11, 2001. The complicity of Serbian government officials in aiding the terrorists in 1914 was, if anything, clearer than the complicity of the Taliban government in the 2001 attacks.) Certainly with the benefit of hindsight, it is hard to see that any good the war achieved outweighed the horrendous toll of at least 9 million dead and millions more wounded. In 1914, no-one expected the war to last four years, or to exact that kind of toll. Two of the extracts in this section – those by Pat Barker and Wilfred Owen – are a response to the trench warfare in France that was part of that conflict.

When there is room for doubt about the justice of going to war, an ethical dilemma arises for the soldiers taking part in the conflict. Is it up to them to judge whether the war is just, or should they simply accept that when their country goes to war, it is their patriotic duty to serve? Since the Christian doctrine of the just war was developed in an age of despotic states and largely uneducated citizens, it is not surprising that – as we see in the second of the two extracts from *Henry V* in this section – the traditional just war doctrine does not encourage soldiers to question the authority of their ruler in declaring the justice of the cause for war. As education spreads, however, soldiers increasingly do challenge the wisdom of their rulers, and they may well feel that, closer to the front lines, they have a better understanding of the costs of war than do the rulers in their comfortable offices far from the battle. Should they come to the conclusion that the war is unjust, they then face an awful dilemma. On the one hand, for a soldier to desert in war is an offense that can mean court-martial and death. On the other hand, to continue to serve may mean killing enemy soldiers who are fighting for a just cause, or at least, one that is no less unjust than one's own side. Similar problems can arise if soldiers receive specific orders – such as to shoot a prisoner, or destroy a village that has civilians in it – that they judge to be wrong. S. Yizhar's story "The Prisoner" deals with one episode in which a soldier must decide whether to follow orders or his conscience. The Nuremberg Tribunal, sitting in judgment on Nazi war criminals after the Second World War, declared that "following orders" does not excuse the killing of innocents. So soldiers are legally entitled to refuse such orders. Doing so, however, especially in the midst of battle, will still require great moral courage.

It may seem that, once war has been declared, anything goes. "War is hell" is one view, and in hell there is surely no ethics. Even a pacifist can agree with that view. Leading to the same conclusion is the distinctly non-pacifist attitude espoused by Prince Andrey in *War and Peace*: that once a nation makes the fateful decision to go to war – which it should only do when there is "something worth facing certain death for" – the only thing that matters is victory, and any means that brings victory closer is justified. Advocates of the traditional just war doctrine disagree with both these views. The just war doctrine not only sets out the principles on which it is right to go to war, it also offers separate principles on how a war may ethically be conducted. The first and most important of these is that even in war, one must not kill the innocent. Since in modern warfare innocent people are always killed, it might seem that this effectively means that no war can be just. But the principle is interpreted in a special way, so that it does not have this consequence. First, the term "innocent" is defined as "noncombatant" rather than in terms of moral innocence. So the fact that an enemy soldier may have been compelled to fight for his country, that he is opposed to the war, and has done his best not to kill anyone, is irrelevant to his innocence, in this sense. If he is a soldier, he is a combatant and may legitimately be killed. Secondly, although the principle says that civilians are not to be directly attacked, it does not say that we may never carry out an attack that we foresee will kill civilians.

Here the doctrine of double effect, which we saw earlier in discussing euthanasia, is employed to distinguish between intending the deaths of civilians, and foreseeing that they will die as a result of what we do. So, for example, the terror bombing of Dresden and Hamburg, with the direct intention of killing German civilians in order to destroy German morale and thus lead to Germany's surrender, violated the traditional just war doctrine. On the other hand, the bombing of a munitions factory in a residential area would not violate it, even if it was known that some civilians lived close to the factory and would inevitably be killed. This is what American military jargon calls "collateral damage." The language used by Henry V, when he discusses the consequences of an attack on the besieged French city of Harfleur, is more poetic, but amounts to much the same thing. The English king knows that if he orders an attack, civilians will be killed, but he denies that he will be responsible for their deaths.

We may also ask, as we did in the medical context, whether the distinction between "intended" and "foreseen" killing is really so morally significant. Assuming that one is fighting for a just cause, and that many of the combatants in a war are morally innocent conscripts, who would prefer not to be fighting, is it more important to target only combatants, or to conduct the war so as to achieve victory with the lowest overall death toll, counting combatants and civilians? Perhaps the best justification for a prohibition on targeting civilians is that, even if on some rare occasions we may save more lives by directly killing civilians, the outcome of breaking down all barriers between combatants and noncombatants would be greater bloodshed in the long run.

47

LEO TOLSTOY

War and Peace

War and Peace was published in separate volumes from 1865 to 1869. The story follows the entangled lives of several noble Russian families – among them the Bolkonskys, the Rostovs, and the Bezukhovs – during the time of the Napoleonic wars.

It is seven years since Prince Andrey Bolkonsky was wounded fighting the French at Austerlitz. Napoleon has invaded Russia and is approaching Moscow. Prince Andrey, who spent the past few years in retreat at his country estate of Bleak Hills, has rejoined the army. This time, instead of being on the staff behind the lines, he has chosen to command a fighting regiment. His friend, Pierre Bezukhov, a civilian, is visiting the Russian forces, which, under the newly appointed Commander Kutuzov, are preparing for the battle at Borodino (August 26, 1812).

The officers would have taken leave, but Prince Andrey, apparently unwilling to be left alone with his friend, pressed them to stay and have some tea. Benches were set, and tea was brought. With some astonishment the officers stared at Pierre's huge, bulky figure, and heard his talk of Moscow, and of the position of our troops, which he had succeeded in getting a view of. Prince Andrey did not speak, and his face was so forbidding that Pierre addressed his remarks more to the simple-hearted Timohin than to Bolkonsky.

"So you understand the whole disposition of the troops?" Prince Andrey put in.

"Yes. At least, how do you mean?" said Pierre. "As I am not a military man, I can't say I do fully; but still I understand the general arrangement."

"Well, then, you know more than anybody else," said Prince Andrey.

"Oh!" said Pierre incredulously, looking over his spectacles at Prince Andrey. "Well, and what do you say of the appointment of Kutuzov?" he asked.

"I was very glad of his appointment; that's all I know," said Prince Andrey.

"Well, tell me your opinion of Barclay de Tolly. In Moscow they are saying all kinds of things about him. What do you think of him?"

"Ask them," said Prince Andrey, indicating the officers.

LEO TOLSTOY, from Book X, Chapter XXV in *War and Peace* (tr. Constance Garnett), first published in 1865–9.

With the condescendingly doubtful smile with which every one addressed him, Pierre looked at Timohin.

"It was a gleam of light in the dark, your excellency, when his highness took the command," said Timohin, stealing shy glances continually at his colonel.

"Why so?" asked Pierre.

"Well, as regards firewood and food, let me tell you. Why, all the way we retreated from Sventsyan not a twig, nor a wisp of hay, nor anything, dare we touch. We were retreating, you see, so *he* would get it, wouldn't he, your excellency?" he said, turning to his prince, "but we mustn't dare to. In our regiment two officers were court-martialled for such things. Well, since his highness is in command, it's all straightforward as regards that. We see daylight . . ."

"Then why did he forbid it?"

Timohin looked round in confusion, at a loss how to answer such a question. Pierre turned to Prince Andrey with the same inquiry.

"Why, so as not to waste the country we were leaving for the enemy," said Prince Andrey, with angry sarcasm. "That's a first principle: never to allow pillage and accustom your men to marauding. And at Smolensk too he very correctly judged that the French were the stronger and might overcome us. But he could not understand," cried Prince Andrey in a voice suddenly shrill, "he could not understand that for the first time we were fighting on Russian soil, that there was a spirit in the men such as I had never seen before, that we had twice in succession beaten back the French, and that success had multiplied our strength tenfold. He ordered a retreat, and all our efforts and our curses were in vain. He had no thought of treachery; he tried to do everything for the best and thought over everything well. But for that very reason he was no good. He is no good now just because he considers everything soundly and accurately as every German must. How can I explain to you. . . . Well, your father has a German valet, say, and he's an excellent valet and satisfies all his requirements better than you can do, and all's well and good; but if your father is sick unto death, you'll send away the valet and wait on your father yourself with your awkward, unpractised hands, and be more comfort to him than a skilful man who's a stranger. That's how we have done with Barclay. While Russia was well, she might be served by a stranger, and an excellent minister he was, but as soon as she's in danger, she wants a man of her own kith and kin. So you in your club have been making him out to be a traitor! They slander him now as a traitor; and afterwards, ashamed of their false accusations, they will suddenly glorify him as a hero or a genius, which would be even more unfair to him. He's an honest and conscientious German . . ."

"They say he's an able general, though," said Pierre.

"I don't know what's meant by an able general," Prince Andrey said ironically.

"An able general," said Pierre; "well, it's one who foresees all contingencies . . . well, divines the enemy's projects."

"But that's impossible," said Prince Andrey, as though of a matter long ago settled.

Pierre looked at him in surprise.

"But you know they say," he said, "that war is like a game of chess."

"Yes," said Prince Andrey, "only with this little difference, that in chess you may think over each move as long as you please, that you are not limited as to time, and with this further difference that a knight is always stronger than a pawn and two pawns are always stronger than one, while in war a battalion is sometimes stronger than a division, and sometimes weaker than a company. No one can ever be certain of the relative strength of armies. Believe me," he said, "if anything did depend on the arrangements made by the staff, I would be there, and helping to make them, but instead of that I have the honour of serving here in the regiment with these gentlemen here, and I consider that the day really depends upon us to-morrow and not on them. . . . Success never has depended and never will depend on position, on arms, nor even on numbers; and, least of all, on position."

"On what then?"

"On the feeling that is in me and him," he indicated Timohin, "and every soldier."

Prince Andrey glanced at Timohin, who was staring in alarm and bewilderment at his colonel. In contrast to his usual reserved taciturnity, Prince Andrey seemed excited now. Apparently he could not refrain from expressing the ideas that suddenly rose to his mind. "The battle is won by the side that has firmly resolved to win. Why did we lose the battle of Austerlitz? Our losses were almost equalled by the French losses; but we said to ourselves very early in the day that we were losing the battle, and we lost it. And we said so because we had nothing to fight for then; we wanted to get out of fighting as quick as we could. 'We are defeated; so let us run!' and we did run. If we had not said that till evening, God knows what might not have happened. But to-morrow we shan't say that. You talk of our position, of the left flank being weak, and the right flank too extended," he went on; "all that's nonsense; that's all nothing. But what awaits us to-morrow? A hundred millions of the most diverse contingencies, which will determine on the instant whether they run or we do; whether one man is killed and then another; but all that's being done now is all mere child's play. The fact is that these people with whom you have been inspecting the positions do nothing towards the progress of things; they are a positive hindrance. They are entirely taken up with their own petty interests."

"At such a moment?" said Pierre reproachfully.

"*At such a moment,*" repeated Prince Andrey. "To them this is simply a moment on which one may score off a rival and win a cross or ribbon the more. To my mind what is before us to-morrow is this: a hundred thousand Russian and a hundred thousand French troops have met to fight, and the fact is that these two hundred thousand men will fight, and the side that fights most desperately and spares itself least will conquer. And if you like, I'll tell you that whatever happens, and whatever mess they make up yonder, we shall win the battle to-morrow; whatever happens we shall win the victory."

"Your excellency, that's the truth of it, the holy truth," put in Timohin; "who would spare himself now! The soldiers in my battalion, would you believe it, wouldn't drink their vodka; this isn't an ordinary day, they say."

All were silent.

The officers rose. Prince Andrey went with them out of the barn, giving the last instructions to the adjutant. When the officers had gone, Pierre came nearer to

Prince Andrey, and was just about to begin talking when they heard the tramp of hoofs not far away on the road, and glancing in that direction Prince Andrey recognised Woltzogen and Klausewitz, accompanied by a Cossack. They rode close by them, still talking, and Pierre and Prince Andrey could not help over-hearing the following phrases in German:

"The war ought to be carried on over a wide extent of country. I cannot sufficiently strongly express that view of the matter," one said in German.

"Oh yes," said another voice, "since the object is to wear out the enemy, one must not consider the losses of private persons."

"Certainly not," acquiesced the first voice.

"Carried into a wide extent of country," Prince Andrey repeated with a wrathful snort, when they had ridden by. "In that open country I had a father and son and sister at Bleak Hills. He doesn't care about that. That's just what I was saying to you: these excellent Germans won't win the battle to-morrow, they will only make a mess of it, so far as they are able, because they have nothing in their German noddles but calculations that are not worth a rotten egg, and they haven't in their hearts the one thing that's wanted for to-morrow, that Timohin has. They have given all Europe up to *him*, and now they have come to teach us – fine teachers!" he added, his voice growing shrill again.

"So you think the battle to-morrow will be a victory," said Pierre.

"Yes, yes," said Prince Andrey absently. "There's one thing I would do, if I were in power," he began again. "I wouldn't take prisoners. What sense is there in taking prisoners? That's chivalry. The French have destroyed my home and are coming to destroy Moscow; they have outraged and are outraging me at every second. They are my enemies, they are all criminals to my way of thinking. And so thinks Timohin, and all the army with him. They must be put to death. Since they are my enemies, they can't be my friends, whatever they may have said at Tilsit."

"Yes, yes," said Pierre, looking with shining eyes at Prince Andrey. "I entirely agree with you!"

The question that had been disturbing Pierre all that day, since the Mozhaisk hill, now struck him as perfectly clear and fully solved. He saw now all the import and all the gravity of the war and the impending battle. All he had seen that day, all the stern, grave faces of which he had had glimpses, appeared to him in a new light now. He saw, to borrow a term from physics, the latent heat of patriotism in all those men he had seen, and saw in it the explanation of the composure and apparent levity with which they were all preparing for death. "We ought not to take prisoners," said Prince Andrey. "That change alone would transform the whole aspect of war and would make it less cruel. But playing at war, that's what's vile; and playing at magnanimity and all the rest of it. That magnanimity and sensibility is like the magnanimity and sensibility of the lady who turns sick at the sight of a slaughtered calf – she is so kindhearted she can't see blood – but eats fricasseed veal with a very good appetite. They talk of the laws of warfare, of chivalry, of flags of truce, and humanity to the wounded, and so on. That's all rubbish. I saw enough in 1805 of chivalry and flags of truce: they duped us, and we duped them. They plunder other people's homes, issue false money, and, worse than all, kill my children, my father, and then talk of the laws of warfare, and generosity to a fallen foe. No prisoners; and go to give and to meet death! Any one who has come to think this as I have, through the same sufferings . . ."

Prince Andrey, who had thought that he did not care whether they took Moscow as they had taken Smolensk, was suddenly pulled up in his speech by a nervous catch in his throat. He walked to and fro several times in silence, but his eyes blazed with feverish brilliance and his lips quivered, as he began to speak again.

"If there were none of this playing at generosity in warfare, we should never go to war, except for something worth facing certain death for, as now. Then there would not be wars because Pavel Ivanitch had insulted Mihail Ivanitch. But if there is war as now, let it be really war. And then the intensity of warfare would be something quite different. All these Westphalians and Hessians Napoleon is leading against us would not have come to fight us in Russia, and we should not have gone to war in Austria and in Prussia without knowing what for. War is not a polite recreation, but the vilest thing in life, and we ought to understand that and not play at war. We ought to accept it sternly and solemnly as a fearful necessity. It all comes to this: have done with lying, and if it's war, then it's war and not a game, or else warfare is simply the favourite pastime of the idle and frivolous. . . . The military is the most honoured calling. And what is war, what is needed for success in war, what are the morals of the military world? The object of warfare is murder; the means employed in warfare – spying, treachery, and the encouragement of it, the ruin of a country, the plundering of its inhabitants and robbery for the maintenance of the army, trickery and lying, which are called military strategy; the morals of the military class – absence of all independence, that is, discipline, idleness, ignorance, cruelty, debauchery, and drunkenness. And in spite of all that, it is the highest class, respected by every one. All sovereigns, except the Chinese, wear a military uniform, and give the greatest rewards to the man who succeeds in killing most people. . . . They meet together to murder one another, as we shall do to-morrow; they slaughter and mutilate tens of thousands of men, and then offer up thanksgiving services for the number of men they have killed (and even add to it in the telling), and glorify the victory, supposing that the more men have been slaughtered the greater the achievement. How God can look down from above and hear them!" shrieked Prince Andrey in a shrill, piercing voice. "Ah, my dear boy, life has been a bitter thing for me of late. I see that I have come to understand too much. And it is not good for man to taste of the tree of the knowledge of good and evil. . . . Ah, well, it's not for long!" he added. "But you are getting sleepy and it's time I was in bed too. Go back to Gorky," said Prince Andrey suddenly.

"Oh no!" answered Pierre, gazing with eyes full of scared sympathy at Prince Andrey.

"You must be off; before a battle one needs to get a good sleep," repeated Prince Andrey. He went quickly up to Pierre, embraced and kissed him. "Good-bye, be off," he cried, "whether we see each other again or not . . ." and turning hurriedly, he went off into the barn.

48

PAT BARKER

Regeneration

Regeneration is the first book in the trilogy of the same name. The story centers on the real-life relationship of poet and war hero Siegfried Sassoon with army psychologist William Rivers.

The novel opens with the text of Sassoon's anti-war declaration as published in the London *Times* in July 1917. Sassoon, instead of being court-martialed, is sent to Craiglockhart War Hospital for shell-shocked officers. Graves is Robert Graves, also a real person, a fellow-poet and friend of Sassoon. Russell is the pacifist activist and philosopher Bertrand Russssell.

Finished with the War
A Soldier's Declaration

I am making this statement as an act of wilful defiance of military authority, because I believe the war is being deliberately prolonged by those who have the power to end it.

I am a soldier, convinced that I am acting on behalf of soldiers. I believe that this war, upon which I entered as a war of defence and liberation, has now become a war of aggression and conquest. I believe that the purposes for which I and my fellow soldiers entered upon this war should have been so clearly stated as to have made it impossible to change them, and that, had this been done, the objects which actuated us would now be attainable by negotiation.

I have seen and endured the suffering of the troops, and I can no longer be a party to prolong these sufferings for ends which I believe to be evil and unjust.

I am not protesting against the conduct of the war, but against the political errors and insincerities for which the fighting men are being sacrificed.

PAT BARKER, extract from Chapters 1 and 2 in *Regeneration*. London: Viking 1991. Copyright © 1991 by Pat Barker. Used by permission of Dutton Signet, a division of Penguin Group (USA) Inc and Penguin Books Ltd.

On behalf of those who are suffering now I make this protest against the deception which is being practised on them; also I believe that I may help to destroy the callous complacence with which the majority of those at home regard the continuance of agonies which they do not share, and which they have not sufficient imagination to realize.

S. Sassoon
July 1917

Bryce waited for Rivers to finish reading before he spoke again. "The 'S' stands for 'Siegfried'. Apparently, he thought that was better left out."

"And I'm sure he was right." Rivers folded the paper and ran his fingertips along the edge. "So they're sending him here?"

Bryce smiled. "Oh, I think it's rather more specific than that. They're sending him to *you*."

Rivers got up and walked across to the window. It was a fine day, and many of the patients were in the hospital grounds, watching a game of tennis. He heard the *pok-pok* of rackets, and a cry of frustration as a ball smashed into the net. "I suppose he is – 'shell-shocked'?"

"According to the Board, yes."

"It just occurs to me that a diagnosis of neurasthenia might not be inconvenient confronted with this." He held up the Declaration.

"Colonel Langdon chaired the Board. *He* certainly seems to think he is."

"Langdon doesn't believe in shell-shock."

Bryce shrugged. "Perhaps Sassoon was gibbering all over the floor."

"'Funk, old boy.' I know Langdon." Rivers came back to his chair and sat down. "He doesn't *sound* as if he's gibbering, does he?"

Bryce said carefully, "Does it matter what his mental state is? Surely it's better for him to be here than in prison?"

"Better for *him*, perhaps. What about the hospital? Can you imagine what our dear Director of Medical Services is going to say, when he finds out we're sheltering 'conchies' as well as cowards, shirkers, scrimshankers and degenerates? We'll just have to hope there's no publicity."

"There's going to be, I'm afraid. The Declaration's going to be read out in the House of Commons next week."

"By?"

"Lees-Smith."

Rivers made a dismissive gesture.

"Yes, well, I know. But it still means the press."

"And the minister will say that no disciplinary action has been taken, because Mr Sassoon is suffering from a severe mental breakdown, and therefore not responsible for his actions. I'm not sure I'd prefer that to prison."

"I don't suppose he was offered the choice. Will you take him?"

"You mean I *am* being offered a choice?"

"In view of your case load, yes."

Rivers took off his glasses and swept his hand down across his eyes. "I suppose they *have* remembered to send the file?"

Sassoon leant out of the carriage window, still half-expecting to see Graves come pounding along the platform, looking even more dishevelled than usual. But further down the train, doors had already begun to slam, and the platform remained empty.

The whistle blew. Immediately, he saw lines of men with grey muttering faces clambering up the ladders to face the guns. He blinked them away.

The train began to move. Too late for Robert now. *Prisoner arrives without escort*, Sassoon thought, sliding open the carriage door.

By arriving an hour early he'd managed to get a window seat. He began picking his way across to it through the tangle of feet. An elderly vicar, two middle-aged men, both looking as if they'd done rather well out of the war, a young girl and an older woman, obviously travelling together. The train bumped over a point. Everybody rocked and swayed, and Sassoon, stumbling, almost fell into the vicar's lap. He mumbled an apology and sat down. Admiring glances, and not only from the women. Sassoon turned to look out of the window, hunching his shoulder against them all.

After a while he stopped pretending to look at the smoking chimneys of Liverpool's back streets and closed his eyes. He needed to sleep, but instead Robert's face floated in front of him, white and twitching as it had been last Sunday, almost a week ago now, in the lounge of the Exchange Hotel.

For a moment, looking up to find that khaki-clad figure standing just inside the door, he thought he was hallucinating again.

"Robert, what on earth are *you* doing here?" He jumped up and ran across the lounge. "Thank God you've come."

"I got myself passed fit."

"Robert, *no*."

"What else could I do? After getting *this*." Graves dug into his tunic pocket and produced a crumpled piece of paper. "A covering letter would have been nice."

"I wrote."

"No, you didn't, Sass. You just sent me this. Couldn't you at least have *talked* about it first?"

"I thought I'd written."

They sat down, facing each other across a small table. Cold northern light streamed in through the high windows, draining Grave's face of the little colour it had.

"Sass, you've got to give this up."

"Give it up? You don't think I've come this far, do you, just to give in now?"

"Look, you've made your protest. For what it's worth, I agree with every word of it. But you've had your say. There's no point making a martyr of yourself."

"The only way I can get publicity is to make them court-martial me."

"They won't do it."

"Oh, yes, they will. It's just a matter of hanging on."

"You're in no state to stand a court-martial." Graves clasped his clenched fist. "If I had Russell here now, I'd *shoot* him."

"It was my idea."

"Oh, pull the other one. And even if it was, do you think anybody's going to understand it? They'll just say you've got cold feet."

"Look, Robert, you think exactly as I do about the war, and you *do . . . nothing*. All right, that's your choice. But don't come here lecturing *me* about *cold feet*. This is the hardest thing I've ever done."

Now, on the train going to Craiglockhart, it still seemed the hardest thing. He shifted in his seat and sighed, looking out over fields of wheat bending to the wind. He remembered the silvery sound of shaken wheat, the shimmer of light on the stalks. He'd have given anything to be out there, away from the stuffiness of the carriage, the itch and constriction of his uniform.

On that Sunday they'd taken the train to Formby and spent the afternoon wandering aimlessly along the beach. A dull, wintry-looking sun cast their shadows far behind them, so that every gesture either of them made was mimicked and magnified.

"They won't *let* you make a martyr of yourself, Sass. You should have accepted the Board."

The discussion had become repetitive. For perhaps the fourth time, Sassoon said, "If I hold out long enough, there's nothing else they can do."

"There's a lot they can do." Graves seemed to come to a decision. "As a matter of fact, I've been pulling a few strings on your behalf."

Sassoon smiled to hide his anger. "Good. If you've been exercising your usual tact, that ought to get me at least two years."

"They won't court-martial you."

In spite of himself, Sassoon began to feel afraid. "What, then?"

"Shut you up in a lunatic asylum for the rest of the war."

"And that's the result of your string-pulling, is it? Thanks."

"No, the result of my string-pulling is to get you another Board. You must take it this time."

"You can't put people in lunatic asylums just like that. You have to have *reasons*."

"They've got reasons."

"Yes, the Declaration. Well, that doesn't prove me insane."

"And the hallucinations? *The corpses in Piccadilly?*"

A long silence. "I had rather hoped my letters to you were private."

"I had to persuade them to give you another Board."

"They won't court-martial me?"

"No. Not in any circumstances. And if you go on refusing to be boarded, they *will* put you away."

"You know, Robert, I wouldn't believe this from anybody else. Will you *swear* it's true?"

"Yes."

"On the Bible?"

Graves held up an imaginary Bible and raised his right hand. "I swear."

Their shadows stretched out behind them, black on the white sand. For a moment Sassoon still hesitated. Then, with an odd little gasp, he said, "All right then, I'll give way."

In the taxi, going to Craiglockhart, Sassoon began to feel frightened. He looked out of the window at the crowded pavements of Princes Street, thinking he was seeing them for the first and last time. He couldn't imagine what awaited him at Craiglockhart, but he didn't for a moment suppose the inmates were let out.

He glanced up and found the taxi-driver watching him in the mirror. All the local people must know the name of the hospital, and what it was for. Sassoon's hand went up to his chest and began pulling at a loose thread where his MC ribbon had been.

For conspicuous gallantry during a raid on the enemy's trenches. He remained for 1½ hours under rifle and bomb fire collecting and bringing in our wounded. Owing to his courage and determination, all the killed and wounded were brought in.

Reading the citation, it seemed to Rivers more extraordinary than ever that Sassoon should have thrown the medal away. Even the most extreme pacifist could hardly be ashamed of a medal awarded for *saving* life. He took his glasses off and rubbed his eyes. He'd been working on the file for over an hour, but, although he was now confident he knew all the facts, he was no closer to an understanding of Sassoon's state of mind. If anything, Graves's evidence to the Board – with its emphasis on hallucinations – seemed to suggest a full-blown psychosis rather than neurasthenia. And yet there was no other evidence for that. Misguided the Declaration might well be, but it was not deluded, illogical or incoherent. Only the throwing away of the medal still struck him as odd. That surely had been the action of a man at the end of his tether.

Well, we've all been there, he thought. The trouble was, he was finding it difficult to examine the evidence impartially. He *wanted* Sassoon to be ill. Admitting this made him pause. He got up and began pacing the floor of his room, from door to window and back again. He'd only ever encountered one similar case, a man who'd refused to go on fighting on religious grounds. Atrocities took place on both sides, he'd said. There was nothing to choose between the British and the Germans.

The case had given rise to heated discussions in the MO's common room – about the freedom of the individual conscience in wartime, and the role of the army psychiatrist in "treating" a man who refused to fight. Rivers, listening to those arguments, had been left in no doubt of the depth and seriousness of the divisions. The controversy had died down only when the patient proved to be psychotic. That was the crux of the matter. A man like Sassoon would always be trouble, but he'd be a lot less trouble if he were ill.

Rivers was roused from these thoughts by the crunch of tyres on gravel. He reached the window in time to see a taxi draw up, and a man, who from his uniform could only be Sassoon, get out. After paying the driver, Sassoon stood for a moment, looking up at the building. Nobody arriving at Craiglockhart for the first time could fail to be daunted by the sheer gloomy, cavernous bulk of the place. Sassoon lingered on the drive for a full minute after the taxi had driven away, then took a deep breath, squared his shoulders, and ran up the steps.

Rivers turned away from the window, feeling almost ashamed of having witnessed that small, private victory over fear.

*

Light from the window behind Rivers's desk fell directly on to Sassoon's face. Pale skin, purple shadows under the eyes. Apart from that, no obvious signs of nervous disorder. No twitches, jerks, blinks, no repeated ducking to avoid a long-exploded shell. His hands, doing complicated things with cup, saucer, plate, sandwiches, cake, sugar tongs and spoon, were perfectly steady. Rivers raised his own cup to his lips and smiled. One of the nice things about serving afternoon tea to newly arrived patients was that it made so many neurological tests redundant.

So far he hadn't looked at Rivers. He sat with his head slightly averted, a posture that could easily have been taken for arrogance, though Rivers was more inclined to suspect shyness. The voice was slightly slurred, the flow of words sometimes hesitant, sometimes rushed. A disguised stammer, perhaps, but a life-long stammer, Rivers thought, not the recent, self-conscious stammer of the neurasthenic.

"While I remember, Captain Graves rang to say he'll be along some time after dinner. He sent his apologies for missing the train."

"He *is* still coming?"

"Yes."

Sassoon looked relieved. "Do you know, I don't think Graves's caught a train in his life? Unless somebody was there to *put* him on it."

"We were rather concerned about you."

"In case the lunatic went missing?"

"I wouldn't put it quite like that."

"I was all right. I wasn't even surprised, I thought he'd slept in. He's been doing a . . . a lot of rushing round on my behalf recently. You've no idea how much work goes into *rigging* a Medical Board."

Rivers pushed his spectacles up on to his forehead and massaged the inner corners of his eyes. "No, I don't suppose I have. You know this may sound naïve but . . . to *me* . . . the accusation that a Medical Board has been rigged is quite a serious one."

"I've no complaints. I was dealt with in a perfectly fair and reasonable way. Probably better than I deserved."

"What kind of questions did they ask?"

Sassoon smiled. "Don't you know?"

"I've read the report, if that's what you mean. I'd still like to hear your version."

"Oh: 'Did I object to fighting on religious grounds?' I said I didn't. It was rather amusing, actually. For a moment I thought they were asking me whether I objected to going on a crusade. 'Did I think I was qualified to decide when the war should end?' I said I hadn't thought about my qualifications." He glanced at Rivers. "*Not true.* And then . . . then Colonel Langdon asked – *said* 'Your friend tells us you're very good at bombing. Don't you still dislike the Germans?'"

A long silence. The net curtain behind Rivers's head billowed out in a glimmering arc, and a gust of cool air passed over their faces.

"And what did you say to that?"

"I don't remember." He sounded impatient now. "It didn't matter what I said."

"It matters now."

"All right." A faint smile. "*Yes*, I am quite good at bombing. *No*, I do not still dislike the Germans."

"Does that mean you once did?"

Sassoon looked surprised. For the first time something had been said that contradicted his assumptions. "Briefly. April and May of last year, to be precise."

A pause. Rivers waited. After a while Sassoon went on, almost reluctantly. "A friend of mine had been killed. For a while I used to go out on patrol every night, looking for Germans to kill. Or rather I told myself that's what I was doing. In the end I didn't know whether I was trying to kill them, or just giving them plenty of opportunities to kill me."

"'Mad Jack.'"

Sassoon looked taken aback. "Graves really *has* talked, hasn't he?"

"It's the kind of thing the Medical Board would need to know." Rivers hesitated. "Taking *unnecessary* risks is one of the first signs of a war neurosis."

"Is it?" Sassoon looked down at his hands. "I didn't know that."

"Nightmares and hallucinations come later."

"What's an 'unnecessary risk' anyway? The maddest thing *I* ever did was done under orders." He looked up, to see if he should continue. "We were told to go and get the regimental badges off a German corpse. They reckoned he'd been dead two days, so obviously if we got the badges they'd know which battalion was opposite. Full moon, not a cloud in sight, *absolutely mad*, but off we went. Well, we got there – eventually – and what do we find? He's been dead a helluva lot longer than two days, and he's French anyway."

"So what did you do?"

"Pulled one of his boots off and sent it back to battalion HQ. With quite a bit of his leg left inside."

Rivers allowed another silence to open up. "I gather we're not going to talk about nightmares?"

"You're in charge."

"Ye-es. But then one of the paradoxes of being an army psychiatrist is that you don't actually get very far by *ordering* your patients to be frank."

"I'll be as frank as you like. I did have nightmares when I first got back from France. I don't have them now."

"And the hallucinations?"

He found this more difficult. "It was just that when I woke up, the nightmares didn't always stop. So I used to see . . ." A deep breath. "Corpses. Men with half their faces shot off, crawling across the floor."

"And you were awake when this happened?"

"I don't know. I must've been, because I could see the sister."

"And was this always at night?"

"No. It happened once during the day. I'd been to my club for lunch, and when I came out I sat on a bench, and . . . I suppose I must've nodded off." He was forcing himself to go on. "When I woke up, the pavement was covered in corpses.

Old ones, new ones, black, green." His mouth twisted. "People were treading on their faces."

Rivers took a deep breath. "You say you'd just woken up?"

"Yes. I used to sleep quite a bit during the day, because I was afraid to go to sleep at night."

"When did all this stop?"

"As soon as I left the hospital. The atmosphere in that place was really terrible. There was one man who used to boast about killing German prisoners. You can imagine what living with *him* was like."

"And the nightmares haven't recurred?"

"No. I do dream, of course, but not about the war. Sometimes a dream seems to go on after I've woken up, so there's a a kind of in-between stage." He hesitated. "I don't know whether that's abnormal."

"I hope not. It happens to me all the time." Rivers sat back in his chair. "When you look back now on your time in the hospital, do *you* think you were 'shell-shocked'?"

"I don't know. Somebody who came to see me told my uncle he thought I was. As against that, I wrote one or two good poems while I was in there. We-ell . . ." He smiled. "*I* was pleased with them."

"You don't think it's possible to write a good poem in a state of shock?"

"No, I don't."

Rivers nodded. "You may be right. Would it be possible for me to see them?"

"Yes, of course. I'll copy them out."

Rivers said, "I'd like to move on now to the . . . thinking behind the Declaration. You say your motives aren't religious?"

"No, not at all."

"Would you describe yourself as a pacifist?"

"I don't think so. I can't possibly say '*No* war is ever justified', because I haven't thought about it enough. Perhaps some wars are. Perhaps this one was when it started. I just don't think our war aims – *whatever they may be* – and we don't know – justify this level of slaughter."

"And you say you *have* thought about your qualifications for saying that?"

"*Yes*. I'm only too well aware of how it sounds. A *second-lieutenant*, no less, saying 'The war must stop'. On the other hand, I have *been* there. I'm at least as well qualified as some of the old men you see sitting around in clubs, cackling on about 'attrition' and 'wastage of manpower' and . . ." His voice became a vicious parody of an old man's voice. "'*Lost heavily in that last scrap.*' You don't talk like that if you've watched them die."

"No intelligent or sensitive person would talk like that anyway."

A slightly awkward pause. "I'm not saying there are no exceptions."

Rivers laughed. "The point is you hate civilians, don't you? The 'callous', the 'complacent', the 'unimaginative'. Or is 'hate' too strong a word?"

"No."

"So. What you felt for the Germans, rather briefly, in the spring of last year, you now feel for the overwhelming majority of your fellow-countrymen?"

"Yes."

"You know, I think you were quite right not to say too much to the Board."

"That wasn't my idea, it was Graves's. He was afraid I'd sound too sane."

"When you said the Board was 'rigged', what did you mean?"

"I meant the decision to send me here, or or somewhere similar, had been taken before I went in."

"And this had all been fixed by Captain Graves?"

"Yes." Sassoon leant forward. "The point is they weren't going to court-martial me. They were just going to lock me up somewhere . . ." He looked round the room. "*Worse* than this."

Rivers smiled. "There *are* worse places, believe me."

"I'm sure there are," Sassoon said politely.

"They were going to certify you, in fact?"

"I suppose so."

"Did anybody on the Board say anything to you about this?"

"No, because it was –"

"All fixed beforehand. Yes, I see."

Sassoon said, "May I ask you a question?"

"Go ahead."

"Do *you* think I'm mad?"

"No, of course you're not mad. Did you think you were going mad?"

"It crossed my mind. You know when you're brought face to face with the fact that, yes, you did see corpses on the pavement . . ."

"Hallucinations in the half-waking state are surprisingly common, you know. They're not the same thing as psychotic hallucinations. Children have them quite frequently."

Sassoon had started pulling at a loose thread on the breast of his tunic. Rivers watched him for a while. "You must've been in agony when you did that."

Sassoon lowered his hand. "No-o. *Agony's* lying in a shell-hole with your legs shot off. I was *upset*." For a moment he looked almost hostile, then he relaxed. "It was a futile gesture. I'm not particularly proud of it."

"You threw it in the Mersey, didn't you?"

"Yes. It wasn't heavy enough to sink, so it just" – a glint of amusement – "*bobbed* around. There was a ship sailing past, quite a long way out, in the estuary, and I looked at this little scrap of ribbon floating and I looked at the ship, and I thought that me trying to stop the war was a bit like trying to stop the ship would have been. You know, all they'd've seen from the deck was this little figure jumping up and down, waving its arms, and they wouldn't've known what on earth it was getting so excited about."

"So you realized *then* that it was futile?"

Sassoon lifted his head. "It still had to be done. You can't just acquiesce."

Rivers hesitated. "Look, I think we've . . . we've got about as far as we can get today. You must be very tired." He stood up. "I'll see you tomorrow morning at ten. Oh, and could you ask Captain Graves to see me as soon as he arrives?"

Sassoon stood up. "You said a bit back you didn't think I was mad."

"I'm quite sure you're not. As a matter of fact I don't even think you've got a war neurosis."

Sassoon digested this. "What have I got, then?"

"You seem to have a very powerful *anti*-war neurosis."

They looked at each other and laughed. Rivers said, "You realize, don't you, that it's my duty to . . . to try to change that? I can't pretend to be neutral."

Sassoon's glance took in both their uniforms. "No, of course not."

49

WILFRED OWEN

S. I. W.

Wilfred Owen's First World War poems deal with the grim ironies of war and question the platitudes people use when describing it, in this case "death before dishonour." "S. I. W." was the abbreviation for an injury officially designated in the records as "Self-Inflicted Wound."

> I will to the King,
> And offer him consolation in his trouble,
> For that man there has set his teeth to die,
> And being one that hates obedience,
> Discipline, and orderliness of life,
> I cannot mourn him.
>
> W. B. YEATS

I. The Prologue

Patting goodbye, doubtless they told the lad
He'd always show the Hun a brave man's face;
Father would sooner him dead than in disgrace, –
Was proud to see him going, ay, and glad.
Perhaps his mother whimpered how she'd fret
Until he got a nice safe wound to nurse.
Sisters would wish girls too could shoot, charge, curse . . .
Brothers – would send his favourite cigarette.
Each week, month after month, they wrote the same,
Thinking him sheltered in some Y. M. Hut,

WILFRED OWEN, "S. I. W.," from *Poems* (with an introduction by Siegfried Sassoon). London. Chatto & Windus, 1920.

---

the Hun – the Germans

Y. M. Hut – large wooden shelters provided by the YMCA

Because he said so, writing on his butt
Where once an hour a bullet missed its aim
And misses teased the hunger of his brain.
His eyes grew old with wincing, and his hand
Reckless with ague. Courage leaked, as sand
From the best sand-bags after years of rain.
But never leave, wound, fever, trench-foot, shock,
Untrapped the wretch. And death seemed still withheld
For torture of lying machinally shelled,
At the pleasure of this world's Powers who'd run amok.

He'd seen men shoot their hands, on night patrol.
Their people never knew. Yet they were vile.
"Death sooner than dishonour, that's the style!"
So Father said.

II. The Action

          One dawn, our wire patrol
Carried him. This time, Death had not missed.
We could do nothing, but wipe his bleeding cough.
Could it be accident? – Rifles go off . . .
Not sniped? No. (Later they found the English ball.)

III. The Poem

It was the reasoned crisis of his soul
Against more days of inescapable thrall,
Against infrangibly wired and blind trench wall
Curtained with fire, roofed in with creeping fire,
Slow grazing fire, that would not burn him whole
But kept him for death's promises and scoff,
And life's half-promising, and both their riling.

IV. The Epilogue

With him they buried the muzzle his teeth had kissed,
And truthfully wrote the Mother, "Tim died smiling."

---

writing on his butt – rifle butt

wire patrol – patrolling the barbed wire in front of the trench

50

WILLIAM SHAKESPEARE

King Henry V (Act III, Scene III)

In *Henry IV*, Shakespeare depicted the maturation of Prince Hal from an irresponsible pleasure-lover to someone worthy of the throne of England. *Henry V* is Shakespeare's portrait of the "perfect king." In pursuit of a tenuous claim to the French throne through the line of his great-grandfather, Edward III, Henry V invades France. In this scene he addresses the Governor and citizens of the French fortress-city of Harfleur, seeking its surrender.

KING HENRY: How yet resolves the governor of the town?
    This is the latest parley we will admit:
    Therefore, to our best mercy give yourselves;
    Or like to men proud of destruction,
    Defy us to our worst: for as I am a soldier –
    A name that, in my thoughts, becomes me best, –
    If I begin the battery once again,
    I will not leave the half-achieved Harfleur
    Till in her ashes she lie buried.
    The gates of mercy shall be all shut up;
    And the flesh'd soldier, – rough and hard of heart, –
    In liberty of bloody hand shall range
    With conscience wide as hell; mowing like grass
    Your fresh-fair virgins and your flowering infants.
    What is it then to me if impious war, –
    Array'd in flames, like to the prince of fiends, –
    Do, with his smirch'd complexion, all fell feats
    Enlink'd to waste and desolation?
    What is't to me when you yourselves are cause,
    If your pure maidens fall into the hand
    Of hot and forcing violation?

WILLIAM SHAKESPEARE, from Act III, Scene III in *Henry V*, first published in 1598.

What rein can hold licentious wickedness
When down the hill he holds his fierce career?
We may as bootless spend our vain command
Upon the enraged soldiers in their spoil,
As send precepts to the Leviathan
To come ashore. Therefore, you men of Harfleur,
Take pity of your town and of your people
Whiles yet my soldiers are in my command;
Whiles yet the cool and temperate wind of grace
O'erblows the filthy and contagious clouds
Of heady murder, spoil, and villany.
If not, why, in a moment look to see
The blind and bloody soldier with foul hand
Defile the locks of your shrill-shrieking daughters;
Your fathers taken by the silver beards,
And their most reverend heads dash'd to the walls;
Your naked infants spitted upon pikes,
Whiles the mad mothers with their howls confus'd
Do break the clouds, as did the wives of Jewry
At Herod's bloody-hunting slaughtermen.
What say you? will you yield, and this avoid?
Or, guilty in defence, be thus destroy'd?
GOVERNOR: Our expectation hath this day an end:
The Dauphin, whom of succour we entreated,
Returns us that his powers are not yet ready
To raise so great a siege. Therefore, great king,
We yield our town and lives to thy soft mercy.
Enter our gates; dispose of us and ours;
For we no longer are defensible.
KING HENRY: Open your gates. – Come, uncle Exeter,
Go you and enter Harfleur; there remain,
And fortify it strongly 'gainst the French:
Use mercy to them all. For us, dear uncle, –
The winter coming on, and sickness growing
Upon our soldiers, – we will retire to Calais.
To-night in Harfleur will we be your guest;
To-morrow for the march are we addrest.

(*Flourish. The* KING, &c., *enter the Town.*)

Leviathan – a monstrous sea creature mentioned in the Bible

51

WILLIAM SHAKESPEARE

King Henry V (Act IV, Scene I)

This scene takes place in the English camp at Agincourt, France. King Henry, in disguise, is going among his troops to get a sense of their morale for the battle to come. Among the men he talks to on this night are Bates, Court, and Williams.

COURT: Brother John Bates, is not that the morning which breaks yonder?

BATES: I think it be: but we have no great cause to desire the approach of day.

WILLIAMS: We see yonder the beginning of the day, but I think we shall never see the end of it. – Who goes there?

KING HENRY: A friend.

WILLIAMS: Under what captain serve you?

KING HENRY: Under Sir Thomas Erpingham.

WILLIAMS: A good old commander and a most kind gentleman: I pray you, what thinks he of our estate?

KING HENRY: Even as men wrecked upon a sand, that look to be washed off the next tide.

BATES: He hath not told his thought to the king?

KING HENRY: No; nor it is not meet he should. For though I speak it to you, I think the king is but a man as I am: the violet smells to him as it doth to me; the element shows to him as it doth to me; all his senses have but human conditions: his ceremonies laid by, in his nakedness he appears but a man; and though his affections are higher mounted than ours, yet, when they stoop, they stoop with the like wing. Therefore when he sees reason of fears, as we do, his fears, out of doubt, be of the same relish as ours are: yet, in reason, no man should possess him with any appearance of fear, lest he, by showing it, should dishearten his army.

BATES: He may show what outward courage he will; but I believe, as cold a night as 'tis, he could wish himself in the Thames up to the neck; – and so I would he were, and I by him, at all adventures, so we were quit here.

WILLIAM SHAKESPEARE, from Act IV, Scene I in *Henry V*, first published in 1598.

KING HENRY: By my troth, I will speak my conscience of the king: I think he would not wish himself anywhere but where he is.

BATES: Then I would he were here alone; so should he be sure to be ransomed, and a many poor men's lives saved.

KING HENRY: I dare say you love him not so ill, to wish him here alone, howsoever you speak this, to feel other men's minds: methinks I could not die anywhere so contented as in the king's company, – his cause being just and his quarrel honourable.

WILLIAMS: That's more than we know.

BATES: Ay, or more than we should seek after; for we know enough if we know we are the king's subjects: if his cause be wrong, our obedience to the king wipes the crime of it out of us.

WILLIAMS: But if the cause be not good, the king himself hath a heavy reckoning to make when all those legs and arms and heads, chopped off in a battle, shall join together at the latter day and cry all, We died at such a place; some swearing; some crying for a surgeon; some upon their wives left poor behind them; some upon the debts they owe; some upon their children rawly left. I am afeared there are few die well that die in a battle; for how can they charitably dispose of anything when blood is their argument? Now, if these men do not die well, it will be a black matter for the king that led them to it; who to disobey were against all proportion of subjection.

KING HENRY: So if a son, that is by his father sent about merchandise do sinfully miscarry upon the sea, the imputation of his wickedness, by your rule, should be imposed upon his father that sent him: or if a servant, under his master's command, transporting a sum of money, be assailed by robbers, and die in many irreconciled iniquities, you may call the business of the master the author of the servant's damnation: – but this is not so: the king is not bound to answer the particular endings of his soldiers, the father of his son, nor the master of his servant; for they purpose not their death when they purpose their services. Besides, there is no king, be his cause never so spotless, if it come to the arbitrement of swords, can try it out with all unspotted soldiers: some peradventure have on them the guilt of premeditated and contrived murder; some of beguiling virgins with the broken seals of perjury; some making the wars their bulwark that have before gored the gentle bosom of peace with pillage and robbery. Now, if these men have defeated the law and outrun native punishment, though they can outstrip men they have no wings to fly from God: war is his beadle, war is his vengeance; so that here men are punished for before-breach of the king's laws in now the king's quarrel: where they feared the death they have borne life away; and where they would be safe they perish: then if they die unprovided, no more is the king guilty of their damnation than he was before guilty of those impieties for the which they are now visited. Every subject's duty is the king's; but every subject's soul is his own. Therefore should every soldier in the wars do as every sick man in his bed, – wash every mote out of his conscience: and dying so, death is to him advantage; or not dying, the time was blessedly lost wherein such preparation was gained: and in him that escapes it were not sin to think that, making God so free an offer, he let him outlive that day to see his greatness, and to teach others how they should prepare.

WILLIAMS: 'Tis certain, every man that dies ill, the ill upon his own head, – the king is not to answer for it.

52

ALFRED TENNYSON

The Charge of the Light Brigade

"The Charge of the Light Brigade" was written in 1854, five weeks after the event it memorializes, which took place during the Crimean War, at the Battle of Balaclava. Of the 637 men involved in the charge, 247 were killed or wounded.

I

Half a league, half a league,
  Half a league onward,
All in the valley of Death
  Rode the six hundred.
"Forward, the Light Brigade!
Charge for the guns!" he said:
Into the valley of Death
  Rode the six hundred.

II

"Forward, the Light Brigade!"
Was there a man dismay'd?
Not tho' the soldier knew
  Some one had blunder'd:
Their's not to make reply,
Their's not to reason why,
Their's but to do and die:
Into the valley of Death
  Rode the six hundred.

ALFRED LORD TENNYSON, "The Charge of the Light Brigade," 1855.

III

Cannon to right of them,
Cannon to left of them,
Cannon in front of them
   Volley'd and thunder'd;
Storm'd at with shot and shell,
Boldly they rode and well,
Into the jaws of Death,
Into the mouth of Hell
   Rode the six hundred.

IV

Flash'd all their sabres bare,
Flash'd as they turn'd in air
Sabring the gunners there,
Charging an army, while
   All the world wonder'd:
Plunged in the battery-smoke
Right thro' the line they broke;
Cossack and Russian
Reel'd from the sabre-stroke
   Shatter'd and sunder'd.
Then they rode back, but not
   Not the six hundred.

V

Cannon to right of them,
Cannon to left of them,
Cannon behind them
   Volley'd and thunder'd;
Storm'd at with shot and shell,
While horse and hero fell,
They that had fought so well
Came thro' the jaws of Death,
Back from the mouth of Hell,
All that was left of them,
   Left of six hundred.

VI

When can their glory fade?
O the wild charge they made!
  All the world wonder'd.
Honour the charge they made!
Honour the Light Brigade,
  Noble six hundred!

53

S. YIZHAR

The Prisoner

"The Prisoner," written in the 1960s, is characteristic of Yizhar's writing, which deals primarily with the time before and immediately after the establishment of the State of Israel. A troop of Israeli soldiers capture an Arab shepherd, Hassan Ahmed, as he peacefully minds his sheep. They bring him in for interrogation. The shepherd knows nothing. The soldiers, becoming increasingly frustrated, move from asking questions to kicking and beating him.

The questioning petered out miserably. The sentry at the door shifting from one foot to another at his post had been peeping out of the doorway from time to time. Maybe he was seeking something in the bright sky that differed from the sheer mess of this dirty room. Now he began to feel apprehensive. Something dreadful was about to happen and there was no other choice. For what could be left, after all, except to have them tell him to take the carcass along and finish him?

"Well, that's the way it is." The examiner stretched back against his chair, wanting to take a breather after all this nonsense. He crushed his cigarette impatiently, dropped it on the floor and crushed it.

"I'll finish him off," suggested bald-head as he flicked his cigarette through the doorway.

"An absolute dumbbell," decided one officer.

"Just pretending to be a dumbbell," said the other.

"What you have to know is how to talk to him," said the chap leaning against the wall, twisting his lips in recognition of a truth which they had presumably doubted and denied.

The prisoner had already sensed that there was an interval. He licked his thick lips, struck out his thick hand and said:

"*Fi sigara, ya sidi?*" (Got a cigarette, mister?)

S. YIZHAR (Yizhar Smilansky), "The Prisoner" (tr. I. M. Lask), pp. 121–8 from Dalia Rabikovitz (ed.), *The New Israeli Writers: Short Stories of the First Generation*. New York: Sabra Brooks, Funk and Wagnalls, 1969. Copyright in the original Hebrew version by S. Yizhar and Zmora Bitan. Thanks to the assistance of the Institute for the Translation of Hebrew Literature.

Of course no one paid any attention to the idiot. He waited a few moments, then drew his outstretched hand back, thought the matter over and stood still again, an absolute donkey for you. And only to himself alone did he moan: *"ahhh, ya rab."* Meaning: Oh, Lord God.

Well, what next? Where to now? To the quarry slopes in the villages? Or maybe to some torture of the kind that opens mouths and restores truth instead of false-hood? Or was there any other way? How were they to get rid of him? Or maybe . . . Suppose they were to give him a cigarette and send the dolt back home? Get the hell out of here and we don't ever want to see you again!

Finally they phoned somewhere or other and spoke to the Assistant Boss him-self; and it was decided to send him on to another camp (at least three of the fellows in the room disgustedly turned their noses up at this shamefaced, civilian, namby-pamby trick); a camp where prisoners were questioned and handled the way they deserved. With this end in view the sentry at the door, the same one who had felt uneasy all the time without knowing why, would go off and fetch the dusty jeep and the growling duty driver who was annoyed at being called out of turn, which was so easily proved by so many facts and also by objurgations. Apart from which, as far as he himself was concerned he did not have the least objection to going off to some place where he could see human beings, but this was a matter of principle, sheer principle. And then another soldier also came and sat down beside the driver, since there was some job which could not be done until now in the absence of transport. He was now given this additional objective of accom-panying the prisoner. And that was the way they would pass through the town, Spandau in front and prisoner behind. Burdened with these two functions in order to make sure that never under any circumstances would this trip be deducted from his leave (that being a separate account), he sat and loaded the machine-gun.

As for the prisoner, after he had been pushed and began groping around and banged against the side of the car and was helped in, the only place left for him was on the floor where he half-lay, half-kneeled and crouched entirely. Two were in front and the former sentry behind him, his pocket bulging with the proper papers and travel orders and chits and all the rest of it. That afternoon, which had begun some time or other between the hills and the trees and the flocks, was now due to finish in a way nobody could forecast.

They were already out of the smelly village and crossing from the wadi to the fields, then on through the fields. The jeep dashed along bouncing on all fours, and stretches of the not-so-distant future began to be transformed into reality. It was nice to sit facing the fields as they bathed in an increasingly reddish light that comprehended everything in a sweep of tiny bright golden clouds, a light rising higher than anything; than all those things which concern you and me so much, even though they did not in the least matter to the driver or his comrade with the mustache beside him. They smoked, whistled and sang, "In the Negev plains a

---

Spandau – a kind of machine gun

wadi – a dry streambed

man defending fell", and, "Your eyes are bright with a green green light", one after the other. There was someone else on the floor of the jeep, but it wasn't easy to know what could be going on inside him since he was blindfolded, beastlike and silent.

A fuzz of dust rose behind them, a smoky wake which wavered and grew pink at the edges. Irrelevant ditches and unimportant potholes in the road made the jeep jump, while fields spread their arms out to infinity and gave themselves up to a twilight that was fuddled with forgetfulness and gentleness – and something so far away, so far away, so dreamlike – until all of a sudden and unexpectedly a strange thought jumped into his head and would not budge. "The woman, she's undoubtedly lost." For up to now it was astonishing where they could have come from, you understand; as though you were thunderstruck to think that here, right here beside you, something was happening; the same thing which in other circumstances is called by other names, and which is also known as Fate.

You'd better take a jump at once, one, two, and get right out from under this bad business. Sing as a second voice to the two in front, set out for distant regions in the twilight through which the sun was burning with a reddish-citron color; only you would at once see again what had so suddenly emerged through the astounding breach.

The fellow here at your feet, his life, his well-being, his home, three souls, the whole thread of his existence with all that was involved, were in your grip somehow or other as though you were some lesser demigod here in the jeep. The man carried along, the collective flock of sheep and several souls in the mountain village, these variegated threads of life were twined together to be cut or grow inextricably involved, all because you were suddenly their master. If you liked you could just stop the jeep and let him go free, and everything would cut up differently. But . . . just a moment. The fellow on the back seat of the little jeep suddenly felt the spirit darting aloft within him. Just a moment: Let the fellow go?

Here we could stop the jeep, here by the wadi. We could let the fellow down, uncover his eyes, face him towards the mountains, point straight ahead and tell him: Go home, man, go straight along. Take care about that hill, there are Jews on it. Take care and don't fall into our hands again. And then he would take his feet over and dash home. He would go back home. Precisely that. And listen, what a story! The dreadful, tense waiting, the fate of a woman and her children (an Arab woman!). Forebodings at the heart that wrestled with the decree of Fate, wondering will he, won't he come back, guessing what might happen next; and then everything solved satisfactorily so that she could breathe easily, he's condemned to life. Hi lad, come and let's let the fellow go!

And why not? What was to stop it? Simple, decent and human. So just get up and tell the driver to stop. No more fine phrases about humanity any longer. This time it's up to you yourself. This time it's not someone else's malice, this time it's your own conscience you're facing. Let him off and you've saved him. Today that alternative, that ominous, tremendous alternative we always used to talk about so nervously, is firmly in your own two hands. There's no dodging it now, not with Soldier, not with Orders, and not with Suppose they caught you, not even with

What will the boys say. You're standing naked, facing your duty. And the choice is all your own, nobody else's.

Then stop the jeep. Stop the driver. Let the poor devil go. You don't have to give any reasons. It's his right and your duty. If there's any meaning or sense in this war, now's the time for it to be seen. Men, men, there was a man and they sent him home. Snap your fingers at all this customary cruelty and send the fellow away. Just release him. Hallelujah! That peasant, that shepherd would go home to his wife.

There could be no alternative. Otherwise years would pass and then in some remarkable way he would go free and return to the mountains to look for his wife and his home. And meanwhile they would be starving refugees going from bad to worse, sick with typhoid, so much human dust. And who would say what that meanwhile would be or where it would be and even that it would be, provided only that meanwhile some fellow somewhere or other doesn't simply knock him off and send him to heaven by sheer chance, or maybe not just by sheer chance.

Why don't you stop the jeep then? It's your duty. You can't dodge it. That has become so clear, it's hard to wait until you decide to do it. This is where you stand up, this is where you do it. Say a word to the driver, tell him and the other fellow it's the order, spin them a yarn, tell them anything – and you don't need to do even that. You don't need to explain, you don't need to tell them anything. No matter what may happen. There was once a man. Just look at the way things are. Let him go. (How can I? He isn't mine. He isn't in my hands. That's not correct, I'm not his master, I'm an agent and nothing more. What have I done wrong? Since when am I responsible for the hard-heartedness of others?)

Stop it! That's shameful evasion. That's how every scamp dodges a decision and hides himself behind a "no alternative" that has gone shabby with use. Where's your sense of honor? Where's that far-famed independence of thought? Where's the freedom, three cheers for freedom, the love of liberty? Let him go! By all means, and then be prepared to give an account of what you've done. It's an honor. All your words, all your complaints, all your dissatisfaction about trifles and oppression, all your thoughts about ways of forcing yourself to move towards truth and freedom – where are they all? Today the account has been presented, it's payday. So pay up my lad, pay up, it's all yours now. (I can't. I'm only an agent. Besides it's wartime and this fellow comes from the other side which is fighting us. Maybe he is a futile victim. Yet as for me I mustn't free him and I haven't the power to do it. Here's a fresh idea for you. Everybody begins releasing and where are we? Or maybe he really does know something important and merely pretends to be a fool?)

Is that the case? Then is the fellow a soldier? Have you caught him with a weapon in hand? Where have you fetched him from? He isn't a fighter. He's a stinking, miserable civilian. All that prisoner-of-war business is a lie, and don't you forget it. It's a crime, it is. Have you questioned him? Then set him free now. More than he has already told they certainly won't get out of him. And the cost of one extra item of information is not worth the suppression of truth in his release.

(Hard for me to decide. I don't dare. Many unpleasant things simply have to be done. Talk to the driver, explain it to the other fellow, face the investigations afterwards, get into a hell of a fix because of some miserable Hassan; quite apart from which it's not at all clear that he must be released here and now, before he has been properly questioned and put through the mill.)

Nonsense! If anybody else knew only a quarter of what you know and the conclusions you've reached about truth and freedom, he would stop the jeep here and now and send the fellow packing. Then go on and forget this business, plain and simple, short and sweet, in the most practical fashion and without patting yourself on the shoulder. But when it comes to you, with all the thousand facts you know and argue about and demonstrate and dream of, you're clearly thinking you won't do it. You have a nice sweet soul, you'll think it over, you'll get all excited, you'll feel sorry, you'll think it over again, and after all that you'll go diving into a sea of deep thought wondering, why didn't I do it? And you'll put the blame for missing this opportunity, for never rounding off your existence, on the whole wide world. It's a crude and ugly world, you'll say. So do something instead. Do something, just this once. Stand up to it. Get out and fight. Of course! (I do feel sorry for him. It's a pity they chose me for this job. I'd do it if I weren't afraid of I don't know what. If at least we were alone here. The business is already thrilling and throbbing in me like an unsatisfied appetite, yet still I can't. I can't begin. It's simply beyond me. When I remember that it will be necessary to explain things; to come to people and argue, to prove myself, to begin to justify myself – no, I simply can't.)

Now listen lad, do you weigh all these miserable trills and tremolos against a human life? How would you like it if you were crouching on the floor of a jeep, if your wife was waiting at home and everything was destroyed, flying about like chaff, lost and done for, waiting and waiting while the heart burns away and you're not at home; waiting with tears, waiting with your fist, with humility, with prayer and protest . . .

He has already said all he has to say. He told us all he has to tell. And now what next? Even if he did lie, even if it was untrue seven times over, still who and what is he more than a miserable nonentity, a withering submissive creature, a face wrapped around with a kerchief, all squeezed up and twisted, worthless, an empty frightened bag, fading away to nothing, abnegating himself, expecting to be kicked and regarding kicks as natural. (Take a kick at an Arab, it doesn't mean anything to him.)

And you, his guard, you simply have to let him go even if he himself laughs at you, even if he or somebody else regards it as sheer incapacity, even if your companions mock you, even if they ask you to prevent his liberation, even if they send you to the Chief Prosecutor because of it, or to a score of prosecutors. It still remains your duty and you had better set about it and escape from this swinish routine. Then there'll have been somebody who was prepared even if he paid for it to get out for once; to get away from the pigsties which rose so high and spread so far and wide while we were good citizens, and which have now officially and solemnly and by general agreement become the way of the world, the practice of everybody who wants to be worthy of the magnificent name of soldier.

We don't get any leave, we can't go home, it's hot here, filthy here, miserable here, dangerous here – so what? Let's take it out on the enemy. Let's do something.

Let's knock off some miserable Arab. (Who asked him to start this damned war anyway?) Let's permit ourselves to do everything we were once forbidden to do.

Ah well, here's a certain Hassan Ahmad. His wife is either Halima or Fatma and he has two daughters and his flock has been stolen and he has been taken away somewhere or other on a bright and sunny afternoon. And who are you and what's your life good for? All a fellow like you is worth is for having all the black bile inside us emptied out on you, and the hell with it.

Of course you're not going to let him go. That's perfectly plain. It's just fine thoughts. It's not even cowardice, it's something worse. You're a partner in the business, that's what you are. Hiding behind that stinking "what's to be done, it's an order", just this time when you have the choice and it's all in your own power, in your very own hands.

The choice is yours. A great day it is. A day of revolt. A day when you have the choice in your own hands at last, and the power to turn it into a decision, to give life back to a misused man. Think it over. To act as your heart desires. In full accordance with your own love and your own truth, in accordance with the greatest of all things – the liberation of a man.

Let him go.

Be a man.

Let him go!

Well, it's quite clear nothing will happen. Fly away, good idea. You'll dodge, that's plain. You'll look the other way. Of course it's all lost. I'm sorry for you, prisoner. He simply doesn't have the strength to do it.

Yet maybe, in spite of everything? Right away, here and now. It would just take this moment. Pull up, driver. Get off, Hassan. Go home. Do something. Talk. Stop the jeep. Say something now, this moment. After all your aching and bellyaching all these long and empty days, be a human being at last the way you want to be.

The fields were one vast shallow pinkish-gold expanse, all the tens of thousands of dunams made up one single enchanted plain without valleys, without hills, without acclivities or declivities, without villages or trees. Everything had been beaten down to one single gold foil, one leveled expanse above which were scattered quivering restless golden dust-blobs around a vast land of gold that stretched on to infinity; even if it were possible that on the other side (where nobody watches) amid the evening mists making their way down from the hills, even if there is some other sadness over there maybe, some misery, some misery of who knows what, some misery of shameful inaction, some waiting woman, some who-can-know-what decree of life, who knows what very very private individual, who knows what else that may be even more universal, which the setting sun is going to leave here, among us, never brought to an end?

---

dunams – four dunams = one acre

54

JOHN FOWLES

The Magus

The Magus was first published in 1965 and has achieved cult status. A revised edition
came out in 1979. A bored young Englishman, Nicholas Urfe, takes a teaching job on
the Greek island of Phraxos. There he meets the reclusive millionaire Maurice Colchis.
Colchis is recounting an incident that occurred under the Nazi occupation after the
killing of Austrian soldiers by Greek partisans.

We were marched to the harbour. The entire village was there, some four
or five hundred people, black and grey and faded blue, crammed on to
the quays with a line of *die Raben* watching them. The village priests,
the women, even little boys and girls. They screamed as we came into sight. Like
some amorphous protoplasm. Trying to break bounds, but unable to.

We went on marching. There is a large house with huge Attic acroteria facing
the harbour – you know it? – in those days there was a taverna on the ground-
floor. On the balcony above I saw Wimmel and behind him Anton, flanked by
men with machine-guns. I was taken from the column and made to stand against
the wall under the balcony, among the chairs and tables. The hostages went
marching on. Up a street and out of sight.

It was very hot. A perfect blue day. The villagers were driven from the quay to
the terrace with the old cannons in front of the taverna. They stood crowded
there. Brown faces upturned in the sunlight, black kerchiefs of the women fluttering in the breeze. I could not see the balcony, but the colonel waited above,
impressing his silence on them, his presence. And gradually they fell absolutely
quiet, a wall of expectant faces. Up in the sky I saw swallows and martins. Like
children playing in a house where some tragedy is taking place among the adults.

JOHN FOWLES, pp. 429–35 from *The Magus: a Revised Version*. Boston: Little, Brown & Co., 1978. Copyright © 1965 by John Fowles Ltd. Reprinted by permission of Little, Brown and Company, Inc. and
Anthony Sheil in association with Gillon Aitken Associates Limited.

die Raben – the ravens, meaning the Blackshirts or SS

Attic acroteria – ancient pedestals for vases or statues forming a part of the roof balustrade

Strange, to see so many Greeks . . . and not a sound. Only the tranquil cries of little birds.

Wimmel began to speak. The collaborationist interpreted.

"You will now see what happens to those . . . those who are the enemies of Germany . . . and to those who help the enemies of Germany . . . by order of a court martial of the German High Command held last night . . . three have been executed . . . two more will now be executed . . ."

All the brown hands darted up, made the four taps of the Cross. Wimmel paused. German is to death what Latin is to ritual religion – entirely appropriate.

"Following that . . . the eighty hostages . . . taken under Occupation law . . . in retaliation for the brutal murder . . . of four innocent members of the German Armed Forces . . ." and yet again he paused . . . "will be executed."

When the interpreter interpreted the last phrase, there was an exhaled groan, as if they had all been struck in the stomach. Many of the women, some of the men, fell to their knees, imploring the balcony. Humanity groping for the non-existent pity of a *deus vindicans*. Wimmel must have withdrawn, because the beseechings turned to lamentations.

Now I was forced out from the wall and marched after the hostages. Soldiers, the Austrians, stood at every entrance to the harbour and forced the villagers back. It horrified me that they could help *die Raben*, could obey Wimmel, could stand there with impassive faces and roughly force back people that I knew, only a day or two before, they did not hate.

The alley curved up between the houses to the square beside the village school. It is a natural stage, inclined slightly to the north, with the sea and the mainland over the lower roofs. With the wall of the village school on the uphill side, and high walls to east and west. If you remember, there is a large plane tree in the garden of the house to the west. The branches come over the wall. As I came to the square that was the first thing I saw. Three bodies hung from the branches, pale in the shadow, as monstrous as Goya etchings. There was the naked body of the cousin with its terrible wound. And there were the naked bodies of the two girls. They had been disembowelled. A slit cut from their breastbones down to their pubic hair and the intestines pulled out. Half-gutted carcasses, swaying slightly in the noon wind.

Beyond those three atrocious shapes I saw the hostages. They had been herded against the school in a pen of barbed wire. The men at the back were just in the shadow of the wall, the front ones in sunlight. As soon as they saw me they began to shout. There were insults of the obvious kind to me, confused cries of appeal – as if anything I could say then would have touched the colonel. He was there, in the centre of the square, with Anton and some twenty of *die Raben*. On the third side of the square, to the east, there is a long wall. You know it? In the middle a gate. Iron grilles. The two surviving guerrillas were lashed to the bars. Not with rope – with barbed wire.

I was halted behind the two lines of men, some twenty yards away from where Wimmel was standing. Anton would not look at me, though Wimmel turned

deus vindicans – avenging god

briefly. Anton – staring into space, as if he had hypnotized himself into believing that none of what he saw existed. As if he no longer existed himself. The colonel beckoned the collaborationist to him. I suppose he wanted to know what the hostages were shouting. He appeared to think for a moment and then he went towards them. They fell silent. Of course they did not know he had already pronounced sentence on them. He said something that was translated to them. What, I could not hear, except that it reduced the village to silence. So it was not the death sentence. The colonel marched back to me.

He said, "I have made an offer to these peasants." I looked at his face. It was absolutely without nervousness, excitation; a man in complete command of himself. He went on, "I will permit them not to be executed. To go to a labour camp. On one condition. That is that you, as mayor of this village, carry out in front of them the execution of the two murderers."

I said, "I am not an executioner."

The village men began to shout frantically at me.

He looked at his watch, and said, "You have thirty seconds to decide."

Of course in such situations one cannot think. All coherence is crowded out of one's mind. You must remember this. From this point on I acted without reason. Beyond reason.

I said, "I have no choice."

He went to the end of one of the ranks of men in front of me. He took a sub-machine-gun from a man's shoulder, appeared to make sure that it was correctly loaded, then came back with it and presented it to me with both hands. As if it was a prize I had won. The hostages cheered, crossed themselves. And then were silent. The colonel watched me. I had a wild idea that I might turn the gun on him. But of course the massacre of the entire village would then have been inevitable.

I walked towards the men wired to the iron gates. I knew why he had done this. It would be widely publicized by the German-controlled newspapers. The pressure on me would not be mentioned, and I would be presented as the Greek who co-operated in the German theory of order. A warning to other mayors. An example to other frightened Greeks everywhere. But those eighty men – how could I condemn them?

I came within about fifteen feet of the two guerillas. So close, because I had not fired a gun for very many years. For some reason I had not looked them in the face till then. I had looked at the high wall with its tiled top, at a pair of vulgar ornamental urns on top of the pillars that flanked the gate, at the fronds of a pepper tree beyond. But then I had to look at them. The younger of the two might have been dead. His head had fallen forward. They had done something to his hands, I could not see what, but there was blood all over the fingers. He was not dead. I heard him groan. Mutter something. He was delirious.

And the other. His mouth had been struck or kicked. The lips were severely contused, reddened. As I stood there and raised the gun he drew back what remained of those lips. All his teeth had been smashed in. The inside of his mouth was like a blackened vulva. But I was too desperate to finish to realize the real cause. He too had had his fingers crushed, or his nails torn out, and I could see multiple burns on his body. But the Germans had made one terrible error. They had not gouged out his eyes.

I raised the gun blindly and pressed the trigger. Nothing happened. A click. I pressed it again. And again, an empty click.

I turned and looked round. Wimmel and my two guards were standing thirty feet or so away, watching. The hostages suddenly began to call. They thought I had lost the will to shoot. I turned back and tried once more. Again, nothing. I turned to the colonel, and gestured with the gun, to show that it would not fire. I felt faint in the heat. Nausea. Yet unable to faint.

He said, "Is something wrong?"

I answered, "The gun will not fire."

"It is a Schmeisser. An excellent weapon."

"I have tried three times."

"It will not fire because it is not loaded. It is strictly forbidden for the civilian population to possess loaded weapons."

I stared at him, then at the gun. Still not understanding. The hostages were silent again.

I said, very helplessly, "How can I kill them?"

He smiled, a smile as thin as a sabre-slash. Then he said, "I am waiting."

I understood then. I was to club them to death. I understood many things. His real self, his real position. And from that came the realization that he was mad, and that he was therefore innocent, as all mad people, even the most cruel, are innocent. He was what life could do if it wanted – an extreme possibility made hideously mind and flesh. Perhaps that was why he could impose himself so strongly, like a black divinity. For there was something superhuman in the spell he cast. And therefore the real evil, the real monstrosity in the situation lay in the other Germans, those less-than-mad lieutenants and corporals and privates who stood silently there watching this exchange.

I walked towards him. The two guards thought I was going to attack him because they sharply raised their guns. But he said something to them and stood perfectly still. I stopped some six feet from him. We stared at each other.

"I beg you in the name of European civilization to stop this barbarity."

"And I command you to continue this punishment."

Without looking down he said, "Refusal to carry out this order will result in your own immediate execution."

I walked back over the dry earth to that gate. I stood in front of those two men. I was going to say to the one who seemed capable of understanding that I had no choice, I must do this terrible thing to him. But I left a fatal pause of a second to elapse. Perhaps because I realized, close to him, what had happened to his mouth. It had been burnt, not simply bludgeoned or kicked. I remembered that man with the iron stake, the electric fire. They had broken in his teeth and branded his tongue, burnt his tongue right down to the roots with red-hot iron. That word he shouted must finally have driven them beyond endurance. And in those astounding five seconds, the most momentous of my life, I understood this guerilla. I mean that I understood far better than he did himself what he was. He helped me. He managed to stretch his head towards me and say the word he could not say. It was almost not a sound, but a contortion in his throat, a five-syllabled choking. But once again, one last time, it was unmistakably that word. And the word was in his eyes, in his being, totally in his being. What did Christ say on the cross? Why hast thou forsaken me? What this man said was something far less sympathetic, far less pitiful, even far less human, but far profounder. He spoke out of a world the very opposite of mine. In mine life had no price. It was so valuable that it was literally priceless. In his, only one thing had that quality of pricelessness. It was *eleutheria*: freedom. He was the immalleable, the essence, the beyond reason, beyond logic, beyond civilization, beyond history. He was not God, because there is no God we can know. But he was a proof that there is a God that we can never know. He was the final right to deny. To be free to choose. He, or what manifested itself through him, even included the insane Wimmel, the despicable German and Austrian troops. He was every freedom, from the very worst to the very best. The freedom to desert on the battlefield of Neuve Chapelle. The freedom to confront a primitive God at Seidevarre. The freedom to disembowel peasant girls and castrate with wire-cutters. He was something that passed beyond morality but sprang out of the very essence of things – that comprehended all, the freedom to do all, and stood against only one thing – the prohibition not to do all.

All this takes many words to say to you. And I have said nothing about how I felt this immalleability, this refusal to cohere, was essentially Greek. That is, I finally assumed my Greekness. All I saw I saw in a matter of seconds, perhaps not in time at all. Saw that I was the only person left in that square who had the freedom left to choose, and that the annunciation and defence of that freedom was more important than common sense, self-preservation, yes, than my own life, than the lives of the eighty hostages. Again and again, since then, those eighty men have risen in the night and accused me. You must remember that I was certain I was going to die too. But all I have to set against their crucified faces are those few transcendent seconds of knowledge. But knowledge like a white heat. My reason has repeatedly told me I was wrong. Yet my total being still tells me I was right.

I stood there perhaps fifteen seconds – I could not tell you, time means nothing in such situations – and then I dropped the gun and stopped beside the guerilla leader. I saw the colonel watching me, and I said, for him and so also for the remnant of a man beside me to hear, the one word that remained to be said.

Somewhere beyond Wimmel I saw Anton moving, walking quickly towards him. But it was too late. The colonel spoke, the sub-machine-guns flashed and I closed my eyes at exactly the moment the first bullets hit me.

X

ANIMALS AND THE ENVIRONMENT

In previous sections we have seen what a more powerful nation or race can do to other humans when it places them outside the boundary of its moral community. Against a history of racism, slavery, genocide, sexism, and religious persecution, the idea that all human beings are equal and possess human rights is a way of widening the circle of equality, and so must be welcomed as a progressive advance and a bulwark against further atrocities. But the human species is not the only one on this planet. When we take the perspective of other beings, we can see that there is another side to the idea of human equality and universal human rights. A fictional work like Desmond Stewart's story "The Limits of Trooghaft" can help us to see what our behavior might look like from the perspective of beings we put beyond the circle of moral concern.

The idea that animals, and nature itself, exist for our use has a long history, especially in the West. Western attitudes to nature grew out of a blend of those of the Hebrew people, as represented in the early books of the Bible, and the philosophy of ancient Greece, particularly that of Aristotle. In contrast to some other ancient traditions, for example those of India, both the Hebrew and the Aristotelian traditions made human beings the centre of the moral universe; indeed, not merely the centre, but very often the entirety of the morally significant features of this world. Aristotle thought that everything in the universe is there for a purpose, and the purpose of the less rational beings is to serve the more rational ones. Plants exist for the sake of animals, and animals serve humans by providing them with meat and skins. (His justification of slavery had the same basis, for he claimed that barbarians are less rational than Greeks.) The Hebrew story of creation, as told in Genesis, makes it very clear that humans – but not other animals – are made in the image of God, and have a God-given dominion "over the fish of the sea, and over the fowl of the air, and over the earth, and over every creeping thing that creepeth upon the earth."[1]

Mainstream Christianity reiterated this view for at least its first eighteen centuries. The most important and influential Christian thinkers – men like Paul, Augustine and Thomas Aquinas – were its hardline advocates. They agreed that human beings are the only morally important members of this world, denied any intrinsic value to nature, and held that the destruction of plants and animals cannot be sinful, unless it brings harm to human beings. There were gentler spirits, certainly, like Basil, John Chrysostom, and (according to tradition) Francis of Assisi, but for most of Christian history they have been on the fringes, lacking any significant impact on the dominant tradition.

Harsh as this tradition is, it does not rule out concern for the preservation of nature, as long as that concern can be related to human well-being. Often, of course, it can be. Many arguments against the pollution of rivers or air, the emission of gases liable to change the climate of our planet, and the destruction of forests can be couched in terms of long-term harm to human health and welfare. Since human beings need an environment in which they can thrive, the preservation of such an environment can be a value within a human-centered moral framework. Though that fact is of immense practical importance, the more philosophically interesting issue is what the moral status of nonhuman animals and the environment should be.

Most of us believe that all humans are equal. As we have seen, the most solid ground on which to rest this claim is that all humans have wants, needs, and desires, for adequate food and shelter, for personal security, and to avoid physical suffering. This is something that we can expect all reasonable people to accept, as long as they can view the question from an impartial perspective, and are not improperly influenced by having a personal interest in the continued exploitation of members of a different race or sex.

Now consider the question of the moral status of nonhuman animals. Nonhuman animals are also capable of feeling pain, as humans are; they can certainly be miserable, and perhaps in some cases their lives could also be described as joyful; and members of many mammalian species can suffer from separation from their family group. Critics of the traditional view argue that the extent to which pain and suffering are intrinsically bad depends on factors like its duration and intensity, not on the species of the being who experiences it. They point out that some human beings – infants, or those with severe intellectual disabilities – are no more rational or self-aware than many nonhuman animals, and yet we treat them as equals. We grant them basic rights, and would be horrified at any suggestion that we are justified in using them in order to conduct the kind of research that we have performed on nonhuman animals – as described by Richard Adams in *The Plague Dogs*. In saying that the joys and sufferings of these and other humans matter more than those of nonhuman animals, we are giving preference to the interests of members of our own species, simply because they are members of our own species. This, the critics say, is "speciesism," a term that is intended to suggest a parallel to racism, because it attempts to put a morally crucial divide in a place that is not justified on any basis other than a preference for "us" over "them." Instead, they argue, we should extend the principle of equal consideration of interests to all beings capable of suffering or feeling pain. Otherwise, if we ourselves disregard or discount the interests of members of other species because they are not members of our own group, how are we to object to those who wish to disregard the interests of members of other races because they are also outside our own group?

It is important to understand the implications of this principle of equal consideration of interests. It does not require us to regard the death of a nonhuman animal as morally equivalent to the death of a normal human being, nor, for that matter, does it require us to see the death of a mouse as equivalent to that of an elephant or a chimpanzee. Humans, when they are beyond infancy and not severely intellectually impaired, are capable of foresight and planning in ways that mice are not. So too, it seems, are chimpanzees, and perhaps dolphins and elephants too. These capacities are surely relevant to the seriousness of death. In the case of a being capable of planning for the future, death will thwart these plans, and thus causes a loss that is different in kind from the loss that death causes to beings incapable even of understanding that they exist over time and have a future. It is also consistent with the principle of equal consideration of interests that we should take into account the greater sense of loss that humans feel when people close to them die; whether nonhuman animals will feel a sense of loss at the death of another animal will depend on the social habits of the species. What the principle does require is that similar interests should be given similar weight. We still have to judge when the interests of beings with different capacities are relevantly similar.

What, though, of living beings or natural objects without any capacity to feel pain? In an oft-quoted essay, the American ecologist Aldo Leopold proposed a new "Land Ethic" according to which: "A thing is right when it tends to preserve the integrity, stability and beauty of the biotic community. It is wrong when it tends otherwise."[2] Defenders of what is sometimes called "biocentrism" or "deep ecology" have said that "richness and diversity" are a source of intrinsic value in nature. They tend to take a holistic view, attributing value to large entities like species or ecosystems. But defenders of this view have to show not only that trees, species, and ecosystems can properly be said to have interests, but that they have morally significant interests. One way of establishing that an interest is morally significant is to ask what it is like for the entity affected to have that interest unsatisfied. Imaginatively, we can put ourselves in the place of that being, and ask: how would I like it if I were in that situation? This works for sentient beings, but it does not work for trees, species, or ecosystems. We may be able to imagine what it is like to be a bear whose habitat is being flooded by the rising waters of a lake created by a dam, but there is nothing we can imagine that corresponds to what it is like to be an ecosystem flooded by a dam, because an ecosystem, as such, has no experiences at all.

The difficulty with a biocentric ethic is that once we abandon the interests of sentient creatures as our source of value, it is no longer clear where we find value at all. As long as we confine ourselves to arguments based on the interests of sentient creatures, present and future, human and nonhuman, we are on familiar philosophical ground, and we can still make a strong case for the preservation of remaining areas of wilderness and of both local and global ecosystems. When we move beyond that ground, and seek to argue for the intrinsic value of plants, or species, or ecosystems, our arguments become more speculative. Take, for example, endangered species. Most of us feel that to allow a species of plant or animal to become extinct is a tragedy, and we go to great lengths to protect members of endangered species, But we give more importance to large, iconic animals like tigers and pandas than we do to endangered grasses or insects. In *The Pioneers*,

James Fenimore Cooper describes events that, repeated all over the United States, led to the extinction of the passenger pigeon. The slaughter is obviously cruel, for many of the birds die slowly. But beyond the suffering and death, we feel a sense of loss that the great flocks of migrating passenger pigeons are no more. What kind of loss is that? Is there more to it than the loss of aesthetic pleasure and interest to humans who would have enjoyed seeing these birds? To answer these questions in terms of ethical argument is difficult, perhaps impossible. We may have reached the point at which aesthetic judgment takes over from ethical argument.

NOTES

1   Genesis 1:26.
2   Aldo Leopold, *A Sand County Almanac*, New York: Ballantine, 1978, p. 262.

55

DESMOND STEWART

The Limits of Trooghaft

The Troogs took one century to master the planet, then another three to restock it with men, its once dominant but now conquered species. Being hierarchical in temper, the Troogs segregated *homo insipiens* into four castes between which there was no traffic except that of bloodshed. The four castes derived from the Troog experience of human beings.

The planet's new masters had an intermittent sense of the absurd; Troog laughter could shake a forest. Young Troogs first captured some surviving children, then tamed them as "housemen," though to their new pets the draughty Troog structures seemed far from house-like. Pet-keeping spread. Whole zoos of children were reared on a bean diet. For housemen, Troogs preferred children with brown or yellow skins, finding them neater and cleaner than others; this preference soon settled into an arbitrary custom. Themselves hermaphrodite, the Troogs were fascinated by the spectacle of marital couplings. Once their pets reached adolescence, they were put in cages whose nesting boxes had glass walls. Troogs would gaze in by the hour. Captivity – and this was an important discovery – did not inhibit the little creatures from breeding, nor, as was feared, did the sense of being watched turn the nursing females to deeds of violence. Cannibalism was rare. Breeders, by selecting partners, could soon produce strains with certain comical features, such as cone-shaped breasts or cushion-shaped rumps.

The practice of keeping pets was fought by senior Troogs; the conservative disapproved of innovations while the fastidious found it objectionable when bean-fed humans passed malodorous wind. After the innovation became too general to suppress, the Troog elders hedged the practice with laws. No pet should be kept alive if it fell sick, and since bronchitis was endemic, pets had short lives. The young Troogs recognised the wisdom behind this rule for they too disliked the sound of coughing. But in some cases they tried to save an invalid favourite from the lethal chamber, or would surrender it only after assurances that the sick were happier dead.

DESMOND STEWART, "The Limits of Trooghaft," from *Encounter*, London. February 1972. Reprinted by permission of Sheil Land Associates Ltd, London.

Adaptability had enabled the Troogs to survive their travels through time and space; it helped them to a catholic approach to the food provided by the planet, different as this was from their previous nourishment. Within two generations they had become compulsive carnivores. The realisation, derived from pet-keeping, that captive men could breed, led to the establishment of batteries of capons, the second and largest human caste. Capons were naturally preferred when young, since their bones were supple; at this time they fetched, as "eat-alls," the highest price for the lowest weight. Those kept alive after childhood were lodged in small cages maintained at a steady 22 degrees; the cage floors were composed of rolling bars through which the filth fell into a sluice. Capons were not permitted to see the sky or smell unfiltered air. Experience proved that a warm pink glow kept them docile and conduced to weight-gain. Females were in general preferred to males and the eradication of the tongue (sold as a separate delicacy) quietened the batteries.

The third category – the ferocious hound-men – were treated even by the Troogs with a certain caution; the barracks in which they were kennelled were built as far as possible from the batteries lest the black predators escape, break in and massacre hundreds. Bred for speed, obedience and ruthlessness, they were underfed. Unleashed they sped like greyhounds. Their unreliable tempers doomed the few surreptitious efforts to employ them as pets. One night they kept their quarters keening in rhythmic sound; next day, they slumped in yellow-eyed sulks, stirring only to lunge at each other or at their keepers' tentacles. None were kept alive after the age of thirty. Those injured in the chase were slaughtered on the spot and minced for the mess bowl.

Paradoxically, the swift hound-men depended for survival on the quarry they despised and hunted: the fourth human caste, the caste most hedged with laws.

The persistence, long into the first Troog period, of lone nomadic rebels, men and women who resisted from remote valleys and caves, had perplexed the planet's rulers. Then they made an advantage out of the setback. The wits and endurance of the defeated showed that the Troogs had suppressed a menace of some mettle. This was a compliment and Troogs, like the gods of fable, found praise enjoyable. They decided to preserve a caste of the uncorralled. This fourth caste, known as quarry-men or game, were protected within limits and seasons. It was forbidden, for example, to hunt pre-adolescents or pregnant females. All members of the caste enjoyed a respite during eight months of each year. Only at the five-yearly Nova Feast – the joyous commemoration of the greatest escape in Troog history – were all rules abandoned: then the demand for protein became overpowering.

Quarry-men excited more interest in their masters than the three other castes put together. On one level, gluttonous Troogs found their flesh more appetising than that of capons. On another, academically minded Troogs studied their behavior-patterns. Moralising Troogs extolled their courage against hopeless odds to a Troog generation inclined to be complacent about its power. The ruins which spiked the planet were testimony to the rudimentary but numerous civilisations which, over ten millennia, men had produced, from the time when they first cultivated grains and domesticated animals till their final achievement of an environment without vegetation (except under glass) and with only synthetic protein.

Men, it was true, had never reached the stage where they could rely on the telepathy that served the Troogs. But this was no reason to despise them. Originally Troogs, too, had conversed through sound hitting a tympanum; they had retained a hieroglyphic system deep into their journey through time; indeed, their final abandonment of what men called writing (and the Troogs "incising") had been an indirect tribute to men: telepathic waves were harder to decipher than symbols. It moved antiquarian Troogs to see that some men still frequented the ruined repositories of written knowledge; and though men never repaired these ancient libraries, this did not argue that they had lost the constructional talents of forebears who had built skyscrapers and pyramids. It showed shrewd sense. To repair old buildings or build new ones would attract the hound-men. Safety lay in dispersal. Libraries were a place of danger for a quarry-man, known to the contemptuous hound-men as a "book-roach." The courageous passion for the little volumes in which great men had compressed their wisdom was admired by Troogs. In their death throes quarry-men often clutched these talismans.

It was through a library that, in the fifth Troog century, the first attempt was made to communicate between the species, the conquerors and the conquered.

Curiosity was a characteristic shared by both species. Quarry-men still debated what the Troogs were and where they had come from. The first generation had known them as Extra-Terrestrials, when Terra, man's planet, was still the normative centre. Just as the natives of central America had welcomed the Spaniards as gods till the stake gave the notion of the godlike a satanic quality, millions of the superstitious had identified the Troogs with angels. But Doomsday was simply Troog's Day. The planet continued spinning, the sun gave out its heat and the empty oceans rolled against their shores. Living on an earth no longer theirs, quarry-men gazed at the glittering laser beams and reflected light which made the Troog-Halls and speculated about their tenants. A tradition declared that the first space vehicles had glowed with strange pictures. The Troogs, it was correctly deduced, had originally conversed by means analogous to language but had discarded speech in order to remain opaque, untappable. This encouraged some would-be rebels. They saw in precaution signs of caution and in caution proof of fallibility. A counter-attack might one day be possible, through science or magic. Some cynics pretended to find the Troogs a blessing. They quoted a long-dead writer who had believed it was better for a man to die on his feet when not too old. This was now the common human lot. Few quarry-men lived past thirty and the diseases of the past, such as cardiac failure and carcinoma, were all but unknown. But most men dreamed simply of a longer and easier existence.

The first human to be approached by a Troog was a short, stocky youth who had survived his 'teens thanks to strong legs, a good wind and the discovery of a cellar underneath one of the world's largest libraries. Because of his enthusiasm for a poet of that name, this book-roach was known to his group as "Blake." He had also studied other idealists such as the Egyptian Akhenaten and the Russian Tolstoy. These inspired him to speculate along the most hazardous paths, in the direction, for example, of the precipice-question: might not the Troogs have something akin to human consciousness, or even conscience? If so, might man perhaps address his conqueror? Against the backspace of an insentient universe one consciousness should greet another. His friends, his woman, laughed at the notion. They had seen what the Troogs had done to their species. Some men were bred to have protuberant eyes or elongated necks; others were kept in kennels on insufficient rations, and then, at the time of the Nova Feast or in the year's open season, unleashed through urban ruins or surrounding savannah to howl after their quarry – those related by blood and experience to Blake and his fellows. "I shall never trust a Troog," said his woman's brother, "even if he gives me a gold safe-conduct."

One Troog, as much an exception among his species as Blake among his, read this hopeful brain. It was still the closed season and some four months before the quinquennial Nova Feast. Quarry-men still relaxed in safety; the hounds sang or sulked; the Troogs had yet to prepare the lights and sounds for their tumultuous celebrations. Each morning Blake climbed to the Library. It was a long, rubbish-encumbered place with aisles still occupied by books, once arranged according to subject, but now higgledy-piggledy in dust and dereliction, thrown down by earthquake or scattered in the hunt. Each aisle had its attendant bust – Plato, Shakespeare, Darwin, Marx – testifying to a regretted time when men, divided by nationality, class or colour, suffered only from their fellows.

In the corner watched by Shakespeare, Blake had his reading place. He had restored the shelves to some order; he had dusted the table. This May morning a Troog's fading odour made him tremble. A new object stood on his table: a large rusty typewriter of the most ancient model. In it was a sheet of paper.

Blake bent to read.

Are you ready to communicate question.

Blake typed the single word: *yes.*

He did not linger but retreated in mental confusion to the unintellectual huddle round babies and potatoes which was his cellar. He half feared that he had begun to go mad, or that some acquaintance was playing him a trick. But few of his group read and no man could duplicate the distinctive Troog smell.

The days that followed constituted a continual seance between "his" Troog and himself. Blake contributed little to the dialogue. His Troog seemed anxious for a listener but little interested in what that listener thought. Blake was an earphone, an admiring confessor. Try as he feebly did, he got no response when he tried to evoke his woman, his children.

"Trooghaft, you are right," wrote the unseen communicator, attested each time by his no longer frightening scent, "was noble once." Blake had made no such suggestion. "The quality of being a Troog was unfrictional as space and as tolerant as time. It has become – almost human."

Then next morning: "To copy the habits of lower creatures is to sink below them. What is natural to carnivores is unnatural to us. We never ate flesh before the Nova; nor on our journey. We adopted the practice from reading the minds of lower creatures, then copying them. Our corruption shows in new diseases; earlier than in the past, older Troogs decompose. It shows in our characters. We quarrel like our quarry. Our forms are not apt for ingesting so much protein. Protein is what alcohol was to humans. It maddens; it corrupts. Protein, not earth's climate, is paling our. . . ."

Here there was a day's gap before the typewriter produced, next morning, the word *complexion*. And after it, *metaphor*. Blake had learnt that the old Troog hieroglyphs were followed by determinants, symbols showing, for example, whether the concept *rule* meant tyranny or order. Complexion could only be used meta-phorically of faceless and largely gaseous creatures.

To one direct question Blake obtained a direct answer: "How," he had typed, "did you first turn against the idea of eating us?"

"My first insight flashed at our last Nova Feast. Like everyone, I had been programmed to revel. Stench of flesh filled every Troog-Hall. Amid the spurt of music, the ancient greetings with which we flare still, the coruscations, I passed a meat-shop where lights pirouetted. I looked. I saw. Hanging from iron hooks – each pierced a foot-palm – were twenty she-capons, what you call women. Each neck was surrounded by a ruffle to hide the knife-cut; a tomato shut each anus. I suddenly shuddered. Nearby, on a slab of marble, smiled a row of jellied heads. Someone had dressed their sugar-hair in the manner of your Roman empresses: 'Flavian Heads.' A mass of piled up, tong-curled hair in front, behind a bun encoiled by a marzipan fillet. I lowered myself and saw as though for the first time great blocks of neutral-looking matter: 'Paté of Burst Liver.' The owner of the shop was glad to explain. They hold the woman down, then stuff nutriment through a V-shaped funnel. The merchant was pleased by my close attention. He displayed his Sucking Capons and Little Loves, as they call the reproductive organs which half of you split creatures wear outside your bodies."

"Was this," I asked in sudden repugnance, "Trooghaft?"

Encouraged by evidence of soul, Blake brought to the Troog's notice, from the miscellaneous volumes on the shelves, quotations from his favourite writers and narrative accounts of such actions as the death of Socrates, the crucifixion of Jesus and the murder of Che Guevara. Now in the mornings he found books and encyclopaedias open on his table as well as typed pages. Sometimes Blake fancied that there was more than one Troog smell; so perhaps his Troog was converting others.

Each evening Blake told Janine, his partner, of his exploits. She was at first scept-ical, then half-persuaded. This year she was not pregnant and therefore could be hunted. For love of her children, the dangers of the Nova season weighed on her spirits. Only her daughter was Blake's; her son had been sired by Blake's friend, a fast-runner who had sprained his ankle and fallen easy victim to the hounds two years before. As the Nova Feast approached, the majority of the quarry-men in the city began to leave for the mountains. Not that valleys and caves were secure; but the mountains were vast and the valleys remote one from another. The hound-men preferred to hunt in the cities; concentrations of people made their game easier.

Blake refused to join them. Out of loyalty Janine stayed with him.

"I shall build," the Troog had written, "a bridge between Trooghaft and Humanity. The universe calls me to revive true Trooghaft. My Troog-Hall shall become a sanctuary, not a shed of butchers."

Blake asked: "Are you powerful? Can you make other Troogs follow your example?"

The Troog answered: "I can at least do as your Akhenaten did."

Blake flushed at the mention of his hero. Then added: "But Akhenaten's experiment lasted briefly. Men relapsed. May not Troogs do likewise?" He longed for reassurance that his Troog was more than a moral dilettante.

Instead of an answer came a statement:

"We can never be equals with *homo insipiens*. But we can accept our two species as unequal productions of one universe. Men are small, but that does not mean they cannot suffer. Not one tongueless woman moves, upside-down, towards the throat-knife, without trembling. I have seen this. I felt pity, *metaphor*. Our young Troogs argue that fear gives flesh a quivering tenderness. I reject such arguments. Why should a complex, if lowly, life – birth, youth, growth to awareness – be sacrificed for one mealtime's pleasure?"

Although Blake recognised that his Troog was soliloquising, the arguments pleased him. Convinced of their sincerity, Blake decided to trust his Troog and remain where he was, not hide or run as on previous occasions. There was a sewer leading from his refuge whose remembered stench was horrible. He would stay in the cellar. On the first day of the Nova Feast he climbed as usual to his corner of the library. But today there was no paper in the typewriter. Instead, books and encyclo-paedias had been pulled from the shelves and left open; they had nothing to do with poetry or the philosophers and the stench was not that of his Troog. Sudden unease seized him. Janine was alone with the children, her brother having left to join the others in the mountains. He returned to his cellar and, as his fear already predicted, found the children alone, wailing in one corner. The elder, the boy, told the doleful tale. Two hound-men had broken in and their mother had fled down the disused sewer.

Blake searched the sewer. It was empty. His one hope, as he too hid there, lay in his Troog's intervention. But neither the next day nor the day after, when he stole to the library, watching every shadow lest it turn to a hound-man, was there any message. This silence was atoned for on the third morning.

"If we still had a written language, I should publish a volume of confessions." The message was remote, almost unrelated to Blake's anguish. He read, "A few fat-fumes blow away a resolution. It was thus, the evening of the Nova Feast's beginning. Three Troog friends, *metaphor*, came to my Hall where no flesh was burning, where instead I was pondering these puny creatures to whom we cause such suffering. 'You cannot exile yourself from your group; Trooghaft is what Troogs do together.' I resisted such blandishments. The lights and sounds of the Nova were enough. I felt no craving for protein. Their laughter at this caused the laser beams to buckle and the lights to quiver. There entered four black hound-men dragging a quarry-female, filthy from the chase, her hands bound behind her. I was impassive. Housemen staggered under a great cauldron; they fetched logs. They placed the cauldron on a tripod and filled it with water; the logs were under it."

Blake shook as he read. This was the moment for his Troog to incarnate pity and save his woman.

"They now unbound and stripped the female, then set her in the water. It was cold and covered her skin with pimples.

"Again laughter, again the trembling lights and the buckling lasers.

"We, too, have been reading, brother. We have studied one of their ways of cooking. *Place the lobster* – their name for a long extinct sea-thing – *in warm water. Bring the water gently to the boil. The lobster will be lulled to sleep, not knowing it is to be killed. Most experts account this the humane way of treating lobster.*

"The logs under the cauldron gave a pleasant aroma as they started to splutter. The female was not lulled. She tried to clamber out: perhaps a reflex action. The hound-men placed an iron mesh over the cauldron."

Blake saw what he could not bear to see, heard the unhearable. The Troog's confession was humble.

"The scent was so persuasive. 'Try this piece,' they flashed, 'it is so tender. It will soften your scruples.' I hesitated. Outside came the noise of young Troogs whirling in the joy of satiety. A Nova Feast comes only once in five years. I dipped my hand, *metaphor*" – (even now the Troog pedantry was present) – "in the cauldron. If one must eat protein, it is better to do so in a civilised fashion. And as for the humanity, *metaphor*, of eating protein – I should write Trooghaft – if we ate no capons, who would bother to feed them? If we hunted no quarry, who would make the game-laws or keep the hound-men? At least now they live, as we do, for a season. And while they live, they are healthy. I must stop. My stomach, *metaphor*, sits heavy as a mountain."

As Blake turned in horror from the ancient typewriter, up from his line of retreat, keening their happiest music, their white teeth flashing, loped three lithe and ruthless hound-men. All around was the squid-like odour of their master.

56

RICHARD ADAMS

The Plague Dogs

The Plague Dogs is the story of two dogs who escape from an animal research laboratory. The Animal Research, Surgical and Experimental (ARSE) facility is a government-
funded institution situated in the north of England. In the first two extracts from the
novel we learn something about the experiments being undertaken there.

T he water in the metal tank slopped sideways and a treacly ripple ran along
the edge, reached the corner and died away. Under the electric lights the
broken surface was faceted as a cracked mirror, a watery harlequin's coat of
tilting planes and lozenges in movement, one moment dull as stone and the next
glittering like scalpels. Here and there, where during the past two hours the water
had been fouled, gilded streaks of urine and floating, spawn-like bubbles of saliva
rocked more turgidly, in a way suggestive – if anyone present had been receptive
to such suggestion – of an illusion that this was not water, but perhaps some
thicker fluid, such as those concoctions of jam and stale beer which are hung up in
glass jars to drown wasps, or the dark puddles splashed through by hooves and
gum-boots on the concrete floors of Lakeland cattle sheds.

Mr Powell, his note-pad ready in hand, leant across the flanged and over-
hanging edge of the tank, wiped his glasses on his sleeve and looked down the two
or three feet to the contents below.

"I think it's packing in, chief," he said. "Oh, no, wait a jiffy." He paused, drew
back the cuff of his white coat to avoid another, though weak, splash and then
bent over the water once more. "No, I was right first time – it *is* going. D'you want
it out now?"

"When it definitely sinks and stops moving," answered Dr Boycott, without
looking up from the papers on the table. Although there was in the room no
draught or air movement whatever, he had placed the two graphs and the log
sheet on top of one another and was using the heavy stop-watch as a paperweight

---

to ensure that they remained where he intended them to remain. "I thought I'd made it clear the other day," he added, in a level, polite tone, "what the precise moment of removal should be."

"But you don't want it to drown, do you?" asked Mr Powell, a shade of anxiety creeping into his voice. "If it —"

"No!" interjected Dr Boycott quickly, as though to check him before he could say more. "It's nothing to do with want," he went on after a moment. "It's not *intended* to drown — not this time anyway; and I think probably not the next time either — depending on results, of course."

There were further sounds of splashing from inside the tank, but faint, like metallic echoes, rather as though a ghost were trying, but failing, to come down and trouble the waters (and indeed, as far as the occupant was concerned, any sort of miracle, being unscientific, was entirely out of the question). Then a choking, bubbling sound was followed by silence, in which the rasping call of a carrion crow came clearly from the fell outside.

Mr Powell stood up, walked across the concrete floor and took down a shepherd's crook which was hanging on a peg. Sitting down once more on the edge of the tank, he began unthinkingly to tap with the butt of the crook the rhythm of a current popular song.

"Er — please, Stephen," said Dr Boycott, with a faint smile.

"Oh, sorry."

The large mongrel dog in the tank was continuing to struggle with its front paws, but so feebly now that its body, from neck to rump, hung almost vertically in the water. The spaniel-like ears were outspread, floating on either side of the head like wings, but the eyes were submerged and only the black, delicately lyrated nose broke the surface. As Mr Powell watched, this too went under, rose again for an instant and then sank. The body, foreshortened by refraction as it descended, seemed to move sideways from its former floating position, finally appearing on the bottom of the tank as an almost flattened mass and disturbing round its sides, as it settled, little clouds of dirty silt. Dr Boycott clicked the stop-watch. Mr Powell, looking quickly back to see whether he had noticed the silt (for his chief was particular about the cleanliness of equipment), made a mental note to insist to Tyson, the caretaker and head-keeper, that the tank should be emptied and cleaned tomorrow. Then, allowing for the refraction with the skill of a certain amount of practice, he plunged in the crook, engaged the dog's collar and began to drag it to the surface. After a moment, however, he faltered, dropped the crook and stood up, wincing, while the body subsided once more to the floor of the tank.

"Christ, it's heavy," he said. "Oh, no, chief, I don't mean it's any heavier than usual, of course, only I pulled a muscle in my wrist last night and it's been giving me a spot of gyppo. Never mind, never say die, here goes."

"I'm sorry," said Dr Boycott. "Let me help you. I wouldn't want you to suffer avoidably."

Together they pulled on the crook, raised the heavy, pelt-sodden body head-first, broke the surface tension with a concerted heave and laid the inert dog on a foam-rubber mattress beside the tank. Here it resembled an enormous, drowned fly – very black, with a compressed shape something like that of a raindrop; and smaller than life, on account of a kind of collapse of the limbs and other excrescences into the central mass of the trunk. Mr Powell began resuscitation; and after a little the dog vomited water and commenced to gasp, though its eyes remained closed.

"Right, that'll do," said Dr Boycott briskly. "Now the usual tests, please, Stephen – pulse, blood sample, body temperature, reflexes – the various things we've been working on – and then plot the graphs. I'll be back in about twenty minutes. I'm just going over to the Christiaan Barnard block to learn what I can about this afternoon's brain surgery work. And please don't smoke while I'm gone," he added, mildly but firmly. "You'll appreciate that that could have an effect on results."

"All right to put its muzzle on, chief?" asked Mr Powell. "Only this one, seven-three-two, 's been known to be a right sod at times and it might come round enough to start in on me – sudden-like, you know."

"Yes, there's no objection to that," replied Dr Boycott, picking up the stop-watch.

"And the time, chief?" enquired Mr Powell in a rather sycophantic tone, as though the time were likely to be something to Dr Boycott's personal credit.

"Two hours, twenty minutes, fifty-three and two fifths seconds," answered Dr Boycott. "Without looking at the papers, I think that's about six and a half minutes longer than Wednesday's test and about twelve minutes longer than the test before that. It's rather remarkable how regular the increase appears to be. At this rate the graph will work out as a straight incline, although obviously we must reach a diminution somewhere. There must come a point where the additional endurance induced by the dog's expectation of removal is counterbalanced by the limits of its physical capacity."

He paused for a moment and then said, "Now, there's another thing I'd like you to see to, please. I forgot to mention it this morning, but Cambridge are anxious for us to go ahead at once with the social deprivation experiment. We have a monkey set aside for that, haven't we?"

"Yeah, I'm pretty certain we have," replied Mr Powell.

"I thought you told me we definitely had?" Dr Boycott's voice was a shade sharper.

"Yes, that's right," said Mr Powell hastily. "We have."

"Good. Well, it can go into the cylinder this evening. Now you're sure that that cylinder excludes all light?"

"Yep. No light, restricted movement, adequate ventilation, wire mesh floor, faeces and urine fall through. It's all checked."

"Right, well, start it off, keep it under twice daily observation and, of course, mark the particulars up in a log. The total number of days should be kept up to date day by day, on a slate beside the cylinder. That's a matter of courtesy to the Director. He'll probably want to see it."

"Where's it to be kept, chief?" asked Mr Powell.

"It doesn't matter, as long as it's somewhere where you can readily keep an eye on it," answered Dr Boycott. "I suggest, near where you normally work, as long as it's not anywhere near any other animals. There should be silence, as far as possible, and no organic smells, of course. That's part of the deprivation, you understand."

"How about the balance-cupboard in Lab. 4, chief?" asked Mr Powell. "Plenty of space in there at the moment and quiet as the grave."

"Yes, that'll do," said Dr Boycott. "Don't forget to tell Tyson about feeding, and keep me informed how it goes on. We'll aim at – well, say – er – forty-five days."

"Is that the lot, chief?"

"Yes," said Dr Boycott, with his hand on the door. "But since it seems necessary to mention it, you'd better see that this tank's cleaned out. There's silt on the bottom which shouldn't be there."

[. . .]

Old Tyson had once been a sailor, then a shepherd, then for several years a road man employed by the county council; but had taken the option of a job with Animal Research because, as he said, there were less weather wi't and aall in't woon plaace like. He was well regarded and indeed valued by the Director and senior staff, being reasonably respectful, if somewhat dour, in his behaviour, reliable, generally conscientious and no more given to sentimentality about animals than any other Lakelander. Also, being well on in middle age, he was steady and regular and not prone to ailments or to odd days off on account of family problems – which in his case had all been solved (or not solved) long ago. He understood dogs well enough, his attitude towards them being equally valid for the purposes of ARSE or for those of a Lakeland hill-farm – namely, that they were pieces of technological equipment which one needed to know how to maintain and use properly. Tourists' and holiday-makers' dogs annoyed him, being useless for any practical purpose, frequently disobedient and a potential danger to sheep.

In spite of what seemed to the dogs his maddening deliberation, Tyson was in fact anxious to be off as soon as he could this evening, for it was Friday, he had been paid and was due to keep an appointment in The Crown at Coniston with a friend from Torver, who had told him that he could put him in the way of a second-hand refrigerator in good condition and going cheap. He was, therefore, in as much of a hurry as was possible for him – the general effect rather resembling that produced in a tortoise when its lettuce is put down on the grass. This is not to suggest, however, that there was anything foolish or absurd in Tyson's demeanour as he went about his task. Tortoises are dignified and self-sufficient and, though admittedly slow, considerably more reliable than – well – than – what comes to mind? – than – er – well, than distracted princes, for example, who give wild assurances about sweeping to revenge on wings as swift as meditation or the thoughts of love.

Tyson entered each pen in turn, emptied the metal drinking-bowls down the gullies and re-filled them from his watering-can. Then he poured away what was left in the can, put it back in its place in the corner and returned to the pails. Four of these were filled with bloody messes of horse-meat and lights, appropriate portions of which (big or small according to the size of the dog) were doled out at Tyson's discretion to all those on "normal diet." As this part of his task progressed, the noise in the block gradually diminished. When it was complete, he set to work to distribute the contents of the other two pails. These contained a number of separate paper packages, marked individually with the numbers of those dogs for whom special rations had been prescribed on account of the experiments in which they were taking part. Tyson took his spectacle-case out of his pocket, opened it, took out the spectacles, held them up to the light, breathed on them, cleaned them on his sleeve, held them up to the light again, put them on, emptied the packets out on the concrete floor and laid them in two rows. This done, he picked up the first and held it, above his head, towards the nearest light-bulb. Once he had read the number he had no need to look about for the destination, since he knew the dogs and their pens as surely as a huntsman his hounds.

Who can describe what drugs, what charms, what conjuration and what mighty magic those packages contained? They were indeed miracles of rare device. Some included, infused with the liver and offal, stimulants able to banish sleep, or to cause the consumer to perform, on the morrow, prodigies of endurance – to fight, to fast, to tear himself, to drink up eisel, eat a crocodile. Others contained paralytics which suspended colour perception, hearing, taste, smell; analgesics destroying the power to feel pain, so that the subject stood wagging his tail while a hot iron was drawn along his ribs; hallucinogenics able to fill the eye of the beholder with more devils than vast hell can hold, to transform the strong to weaklings, the resolute to cowards, to plunge the intelligent and alert head over ears into idiocy. Some induced disease, madness, or mortification of specific parts of the body; others cured, alleviated, or failed either to cure or to alleviate, diseases already induced. Some destroyed the unborn foetus in the womb, others the power to ovulate, the power to beget, to conceive, to gestate. One might indeed believe that graves, at Dr Boycott's command, would wake their sleepers, ope, and let 'em forth.

Actually that is pitching it a bit high – drawing the long bow, as they say – but at any rate no one could say of Dr Boycott that he would not have attempted resurrection if he had thought there was a sporting chance. He was a qualified expert, initiative was expected of him, his subjects had no legal rights; and intellectual curiosity is, after all, a desire like any other. Besides, who in his senses could reasonably expect Dr Boycott to ask himself, on behalf of the human race, not "How much knowledge can I discover?" but "How much knowledge am I justified in seeking?" Experimental science is the last flower of asceticism and Dr Boycott was indeed an ascetic, an observer of events upon which he passed no value judgements. He represented, in fact, a most ingenious paradox, noble in reason, express and admirable in action, his undemonstrative heart committed with the utmost detachment to the benefit of humanity. Something too much of this.

As he worked, Tyson spoke a few words to each dog – "Well, that's for thee, then. Get yon down." "Hey oop, old lad. Layin' on straw'll get thee nowheer" – much unlike the common way of Lakelanders, who seldom or never speak to dogs except to summon them or to give them an order or reproof. More extraordinary still, he more than once patted a dog or actually stooped down for a moment to scratch its ears. Though he himself could not have said why he acted in this uncharacteristic way, and if asked would have shrugged his shoulders to indicate that the question was not worth serious consideration, it is, of course, beyond argument that he understood very well, on his own level, the work and general purpose of the research station and the kind of effects upon animals which that work commonly had. Not even Dr Freud, however, armed with the longest and most symbolical shepherd's crook in all Vienna, could have dragged from the silt to the surface any guilt which Tyson may, as an individual, unconsciously have felt; for clearly the Director and his colleagues knew more than he, both about the world's needs and about animals' capacity for suffering, and his orders, like his wages, came from them. If each of us insisted on stopping to weigh in every case the relative pros and cons of distress to others, whether human or animal, brought about by obeying our instructions, the world could never be run at all. Life is, as they say, too short.

We take up the story again after the dogs have escaped. Journalist Digby Driver is questioning Dr Boycott.

Digby Driver, fuming inwardly, decided to come in on another beam.

"What experiments were these dogs being used for?" he asked.

Oddly enough, this took Dr Boycott unawares. It was plain that he had not expected the question and was unable to decide, all in a moment, whether or not there was likely to be any harm in answering it.

"I don't see why you shouldn't know *that*," he replied at length, thereby inadvertently suggesting that there were things which he thought Digby Driver should not know. "One was taking part in certain tests connected with physiological and psychological reactions to stress; and the other was a brain surgery subject."

"What specific benefits were expected to result from these tests – experiments – whatever you call them?"

"I think the best way I can answer that," replied Dr Boycott, "is to refer you to paragraph – er – 270, I think – yes, here it is – of the 1965 Report of the Littlewood Committee, the Home Office Departmental Committee on Experiments on Animals. 'From our study of the evidence about unnecessary experiments and the complexity of biological science, we conclude that it is impossible to tell what practical applications any new discovery in biological knowledge may have later for the benefit of man or animal. Accordingly, we recommend that there should be no general barrier to the use of animal experimentation in seeking new biological knowledge, even if it cannot be shown to be of immediate or foreseeable value.'"

"In other words there wasn't any specific purpose. You just do these things to animals to see what's going to happen?"

"The specific purpose of a test," said Dr Boycott, with an air of grave responsibility, "is *always* the advancement of knowledge with a view to the ultimate benefit both of man and of animals."

57

DOUGLAS ADAMS

The Restaurant at the End of the Universe

The Restaurant at the End of the Universe is the second in the series that began with *The Hitchhiker's Guide to the Galaxy*. Arthur Dent, together with galactic travel writer Ford Prefect, the three-armed, two-headed space pirate Zaphod Beeblebrox, and ex-Earthwoman Trillian, has arrived at a restaurant that is chronologically, rather than spatially, at the end of the universe. They and other patrons have gathered to watch the universe blow up, with a bang and not a whimper. (Thanks to time-travel, however, they will be able to leave before the very end.)

A large dairy animal approached Zaphod Beeblebrox's table, a large fat meaty quadruped of the bovine type with large watery eyes, small horns and what might almost have been an ingratiating smile on its lips.

"Good evening," it lowed and sat back heavily on its haunches, "I am the main Dish of the Day. May I interest you in parts of my body?" It harrumphed and gurgled a bit, wriggled its hind quarters into a more comfortable position and gazed peacefully at them.

Its gaze was met by looks of startled bewilderment from Arthur and Trillian, a resigned shrug from Ford Prefect and naked hunger from Zaphod Beeblebrox.

"Something off the shoulder perhaps?" suggested the animal. "Braised in a white wine sauce?"

"Er, *your* shoulder?" said Arthur in a horrified whisper.

"But naturally my shoulder, sir," mooed the animal contentedly, "nobody else's is mine to offer."

Zaphod leapt to his feet and started prodding and feeling the animal's shoulder appreciatively.

"Or the rump is very good," murmured the animal. "I've been exercising it and eating plenty of grain, so there's a lot of good meat there." It gave a mellow grunt, gurgled again and started to chew the cud. It swallowed the cud again.

"Or a casserole of me perhaps?" it added.

"You mean this animal actually wants us to eat it?" whispered Trillian to Ford.

"Me?" said Ford, with a glazed look in his eyes. "I don't mean anything."

"That's absolutely horrible," exclaimed Arthur, "the most revolting thing I've ever heard."

"What's the problem, Earthman?" said Zaphod, now transferring his attention to the animal's enormous rump.

"I just don't want to eat an animal that's standing there inviting me to," said Arthur. "It's heartless."

"Better than eating an animal that doesn't want to be eaten," said Zaphod.

"That's not the point," Arthur protested. Then he thought about it for a moment. "All right," he said, "maybe it is the point. I don't care, I'm not going to think about it now. I'll just . . . er . . ."

The Universe raged about him in its death throes.

"I think I'll just have a green salad," he muttered.

"May I urge you to consider my liver?" asked the animal, "it must be very rich and tender by now, I've been force-feeding myself for months."

"A green salad," said Arthur emphatically.

"A green salad?" said the animal, rolling his eyes disapprovingly at Arthur.

"Are you going to tell me," said Arthur, "that I shouldn't have green salad?"

"Well," said the animal, "I know many vegetables that are very clear on that point. Which is why it was eventually decided to cut through the whole tangled problem and breed an animal that actually wanted to be eaten and was capable of saying so clearly and distinctly. And here I am."

It managed a very slight bow.

"Glass of water please," said Arthur.

"Look," said Zaphod, "we want to eat, we don't want to make a meal of the issues. Four rare steaks please, and hurry. We haven't eaten in five hundred and seventy-six thousand million years."

The animal staggered to its feet. It gave a mellow gurgle.

"A very wise choice, sir, if I may say so. Very good," it said. "I'll just nip off and shoot myself."

He turned and gave a friendly wink to Arthur.

"Don't worry, sir," he said, "I'll be very humane."

It waddled unhurriedly off to the kitchen.

A matter of minutes later the waiter arrived with four huge steaming steaks. Zaphod and Ford wolfed straight into them without a second's hesitation. Trillian paused, then shrugged and started into hers.

Arthur stared at his feeling slightly ill.

"Hey, Earthman," said Zaphod with a malicious grin on the face that wasn't stuffing itself, "what's eating you?"

And the band played on.

58

JAMES FENIMORE COOPER

The Pioneers

The Pioneers is the first of the series of novels featuring Natty Bumppo (Leather-stocking) and was Fenimore Cooper's third novel. It draws on the author's experience growing up in the frontier village of Cooperstown in upstate New York and is set in the era before the American War of Independence. Forest clearing farmers are taking up the land that was once home to wild animals, Native Americans, and white hunters. It is the end of April. Spring is coming to the Valley of Templeton, and with spring come the migrating pigeons.

The following morning Elizabeth was awakened by the exhilarating sounds of the martins, who were quarreling and chattering around the little boxes suspended above her windows, and the cries of Richard, who was calling, in tones animating as the signs of the season itself –

"Awake! awake! my fair lady! the gulls are hovering over the lake already, and the heavens are alive with pigeons. You may look an hour before you can find a hole, through which, to get a peep at the sun. Awake! awake! lazy ones! Benjamin is overhauling the ammunition, and we only wait for our breakfasts, and away for the mountains and pigeon-shooting."

There was no resisting this animated appeal, and in a few minutes Miss Temple and her friend descended to the parlour. The doors of the hall were thrown open, and the mild, balmy air of a clear spring morning was ventilating the apartment, where the vigilance of the ex-steward had been so long maintaining an artificial heat, with such unremitted diligence. The gentlemen were impatiently waiting for their morning's repast, each equipt in the garb of a sportsman. Mr Jones made many visits to the southern door, and would cry –

"See, cousin Bess! see, 'duke! the pigeon-roosts of the south have broken up! They are growing more thick every instant. Here is a flock that the eye cannot see the end of. There is food enough in it to keep the army of Xerxes for a month, and feathers enough to make beds for the whole country. Xerxes, Mr Edwards, was a Grecian king, who – no, he was a Turk, or a Persian, who wanted to conquer

JAMES FENIMORE COOPER, from Chapter XXII in *The Pioneers*, first published in 1823.

Greece, just the same as these rascals will overrun our wheat-fields, when they come back in the fall. – Away! away! Bess; I long to pepper them."

In this wish both Marmaduke and young Edwards seemed equally to participate, for the sight was exhilarating to a sportsman; and the ladies soon dismissed the party, after a hasty breakfast.

If the heavens were alive with pigeons, the whole village seemed equally in motion, with men, women, and children. Every species of fire-arms, from the French ducking-gun, with a barrel near six feet in length, to the common horseman's pistol, was to be seen in the hands of the men and boys; while bows and arrows, some made of the simple stick of a walnut sapling, and others in a rude imitation of the ancient cross-bows, were carried by many of the latter.

The houses, and the signs of life apparent in the village, drove the alarmed birds from the direct line of their flight, towards the mountains, along the sides and near the bases of which they were glancing in dense masses, equally wonderful by the rapidity of their motion, and their incredible numbers.

We have already said, that across the inclined plane which fell from the steep ascent of the mountain to the banks of the Susquehanna, ran the highway, on either side of which a clearing of many acres had been made, at a very early day. Over those clearings, and up the eastern mountain, and along the dangerous path that was cut into its side, the different individuals posted themselves, and in a few moments the attack commenced.

Amongst the sportsmen was the tall, gaunt form of Leather-stocking, walking over the field, with his rifle hanging on his arm, his dogs at his heels; the latter now scenting the dead or wounded birds, that were beginning to tumble from the flocks, and then crouching under the legs of their master, as if they participated in his feelings, at this wasteful and unsportsmanlike execution.

The reports of the fire-arms became rapid, whole volleys rising from the plain, as flocks of more than ordinary numbers darted over the opening, shadowing the field, like a cloud; and then the light smoke of a single piece would issue from among the leafless bushes on the mountain, as death was hurled on the retreat of the affrighted birds, who were rising from a volley, in a vain effort to escape. Arrows, and missiles of every kind, were in the midst of the flocks; and so numerous were the birds, and so low did they take their flight, that even long poles, in the hands of those on the sides of the mountain, were used to strike them to the earth.

During all this time, Mr Jones, who disdained the humble and ordinary means of destruction used by his companions, was busily occupied, aided by Benjamin, in making arrangements for an assault of a more than ordinarily fatal character. Among the relics of the old military excursions, that occasionally are discovered throughout the different districts of the western part of New-York, there had been found in Templeton, at its settlement, a small swivel, which would carry a ball of a pound weight. It was thought to have been deserted by a war-party of the whites, in one of their inroads into the Indian settlements, when, perhaps, convenience or their necessity induced them to leave such an encumbrance behind them in the woods. This miniature cannon had been released from the rust, and being mounted on little wheels, was now in a state for actual service. For several years, it was the sole organ for extraordinary rejoicings used in those mountains. On the mornings of the Fourths of July, it would be heard ringing among the hills, and even Captain Hollister, who was the highest authority in that part of the country on all such occasions, affirmed that, considering its dimensions, it was no despicable gun for a salute. It was somewhat the worse for the service it had performed, it is true, there being but a trifling difference in size between the touch-hole and the muzzle. Still, the grand conceptions of Richard had suggested the importance of such an instrument, in hurling death at his nimble enemies. The swivel was dragged by a horse into a part of the open space, that the Sheriff thought most eligible for planting a battery of the kind, and Mr Pump proceeded to load it. Several handfuls of duck-shot were placed on top of the powder, and the Major-domo announced that his piece was ready for service.

The sight of such an implement collected all the idle spectators to the spot, who, being mostly boys, filled the air with cries of exultation and delight. The gun was pointed high, and Richard, holding a coal of fire in a pair of tongs, patiently took his seat on a stump, awaiting the appearance of a flock worthy of his notice.

So prodigious was the number of the birds, that the scattering fire of the guns, with the hurling of missiles, and the cries of the boys, had no other effect than to break off small flocks from the immense masses that continued to dart along the valley, as if the whole of the feathered tribe were pouring through that one pass. None pretended to collect the game, which lay scattered over the fields in such profusion, as to cover the very ground with the fluttering victims.

Leather-stocking was a silent, but uneasy spectator of all these proceedings, but was able to keep his sentiments to himself until he saw the introduction of the swivel into the sports.

"This comes of settling a country!" he said – "here have I known the pigeons to fly for forty long years, and, till you made your clearings, there was nobody to skear or to hurt them. I loved to see them come into the woods, for they were company to a body; hurting nothing; being, as it was, as harmless as a garter-snake. But now it gives me sore thoughts when I hear the frighty things whizzing through the air, for I know it's only a motion to bring out all the brats in the village. Well! the Lord won't see the waste of his creaters for nothing, and right will be done to the pigeons, as well as others, by-and-by. – There's Mr Oliver, as bad as the rest of them, firing into the flocks as if he was shooting down nothing but Mingo warriors."

Among the sportsmen was Billy Kirby, who, armed with an old musket, was loading, and, without even looking into the air, was firing, and shouting as his victims fell even on his own person. He heard the speech of Natty, and took upon himself to reply –

"What! old Leather-stocking," he cried, "grumbling at the loss of a few pigeons! If you had to sow your wheat twice, and three times, as I have done, you wouldn't be so massyfully feeling'd to'ards the divils. – Hurrah, boys! scatter the feathers. This is better than shooting at a turkey's head and neck, old fellow."

"It's better for you, maybe, Billy Kirby," replied the indignant old hunter, "and all them that don't know how to put a ball down a rifle-barrel, or how to bring it up ag'in with a true aim; but it's wicked to be shooting into flocks in this wastey manner; and none do it, who know how to knock over a single bird. If a body has a craving for pigeon's flesh, why! it's made the same as all other creater's, for man's eating, but not to kill twenty and eat one. When I want such a thing, I go into the woods till I find one to my liking, and then I shoot him off the branches without touching a feather of another, though there might be a hundred on the same tree. You couldn't do such a thing, Billy Kirby – you couldn't do it if you tried."

"What's that, old corn-stalk! you sapless stub!" cried the wood-chopper. "You've grown wordy, since the affair of the turkey; but if you're for a single shot, here goes at that bird which comes on by himself."

The fire from the distant part of the field had driven a single pigeon below the flock to which it belonged, and, frightened with the constant reports of the muskets, it was approaching the spot where the disputants stood, darting first from one side, and then to the other, cutting the air with the swiftness of lightning, and making a noise with its wings, not unlike the rushing of a bullet. Unfortunately for the wood-chopper, notwithstanding his vaunt, he did not see this bird until it was too late to fire as it approached, and he pulled his trigger at the unlucky moment when it was darting immediately over his head. The bird continued its course with the usual velocity.

Natty lowered the rifle from his arm, when the challenge was made, and, waiting a moment, until the terrified victim had got in a line with his eye, and had dropped near the bank of the lake, he raised it again with uncommon rapidity, and fired. It might have been chance, or it might have been skill, that produced the result; it was probably a union of both; but the pigeon whirled over in the air, and fell into the lake, with a broken wing. At the sound of his rifle, both his dogs started from his feet, and in a few minutes the "slut" brought out the bird, still alive.

The wonderful exploit of Leather-stocking was noised through the field with great rapidity, and the sportsmen gathered in to learn the truth of the report.

"What," said young Edwards, "have you really killed a pigeon on the wing, Natty, with a single ball?"

"Haven't I killed loons before now, lad, that dive at the flash?" returned the hunter. "It's much better to kill only such as you want, without wasting your powder and lead, than to be firing into God's creaters in this wicked manner. But I come out for a bird, and you know the reason why I like small game, Mr Oliver, and now I have got one I will go home, for I don't relish to see these wasty ways that you are all practysing, as if the least thing was not made for use, and not to destroy."

"Thou sayest well, Leather-stocking," cried Marmaduke, "and I begin to think it time to put an end to this work of destruction."

"Put an ind, Judge, to your clearings. An't the woods his work as well as the pigeons? Use, but don't waste. Wasn't the woods made for the beasts and birds to harbour in? and when man wanted their flesh, their skins, or their feathers, there's

---

slut – female dog

the place to seek them. But I'll go to the hut with my own game, for I wouldn't touch one of the harmless things that kiver the ground here, looking up with their eyes on me, as if they only wanted tongues to say their thoughts."

With this sentiment in his mouth, Leather-stocking threw his rifle over his arm, and, followed by his dogs, stepped across the clearing with great caution, taking care not to tread on one of the wounded birds in his path. He soon entered the bushes on the margin of the lake, and was hid from view.

Whatever impression the morality of Natty made on the Judge, it was utterly lost on Richard. He availed himself of the gathering of the sportsmen, to lay a plan for one "fell swoop" of destruction. The musketmen were drawn up in battle array, in a line extending on each side of his artillery, with orders to await the signal of firing from himself.

"Stand by, my lads," said Benjamin, who acted as an aide-de-camp, on this occasion, "stand by, my hearties, and when Squire Dickens heaves out the signal to begin the firing, d'ye see, you may open upon them in a broadside. Take care and fire low, boys, and you'll be sure to hull the flock."

"Fire low!" shouted Kirby – "hear the old fool! If we fire low, we may hit the stumps, but not ruffle a pigeon."

"How should you know, you lubber?" cried Benjamin, with a very unbecoming heat, for an officer on the eve of battle – "how should you know, you grampus? Havn't I sailed aboard of the Boadishy for five years? and wasn't it a standing order to fire low, and to hull your enemy? Keep silence at your guns, boys, and mind the order that is passed."

The loud laughs of the musketmen were silenced by the more authoritative voice of Richard, who called for attention and obedience to his signals.

Some millions of pigeons were supposed to have already passed, that morning, over the valley of Templeton; but nothing like the flock that was now approaching had been seen before. It extended from mountain to mountain in one solid blue mass, and the eye looked in vain over the southern hills to find its termination. The front of this living column was distinctly marked by a line, but very slightly indented, so regular and even was the flight. Even Marmaduke forgot the morality of Leather-stocking as it approached, and, in common with the rest, brought his musket to a poise.

"Fire!" cried the Sheriff, clapping a coal to the priming of the cannon. As half of Benjamin's charge escaped through the touch-hole, the whole volley of the musketry preceded the report of the swivel. On receiving this united discharge of small-arms, the front of the flock darted upward, while, at the same instant, myriads of those in the rear rushed with amazing rapidity into their places, so that when the column of white smoke gushed from the mouth of the little cannon, an accumulated mass of objects was gliding over its point of direction. The roar of the gun echoed along the mountains, and died away to the north, like distant thunder, while the whole flock of alarmed birds seemed, for a moment, thrown into one disorderly and agitated mass. The air was filled with their irregular flight, layer rising above layer, far above the tops of the highest pines, none daring to advance beyond the dangerous pass; when, suddenly, some of the leaders of the feathered tribe shot across the valley, taking their flight directly over the village, and hundreds of thousands in their rear followed the example, deserting the eastern side of the plain to their persecutors and the slain.

"Victory!" shouted Richard, "victory! we have driven the enemy from the field."

"Not so, Dickon," said Marmaduke; "the field is covered with them; and, like the Leather-stocking, I see nothing but eyes, in every direction, as the innocent sufferers turn their heads in terror. Full one half of those that have fallen are yet alive: and I think it is time to end the sport; if sport it be."

"Sport!" cried the Sheriff; "it is princely sport. There are some thousands of the blue-coated boys on the ground, so that every old woman in the village may have a pot-pie for the asking."

"Well, we have happily frightened the birds from this side of the valley," said Marmaduke, "and the carnage must of necessity end, for the present. – Boys, I will give thee sixpence a hundred for the pigeons' heads only; so go to work, and bring them into the village."

This expedient produced the desired effect, for every urchin on the ground went industriously to work to wring the necks of the wounded birds. Judge Temple retired towards his dwelling with that kind of feeling, that many a man has experienced before him, who discovers, after the excitement of the moment has passed, that he has purchased pleasure at the price of misery to others. Horses were loaded with the dead; and, after this first burst of sporting, the shooting of pigeons became a business, with a few idlers, for the remainder of the season. Richard, however, boasted for many a year, of his shot with the "cricket;" and Benjamin gravely asserted, that he thought they killed nearly as many pigeons on that day, as there were Frenchmen destroyed on the memorable occasion of Rodney's victory.

Rodney's – British Admiral George Rodney beat the French forces into surrender in the Caribbean in 1782

XI

DUTIES TO GOD

I f there is a God, do we have duties to him, or her? What if we come to believe that God commands us to do something that seems terribly wrong? Should we nevertheless obey? Does our duty to God override our own conscience?

Different cultures have different conceptions of God, or of the gods. For the ancient Greeks, the gods could be spiteful or jealous of rivals, and so the idea of courageously defying the gods made sense. Those who follow Christianity, Islam, or Judaism have difficulty in understanding that idea. They would reject the idea that God could command us to do what is wrong. Yet the Bible has several instances in which God appears to command something that is morally wrong. Believers in the literal truth of the Bible would need to explain how this view can be reconciled with — to give just one of several possible examples — God's commands to the Israelites to "smite Amalek, and utterly destroy all that they have, and spare them not, but slay both man and woman, infant and suckling, ox and sheep, camel and ass."[1] Is genocide right when God commands it?

Some theists hold that God can never command what is wrong, because "good" has meaning only through the existence of God. What he commands is good, what he forbids is bad. If this is true, then the idea that he could command us to do what is wrong is a contradiction in terms. But this view, known to philosophers as the "divine command" theory of the meaning of "good," faces serious difficulties. It implies that there is no intrinsic difference between loving your neighbors and knocking them to the ground and kicking them to death, except that God commands us to do the former and forbids the latter. If God were to reverse his commands, it would be good to kill your neighbors and bad to love them. God, on this view, seems to be an arbitary tyrant who does as he pleases, independently of any external standards of good or evil. The only reason for obeying him is that we fear his wrath if we do not.

The theist might reply that this misconstrues the divine command theory. Since God is good, he could never command us to kill our neighbors. But on the divine command theory, it is meaningless to assert that God's nature is good. Since "good" means "commanded by God," that claim tells us only that God is commanded by God. We still have no reason to deny that God could as easily command us to kill our neighbors as to love them. And some orthodox Jews do believe

427

that the ancient Israelites were justified in slaughtering the Amalekites precisely because it was God's command that they did so.

On the other hand, most monotheists think that God is good, and frequently praise him. For that to make sense, they must have a standard of what is good that is independent of him and his commands. If that is so, then they do not need to know what God wants in order to know what is good and bad. They can form their own opinion, based on the independent standard. Where that standard comes from is a question that everyone must face, except those theists who are prepared to take God's commands as the standard of goodness, and therefore to cease to describe him as good. Of course, the independent standard may still be a religious one, based on a religious text, like the New Testament. But then the text must stand on its own merits, on the wisdom or inspiration or cogency its words would have, no matter what their source. If we assert that scripture is beyond criticism because it is the word of God, we have still not escaped the tight logical circle in which we lack an independent standard for saying that God is good.

Despite the fact that even theists need an independent standard of goodness to give us a reason for obeying God (unless they are prepared to say that we should obey God simply because he is more powerful than we are), many people believe that there can be no ethics without God. That view is put by Ivan Karamazov, in *The Brothers Karamazov*. Perhaps it derives from a confused idea that God must be the source of our ideas of right and wrong. It is also possible, however, that the view is based not so much on a doubt about whether there can be such a thing as right or wrong in the absence of God, but rather on the sense that without God, and a scheme of reward and punishment in an afterlife, there is no motivation for doing good. It is obviously true that those who believe that God rewards those who do good and punishes those who do what is bad have a motivation for doing good that others do not have. But do we really need this motivation? We tend to think less of people who do what is right only because there is a reward for doing so. If we praise someone for helping an elderly neighbor, we will withdraw our praise when we learn that he only helps wealthy elderly people, and encourages them to remember him in their wills. Shouldn't we feel the same about people who do what is right only because they believe that God will reward them for doing so? As we saw in the introduction to Section I, Immanuel Kant said that for an action to have true moral worth, it must be done because it is the right thing to do, and not for some external reward. He thought that to encourage people to do what is right because of the hope of reward or the fear of punishment in an afterlife is to degrade morality.

Since there must be a standard of goodness that is independent of God's will, and there can be sufficient motivation to do what is right independently of divine reward and punishment, ethics is independent of religion. It is therefore not surprising that many atheists and agnostics live highly ethical lives. It also would follow that if there is a God, we cannot simply assume that our duties to him override all our other duties. Prometheus was right to defy Zeus, and we can at least raise the question whether Abraham should have been so obedient to

God that he would have murdered Isaac had God not countermanded his order to do so.

NOTE

1　I Samuel 15:3.

59

AESCHYLUS

Prometheus Bound

As punishment for stealing fire from the gods and giving it to humans, Prometheus has been chained to a rock on Mount Caucasus. In this, the final scene of the play, Zeus has sent his messenger, Hermes, to persuade, or intimidate, Prometheus into telling his secret – the name of the woman who can bring about Zeus' downfall.

CHORUS: These threats against Zeus surely voice but your own wish.
PROMETHEUS: I speak what shall prove true – and my own wish as well.
CHORUS: Must we expect one who shall bring Zeus to his knees?
PROMETHEUS: Yes; Zeus's neck shall bow beneath worse pains than mine.
CHORUS: Why are you not afraid to fling such taunting words?
PROMETHEUS: Why should I fear? My destiny is not to die.
CHORUS: Zeus might invent for you some still worse agony.
PROMETHEUS: Then let him do it! I am prepared for everything.
CHORUS: A wise man will speak humbly, and fear Nemesis.
PROMETHEUS: Bow! Pray! As always, fawn upon the powerful hand!
    For great Zeus I care less than nothing. Let him do
    And govern as he wills, for the short time he has.
    He will not govern long among the gods. – Why, look!
    Here comes his runner, the new tyrant's lickspittle.
    No doubt he brings some message.

(*Enter* HERMES.)

HERMES: I speak to you – the master-mind, with heart more sour
    Than sourness; you who honoured creatures of a day
    And sinned against immortals; you, the thief of fire:
    The Father bids you tell him what this marriage is
    Through which you boast that he shall fall from power. Now speak
    No clever riddles, but set forth the detailed truth.

AESCHYLUS, pp. 47–52 from *Prometheus Bound and Other Plays* (tr. Philip Vellacott). London: Penguin, 1961. Copyright © 1961 by Philip Vellacott.

Do not, Prometheus, make me travel all this way
   Again; Zeus is not mollified by such replies.
PROMETHEUS: This underling of gods makes a high-sounding speech
   Crammed with importance. – You and all your crew are young;
   So is your power; and you imagine that you hold
   An unassailable citadel. But I have seen
   Two dynasties already hurled from those same heights;
   And I shall see the third, today's king, fall to earth
   More shamefully than his precursors, and more soon.
   Do you think I quake and cower before these upstart gods?
   Not much, nor little – not one slightest thought! Now you
   Trot back the way you came; you'll find out nothing here.
HERMES: Conduct like this, both obstinate and insolent,
   Has once already brought you to a painful plight.
PROMETHEUS: Understand this: I would not change my painful plight,
   On any terms, for your servile humility.
HERMES: Being bondslave to this rock is preferable, no doubt,
   To being the trusted messenger of Father Zeus.
PROMETHEUS: You use the fitting language of the insolent.
HERMES: It seems you find your present state a luxury.
PROMETHEUS: You think so? May I one day see my enemies,
   And you among them, in such luxury as this!
HERMES: What, I? Do you blame me too for your sufferings?
PROMETHEUS: In one word, I detest all gods who could repay
   My benefits with such outrageous infamy.
HERMES: It's plain that your insanity is far advanced.
PROMETHEUS: Perhaps – if to hate enemies is insanity.
HERMES: Now you, free and in power, would be unbearable.
PROMETHEUS: Alas!
HERMES: Alas? That word is one which Zeus has never known.
PROMETHEUS: But Time, as he grows older, teaches everything.
HERMES: Time has not taught *you* self-control or prudence – yet.
PROMETHEUS: No – or I would not argue with an underling.
HERMES: It seems you'll tell nothing of what Zeus wants to know.
PROMETHEUS: And yet I owe him much – that I would gladly pay.
HERMES: You banter with me – do you think I am a child?
PROMETHEUS: Are you not then a child, or worse than childish, if
   You still expect to get an answer out of me?
   There is no torture, no ingenuity, by which
   Zeus can persuade me to reveal my secret, till
   The injury of these bonds is loosed from me. Therefore
   Let scorching flames be flung from heaven; let the whole earth
   With white-winged snowstorms, subterranean thunderings,
   Heave and convulse: nothing will force me to reveal
   By whose hand Fate shall hurl Zeus from his tyranny.
HERMES: Consider now whether this course seems profitable.

PROMETHEUS: I have long ago considered all this, and resolved.
HERMES: Come, bring yourself, perverse fool, while there is still time,
   To weigh your situation, and so turn to sense.
PROMETHEUS: You waste your breath; you may as well exhort the waves.
   Never persuade yourself that I, through fear of what
   Zeus may intend, will show a woman's mind, or kneel
   To my detested enemy, with womanish hands
   Outspread in supplication for release. No, never!
HERMES: My words lead only to more words, without effect;
   Beg as I may, nothing can soothe or soften you.
   Like an unbroken colt you try your strength, and take
   The bit between your teeth, and fight against the reins.
   Yet all your violence springs from feeble reckoning;
   For obstinacy in a fool has by itself
   No strength at all. Consider now what punishments
   Will burst inevitably upon you like a storm
   Of mountainous waves, if you refuse to listen to me.

      First, Zeus will split this rugged chasm with the shock
   And flame of lightning, and entomb you underground
   Still clamped on this embracing rock. When a long age
   Has passed, you will return into the light; and then
   The dark-winged hound of Zeus will come, the savage eagle,
   An uninvited banqueter, and all day long
   Will rip your flesh in rags and feast upon your liver,
   Gnawing it black. And you may hope for no release
   From such a torment, till some god be found to take
   Your pains upon him, and of his own will descend
   To sunless Hades and the black depths of Tartarus.

      So think again; this is no fabricated boast,
   But truth as Zeus has spoken it, who cannot lie,
   But will accomplish every word his mouth has uttered.
   Look every way; consider; and be sure of this:
   Wise counsel always is worth more than stubbornness.
CHORUS: To us it seems that Hermes' words are sensible.
   He bids you quit resistance and seek good advice.
   Do so; a wise man's folly forfeits dignity.
PROMETHEUS: I knew what Hermes had to say
   Before he made his brag. It is no dishonour
   For an enemy to suffer at his enemy's hands.
   So let the pronged locks of lightning be launched at me,
   Let the air be roused with thunder and convulsion of wild winds,
   Let hurricanes upheave by the roots the base of the earth,

---

Tartarus – fabled place of punishment in a lower world

Let the sea-waves' roaring savagery
Confound the courses of the heavenly stars;
Let him lift me high and hurl me to black Tartarus
On ruthless floods of irresistible doom:
I am one whom he cannot kill.
HERMES: Thoughts and words like these
Are what one may hear from lunatics.
This prayer of his shows all the features of frenzy;
And I see no sign of improvement.
(*to the* CHORUS) You, however, who sympathize with his sufferings,
Get away quickly from this place,
Lest the intolerable roar of thunder stun your senses.
CHORUS: If you want to persuade me, use a different tone
And give other advice. You speak too hastily,
Bidding me do what I could not think of doing.
Would you have me practise cowardice?
I will stay with Prometheus, come what must.
I was taught to hate those who desert their friends;
And there is no infamy I more despise.
HERMES: Then remember my warning;
And when you are caught by calamity
Don't lay the blame on Fortune, or say that Zeus
Plunged you in suffering unforeseen;
Not Zeus but yourselves will be to blame.
You know what is coming; it is neither sudden nor secret.
Only your own folly will entangle you
In the inextricable net of destruction.

(*Exit* HERMES.)

PROMETHEUS: Now it is happening: threat gives place to performance.
The earth rocks; thunder, echoing from the depth,
Roars in answer; fiery lightnings twist and flash.
Dust dances in a whirling fountain;
Blasts of the four winds skirmish together,
Set themselves in array for battle;
Sky and sea rage indistinguishably.
The cataclysm advances visibly upon me,
Sent by Zeus to make me afraid.

O Earth, my holy mother,
O Sky, where sun and moon
Give light to all in turn,
You see how I am wronged!

(*The rock collapses and disappears, as the* CHORUS *scatter in all directions.*)

60

Genesis 22

God answered the prayers of Abraham and his wife Sarah for a son. Isaac was born when Abraham was 100 years old.

The time came when God put Abraham to the test. "Abraham", he called, and Abraham replied, "Here I am." God said, "Take your son Isaac, your only son, whom you love, and go to the land of Moriah. There you shall offer him as a sacrifice on one of the hills which I will show you." So Abraham rose early in the morning and saddled his ass, and he took with him two of his men and his son Isaac; and he split the firewood for the sacrifice, and set out for the place of which God had spoken. On the third day Abraham looked up and saw the place in the distance. He said to his men, "Stay here with the ass while I and the boy go over there; and when we have worshipped we will come back to you." So Abraham took the wood for the sacrifice and laid it on his son Isaac's shoulder; he himself carried the fire and the knife, and the two of them went on together. Isaac said to Abraham, "Father", and he answered, "What is it, my son?" Isaac said, "Here are the fire and the wood, but where is the young beast for the sacrifice?" Abraham answered, "God will provide himself with a young beast for a sacrifice, my son." And the two of them went on together and came to the place of which God had spoken. There Abraham built an altar and arranged the wood. He bound his son Isaac and laid him on the altar on top of the wood. Then he stretched out his hand and took the knife to kill his son; but the angel of the LORD called to him from heaven, "Abraham, Abraham." He answered, "Here I am." The angel of the LORD said, "Do not raise your hand against the boy; do not touch him. Now I know that you are a God-fearing man. You have not withheld from me your son, your only son." Abraham looked up, and there he saw a ram caught by its horns in a thicket. So he went and took the ram and offered it as a sacrifice instead of his son.

GENESIS, Chapter 22, p.16 from *The New English Bible* 1972. New English Bible © by Oxford University Press and Cambridge University Press, 1961, 1970. Reprinted by permission of Cambridge University Press.

Abraham named that place Jehovah-jireh; and to this day the saying is: "In the mountain of the LORD it was provided." Then the angel of the LORD called from heaven a second time to Abraham, "This is the word of the LORD: By my own self I swear: inasmuch as you have done this and have not withheld your son, your only son, I will bless you abundantly and greatly multiply your descendants until they are as numerous as the stars in the sky and the grains of sand on the sea-shore. Your descendants shall possess the cities of their enemies. All nations on earth shall pray to be blessed as your descendants are blessed, and this because you have obeyed me."

Jehovah-jireh – the Lord will provide

61

FYODOR DOSTOYEVSKY

The Brothers Karamazov

The Brothers Karamazov is Dostoyevsky's final novel. It centers on the search for God through the dramatic story of three brothers and the alleged patricide of their father, Fyodor Pavlovitch. The youngest brother, Alyosha, has a saint-like innocence, while Ivan is a more sceptical intellectual. Dimitri, the oldest brother, is ruled by his animal instincts. At this point in the story the Karamazovs are at a nearby monastery, with the elder, Father Zossima, who they hope will be able to resolve the bitter differences between Dimitri and his father. Father Paissy is another monk at the monastery. Miusov, an anti-clerical local landowner distantly related to the Karamazovs, is recounting an argument that Ivan proposed.

"Only five days ago, in a gathering here, principally of ladies, he solemnly declared in argument that there was nothing in the whole world to make men love their neighbours. That there was no law of nature that man should love mankind, and that, if there had been any love on earth hitherto, it was not owing to a natural law, but simply because men have believed in immortality. Ivan Fyodorovitch added in parenthesis that the whole natural law lies in that faith, and that if you were to destroy in mankind the belief in immortality, not only love but every living force maintaining the life of the world would at once be dried up. Moreover, nothing then would be immoral, everything would be lawful, even cannibalism. That's not all. He ended by asserting that for every individual, like ourselves, who does not believe in God or immortality, the moral law of nature must immediately be changed into the exact contrary of the former religious law, and that egoism, even to crime, must become not only lawful but even recognised as the inevitable, the most rational, even honourable outcome of his position. From this paradox, gentlemen, you can judge of the rest of our eccentric and paradoxical friend Ivan Fyodorovitch's theories."

"Excuse me," Dimitri cried suddenly; "if I've heard aright, crime must not only be permitted but even recognised as the inevitable and the most rational outcome of his position for every infidel! Is that so or not?"

FYODOR DOSTOYEVSKY, extract from Part 1, Book 2, Chapter 6 in *The Brothers Karamazov* (tr. Constance Garnett), first published in 1879–80.

"Quite so," said Father Paissy.

"I'll remember it."

Having uttered these words Dmitri ceased speaking as suddenly as he had begun. Everyone looked at him with curiosity.

"Is that really your conviction as to the consequences of the disappearance of the faith in immortality?" the elder asked Ivan suddenly.

"Yes. That was my contention. There is no virtue if there is no immortality."

"You are blessed in believing that, or else most unhappy."

"Why unhappy?" Ivan asked smiling.

"Because, in all probability you don't believe yourself in the immortality of your soul, nor in what you have written yourself in your article on Church Jurisdiction."

"Perhaps you are right! . . . But I wasn't altogether joking," Ivan suddenly and strangely confessed, flushing quickly.

"You were not altogether joking. That's true. The question is still fretting your heart, and not answered. But the martyr likes sometimes to divert himself with his despair, as it were driven to it by despair itself. Meanwhile, in your despair, you, too, divert yourself with magazine articles, and discussions in society, though you don't believe your own arguments, and with an aching heart mock at them inwardly. . . . That question you have not answered, and it is your great grief, for it clamours for an answer."

"But can it be answered by me? Answered in the affirmative?" Ivan went on asking strangely, still looking at the elder with the same inexplicable smile.

"If it can't be decided in the affirmative, it will never be decided in the negative. You know that that is the peculiarity of your heart, and all its suffering is due to it. But thank the Creator who has given you a lofty heart capable of such suffering; of thinking and seeking higher things, for our dwelling is in the heavens. God grant that your heart will attain the answer on earth, and may God bless your path."

The elder raised his hand and would have made the sign of the cross over Ivan from where he stood. But the latter rose from his seat, went up to him, received his blessing, and kissing his hand went back to his place in silence. His face looked firm and earnest. This action and all the preceding conversation, which was so surprising from Ivan, impressed everyone by its strangeness and a certain solemnity, so that all were silent for a moment, and there was a look almost of apprehension in Alyosha's face.

XII

NEW LIFE FORMS

In February 1997, a research team from Edinburgh, Scotland, caused a media frenzy when it announced that it had produced a lamb, Dolly, who was cloned from an adult sheep. The excitement, however, was not about sheep. *Newsweek's* cover on March 10 that year pictured three identical human babies standing inside glass laboratory beakers. Against a background created by films like *The Boys from Brazil* (about cloning Hitler), it was the prospect of cloning humans, not sheep, that rang alarms. "Do we really want to play God?" *Newsweek* asked. Commentators seized on Mary Shelley's *Frankenstein* as the literary model most relevant to the prospect of cloning, though Aldous Huxley's vision, in *Brave New World*, of new ways of creating similar human beings might have been a little closer. Political leaders called for the cloning of humans to be banned, and governments set up committees to investigate ways of doing this. The European Parliament resolved that human cloning must be prohibited because each individual has a right to his or her own genetic identity.[1] Few asked from where this right comes, or whether giving birth to identical twins violates the right of each of them to his or her own genetic identity.

Why are we so fearful of new means of creating life? Although Nietzsche thought that we have more faith in science than the utility of its results can justify,[2] the popularity of Mary Shelley's *Frankenstein* and of films about evil or obsessive scientists bringing disaster on us all suggests that there is also a wide-spread fear of humans taking a step too far, of science running amok, and of a new breed of monsters who escape our control. Cloning is not the only way in which this could happen. Genetically modified crops are now in widespread commercial use, despite concerns that they could escape into the natural environment and change ecosystems forever. By inserting the genes of one species of animal into another, scientists have created transgenic animals, including sheep and goats who produce valuable pharmaceuticals in their milk, and mice who grow twice as large as they would naturally. Since genetically modified animals can be patented, we will no doubt see more of them as the scientific – and hence commercial – possibilities expand. Rapid advances in artificial intelligence hold other possibilities. In *The Age of Spiritual Machines*,[3] Ray Kurzweil holds out the prospect of human beings achieving their age-old dream of overcoming death by using new forms of technology to replace our biological parts, while retaining our consciousness. A less optimistic scenario is sketched by computer expert Bill Joy, who, in an essay entitled "Why the Future Doesn't Need Us," has speculated about an era in which intelligent machines escape our control and become our masters.[4]

The fear of unleashing something we can't control undoubtedly fuels part of the concern about creating new forms of life or altering human genetics, but the prospect raises other issues too. *Newsweek*'s question about "playing God" implies that we should avoid the creation of new forms of life because it is God's business, not ours. Those who say this rarely explain exactly what we may do, and what we must leave to God. If we do not believe in the existence of God, the objection to "playing God" must either be abandoned or at least rephrased, perhaps in terms of an objection to artificial or unnatural ways of creating life. But the problem of selecting a morally significant boundary line between what we may and may not do remains the same, whether we see it as separating God's exclusive sphere of action from our own, or as distinguishing what is natural from what is unnatural. Every day, people create life or decide not to create it by using or discontinuing the use of contraceptives, or consulting a calendar in order to avoid having sex when a woman is most likely to be fertile. Infertile couples use new techniques in order to have a child, like artificial insemination, or *in vitro* fertilization, perhaps involving a donated egg, or an embryo that has been frozen and stored for several years. Couples at risk of having a child with a genetic disease can now resort to *in vitro* fertilization in order to select, from several of their embryos, one that does not carry the disease. If these acts are not "playing God," or to be condemned as "unnatural," why is cloning?

Our ability to create new life forms, and to modify the nature of our own offspring, has also been seen as a threat to human dignity. When we genetically modify and patent animals, we treat them as machines that can be redesigned. We also treat them as commodities, or things. Of course, with animals, this is not new. In every economy, they *are* commodities. As we have seen in Section X, there are strong moral reasons to object to this, but so far those reasons have not resulted in the abolition of the commodity status of animals. The fact that these genetic techniques can be applied to animals, however, suggests that they would also work with human beings. It is increasingly hard to resist the fact that we are biological machines, and not only our bodies, but also some of our abilities and our most personal characteristics are the outcome of a set of biological instructions encoded in DNA. That frightens those who prefer to think of us as a creation made in the image of God, a spirit transmitted by a divine spark, as Michelangelo depicted it on the ceiling of the Sistine Chapel. Others, however, welcome the prospect of modifying early embryos. They seek not only the avoidance of genetic diseases, but also the insertion of genetic information that will lead to qualities beyond the normal range of human genetic variation. They point out that the history of humanity does not support the claim that there is no room for improving our species, and they look forward to the first genetically engineered "post-human" beings with qualities and capacities far superior to our own.

The question whether we should allow scientists and parents to redesign future generations of human beings looms as one of the key issues for the twenty-first century – one that poses great dangers, but may also offer great opportunities for creating a better world.

NOTES

1 The European Parliament. Resolution on cloning motion dated March 11, 1997, passed March 13, 1997; quoted from John Harris, "Goodbye Dolly," *Journal of Medical Ethics*, vol. 23 (1997).

2 Friedrich Nietzsche, *The Gay Science*, Book V.

3 Ray Kurzweil, *The Age of Spiritual Machines*, New York: Viking Press, 1999.

4 Bill Joy, "Why the Future Doesn't Need Us," *Wired*, April 2000. *http://www.wirednews.com/wired/archive/8.04/joy_pr.html*

62

MARY SHELLEY

Frankenstein

The novel is narrated by Victor Frankenstein, a young Swiss student, who discovers how to animate lifeless matter.

After days and nights of incredible labour and fatigue, I succeeded in discovering the cause of generation and life; nay, more, I became myself capable of bestowing animation upon lifeless matter.

The astonishment which I had at first experienced on this discovery soon gave place to delight and rapture. After so much time spent in painful labour, to arrive at once at the summit of my desires, was the most gratifying consummation of my toils. But this discovery was so great and overwhelming, that all the steps by which I had been progressively led to it were obliterated, and I beheld only the result. What had been the study and desire of the wisest men since the creation of the world was now within my grasp. Not that, like a magic scene, it all opened upon me at once: the information I had obtained was of a nature rather to direct my endeavours so soon as I should point them towards the object of my search, than to exhibit that object already accomplished. I was like the Arabian who had been buried with the dead, and found a passage to life, aided only by one glimmering, and seemingly ineffectual, light.

I see by your eagerness, and the wonder and hope which your eyes express, my friend, that you expect to be informed of the secret with which I am acquainted; that cannot be: listen patiently until the end of my story, and you will easily perceive why I am reserved upon that subject. I will not lead you on, unguarded and ardent as I then was, to your destruction and infallible misery. Learn from me, if not by my precepts, at least by my example, how dangerous is the acquirement of knowledge, and how much happier that man is who believes his native town to be the world, than he who aspires to become greater than his nature will allow.

MARY SHELLEY, *Frankenstein*, extracts from Chapters IV, V, X, XVII, and XX in *Frankenstein*, first published in 1818.

"like the Arabian who had been buried with the dead" – Sinbad in *The Arabian Nights* was, as was the custom in that country, buried with his wife when she died

When I found so astonishing a power placed within my hands, I hesitated a long time concerning the manner in which I should employ it. Although I possessed the capacity of bestowing animation, yet to prepare a frame for the reception of it, with all its intricacies of fibres, muscles, and veins, still remained a work of inconceivable difficulty and labour. I doubted at first whether I should attempt the creation of a being like myself, or one of simpler organization; but my imagination was too much exalted by my first success to permit me to doubt of my ability to give life to an animal as complex and wonderful as man. The materials at present within my command hardly appeared adequate to so arduous an undertaking; but I doubted not that I should ultimately succeed. I prepared myself for a multitude of reverses; my operations might be incessantly baffled, and at last my work be imperfect: yet, when I considered the improvement which every day takes place in science and mechanics, I was encouraged to hope my present attempts would at least lay the foundations of future success. Nor could I consider the magnitude and complexity of my plan as any argument of its impracticability. It was with these feelings that I began the creation of a human being. As the minuteness of the parts formed a great hindrance to my speed, I resolved, contrary to my first intention, to make the being of a gigantic stature; that is to say, about eight feet in height, and proportionably large. After having formed this determination, and having spent some months in successfully collecting and arranging my materials, I began.

[. . .]

It was on a dreary night of November, that I beheld the accomplishment of my toils. With an anxiety that almost amounted to agony, I collected the instruments of life around me, that I might infuse a spark of being into the lifeless thing that lay at my feet. It was already one in the morning; the rain pattered dismally against the panes, and my candle was nearly burnt out, when, by the glimmer of the half-extinguished light, I saw the dull yellow eye of the creature open; it breathed hard, and a convulsive motion agitated its limbs.

How can I describe my emotions at this catastrophe, or how delineate the wretch whom with such infinite pains and care I had endeavoured to form? His limbs were in proportion, and I had selected his features as beautiful. Beautiful! – Great God! His yellow skin scarcely covered the work of muscles and arteries beneath; his hair was of a lustrous black, and flowing; his teeth of a pearly whiteness; but these luxuriances only formed a more horrid contrast with his watery eyes, that seemed almost of the same colour as the dun white sockets in which they were set, his shrivelled complexion and straight black lips.

The different accidents of life are not so changeable as the feelings of human nature. I had worked hard for nearly two years, for the sole purpose of infusing life into an inanimate body. For this I had deprived myself of rest and health. I had desired it with an ardour that far exceeded moderation; but now that I had finished, the beauty of the dream vanished, and breathless horror and disgust filled my heart. Unable to endure the aspect of the being I had created, I rushed out of the room, and continued a long time traversing my bed-chamber, unable to compose my mind to sleep. At length lassitude succeeded to the tumult I had before endured; and I threw myself on the bed in my clothes, endeavouring to seek a few moments of forgetfulness. But it was in vain: I slept, indeed, but I was disturbed by the wildest dreams. I thought I saw Elizabeth, in the bloom of health, walking in the streets of Ingolstadt. Delighted and surprised, I embraced her; but as I imprinted the first kiss on her lips, they became livid with the hue of death; her features appeared to change, and I thought that I held the corpse of my dead mother in my arms; a shroud enveloped her form, and I saw the grave-worms crawling in the folds of the flannel. I started from my sleep with horror; a cold dew covered my forehead, my teeth chattered, and every limb became convulsed: when, by the dim and yellow light of the moon, as it forced its way through the window shutters, I beheld the wretch – the miserable monster whom I had created. He held up the curtain of the bed; and his eyes, if eyes they may be called, were fixed on me. His jaws opened, and he muttered some inarticulate sounds, while a grin wrinkled his cheeks. He might have spoken, but I did not hear; one hand was stretched out, seemingly to detain me, but I escaped, and rushed down stairs. I took refuge in the courtyard belonging to the house which I inhabited; where I remained during the rest of the night, walking up and down in the greatest agitation, listening attentively, catching and fearing each sound as if it were to announce the approach of the demoniacal corpse to which I had so miserably given life.

After his "monster" murdered his younger brother, Frankenstein ran away and is now in a remote area of the French Alps.

I suddenly beheld the figure of a man, at some distance, advancing towards me with superhuman speed. He bounded over the crevices in the ice, among which I had walked with caution; his stature, also, as he approached, seemed to exceed that of man. I was troubled: a mist came over my eyes, and I felt a faintness seize me; but I was quickly restored by the cold gale of the mountains. I perceived, as the shape came nearer (sight tremendous and abhorred?) that it was the wretch whom I had created. I trembled with rage and horror, resolving to wait his approach, and then close with him in mortal combat. He approached; his countenance bespoke bitter anguish, combined with disdain and malignity, while its unearthly ugliness rendered it almost too horrible for human eyes. But I scarcely observed this; rage and hatred had at first deprived me of utterance, and I recovered only to overwhelm him with words expressive of furious detestation and contempt.

"Devil," I exclaimed, "do you dare approach me? and do not you fear the fierce vengeance of my arm wreaked on your miserable head? Begone, vile insect! or rather, stay, that I may trample you to dust! and, oh! that I could, with the extinction of your miserable existence, restore those victims whom you have so diabolically murdered!"

"I expected this reception," said the dæmon. "All men hate the wretched; how, then, must I be hated, who am miserable beyond all living things! Yet you, my creator, detest and spurn me, thy creature, to whom thou art bound by ties only dissoluble by the annihilation of one of us. You purpose to kill me. How dare you sport thus with life? Do your duty towards me, and I will do mine towards you and the rest of mankind. If you will comply with my conditions, I will leave them and you at peace; but if you refuse, I will glut the maw of death, until it be satiated with the blood of your remaining friends."

"Abhorred monster! fiend that thou art! the tortures of hell are too mild a vengeance for thy crimes. Wretched devil! you reproach me with your creation; come on, then, that I may extinguish the spark which I so negligently bestowed."

My rage was without bounds; I sprang on him, impelled by all the feelings which can arm one being against the existence of another.

He easily eluded me, and said –

"Be calm! I entreat you to hear me, before you give vent to your hatred on my devoted head. Have I not suffered enough, that you seek to increase my misery? Life, although it may only be an accumulation of anguish, is dear to me, and I will defend it. Remember, thou hast made me more powerful than thyself; my height is superior to thine; my joints more supple. But I will not be tempted to set myself in opposition to thee. I am thy creature, and I will be even mild and docile to my natural lord and king, if thou wilt also perform thy part, the which thou owest me. Oh, Frankenstein, be not equitable to every other, and trample upon me alone, to whom thy justice, and even thy clemency and affection, is most due. Remember, that I am thy creature; I ought to be thy Adam; but I am rather the fallen angel whom thou drivest from joy for no misdeed. Every where I see bliss, from which I alone am irrevocably excluded. I was benevolent and good; misery made me a fiend. Make me happy, and I shall again be virtuous."

"Begone! I will not hear you. There can be no community between you and me; we are enemies. Begone, or let us try our strength in a fight, in which one must fall."

"How can I move thee? Will no entreaties cause thee to turn a favourable eye upon thy creature, who implores thy goodness and compassion? Believe me, Frankenstein: I was benevolent; my soul glowed with love and humanity: but am I not alone, miserably alone? You, my creator, abhor me; what hope can I gather from your fellow-creatures, who owe me nothing? they spurn and hate me. The desert mountains and dreary glaciers are my refuge. I have wandered here many days; the caves of ice, which I only do not fear, are a dwelling to me, and the only one which man does not grudge. These bleak skies I hail, for they are kinder to me than your fellow-beings. If the multitude of mankind knew of my existence, they would do as you do, and arm themselves for my destruction. Shall I not then hate them who abhor me? I will keep no terms with my enemies. I am miserable, and they shall share my wretchedness. Yet it is in your power to recompense me, and deliver them from an evil which it only remains for you to make so great, that not only you and your family, but thousands of others, shall be swallowed up in the whirlwinds of its rage. Let your compassion be moved, and do not disdain me. Listen to my tale: when you have heard that, abandon or commiserate me, as you shall judge that I deserve. But hear me. The guilty are allowed, by human laws, bloody as they are, to speak in their own defence before they are condemned. Listen to me, Frankenstein. You accuse me of murder; and yet you would, with a satisfied conscience, destroy your own creature. Oh, praise the eternal justice of man! Yet I ask you not to spare me: listen to me; and then, if you can, and if you will, destroy the work of your hands."

"Why do you call to my remembrance," I rejoined, "circumstances, of which I shudder to reflect, that I have been the miserable origin and author? Cursed be the day, abhorred devil, in which you first saw light! Cursed (although I curse myself) be the hands that formed you! You have made me wretched beyond expression. You have left me no power to consider whether I am just to you, or not. Begone! relieve me from the sight of your detested form."

"Thus I relieve thee, my creator," he said, and placed his hated hands before my eyes, which I flung from me with violence; "thus I take from thee a sight which you abhor. Still thou canst listen to me, and grant me thy compassion. By the virtues that I once possessed, I demand this from you. Hear my tale; it is long and strange, and the temperature of this place is not fitting to your fine sensations; come to the hut upon the mountain. The sun is yet high in the heavens; before it descends to hide itself behind yon snowy precipices, and illuminate another world, you will have heard my story, and can decide. On you it rests, whether I quit for ever the neighbourhood of man, and lead a harmless life, or become the scourge of your fellow-creatures, and the author of your own speedy ruin."

As he said this, he led the way across the ice: I followed. My heart was full, and I did not answer him; but, as I proceeded, I weighed the various arguments that he had used, and determined at least to listen to his tale. I was partly urged by curiosity, and compassion confirmed my resolution. I had hitherto supposed him to be the murderer of my brother, and I eagerly sought a confirmation or denial of this opinion. For the first time, also, I felt what the duties of a creator towards his creature were, and that I ought to render him happy before I complained of his wickedness.

[. . .]

The being finished speaking, and fixed his looks upon me in expectation of a reply. But I was bewildered, perplexed, and unable to arrange my ideas sufficiently to understand the full extent of his proposition. He continued –

"You must create a female for me, with whom I can live in the interchange of those sympathies necessary for my being. This you alone can do; and I demand it of you as a right which you must not refuse to concede."

The latter part of his tale had kindled anew in me the anger that had died away while he narrated his peaceful life among the cottagers, and, as he said this, I could no longer suppress the rage that burned within me.

"I do refuse it," I replied; "and no torture shall ever extort a consent from me. You may render me the most miserable of men, but you shall never make me base in my own eyes. Shall I create another like yourself, whose joint wickedness might desolate the world? Begone! I have answered you; you may torture me, but I will never consent."

"You are in the wrong," replied the fiend; "and, instead of threatening, I am content to reason with you. I am malicious because I am miserable. Am I not shunned and hated by all mankind? You, my creator, would tear me to pieces, and triumph; remember that, and tell me why I should pity man more than he pities me? You would not call it murder, if you could precipitate me into one of those ice-rifts, and destroy my frame, the work of your own hands. Shall I respect man, when he contemns me? Let him live with me in the interchange of kindness; and, instead of injury, I would bestow every benefit upon him with tears of gratitude at his acceptance. But that cannot be; the human senses are insurmountable barriers to our union. Yet mine shall not be the submission of abject slavery. I will revenge my injuries: if I cannot inspire love, I will cause fear; and chiefly towards you my arch-enemy, because my creator, do I swear inextinguishable hatred. Have a care: I will work at your destruction, nor finish until I desolate your heart, so that you shall curse the hour of your birth."

A fiendish rage animated him as he said this; his face was wrinkled into contortions too horrible for human eyes to behold; but presently he calmed himself and proceeded –

"I intended to reason. This passion is detrimental to me; for you do not reflect that *you* are the cause of its excess. If any being felt emotions of benevolence towards me, I should return them an hundred and an hundred fold; for that one creature's sake, I would make peace with the whole kind! But I now indulge in dreams of bliss that cannot be realised. What I ask of you is reasonable and moderate; I demand a creature of another sex, but as hideous as myself; the gratification is small, but it is all that I can receive, and it shall content me. It is true, we shall be monsters, cut off from all the world; but on that account we shall be more attached to one another. Our lives will not be happy, but they will be harmless, and free from the misery I now feel. Oh! my creator, make me happy; let me feel gratitude towards you for one benefit! Let me see that I excite the sympathy of some existing thing; do not deny me my request!"

I was moved. I shuddered when I thought of the possible consequences of my consent; but I felt that there was some justice in his argument. His tale, and the feelings he now expressed, proved him to be a creature of fine sensations; and did I not, as his maker, owe him all the portion of happiness that it was in my power to bestow? He saw my change of feeling, and continued –

"If you consent, neither you nor any other human being shall ever see us again: I will go to the vast wilds of South America. My food is not that of man; I do not destroy the lamb and the kid to glut my appetite; acorns and berries afford me sufficient nourishment. My companion will be of the same nature as myself, and will be content with the same fare. We shall make our bed of dried leaves; the sun will shine on us as on man, and will ripen our food. The picture I present to you is peaceful and human, and you must feel that you could deny it only in the wantonness of power and cruelty. Pitiless as you have been towards me, I now see compassion in your eyes; let me seize the favourable moment, and persuade you to promise what I so ardently desire."

"You propose," replied I, "to fly from the habitations of man, to dwell in those wilds where the beasts of the field will be your only companions. How can you, who long for the love and sympathy of man, persevere in this exile? You will return, and again seek their kindness, and you will meet with their detestation; your evil passions will be renewed, and you will then have a companion to aid you in the task of destruction. This may not be: cease to argue the point, for I cannot consent."

"How inconstant are your feelings! but a moment ago you were moved by my representations, and why do you again harden yourself to my complaints? I swear to you, by the earth which I inhabit, and by you that made me, that, with the companion you bestow, I will quit the neighbourhood of man, and dwell as it may chance, in the most savage of places. My evil passions will have fled, for I shall meet with sympathy! my life will flow quietly away, and, in my dying moments, I shall not curse my maker."

His words had a strange effect upon me. I compassioned him, and sometimes felt a wish to console him; but when I looked upon him, when I saw the filthy mass that moved and talked, my heart sickened, and my feelings were altered to those of horror and hatred. I tried to stifle these sensations; I thought, that as I could not sympathise with him, I had no right to withhold from him the small portion of happiness which was yet in my power to bestow.

"You swear," I said, "to be harmless; but have you not already shown a degree of malice that should reasonably make me distrust you? May not even this be a feint that will increase your triumph by affording a wider scope for your revenge?"

"How is this? I must not be trifled with: and I demand an answer. If I have no ties and no affections, hatred and vice must be my portion; the love of another will destroy the cause of my crimes, and I shall become a thing, of whose existence every one will be ignorant. My vices are the children of a forced solitude that I abhor; and my virtues will necessarily arise when I live in communion with an equal. I shall feel the affections of a sensitive being, and become linked to the chain of existence and events, from which I am now excluded."

I paused some time to reflect on all he had related, and the various arguments which he had employed. I thought of the promise of virtues which he had displayed on the opening of his existence, and the subsequent blight of all kindly feeling by the loathing and scorn which his protectors had manifested towards him. His power and threats were not omitted in my calculations: a creature who could exist in the ice-caves of the glaciers, and hide himself from pursuit among the ridges of inaccessible precipices, was a being possessing faculties it would be vain to cope with. After a long pause of reflection, I concluded that the justice due both to him and my fellow-creatures demanded of me that I should comply with his request. Turning to him, therefore, I said –

"I consent to your demand, on your solemn oath to quit Europe for ever, and every other place in the neighbourhood of man, as soon as I shall deliver into your hands a female who will accompany you in your exile."

"I swear," he cried, "by the sun, and by the blue sky of Heaven, and by the fire of love that burns my heart, that if you grant my prayer, while they exist you shall never behold me again. Depart to your home, and commence your labours: I shall watch their progress with unutterable anxiety; and fear not but that when you are ready I shall appear."

Saying this, he suddenly quitted me, fearful, perhaps, of any change in my sentiments. I saw him descend the mountain with greater speed than the flight of an eagle, and quickly lost him among the undulations of the sea of ice.

[. . .]

I sat one evening in my laboratory; the sun had set, and the moon was just rising from the sea; I had not sufficient light for my employment, and I remained idle, in a pause of consideration of whether I should leave my labour for the night, or hasten its conclusion by an unremitting attention to it. As I sat, a train of reflection occurred to me, which led me to consider the effects of what I was now doing. Three years before I was engaged in the same manner, and had created a fiend whose unparalleled barbarity had desolated my heart, and filled it for ever with the bitterest remorse. I was now about to form another being, of whose dispositions I was alike ignorant; she might become ten thousand times more malignant than her mate, and delight, for its own sake, in murder and wretchedness. He had sworn to quit the neighbourhood of man, and hide himself in deserts; but she had not; and she, who in all probability was to become a thinking and reasoning animal, might refuse to comply with a compact made before her creation. They might even hate each other; the creature who already lived loathed his own deformity, and might he not conceive a greater abhorrence for it when it came before his eyes in the female form? She also might turn with disgust from him to the superior beauty of man; she might quit him, and he be again alone, exasperated by the fresh provocation of being deserted by one of his own species.

Even if they were to leave Europe, and inhabit the deserts of the new world, yet one of the first results of those sympathies for which the dæmon thirsted would be children, and a race of devils would be propagated upon the earth, who might make the very existence of the species of man a condition precarious and full of terror. Had I a right, for my own benefit, to inflict this curse upon everlasting generations? I had before been moved by the sophisms of the being I had created; I had been struck senseless by his fiendish threats: but now, for the first time, the wickedness of my promise burst upon me; I shuddered to think that future ages might curse me as their pest, whose selfishness had not hesitated to buy its own peace at the price, perhaps, of the existence of the whole human race.

I trembled, and my heart failed within me; when, on looking up, I saw, by the light of the moon, the dæmon at the casement. A ghastly grin wrinkled his lips as he gazed on me, where I sat fulfilling the task which he had allotted to me. Yes, he had followed me in my travels; he had loitered in forests, hid himself in caves, or taken refuge in wide and desert heaths; and he now came to mark my progress, and claim the fulfilment of my promise.

As I looked on him, his countenance expressed the utmost extent of malice and treachery. I thought with a sensation of madness on my promise of creating another like to him, and trembling with passion, tore to pieces the thing on which I was engaged. The wretch saw me destroy the creature on whose future existence he depended for happiness, and, with a howl of devilish despair and revenge, withdrew.

I left the room, and, locking the door, made a solemn vow in my own heart never to resume my labours; and then, with trembling steps, I sought my own apartment. I was alone; none were near me to dissipate the gloom, and relieve me from the sickening oppression of the most terrible reveries.

63

KAREL ČAPEK

The Makropulos Secret

The Makropulos Secret was first produced in 1922. In this final scene from the play, the famous singer Emilia Marty (really Elina Makropulos) has been drugged and has revealed her long-kept secret.

DR KOLENATY (*making sure both doors are closed and locked*): And now, gentlemen, put your brains to work. What are we going to do with it?

GREGOR: With what?

DR KOLENATY: With the Makropulos formula. Somewhere very nearby is a recipe for 300 years of life. We can lay our hands on it very easily.

PRUS: It is in her bosom.

DR KOLENATY (*shrugs*): That is hardly a major problem, gentlemen. Here is a thing . . . of unimaginable importance. What are we going to do with it?

GREGOR: You're not going to do a goddam thing with it. The formula belongs to me. I am her heir.

DR KOLENATY: Think! As long as she is alive, you are not an heir, and she can live for another 300 years if she wants to. But we can get hold of it. Do you follow me?

GREGOR: By theft.

DR KOLENATY: If necessary. But this is something of such importance . . . for us . . . for the entire human race, that . . . hmmm. Gentlemen, you do understand me? Are we to leave it to her? Should she be the only one who profits from it? She, or some kind of a crook like that Bombita person? Who will get it?

GREGOR: First of all, her descendants.

DR KOLENATY: Well, we certainly can find a lot of those! Don't count on getting it for yourself. Let's take Prus, here. If you had that formula in your hands, would you lend it to me? You know, so I could live for 300 years?

PRUS: Certainly not.

KAREL ČAPEK, *The Makropulos Secret* (tr. Yveta Synek Graff and Robert T. Jones), pp. 167–77 from Peter Kussi (ed.), *Toward the Radical Center, A Karel Čapek Reader.* Highland Park, NJ: Catbird Press, 1990. Reprinted by permission of the publisher and the translators.

Dr Kolenaty: So you see, gentlemen. We have to come to some understanding between ourselves. What are we going to do with it?

Vitek (*gets up*): We will make it public, this Makropulos formula.

Dr Kolenaty: I hope nothing that foolish.

Vitek: We will give it to everybody, to all humanity! Everybody, but everybody, has the same right to life. God, we live such a short time. It means so little to be a human being!

Dr Kolenaty: None of this matters.

Vitek: But it does! It is a matter for weeping! Just think: the human soul, the thirst for knowledge, the intellect, the work, love, creativity, everything! My God, what can a man do in a mere sixty years of life? How much can he enjoy? How much can he learn? He can't even harvest the fruit from the tree he plants. He never learns what his ancestors knew. He dies before he begins to live! God in Heaven, we live so briefly!

Dr Kolenaty: Really, Vitek . . .

Vitek: We don't have time for happiness, or even thinking. We don't have time for anything but this eternal scratching for a piece of bread. We never see anything, never know anything, never learn anything, never complete anything – not even ourselves. We are just fragments of something else. Why do we live? Is it worth it?

Dr Kolenaty: Are you trying to make me cry?

Vitek: We die like animals. What is life after death? Immortality of the soul? Only a desperate protest against the shortness of life. Man has never accepted this animal part of life. He cannot accept it because it is too unjust to live for such a short time. A man should be a little more than a turtle or a raven. A man needs more time to live. Sixty years! That is serfdom. It is weakness, an animal life, ignorance.

Hauk-Sendorf: And already I'm seventy-six.

Vitek: Let's give everybody 300 years of life! This will be the greatest event since the creation. It will be a liberation and a new beginning. God, what can be done with a man in 300 years! Fifty years to be a child and a student, fifty years to understand the world, a hundred years to work and be useful, then a hundred years to be wise and understanding, to rule, to teach and give example! Oh, how valuable would a human life be if it lasted 300 years! There would be no wars, no more of that dreadful hunt for bread, no fear, no selfishness. Everyone would have dignity and wisdom. (*He clasps his hands in ecstasy.*) How sovereign and perfect man would be, a real son of God and no longer just a miscarriage of God's justice. Let us give people life! Let us give them a full and long human life!

Dr Kolenaty: Bravo, Vitek, bravo. That was very nice. Very nice indeed.

Gregor (*interrupting*): Thank you very much. 300 years to be a filing clerk. 300 years to knit stockings!

Vitek: But . . .

Gregor: To be powerful and knowing . . . when most human occupations are bearable only because of ignorance.

Dr Kolenaty: You had better realize, Vitek, that all you have said is legally and economically ridiculous. Our social system is founded upon a brief life span:

contracts, pensions, insurance policies, salaries, inheritance laws, and I don't know what all. And marriage! Ha! Nobody would get married for 300 years! Nobody would make any kind of commitment for 300 years! You! You are an anarchist! You want to topple all our social systems!

HAUK-SENDORF: And . . . permit me . . . then after 300 years everybody could get young all over again.

DR KOLENATY: . . . and, in fact, live forever. Such a thing is simply impossible.

VITEK: Please, that could be forbidden. After 300 years, everybody would have to die.

DR KOLENATY: Marvelous. He loves humanity so much that he wants to condemn everybody to death!

HAUK-SENDORF: Excuse me. I . . . I think that the secret could be divided into doses.

DR KOLENATY: Doses?

HAUK-SENDORF: Well, understand me, divided into years. One dose would equal ten years of life. 300 years is a little too much. Not everybody would want that. But ten years, everybody would buy that, wouldn't they?

DR KOLENATY (*drawing out the word*): B-u-y? We could start a business with years. What an idea! I can just see it: "Send immediately: 1,200 years of life, in your best gift wrap. Kohn and Company." "Send express, two million years, top quality, luxury wrapping, FOB Vienna." Hauk, it's a great idea.

HAUK-SENDORF: Please, I am not a businessman. I . . . you know? But when one gets older, it would be nice to buy . . . a little extra . . . but 300 years is too much. No?

VITEK: For self-improvement, no.

HAUK-SENDORF: Nobody wants to buy ten years of self-improvement. But ten years of pleasure? Yes. Definitely yes.

MAID (*entering*): Here is the prescription, sir.

DR KOLENATY: Thank you. How long would you like to go on living?

MAID: Me? (*She giggles.*): Oh, another thirty years.

DR KOLENATY: No more?

MAID: Oh no, sir. What would I do with it?

DR KOLENATY: You see, Vitek?

(MAID *leaves.* DR KOLENATY *knocks on the bedroom door. The* DOCTOR *opens it.*)

DOCTOR: Yes? Oh, good. (*He takes the prescription.*)

HAUK-SENDORF: How is Madame Marty?

DOCTOR: Sick. (*He goes back into the bedroom and shuts the door.*)

HAUK-SENDORF: Poor girl.

PRUS (*rising*): Gentlemen, a strange chain of events has placed in our hands a certain secret. It concerns the indefinite prolongation of life. Let's assume that it works, that it is possible. None of us, I trust, is thinking of using it for himself.

VITEK: I should say not! We must prolong life for all humanity!

PRUS: No, only for the strong. The life of the most capable. For the mediocre human mob, even the life of an ephemera is too long.

VITEK: Oh, permit me!

PRUS: Please, I do not want to argue. But, if I may: the ordinary, small, stupid human being never dies. A small person is everlasting, even without your help. Smallness multiplies without rest, like flies or mice. Only greatness dies. Only strength and talent die, because they cannot be replaced. It may be in our grasp to keep that alive. We can begin an aristocracy of the everlasting.

VITEK: An aristocracy! You hear that? The privilege of life!

PRUS: Correct. Only the best are important in life. Only the leaders, only productive, efficient men. I don't even talk about women. But there are in this world about ten or twenty thousand men who are irreplaceable. We can preserve them. In these men we can develop superhuman brains and supernormal powers. We can breed ten or twenty thousand supermen, leaders and creators.

VITEK: A race of supermen!

PRUS: Exactly. Choice men who have the right to unlimited life.

DR KOLENATY: And tell me, if you will, who is going to choose the chosen? Governments? Voters? The Swedish Academy?

PRUS: No stupid voting. From hand to hand they would pass on life, the strongest to the strongest. Masters of the material to masters of the mind. Inventors to soldiers, builders to despots. It would be a dynasty of the masters of life, a dynasty that would not depend on any kind of mob opinion.

VITEK: Until the mob decides to claim its own right to life!

PRUS: Let them. Revolution is the privilege of all slaves, but the right to life is not. A few people will have to be killed from time to time. That is of no importance. After all, the only progress in the world is the progression from small and weak despots to big and strong ones. Look at it this way: a long and privileged life will be the despotism of the chosen – that is, the rule of reason. Superhuman authority given by superhuman knowledge and ability. The long-living would become the natural leaders of nations. You have it in your hands, gentlemen. You can use it, or you can abuse it. I have finished. (*He sits down.*)

DR KOLENATY: Hmmm. Do I belong to those chosen ones, just for example? Do I? Does Gregor?

PRUS: I'm afraid not.

GREGOR: But you do.

PRUS: After today, no.

GREGOR: Let's stop this talking. The Makropulos formula is owned by the Makropulos family, and that's all there is to it. Let them do what they want with it.

VITEK: And what is that, please?

GREGOR: Whatever the descendants of Elina Makropulos decide.

DR KOLENATY: And they will live forever, because they were born to some vagrant baron and some hysterical soprano. This family inheritance is something outrageous.

GREGOR: That's none of your concern.

DR KOLENATY: We are lucky enough to know one gentleman from that family. He is, you will forgive me, my dear sir – and may he be damned – a useless, lazy person. From a "fine" family.

GREGOR: That is your opinion. But we may be fools, or baboons, or depraved and overweight and crippled, helpless idiots or anything you say. We may be as evil as Satan himself, but that doesn't change a thing. We own the Makropulos formula. And that, my friend, is that.

DR KOLENATY: Incredible.

DOCTOR (*coming out of the bedroom*): She is all right now. Let her sleep.

HAUK-SENDORF: Yes, yes. Sleep. That is good for her.

DOCTOR: Come home now, Mr. Hauk-Sendorf. I will take you.

HAUK-SENDORF: But we are having a most important discussion here, isn't that so? Please let me stay a little longer. I . . . I . . . surely . . .

DOCTOR: Well, somebody is waiting for you outside. No more fooling around, old man, or . . . well, I'll be waiting. (*He leaves.*)

DR KOLENATY: Gregor. Did you mean what you just said?

GREGOR: I certainly did.

KRISTA (*coming out of the bedroom*): Keep your voices down. She needs to sleep.

DR KOLENATY: Kristinka, dear. Come here. Would you like to live for 300 years?

KRISTA: No.

DR KOLENATY: And if you had a formula for such a long life, what would you do with it?

KRISTA: I have no idea.

VITEK: You would give it to all the world, wouldn't you?

KRISTA: I don't know. Would the world be happier if everyone lived such a long time?

DR KOLENATY: Little girl, no matter what anyone says, life is still a very great happiness.

KRISTA: No . . . I don't know. Don't ask me.

HAUK-SENDORF: Oh Miss Kristina, one does want so much to live!

KRISTA (*hiding her eyes*): Sometimes one does . . . and sometimes . . . not.

PRUS (*after a pause*): Thank you. For Janek.

KRISTA: Why?

PRUS: For thinking of him now.

KRISTA: Thinking of him? How can I think of anything else?

DR KOLENATY: And here we are quarreling about eternal life.

(EMILIA *comes out of the bedroom like a shadow, with her head in compresses. Everyone stands.*)

EMILIA: Forgive me for . . . leaving you . . . for a little . . .

GREGOR: How are you feeling?

EMILIA: My head hurts. Dreadfully.

HAUK-SENDORF: Oh, that will soon go away.

EMILIA: It will not. It will never go away. I have had it for 200 years.

DR KOLENATY: What have you had?

EMILIA: Boredom. No, it isn't even boredom. It is . . . it is . . . oh, you people, you have no name for it. No language on earth has a name for it. Bombita talked about it too. It is horrible.

GREGOR: What is it?

EMILIA: I don't know. Everything is so pointless, so empty, so meaningless. You are all here? It seems as if you are not. As if you are only things . . . or shadows . . . What am I to do with you?

DR KOLENATY: Perhaps we should leave you alone?

EMILIA: It doesn't really matter. To die, or just to hide behind a door, it's all the same. Everything is the same, whether it is, or is not. And you people make so much fuss about every little death! You are so funny. Ah . . .

VITEK: What is wrong?

EMILIA: One should not, should not, should not live so long!

VITEK: But why not?

EMILIA: One cannot stand it. For 100, 130 years, one can go on. But then . . . then . . . one finds out . . . that . . . and then one's soul dies.

VITEK: One finds out what?

EMILIA: God, there are no words for it. One finds out that one cannot believe in anything. Anything. And from that comes this cold emptiness. You know, Berti, you said that I sing as if I were frozen. You see, art only has meaning when one does not know everything. Once you know it all, know it completely, you realize that art is useless. It is all in vain, Krista, all in vain. To sing is the same as to be silent. There is no difference.

VITEK: That's not true. When you sing, people are moved to higher and better things.

EMILIA: People are never better. Nothing can ever be changed. Nothing, nothing, nothing ever really matters. If at this moment there were to be shooting or an earthquake or the end of the world, or whatever, still nothing would matter. Even I do not matter. You are here, and I am very far away . . . from every-thing . . . 300 years! Oh God, if you knew how easy it is for you to live!

DR KOLENATY: Why?

EMILIA: You are so near to everything! For you, everything has meaning. For you, everything has value because for the few years that you are here, you don't have time to live enough. God, if I could only once more . . . (*She wrings her hands.*) Idiots! You are so happy! You disgust me with your incessant happiness. And all because of this silly chance, that you are going to die soon! Everything interests you – you're like monkeys! You believe in everything: in love, in yourselves, in honor, in progress, in humanity, I don't know what all. Maxi, you believe in pleasure. You, Krista, in love and faithfulness. Prus believes in power. You, Vitek, believe in foolishness. Everybody, everybody believes in something. You can live happily, you . . . fools!

VITEK (*excited*): Excuse me, please, but there are still higher values . . . ideals . . . aspirations . . .

EMILIA: There are, but only for you. How can I explain it to you? There may be love, but only for you. As soon as love has gone from your minds, then it is nowhere, nowhere in the whole universe. And no one can love for 300 years – it cannot last. And then everything tires one. It tires one to be good, it tires one to be bad. The earth itself tires one. And then you find out that there is nothing at all: no sin, no pain, no earth, nothing. The only thing that exists is a thing with meaning, and for you all things have meaning. My God, I was once like you. I was a girl, I was a woman, I was happy. I . . . I . . . was a human. God in Heaven!

HAUK-SENDORF: What is it? What happened to you?

EMILIA: If you only knew what Bombita told me! We . . . we old ones . . . we know too much. But you know much more than us, you fools, infinitely more! You know love, greatness, purpose. You have it all. You could not wish for anything more. You live, but in us all life has stopped. Pater hemon! And it goes on, goes on, goes on. Ah, this terrible loneliness.

PRUS: Then why did you come here for the Makropulos formula? Why do you want to have another 300 years?

EMILIA: Because I am afraid of death.

PRUS: Then not even the immortals are spared that?

EMILIA: They are not.

(Long pause.)

PRUS: Elina Makropulos, we have been cruel to you.

EMILIA: I do not feel that. And you were right. It is undignified to be so old. Do you know that children are frightened of me? Krista, you loathe me, don't you?

KRISTA: No. I am . . . very sorry for you.

EMILIA: Sorry? That's all you feel for me? You don't even envy me? *(She pauses and takes the folded parchment from her bosom.)* Here it is written: "Ego Hieronymus Makropulos, iatres kaisaros Rodolfo . . ." And so on, and so on. Word after word. Exactly what to do. *(She rises.)* Take it, Berti. I don't want it anymore.

GREGOR: Thank you. But I don't want it either.

EMILIA: No? Then you, Maxi. You love to live. You will be able to love, you know? Take it.

HAUK-SENDORF: Please . . . can one die from it? And it hurts when . . . when it works?

EMILIA: Yes, it hurts. Are you afraid?

HAUK-SENDORF: Yes.

EMILIA: But you will live for 300 years!

HAUK-SENDORF: If . . . if it did not hurt. *(He giggles nervously.)* I don't want it.

EMILIA: Doctor, you are a knowledgeable man. You will consider . . . what it might be useful for. Do you want it?

DR KOLENATY: You are very kind. I want nothing to do with it.

EMILIA: You are a foolish little man. Vitek, I will give it to you. Who knows? You might make all humanity happier with it.

VITEK *(backing away)*: No, please. I think . . . that . . . that . . . it is better not.

EMILIA: Prus, you are such a strong person. Are you also afraid to live 300 years?

PRUS: Yes.

EMILIA: I cannot believe this. Nobody wants it? Nobody cares for it? What about you, Krista? You haven't made a sound. My dear girl, I took your lover from you

---

Pater hemon – Our Father – the beginning of the Lord's Prayer

— you take it. You are beautiful, you will live for 300 years. You will sing like
Emilia Marty. You will be famous. Think about it. In a few short years, you will
begin to grow old, and then you will be sorry. Take it, child.

KRISTA *(takes the paper)*: Thank you.

VITEK: What will you do with it, Krista?

KRISTA *(opening the document)*: I don't know.

GREGOR: Are you going to try it?

DR KOLENATY: Good Lord, she isn't afraid? Give it back!

VITEK: Give it back to her!

EMILIA: Let her be!

(KRISTA silently places the paper over the burning candle.)

VITEK: Don't burn it! It is a historical document!

DR KOLENATY: Careful!

HAUK-SENDORF: Good God.

PRUS *(holds them all back)*: Let her deal with it herself.

(A stunned silence.)

HAUK-SENDORF: Look at that. It doesn't want to burn.

GREGOR: It's parchment.

DR KOLENATY: How slowly it's getting black. Don't burn yourself, Krista.

HAUK-SENDORF: Let me have just a little piece! Just a little piece!

(Silence.)

VITEK: Everlasting Life. Mankind will always be searching for it. And
here . . . here . . . we may have held it . . .

DR KOLENATY: And we might have lived forever.

PRUS: Eternal life. Do you have any children?

DR KOLENATY: I have.

PRUS: So there you are: Eternal Life. If we only thought of birth instead of
death . . . Life is not so short, so long as we can be the cause of new life.

GREGOR: It's burning out. After all, it was a wild idea, to live forever. God, I feel
lonely, but a bit lighter, knowing it isn't possible anymore . . .

DR KOLENATY: We're no longer young, any of us. Only youth could burn such a
thing so fearlessly. You did well, child.

HAUK-SENDORF: Excuse me, but there is such a strange smell in here . . . a smell
like . . .

VITEK *(opening a window)*: Like burning.

EMILIA *(laughs)*: The end of immortality!

PART THREE

REFLECTING ON ETHICS

XIII

THE NATURE OF ETHICS

M any societies resort to myth or story to explain the origins of ethics. In these myths it is usually God, or the gods, who hands humans a set of ethical rules. The biblical account of God giving the Ten Commandments to Moses on Mount Sinai is one example. Plato, in his *Protagoras*, tells of the myth that Zeus pitied humans, for they lacked the strong teeth and claws of other beasts, and did not even have the speed to get away from them. So Zeus gave humans a moral sense and the capacity for law and justice, which made it possible for them to combine their individual strength and work cooperatively in larger communities. (Some of the problems with religious accounts of the origins of ethics have already been discussed in Section XI.) In E. Pauline Johnson's re-telling of the Native American story of the sea-serpent, we have an interesting reversal of the usual myth, for here a more harmonious social existence is taken as self-evident, and it is the existence of greed that has to be explained.

In addition to these mythical accounts, for at least 2,500 years philosophers have discussed and written about the nature of ethics. Plato himself was evidently not content with the account he offered in *Protagoras*, for in other works he offers a variety of different possibilities. In *The Republic* alone, we have three different possibilities. Thrasymachus insists that "justice" is a kind of fraud that the strong perpetrate against the weak, so as to persuade them that they should act in ways that are not in their own interests, but are in the interests of those who have concocted this idea. Glaucon, on the other hand, offers a precursor to the social contract theory developed later by Thomas Hobbes and John Locke. He sees the origin of justice in an agreement that is in everyone's interests. Each of us agrees not to rob, assault, or kill others, in return for everyone doing the same. Socrates, obviously speaking for Plato, does not accept this account of justice as a social convention, for, on Glaucon's view, the reason for acting justly is that I will be punished in some way for breaking the agreement. Socrates wants a view that gives everyone a reason for doing what is just, independently of whether others come to know what they have done and are able to reward or punish them for it. He argues that justice is having the different parts of our nature in harmony, and it is only by living in this way that we can have a happy and successful life.

The eighteenth-century French philosopher Rousseau views ethics as the outcome of natural feelings, such as benevolence and sympathy for others. He presents us with the classic portrait of the "noble savage," a human being whose simple needs are satisfied by the bounty of nature, and who has no cause to quarrel with the other inhabitants of his forest. Indeed, these "savages" are, for Rousseau, anything but savage; their innate feelings of compassion make them naturally ethical beings. In Rousseau's view it is civilization, and particularly the introduction of property, that introduces evil into the world. The Native American Chief in E. Pauline Johnson's story of the sea-serpent would agree. So might Mark Twain. Huck Finn's natural instincts are much better than his conscience, which has been formed by the time and place in which he has grown up.

Today the most plausible account of the origins of ethics starts with an evolutionary understanding of our behavior, allowing a role for culture and for our capacity for reason. We know that morality is not entirely a matter of human culture, for we share some elements of it with other social mammals, especially with primates. It is common for them to have strong ties between kin, and to reciprocate favors. They even show signs of an elementary sense of justice. Chimpanzees become angry when someone to whom they have done a favor does not return the favor when circumstances make it appropriate to do so. Capuchin monkeys resent receiving a lesser reward than another monkey for doing the same task.[1] Starting with these patterns of primate behavior, and given our superior powers of reasoning and communicating, it is not difficult to see how ethics has developed.

Though we now have a better understanding of the origins of ethics than earlier philosophers, many views about the nature of ethics remain contentious. One of them is Socrates' claim that justice is necessary for a happy and successful life. Can we be confident that someone like Harry Lime in Graham Greene's *The Third Man* will not benefit from his ill-gotten gains? If Lime lacks the benevolent and sympathetic feelings most of us have, is there any further argument that can cogently persuade him to care about others?

Another longstanding debate is whether our ethical judgments are inextricably bound up with our own culture. The Greek historian Herodotus tells how Darius, King of Persia, once asked some Greeks how much he would have to pay to induce them to eat their fathers' dead bodies. They were shocked by the question. They insisted that no sum would suffice: the bodies of their fathers must be cremated. Darius then called in some Indians, whose custom it was to eat the bodies of their parents, and asked them what amount they wanted to burn their fathers' bodies. The Indians implored Darius not to mention so horrid a deed.

That story is relevant to Robinson Crusoe's reasoning when he encounters cannibals. Should we simply say that what is "right" is always relative to a particular culture and, since no-one can judge from a standpoint independent of all cultures, when cultures differ, there is no way to judge between them? In the late nineteenth and early twentieth century, many anthropologists supported cultural relativism as a bulwark against the arrogance of European imperialism. They did so by holding that since morality is relative to culture, no culture can have any basis for regarding its morality as superior to any other culture. Although this view may have been adopted for admirable motives, it has implications that few would want to embrace. Cultural relativism in ethics means that when people from two different cultures disagree about an ethical issue, it is impossible to say that one is right and the other is wrong. They are each simply reporting the views of their own culture, and both sides may be doing this quite accurately. This holds not only for the standards of sexual behavior that missionaries sought to impose on so-called "primitive" cultures, but also for such culturally diverse practices as female genital mutilation, slavery, and the burning of widows on the funeral pyres of their husbands.

These examples are enough to show how unpalatable ethical relativism is; but in fact the position as usually stated is not only unpalatable, but incoherent too. Ethical relativists have typically wanted to say: "It is wrong for one culture to impose its values on another." Since this is itself an ethical judgment, it can only purport to state the ethical views of the culture to which the anthropologist belongs. In many cultures – including those of nineteenth-century Europe, home to many of the anthropologists who made such statements – this may well not even have been an accurate description of the views of the anthropologist's own culture. Suppose, however, that in our culture we do hold that it is wrong to impose our values on another culture. If there is another culture that holds that it has an obligation to spread its values to all parts of the globe, we will be unable to argue to members of that culture that our more tolerant view is ethically superior. All we will be able to say is – tautologously – that we hold our view and they hold a different view. An understanding of these objections means that today few philosophers are cultural relativists, but the rise of postmodernist thinking, with its critique of the universalist ideas of the Enlightenment, has made relativism more popular among students of literary theory and culture, who are often unaware of how uncongenial and paradoxical the implications of relativism really are.

Some philosophers hold that ethics is entirely a matter of subjective, rather than cultural, preferences, but this view has trouble in explaining how reasoning can play any role at all in ethics. The Oxford philosopher R. M. Hare has put forward a more promising account. Starting from Hume's idea that ethical judgments are intended to move us to action, and cannot be statements of fact, he suggested that ethical judgments should be seen as a special kind of imperative. A command such as "Please shut the door" does not describe anything, and so it would be odd to respond by saying "That's true" or "That's false." Nevertheless, Hare argues, we can reason about ethical judgments because they must be universalizable. If I make an ethical judgment, I must be prepared to state it in universal terms, and apply it to all relevantly similar situations. I must put myself in the position of all those affected by it and see if I would still be able to accept that judgment if I were to occupy these positions. For example, if the villagers of Eyam in the circumstances described in Geraldine Brooks' *Year of Wonders* (Section VI) want to know whether they ought to stay in the village despite the high risk of catching the Plague, they should put themselves in the position of all those who may be affected by the Plague if they leave the village, and weigh that against their own interests – and those of their families – in leaving. Doing so is likely to lead to the conclusion that, if they were to live the lives of all those affected, they would prefer the villagers to remain isolated in Eyam. That is, then, what the villagers ought to do.

To decide on the right thing to do is a process that requires factual information, empathy, and reasoning.

The moral horrors of the twentieth century have challenged the idea that humans are inherently ethical beings. The Nazi extermination camps, described here from the inside in Tadeusz Borowski's short story, seem almost a purpose-built challenge to the idea that ethics puts constraints on what humans can do to each other. But perhaps what they show is that for ethics to have a pull on us, we must feel that the "others" are sufficiently like ourselves to be able to put ourselves in their situation and take their interests into account. By putting Jews into the category of "sub-humans," the Nazis cut off empathy for them, and for ordinary Germans it became possible to think of Jews as Harry Lime thought of the "dots."

The camps can also be seen as a testing ground for the hypothesis that ethics is a luxury that is possible only when our own survival, or that of our close kin, is not at stake. As we saw earlier in this introduction, there are some who dismiss ethics and follow their own interests exclusively even when their survival is not at stake, so it is scarcely surprising that, in the camps, many prisoners acted with ruthless selfishness. Yet others went out of their way to help their fellow-prisoners, sharing food, taking risks for them, and choosing to die rather than abandon their ethical standards. The camps provide evidence, not that humans are inherently evil, but that they are diverse and their behavior is unpredictable.

NOTE

1   F. de Waal. *Chimpanzee Politics*, rev. edn, Baltimore: Johns Hopkins University Press, 1998; S. Brosnan and F. de Waal, "Monkeys Reject Unequal Pay," *Nature*, vol. 425 (2003), pp. 297–9.

64

E. PAULINE JOHNSON

The Sea-Serpent

There is one vice that is absolutely unknown to the red man; he was born without it, and amongst all the deplorable things he has learned from the white races, this, at least, he has never acquired. That is the vice of avarice. That the Indian looks upon greed of gain, miserliness, avariciousness, and wealth accumulated above the head of his poorer neighbour as one of the lowest degradations he can fall to is perhaps more aptly illustrated than anything I could quote to demonstrate his horror of what he calls "the white man's unkindness." In a very wide and varied experience with many tribes, I have yet to find even one instance of avarice, and I have encountered but one single case of a "stingy Indian," and this man was so marked amongst his fellows that at mention of his name his tribespeople jeered and would remark contemptuously that he was like a white man – hated to share his money and his possessions. All red races are born Socialists, and most tribes carry out their communistic ideas to the letter. Amongst the Iroquois it is considered disgraceful to have food if your neighbour has none. To be a creditable member of the nation you must divide your possessions with your less fortunate fellows. I find it much the same amongst the Coast Indians, though they are less bitter in their hatred of the extremes of wealth and poverty than are the Eastern tribes. Still, the very fact that they have preserved this legend, in which they liken avarice to a slimy sea-serpent, shows the trend of their ideas; shows, too, that an Indian is an Indian, no matter what his tribe; shows that he cannot, or will not, hoard money; shows that his native morals demand that the spirit of greed must be strangled at all cost.

The chief and I had sat long over our luncheon. He had been talking of his trip to England and of the many curious things he had seen. At last, in an outburst of enthusiasm, he said: "I saw everything in the world – everything but a sea-serpent!"

"But there is no such thing as a sea-serpent," I laughed, "so you must have really seen everything in the world."

His face clouded; for a moment he sat in silence; then, looking directly at me, said, "Maybe none now, but long ago there was one here – in the Inlet."

E. PAULINE JOHNSON, 'The Sea-Serpent,' pp. 245–7 from Karen L. Kilcup (ed.), *Native American Women's Writing c.1800–1924: An Anthology*. Oxford: Blackwell, 2000.

"How long ago?" I asked.

"When first the white gold-hunters came," he replied. "Came with greedy, clutching fingers, greedy eyes, greedy hearts. The white men fought, murdered, starved, went mad with love of that gold far up the Fraser River. Tillicums were tillicums no more, brothers were foes, fathers and sons were enemies. Their love of the gold was a curse."

"Was it then the sea-serpent was seen?" I asked, perplexed with the problem of trying to connect the goldseekers with such a monster.

"Yes, it was then, but –" he hesitated, then plunged into the assertion, "but you will not believe the story if you think there is no such thing as a sea-serpent."

"I shall believe whatever you tell me, Chief," I answered. "I am only too ready to believe. You know I come of a superstitious race, and all my association with the Pale-faces has never yet robbed me of my birthright to believe strange traditions."

"You always understand," he said after a pause.

"It's my heart that understands," I remarked quietly.

He glanced up quickly, and with one of his all too few radiant smiles, he laughed.

"Yes, skookum tum-tum." Then without further hesitation he told the tradition, which, although not of ancient happening, is held in great reverence by his tribe. During its recital he sat with folded arms, leaning on the table, his head and shoulders bending eagerly towards me as I sat at the opposite side. It was the only time he ever talked to me when he did not use emphasizing gesticulations, but his hands never once lifted: his wonderful eyes alone gave expression to what he called "The Legend of the 'Salt-chuck Oluk'" (sea-serpent).

"Yes, it was during the first gold craze, and many of our young men went as guides to the whites far up the Fraser. When they returned they brought these tales of greed and murder back with them, and our old people and our women shook their heads and said evil would come of it. But all our young men, except one, returned as they went – kind to the poor, kind to those who were foodless, sharing whatever they had with their tillicums. But one, by name Shak-shak (The Hawk), came back with hoards of gold nuggets, chickimin, everything; he was rich like the white men, and, like them, he kept it. He would count his chickimin, count his nuggets, gloat over them, toss them in his palms. He rested his head on them as he slept, he packed them about with him through the day. He loved them better than food, better than his tillicums, better than his life. The entire tribe arose. They said Shak-shak had the disease of greed; that to cure it he must give a great potlatch, divide his riches with the poorer ones, share them with the old, the sick, the foodless. But he jeered and laughed and told them No, and went on loving and gloating over his gold.

"Then the Sagalie Tyee spoke out of the sky and said, 'Shak-shak, you have made of yourself a loathsome thing; you will not listen to the cry of the hungry, to the call of the old and sick; you will not share your possessions; you have made of

---

tillicums – members of one's own tribe or people

chickimin – money

yourself an outcast from your tribe and disobeyed the ancient laws of your people. Now I will make of you a thing loathed and hated by all men, both white and red. You will have two heads, for your greed has two mouths to bite. One bites the poor, and one bites your own evil heart; and the fangs in these mouths are poison – poison that kills the hungry, and poison that kills your own manhood. Your evil heart will beat in the very centre of your foul body, and he that pierces it will kill the disease of greed for ever from amongst his people.' And when the sun arose above the North Arm the next morning the tribes-people saw a gigantic sea-serpent stretched across the surface of the waters. One hideous head rested on the bluffs at Brockton Point, the other rested on a group of rocks just below the Mission, at the western edge of North Vancouver. If you care to go there some day I will show you the hollow in one great stone where that head lay. The tribes-people were stunned with horror. They loathed the creature, they hated it, they feared it. Day after day it lay there, its monstrous heads lifted out of the waters, its mile-long body blocking all entrance from the Narrows, all outlet from the North Arm. The chiefs made council, the medicine-men danced and chanted, but the salt-chuck oluk never moved. It could not move, for it was the hated totem of what now rules the white man's world – greed and love of chickimin. No one can ever move the love of chickimin from the white man's heart, no one can ever make him divide all with the poor. But after the chiefs and medicine-men had done all in their power and still the salt-chuck oluk lay across the waters, a handsome boy of sixteen approached them and reminded them of the words of the Sagalie Tyee, 'that he that pierced the monster's heart would kill the disease of greed for ever amongst his people.'

"'Let me try to find this evil heart, oh! great men of my tribe,' he cried. 'Let me war upon this creature; let me try to rid my people of this pestilence.'

"The boy was brave and very beautiful. His tribes-people called him the Tenas Tyee (Little Chief) and they loved him. Of all his wealth of fish and furs, of game and hykwa (large shell-money) he gave to the boys who had none; he hunted food for the old people; he tanned skins and furs for those whose feet were feeble, whose eyes were fading, whose blood ran thin with age.

"'Let him go!' cried the tribes-people. 'This unclean monster can only be over-come by cleanliness, this creature of greed can only be overthrown by generosity. Let him go!' The chiefs and the medicine-men listened, then consented. 'Go,' they commanded, 'and fight this thing with your strongest weapons – cleanliness and generosity.'

"The Tenas Tyee turned to his mother. 'I shall be gone four days,' he told her, 'and I shall swim all that time. I have tried all my life to be generous, but the people say I must be clean also to fight this unclean thing. While I am gone put fresh furs on my bed every day, even if I am not here to lie on them; if I know my bed, my body, and my heart are all clean I can overcome this serpent.'

"'Your bed shall have fresh furs every morning,' his mother said simply.

"The Tenas Tyee then stripped himself, and, with no clothing save a buckskin belt into which he thrust his hunting-knife, he flung his lithe young body into the sea. But at the end of four days he did not return. Sometimes his people could see him swimming far out in midchannel, endeavouring to find the exact centre of the

serpent, where lay its evil, selfish heart; but on the fifth morning they saw him rise
out of the sea, climb to the summit of Brockton Point, and greet the rising sun
with outstretched arms. Weeks and months went by, still the Tenas Tyee would
swim daily searching for that heart of greed; and each morning the sunrise glinted
on his slender young copper-coloured body as he stood with outstretched arms at
the tip of Brockton Point, greeting the coming day and then plunging from the
summit into the sea.

"And at his home on the north shore his mother dressed his bed with fresh furs
each morning. The seasons drifted by; winter followed summer, summer followed
winter. But it was four years before the Tenas Tyee found the centre of the great
salt-chuck oluk and plunged his hunting-knife into its evil heart. In its death-
agony it writhed through the Narrows, leaving a trail of blackness on the waters.
Its huge body began to shrink, to shrivel; it became dwarfed and withered, until
nothing but the bones of its back remained, and they, sea-bleached and lifeless,
soon sank to the bed of the ocean leagues off from the run of land. But as the
Tenas Tyee swam homeward and his clean young body crossed through the black
stain left by the serpent, the waters became clear and blue and sparkling. He had
overcome even the trail of the salt-chuck oluk.

"When at last he stood in the doorway of his home he said, 'My mother, I could
not have killed the monster of greed amongst my people had you not helped me
by keeping one place for me at home fresh and clean for my return.'

"She looked at him as only mothers look. 'Each day, these four years, fresh furs
have I laid for your bed. Sleep now, and rest, oh! my Tenas Tyee,' she said."

The chief unfolded his arms, and his voice took another tone as he said, 'What do
you call that story – a legend?"

"The white people would call it an allegory," I answered. He shook his head.

"No savvy," he smiled.

I explained as simply as possible, and with his customary alertness he immediately understood. "That's right," he said. "That's what we say it means, we Squamish,
that greed is evil and not clean, like the salt-chuck oluk. That it must be stamped
out amongst our people, killed by cleanliness and generosity. The boy that over-
came the serpent was both these things."

What became of this splendid boy?" I asked.

"The Tenas Tyee? Oh! some of our old, old people say they sometimes see him
now, standing on Brockton Point, his bare young arms outstretched to the rising
sun," he replied.

"Have you ever seen him, Chief?" I questioned.

"No," he answered simply. But I have never heard such poignant regret as his
wonderful voice crowded into that single word.

65

DANIEL DEFOE

Robinson Crusoe

Robinson Crusoe tells of a man shipwrecked alone on an island. The story was based partly on the memoirs of voyagers and castaways such as Alexander Selkirk. When first published in 1719, it was presented as being "written by himself," as if Crusoe were a real person. It is sometimes said to be the first novel in the English language.

Crusoe has discovered that the far side of his island is occasionally visited by people from a neighboring island, who come in order to kill, cook, and feast on other humans, apparently captives they have taken in war.

For Night and Day, I could think of nothing but how I might destroy some of these Monsters in their cruel bloody Entertainment, and if possible, save the Victim they should bring hither to destroy. It would take up a larger Volume than this whole Work is intended to be, to set down all the Contrivances I hatch'd, or rather brooded upon in my Thought, for the destroying these Creatures, or at least frightening them, so as to prevent their coming hither any more; but all was abortive, nothing could be possible to take effect, unless I was to be there to do it my self; and what could one Man do among them, when perhaps there might be twenty or thirty of them together, with their Darts, or their Bows and Arrows, with which they could shoot as true to a Mark, as I could with my Gun?

Sometimes I contriv'd to dig a Hole under the Place where they made their Fire, and put in five or six Pound of Gun-Powder, which when they kindled their Fire, would consequently take Fire, and blow up all that was near it: but as in the first place I should be very loth to wast so much Powder upon them, my Store being now within the Quantity of one Barrel; so neither could I be sure of its going off, at any certain Time; when it might surprise them, and at best, that it would do little more than just blow the Fire about their Ears and fright them, but not sufficient to make them forsake the Place; so I laid it aside, and then propos'd, that I would place my self in Ambush, in some convenient Place, with my three Guns, all double loaded; and in the middle of their bloody Ceremony, let fly at them,

---

DANIEL DEFOE, from Part V of *Robinson Crusoe*, first published in 1719.

when I should be sure to kill or wound perhaps two or three at every shoot; and then falling in upon them with my three Pistols, and my Sword, I made no doubt, but that if there was twenty I should kill them all: This Fancy pleas'd my Thoughts for some Weeks, and I was so full of it, that I often dream'd of it; and sometimes that I was just going to let fly at them in my Sleep.

I went so far with it in my Imagination, that I employ'd my self several Days to find out proper Places to put my self in Ambuscade, as I said, to watch for them; and I went frequently to the Place it self, which was now grown more familiar to me; and especially while my Mind was thus fill'd with Thoughts of Revenge, and of a bloody putting twenty or thirty of them to the Sword, as I may call it; the Horror I had at the Place, and at the Signals of the barbarous Wretches devouring one another, abated my Malice.

Well, at length I found a Place in the Side of the Hill, where I was satisfy'd I might securely wait, till I saw any of their Boats coming, and might then, even before they would be ready to come on Shore, convey my self unseen into Thickets of Trees, in one of which there was a Hollow large enough to conceal me entirely; and where I might sit and observe all their bloody Doings, and take my full aim at their Heads, when they were so close together, as that it would be next to impossible that I should miss my Shoot, or that I could fail wounding three or four of them at the first Shoot.

In this Place then I resolv'd to fix my Design, and accordingly I prepar'd two Muskets, and my ordinary Fowling Piece. The two Muskets I loaded with a Brace of Slugs each, and four or five smaller Bullets, about the Size of Pistol Bullets; and the Fowling Piece I loaded with near a Handful of Swan-shot, of the largest Size; I also loaded my Pistols with about four Bullets each, and in this Posture, well provided with Ammunition for a second and third Charge, I prepar'd my self for my Expedition.

After I had thus laid the Scheme of my Design, and in my Imagination put it in Practice, I continually made my Tour every Morning up to the Top of the Hill, which was from my Castle, as I call'd it, about three Miles, or more, to see if I cou'd observe any Boats upon the Sea, coming near the Island, or standing over towards it; but I began to tire of this hard Duty; after I had for two or three Months constantly kept my Watch; but came always back without any Discovery, there having not in all that Time been the least Appearance, not only on, or near the Shore; but not on the whole Ocean, so far as my Eyes or Glasses could reach every Way.

As long as I kept up my daily Tour to the Hill, to look out; so long also I kept up the Vigour of my Design, and my Spirits seem'd to be all the while in a suitable Form, for so outragious an Execution as the killing twenty or thirty naked Savages, for an Offence which I had not at all entred into a Discussion of in my Thoughts, any farther than my Passions were at first fir'd by the Horror I conceiv'd at the unnatural Custom of that People of the Country, who it seems had been suffer'd by Providence in his wise Disposition of the World, to have no other Guide than that of their own abominable and vitiated Passions; and consequently were left, and perhaps had been so for some Ages, to act such horrid Things, and receive such dreadful Customs, as nothing but Nature entirely abandon'd of Heaven, and acted by some hellish Degeneracy, could have run them into: But now, when as I have said, I began to be weary of the fruitless Excursion, which I had made so long, and so far, every Morning in vain, so my Opinion of the Action it self began to alter, and I began with cooler and calmer Thoughts to consider what it was I was going to engage in. What Authority, or Call I had, to pretend to be Judge and Executioner upon these Men as Criminals, whom Heaven had thought fit for so many Ages to suffer unpunish'd, to go on, and to be as it were, the Executioners of his Judgments one upon another. How far these People were Offenders against me, and what Right I had to engage in the Quarrel of that Blood, which they shed promiscuously one upon another. I debated this very often with my self thus; How do I know what God himself judges in this particular Case; it is certain these People either do not commit this as a Crime; it is not against their own Consciences reproving, or their Light reproaching them. They do not know it be an Offence, and then commit it in Defiance of Divine Justice, as we do in almost all the Sins we commit, They think it no more a Crime to kill a Captive taken in War, than we do to kill an Ox; nor to eat humane Flesh, than we do to eat Mutton.

When I had consider'd this a little, it follow'd necessarily, that I was certainly in the Wrong in it, that these People were not Murtherers, in the Sense that I had before condemn'd them, in my Thoughts; any more than those Christians were Murtherers, who often put to Death the Prisoners taken in Battle; or more frequently, upon many Occasions, put whole Troops of Men to the Sword, without giving Quarter, though they threw down their Arms and submitted.

In the next Place it occurr'd to me, that albeit the Usage they thus gave one another, was thus brutish and inhumane; yet it was really nothing to me: These People had done me no Injury. That if they attempted me, or I saw it necessary for my immediate Preservation to fall upon them, something might be said for it; but that as I was yet out of their Power, and they had really no Knowledge of me, and consequently no Design upon me; and therefore it could not be just for me to fall upon them. That this would justify the Conduct of the *Spaniards* in all their Barbarities practis'd in *America*, where they destroy'd Millions of these People, who however they were Idolaters and Barbarians, and had several bloody and barbarous Rites in their Customs, such as sacrificing human Bodies to their Idols, were yet, as to the *Spaniards*, very innocent People; and that the rooting them out of the Country, is spoken of with the utmost Abhorrence and Detestation, by even the *Spaniards* themselves, at this Time; and by all other Christian Nations of *Europe*, as a meer Butchery, a bloody and unnatural Piece of Cruelty, unjustifiable either to God or Man; and such, as for which the very Name of a *Spaniard* is reckon'd to be frightful and terrible to all People of Humanity, or of Christian Compassion: As if the Kingdom of *Spain* were particularly Eminent for the Product of a Race of Men, who were without Principles of Tenderness, or the common Bowels of Pity to the Miserable, which is reckon'd to be a Mark of generous Temper in the Mind.

These Considerations really put me to a Pause, and to a kind of a Full-stop; and I began by little and little to be off of my Design, and to conclude, I had taken wrong Measures in my Resolutions to attack the Savages; that it was not my Business to meddle with them, unless they first attack'd me, and this it was my Business if possible to prevent; but that if I were discover'd, and attack'd, then I knew my Duty.

66

MARK TWAIN

The Adventures of Huckleberry Finn

Set in the time before the American Civil War, *The Adventures of Huckleberry Finn* is a sequel to *Tom Sawyer*. Huck narrates his travels down the mighty Mississippi river on a raft with Jim, a slave seeking to escape to the North. The raft is drifting down the Mississippi from Hannibal in the slave-owning state of Missouri. Jim wants to get to Cairo, situated at the southernmost tip of Illinois, a state in which slave-owning is outlawed.

From the outset the novel was controversial. Initially banned by many libraries for its use of dialect and for being "low class," more recently it has been considered unsuitable because of its use of the word "nigger."

We slept most all day, and started out at night, a little ways behind a monstrous long raft that was as long going by as a procession. She had four long sweeps at each end, so we judged she carried as many as thirty men, likely. She had five big wigwams aboard, wide apart, and an open camp fire in the middle, and a tall flag-pole at each end. There was a power of style about her. It amounted to something being a raftsman on such a craft as that.

We went drifting down into a big bend, and the night clouded up and got hot. The river was very wide, and was walled with solid timber on both sides; you couldn't see a break in it hardly ever, or a light. We talked about Cairo, and wondered whether we would know it when we got to it. I said likely we wouldn't, because I had heard say there warn't but about a dozen houses there, and if they didn't happen to have them lit up, how was we going to know we was passing a town? Jim said if the two big rivers joined together there, that would show. But I said maybe we might think we was passing the foot of an island and coming into the same old river again. That disturbed Jim — and me too. So the question was, what to do? I said, paddle ashore the first time a light showed, and tell them pap was behind, coming along with a trading-scow, and was a green hand at the

---

MARK TWAIN, from Chapter XVI in *The Adventures of Huckleberry Finn*, first published in 1885.

---

trading-scow – a large flatbottom boat with square ends, usually used for freight

business, and wanted to know how far it was to Cairo. Jim thought it was a good idea, so we took a smoke on it and waited.

There warn't nothing to do, now, but to look out sharp for the town, and not pass it without seeing it. He said he'd be mighty sure to see it, because he'd be a free man the minute he seen it, but if he missed it he'd be in the slave country again and no more show for freedom. Every little while he jumps up and says:

"Dah she is!"

But it warn't. It was Jack-o-lanterns, or lightning-bugs; so he set down again, and went to watching, same as before. Jim said it made him all over trembly and feverish to be so close to freedom. Well, I can tell you it made me all over trembly and feverish, too, to hear him, because I begun to get it through my head that he was most free — and who was to blame for it? Why, me. I couldn't get that out of my conscience, no how nor no way. It got to troubling me so I couldn't rest; I couldn't stay still in one place. It hadn't ever come home to me before, what this thing was that I was doing. But now it did; and it staid with me, and scorched me more and more. I tried to make out to myself that I warn't to blame, because I didn't run Jim off from his rightful owner; but it warn't no use, conscience up and says, every time, "But you knowed he was running for his freedom, and you could a paddled ashore and told somebody." That was so — I couldn't get around that, no way. That was where it pinched. Conscience says to me, "What had poor Miss Watson done to you, that you could see her nigger go off right under your eyes and never say one single word? What did that poor old woman do to you, that you could treat her so mean? Why, she tried to learn you your book, she tried to learn you your manners, she tried to be good to you every way she knowed how. That's what she done."

I got to feeling so mean and so miserable I most wished I was dead. I fidgeted up and down the raft, abusing myself to myself, and Jim was fidgeting up and down past me. We neither of us could keep still. Every time he danced around and says, "Dah's Cairo!" it went through me like a shot, and I thought if it was Cairo I reckoned I would die of miserableness.

Jim talked out loud all the time while I was talking to myself. He was saying how the first thing he would do when he got to a free State he would go to saving up money and never spend a single cent, and when he got enough he would buy his wife, which was owned on a farm close to where Miss Watson lived; and then they would both work to buy the two children, and if their master wouldn't sell them, they'd get an Ab'litionist to go and steal them.

It most froze me to hear such talk. He wouldn't ever dared to talk such talk in his life before. Just see what a difference it made in him the minute he judged he was about free. It was according to the old saying, "give a nigger an inch and he'll take an ell." Thinks I, this is what comes of my not thinking. Here was this nigger which I had as good as helped to run away, coming right out flat-footed and saying he would steal his children — children that belonged to a man I didn't even know; a man that hadn't ever done me no harm.

Jack-o-lanterns — elusive or mysterious lights

I was sorry to hear Jim say that, it was such a lowering of him. My conscience got to stirring me up hotter than ever, until at last I says to it, "Let up on me – it ain't too late, yet – I'll paddle ashore at the first light and tell." I felt easy, and happy, and light as a feather, right off. All my troubles was gone. I went to looking out sharp for a light, and sort of singing to myself. By-and-by one showed. Jim sings out:

"We's safe, Huck, we's safe! Jump up and crack yo' heels, dat's de good ole Cairo at las', I jis knows it!"

I says:

"I'll take the canoe and go see, Jim. It mightn't be, you know."

He jumped and got the canoe ready, and put his old coat in the bottom for me to set on, and give me the paddle; and as I shoved off, he says:

"Pooty soon I'll be a-shout'n for joy, en I'll say, it's all on accounts o' Huck; I's a free man, en I couldn't ever ben free ef it hadn't ben for Huck; Huck done it. Jim won't ever forgit you, Huck; you's de bes' fren' Jim's ever had; en you's de only fren' ole Jim's got now."

I was paddling off, all in a sweat to tell on him; but when he says this, it seemed to kind of take the tuck all out of me. I went along slow then, and I warn't right down certain whether I was glad I started or whether I warn't. When I was fifty yards off, Jim says:

"Dah you goes, de ole true Huck; de on'y white genlman dat ever kep' his promise to ole Jim."

Well, I just felt sick. But I says, I got to do it – I can't get out of it. Right then, along comes a skiff with two men in it, with guns, and they stopped and I stopped. One of them says:

"What's that, yonder?"

"A piece of a raft," I says.

"So you belong on it?"

"Yes, sir."

"Any men on it?"

"Only one, sir."

"Well, there's five niggers run off to-night, up yonder above the head of the bend. Is your man white or black?"

I didn't answer up prompt. I tried to, but the words wouldn't come. I tried, for a second or two, to brace up and out with it, but I warn't man enough – hadn't the spunk of a rabbit. I see I was weakening; so I just give up trying, and up and say –

"He's white."

"I reckon we'll go and see for ourselves."

"I wish you would," says I, "because it's pap that's there, and maybe you'd help me tow the raft ashore where the light is. He's sick – and so is mam and Mary Ann."

"Oh, the devil! we're in a hurry, boy. But I s'pose we've got to. Come – buckle to your paddle, and let's get along."

I buckled to my paddle and they laid to their oars. When we had made a stroke or two, I says:

"Pap'll be mighty much obleeged to you, I can tell you. Everybody goes away when I want them to help me tow the raft ashore, and I can't do it by myself."

"Well, that's infernal mean. Odd, too. Say, boy, what's the matter with your father?"

"It's the – a – the – well, it ain't anything, much."

They stopped pulling. It warn't but a mighty little ways to the raft, now. One says:

"Boy, that's a lie. What is the matter with your pap? Answer up square, now, and it'll be the better for you."

"I will, sir, I will, honest – but don't leave us, please. It's the – the – gentlemen, if you'll only pull ahead, and let me heave you the head-line, you won't have to come a-near the raft – please do."

"Set her back, John, set her back!" says one. They backed water. "Keep away, boy – keep to looard. Confound it, I just expect the wind has blowed it to us. Your pap's got the smallpox, and you know it precious well. Why didn't you come out and say so? Do you want to spread it all over?"

"Well," says I, a-blubbering, "I've told everybody before, and then they just went away and left us."

"Poor devil, there's something in that. We are right down sorry for you, but we – well, hang it, we don't want the smallpox, you see. Look here, I'll tell you what to do. Don't you try to land by yourself, and you'll smash everything to pieces. You float along down about twenty miles and. you'll come to a town on the left-hand side of the river. It will be long after sun-up, then, and when you ask for help, you tell them your folks are all down with chills and fever. Don't be a fool again, and let people guess what is the matter. Now we're trying to do you a kindness; so you just put twenty miles between us, that's a good boy. It wouldn't do any good to land yonder where the light is – it's only a wood-yard. Say – I reckon your father's poor, and I'm bound to say he's in pretty hard luck. Here – I'll put a twenty dollar gold piece on this board, and you get it when it floats by. I feel mighty mean to leave you, but my kingdom! it won't do to fool with smallpox, don't you see?"

"Hold on, Parker," says the other man, "here's a twenty to put on the board for me. Good-bye, boy, you do as Mr Parker told you, and you'll be all right."

"That's so, my boy – good-bye, good-bye. If you see any runaway niggers, you get help and nab them, and you can make some money by it."

"Good-bye, sir," says I, "I won't let no runaway niggers get by me if I can help it."

They went off, and I got aboard the raft, feeling bad and low, because I knowed very well I had done wrong, and I see it warn't no use for me to try to learn to do right; a body that don't get started right when he's little, ain't got no show – when the pinch comes there ain't nothing to back him up and keep him to his work, and so he gets beat. Then I thought a minute, and says to myself, hold on – s'pose you'd a done right and give Jim up; would you felt better than what you do now? No, says I, I'd feel bad – I'd feel just the same way I do now. Well, then, says I, what's the use you learning to do right, when it's troublesome to do right and ain't no trouble to do wrong, and the wages is just the same? I was stuck. I couldn't answer that. So I reckoned I wouldn't bother no more about it, but after this always do whichever comes handiest at the time.

67

GRAHAM GREENE

The Third Man

Graham Greene originally wrote *The Third Man* as a screenplay. The film, directed by Carol Reed and starring Joseph Cotten and Orson Welles, is better known than the book.

Pulp fiction writer Rollo Martins arrives in Vienna after the end of World War II, looking for his old friend Harry Lime, who is supposed to be dead. He finds murder, corruption, and mystery. At this point in the story Rollo has discovered that Lime is alive and hiding in the Russian-occupied zone of Vienna, apparently involved in selling adulterated penicillin. He has arranged a meeting at Vienna's famous giant Ferris wheel in the Prater, a large park.

Somewhere behind the cake stall a man was whistling, and Martins knew the tune. He turned and waited. Was it fear or excitement that made his heart beat – or just the memories that tune ushered in, for life had always quickened when Harry came, came just as he came now, as though nothing much had happened, nobody had been lowered into a grave or found with cut throat in a basement, came with his amused deprecating take-it-or-leave-it manner – and of course one always took it.

"Harry."

"Hullo, Rollo."

Don't picture Harry Lime as a smooth scoundrel. He wasn't that. The picture I have of him on my files is an excellent one: he is caught by a street photographer with his stocky legs apart, big shoulders a little hunched, a belly that has known too much good food too long, on his face a look of cheerful rascality, a geniality, a recognition that his happiness will make the world's day. Now he didn't make the mistake of putting out a hand that might have been rejected, but instead just patted Martins on the elbow and said, "How are things?"

"We've got to talk, Harry."

"Of course."

"Alone."

"We couldn't be more alone than here."

He had always known the ropes, and even in the smashed pleasure park he knew them, tipping the woman in charge of the Wheel, so that they might have a car to themselves. He said, "Lovers used to do this in the old days, but they haven't the money to spare, poor devils, now," and he looked out of the window of the swaying, rising car at the figures diminishing below with what looked like genuine commiseration.

Very slowly on one side of them the city sank; very slowly on the other the great cross girders of the Wheel rose into sight. As the horizon slid away the Danube became visible, and the piers of the Kaiser Friedrich Brücke lifted above the houses. "Well," Harry said, "it's good to see you, Rollo."

"I was at your funeral."

"That was pretty smart of me, wasn't it?"

"Not so smart for your girl. She was there too – in tears."

"She's a good little thing," Harry said. "I'm very fond of her."

"I didn't believe the police when they told me about you."

Harry said, "I wouldn't have asked you to come if I'd known what was going to happen, but I didn't think the police were on to me."

"Were you going to cut me in on the spoils?"

"I've never kept you out of anything, old man, yet." He stood with his back to the door as the car swung upwards, and smiled back at Rollo Martins, who could remember him in just such an attitude in a secluded corner of the school quad, saying, "I've learned a way to get out at night. It's absolutely safe. You are the only one I'm letting in on it." For the first time Rollo Martins looked back through the years without admiration, as he thought, He's never grown up. Marlowe's devils wore squibs attached to their tails: evil was like Peter Pan – it carried with it the horrifying and horrible gift of eternal youth.

Martins said, "Have you ever visited the children's hospital? Have you seen any of your victims?"

Harry took a look at the toy landscape below and came away from the door. "I never feel quite safe in these things," he said. He felt the back of the door with his hand, as though he were afraid that it might fly open and launch him into that iron-ribbed space. "Victims?" he asked. "Don't be melodramatic, Rollo. Look down there," he went on, pointing through the window at the people moving like black flies at the base of the Wheel. "Would you really feel any pity if one of those dots stopped moving – forever? If I said you can have twenty thousand pounds for every dot that stops, would you really, old man, tell me to keep my money – without hesitation? Or would you calculate how many dots you could afford to spare? Free of income tax, old man. Free of income tax." He gave his boyish conspiratorial smile. "It's the only way to save nowadays."

"Couldn't you have stuck to tires?"

"Like Cooler? No, I've always been ambitious.

"But they can't catch me, Rollo, you'll see. I'll pop up again. You can't keep a good man down." The car swung to a standstill at the highest point of the curve and Harry turned his back and gazed out of the window. Martins thought: one good shove and I could break the glass, and he pictured the body dropping among the flies. He said, "You know the police are planning to dig up your body. What will they find?"

"Harbin," Harry replied with simplicity. He turned away from the window and said, "Look at the sky."

The car had reached the top of the Wheel and hung there motionless, while the stain of the sunset ran in streaks over the wrinkled papery sky beyond the black girders.

"Why did the Russians try to take Anna Schmidt?"

"She had false papers, old man."

"I thought perhaps you were just trying to get her here – because she was your girl? Because you wanted her?"

Harry smiled. "I haven't all that influence."

"What would have happened to her?"

"Nothing very serious. She'd have been sent back to Hungary. There's nothing against her really. She'd be infinitely better off in her own country than being pushed around by the British police."

"She hasn't told them anything about you."

"She's a good little thing," Harry repeated with complacent pride.

"She loves you."

"Well, I gave her a good time while it lasted."

"And I love her."

"That's fine, old man. Be kind to her. She's worth it. I'm glad." He gave the impression of having arranged everything to everybody's satisfaction. "And you can help to keep her mouth shut. Not that she knows anything that matters."

"I'd like to knock you through the window."

"But you won't, old man. Our quarrels never last long. You remember that fearful one in the Monaco, when we swore we were through. I'd trust you anywhere, Rollo. Kurtz tried to persuade me not to come but I know you. Then he tried to persuade me to, well, arrange an accident. He told me it would be quite easy in this car."

"Except that I'm the stronger man."

"But I've got the gun. You don't think a bullet wound would show when you hit *that* ground?" Again the car began to move, sailing slowly down, until the flies were midgets, were recognizable human beings. "What fools we are, Rollo, talking like this, as if I'd do that to you – or you to me." He turned his back and leaned his face against the glass. One thrust . . . "How much do you earn a year with your Westerns, old man?"

"A thousand."

"Taxed. I earn thirty thousand free. It's the fashion. In these days, old man, nobody thinks in terms of human beings. Governments don't, so why should we? They talk of the people and the proletariat, and I talk of the mugs. It's the same thing. They have their five-year plans and so have I."

"You used to be a Catholic."

"Oh, I still *believe*, old man. In God and mercy and all that. I'm not hurting anybody's soul by what I do. The dead are happier dead. They don't miss much here, poor devils," he added with that odd touch of genuine pity, as the car reached the platform and the faces of the doomed-to-be-victims, the tired pleasure-hoping Sunday faces, peered in at them. "I could cut you in, you know. It would be useful. I have no one left in the Inner City."

"Except Cooler? And Winkler?"

"You really mustn't turn policeman, old man." They passed out of the car and he put his hand again on Martins' elbow. "That was a joke, I know you won't. Have you heard anything of old Bracer recently?"

"I had a card at Christmas."

"Those were the days, old man. Those were the days. I've got to leave you here. We'll see each other — sometime. If you are in a jam, you can always get me at Kurtz's." He moved away and, turning, waved the hand he had had the tact not to offer: it was like the whole past moving off under a cloud. Martins suddenly called after him, "Don't trust me, Harry," but there was too great a distance now between them for the words to carry.

68

TADEUSZ BOROWSKI

This Way for the Gas, Ladies and Gentlemen

All of us walk around naked. The delousing is finally over, and our striped suits are back from the tanks of Cyclone B solution, an efficient killer of lice in clothing and of men in gas chambers. Only the inmates in the blocks cut off from ours by the "Spanish goats" still have nothing to wear. But all the same, all of us walk around naked: the heat is unbearable. The camp has been sealed off tight. Not a single prisoner, not one solitary louse, can sneak through the gate. The labour Kommandos have stopped working. All day, thousands of naked men shuffle up and down the roads, cluster around the squares, or lie against the walls and on top of the roofs. We have been sleeping on plain boards, since our mattresses and blankets are still being disinfected. From the rear blockhouses we have a view of the FKL – *Frauen Konzentration Lager;* there too the delousing is in full swing. Twenty-eight thousand women have been stripped naked and driven out of the barracks. Now they swarm around the large yard between the block-houses.

The heat rises, the hours are endless. We are without even our usual diversion: the wide roads leading to the crematoria are empty. For several days now, no new transports have come in. Part of "Canada" has been liquidated and detailed to a labour Kommando – one of the very toughest – at Harmenz. For there exists in the camp a special brand of justice based on envy: when the rich and mighty fall, their friends see to it that they fall to the very bottom. And Canada, our Canada, which smells not of maple forests but of French perfume, has amassed great fortunes in diamonds and currency from all over Europe.

TADEUSZ BOROWSKI, "This Way For the Gas, Ladies and Gentlemen," pp. 29–49 from *This Way for the Gas, Ladies and Gentlemen* (tr. Barbara Vedder), New York: Penguin Books, 1976. First published in the USA by Viking Penguin, Inc., 1967. Copyright © 1967 by Penguin Books Ltd. Original text copyright © 1959 by Maria Borowski. Used by permission of Viking Penguin, a division of Penguin Group (USA).

"Spanish goats" – crossed wooden beams wrapped in barbed wire

"Canada" – designated wealth and well-being in the camp; more specifically, it referred to the members of the labor gang, or Kommando, who helped to unload the incoming transports of people destined for the gas chambers

Several of us sit on the top bunk, our legs dangling over the edge. We slice the neat loaves of crisp, crunchy bread. It is a bit coarse to the taste, the kind that stays fresh for days. Sent all the way from Warsaw – only a week ago my mother held this white loaf in her hands . . . dear Lord, dear Lord . . .

We unwrap the bacon, the onion, we open a can of evaporated milk. Henri, the fat Frenchman, dreams aloud of the French wine brought by the transports from Strasbourg, Paris, Marseille . . . Sweat streams down his body.

"Listen, *mon ami*, next time we go up on the loading ramp, I'll bring you real champagne. You haven't tried it before, eh?"

"No. But you'll never be able to smuggle it through the gate, so stop teasing. Why not try and 'organize' some shoes for me instead – you know, the perforated kind, with a double sole, and what about that shirt you promised me long ago?"

"*Patience, patience.* When the new transports come, I'll bring all you want. We'll be going on the ramp again!"

"And what if there aren't any more 'cremo' transports?" I say spitefully. "Can't you see how much easier life is becoming around here: no limit on packages, no more beatings? You even write letters home . . . One hears all kind of talk, and, dammit, they'll run out of people!"

"Stop talking nonsense." Henri's serious fat face moves rhythmically, his mouth is full of sardines. We have been friends for a long time, but I do not even know his last name. "Stop talking nonsense," he repeats, swallowing with effort. "They can't run out of people, or we'll starve to death in this blasted camp. All of us live on what they bring."

"All? We have our packages . . ."

"Sure, you and your friend, and ten other friends of yours. Some of you Poles get packages. But what about us, and the Jews, and the Russkis? And what if we had no food, no 'organization' from the transports, do you think you'd be eating those packages of yours in peace? We wouldn't let you!"

"You would, you'd starve to death like the Greeks. Around here, whoever has grub, has power."

"Anyway, you have enough, we have enough, so why argue?"

Right, why argue? They have enough, I have enough, we eat together and we sleep on the same bunks. Henri slices the bread, he makes a tomato salad. It tastes good with the commissary mustard.

Below us, naked, sweat-drenched men crowd the narrow barracks aisles or lie packed in eights and tens in the lower bunks. Their nude, withered bodies stink of sweat and excrement; their cheeks are hollow. Directly beneath me, in the bottom bunk, lies a rabbi. He has covered his head with a piece of rag torn off a blanket and reads from a Hebrew prayer book (there is no shortage of this type of literature at the camp), wailing loudly, monotonously.

"Can't somebody shut him up? He's been raving as if he'd caught God himself by the feet."

"I don't feel like moving. Let him rave. They'll take him to the oven that much sooner."

"Religion is the opium of the people," Henri, who is a Communist and a *rentier*, says sententiously. "If they didn't believe in God and eternal life, they'd have smashed the crematoria long ago."

"Why haven't you done it then?"

The question is rhetorical; the Frenchman ignores it.

"Idiot," he says simply, and stuffs a tomato in his mouth.

Just as we finish our snack, there is a sudden commotion at the door. The Muslims scurry in fright to the safety of their bunks, a messenger runs into the Block Elder's shack. The Elder, his face solemn, steps out at once.

"Canada! *Antreten!* But fast! There's a transport coming!"

"Great God!" yells Henri, jumping off the bunk. He swallows the rest of his tomato, snatches his coat, screams *"Raus"* at the men below, and in a flash is at the door. We can hear a scramble in the other bunks. Canada is leaving for the ramp.

"Henri, the shoes!" I call after him.

"Keine Angst!" he shouts back, already outside.

I proceed to put away the food. I tie a piece of rope around the suitcase where the onions and the tomatoes from my father's garden in Warsaw mingle with Portuguese sardines, bacon from Lublin (that's from my brother), and authentic sweetmeats from Salonica. I tie it all up, pull on my trousers, and slide off the bunk.

"Platz!" I yell, pushing my way through the Greeks. They step aside. At the door I bump into Henri.

"Was ist los?"

"Want to come with us on the ramp?"

"Sure, why not?"

"Come along then, grab your coat! We're short of a few men. I've already told the Kapo," and he shoves me out of the barracks door.

We line up. Someone has marked down our numbers, someone up ahead yells, "March, march," and now we are running towards the gate, accompanied by the shouts of a multilingual throng that is already being pushed back to the barracks. Not everybody is lucky enough to be going on the ramp . . . We have almost reached the gate. *Links, zwei, drei, vier! Mützen ab!* Erect, arms stretched stiffly along our hips, we march past the gate briskly, smartly, almost gracefully. A sleepy SS man with a large pad in his hand checks us off, waving us ahead in groups of five.

"Hundert!" he calls after we have all passed.

"Stimmt!" comes a hoarse answer from out front.

We march fast, almost at a run. There are guards all around, young men with automatics. We pass camp II B, then some deserted barracks and a clump of unfamiliar green – apple and pear trees. We cross the circle of watch-towers and,

---

rentier – landlord, someone who lives off rental income

"Muslim" – camp name for a prisoner who had been destroyed physically and spiritually, and who had neither the strength nor the will to go on living – a man ripe for the gas chamber

Kapo – a supervisor of inmates in a concentration camp who was, usually, chosen by the Nazis from among the prisoners

running, burst on to the highway. We have arrived. Just a few more yards. There, surrounded by trees, is the ramp.

A cheerful little station, very much like any other provincial railway stop: a small square framed by tall chestnuts and paved with yellow gravel. Not far off, beside the road, squats a tiny wooden shed, uglier and more flimsy then the ugliest and flimsiest railway shack; farther along lie stacks of old rails, heaps of wooden beams, barracks parts, bricks, paving stones. This is where they load freight for Birkenau: supplies for the construction of the camp, and people for the gas chambers. Trucks drive around, load up lumber, cement, people – a regular daily routine.

And now the guards are being posted along the rails, across the beams, in the green shade of the Silesian chestnuts, to form a tight circle around the ramp. They wipe the sweat from their faces and sip out of their canteens. It is unbearably hot; the sun stands motionless at its zenith.

"Fall out!"

We sit down in the narrow streaks of shade along the stacked rails. The hungry Greeks (several of them managed to come along, God only knows how) rummage underneath the rails. One of them finds some pieces of mildewed bread, another a few half-rotten sardines. They eat.

"*Schweinedreck,*" spits a young, tall guard with corn-coloured hair and dreamy blue eyes. "For God's sake, any minute you'll have so much food to stuff down your guts, you'll bust!" He adjusts his gun, wipes his face with a handkerchief.

"Hey you, fatso!" His boot lightly touches Henri's shoulder. "*Pass mal auf,* want a drink?"

"Sure, but I haven't got any marks," replies the Frenchman with a professional air.

"*Schade,* too bad."

"Come, come, Herr Posten, isn't my word good enough any more? Haven't we done business before? How much?"

"One hundred. *Gemacht?*"

"*Gemacht.*"

We drink the water, lukewarm and tasteless. It will be paid for by the people who have not yet arrived.

"Now you be careful," says Henri, turning to me. He tosses away the empty bottle. It strikes the rails and bursts into tiny fragments. "Don't take any money, they might be checking. Anyway, who the hell needs money? You've got enough to eat. Don't take suits, either, or they'll think you're planning to escape. Just get a shirt, silk only, with a collar. And a vest. And if you find something to drink, don't bother calling me. I know how to shift for myself, but you watch your step or they'll let you have it."

"Do they beat you up here?"

"Naturally. You've got to have eyes in your ass. *Arschaugen.*"

Birkenau – Auschwitz-Birkenau camp, established by the Nazis in 1940 in south-west Poland, not far from Cracow. Initially the concentration camp held Gypsies, Soviet prisoners of war, and Polish "undesirables." From 1942 Jews from all over Europe were transported there. Most of the Jews went directly from the train to the gas chambers in Birkenau.

Around us sit the Greeks, their jaws working greedily, like huge human insects. They munch on stale lumps of bread. They are restless, wondering what will happen next. The sight of the large beams and the stacks of rails has them worried. They dislike carrying heavy loads.

"*Was wir arbeiten?*" they ask.

"*Niks. Transport kommen, alles Krematorium, compris?*"

"*Alles verstehen*," they answer in crematorium Esperanto. All is well – they will not have to move the heavy rails or carry the beams.

In the meantime, the ramp has become increasingly alive with activity, increasingly noisy. The crews are being divided into those who will open and unload the arriving cattle cars and those who will be posted by the wooden steps. They receive instructions on how to proceed most efficiently. Motor cycles drive up, delivering SS officers, bemedalled, glittering with brass, beefy men with highly polished boots and shiny, brutal faces. Some have brought their briefcases, others hold thin, flexible whips. This gives them an air of military readiness and agility. They walk in and out of the commissary – for the miserable little shack by the road serves as their commissary, where in the summertime they drink mineral water, *Studentenquelle*, and where in winter they can warm up with a glass of hot wine. They greet each other in the state-approved way, raising an arm Roman fashion, then shake hands cordially, exchange warm smiles, discuss mail from home, their children, their families. Some stroll majestically on the ramp. The silver squares on their collars glitter, the gravel crunches under their boots, their bamboo whips snap impatiently.

We lie against the rails in the narrow streaks of shade, breathe unevenly, occasionally exchange a few words in our various tongues, and gaze listlessly at the majestic men in green uniforms, at the green trees, and at the church steeple of a distant village.

"The transport is coming," somebody says. We spring to our feet, all eyes turn in one direction. Around the bend, one after another, the cattle cars begin rolling in. The train backs into the station, a conductor leans out, waves his hand, blows a whistle. The locomotive whistles back with a shrieking noise, puffs, the train rolls slowly alongside the ramp. In the tiny barred windows appear pale, wilted, exhausted human faces, terror-stricken women with tangled hair, unshaven men. They gaze at the station in silence. And then, suddenly, there is a stir inside the cars and a pounding against the wooden boards.

"Water! Air!" – weary, desperate cries.

Heads push through the windows, mouths gasp frantically for air. They draw a few breaths, then disappear; others come in their place, then also disappear. The cries and moans grow louder.

A man in a green uniform covered with more glitter than any of the others jerks his head impatiently, his lips twist in annoyance. He inhales deeply, then with a rapid gesture throws his cigarette away and signals to the guard. The guard removes the automatic from his shoulder, aims, sends a series of shots along the train. All is quiet now. Meanwhile, the trucks have arrived, steps are being drawn up, and the Canada men stand ready at their posts by the train doors. The SS officer with the briefcase raises his hand.

"Whoever takes gold, or anything at all besides food, will be shot for stealing Reich property. Understand? *Verstanden?*"

"*Jawohl!*" we answer eagerly.

"*Also los!* Begin!"

The bolts crack, the doors fall open. A wave of fresh air rushes inside the train. People . . . inhumanly crammed, buried under incredible heaps of luggage, suitcases, trunks, packages, crates, bundles of every description (everything that had been their past and was to start their future). Monstrously squeezed together, they have fainted from heat, suffocated, crushed one another. Now they push towards the opened doors, breathing like fish cast out on the sand.

"Attention! Out, and take your luggage with you! Take out everything. Pile all your stuff near the exits. Yes, your coats too. It is summer. March to the left. Understand?"

"Sir, what's going to happen to us?" They jump from the train on to the gravel, anxious, worn-out.

"Where are you people from?"

"Sosnowiec-Będzin. Sir, what's going to happen to us?" They repeat the question stubbornly, gazing into our tired eyes.

"I don't know, I don't understand Polish."

It is the camp law: people going to their death must be deceived to the very end. This is the only permissible form of charity. The heat is tremendous. The sun hangs directly over our heads, the white, hot sky quivers, the air vibrates, an occasional breeze feels like a sizzling blast from a furnace. Our lips are parched, the mouth fills with the salty taste of blood, the body is weak and heavy from lying in the sun. Water!

A huge, multicoloured wave of people loaded down with luggage pours from the train like a blind, mad river trying to find a new bed. But before they have a chance to recover, before they can draw a breath of fresh air and look at the sky, bundles are snatched from their hands, coats ripped off their backs, their purses and umbrellas taken away.

"But please, sir, it's for the sun, I cannot . . ."

"*Verboten!*" one of us barks through clenched teeth. There is an SS man standing behind your back, calm, efficient, watchful.

"*Meine Herrschaften*, this way, ladies and gentlemen, try not to throw your things around, please. Show some goodwill," he says courteously, his restless hands playing with the slender whip.

"Of course, of course," they answer as they pass, and now they walk alongside the train somewhat more cheerfully. A woman reaches down quickly to pick up her handbag. The whip flies, the woman screams, stumbles, and falls under the feet of the surging crowd. Behind her, a child cries in a thin little voice "Mamele!" – a very small girl with tangled black curls.

The heaps grow. Suitcases, bundles, blankets, coats, handbags that open as they fall, spilling coins, gold, watches; mountains of bread pile up at the exits, heaps of marmalade, jams, masses of meat, sausages; sugar spills on the gravel. Trucks, loaded with people, start up with a deafening roar and drive off amidst the wailing and screaming of the women separated from their children, and the stupefied silence of the men left behind. They are the ones who had been ordered to step to the right – the healthy and the young who will go to the camp. In the end, they too will not escape death, but first they must work.

Trucks leave and return, without interruption, as on a monstrous conveyor belt. A Red Cross van drives back and forth, back and forth, incessantly: it transports the gas that will kill these people. The enormous cross on the hood, red as blood, seems to dissolve in the sun.

The Canada men at the trucks cannot stop for a single moment, even to catch their breath. They shove the people up the steps, pack them in tightly, sixty per truck, more or less. Nearby stands a young, cleanshaven "gentleman", an SS officer with a notebook in his hand. For each departing truck he enters a mark; sixteen gone means one thousand people, more or less. The gentleman is calm, precise. No truck can leave without a signal from him, or a mark in his notebook: *Ordnung muss sein*. The marks swell into thousands, the thousands into whole transports, which afterwards we shall simply call "from Salonica", "from Strasbourg", "from Rotterdam". This one will be called "Sosnowiec-Będzin". The new prisoners from Sosnowiec-Będzin will receive serial numbers 131–2 – thousand, of course, though afterwards we shall simply say 131–2, for short.

The transports swell into weeks, months, years. When the war is over, they will count up the marks in their notebooks – all four and a half million of them. The bloodiest battle of the war, the greatest victory of the strong, united Germany. *Ein Reich, ein Volk, ein Führer* – and four crematoria.

The train has been emptied. A thin, pock-marked SS man peers inside, shakes his head in disgust and motions to our group, pointing his finger at the door.

"*Rein*. Clean it up!"

We climb inside. In the corners amid human excrement and abandoned wrist-watches lie squashed, trampled infants, naked little monsters with enormous heads and bloated bellies. We carry them out like chickens, holding several in each hand.

"Don't take them to the trucks, pass them on to the women," says the SS man, lighting a cigarette. His cigarette lighter is not working properly; he examines it carefully.

"Take them, for God's sake!" I explode as the women run from me in horror, covering their eyes.

The name of God sounds strangely pointless, since the women and the infants will go on the trucks, every one of them, without exception. We all know what this means, and we look at each other with hate and horror.

"What, you don't want to take them?" asks the pock-marked SS man with a note of surprise and reproach in his voice, and reaches for his revolver.

"You mustn't shoot, I'll carry them." A tall, grey-haired woman takes the little corpses out of my hands and for an instant gazes straight into my eyes.

"My poor boy," she whispers and smiles at me. Then she walks away, staggering along the path. I lean against the side of the train. I am terribly tired. Someone pulls at my sleeve.

"*En avant*, to the rails, come on!"

I look up, but the face swims before my eyes, dissolves, huge and transparent, melts into the motionless trees and the sea of people . . . I blink rapidly: Henri.

"Listen, Henri, are we good people?"

"That's stupid. Why do you ask?"

"You see, my friend, you see, I don't know why, but I am furious, simply furious with these people – furious because I must be here because of them. I feel no pity. I am not sorry they're going to the gas chamber. Damn them all! I could throw myself at them, beat them with my fists. It must be pathological, I just can't understand . . ."

"Ah, on the contrary, it is natural, predictable, calculated. The ramp exhausts you, you rebel – and the easiest way to relieve your hate is to turn against someone weaker. Why, I'd even call it healthy. It's simple logic, *compris?*" He props himself up comfortably against the heap of rails. "Look at the Greeks, they know how to make the best of it! They stuff their bellies with anything they find. One of them has just devoured a full jar of marmalade."

"Pigs! Tomorrow half of them will die of the shits."

"Pigs? You've been hungry."

"Pigs!" I repeat furiously. I close my eyes. The air is filled with ghastly cries, the earth trembles beneath me, I can feel sticky moisture on my eyelids. My throat is completely dry.

The morbid procession streams on and on – trucks growl like mad dogs. I shut my eyes tight, but I can still see corpses dragged from the train, trampled infants, cripples piled on top of the dead, wave after wave . . . freight cars roll in, the heaps of clothing, suitcases and bundles grow, people climb out, look at the sun, take a few breaths, beg for water, get into the trucks, drive away. And again freight cars roll in, again people . . . The scenes become confused in my mind – I am not sure if all of this is actually happening, or if I am dreaming. There is a humming inside my head; I feel that I must vomit.

Henri tugs at my arm.

"Don't sleep, we're off to load up the loot."

All the people are gone. In the distance, the last few trucks roll along the road in clouds of dust, the train has left, several SS officers promenade up and down the ramp. The silver glitters on their collars. Their boots shine, their red, beefy faces shine. Among them there is a woman – only now I realize she has been here all along – withered, flat-chested, bony, her thin, colourless hair pulled back and tied in a "Nordic" knot; her hands are in the pockets of her wide skirt. With a rat-like, resolute smile glued on her thin lips she sniffs around the corners of the ramp. She detests feminine beauty with the hatred of a woman who is herself repulsive, and knows it. Yes, I have seen her many times before and I know her well: she is the commandant of the FKL. She has come to look over the new crop of women, for some of them, instead of going on the trucks, will go on foot – to the concentration camp. There our boys, the barbers from Zauna, will shave their heads and will have a good laugh at their "outside world" modesty.

We proceed to load the loot. We lift huge trunks, heave them on to the trucks. There they are arranged in stacks, packed tightly. Occasionally somebody slashes one open with a knife, for pleasure or in search of vodka and perfume. One of the crates falls open; suits, shirts, books drop out on the ground . . . I pick up a small, heavy package. I unwrap it – gold, about two handfuls, bracelets, rings, brooches, diamonds . . .

"*Gib hier*," an SS man says calmly, holding up his briefcase already full of gold and colourful foreign currency. He locks the case, hands it to an officer, takes another, an empty one, and stands by the next truck, waiting. The gold will go to the Reich.

It is hot, terribly hot. Our throats are dry, each word hurts. Anything for a sip of water! Faster, faster, so that it is over, so that we may rest. At last we are done, all the trucks have gone. Now we swiftly clean up the remaining dirt: there must be "no trace left of the *Schweinerei*". But just as the last truck disappears behind the trees and we walk, finally, to rest in the shade, a shrill whistle sounds around the bend. Slowly, terribly slowly, a train rolls in, the engine whistles back with a deafening shriek. Again weary, pale faces at the windows, flat as though cut out of paper, with huge, feverishly burning eyes. Already trucks are pulling up, already the composed gentleman with the notebook is at his post, and the SS men emerge from the commissary carrying briefcases for the gold and money. We unseal the train doors.

It is impossible to control oneself any longer. Brutally we tear suitcases from their hands, impatiently pull off their coats. Go on, go on, vanish! They go, they vanish. Men, women, children. Some of them know.

Here is a woman – she walks quickly, but tries to appear calm. A small child with a pink cherub's face runs after her and, unable to keep up, stretches out his little arms and cries: "Mama! Mama!"

"Pick up your child, woman!"

"It's not mine, sir, not mine!" she shouts hysterically and runs on, covering her face with her hands. She wants to hide, she wants to reach those who will not ride the trucks, those who will go on foot, those who will stay alive. She is young, healthy, good-looking, she wants to live.

But the child runs after her, wailing loudly: "Mama, mama, don't leave me!"

"It's not mine, not mine, no!"

Andrei, a sailor from Sevastopol, grabs hold of her. His eyes are glassy from vodka and the heat. With one powerful blow he knocks her off her feet, then, as she falls, takes her by the hair and pulls her up again. His face twitches with rage.

"Ah, you bloody Jewess! So you're running from your own child! I'll show you, you whore!" His huge hand chokes her, he lifts her in the air and heaves her on to the truck like a heavy sack of grain.

"Here! And take this with you, bitch!" and he throws the child at her feet.

"*Gut gemacht*, good work. That's the way to deal with degenerate mothers," says the SS man standing at the foot of the truck. "*Gut, gut, Russki*."

"Shut your mouth," growls Andrei through clenched teeth, and walks away. From under a pile of rags he pulls out a canteen, unscrews the cork, takes a few deep swallows, passes it to me. The strong vodka burns the throat. My head swims, my legs are shaky, again I feel like throwing up.

And suddenly, above the teeming crowd pushing forward like a river driven by an unseen power, a girl appears. She descends lightly from the train, hops on to the gravel, looks around inquiringly, as if somewhat surprised. Her soft, blonde hair has fallen on her shoulders in a torrent, she throws it back impatiently. With a natural gesture she runs her hands down her blouse, casually straightens her skirt. She stands like this for an instant, gazing at the crowd, then turns and with a gliding look examines our faces, as though searching for someone. Unknowingly, I continue to stare at her, until our eyes meet.

"Listen, tell me, where are they taking us?"

I look at her without saying a word. Here, standing before me, is a girl, a girl with enchanting blonde hair, with beautiful breasts, wearing a little cotton blouse, a girl with a wise, mature look in her eyes. Here she stands, gazing straight into my face, waiting. And over there is the gas chamber: communal death, disgusting and ugly. And over in the other direction is the concentration camp: the shaved head, the heavy Soviet trousers in sweltering heat, the sickening, stale odour of dirty, damp female bodies, the animal hunger, the inhuman labour, and later the same gas chamber, only an even more hideous, more terrible death . . .

Why did she bring it? I think to myself, noticing a lovely gold watch on her delicate wrist. They'll take it away from her anyway.

"Listen, tell me," she repeats.

I remain silent. Her lips tighten.

"I know," she says with a shade of proud contempt in her voice, tossing her head. She walks off resolutely in the direction of the trucks. Someone tries to stop her; she boldly pushes him aside and runs up the steps. In the distance I can only catch a glimpse of her blonde hair flying in the breeze.

I go back inside the train; I carry out dead infants; I unload luggage. I touch corpses, but I cannot overcome the mounting, uncontrollable terror. I try to escape from the corpses, but they are everywhere: lined up on the gravel, on the cement edge of the ramp, inside the cattle cars. Babies, hideous naked women, men twisted by convulsions. I run off as far as I can go, but immediately a whip slashes across my back. Out of the corner of my eye I see an SS man, swearing profusely. I stagger forward and run, lose myself in the Canada group. Now, at last, I can once more rest against the stack of rails. The sun has leaned low over the horizon and illuminates the ramp with a reddish glow; the shadows of the trees have become elongated, ghostlike. In the silence that settles over nature at this time of day, the human cries seem to rise all the way to the sky.

Only from this distance does one have a full view of the inferno on the teeming ramp. I see a pair of human beings who have fallen to the ground locked in a last desperate embrace. The man has dug his fingers into the woman's flesh and has caught her clothing with his teeth. She screams hysterically, swears, cries, until at last a large boot comes down over her throat and she is silent. They are pulled apart and dragged like cattle to the truck. I see four Canada men lugging a corpse: a huge, swollen female corpse. Cursing, dripping wet from the strain, they kick out of their way some stray children who have been running all over the ramp, howling like dogs. The men pick them up by the collars, heads, arms, and toss them inside the trucks, on top of the heaps. The four men have trouble lifting the fat corpse on to the car, they call others for help, and all together they hoist up the mound of meat. Big, swollen, puffed-up corpses are being collected from all over the ramp; on top of them are piled the invalids, the smothered, the sick, the unconscious. The heap seethes, howls, groans. The driver starts the motor, the truck begins rolling.

"Halt! Halt!" an SS man yells after them. "Stop, damn you!"

They are dragging to the truck an old man wearing tails and a band around his arm. His head knocks against the gravel and pavement; he moans and wails in an uninterrupted monotone: *"Ich will mit dem Herrn Kommandanten sprechen — I wish to speak with the commandant . . ."* With senile stubbornness he keeps repeating these words all the way. Thrown on the truck, trampled by others, choked, he still wails: *"Ich will mit dem . . ."*

"Look here, old man!" a young SS man calls, laughing jovially. "In half an hour you'll be talking with the top commandant! Only don't forget to greet him with a *Heil Hitler!*'

Several other men are carrying a small girl with only one leg. They hold her by the arms and the one leg. Tears are running down her face and she whispers faintly: "Sir, it hurts, it hurts . . ." They throw her on the truck on top of the corpses. She will burn alive along with them.

The evening has come, cool and clear. The stars are out. We lie against the rails. It is incredibly quiet. Anaemic bulbs hang from the top of the high lamp-posts; beyond the circle of light stretches an impenetrable darkness. Just one step, and a man could vanish for ever. But the guards are watching, their automatics ready.

"Did you get the shoes?" asks Henri.

"No."

"Why?"

"My God, man, I am finished, absolutely finished!"

"So soon? After only two transports? Just look at me, I . . . since Christmas, at least a million people have passed through my hands. The worst of all are the transports from around Paris — one is always bumping into friends."

"And what do you say to them?"

'That first they will have a bath, and later we'll meet at the camp. What would you say?"

I do not answer. We drink coffee with vodka; somebody opens a tin of cocoa and mixes it with sugar. We scoop it up by the handful, the cocoa sticks to the lips. Again coffee, again vodka.

"Henri, what are we waiting for?"

'There'll be another transport."

"I'm not going to unload it! I can't take any more."

"So, it's got you down? Canada is nice, eh?" Henri grins indulgently and disappears into the darkness. In a moment he is back again.

"All right. Just sit here quietly and don't let an SS man see you. I'll try to find you your shoes."

"Just leave me alone. Never mind the shoes." I want to sleep. It is very late.

Another whistle, another transport. Freight cars emerge out of the darkness, pass under the lamp-posts, and again vanish in the night. The ramp is small, but the circle of lights is smaller. The unloading will have to be done gradually. Somewhere the trucks are growling. They back up against the steps, black, ghostlike, their searchlights flash across the trees. *Wasser! Luft!* The same all over again, like a late showing of the same film: a volley of shots, the train falls silent. Only this time a little girl pushes herself halfway through the small window and, losing her balance, falls out on to the gravel. Stunned, she lies still for a moment, then stands up and begins walking around in a circle, faster and faster, waving her rigid arms in the air, breathing loudly and spasmodically, whining in a faint voice. Her mind has given way in the inferno inside the train. The whining is hard on the nerves: an SS man approaches calmly, his heavy boot strikes between her shoulders. She falls. Holding her down with his foot, he draws his revolver, fires once, then again. She remains face down, kicking the gravel with her feet, until she stiffens. They proceed to unseal the train.

I am back on the ramp, standing by the doors. A warm, sickening smell gushes from inside. The mountain of people filling the car almost halfway up to the ceiling is motionless, horribly tangled, but still steaming.

"Ausladen!" comes the command. An SS man steps out from the darkness. Across his chest hangs a portable searchlight. He throws a stream of light inside.

"Why are you standing about like sheep? Start unloading!" His whip flies and falls across our backs. I seize a corpse by the hand; the fingers close tightly around mine. I pull back with a shriek and stagger away. My heart pounds, jumps up to my throat. I can no longer control the nausea. Hunched under the train I begin to vomit. Then, like a drunk, I weave over to the stack of rails.

I lie against the cool, kind metal and dream about returning to the camp, about my bunk, on which there is no mattress, about sleep among comrades who are not going to the gas tonight. Suddenly I see the camp as a haven of peace. It is true, others may be dying, but one is somehow still alive, one has enough food, enough strength to work . . .

The lights on the ramp flicker with a spectral glow, the wave of people – feverish, agitated, stupefied people – flows on and on, endlessly. They think that now they will have to face a new life in the camp, and they prepare themselves emotionally for the hard struggle ahead. They do not know that in just a few moments they will die, that the gold, money, and diamonds which they have so prudently hidden in their clothing and on their bodies are now useless to them. Experienced professionals will probe into every recess of their flesh, will pull the gold from under the tongue and the diamonds from the uterus and the colon. They will rip out gold teeth. In tightly sealed crates they will ship them to Berlin.

The SS men's black figures move about, dignified, businesslike. The gentleman with the notebook puts down his final marks, rounds out the figures: fifteen thousand.

Many, very many, trucks have been driven to the crematoria today.

It is almost over. The dead are being cleared off the ramp and piled into the last truck. The Canada men, weighed down under a load of bread, marmalade and sugar, and smelling of perfume and fresh linen, line up to go. For several days the entire camp will live off this transport. For several days the entire camp will talk about "Sosnowiec-Będzin". "Sosnowiec-Będzin" was a good, rich transport.

The stars are already beginning to pale as we walk back to the camp. The sky grows translucent and opens high above our heads – it is getting light.

Great columns of smoke rise from the crematoria and merge up above into a huge black river which very slowly floats across the sky over Birkenau and disappears beyond the forests in the direction of Trzebinia. The "Sosnowiec-Będzin" transport is already burning.

We pass a heavily armed SS detachment on its way to change guard. The men march briskly, in step, shoulder to shoulder, one mass, one will.

"Und morgen die ganze Welt . . ." they sing at the top of their lungs.

"Rechts ran! To the right march!" snaps a command from up front. We move out of their way.

XIV

RULES, RIGHTS, DUTIES, AND THE GREATER GOOD

I n *The Brothers Karamazov*, Ivan puts an ethical question that forces us to choose between two contrasting perspectives on what we ought to do.

> Imagine that you are creating a fabric of human destiny with the object of making men happy in the end, giving them peace and rest at last, but that it was essential and inevitable to torture to death only one tiny creature – that baby beating its breast with its fist, for instance – and to found that edifice on its unavenged tears, would you consent to be the architect on those conditions? Tell me, and tell the truth.[1]

Most would refuse to torture the child. That some acts are always wrong has, for most of Western history, been the prevailing approach to morality, at least at the level of what has been officially taught and approved by the institutions of church and state. The ten commandments of the Hebrew scriptures served as a model for much of the Christian era. The Roman Catholic church built up an elaborate system of morality based on rules to which no exceptions were allowed. These acts range from intentionally killing an innocent human being to acting against the reproductive capacity of our sexual behavior by using contraceptives. But no matter what the particular ethic we hold, if anything at all is always wrong, what can be more clearly wrong than torturing an innocent child?

Immanuel Kant also held that some things are always wrong. He based this view on his "categorical imperative," which he states in several distinct formulations. One is that we must always act so that we can will the maxim of our action to be a universal law. While these formulations of the categorical imperative might be applied in various ways, in Kant's hands they lead to inviolable rules, for example against telling a lie. In response to a critic who suggested that this rule has exceptions, Kant said that it would be wrong to lie even if someone had taken refuge in your house, and a person seeking to murder him came to your door and asked where he was.

Few people are as rigid as Kant in condemning lying under all circumstances. Lovers may forgive each other's flattering lies, and both be better off for it, as Shakespeare so cleverly describes in Sonnet 138. Life would be difficult if we never told lies. When a friend invites us to a party that we are sure will be dull, is it wrong to say we are already committed for that evening, even if that is untrue? Would it be better to say: "No thanks, your parties are a bore"? The duty of a sheriff or other officer of the law to tell the truth would normally be considered even more inviolable than the ordinary duty not to lie, but the extract from *To Kill a Mockingbird* forces us to reconsider this assumption.

"Let justice be done, though the heavens fall," the saying goes. But is there any point in acting justly if it makes no-one better off? In Anthony Trollope's *Dr Wortle's School*, the title character grapples with his duty towards someone who has violated what Wortle takes to be a serious moral rule. Yet Wortle acknowledges that the rule-breaker is a good person, that his initial violation of the rule was unintentional, and that had he, on discovering his error, ceased to violate the rule, he would have caused great hardship, not only to himself but also to the person he most loves – and all that without benefiting anyone else. Do we really want rules that allow for no exceptions?

In addition to leading to avoidable harm without any offsetting benefit, an ethic based on rules requires some basis for deciding what is to count as a breach of a rule, and here there is an opportunity for self-serving decision-making. In his poem "The Latest Decalogue,"[2] A. H. Clough wrote about one way of narrowing the scope of a well-known moral rule:

> Thou shalt not kill; but need'st not strive
> Officiously to keep alive.

Clough's couplet provides an amusing example of the misuse of literary works in ethical debates. In discussions of medical ethics, it is sometimes uttered in revered tones, as if it were the words of an ancient sage. One doctor, writing in *The Lancet* to defend the non-treatment of infants born with a disability that often causes paralysis, referred to the couplet as "the old dictum we were taught as medical students."[3] Read the remainder of "The Latest Decalogue," however, and it is immediately apparent that the poet's intention is to satirize our failure to heed the spirit of the original Ten Commandments. Clough obviously thought that merely avoiding killing is not enough. If we fail to strive to keep people alive, we may not have broken the rule against killing, but we are still responsible for their deaths.

The distinction between not preserving life and killing is relevant to Section IV's extract from *Whose Life Is It Anyway?* The law allows physicians to "not strive to keep alive" when a patient requests it, even though they know that without the treatment the patient will die. Except in the Netherlands and Belgium, however, it would be murder for a doctor to give a patient a lethal injection, even if the patient requests it. In the extract from *Middlemarch* in this section, we see examples of even finer distinctions between failing to do everything possible to prevent a man's death, and taking steps that contribute positively to that death. If it is wrong to kill, is it also wrong deliberately to omit to do an act that would save the life of an innocent person? If so, the rule against killing is extremely demanding, as we saw in the introduction to Section VI. But if not, where is the line between acts and omissions to be drawn?

Utilitarianism, an approach to ethics developed by the English philosopher and political reformer Jeremy Bentham in the late eighteenth and early nineteenth centuries, has no need of such niceties as the distinction between acts and omissions, for it considers the consequences of our actions, rather than whether they conform to a set of moral rules. Bentham held that an action is right if it leads to a greater surplus of happiness over misery than any possible alternative, and wrong if it does not. By "greater surplus of happiness," Bentham and later utilitarians had in mind the idea of adding up all the pleasure or happiness that resulted from the action and subtracting from that total all the pain or misery to which the action gave rise.

It is at utilitarians, broadly speaking, that Ivan's question is aimed. If one really could be certain that torturing a single child was the only way, and a sure way, of bringing lasting happiness to all the people of the world, a utilitarian would have to do it, for the suffering of that child, terrible and wholly undeserved as it is, will otherwise be inflicted tens of millions of times over the next century on other children, just as innocent, who are victims of starvation, disease, and brutality. Denying the moral significance of the distinction between acts and omissions, the utilitarian will say that to refuse to torture the child is to be responsible for that vastly larger quantity of undeserved suffering.

The utilitarian view is striking in many ways. It puts forward a single principle that it claims can provide the right answer to all ethical dilemmas, if only we can predict what the consequences of our actions will be. It de-mystifies ethics because it bases ethical decisions on happiness, or, in some versions, on the satisfaction of preferences, things that everyone understands and values. And its single principle is applied universally, without fear or favor. Bentham said: "Each to count for one and none for more than one,"[4] by which he meant that the happiness of a peasant counts for as much as that of a noble, and the happiness of an African is no less important than that of a European. At a time when morality was still very largely based on inflexible rules, and the slave trade was a profitable part of Britain's commerce, these were very progressive ideas.

So radical were Bentham's views that later utilitarians have spent a good deal of time trying to modify them in order to avoid some implications with which they were decidedly uncomfortable. One of these is the objection that following utilitarianism would mean lying, stealing, and even murder, whenever they would bring about more good than any alternative action. How are we to decide when murder will bring about more good than anything else we can do? Might doing away with moral rules make it easier for people to persuade themselves that murder is the way to bring about the greatest good for all – as Dostoyevsky portrays Raskolnikov persuading himself, in *Crime and Punishment*? Surely it is better to insist on absolute obedience to the rule against murder than to rely on individuals making such judgments? But then, consider Cath's killing of her demented husband in *Moral Hazard* (Section IV). Do we also want to insist on absolute obedience to the rule against killing in those circumstances?

Perhaps the best utilitarian response to this problem of whether judgments should be left to individuals without giving them rules to obey is what is known as a "two-level" utilitarian theory. At the level of everyday moral decision-making, on this view, we should adopt general moral rules that have been shown over time to have the best consequences in most circumstances. These rules will prohibit lying, stealing, and murder, among other things. Normally we should stick to the rules, because to try to calculate the consequences of every act within the constraints of everyday life is barely feasible, and even if it were, we would still be in danger of being led astray by our own interests, or by particular emotions or biases that might distort our calculation. On the other hand, there may be rare occasions when following the rules will clearly lead to worse consequences than breaking them, and we have the time and ability to reflect carefully on this and be sure that our judgment is sound. Then we may be justified in breaking the rules. Perhaps that was the situation of Sheriff Tate in *To Kill a Mockingbird*, or of the unfortunate Peacockes in *Dr Wortle's School* when they discovered that Mrs Peacocke's first husband was still alive, and yet decided to continue to live together as man and wife.

There are many possible systems of ethics other than a strict ethic of rules and a utilitarian ethic that judges everything by its consequences. As we saw in the introduction to Section I, F. H. Bradley thought that everyone has a role, or station, in life, and this station comes with its own set of duties. The role may be a grand one, for example that of president of a nation, or it may be a more humble one, like that of the butler in Kazuo Ishiguro's *The Remains of the Day*. But the role will come with specific duties that override the general obligation to do what will produce the best consequences for everyone. Here again, however, the question is whether these duties are inviolable, or can be overriden by a greater good, or by the need to avoid doing a greater wrong.

Although some see individual rights, moral rules, or the duties of one's station as absolutely inviolable, no matter what, it is also possible to take a softer approach to such rights, rules, and duties. They can be regarded as something that must be taken into account, but can be overridden in certain circumstances. The problem then is to judge what rights or duties people have, and when they may be over-ridden. Very often, the attempt to find coherent principles for such judgments leads back to a kind of two-level utilitarianism, for it is hard to find other coherent approaches to balancing individual rights, obedience to rules, or the duties of one's role, with the greater good. The readings in this section illustrate the problem of striking this balance.

NOTES

1   Fyodor Dostoevsky, *The Brothers Karamazov* (tr. Constance Garnett), Vol. 1, Pt. 2, Bk 5, Ch. 4. First published in 1879–80.

2   Clough's "The Latest Decalogue" can be found in Helen Gardner (ed.), *The New Oxford Book of English Verse*, Oxford: Oxford University Press, 1978.

3   Dr L. Haas, from a letter in *The Lancet*, 1968; quoted from S. Gorovitz (ed.), *Moral Problems in Medicine*, Englewood Cliffs, NJ: Prentice-Hall, 1976, p. 351.

4   Jeremy Bentham, *An Introduction to the Principles of Morals and Legislation*, 2nd edn, 1823; New York: Hafner, 1948, Ch. 1, n. 4.

69

URSULA K. LE GUIN

The Ones Who Walk Away from Omelas

With a clamor of bells that set the swallows soaring, the Festival of Summer came to the city Omelas, bright-towered by the sea. The rigging of the boats in harbor sparkled with flags. In the streets between houses with red roofs and painted walls, between old moss-grown gardens and under avenues of trees, past great parks and public buildings, processions moved. Some were decorous: old people in long stiff robes of mauve and grey, grave master workmen, quiet, merry women carrying their babies and chatting as they walked. In other streets the music beat faster, a shimmering of gong and tambourine, and the people went dancing, the procession was a dance. Children dodged in and out, their high calls rising like the swallows' crossing flights over the music and the singing. All the processions wound towards the north side of the city, where on the great water-meadow called the Green Fields boys and girls, naked in the bright air, with mud-stained feet and ankles and long, lithe arms, exercised their restive horses before the race. The horses wore no gear at all but a halter without bit. Their manes were braided with streamers of silver, gold, and green. They flared their nostrils and pranced and boasted to one another; they were vastly excited, the horse being the only animal who has adopted our ceremonies as his own. Far off to the north and west the mountains stood up half encircling Omelas on her bay. The air of morning was so clear that the snow still crowning the Eighteen Peaks burned with white-gold fire across the miles of sunlit air, under the dark blue of the sky. There was just enough wind to make the banners that marked the racecourse snap and flutter now and then. In the silence of the broad green meadows one could hear the music winding through the city streets, farther and nearer and ever approaching, a cheerful faint sweetness of the air that from time to time trembled and gathered together and broke out into the great joyous clanging of the bells.

Joyous! How is one to tell about joy? How describe the citizens of Omelas?

They were not simple folk, you see, though they were happy. But we do not say the words of cheer much any more. All smiles have become archaic. Given a

---

description such as this one tends to make certain assumptions. Given a description such as this one tends to look next for the King, mounted on a splendid stallion and surrounded by his noble knights, or perhaps in a golden litter borne by great-muscled slaves. But there was no king. They did not use swords, or keep slaves. They were not barbarians. I do not know the rules and laws of their society, but I suspect that they were singularly few. As they did without monarchy and slavery, so they also got on without the stock exchange, the advertisement, the secret police, and the bomb. Yet I repeat that these were not simple folk, not dulcet shepherds, noble savages, bland utopians. They were not less complex than us. The trouble is that we have a bad habit, encouraged by pedants and sophisticates, of considering happiness as something rather stupid. Only pain is intellectual, only evil interesting. This is the treason of the artist: a refusal to admit the banality of evil and the terrible boredom of pain. If you can't lick 'em, join 'em. If it hurts, repeat it. But to praise despair is to condemn delight, to embrace violence is to lose hold of everything else. We have almost lost hold; we can no longer describe a happy man, nor make any celebration of joy. How can I tell you about the people of Omelas? They were not naïve and happy children – though their children were, in fact, happy. They were mature, intelligent, passionate adults whose lives were not wretched. O miracle! but I wish I could describe it better. I wish I could convince you. Omelas sounds in my words like a city in a fairy tale, long ago and far away, once upon a time. Perhaps it would be best if you imagined it as your own fancy bids, assuming it will rise to the occasion, for certainly I cannot suit you all. For instance, how about technology? I think that there would be no cars or helicopters in and above the streets; this follows from the fact that the people of Omelas are happy people. Happiness is based on a just discrimination of what is necessary, what is neither necessary nor destructive, and what is destructive. In the middle category, however – that of the unnecessary but undestructive, that of comfort, luxury, exuberance, etc. – they could perfectly well have central heating, subway trains, washing machines, and all kinds of marvelous devices not yet invented here, floating light-sources, fuelless power, a cure for the common cold. Or they could have none of that: it doesn't matter. As you like it. I incline to think that people from towns up and down the coast have been coming in to Omelas during the last days before the Festival on very fast little trains and double-decked trams, and that the train station of Omelas is actually the handsomest building in town, though plainer than the magnificent Farmers' Market. But even granted trains, I fear that Omelas so far strikes some of you as goody-goody. Smiles, bells, parades, horses, bleh. If so, please add an orgy. If an orgy would help, don't hesitate. Let us not, however, have temples from which issue beautiful nude priests and priestesses already half in ecstasy and ready to copulate with any man or woman, lover or stranger, who desires union with the deep godhead of the blood, although that was my first idea. But really it would be better not to have any temples in Omelas – at least, not manned temples. Religion yes, clergy no. Surely the beautiful nudes can just wander about, offering themselves like divine soufflés to the hunger of the needy and the rapture of the flesh. Let them join the processions. Let tambourines be struck above the copulations, and the glory of desire be proclaimed upon the gongs, and (a not unimportant point) let the offspring of these delightful rituals be beloved and looked after by all. One thing I know there is none of in Omelas is guilt. But what else should there be? I thought at first there were no drugs, but that is puritanical. For those who like it, the faint insistent sweetness of *drooz* may perfume the ways of the city, *drooz* which first brings a great lightness and brilliance to the mind and limbs, and then after some hours a dreamy languor, and wonderful visions at last of the very arcana and inmost secrets of the Universe, as well as exciting the pleasure of sex beyond all belief; and it is not habit-forming. For more modest tastes I think there ought to be beer. What else, what else belongs in the joyous city? The sense of victory, surely, the celebration of courage. But as we did without clergy, let us do without soldiers. The joy built upon successful slaughter is not the right kind of joy; it will not do; it is fearful and it is trivial. A boundless and generous contentment, a magnanimous triumph felt not against some outer enemy but in communion with the finest and fairest in the souls of all men everywhere and the splendor of the world's summer: this is what swells the hearts of the people of Omelas, and the victory they celebrate is that of life. I really don't think many of them need to take *drooz*.

Most of the processions have reached the Green Fields by now. A marvelous smell of cooking goes forth from the red and blue tents of the provisioners. The faces of small children are amiably sticky; in the benign grey beard of a man a couple of crumbs of rich pastry are entangled. The youths and girls have mounted their horses and are beginning to group around the starting line of the course. An old woman, small, fat, and laughing, is passing out flowers from a basket, and tall young men wear her flowers in their shining hair. A child of nine or ten sits at the edge of the crowd, alone, playing on a wooden flute. People pause to listen, and they smile, but they do not speak to him, for he never ceases playing and never sees them, his dark eyes wholly rapt in the sweet, thin magic of the tune.

He finishes, and slowly lowers his hands holding the wooden flute.

As if that little private silence were the signal, all at once a trumpet sounds from the pavilion near the starting line: imperious, melancholy, piercing. The horses rear on their slender legs, and some of them neigh in answer. Sober-faced, the young riders stroke the horses' necks and soothe them, whispering, "Quiet, quiet, there my beauty, my hope. . . ." They begin to form in rank along the starting line. The crowds along the racecourse are like a field of grass and flowers in the wind. The Festival of Summer has begun.

Do you believe? Do you accept the festival, the city, the joy? No? Then let me describe one more thing.

In a basement under one of the beautiful public buildings of Omelas, or perhaps in the cellar of one of its spacious private homes, there is a room. It has one locked door, and no window. A little light seeps in dustily between cracks in the boards, secondhand from a cobwebbed window somewhere across the cellar. In one corner of the little room a couple of mops, with stiff, clotted, foul-smelling heads, stand near a rusty bucket. The floor is dirt, a little damp to the touch, as cellar dirt usually is. The room is about three paces long and two wide: a mere broom closet or disused tool room. In the room a child is sitting. It could be a boy or a girl. It looks about six, but actually is nearly ten. It is feeble-minded. Perhaps it was born defective, or perhaps it has become imbecile through fear, malnutrition, and neglect. It picks its nose and occasionally fumbles vaguely with its toes or genitals, as it sits hunched in the corner farthest from the bucket and the two mops. It is afraid of the mops. It finds them horrible. It shuts its eyes, but it knows the mops are still standing there; and the door is locked; and nobody will come. The door is always locked; and nobody ever comes, except that sometimes – the child has no under-standing of time or interval – sometimes the door rattles terribly and opens, and a person, or several people, are there. One of them may come in and kick the child to make it stand up. The others never come close, but peer in at it with frightened, disgusted eyes. The food bowl and the water jug are hastily filled, the door is locked, the eyes disappear. The people at the door never say anything, but the child, who has not always lived in the tool room, and can remember sunlight and its mother's voice, sometimes speaks. "I will be good," it says. "Please let me out. I will be good!" They never answer. The child used to scream for help at night, and cry a good deal, but now it only makes a kind of whining, "eh-haa, eh-haa," and it speaks less and less often. It is so thin there are no calves to its legs; its belly protrudes; it lives on a half-bowl of corn meal and grease a day. It is naked. Its buttocks and thighs are a mass of festered sores, as it sits in its own excrement continually.

They all know it is there, all the people of Omelas. Some of them have come to see it, others are content merely to know it is there. They all know that it has to be there. Some of them understand why, and some do not, but they all understand that their happiness, the beauty of their city, the tenderness of their friendships, the health of their children, the wisdom of their scholars, the skill of their makers, even the abundance of their harvest and the kindly weathers of their skies, depend wholly on this child's abominable misery.

This is usually explained to children when they are between eight and twelve, whenever they seem capable of understanding; and most of those who come to see the child are young people, though often enough an adult comes, or comes back, to see the child. No matter how well the matter has been explained to them, these young spectators are always shocked and sickened at the sight. They feel disgust, which they had thought themselves superior to. They feel anger, outrage, impot-ence, despite all the explanations. They would like to do something for the child. But there is nothing they can do. If the child were brought up into the sunlight out of that vile place, if it were cleaned and fed and comforted, that would be a good thing, indeed; but if it were done, in that day and hour all the prosperity and beauty and delight of Omelas would wither and be destroyed. Those are the terms. To exchange all the goodness and grace of every life in Omelas for that single, small improvement: to throw away the happiness of thousands for the chance of the happiness of one: that would be to let guilt within the walls indeed.

The terms are strict and absolute; there may not even be a kind word spoken to the child.

Often the young people go home in tears, or in a tearless rage, when they have seen the child and faced this terrible paradox. They may brood over it for weeks or years. But as time goes on they begin to realize that even if the child could be released, it would not get much good of its freedom: a little vague pleasure of warmth and food, no doubt, but little more. It is too degraded and imbecile to know any real joy. It has been afraid too long ever to be free of fear. Its habits are too uncouth for it to respond to humane treatment. Indeed, after so long it would probably be wretched without walls about it to protect it, and darkness for its eyes, and its own excrement to sit in. Their tears at the bitter injustice dry when they begin to perceive the terrible justice of reality, and to accept it. Yet it is their tears and anger, the trying of their generosity and the acceptance of their helplessness, which are perhaps the true source of the splendor of their lives. Theirs is no vapid, irresponsible happiness. They know that they, like the child, are not free. They know compassion. It is the existence of the child, and their knowledge of its existence, that makes possible the nobility of their architecture, the poignancy of their music, the profundity of their science. It is because of the child that they are so gentle with children. They know that if the wretched one were not there snivelling in the dark, the other one, the flute-player, could make no joyful music as the young riders line up in their beauty for the race in the sunlight of the first morning of summer.

Now do you believe in them? Are they not more credible? But there is one more thing to tell, and this is quite incredible.

At times one of the adolescent girls or boys who go to see the child does not go home to weep or rage, does not, in fact, go home at all. Sometimes also a man or woman much older falls silent for a day or two, and then leaves home. These people go out into the street, and walk down the street alone. They keep walking, and walk straight out of the city of Omelas, through the beautiful gates. They keep walking across the farmlands of Omelas. Each one goes alone, youth or girl, man or woman. Night falls; the traveler must pass down village streets, between the houses with yellow-lit windows, and on out into the darkness of the fields. Each alone, they go west or north, towards the mountains. They go on. They leave Omelas, they walk ahead into the darkness, and they do not come back. The place they go towards is a place even less imaginable to most of us than the city of happiness. I cannot describe it at all. It is possible that it does not exist. But they seem to know where they are going, the ones who walk away from Omelas.

70

FYODOR DOSTOYEVSKY

Crime and Punishment

Crime and Punishment tells of a desperate plan, and its consequences. Raskolnikov, a destitute former student, plots the perfect crime of principle.

Raskolnikov had become superstitious of late. The traces of superstition remained in him long after, and were almost ineradicable. And in all this he was always afterwards disposed to see something strange and mysterious, as it were the presence of some peculiar influences and coincidences. In the previous winter a student he knew called Pokorev, who had left for Harkov, had chanced in conversation to give him the address of Alyona Ivanovna, the old pawnbroker, in case he might want to pawn anything. For a long while he did not go to her, for he had lessons and managed to get along somehow. Six weeks ago he had remembered the address; he had two articles that could be pawned: his father's old silver watch and a little gold ring with three red stones, a present from his sister at parting. He decided to take the ring. When he found the old woman he had felt an insurmountable repulsion for her at the first glance, though he knew nothing special about her. He got two roubles from her and went into a miserable little tavern on his way home. He asked for tea, sat down and sank into deep thought. A strange idea was pecking at his brain like a chicken in the egg, and very, very much absorbed him.

Almost beside him at the next table there was sitting a student, whom he did not know and had never seen, and with him a young officer. They had played a game of billiards and began drinking tea. All at once he heard the student mention to the officer the pawnbroker Alyona Ivanovna and give him her address. This of itself seemed strange to Raskolnikov; he had just come from her and here at once he heard her name. Of course it was a chance, but he could not shake off a very extraordinary impression, and here some one seemed to be speaking expressly for him; the student began telling his friend various details about Alyona Ivanovna.

"She is first rate," he said. "You can always get money from her. She is as rich as a Jew, she can give you five thousand roubles at a time and she is not above taking

---

Fyodor Dostoyevsky, from Chapter VI in *Crime and Punishment*, first published in 1866.

a pledge for a rouble. Lots of our fellows have had dealings with her. But she is an awful old harpy. . . ."

And he began describing how spiteful and uncertain she was, how if you were only a day late with your interest the pledge was lost; how she gave a quarter of the value of an article and took five and even seven percent a month on it and so on. The student chattered on, saying that she had a sister Lizaveta, whom the wretched little creature was continually beating, and kept in complete bondage like a small child, though Lizaveta was at least six feet high.

"There's a phenomenon for you," cried the student and he laughed.

They began talking about Lizaveta. The student spoke about her with a peculiar relish and was continually laughing and the officer listened with great interest and asked him to send Lizaveta to do some mending for him. Raskolnikov did not miss a word and learned everything about her. Lizaveta was younger than the old woman and was her half-sister, being the child of a different mother. She was thirty-five. She worked day and night for her sister, and besides doing the cooking and the washing, she did sewing and worked as a charwoman and gave her sister all she earned. She did not dare to accept an order or job of any kind without her sister's permission. The old woman had already made her will, and Lizaveta knew of it, and by this will she would not get a farthing; nothing but the movables, chairs and so on; all the money was left to a monastery in the province of N———, that prayers might be said for her in perpetuity. Lizaveta was of lower rank than her sister, unmarried and awfully uncouth in appearance, remarkably tall with long feet that looked as if they were bent outwards. She always wore battered goatskin shoes, and was clean in her person. What the student expressed most surprise and amusement about was the fact that Lizaveta was continually with child.

"But you say she is hideous?" observed the officer.

"Yes, she is so dark-skinned and looks like a soldier dressed up, but you know she is not at all hideous. She has such a good-natured face and eyes. Strikingly so. And the proof of it is that lots of people are attracted by her. She is such a soft, gentle creature, ready to put up with anything, always willing, willing to do anything. And her smile is really very sweet."

"You seem to find her attractive yourself," laughed the officer.

"From her queerness. No, I'll tell you what. I could kill that damned old woman and make off with her money, I assure you, without the faintest conscience-prick," the student added with warmth. The officer laughed again while Raskolnikov shuddered. How strange it was!

"Listen, I want to ask you a serious question," the student said hotly. "I was joking of course, but look here; on one side we have a stupid, senseless, worthless, spiteful, ailing, horrid old woman, not simply useless but doing actual mischief, who has not an idea what she is living for herself, and who will die in a day or two in any case. You understand? You understand?"

"Yes, yes, I understand," answered the officer, watching his excited companion attentively.

"Well, listen then. On the other side, fresh young lives thrown away for want of help and by thousands, on every side! A hundred thousand good deeds could be done and helped, on that old woman's money which will be buried in a monastery! Hundreds, thousands perhaps, might be set on the right path; dozens of families saved from destitution, from ruin, from vice, from the Lock hospitals – and all with her money. Kill her, take her money and with the help of it devote oneself to the service of humanity and the good of all. What do you think, would not one tiny crime be wiped out by thousands of good deeds? For one life thousands would be saved from corruption and decay. One death, and a hundred lives in exchange – it's simple arithmetic! Besides, what value has the life of that sickly, stupid, ill-natured old woman in the balance of existence! No more than the life of a louse, of a black beetle, less in fact because the old woman is doing harm. She is wearing out the lives of others; the other day she bit Lizaveta's finger out of spite; it almost had to be amputated."

"Of course she does not deserve to live," remarked the officer, "but there it is, it's nature."

"Oh, well, brother, but we have to correct and direct nature, and, but for that, we should drown in an ocean of prejudice. But for that, there would never have been a single great man. They talk of duty, conscience – I don't want to say anything against duty and conscience; – but the point is what do we mean by them. Stay, I have another question to ask you. Listen!"

"No, you stay, I'll ask you a question. Listen!"

"Well?"

"You are talking and speechifying away, but tell me, would you kill the old woman *yourself?*"

"Of course not! I was only arguing the justice of it. . . . It's nothing to do with me. . . ."

"But I think, if you would not do it yourself, there's no justice about it. . . . Let us have another game."

Raskolnikov was violently agitated. Of course, it was all ordinary youthful talk and thought, such as he had often heard before in different forms and on different themes. But why had he happened to hear such a discussion and such ideas at the very moment when his own brain was just conceiving . . . *the very same ideas?* And why, just at the moment when he had brought away the embryo of his idea from the old woman had he dropped at once upon a conversation about her? This coincidence always seemed strange to him. This trivial talk in a tavern had an immense influence on him in his later action; as though there had really been in it something preordained, some guiding hint. . . .

That night and for the whole of the following day Raskolnikov is feverish and sleeps a great deal.

Suddenly he heard a clock strike. He started, roused himself, raised his head, looked out of the window, and seeing how late it was, suddenly jumped up wide awake as though some one had pulled him off the sofa. He crept on tiptoe to the door, stealthily opened it and began listening on the staircase. His heart beat terribly. But all was quiet on the stairs as if every one was asleep. . . . It seemed to him strange and monstrous that he could have slept in such forgetfulness from the previous day and had done nothing, had prepared nothing yet. . . . And meanwhile perhaps it had struck six. And his drowsiness and stupefaction were followed by an extraordinary, feverish, as it were, distracted, haste. But the preparations to be made were few. He concentrated all his energies on thinking of everything and forgetting nothing; and his heart kept beating and thumping so that he could hardly breathe. First he had to make a noose and sew it into his overcoat – a work of a moment. He rummaged under his pillow and picked out amongst the linen stuffed away under it, a worn out, old unwashed shirt. From its rags he tore a long strip, a couple of inches wide and about sixteen inches long. He folded this strip in two, took off his wide, strong summer overcoat of some stout cotton material (his only outer garment) and began sewing the two ends of the rag on the inside, under the left armhole. His hands shook as he sewed, but he did it successfully so that nothing showed outside when he put the coat on again. The needle and thread he had got ready long before and they lay on his table in a piece of paper. As for the noose, it was a very ingenious device of his own; the noose was intended for the axe. It was impossible for him to carry the axe through the street in his hands. And if hidden under his coat he would still have had to support it with his hand, which would have been noticeable. Now he had only to put the head of the axe in the noose, and it would hang quietly under his arm on the inside. Putting his hand in his coat pocket, he could hold the end of the handle all the way, so that it did not swing; and as the coat was very full, a regular sack in fact, it could not be seen from outside that he was holding something with the hand that was in the pocket. This noose, too, he had designed a fortnight before.

When he had finished with this, he thrust his hand into a little opening between his sofa and the floor, fumbled in the left corner and drew out the *pledge*, which he had got ready long before and hidden there. This pledge was, however, only a smoothly planed piece of wood the size and thickness of a silver cigarette case. He picked up this piece of wood in one of his wanderings in a courtyard where there was some sort of a workshop. Afterwards he had added to the wood a thin smooth piece of iron, which he had also picked up at the same time in the street. Putting the iron which was a little the smaller on the piece of wood, he fastened them very firmly, crossing and re-crossing the thread round them; then wrapped them carefully and daintily in clean white paper and tied up the parcel so that it would be very difficult to untie it. This was in order to divert the attention of the old woman for a time, while she was trying to undo the knot, and so to gain a moment. The iron strip was added to give weight, so that the woman might not guess the first minute that the "thing" was made of wood. All this had been stored by him beforehand under the sofa. He had only just got the pledge out when he heard some one suddenly about in the yard.

"It struck six long ago."

"Long ago! My God!"

He rushed to the door, listened, caught up his hat and began to descend his thirteen steps cautiously, noiselessly, like a cat. He had still the most important thing to do – to steal the axe from the kitchen. That the deed must be done with an axe he had decided long ago. He had also a pocket pruning-knife, but he could not rely on the knife and still less on his own strength, and so resolved finally on the axe. We may note in passing, one peculiarity in regard to all the final resolutions taken by him in the matter; they had one strange characteristic: the more final they were, the more hideous and the more absurd they at once became in his eyes. In spite of all his agonising inward struggle, he never for a single instant all that time could believe in the carrying out of his plans.

And, indeed, if it had ever happened that everything to the least point could have been considered and finally settled, and no uncertainty of any kind had remained, he would, it seems, have renounced it all as something absurd, monstrous and impossible. But a whole mass of unsettled points and uncertainties remained. As for getting the axe, that trifling business cost him no anxiety, for nothing could be easier. Nastasya was continually out of the house, especially in the evenings; she would run in to the neighbours or to a shop, and always left the door ajar. It was the one thing the landlady was always scolding her about. And so when the time came, he would only have to go quietly into the kitchen and to take the axe, and an hour later (when everything was over) go in and put it back again. But these were doubtful points. Supposing he returned an hour later to put it back, and Nastasya had come back and was on the spot. He would of course have to go by and wait till she went out again. But supposing she were in the meantime to miss the axe, look for it, make an outcry – that would mean suspicion or at least grounds for suspicion.

But those were all trifles which he had not even begun to consider, and indeed he had no time. He was thinking of the chief point, and put off trifling details, until he *could believe in it all*. But that seemed utterly unattainable. So it seemed to himself at least. He could not imagine, for instance, that he would sometime leave off thinking, get up and simply go there. . . . Even his late experiment (*i.e.* his visit with the object of a final survey of the place) was simply an attempt at an experiment, far from being the real thing, as though one should say "come, let us go and try it – why dream about it!" – and at once he had broken down and had run away cursing, in a frenzy with himself. Meanwhile it would seem, as regards the moral question, that his analysis was complete; his casuistry had become keen as a razor, and he could not find rational objections in himself. But in the last resort he simply ceased to believe in himself, and doggedly, slavishly sought arguments in all directions, fumbling for them, as though some one were forcing and drawing him to it.

At first – long before indeed – he had been much occupied with one question; why almost all crimes are so badly concealed and so easily detected, and why almost all criminals leave such obvious traces? He had come gradually to many different and curious conclusions, and in his opinion the chief reason lay not so much in the material impossibility of concealing the crime, as in the criminal himself. Almost every criminal is subject to a failure of will and reasoning power by a childish and phenomenal heedlessness, at the very instant when prudence and caution are most essential. It was his conviction that this eclipse of reason and failure of will power attacked a man like a disease, developed gradually and reached its highest point just before the perpetration of the crime, continued with equal violence at the moment of the crime and for a longer or shorter time after, according to the individual case, and then passed off like any other disease. The question whether the disease gives rise to the crime, or whether the crime from its own peculiar nature is always accompanied by something of the nature of disease, he did not yet feel able to decide.

When he reached these conclusions, he decided that in his own case there could not be such a morbid reaction, that his reason and will would remain unimpaired at the time of carrying out his design, for the simple reason that his design was "not a crime. . . ." We will omit all the process by means of which he arrived at this last conclusion; we have run too far ahead already. . . . We may add only that the practical, purely material difficulties of the affair occupied a secondary position in his mind. "One has but to keep all one's will power and reason to deal with them, and they will all be overcome at the time when once one has familiarised oneself with the minutest details of the business. . . ." But this preparation had never been begun. His final decisions were what he came to trust least, and when the hour struck, it all came to pass quite differently, as it were accidentally and unexpectedly.

One trifling circumstance upset his calculations, before he had even left the staircase. When he reached the landlady's kitchen, the door of which was open as usual, he glanced cautiously in to see whether, in Nastasya's absence, the landlady herself was there, or if not, whether the door to her own room was closed, so that she might not peep out when he went in for the axe. But what was his amazement when he suddenly saw that Nastasya was not only at home in the kitchen, but was occupied there, taking linen out of a basket and hanging it on a line. Seeing him, she left off hanging the clothes, turned to him and stared at him all the time he was passing. He turned away his eyes, and walked past as though he noticed nothing. But it was the end of everything; he had not the axe! He was overwhelmed.

"What made me think," he reflected, as he went under the gateway, "what made me think that she would be sure not to be at home at that moment! Why, why, why did I assume this so certainly?"

He was crushed and even humiliated. He could have laughed at himself in his anger. . . . A dull animal rage boiled within him.

He stood hesitating in the gateway. To go into the street, to go for a walk for appearance sake was revolting; to go back to his room, even more revolting. "And what a chance I have lost for ever!" he muttered, standing aimlessly in the gateway, just opposite the porter's little dark room, which was also open. Suddenly he started. From the porter's room, two paces away from him, something shining under the bench to the right caught his eye. . . . He looked about him – nobody. He approached the room on tiptoe, went down two steps into it and in a faint voice called the porter. "Yes, not at home! Somewhere near though, in the yard, for the door is wide open." He dashed to the axe (it was an axe) and pulled it out from under the bench, where it lay between two chunks of wood; at once before going out, he made it fast in the noose, he thrust both hands into his pockets and went out of the room; no one had noticed him! "When reason fails, the devil helps!" he thought with a strange grin. This chance raised his spirits extraordinarily.

He walked along quietly and sedately, without hurry, to avoid awakening suspicion. He scarcely looked at the passers-by, tried to escape looking at their faces at all, and to be as little noticeable as possible. Suddenly he thought of his hat. "Good heavens! I had the money the day before yesterday and did not get a cap to wear instead!" A curse rose from the bottom of his soul.

Glancing out of the corner of his eye into a shop, he saw by a clock on the wall that it was ten minutes past seven. He had to make haste and at the same time to go someway round, so as to approach the house from the other side. . . .

When he had happened to imagine all this beforehand, he had sometimes thought that he would be very much afraid. But he was not very much afraid now, was not afraid at all, indeed. His mind was even occupied by irrelevant matters, but by nothing for long. As he passed the Yusupov garden, he was deeply absorbed in considering the building of great fountains, and of their refreshing effect on the atmosphere in all the squares. By degrees he passed to the conviction that if the summer garden were extended to the field of Mars, and perhaps joined to the garden of the Mihailovsky Palace, it would be a splendid thing and a great benefit to the town. Then he was interested by the question why in all great towns men are not simply driven by necessity, but in some peculiar way inclined to live in those parts of the town where there are no gardens nor fountains; where there is most dirt and smell and all sorts of nastiness. Then his own walks through the Hay Market came back to his mind, and for a moment he waked up to reality. "What nonsense!" he thought, "better think of nothing at all!"

"So probably men led to execution clutch mentally at every object that meets them on the way," flashed through his mind, but simply flashed, like lightning; he made haste to dismiss this thought. . . . And by now he was near; here was the house, here was the gate. Suddenly a clock somewhere struck once. "What! can it be half-past seven? Impossible, it must be fast!"

Luckily for him, everything went well again at the gates. At that very moment, as though expressly for his benefit, a huge waggon of hay had just driven in at the gate, completely screening him as he passed under the gateway, and the waggon had scarcely had time to drive through into the yard, before he had slipped in a flash to the right. On the other side of the waggon he could hear shouting and quarrelling; but no one noticed him and no one met him. Many windows looking into that huge quadrangular yard were open at that moment, but he did not raise his head – he had not the strength to. The staircase leading to the old woman's room was close by, just on the right of the gateway. He was already on the stairs. . . .

Drawing a breath, pressing his hand against his throbbing heart, and once more feeling for the axe and setting it straight, he began softly and cautiously ascending the stairs, listening every minute. But the stairs, too, were quite deserted; all the doors were shut; he met no one. One flat indeed on the first floor was wide open and painters were at work in it, but they did not glance at him. He stood still, thought a minute and went on. "Of course it would be better if they had not been here, but . . . it's two storeys above them."

And there was the fourth storey, here was the door, here was the flat opposite, the empty one. The flat underneath the old woman's was apparently empty also; the visiting card nailed on the door had been torn off – they had gone away! . . . He was out of breath. For one instant the thought floated through his mind "Shall I go back?" But he made no answer and began listening at the old woman's door, a dead silence. Then he listened again on the staircase, listened long and intently . . . then looked about him for the last time, pulled himself together, drew himself up, and once more tried the axe in the noose. "Am I very pale?" he wondered. "Am I not evidently agitated? She is mistrustful. . . . Had I better wait a little longer . . . till my heart leaves off thumping?"

But his heart did not leave off. On the contrary, as though to spite him, it throbbed more and more violently. He could stand it no longer, he slowly put out his hand to the bell and rang. Half a minute later he rang again, more loudly.

No answer. To go on ringing was useless and out of place. The old woman was, of course, at home, but she was suspicious and alone. He had some knowledge of her habits . . . and once more he put his ear to the door. Either his senses were peculiarly keen (which it is difficult to suppose), or the sound was really very distinct. Anyway, he suddenly heard something like the cautious touch of a hand on the lock and the rustle of a skirt at the very door. Some one was standing stealthily close to the lock and just as he was doing on the outside was secretly listening within, and seemed to have her ear to the door. . . . He moved a little on purpose and muttered something aloud that he might not have the appearance of hiding, then rang a third time, but quietly, soberly and without impatience, Recalling it afterwards, that moment stood out in his mind vividly, distinctly, forever; he could not make out how he had had such cunning, for his mind was as it were clouded at moments and he was almost unconscious of his body. . . . An instant later he heard the latch unfastened.

71

KAZUO ISHIGURO

The Remains of the Day

In *The Remains of the Day*, Stevens, an elderly butler, reflects on his thirty years of service to Lord Darlington. The reserved Stevens looks back, through the blinkers of memory, at the missed opportunities and losses of his past.

I feel I should perhaps return a moment to the question of his lordship's attitude to Jewish persons, since this whole issue of anti-Semitism, I realize, has become a rather sensitive one these days. In particular, let me clear up this matter of a supposed bar against Jewish persons on the staff at Darlington Hall. Since this allegation falls very directly into my own realm, I am able to refute it with absolute authority. There were many Jewish persons on my staff throughout all my years with his lordship, and let me say furthermore that they were never treated in any way differently on account of their race. One really cannot guess the reason for these absurd allegations – unless, quite ludicrously, they originate from that brief, entirely insignificant few weeks in the early thirties when Mrs Carolyn Barnet came to wield an unusual influence over his lordship.

Mrs Barnet, the widow of Mr Charles Barnet, was at that point in her forties – a very handsome, some might say glamorous lady. She had a reputation for being formidably intelligent, and in those days one often tended to hear of how she had humiliated this or that learned gentleman at dinner over some important contemporary issue. For much of the summer of 1932, she was a regular presence at Darlington Hall, she and his lordship often spending hour after hour deep in conversation, typically of a social or political nature. And it was Mrs Barnet, as I recall, who took his lordship on those "guided inspections" of the poorest areas of London's East End, during which his lordship visited the actual homes of many of the families suffering the desperate plight of those years. That is to say, Mrs Barnet, in all likelihood, made some sort of contribution to Lord Darlington's developing concern for the poor of our country and as such, her influence cannot

KAZUO ISHIGURO, pp.145–54 from *The Remains of the Day*. London: Faber & Faber, 1989. Copyright © 1989 by Kazuo Ishiguro. Used by permission of Alfred A. Knopf, a division of Random House, Inc. and Faber & Faber Ltd.

be said to have been entirely negative. But she was too, of course, a member of Sir Oswald Mosley's "blackshirts" organization, and the very little contact his lordship ever had with Sir Oswald occurred during those few weeks of that summer. And it was during those same weeks that those entirely untypical incidents took place at Darlington Hall which must, one supposes, have provided what flimsy basis exists for these absurd allegations.

I call them "incidents" but some of these were extremely minor. For instance, I recall overhearing at dinner one evening, when a particular newspaper had been mentioned, his lordship remarking: "Oh, you mean that Jewish propaganda sheet." And then on another occasion around that time, I remember his instructing me to cease giving donations to a particular local charity which regularly came to the door on the grounds that the management committee was "more or less homogeneously Jewish". I have remembered these remarks because they truly surprised me at the time, his lordship never previously having shown any antagonism whatsoever towards the Jewish race.

Then, of course, came that afternoon his lordship called me into his study. Initially, he made rather general conversation, inquiring if all was well around the house and so on. Then he said:

"I've been doing a great deal of thinking, Stevens. A great deal of thinking. And I've reached my conclusion. We cannot have Jews on the staff here at Darlington Hall."

"Sir?"

"It's for the good of this house, Stevens. In the interests of the guests we have staying here. I've looked into this carefully, Stevens, and I'm letting you know my conclusion."

"Very well, sir."

"Tell me, Stevens, we have a few on the staff at the moment, don't we? Jews, I mean."

"I believe two of the present staff members would fall into that category, sir."

"Ah." His lordship paused for a moment, staring out of his window. "Of course, you'll have to let them go."

"I beg your pardon, sir?"

"It's regrettable, Stevens, but we have no choice. There's the safety and well-being of my guests to consider. Let me assure you, I've looked into this matter and thought it through thoroughly. It's in all our best interests."

The two staff members concerned were, in fact, both housemaids. It would hardly have been proper, then, to have taken any action without first informing Miss Kenton of the situation, and I resolved to do just this that same evening when I met her for cocoa in her parlour. I should perhaps say a few words here concerning these meetings in her parlour at the end of each day. These were, let me say, overwhelmingly professional in tone – though naturally we might discuss some informal topics from time to time. Our reason for instituting such meetings was simple: we had found that our respective lives were often so busy, several days could go by without our having an opportunity to exchange even the most basic of information. Such a situation, we recognized, seriously jeopardized the smooth running of operations, and to spend fifteen minutes or so together at the end of the day in the privacy of Miss Kenton's parlour was the most straightforward remedy. I must reiterate, these meetings were predominantly professional in character; that is to say, for instance, we might talk over the plans for a forthcoming event, or else discuss how a new recruit was settling in.

In any case, to return to my thread, you will appreciate I was not unperturbed at the prospect of telling Miss Kenton I was about to dismiss two of her maids. Indeed, the maids had been perfectly satisfactory employees and – I may as well say this since the Jewish issue has become so sensitive of late – my every instinct opposed the idea of their dismissal. Nevertheless, my duty in this instance was quite clear, and as I saw it, there was nothing to be gained at all in irresponsibly displaying such personal doubts. It was a difficult task, but as such, one that demanded to be carried out with dignity. And so it was that when I finally raised the matter towards the end of our conversation that evening, I did so in as concise and businesslike a way as possible, concluding with the words:

"I will speak to the two employees in my pantry tomorrow morning at ten thirty. I would be grateful then, Miss Kenton, if you would send them along. I leave it entirely to yourself whether or not you inform them beforehand as to the nature of what I am going to say to them."

At this point, Miss Kenton seemed to have nothing to say in response. So I continued: "Well, Miss Kenton, thank you for the cocoa. It's high time I was turning in. Another busy day tomorrow."

It was then that Miss Kenton said: "Mr Stevens, I cannot quite believe my ears. Ruth and Sarah have been members of my staff for over six years now. I trust them absolutely and indeed they trust me. They have served this house excellently."

"I am sure that is so, Miss Kenton. However, we must not allow sentiment to creep into our judgement. Now really, I must bid you good night . . ."

"Mr Stevens, I am outraged that you can sit there and utter what you have just done as though you were discussing orders for the larder. I simply cannot believe it. You are saying Ruth and Sarah are to be dismissed on the grounds that they are Jewish?"

"Miss Kenton, I have just this moment explained the situation to you fully. His lordship has made his decision and there is nothing for you and I to debate over."

"Does it not occur to you, Mr Stevens, that to dismiss Ruth and Sarah on these grounds would be simply – *wrong*? I will not stand for such things. I will not work in a house in which such things can occur."

"Miss Kenton, I will ask you not to excite yourself and to conduct yourself in a manner befitting your position. This is a very straightforward matter. If his lordship wishes these particular contracts to be discontinued, then there is little more to be said."

"I am warning you, Mr Stevens, I will not continue to work in such a house. If my girls are dismissed, I will leave also."

"Miss Kenton, I am surprised to find you reacting in this manner. Surely I don't have to remind you that our professional duty is not to our own foibles and sentiments, but to the wishes of our employer."

"I am telling you, Mr Stevens, if you dismiss my girls tomorrow, it will be wrong, a sin as any sin ever was one and I will not continue to work in such a house."

"Miss Kenton, let me suggest to you that you are hardly well placed to be passing judgements of such a high and mighty nature. The fact is, the world of today is a very complicated and treacherous place. There are many things you and I are simply not in a position to understand concerning, say, the nature of Jewry. Whereas his lordship, I might venture, is somewhat better placed to judge what is for the best. Now, Miss Kenton, I really must retire. I thank you again for the cocoa. Ten thirty tomorrow morning. Send the two employees concerned, please."

It was evident from the moment the two maids stepped into my pantry the following morning that Miss Kenton had already spoken to them, for they both came in sobbing. I explained the situation to them as briefly as possible, underlining that their work had been satisfactory and that they would, accordingly, receive good references. As I recall, neither of them said anything of note throughout the whole interview, which lasted perhaps three or four minutes, and they left sobbing just as they had arrived.

Miss Kenton was extremely cold towards me for some days following the dismissal of the employees. Indeed, at times she was quite rude to me, even in the presence of staff. And although we continued our habit of meeting for cocoa in the evening, the sessions tended to be brief and unfriendly. When there had been no sign of her behaviour abating after a fortnight or so, I think you will understand that I started to become a little impatient. I thus said to her during one of our cocoa sessions, in an ironic tone of voice:

"Miss Kenton, I'd rather expected you to have handed in your notice by now," accompanying this with a light laugh. I did, I suppose, hope that she might finally relent a little and make some conciliatory response or other, allowing us once and for all to put the whole episode behind us. Miss Kenton, however, simply looked at me sternly and said:

"I still have every intention of handing in my notice, Mr Stevens. It is merely that I have been so busy, I have not had time to see to the matter."

This did, I must admit, make me a little concerned for a time that she was serious about her threat. But then as week followed week, it became clear that there was no question of her leaving Darlington Hall, and as the atmosphere between us gradually thawed, I suppose I tended to tease her every now and again by reminding her of her threatened resignation. For instance, if we were discussing some future large occasion to be held at the house, I might put in: "That is, Miss Kenton, assuming you are still with us at that stage." Even months after the event, such remarks still tended to make Miss Kenton go quiet – though by this stage, I fancy, this was due more to embarrassment than anger.

Eventually, of course, the matter came to be, by and large, forgotten. But I remember it coming up one last time well over a year after the dismissal of the two maids.

It was his lordship who initially revived the matter one afternoon when I was serving his tea in the drawing room. By then, Mrs Carolyn Barnet's days of influence over his lordship were well over – indeed, the lady had ceased to be a visitor

at Darlington Hall altogether. It is worth pointing out, furthermore, that his lordship had by that time severed all links with the "blackshirts", having witnessed the
true, ugly nature of that organization.

"Oh, Stevens," he had said to me. "I've been meaning to say to you. About that
business last year. About the Jewish maids. You recall the matter?"

"Indeed, sir."

"I suppose there's no way of tracing them now, is there? It was wrong what
happened and one would like to recompense them somehow."

"I will certainly look into the matter, sir. But I am not at all certain it will be
possible to ascertain their whereabouts at this stage."

"See what you can do. It was wrong, what occurred."

I assumed this exchange with his lordship would be of some interest to Miss
Kenton, and I decided it only proper to mention it to her — even at the risk of
getting her angry again. As it turned out, my doing so on that foggy afternoon I
encountered her in the summerhouse produced curious results.

I recall a mist starting to set in as I crossed the lawn that afternoon. I was making
my way up to the summerhouse for the purpose of clearing away the remains of
his lordship's taking tea there with some guests a little while earlier. I can recall
spotting from some distance — long before reaching the steps where my father had
once fallen — Miss Kenton's figure moving about inside the summerhouse. When I
entered she had seated herself on one of the wicker chairs scattered around its
interior, evidently engaged in some needlework. On closer inspection, I saw she
was performing repairs to a cushion. I went about gathering up the various items of
crockery from amidst the plants and the cane furniture, and as I did so, I believe
we exchanged a few pleasantries, perhaps discussed one or two professional matters. For the truth was, it was extremely refreshing to be out in the summerhouse
after many continuous days in the main building and neither of us was inclined
to hurry with our tasks. Indeed, although one could not see out far that day
on account of the encroaching mist, and the daylight too was rapidly fading by
this stage, obliging Miss Kenton to hold her needlework up to the last of it, I
remember our often breaking off from our respective activities simply to gaze out
at the views around us. In fact, I was looking out over the lawn to where the mist
was thickening down around the poplar trees planted along the cart-track, when
I finally introduced the topic of the previous year's dismissals. Perhaps a little
predictably, I did so by saying:

"I was just thinking earlier, Miss Kenton. It's rather funny to remember now, but
you know, only this time a year ago, you were still insisting you were going to
resign. It rather amused me to think of it." I gave a laugh, but behind me Miss
Kenton remained silent. When I finally turned to look at her, she was gazing
through the glass at the great expanse of fog outside.

"You probably have no idea, Mr Stevens," she said eventually, "how seriously I
really thought of leaving this house. I felt so strongly about what happened. Had
I been anyone worthy of any respect at all, I dare say I would have left Darlington
Hall long ago." She paused for a while, and I turned my gaze back out to the
poplar trees down in the distance. Then she continued in a tired voice: "It was

cowardice, Mr Stevens. Simple cowardice. Where could I have gone? I have no family. Only my aunt. I love her dearly, but I can't live with her for a day without feeling my whole life is wasting away. I did tell myself, of course, I would soon find some new situation. But I was so frightened, Mr Stevens. Whenever I thought of leaving, I just saw myself going out there and finding nobody who knew or cared about me. There, that's all my high principles amount to. I feel so ashamed of myself. But I just couldn't leave, Mr Stevens. I just couldn't bring myself to leave."

Miss Kenton paused again and seemed to be deep in thought. I thus thought it opportune to relate at this point, as precisely as possible, what had taken place earlier between myself and Lord Darlington. I proceeded to do so and concluded by saying:

"What's done can hardly be undone. But it is at least a great comfort to hear his lordship declare so unequivocally that it was all a terrible misunderstanding. I just thought you'd like to know, Miss Kenton, since I recall you were as distressed by the episode as I was."

"I'm sorry, Mr Stevens," Miss Kenton said behind me in an entirely new voice, as though she had just been jolted from a dream, "I don't understand you." Then as I turned to her, she went on: "As I recall, you thought it was only right and proper that Ruth and Sarah be sent packing. You were positively cheerful about it."

"Now really, Miss Kenton, that is quite incorrect and unfair. The whole matter caused me great concern, great concern indeed. It is hardly the sort of thing I like to see happen in this house."

"Then why, Mr Stevens, did you not tell me so at the time?"

I gave a laugh, but for a moment was rather at a loss for an answer. Before I could formulate one, Miss Kenton put down her sewing and said:

"Do you realize, Mr Stevens, how much it would have meant to me if you had thought to share your feelings last year? You knew how upset I was when my girls were dismissed. Do you realize how much it would have helped me? Why, Mr Stevens, why, why, why do you always have to *pretend*?"

I gave another laugh at the ridiculous turn the conversation had suddenly taken. "Really, Miss Kenton," I said, "I'm not sure I know what you mean. Pretend? Why, really . . ."

"I suffered so much over Ruth and Sarah leaving us. And I suffered all the more because I believed I was alone."

"Really, Miss Kenton . . ." I picked up the tray on which I had gathered together the used crockery. "Naturally, one disapproved of the dismissals. One would have thought that quite self-evident."

She did not say anything, and as I was leaving I glanced back towards her. She was again gazing out at the view, but it had by this point grown so dark inside the summerhouse, all I could see of her was her profile outlined against a pale and empty background. I excused myself and proceeded to make my exit.

72

ANTHONY TROLLOPE

Dr Wortle's School

One of Trollope's last novels, this deals with the scandal arising from the revelation of the bigamous marriage of Mr Peacocke, a teacher in Dr Wortle's school.

O ur mystery is going to be revealed in the next paragraph, – in the next half-dozen words. Mr and Mrs Peacocke were not man and wife.

The story how it came to be so need not be very long; – nor will it, as I think, entail any great degree of odious criminality either upon the man or upon the woman. At St Louis Mrs Peacocke had become acquainted with two brothers named Lefroy, who had come up from Louisiana, and had achieved for themselves characters which were by no means desirable. They were sons of a planter who had been rich in extent of acres and number of slaves before the war of the Secession. General Lefroy had been in those days a great man in his State, had held command during the war, and had been utterly ruined. When the war was over the two boys, – then seventeen and sixteen years of age, – were old enough to remember and to regret all that they had lost, to hate the idea of Abolition, and to feel that the world had nothing left for them but what was to be got by opposition to the laws of the Union, which was now hateful to them. They were both handsome, and, in spite of the sufferings of their State, an attempt had been made to educate them like gentlemen. But no career of honour had been open to them, and they had fallen by degrees into dishonour, dishonesty, and brigandage.

The elder of these, when he was still little more than a stripling, had married Ella Beaufort, the daughter of another ruined planter in his State. She had been only sixteen when her father died, and not seventeen when she married Ferdinand Lefroy. It was she who afterwards came to England under the name of Mrs Peacocke.

Mr Peacocke was Vice-president of the College at Missouri when he first saw her, and when he first became acquainted with the two brothers, each of whom was called Colonel Lefroy. Then there arose a great scandal in the city as to the treatment which the wife received from her husband. He was about to go away

---

Anthony Trollope, extracts from Chapters III, IX, and XIX in *Dr Wortle's School*, first published in 1880.

South, into Mexico, with the view of pushing his fortune there with certain desperadoes, who were maintaining a perpetual war against the authorities of the United States on the borders of Texas, and he demanded that his wife should accompany him. This she refused to do, and violence was used to force her. Then it came to pass that certain persons in St Louis interfered on her behalf, and among these was the Reverend Mr Peacocke, the Vice-President of the College, upon whose feelings the singular beauty and dignified demeanour of the woman, no doubt, had had much effect. The man failed to be powerful over his wife, and then the two brothers went away together. The woman was left to provide for herself, and Mr Peacocke was generous in the aid he gave to her in doing so.

It may be understood that in this way an intimacy was created, but it must not be understood that the intimacy was of such a nature as to be injurious to the fair fame of the lady. Things went on in this way for two years, during which Mrs Lefroy's conduct drew down upon her reproaches from no one. Then there came tidings that Colonel Lefroy had perished in making one of those raids in which the two brothers were continually concerned. But which Colonel Lefroy had perished? If it were the younger brother, that would be nothing to Mr Peacocke. If it were the elder, it would be everything. If Ferdinand Lefroy were dead, he would not scruple at once to ask the woman to be his wife. That which the man had done, and that which he had not done, had been of such a nature as to solve all bonds of affection. She had already allowed herself to speak of the man as one whose life was a blight upon her own; and though there had been no word of out-spoken love from her lips to his ears, he thought that he might succeed if it could be made certain that Ferdinand Lefroy was no longer among the living.

"I shall never know," she said in her misery. "What I do hear I shall never believe. How can one know anything as to what happens in a country such as that?"

Then he took up his hat and staff, and, vice-president, professor, and clergyman as he was, started off for the Mexican border. He did tell her that he was going, but barely told her. "It's a thing that ought to be found out," he said, "and I want a turn of travelling. I shall be away three months." She merely bade God bless him, but said not a word to hinder or to encourage his going.

He was gone just the three months which he had himself named, and then returned elate with his news. He had seen the younger brother, Robert Lefroy, and had learnt from him that the elder Ferdinand had certainly been killed. Robert had been most ungracious to him, having even on one occasion threatened his life; but there had been no doubt that he, Robert, was alive, and that Ferdinand had been killed by a party of United States soldiers.

Then the clergyman had his reward, and was accepted by the widow with a full and happy heart. Not only had her release been complete, but so was her present joy; and nothing seemed wanting to their happiness during the six first months after their union. Then one day, all of a sudden, Ferdinand Lefroy was standing within her little drawing-room at the College of St Louis.

Dead? Certainly he was not dead! He did not believe that any one had said that he was dead! He might be lying or not, – he did not care; he, Peacocke, certainly had lied; – so said the Colonel. He did not believe that Peacocke had ever seen his brother Robert. Robert was dead, – must have been dead, indeed, before the date given for that interview. The woman was a bigamist, – that is, if any second marriage had ever been perpetrated. Probably both had wilfully agreed to the falsehood. For himself he should resolve at once what steps he meant to take. Then he departed, it being at that moment after nine in the evening. In the morning he was gone again, and from that moment they had never either heard of him or seen him.

How was it to be with them? They could have almost brought themselves to think it a dream, were it not that others besides themselves had seen the man, and known that Colonel Ferdinand Lefroy had been in St Louis. Then there came to him an idea that even she might disbelieve the words which he had spoken; – that even she might think his story to have been false. But to this she soon put an end. "Dearest," she said, "I never knew a word that was true to come from his mouth, or a word that was false from yours."

Should they part? There is no one who reads this but will say that they should have parted. Every day passed together as man and wife must be a falsehood and a sin. There would be absolute misery for both in parting; – but there is no law from God or man entitling a man to escape from misery at the expense of false-hood and sin. Though their hearts might have burst in the doing of it, they should have parted. Though she would have been friendless, alone, and utterly despicable in the eyes of the world, abandoning the name which she cherished, as not her own, and going back to that which she utterly abhorred, still she should have done it. And he, resolving, as no doubt he would have done under any circum-stances, that he must quit the city of his adoption, – he should have left her with such material sustenance as her spirit would have enabled her to accept, should have gone his widowed way, and endured as best he might the idea that he had left the woman whom he loved behind, in the desert, all alone! That he had not done so the reader is aware. That he had lived a life of sin, – that he and she had continued in one great falsehood, – is manifest enough.

Dr Wortle has discovered that the Peacockes' marriage is bigamous and must decide what to do.

For an hour or two before his dinner, the Doctor went out on horseback, and roamed about among the lanes, endeavouring to make up his mind. He was hitherto altogether at a loss as to what he should do in this present uncom-fortable emergency. He could not bring his conscience and his inclination to come square together. And even when he counselled himself to yield to his conscience, his very conscience, – a second conscience, as it were, – revolted against the first. His first conscience told him that he owed a primary duty to his parish, a second duty to his school, and a third to his wife and daughter. In the performance of all these duties he would be bound to rid himself of Mr Peacocke. But then there came that other conscience, telling him that the man had been more "sinned against than sinning", – that common humanity required him to stand by a man who had suffered so much, and had suffered so unworthily. Then this second conscience went on to remind him that the man was pre-eminently fit for the duties which he had undertaken, – that the man was a God-fearing, moral, and especially intellectual assistant in his school, – that were he to lose him he could not hope to find any one that would be his equal, or at all approaching to him in capacity. This second conscience went further, and assured him that the man's excellence as a schoolmaster was even increased by the peculiarity of his position. Do we not all know that if a man be under a cloud the very cloud will make him more attentive to his duties than another? If a man, for the wages which he receives, can give to his employer high character as well as work, he will think that he may lighten his work because of his character. And as to this man, who was the very phœnix of school assistants, there would really be nothing amiss with his character if only this piteous incident as to his wife were unknown. In this way his second conscience almost got the better of the first.

But then it would be known. It would be impossible that it should not be known. He had already made up his mind to tell Mr Puddicombe, absolutely not daring to decide in such an emergency without consulting some friend. Mr Puddicombe would hold his peace if he were to promise to do so. Certainly he might be trusted to do that. But others would know it; the Bishop would know it; Mrs Stantiloup would know it. That man, of course, would take care that all Broughton, with its close full of cathedral clergymen, would know it. When Mrs Stantiloup should know it there would not be a boy's parent through all the school who would not know it. If he kept the man he must keep him resolving that all the world should know that he kept him, that all the world should know of what nature was the married life of the assistant in whom he trusted. And he must be prepared to face all the world, confiding in the uprightness and the humanity of his purpose.

In such case he must say something of this kind to all the world; "I know that they are not married. I know that their condition of life is opposed to the law of God and man. I know that she bears a name that is not, in truth, her own; but I think that the circumstances in this case are so strange, so peculiar, that they excuse a disregard even of the law of God and man." Had he courage enough for this? And if the courage were there, was he high enough and powerful enough to carry out such a purpose? Could he beat down the Mrs Stantiloups? And, indeed, could he beat down the Bishop and the Bishop's phalanx; – for he knew that the Bishop and the Bishop's phalanx would be against him? They could not touch him in his living, because Mr Peacocke would not be concerned in the services of the church; but would not his school melt away to nothing in his hands, if he were to attempt to carry it on after this fashion? And then would he not have destroyed himself without advantage to the man whom he was anxious to assist?

To only one point did he make up his mind certainly during that ride. Before he slept that night he would tell the whole story to his wife. He had at first thought that he would conceal it from her. It was his rule of life to act so entirely on his own will, that he rarely consulted her on matters of any importance. As it was, he could not endure the responsibility of acting by himself. People would say of him that he had subjected his wife to contamination, and had done so without giving her any choice in the matter. So he resolved that he would tell his wife.

"Not married," said Mrs Wortle, when she heard the story.

"Married; yes. They were married. It was not their fault that the marriage was nothing. What was he to do when he heard that they had been deceived in this way?"

"Not married properly! Poor woman!"

"Yes, indeed. What should I have done if such had happened to me when we had been six months married?"

"It couldn't have been."

"Why not to you as well as to another?"

"I was only a young girl."

"But if you had been a widow?"

"Don't, my dear; don't! It wouldn't have been possible."

"But you pity her?"

"Oh yes."

"And you see that a great misfortune has fallen upon her, which she could not help?"

"Not till she knew it," said the wife who had been married quite properly.

"And what then? What should she have done then?"

"Gone," said the wife, who had no doubt as to the comfort, the beauty, the perfect security of her own position.

"Gone?"

"Gone away at once."

"Whither should she go? Who would have taken her by the hand? Who would have supported her? Would you have had her lay herself down in the first gutter and die?"

"Better that than what she did do," said Mrs Wortle.

"Then, by all the faith I have in Christ, I think you are hard upon her. Do you think what it is to have to go out and live alone; – to have to look for your bread in desolation?"

"I have never been tried, my dear," said she, clinging close to, him. "I have never had anything but what was good."

"Ought we not to be kind to one to whom Fortune has been so unkind?"

"If we can do so without sin."

"Sin! I despise the fear of sin which makes us think that its contact will soil us. Her sin, if it be sin, is so near akin to virtue, that I doubt whether we should not learn of her rather than avoid her."

"A woman should not live with a man unless she be his wife." Mrs Wortle said this with more of obstinacy than he had expected.

"She was his wife, as far as she knew."

"But when she knew that it was not so any longer, – then she should have left him."

"And have starved?"

"I suppose she might have taken bread from him."

"You think, then, that she should go away from here?"

"Do not you think so? What will Mrs Stantiloup say?"

"And I am to turn them out into the cold because of a virago such as she is? You would have no more charity than that?"

"Oh, Jeffrey! what would the Bishop say?"

"Cannot you get beyond Mrs Stantiloup and beyond the Bishop, and think what Justice demands?"

"The boys would all be taken away. If you had a son, would you send him where there was a schoolmaster living, – living – Oh, you wouldn't."

It is very clear to the Doctor that his wife's mind was made up on the subject; and yet there was no softer-hearted woman than Mrs Wortle anywhere in the diocese, or one less likely to be severe upon a neighbour. Not only was she a kindly, gentle woman, but she was one who always had been willing to take her husband's opinion on all questions of right and wrong. She, however, was decided that they must go.

On the next morning, after service, which the schoolmaster did not attend, the Doctor saw Mr Peacocke, and declared his intention of telling the story to Mr Puddicombe. "If you bid me hold my tongue," he said, "I will do so. But it will be better that I should consult another clergyman. He is a man who can keep a secret." Then Mr Peacocke gave him full authority to tell everything to Mr Puddicombe. He declared that the Doctor might tell the story to whom he would. Everybody might know it now. He had, he said, quite made up his mind about that. What was the good of affecting secrecy when this man Lefroy was in the country?

In the afternoon, after service, Mr Puddicombe came up to the house, and heard it all. He was a dry, thin, apparently unsympathetic man, but just withal, and by no means given to harshness. He could pardon whenever he could bring himself to believe that pardon would have good results; but he would not be driven by impulses and softness of heart to save the faulty one from the effect of his fault, merely because that effect would be painful. He was a man of no great mental calibre, – not sharp, and quick, and capable of repartee as was the Doctor, but rational in all things, and always guided by his conscience. "He has behaved very badly to you," he said, when he heard the story.

"I do not think so; I have no such feeling myself."

"He behaved very badly in bringing her here without telling you all the facts. Considering the position that she was to occupy, he must have known that he was deceiving you."

"I can forgive all that," said the Doctor vehemently. "As far as I myself am concerned, I forgive everything."

"You are not entitled to do so."

"How – not entitled?"

"You must pardon me if I seem to take a liberty in expressing myself too boldly in this matter. Of course I should not do so unless you asked me."

"I want you to speak freely, – all that you think."

"In considering his conduct, we have to consider it all. First of all there came a great and terrible misfortune which cannot but excite our pity. According to his own story, he seems, up to that time, to have been affectionate and generous."

"I believe every word of it," said the Doctor.

"Allowing for a man's natural bias on his own side, so do I. He had allowed himself to become attached to another man's wife; but we need not, perhaps, insist upon that." The Doctor moved himself uneasily in his chair, but said nothing. "We will grant that he put himself right by his marriage, though in that, no doubt, there should have been more of caution. Then came his great misfortune. He knew that his marriage had been no marriage. He saw the man and had no doubt."

"Quite so; quite so," said the Doctor, impatiently.

"He should, of course, have separated himself from her. There can be no doubt about it. There is no room for any quibble."

"Quibble!" said the Doctor.

"I mean that no reference in our own minds to the pity of the thing, to the softness of the moment, – should make us doubt about it. Feelings such as these should induce us to pardon sinners, even to receive them back into our friendship and respect – when they have seen the error of their ways and have repented."

"You are very hard."

"I hope not. At any rate I can only say as I think. But, in truth, in the present emergency you have nothing to do with all that. If he asked you for counsel you might give it to him, but that is not his present position. He has told you his story, not in a spirit of repentance, but because such telling had become necessary."

"He would have told it all the same though this man had never come."

"Let us grant that it is so, there still remains his relation to you. He came here under false pretences, and has done you a serious injury."

"I think not," said the Doctor.

"Would you have taken him into your establishment had you known it all before? Certainly not. Therefore I say that he has deceived you. I do not advise you to speak to him with severity; but he should, I think, be made to know that you appreciate what he has done."

"And you would turn him off; – send him away at once, out about his business?"

"Certainly I would send him away."

"You think him such a reprobate that he should not be allowed to earn his bread anywhere?"

"I have not said so. I know nothing of his means of earning his bread. Men living in sin earn their bread constantly. But he certainly should not be allowed to earn his here."

"Not though that man who was her husband should now be dead, and he should again marry, – legally marry, – this woman to whom he has been so true and loyal?"

"As regards you and your school," said Mr Puddicombe, "I do not think it would alter his position."

With this the conference ended, and Mr Puddicombe took his leave. As he left the house the Doctor declared to himself that the man was a strait-laced, fanatical, hard-hearted bigot. But though he said so to himself, he hardly thought so; and was aware that the man's words had had effect upon him.

Mrs Peacocke has just informed Mrs Wortle that Mr Peacocke, now traveling to America, has proof that Ferdinand Lefroy is really dead.

The two women, when they parted on that morning, kissed each other, which they had not done before; and Mrs Wortle had been made to doubt whether, after all, the sin had been so very sinful. She did endeavour to ask herself whether she would not have done the same in the same circumstances. The woman, she thought, must have been right to have married the man whom she loved, when she heard that that first horrid husband was dead. There could, at any rate, have been no sin in that. And then, what ought she to have done when the dead man, – dead as he was supposed to have been, – burst into her room? Mrs Wortle, – who found it indeed extremely difficult to imagine herself to be in such a position, – did at last acknowledge that, in such circumstances, she certainly would have done whatever Dr Wortle had told her. She could not bring it nearer to herself than that. She could not suggest to herself two men as her own husbands. She could not imagine that the Doctor had been either the bad husband, who had unexpectedly come to life, – or the good husband, who would not, in truth, be her husband at all; but she did determine, in her own mind, that, however all that might have been, she would clearly have done whatever the Doctor told her. She would have sworn to obey him, even though, when swearing, she should not have really married him. It was terrible to think of, – so terrible that she could not quite think of it; but in struggling to think of it her heart was softened towards this other woman. After that day she never spoke further of the woman's sin.

Of course she told it all to the Doctor, – not indeed explaining the working of her own mind as to that suggestion that he should have been, in his first condition, a very bad man, and have been reported dead, and have come again, in a second shape, as a good man. She kept that to herself. But she did endeavour to describe the effect upon herself of the description the woman had given her of her own conduct.

"I don't quite know how she could have done otherwise," said Mrs Wortle.

"Nor I either, I have always said so."

"It would have been so very hard to go away, when he told her not."

"It would have been very hard to go away," said the Doctor, "if he had told her to do so. Where was she to go? What was she to do? They had been brought together by circumstances, in such a manner that it was, so to say, impossible that they should part. It is not often that one comes across events like these, so altogether out of the ordinary course that the common rules of life seem to be insufficient for guidance. To most of us it never happens; and it is better for us that it should not happen. But when it does, one is forced to go beyond the common rules."

73

HARPER LEE

To Kill a Mockingbird

Set in a small Alabama town, the story is narrated by Scout (Jean Louise) Finch, who is 8 years old by the end of the novel. She lives with her older brother Jem, her aunt, and her father Atticus. Her father agrees to defend an innocent black man accused of raping a white woman, the daughter of Bob Ewell. One subplot centers on their reclusive neighbor Arthur (Boo) Radley. This extract begins as Jem and Scout come back late at night from a Halloween pageant at the school. Scout is still wearing her costume – that of a ham.

We went through the auditorium to the hallway, then down the steps. It was still black dark. The remaining cars were parked on the other side of the building, and their headlights were little help. "If some of 'em were goin' in our direction we could see better," said Jem. "Here Scout, let me hold onto your – hock. You might lose your balance."

"I can see all right."

"Yeah, but you might lose your balance." I felt a slight pressure on my head, and assumed that Jem had grabbed that end of the ham. "You got me?"

"Uh huh."

We began crossing the black schoolyard, straining to see our feet. "Jem," I said, "I forgot my shoes, they're back behind the stage."

"Well let's go get 'em." But as we turned around the auditorium lights went off. "You can get 'em tomorrow," he said.

"But tomorrow's Sunday," I protested, as Jem turned me homeward.

"You can get the Janitor to let you in . . . Scout?"

"Hm?"

"Nothing."

Jem hadn't started that in a long time. I wondered what he was thinking. He'd tell me when he wanted to, probably when we got home. I felt his fingers press the top of my costume, too hard, it seemed. I shook my head. "Jem, you don't hafta –"

HARPER LEE, pp. 262–79 from *To Kill a Mockingbird*. New York: Popular Library, 1962. Copyright © 1960 by Harper Lee. Copyright renewed © 1988 by Harper Lee. Reprinted by permission of HarperCollins Publishers Inc. and Random House Group Limited.

"Hush a minute, Scout," he said, pinching me.

We walked along silently. "Minute's up," I said, "Whatcha thinkin' about?" I turned to look at him, but his outline was barely visible.

"Thought I heard something," he said. "Stop a minute."

We stopped.

"Hear anything?" he asked.

"No."

We had not gone five paces before he made me stop again.

"Jem, are you tryin' to scare me? You know I'm too old –"

"Be quiet," he said, and I knew he was not joking.

The night was still. I could hear his breath coming easily beside me. Occasionally there was a sudden breeze that hit my bare legs, but it was all that remained of a promised windy night. This was the stillness before a thunderstorm. We listened.

"Heard an old dog just then," I said.

"It's not that," Jem answered. "I hear it when we're walkin' along, but when we stop I don't hear it."

"You hear my costume rustlin'. Aw, it's just Halloween got you. . . ."

I said it more to convince myself than Jem, for sure enough, as we began walking, I heard what he was talking about. It was not my costume.

"It's just old Cecil," said Jem presently. "He won't get us again. Let's don't let him think we're hurrying."

We slowed to a crawl. I asked Jem how Cecil could follow us in this dark, looked to me like he'd bump into us from behind.

"I can see you, Scout," Jem said.

"How? I can't see you."

"Your fat streaks are showin'. Mrs. Crenshaw painted 'em with some of that shiny stuff so they'd show up under the footlights. I can see you pretty well, an' I expect Cecil can see you well enough to keep his distance."

I would show Cecil that we knew he was behind us and we were ready for him. "Cecil Jacobs is a big wet he-en!" I yelled suddenly, turning around.

We stopped. There was no acknowledgement save he-en bouncing off the distant schoolhouse wall.

"I'll get him," said Jem. "*He-y!*"

Hay-e-hay-e-hay-ey, answered the schoolhouse wall.

It was unlike Cecil to hold out for so long; once he pulled a joke he'd repeat it time and again. We should have been leapt at already. Jem signaled for me to stop again.

He said softly, "Scout, can you take that thing off?"

"I think so, but I ain't got anything on under it much."

"I've got your dress here."

"I can't get it on in the dark."

"Okay," he said, "never mind."

"Jem, are you afraid?"

"No. Think we're almost to the tree now. Few yards from that, an' we'll be to the road. We can see the street light then." Jem was talking in an unhurried, flat toneless voice. I wondered how long he would try to keep the Cecil myth going.

"You reckon we oughta sing, Jem?"

"No. Be real quiet again, Scout."

We had not increased our pace. Jem knew as well as I that it was difficult to walk fast without stumping a toe, tripping on stones, and other inconveniences, and I was barefooted. Maybe it was the wind rustling the trees. But there wasn't any wind and there weren't any trees except the big oak.

Our company shuffled and dragged his feet, as if wearing heavy shoes. Whoever it was wore thick cotton pants; what I thought were trees rustling was the soft swish of cotton on cotton, wheek, wheek, with every step.

I felt the sand go cold under my feet and I knew we were near the big oak. Jem pressed my head. We stopped and listened.

Shuffle-foot had not stopped with us this time. His trousers swished softly and steadily. Then they stopped. He was running, running toward us with no child's steps.

"Run, Scout! Run! Run!" Jem screamed.

I took one giant step and found myself reeling: my arms useless, in the dark, I could not keep my balance.

"Jem, Jem, help me, Jem!"

Something crushed the chicken wire around me. Metal ripped on metal and I fell to the ground and rolled as far as I could, floundering to escape my wire prison. From somewhere near by came scuffling, kicking sounds, sounds of shoes and flesh scraping dirt and roots. Someone rolled against me and I felt Jem. He was up like lightning and pulling me with him but, though my head and shoulders were free, I was so entangled we didn't get very far.

We were nearly to the road when I felt Jem's hand leave me, felt him jerk backwards to the ground. More scuffling, and there came a dull crunching sound and Jem screamed.

I ran in the direction of Jem's scream and sank into a flabby male stomach. Its owner said, "Uff!" and tried to catch my arms, but they were tightly pinioned. His stomach was soft but his arms were like steel. He slowly squeezed the breath out of me. I could not move. Suddenly he was jerked backwards and flung on the ground, almost carrying me with him. I thought, Jem's up.

One's mind works very slowly at times. Stunned, I stood there dumbly. The scuffling noises were dying; someone wheezed and the night was still again.

Still but for a man breathing heavily, breathing heavily and staggering. I thought he went to the tree and leaned against it. He coughed violently, a sobbing, bone-shaking cough.

"Jem?"

There was no answer but the man's heavy breathing.

"Jem?"

Jem didn't answer.

The man began moving around, as if searching for something. I heard him groan and pull something heavy along the ground. It was slowly coming to me that there were now four people under the tree.

"Atticus . . . ?"

The man was walking heavily and unsteadily toward the road.

I went to where I thought he had been and felt frantically along the ground, reaching out with my toes. Presently I touched someone.

"Jem?"

My toes touched trousers, a belt buckle, buttons, something I could not identify, a collar, and a face. A prickly stubble on the face told me it was not Jem's. I smelled stale whiskey.

I made my way along in what I thought was the direction of the road. I was not sure, because I had been turned around so many times. But I found it and looked down to the street light. A man was passing under it. The man was walking with the staccato steps of someone carrying a load too heavy for him. He was going around the corner. He was carrying Jem. Jem's arm was dangling crazily in front of him.

By the time I reached the corner the man was crossing our front yard. Light from our front door framed Atticus for an instant; he ran down the steps, and together, he and the man took Jem inside.

I was at the front door when they were going down the hall. Aunt Alexandra was running to meet me. "Call Dr Reynolds!" Atticus's voice came sharply from Jem's room. "Where's Scout?"

"Here she is," Aunt Alexandra called, pulling me along with her to the telephone. She tugged at me anxiously. "I'm all right, Aunty," I said, "you better call."

She pulled the receiver from the hook and said, "Eula May, get Dr Reynolds, quick!"

"Agnes, is your father home? Oh God, where is he? Please tell him to come over here as soon as he comes in. Please, it's urgent!"

There was no need for Aunt Alexandra to identify herself; people in Maycomb knew each other's voices.

Atticus came out of Jem's room. The moment Aunt Alexandra broke the connection, Atticus took the receiver from her. He rattled the hook, then said, "Eula May, get me the sheriff, please."

"Heck? Atticus Finch. Someone's been after my children. Jem's hurt. Between here and the schoolhouse. I can't leave my boy. Run out there for me, please, and see if he's still around. Doubt if you'll find him now, but I'd like to see him if you do. Got to go now. Thanks, Heck."

"Atticus, is Jem dead?"

"No, Scout. Look after her, sister," he called, as he went down the hall.

Aunt Alexandra's fingers trembled as she unwound the crushed fabric and wire from around me. "Are you all right, darling?" she asked over and over as she worked me free.

It was a relief to be out. My arms were beginning to tingle, and they were red with small hexagonal marks. I rubbed them, and they felt better.

"Aunty, is Jem dead?"

"No – no, darling, he's unconscious. We won't know how badly he's hurt until Dr Reynolds gets here. Jean Louise, what happened?"

"I don't know."

She left it at that. She brought me something to put on, and had I thought about it then, I would have never let her forget it: in her distraction, Aunty brought me my overalls. "Put these on, darling," she said, handing me the garments she most despised.

She rushed back to Jem's room, then came to me in the hall. She patted me vaguely, and went back to Jem's room.

A car stopped in front of the house. I knew Dr Reynolds's step almost as well as my father's. He had brought Jem and me into the world, had led us through every childhood disease known to man including the time Jem fell out of the treehouse, and he had never lost our friendship. Dr Reynolds said if we had been boil-prone things would have been different, but we doubted it.

He came in the door and said, "Good Lord." He walked toward me, said, "You're still standing," and changed his course. He knew every room in the house. He also knew that if I was in bad shape, so was Jem.

After ten forevers Dr Reynolds returned. "Is Jem dead?" I asked.

"Far from it," he said, squatting down to me. "He's got a bump on the head just like yours, and a broken arm. Scout, look that way — no, don't turn your head, roll your eyes. Now look over yonder. He's got a bad break, so far as I can tell now it's in the elbow. Like somebody tried to wring his arm off . . . now look at me."

"Then he's not dead?"

"No-o!" Dr Reynolds got to his feet. "We can't do much tonight," he said, "except try to make him as comfortable as we can. We'll have to X-ray his arm — looks like he'll be wearing his arm 'way out by his side for a while. Don't worry, though, he'll be as good as new. Boys his age bounce."

While he was talking, Dr Reynolds had been looking keenly at me, lightly fingering the bump that was coming on my forehead. "You don't feel broke anywhere, do you?"

Dr Reynolds's small joke made me smile. "Then you don't think he's dead, then?"

He put on his hat. "Now I may be wrong, of course, but I think he's very alive. Shows all the symptoms of it. Go have a look at him, and when I come back we'll get together and decide."

Dr Reynolds's step was young and brisk. Mr Heck Tate's was not. His heavy boots punished the porch and he opened the door awkwardly, but he said the same thing Dr Reynolds said when he came in. "You all right, Scout?" he added.

"Yes sir, I'm goin' in to see Jem. Atticus'n'them's in there."

"I'll go with you," said Mr Tate.

Aunt Alexandra had shaded Jem's reading light with a towel, and his room was dim. Jem was lying on his back. There was an ugly mark along one side of his face. His left arm lay out from his body; his elbow was bent slightly, but in the wrong direction. Jem was frowning.

"Jem . . . ?"

Atticus spoke. "He can't hear you, Scout, he's out like a light. He was coming around, but Dr Reynolds put him out again."

"Yes sir." I retreated. Jem's room was large and square. Aunt Alexandra was sitting in a rocking-chair by the fireplace. The man who brought Jem in was standing in a corner, leaning against the wall. He was some countryman I did not know. He had probably been at the pageant, and was in the vicinity when it happened. He must have heard our screams and come running.

Atticus was standing by Jem's bed.

Mr Heck Tate stood in the doorway. His hat was in his hand, and a flashlight bulged from his pants pocket. He was in his working clothes.

"Come in, Heck," said Atticus. "Did you find anything? I can't conceive of anyone low-down enough to do a thing like this, but I hope you found him."

Mr Tate sniffed. He glanced sharply at the man in the corner, nodded to him, then looked around the room – at Jem, at Aunt Alexandra, then at Atticus.

"Sit down, Mr Finch," he said pleasantly.

Atticus said, "Let's all sit down. Have that chair, Heck. I'll get another one from the livingroom."

Mr Tate sat in Jem's desk chair. He waited until Atticus returned and settled himself. I wondered why Atticus had not brought a chair for the man in the corner, but Atticus knew the ways of country people far better than I. Some of his rural clients would park their long-eared steeds under the chinaberry trees in the back yard, and Atticus would often keep appointments on the back steps. This one was probably more comfortable where he was.

"Mr Finch," said Mr Tate, "tell you what I found. I found a little girl's dress – it's out there in my car. That your dress, Scout?"

"Yes sir, if it's a pink one with smockin'," I said. Mr Tate was behaving as if he were on the witness stand. He liked to tell things his own way, untrammeled by state or defense, and sometimes it took him a while.

"I found some funny-looking pieces of muddy-colored cloth –"

"That's m'costume, Mr Tate."

Mr Tate ran his hands down his thighs. He rubbed his left arm and investigated Jem's mantelpiece, then he seemed to be interested in the fireplace. His fingers sought his long nose.

"What is it, Heck?" said Atticus.

Mr Tate found his neck and rubbed it. "Bob Ewell's lyin' on the ground under that tree down yonder with a kitchen knife stuck up under his ribs. He's dead, Mr Finch."

*

Aunt Alexandra got up and reached for the mantelpiece. Mr Tate rose, but she declined assistance. For once in his life, Atticus's instinctive courtesy failed him: he sat where he was.

Somehow, I could think of nothing but Mr Bob Ewell saying he'd get Atticus if it took him the rest of his life. Mr Ewell almost got him, and it was the last thing he did.

"Are you sure?" Atticus said bleakly.

"He's dead all right," said Mr Tate. "He's good and dead. He won't hurt these children again."

"I didn't mean that." Atticus seemed to be talking in his sleep. His age was beginning to show, his one sign of inner turmoil: the strong line of his jaw melted a little, one became aware of telltale creases forming under his ears, one noticed not his jet-black hair but the gray patches growing at his temples.

"Hadn't we better go to the livingroom?" Aunt Alexandra said at last.

"If you don't mind," said Mr Tate, "I'd rather us stay in here if it won't hurt Jem any. I want to have a look at his injuries while Scout . . . tells us about it."

"Is it all right if I leave?" she asked. "I'm just one person too many in here. I'll be in my room if you want me, Atticus." Aunt Alexandra went to the door, but she stopped and turned. "Atticus, I had a feeling about this tonight – I – this is my fault," she began. "I should have –"

Mr Tate held up his hand. "You go ahead, Miss Alexandra, I know it's been a shock to you. And don't you fret yourself about anything – why, if we followed our feelings all the time we'd be like cats chasin' their tails. Miss Scout, see if you can tell us what happened, while it's still fresh in your mind. You think you can? Did you see him following you?"

I went to Atticus and felt his arms go around me. I buried my head in his lap. "We started home. I said Jem, I've forgot m'shoes. Soon's we started back for 'em the lights went out. Jem said I could get 'em tomorrow. . . ."

"Scout, raise up so Mr Tate can hear you," Atticus said. I crawled into his lap.

"Then Jem said hush a minute. I thought he was thinkin' – he always wants you to hush so he can think – then he said he heard somethin'. We thought it was Cecil."

"Cecil?"

"Cecil Jacobs. He scared us once tonight, an' we thought it was him again. He had on a sheet. They gave a quarter for the best costume, I don't know who won it –"

"Where were you when you thought it was Cecil?"

"Just a little piece from the schoolhouse. I yelled somethin' at him –"

"You yelled, what?"

"Cecil Jacobs is a big fat hen, I think. We didn't hear nothin' – then Jem yelled hello or somethin' loud enough to wake the dead –"

"Just a minute, Scout," said Mr Tate. "Mr Finch, did you hear them?"

Atticus said he didn't. He had the radio on. Aunt Alexandra had hers going in her bedroom. He remembered because she told him to turn his down a bit so she could hear hers. Atticus smiled. "I always play a radio too loud."

"I wonder if the neighbors heard anything. . . ." said Mr Tate.

"I doubt it, Heck. Most of them listen to their radios or go to bed with the chickens. Maudie Atkinson may have been up, but I doubt it."

"Go ahead, Scout," Mr Tate said.

"Well, after Jem yelled we walked on. Mr Tate, I was shut up in my costume but I could hear it myself, then. Footsteps, I mean. They walked when we walked and stopped when we stopped. Jem said he could see me because Mrs Crenshaw put some kind of shiny paint on my costume. I was a ham."

"How's that?" asked Mr Tate, startled.

Atticus described my role to Mr Tate, plus the construction of my garment. "You should have seen her when she came in," he said, "it was crushed to a pulp."

Mr Tate rubbed his chin. "I wondered why he had those marks on him. His sleeves were perforated with little holes. There were one or two little puncture marks on his arms to match the holes. Let me see that thing if you will, sir."

Atticus fetched the remains of my costume. Mr Tate turned it over and bent it around to get an idea of its former shape. "This thing probably saved her life," he said. "Look."

He pointed with a long forefinger. A shiny clean line stood out on the dull wire. "Bob Ewell meant business," Mr Tate muttered.

"He was out of his mind," said Atticus.

"Don't like to contradict you, Mr Finch – wasn't crazy, mean as hell. Low-down skunk with enough liquor in him to make him brave enough to kill children. He'd never have met you face to face."

Atticus shook his head. "I can't conceive of a man who'd –"

"Mr Finch, there's just some kind of men you have to shoot before you can say hidy to 'em. Even then, they ain't worth the bullet it takes to shoot 'em. Ewell 'as one of 'em."

Atticus said, "I thought he got it all out of him the day he threatened me. Even if he hadn't, I thought he'd come after me."

"He had guts enough to pester a poor colored woman, he had guts enough to pester Judge Taylor when he thought the house was empty, so do you think he'da met you to your face in daylight?" Mr Tate sighed. "We'd better get on. Scout, you heard him behind you –"

"Yes sir. When we got under the tree –"

"How'd you know you were under the tree, you couldn't see thunder out there."

"I was barefooted, and Jem says the ground's always cooler under a tree."

"We'll have to make him a deputy, go ahead."

"Then all of a sudden somethin' grabbed me an' mashed my costume . . . think I ducked on the ground . . . heard a tusslin' under the tree sort of . . . they were bammin' against the trunk, sounded like. Jem found me and started pullin' me toward the road. Some – Mr Ewell yanked him down, I reckon. They tussled some more and then there was this funny noise – Jem hollered . . ." I stopped. That was Jem's arm.

"Anyway, Jem hollered and I didn't hear him any more an' the next thing – Mr Ewell was tryin' to squeeze me to death, I reckon . . . then somebody yanked Mr Ewell down. Jem must have got up, I guess. That's all I know . . ."

"And then?" Mr Tate was looking at me sharply.

"Somebody was staggerin' around and pantin' and – coughing fit to die. I thought it was Jem at first, but it didn't sound like him, so I went lookin' for Jem on the ground. I thought Atticus had come to help us and had got wore out –"

"Who was it?"

"Why there he is, Mr Tate, he can tell you his name."

As I said it, I half pointed to the man in the corner, but brought my arm down quickly lest Atticus reprimand me for pointing. It was impolite to point.

He was still leaning against the wall. He had been leaning against the wall when I came into the room, his arms folded across his chest. As I pointed he brought his arms down and pressed the palms of his hands against the wall. They were white hands, sickly white hands that had never seen the sun, so white they stood out garishly against the dull cream wall in the dim light of Jem's room.

I looked from his hands to his sand-stained khaki pants; my eyes traveled up his thin frame to his torn denim shirt. His face was as white as his hands, but for a shadow on his jutting chin. His cheeks were thin to hollowness; his mouth was wide; there were shallow, almost delicate indentations at his temples, and his gray eyes were so colorless I thought he was blind. His hair was dead and thin, almost feathery on top of his head.

When I pointed to him his palms slipped slightly, leaving greasy sweat streaks on the wall, and he hooked his thumbs in his belt. A strange small spasm shook him, as if he heard fingernails scrape slate, but as I gazed at him in wonder the tension slowly drained from his face. His lips parted into a timid smile, and our neighbor's image blurred with my sudden tears.

"Hey, Boo," I said.

*

"Mr Arthur, honey," said Atticus, gently correcting me. "Jean Louise, this is Mr Arthur Radley. I believe he already knows you."

If Atticus could blandly introduce me to Boo Radley at a time like this, well – that was Atticus.

Boo saw me run instinctively to the bed where Jem was sleeping, for the same shy smile crept across his face. Hot with embarrassment, I tried to cover up by covering Jem up.

"Ah-ah, don't touch him," Atticus said.

Mr Heck Tate sat looking intently at Boo through his horn-rimmed glasses. He was about to speak when Dr Reynolds came down the hall.

"Everybody out," he said, as he came in the door. "Evenin', Arthur, didn't notice you the first time I was here."

Dr Reynolds's voice was as breezy as his step, as though he had said it every evening of his life, an announcement that astounded me even more than being in the same room with Boo Radley. Of course . . . even Boo Radley got sick sometimes, I thought. But on the other hand I wasn't sure.

Dr Reynolds was carrying a big package wrapped in newspaper. He put it down on Jem's desk and took off his coat. "You're quite satisfied he's alive, now? Tell you how I knew. When I tried to examine him he kicked me. Had to put him out good and proper to touch him. So scat," he said to me.

"Er –" said Atticus, glancing at Boo. "Heck, let's go out on the front porch. There are plenty of chairs out there, and it's still warm enough."

I wondered why Atticus was inviting us to the front porch instead of the livingroom, then I understood. The livingroom lights were awfully strong.

We filed out, first Mr Tate – Atticus was waiting at the door for him to go ahead of him. Then he changed his mind and followed Mr Tate.

People have a habit of doing everyday things even under the oddest conditions. I was no exception: "Come along, Mr Arthur," I heard myself saying, "you don't know the house real well. I'll just take you to the porch, sir."

He looked down at me and nodded.

I led him through the hall and past the livingroom.

"Won't you have a seat, Mr Arthur? This rocking-chair's nice and comfortable."

My small fantasy about him was alive again: he would be sitting on the porch . . . right pretty spell we're having, isn't it, Mr Arthur?

Yes, a right pretty spell. Feeling slightly unreal, I led him to the chair farthest from Atticus and Mr Tate. It was in deep shadow. Boo would feel more comfortable in the dark.

Atticus was sitting in the swing, and Mr Tate was in a chair next to him. The light from the livingroom windows was strong on them. I sat beside Boo.

"Well, Heck," Atticus was saying, "I guess the thing to do – good Lord, I'm losing my memory . . ." Atticus pushed up his glasses and pressed his fingers to his eyes. "Jem's not quite thirteen . . . no, he's already thirteen – I can't remember. Anyway, it'll come before county court –"

"What will, Mr Finch?" Mr Tate uncrossed his legs and leaned forward.

"Of course it was clear-cut self defense, but I'll have to go to the office and hunt up –"

"Mr Finch, do you think Jem killed Bob Ewell? Do you think that?"

"You heard what Scout said, there's no doubt about it. She said Jem got up and yanked him off her – he probably got hold of Ewell's knife somehow in the dark . . . we'll find out tomorrow."

"Mis-ter Finch, hold on," said Mr Tate. "Jem never stabbed Bob Ewell."

Atticus was silent for a moment. He looked at Mr Tate as if he appreciated what he said. But Atticus shook his head.

"Heck, it's mighty kind of you and I know you're doing it from that good heart of yours, but don't start anything like that."

Mr Tate got up and went to the edge of the porch. He spat into the shrubbery, then thrust his hands into his hip pockets and faced Atticus. "Like what?" he said.

"I'm sorry if I spoke sharply, Heck," Atticus said simply, "but nobody's hushing this up. I don't live that way."

"Nobody's gonna hush anything up, Mr Finch."

Mr Tate's voice was quiet, but his boots were planted so solidly on the porch floorboards it seemed that they grew there. A curious contest, the nature of which eluded me, was developing between my father and the sheriff.

It was Atticus's turn to get up and go to the edge of the porch. He said, "H'rm," and spat dryly into the yard. He put his hands in his pockets and faced Mr Tate.

"Heck, you haven't said it, but I know what you're thinking. Thank you for it. Jean Louise –" he turned to me. "You said Jem yanked Mr Ewell off you?"

"Yes sir, that's what I thought . . . I –"

"See there, Heck? Thank you from the bottom of my heart, but I don't want my boy starting out with something like this over his head. Best way to clear the air is to have it all out in the open. Let the county come and bring sandwiches. I don't want him growing up with a whisper about him, I don't want anybody saying,

'Jem Finch . . . his daddy paid a mint to get him out of that.' Sooner we get this over with the better."

"Mr Finch," Mr Tate said stolidly, "Bob Ewell fell on his knife. He killed himself."

Atticus walked to the corner of the porch. He looked at the wisteria vine. In his own way, I thought, each was as stubborn as the other. I wondered who would give in first. Atticus's stubbornness was quiet and rarely evident, but in some ways he was as set as the Cunninghams. Mr Tate's was unschooled and blunt, but it was equal to my father's.

"Heck," Atticus's back was turned. "If this thing's hushed up it'll be a simple denial to Jem of the way I've tried to raise him. Sometimes I think I'm a total failure as a parent, but I'm all they've got. Before Jem looks at anyone else he looks at me, and I've tried to live so I can look squarely back at him . . . if I connived at something like this, frankly I couldn't meet his eye, and the day I can't do that I'll know I've lost him. I don't want to lose him and Scout, because they're all I've got."

"Mr Finch." Mr Tate was still planted to the floorboards. "Bob Ewell fell on his knife. I can prove it."

Atticus wheeled around. His hands dug in to his pockets. "Heck, can't you even try to see it my way? You've got children of your own, but I'm older than you. When mine are grown I'll be an old man if I'm still around, but right now I'm – if they don't trust me they won't trust anybody. Jem and Scout know what happened. If they hear of me saying down town something different happened – Heck, I won't have them any more. I can't live one way in town and another way in my home."

Mr Tate rocked on his heels and said patiently, "He'd flung Jem down, he stumbled over a root under that tree and – look, I can show you."

Mr Tate reached in his side pocket and withdrew a long switchblade knife. As he did so, Dr Reynolds came to the door. "The son – deceased's under that tree, doctor, just inside the schoolyard. Got a flashlight? Better have this one."

"I can ease around and turn my car lights on," said Dr Reynolds, but he took Mr Tate's flashlight. "Jem's all right. He won't wake up tonight, I hope, so don't worry. That the knife that killed him, Heck?"

"No sir, still in him. Looked like a kitchen knife from the handle. Ken oughta be there with the hearse by now, doctor, 'night."

Mr Tate flicked open the knife. "It was like this," he said. He held the knife and pretended to stumble; as he leaned forward his left arm went down in front of him. "See there? Stabbed himself through that soft stuff between his ribs. His whole weight drove it in."

Mr Tate closed the knife and jammed it back in his pocket. "Scout is eight years old," he said. "She was too scared to know exactly what went on."

"You'd be surprised," Atticus said grimly.

"I'm not sayin' she made it up, I'm sayin' she was too scared to know exactly what happened. It was mighty dark out there, black as ink. 'd take somebody mighty used to the dark to make a competent witness . . ."

"I won't have it," Atticus said softly.

"*God damn it, I'm not thinking of Jem!*"

Mr Tate's boot hit the floorboards so hard the lights in Miss Maudie's bedroom went on. Miss Stephanie Crawford's lights went on. Atticus and Mr Tate looked across the street, then at each other. They waited.

When Mr Tate spoke again his voice was barely audible. "Mr Finch, I hate to fight you when you're like this. You've been under a strain tonight no man should ever have to go through. Why you ain't in the bed from it I don't know, but I do know that for once you haven't been able to put two and two together, and we've got to settle this tonight because tomorrow'll be too late. Bob Ewell's got a kitchen knife in his craw."

Mr Tate added that Atticus wasn't going to stand there and maintain that any boy Jem's size with a busted arm had fight enough left in him to tackle and kill a grown man in the pitch dark.

"Heck," said Atticus abruptly, "that was a switchblade you were waving. Where'd you get it?"

"Took it off a drunk man," Mr Tate answered coolly.

I was trying to remember. Mr Ewell was on me . . . then he went down. . . . Jem must have gotten up. At least I thought . . .

"Heck?"

"I said I took it off a drunk man downtown tonight. Ewell probably found that kitchen knife in the dump somewhere. Honed it down and bided his time . . . just bided his time."

Atticus made his way to the swing and sat down. His hands dangled limply between his knees. He was looking at the floor. He had moved with the same slowness that night in front of the jail, when I thought it took him forever to fold his newspaper and toss it in his chair.

Mr Tate clumped softly around the porch. "It ain't your decision, Mr Finch, it's all mine. It's my decision and my responsibility. For once, if you don't see it my way, there's not much you can do about it. If you wanta try, I'll call you a liar to your face. Your boy never stabbed Bob Ewell," he said slowly, "didn't come near a mile of it and now you know it. All he wanted to do was get him and his sister safely home."

Mr Tate stopped pacing. He stopped in front of Atticus, and his back was to us. "I'm not a very good man, sir, but I am sheriff of Maycomb County. Lived in this town all my life an' I'm goin' on forty-three years old. Know everything that's happened here since before I was born. There's a black boy dead for no reason, and the man responsible for it's dead. Let the dead bury the dead this time, Mr Finch. Let the dead bury the dead."

Mr Tate went to the swing and picked up his hat. It was lying beside Atticus. Mr Tate pushed back his hair and put his hat on.

"I never heard tell that it's against the law for a citizen to do his utmost to prevent a crime from being committed, which is exactly what he did, but maybe you'll say it's my duty to tell the town all about it and not hush it up. Know what'd happen then? All the ladies in Maycomb includin' my wife'd be knocking on his door bringing angel food cakes. To my way of thinkin', Mr Finch, taking the one man who's done you and this town a great service an' draggin' him with his shy ways into the limelight – to me, that's a sin. It's a sin and I'm not about to have it on my head. If it was any other man it'd be different. But not this man, Mr Finch."

Mr Tate was trying to dig a hole in the floor with the toe of his boot. He pulled his nose, then he massaged his left arm. "I may not be much, Mr Finch, but I'm still sheriff of Maycomb County and Bob Ewell fell on his knife. Good night, sir."

Mr Tate stamped off the porch and strode across the front yard. His car door slammed and he drove away.

Atticus sat looking at the floor for a long time. Finally he raised his head. "Scout," he said, "Mr Ewell fell on his knife. Can you possibly understand?"

Atticus looked like he needed cheering up. I ran to him and hugged him and kissed him with all my might. "Yes sir, I understand," I reassured him. "Mr Tate was right."

Atticus disengaged himself and looked at me. "What do you mean?"

"Well, it'd be sort of like shootin' a mockingbird, wouldn't it?"

Atticus put his face in my hair and rubbed it. When he got up and walked across the porch into the shadows, his youthful step has returned. Before he went inside the house, he stopped in front of Boo Radley. "Thank you for my children, Arthur," he said.

"Well, it'd be sort of like shootin' a mockingbird, wouldn't it?" – earlier in the novel, Atticus said that it is a sin to kill a mockingbird because they do no harm and make music for people to enjoy

74

WILLIAM SHAKESPEARE

Sonnet 138

When my love swears that she is made of truth
I do believe her though I know she lies,
That she might think me some untutored youth
Unlearned in the world's false subtleties.
Thus vainly thinking that she thinks me young,
Although she knows my days are past the best,
Simply I credit her false-speaking tongue;
On both sides thus is simple truth suppressed.
But wherefore says she not she is unjust,
And wherefore say not I that I am old?
O, love's best habit is in seeming trust,
And age in love loves not to have years told.
Therefore I lie with her, and she with me,
And in our faults by lies we flattered be.

WILLIAM SHAKESPEARE, Sonnet 138, first published in 1609.

75

GEORGE ELIOT

Middlemarch

Among the subplots in George Eliot's *Middlemarch* is that of Mr Bulstrode the banker and how his past catches up with him. John Raffles is part of this shady past that Mr Bulstrode wants kept secret. Raffles has tracked him down and, when drunk, has already let drop stories of Bulstrode's previous life. Raffles is now very ill and Bulstrode calls Dr Lydgate in to this patient.

Dr Lydgate is badly in debt. He sought a loan from Bulstrode, but was refused. The bailiffs have taken away his furniture, and his wife Rosamund has gone to live with her parents.

In less than an hour Lydgate arrived. Bulstrode met him outside the wainscoted parlour, where Raffles was, and said –

"I have called you in, Mr Lydgate, to an unfortunate man who was once in my employment many years ago. Afterwards he went to America, and returned I fear to an idle dissolute life. Being destitute, he has a claim on me. He was slightly connected with Rigg, the former owner of this place, and in consequence found his way here. I believe he is seriously ill: apparently his mind is affected; I feel bound to do the utmost for him."

Lydgate, who had the remembrance of his last conversation with Bulstrode strongly upon him, was not disposed to say an unnecessary word to him, and bowed slightly in answer to this account; but just before entering the room he turned automatically and said, "What is his name?" – to know names being as much a part of the medical man's accomplishment as of the practical politician's.

"Raffles, John Raffles," said Bulstrode, who hoped that whatever became of Raffles, Lydgate would never know any more of him.

When he had thoroughly examined and considered the patient, Lydgate ordered that he should go to bed, and be kept there in as complete quiet as possible, and then went with Bulstrode into another room.

"It is a serious case, I apprehend," said the banker, before Lydgate began to speak.

GEORGE ELIOT, from Book VII, Chapters LXIX and LXX in *Middlemarch*, first published in 1872.

"No – and yes," said Lydgate, half dubiously. "It is difficult to decide as to the possible effect of long-standing complications; but the man had a robust constitution to begin with. I should not expect this attack to be fatal, though of course the system is in a ticklish state. He should be well watched and attended to."

"I will remain here myself," said Bulstrode. "Mrs Abel and her husband are inexperienced. I can easily remain here for the night, if you will oblige me by taking a note for Mrs Bulstrode."

"I should think that is hardly necessary," said Lydgate. "He seems tame and terrified enough. He might become more unmanageable. But there is a man here – is there not?"

"I have more than once stayed here a few nights for the sake of seclusion," said Bulstrode, indifferently; "I am quite disposed to do so now. Mrs Abel and her husband can relieve or aid me, if necessary."

"Very well. Then I need give my directions only to you," said Lydgate, not feeling surprised at a little peculiarity in Bulstrode.

"You think, then, that the case is hopeful?" said Bulstrode, when Lydgate had ended giving his orders.

"Unless there turn out to be further complications, such as I have not at present detected – yes," said Lydgate. "He may pass on to a worse stage; but I should not wonder if he got better in a few days, by adhering to the treatment I have prescribed. There must be firmness. Remember, if he calls for liquors of any sort, not to give them to him. In my opinion, men in his condition are oftener killed by treatment than by the disease. Still, new symptoms may arise. I shall come again tomorrow morning."

After waiting for the note to be carried to Mrs Bulstrode, Lydgate rode away, forming no conjectures, in the first instance, about the history of Raffles, but rehearsing the whole argument which had lately been much stirred by the publication of Dr Ware's abundant experience in America, as to the right way of treating cases of alcoholic poisoning such as this. Lydgate, when abroad, had already been interested in this question: he was strongly convinced against the prevalent practice of allowing alcohol and persistently administering large doses of opium; and he had repeatedly acted on this conviction with a favourable result.

"The man is in a diseased state," he thought, "But there's a good deal of wear in him still, I suppose he is an object of charity to Bulstrode. It is curious what patches of hardness and tenderness lie side by side in men's dispositions. Bulstrode seems the most unsympathetic fellow I ever saw about some people, and yet he has taken no end of trouble, and spent a great deal of money, on benevolent objects. I suppose he has some test by which he finds out whom Heaven cares for – he has made up his mind that it doesn't care for me."

[. . .]

Bulstrode's first object after Lydgate had left Stone Court was to examine Raffles' pockets, which he imagined were sure to carry signs in the shape of hotel-bills of the places he had stopped in, if he had not told the truth in saying that he had come straight from Liverpool because he was ill and had no money. There were various bills crammed into his pocket-book, but none of a later date than Christmas at any other place, except one, which bore date that morning. This was crumpled up with a handbill about a horse-fair in one of his tail-pockets and represented the cost of three days' stay at an inn at Bilkley, where the fair was held – a town at least forty miles from Middlemarch. The bill was heavy, and since Raffles had no luggage with him, it seemed probable that he had left his portmanteau behind in payment, in order to save money for his travelling fare; for his purse was empty, and he had only a couple of sixpences and some loose pence in his pockets.

Bulstrode gathered a sense of safety from these indications that Raffles had really kept at a distance from Middlemarch since his memorable visit at Christmas. At a distance and among people who were strangers to Bulstrode, what satisfaction could there be to Raffles' tormenting, self-magnifying vein in telling old scandalous stories about a Middlemarch banker? And what harm if he did talk? The chief point now was to keep watch over him as long as there was any danger of that intelligible raving, that unaccountable impulse to tell, which seemed to have acted towards Caleb Garth; and Bulstrode felt much anxiety lest some such impulse should come over him at the sight of Lydgate. He sat up alone with him through the night, only ordering the housekeeper to lie down in her clothes, so as to be ready when he called her, alleging his own indisposition to sleep, and his anxiety to carry out the doctor's orders. He did carry them out faithfully, although Raffles was incessantly asking for brandy, and declaring that he was sinking away – that the earth was sinking away from under him. He was restless and sleepless, but still quailing and manageable. On the offer of the food ordered by Lydgate, which he refused, and the denial of other things which he demanded, he seemed to concentrate all his terror on Bulstrode, imploringly deprecating his anger, his revenge on him by starvation, and declaring with strong oaths that he had never told any mortal a word against him. Even this Bulstrode felt that he would not have liked Lydgate to hear; but a more alarming sign of fitful alternation in his delirium was, that in the morning twilight Raffles suddenly seemed to imagine a doctor present, addressing him and declaring that Bulstrode wanted to starve him to death out of revenge for telling, when he never had told.

Bulstrode's native imperiousness and strength of determination served him well. This delicate-looking man, himself nervously perturbed, found the needed stimulus in his strenuous circumstances, and through that difficult night and morning, while he had the air of an animated corpse returned to movement without warmth, holding the mastery by its chill impassibility, his mind was intensely at work thinking of what he had to guard against and what would win him security. Whatever prayers he might lift up, whatever statements he might inwardly make of this man's wretched spiritual condition, and the duty he himself was under to submit to the punishment divinely appointed for him rather than to wish for evil to another – through all this effort to condense words into a solid mental state, there pierced and spread with irresistible vividness the images of the events he desired. And in the train of those images came their apology. He could not but see the death of Raffles, and see in it his own deliverance. What was the removal of this wretched creature? He was impenitent – but were not public criminals impenitent? – yet the law decided on their fate. Should Providence in this case award death, there was no sin in contemplating death as the desirable issue – if he kept his hands from hastening it – if he scrupulously did what was prescribed. Even here there might be a mistake: human prescriptions were fallible things: Lydgate had said that treatment had hastened death, – why not his own method of treatment? But of course intention was everything in the question of right and wrong.

And Bulstrode set himself to keep his intention separate from his desire. He inwardly declared that he intended to obey orders. Why should he have got into any argument about the validity of these orders? It was only the common trick of desire – which avails itself of any irrelevant scepticism, finding larger room for itself in all uncertainty about effects, in every obscurity that looks like the absence of law. Still, he did obey the orders.

His anxieties continually glanced towards Lydgate, and his remembrance of what had taken place between them the morning before was accompanied with sensibilities which had not been roused at all during the actual scene. He had then cared but little about Lydgate's painful impressions with regard to the suggested change in the Hospital, or about the disposition towards himself which what he held to be his justifiable refusal of a rather exorbitant request might call forth. He recurred to the scene now with a perception that he had probably made Lydgate his enemy, and with an awakened desire to propitiate him, or rather to create in him a strong sense of personal obligation. He regretted that he had not at once made even an unreasonable money-sacrifice. For in case of unpleasant suspicions or even knowledge gathered from the raving of Raffles, Bulstrode would have felt that he had a defence in Lydgate's mind by having conferred a momentous benefit on him. But the regret had perhaps come too late.

Strange, piteous conflict in the soul of this unhappy man, who had longed for years to be better than he was – who had taken his selfish passions into discipline and clad them in severe robes, so that he had walked with them as a devout quire, till now that a terror had risen among them, and they could chant no longer, but threw out their common cries for safety.

It was nearly the middle of the day before Lydgate arrived: he had meant to come earlier, but had been detained, he said; and his shattered looks were noticed by Bulstrode. But he immediately threw himself into the consideration of the patient, and inquired strictly into all that had occurred. Raffles was worse, would take hardly any food, was persistently wakeful and restlessly raving; but still not violent. Contrary to Bulstrode's alarmed expectation, he took little notice of Lydgate's presence, and continued to talk or murmur incoherently.

"What do you think of him?" said Bulstrode, in private.

"The symptoms are worse."

"You are less hopeful?"

"No; I still think he may come round. Are you going to stay here yourself?" said Lydgate, looking at Bulstrode with an abrupt question, which made him uneasy, though in reality it was not due to any suspicious conjecture.

"Yes, I think so," said Bulstrode, governing himself and speaking with delibera-tion. "Mrs Bulstrode is advised of the reasons which detain me. Mrs Abel and her husband are not experienced enough to be left quite alone, and this kind of responsibility is scarcely included in their service of me. You have some fresh instructions, I presume."

The chief new instruction that Lydgate had to give was on the administration of extremely moderate doses of opium, in case of the sleeplessness continuing after several hours. He had taken the precaution of bringing opium in his pocket, and he gave minute directions to Bulstrode as to the doses, and the point at which they should cease. He insisted on the risk of not ceasing; and repeated his order that no alcohol should be given.

"From what I see of the case," he ended, "narcotism is the only thing I should be much afraid of. He may wear through even without much food. There's a good deal of strength in him."

"You look ill yourself, Mr Lydgate – a most unusual, I may say unprecedented thing in my knowledge of you," said Bulstrode, showing a solicitude as unlike his indifference the day before, as his present recklessness about his own fatigue was unlike his habitual self-cherishing anxiety. "I fear you are harassed."

"Yes, I am," said Lydgate, brusquely, holding his hat, and ready to go.

"Something new, I fear," said Bulstrode, inquiringly. "Pray be seated."

"No, thank you," said Lydgate, with some *hauteur*. "I mentioned to you yesterday what was the state of my affairs. There is nothing to add, except that the execution has since then been actually put into my house. One can tell a good deal of trouble in a short sentence. I will say good-morning."

"Stay, Mr Lydgate, stay," said Bulstrode; "I have been reconsidering this subject. I was yesterday taken by surprise and saw it superficially. Mrs Bulstrode is anxious for her niece, and I myself should grieve at a calamitous change in your position. Claims on me are numerous, but on reconsideration, I esteem it right that I should incur a small sacrifice rather than leave you unaided. You said, I think, that a thousand pounds would suffice entirely to free you from your burthens, and enable you to recover a firm stand?"

"Yes," said Lydgate, a great leap of joy within him surmounting every other feeling; "that would pay all my debts, and leave me a little on hand. I could set about economising in our way of living. And by-and-by my practice might look up."

"If you will wait a moment, Mr Lydgate, I will draw a cheque to that amount. I am aware that help, to be effectual in these cases, should be thorough."

While Bulstrode wrote, Lydgate turned to the window thinking of his home – thinking of his life with its good start saved from frustration, its good purposes still unbroken.

"You can give me a note of hand for this, Mr Lydgate," said the banker, advancing towards him with the cheque. "And by-and-by, I hope, you may be in circumstances gradually to repay me. Meanwhile, I have great pleasure in thinking that you will be released from further difficulty."

"I am deeply obliged to you," said Lydgate. "You have restored to me the prospect of working with some happiness and some chance of good."

It appeared to him a very natural movement in Bulstrode that he should have reconsidered his refusal: it corresponded with the more munificent side of his character. But as he put his hack into a canter, that he might get the sooner home, and tell the good news to Rosamond, and get cash at the bank to pay over to Dover's agent, there crossed his mind, with an unpleasant impression, as from a dark-winged flight of evil augury across his vision, the thought of that contrast in himself which a few months had brought – that he should be overjoyed at being under a strong personal obligation – that he should be overjoyed at getting money for himself from Bulstrode.

The banker felt that he had done something to nullify one cause of uneasiness, and yet he was scarcely the easier. He did not measure the quantity of diseased motive which had made him wish for Lydgate's goodwill, but the quantity was none the less actively there, like an irritating agent in his blood. A man vows, and yet will not cast away the means of breaking his vow. Is it that he distinctly means to break it? Not at all; but the desires which tend to break it are at work in him dimly, and make their way into his imagination, and relax his muscles in the very moments when he is telling himself over again the reasons for his vow. Raffles, recovering quickly, returning to the free use of his odious powers – how could Bulstrode wish for that? Raffles dead was the image that brought release, and indirectly he prayed for that way of release, beseeching that, if it were possible, the rest of his days here below might be freed from the threat of an ignominy which would break him utterly as an instrument of God's service. Lydgate's opinion was not on the side of promise that this prayer would be fulfilled; and as the day advanced, Bulstrode felt himself getting irritated at the persistent life in this man, whom he would fain have seen sinking in to the silence of death: imperious will stirred murderous impulses towards this brute life, over which will, by itself, had no power. He said inwardly that he was getting too much worn; he would not sit up with the patient to-night, but leave him to Mrs Abel, who, if necessary, could call her husband.

At six o'clock, Raffles, having had only fitful perturbed snatches of sleep, from which he waked with fresh restlessness and perpetual cries that he was sinking away, Bulstrode began to administer the opium according to Lydgate's directions. At the end of half an hour or more he called Mrs Abel and told her that he found himself unfit for further watching. He must now consign the patient to her care; and he proceeded to repeat to her Lydgate's directions as to the quantity of each dose. Mrs Abel had not before known anything of Lydgate's prescriptions; she had simply prepared and brought whatever Bulstrode ordered, and had done what he pointed out to her. She began now to ask what else she should do besides administering the opium.

"Nothing at present, except the offer of the soup or the soda-water: you can come to me for further directions. Unless there is any important change, I shall not come into the room again to-night. You will ask your husband for help, if necessary. I must go to bed early."

"You've much need, sir, I'm sure," said Mrs Abel, "and to take something more strengthening than what you've done."

Bulstrode went away now without anxiety as to what Raffles might say in his raving, which had taken on a muttering incoherence not likely to create any dangerous belief. At any rate he must risk this. He went down into the wainscoted parlour first, and began to consider whether he would not have his horse saddled and go home by the moonlight, and give up caring for earthly consequences. Then, he wished that he had begged Lydgate to come again that evening. Perhaps he might deliver a different opinion, and think that Raffles was getting into a less hopeful state. Should he send for Lydgate? If Raffles were really getting worse, and slowly dying, Bulstrode felt that he could go to bed and sleep in gratitude to Providence. But was he worse? Lydgate might come and simply say that he was going on as he expected, and predict that he would by-and-by fall into a good sleep, and get well. What was the use of sending for him? Bulstrode shrank from that result. No ideas or opinions could hinder him from seeing the one probability to be, that Raffles recovered would be just the same man as before, with his strength as a tormentor renewed, obliging him to drag away his wife to spend her years apart from her friends and native place, carrying an alienating suspicion against him in her heart.

He had sat an hour and a half in this conflict by the firelight only, when a sudden thought made him rise and light the bed-candle, which he had brought down with him. The thought was, that he had not told Mrs Abel when the doses of opium must cease.

He took hold of the candlestick, but stood motionless for a long while. She might already have given him more than Lydgate had prescribed. But it was excusable in him, that he should forget part of an order, in his present wearied condition. He walked up-stairs, candle in hand, not knowing whether he should straightway enter his own room and go to bed, or turn to the patient's room and rectify his omission. He paused in the passage, with his face turned towards Raffles' room, and he could hear him moaning and murmuring. He was not asleep, then. Who could know that Lydgate's prescription would not be better disobeyed than followed, since there was still no sleep?

He turned into his own room. Before he had quite undressed, Mrs Abel rapped at the door; he opened it an inch, so that he could hear her speak low.

"If you please, sir, should I have no brandy nor nothing to give the poor creetur? He feels sinking away, and nothing else will he swaller – and but little strength in it, if he did – only the opium. And he says more and more he's sinking down through the earth."

To her surprise, Mr Bulstrode did not answer. A struggle was going on within him.

"I think he must die for want o' support, if he goes on in that way. When I nursed my poor master, Mr Robisson, I had to give him port-wine and brandy constant, and a big glass at a time," added Mrs Abel, with a touch of remonstrance in her tone.

But again Mr Bulstrode did not answer immediately, and she continued, "It's not a time to spare when people are at death's door, nor would you wish it, sir, I'm sure. Else I should give him our own bottle o' rum as we keep by us. But a sitter-up so as you've been, and doing everything as laid in your power –"

Here a key was thrust through the inch of doorway, and Mr Bulstrode said huskily, "That is the key of the wine-cooler. You will find plenty of brandy there."

Early in the morning – about six – Mr Bulstrode rose and spent some time in prayer. Does any one suppose that private prayer is necessarily candid – necessarily goes to the roots of action! Private prayer is inaudible speech, and speech is representative: who can represent himself just as he is, even in his own reflections? Bulstrode had not yet unravelled in his thought the confused promptings of the last four-and-twenty hours.

He listened in the passage, and could hear hard stertorous breathing. Then he walked out in the garden, and looked at the early rime on the grass and fresh spring leaves. When he re-entered the house, he felt startled at the sight of Mrs Abel.

"How is your patient – asleep, I think?" he said, with an attempt at cheerfulness in his tone.

"He's gone very deep, sir," said Mrs Abel. "He went off gradual between three and four o'clock. Would you please to go and look at him? I thought it no harm to leave him. My man's gone afield, and the little girl's seeing to the kettles."

Bulstrode went up. At a glance he knew that Raffles was not in the sleep which brings revival, but in the sleep which streams deeper and deeper into the gulf of death.

He looked round the room and saw a bottle with some brandy in it, and the almost empty opium phial. He put the phial out of sight, and carried the brandy-bottle down-stairs with him, locking it again in the wine-cooler.

While breakfasting he considered whether he should ride to Middlemarch at once, or wait for Lydgate's arrival. He decided to wait, and told Mrs Abel that she might go about her work – he could watch in the bed-chamber.

As he sat there and beheld the enemy of his peace going irrevocably into silence, he felt more at rest than he had done for many months. His conscience was soothed by the enfolding wing of secrecy, which seemed just then like an angel sent down for his relief. He drew out his pocket-book to review various memoranda there as to the arrangements he had projected and partly carried out in the prospect of quitting Middlemarch, and considered how far he would let them stand or recall them, now that his absence would be brief. Some economies which he felt desirable might still find a suitable occasion in his temporary withdrawal from management, and he hoped still that Mrs Casaubon would take a large share in the expenses of the Hospital. In that way the moments passed, until a change in the stertorous breathing was marked enough to draw his attention wholly to the bed, and forced him to think of the departing life, which had once been subservient to his own – which he had once been glad to find base enough for him to act as he would. It was his gladness then which impelled him now to be glad that the life was at an end.

And who could say that the death of Raffles had been hastened? Who knew what would have saved him?

Lydgate arrived at half-past ten, in time to witness the final pause of the breath. When he entered the room Bulstrode observed a sudden expression in his face, which was not so much surprise as a recognition that he had not judged correctly. He stood by the bed in silence for some time, with his eyes turned on the dying man, but with that subdued activity of expression which showed that he was carrying on an inward debate.

"When did this change begin?" said he, looking at Bulstrode.

"I did not watch by him last night," said Bulstrode. "I was overworn, and left him under Mrs Abel's care. She said that he sank into sleep between three and four o'clock. When I came in before eight he was nearly in this condition."

Lydgate did not ask another question, but watched in silence until he said, "It's all over."

This morning Lydgate was in a state of recovered hope and freedom. He had set out on his work with all his old animation, and felt strong enough to bear all the deficiencies of his married life. And he was conscious that Bulstrode had been a benefactor to him. But he was uneasy about this case. He had not expected it to terminate as it had done. Yet he hardly knew how to put a question on the subject to Bulstrode without appearing to insult him; and if he examined the housekeeper – why, the man was dead. There seemed to be no use in implying that somebody's ignorance or imprudence had killed him. And after all, he himself might be wrong.

He and Bulstrode rode back to Middlemarch together, talking of many things – chiefly cholera and the chances of the Reform Bill in the House of Lords, and the firm resolve of the Political Unions. Nothing was said about Raffles, except that Bulstrode mentioned the necessity of having a grave for him in Lowick churchyard and observed that, so far as he knew, the poor man had no connections, except Rigg, whom he had stated to be unfriendly towards him.

XV

ULTIMATE VALUES

When Robinson Crusoe took stock of his situation after four years on his desert island, he did not consider the money he had to be an asset. In modern society money is valuable, but only as a means for obtaining something else. Hence we say it is of instrumental value, but not of intrinsic value. On Crusoe's island, since there was nothing to buy, the instrumental value of money was nil. Carrot seeds, too, are only of instrumental value, but if there had been any on the island, their instrumental value to Crusoe would have been high, because he could have planted them. Given his limited diet, he would very much have liked to have a few carrots.

Philosophers distinguish things that are of instrumental value, which we want as a means to something else, from things of intrinsic or ultimate value, which we want for their own sake. The pleasure that Crusoe would have gained from eating carrots is something he wanted for its own sake, not because it would lead to anything else. Jeremy Bentham, the founding father of utilitarianism, thought that pleasure or happiness is the ultimate value, and that the goodness or badness of every act comes down to its tendency to increase or diminish the total amount of happiness in the world. Utilitarianism was attacked as a philosophy suited for swine, rather than cultivated human beings, but Bentham did not budge. If poetry and the then-popular game of push-pin produce equal quantities of pleasure, Bentham said, push-pin is as good as poetry.[1]

John Stuart Mill, Bentham's godson and the leading philosopher of the next generation of utilitarians, was troubled by Bentham's refusal to give greater weight to the higher, more intellectual, or aesthetically refined aspects of human life than to the lower, more animal-like pleasures. He eventually satisfied himself that utilitarianism can distinguish "higher" quality pleasures and "lower" quality pleasures. He attempted to reconcile utilitarianism and his own instincts by claiming that the higher pleasures are simply more pleasurable than the lower pleasures. So, he wrote, it is "better to be Socrates dissatisfied than a fool satisfied."[2] If the fool is of a different opinion, he argued, that is because the fool does not know both sides of the question. But to most readers, this is a dubious attempt to reconcile utilitarianism with values that are really independent of pleasure or happiness. Better, surely, either to accept Bentham's classical form of utilitarianism with its refusal to attribute special value to the pleasures of the intellect, or of artistic achievement, or to reject classical utilitarianism and admit that there are independent values, like the value of striving to understand the world we live in, or of creating great works of art, which are independent of the happiness such actitivities produce.

Pleasure and happiness are forms of consciousness, or states of mind. For the classical utilitarians, it is only states of mind – and not all of them – that can have intrinsic value. Robert Nozick has suggested that it must follow from this view that the best possible world would be one in which everyone was linked up to an "experience machine" that gave them the illusion that they were doing whatever they most enjoyed or most wanted to do, although in reality they were just lying in a bed.[3] If what they most enjoyed was sunning themselves on a tropical beach, the machine could give them exactly that state of mind. If it was the thrill of climbing Everest, the pleasures of passionate love-making, or the satisfaction of writing a major novel, the experience machine could give you those states of mind too. If only the entire population of the world could be maintained on such machines, wouldn't that be, for the classical utilitarian, the best possible state of affairs? And yet, to most of us, it is far from that. The Savage in Aldous Huxley's *Brave New World* speaks for those who object to the idea that pleasure is the ultimate value.

The English philosopher G. E. Moore, writing at the beginning of the twentieth century, also objected to pleasure as the ultimate end. He asked his readers to imagine two worlds, one full of the most beautiful things one can imagine, and the other "simply one heap of filth." But in neither world is there, nor will there ever be, anyone who can appreciate the beauty of one or be repulsed by the ugliness of the other. Nevertheless, Moore thought, it is self-evidently better that the beautiful world should exist than that the ugly one should exist.[4] Moore was saying, obviously, that beauty has intrinsic, not merely instrumental, value. But since he thought this self-evident, he did not offer any argument for it. Others have thought it equally self-evident that in the absence of consciousness there can be no value. At this point argument stops and we seem to be at an impasse.

Many modern utilitarians agree with Bentham and Mill that nothing apart from the feelings or attitudes of conscious beings can be intrinsically good, but they do not identify intrinsic good with pleasure or happiness. Following a view held by the American philosopher William James – the brother of Henry James – and later by Ralph Barton Perry, they say, instead, that value exists in the world only because there are beings with wants, or preferences. Something is good if, on the whole, it satisfies more wants than it thwarts and it is bad if it thwarts more wants than it satisfies. (We must, of course, allow for differences in intensity of preference. More intense preferences can outweigh a larger number of less intense preferences.) This position, known as preference utilitarianism, is broader in scope than the classical form of utilitarianism, for we can have preferences for almost anything, and not only for pleasure or happiness. If a woman turns her back on what she knows would be a very enjoyable life as a well-paid writer of advertising copy, and instead prefers the poverty-stricken existence of a struggling poet, then it is good that she should have what she prefers, even if she will be less happy as a result. In contrast to the classical utilitarian, the preference utilitarian does not try to persuade everyone that happiness is the only thing worth wanting.

Another advantage of preference utilitarianism is that it does not imply that the best world is one in which we are all connected to experience machines – if what we prefer is facing reality, with all its hardships and without illusions, then putting us on experience machines is not going to satisfy our preferences.

Both the classical and the preference-based version of utilitarianism have a form of egalitarianism built into them. Whether it is pleasures or preferences that are of ultimate value, they are to be given the same weight irrespective of the race, sex, social class, intelligence, education, or even species of the being whose pleasures or preferences they are. That kind of egalitarianism is seen in Bentham's equation of push-pin and poetry. But utilitarianism is also compatible with substantive inegalitarianism if, for example, members of one category of beings are able to obtain more pleasure or preference satisfaction than members of another category. Mill's claim that the pleasures of philosophy are, because they are of higher quality, greater than the pleasures to be obtained from the activities of more foolish people would, if sound, be a justification for doing more to promote intellectual pursuits than simpler enjoyments. If it also is true that only a minority with superior intellectual capacities are capable of enjoying the higher pleasures of philosophy, then Mill's distinction will justify promoting the pleasures of the elite rather than those of the masses. Even without a distinction between higher and lower pleasures, any form of utilitarianism will be sensitive to differences in the capacities of different people, or beings, to experience pleasure or to suffer, or to have particularly intense preferences.

Ethical views that find intrinsic value outside the experiences or preferences of sentient beings can be more directly dismissive of the interests of most, or perhaps all, human beings, and hence are more open to the accusation of elitism. If beauty is an intrinsic good, and human suffering is not, then there seems no limit to the amount of human suffering that can be justified in order to build a magnificent cathedral or splendid palace. One of the two extracts from Henry James, that from *The Princess Casamassima*, suggests that view; the other, from *The Portrait of a Lady*, points to a different kind of intrinsic value, but both have in them some sympathy for the tastes and activities of an elite, rather than for relieving the suffering and hardship of ordinary people.

NOTES

1   Jeremy Bentham, *The Rationale of Reward*, Bk III, Ch. 1, online at *http://www.la.texas.edu/labyrinth/rr*; first published London: John and H. L. Hunt, 1825.
2   J. S. Mill, *Utilitarianism*, London: J. M. Dent, 1962, p. 9.
3   Robert Nozick, *Anarchy, State and Utopia*, New York: Basic Books, 1974, p. 42.
4   G. E. Moore, *Principia Ethica*, Cambridge: Cambridge University Press, 1922, pp. 83–5.

76

DANIEL DEFOE

Robinson Crusoe

In this extract Robinson Crusoe is reflecting on his life after four years of solitude on his island.

In the middle of this Work, I finish'd my fourth Year in this Place, and kept my Anniversary with the same Devotion, and with as much Comfort as ever before; for by a constant Study, and serious Application of the Word of God, and by the Assistance of his Grace, I gain'd a different Knowledge from what I had before. I entertain'd different Notions of Things. I look'd now upon the World as a Thing remote, which I had nothing to do with, no Expectation from, and indeed no Desires about: In a Word, I had nothing indeed to do with it, nor was ever like to have; so I thought it look'd as we may perhaps look upon it hereafter, *viz.* as a Place I had liv'd in, but was come out of it; and well might I say, as Father *Abraham* to *Dives, Between me and thee is a great Gulph fix'd.*

In the first Place, I was remov'd from all the Wickedness of the World here. I had neither the *Lust of the Flesh, the Lust of the Eye, or the Pride of Life.* I had nothing to covet; for I had all that I was now capable of enjoying: I was Lord of the whole Manor; or if I pleas'd, I might call my self King, or Emperor over the whole Country which I had Possession of. There were no Rivals. I had no Competitor, none to dispute Sovereignty or Command with me. I might have rais'd Ship Loadings of Corn; but I had no use for it; so I let as little grow as I thought enough for my Occasion. I had Tortoise or Turtles enough; but now and then one, was as much as I could put to any use. I had Timber enough to have built a Fleet of Ships. I had Grapes enough to have made Wine, or to have cur'd into Raisins, to have loaded that Fleet, when they had been built.

But all I could make use of, was, All that was valuable. I had enough to eat, and to supply my Wants, and, what was all the rest to me? If I kill'd more Flesh than I could eat, the Dog must eat it, or the Vermin. If I sow'd more Corn than I could eat, it must be spoil'd. The Trees that I cut down, were lying to rot on the Ground.

DANIEL DEFOE, from Part III of *Robinson Crusoe*, first published in 1719.

I could make no more use of them than for Fewel; and that I had no Occasion for, but to dress my Food.

In a Word, The Nature and Experience of Things dictated to me upon just Reflection, That all the good Things of this World, are no farther good to us, than they are for our Use; and that whatever we may heap up indeed to give others, we enjoy just as much as we can use, and no more. The most covetous griping Miser in the World would have been cur'd of the Vice of Covetousness, if he had been in my Case; for I possess'd infinitely more than I knew what to do with. I had no room for Desire, except it was of Things which I had not, and they were but Trifles, though indeed of great Use to me. I had, as I hinted before, a Parcel of Money, as well Gold as Silver, about thirty six Pounds Sterling: Alas! There the nasty sorry useless Stuff lay; I had no manner of Business for it; and I often thought with my self, That I would have given a Handful of it for a Gross of Tobacco-Pipes, or for a Hand-Mill to grind my Corn; nay, I would have given it all for Sixpenny worth of *Turnip* and *Carrot* Seed out of *England*, or for a Handful of *Pease* and *Beans*, and a Bottle of Ink: *As it was*, I had not the least Advantage by it, or Benefit from it; but there it lay in a Drawer, and grew mouldy with the Damp of the Cave, in the wet Season; and if I had had the Drawer full of Diamonds, it had been the same Case; and they had been of no manner of Value to me, because of no Use.

77

HENRY JAMES

The Portrait of a Lady

Isabel Archer, heroine of *The Portrait of a Lady*, is considered to be Henry James's most engaging character. This young, headstrong American with looks, wit, and imagination has recently arrived in Europe. Isabel has already refused two suitors. She is staying with her relatives, the Touchetts. The wealthy, and gravely ill, Daniel Touchett initiates a conversation with his son about the money Ralph will soon inherit.

"You'll be very well off."

"Yes," said Ralph, "I know that. But I hope you've not forgotten the talk we had a year ago – when I told you exactly what money I should need and begged you to make some good use of the rest."

"Yes, yes, I remember. I made a new will – in a few days. I suppose it was the first time such a thing had happened – a young man trying to get a will made against him."

"It is not against me," said Ralph. "It would be against me to have a large property to take care of. It's impossible for a man in my state of health to spend much money, and enough is as good as a feast."

"Well, you'll have enough – and something over. There will be more than enough for one – there will be enough for two."

"That's too much," said Ralph.

"Ah, don't say that. The best thing you can do, when I'm gone, will be to marry."

Ralph had foreseen what his father was coming to, and this suggestion was by no means fresh. It had long been Mr Touchett's most ingenious way of taking the cheerful view of his son's possible duration. Ralph had usually treated it facetiously; but present circumstances proscribed the facetious. He simply fell back in his chair and returned his father's appealing gaze.

"If I, with a wife who hasn't been very fond of me, have had a very happy life," said the old man, carrying his ingenuity further still, "what a life mightn't you have if you should marry a person different from Mrs Touchett. There are more

---

HENRY JAMES, from Chapter XVIII in *The Portrait of a Lady*, first published in 1881.

different from her than there are like her." Ralph still said nothing; and after a pause his father resumed softly: "What do you think of your cousin?"

At this Ralph started, meeting the question with a strained smile. "Do I understand you to propose that I should marry Isabel?"

"Well, that's what it comes to in the end. Don't you like Isabel?"

"Yes, very much." And Ralph got up from his chair and wandered over to the fire. He stood before it an instant and then he stooped and stirred it mechanically. "I like Isabel very much," he repeated.

"Well," said his father, "I know she likes you. She has told me how much she likes you."

"Did she remark that she would like to marry me?"

"No, but she can't have anything against you. And she's the most charming young lady I've ever seen. And she would be good to you. I have thought a great deal about it."

"So have I," said Ralph, coming back to the bedside again. "I don't mind telling you that."

"You *are* in love with her then? I should think you would be. It's as if she came over on purpose."

"No, I'm not in love with her; but I should be if – if certain things were different."

"Ah, things are always different from what they might be," said the old man. "If you wait for them to change you'll never do anything. I don't know whether you know," he went on; "but I suppose there's no harm in my alluding to it at such an hour as this: there was some one wanted to marry Isabel the other day, and she wouldn't have him."

"I know she refused Warburton: he told me himself."

"Well, that proves there's a chance for somebody else."

"Somebody else took his chance the other day in London – and got nothing by it."

"Was it you?" Mr Touchett eagerly asked.

"No, it was an older friend; a poor gentleman who came over from America to see about it."

"Well, I'm sorry for him, whoever he was. But it only proves what I say – that the way's open to you."

"If it is, dear father, it's all the greater pity that I'm unable to tread it. I haven't many convictions; but I have three or four that I hold strongly. One is that people, on the whole, had better not marry their cousins. Another is that people in an advanced stage of pulmonary disorder had better not marry at all."

The old man raised his weak hand and moved it to and fro before his face. "What do you mean by that? You look at things in a way that would make everything wrong. What sort of a cousin is a cousin that you had never seen for more than twenty years of her life? We're all each other's cousins, and if we stopped at that the human race would die out. It's just the same with your bad lung. You're a great deal better than you used to be. All you want is to lead a natural life. It is a great deal more natural to marry a pretty young lady that you're in love with than it is to remain single on false principles."

"I'm not in love with Isabel," said Ralph.

"You said just now that you would be if you didn't think it wrong. I want to prove to you that it isn't wrong."

"It will only tire you, dear daddy," said Ralph, who marvelled at his father's tenacity and at his finding strength to insist. "Then where shall we all be?"

"Where shall you be if I don't provide for you? You won't have anything to do with the bank, and you won't have me to take care of. You say you've so many interests; but I can't make them out."

Ralph leaned back in his chair with folded arms; his eyes were fixed for some time in meditation. At last, with the air of a man fairly mustering courage, "I take a great interest in my cousin," he said, "but not the sort of interest you desire. I shall not live many years; but I hope I shall live long enough to see what she does with herself. She's entirely independent of me; I can exercise very little influence upon her life. But I should like to do something for her."

"What should you like to do?"

"I should like to put a little wind in her sails."

"What do you mean by that?"

"I should like to put it into her power to do some of the things she wants. She wants to see the world for instance. I should like to put money in her purse."

"Ah, I'm glad you've thought of that," said the old man. "But I've thought of it too. I've left her a legacy – five thousand pounds."

"That's capital; it's very kind of you. But I should like to do a little more."

Something of that veiled acuteness with which it had been on Daniel Touchett's part the habit of a lifetime to listen to a financial proposition still lingered in the face in which the invalid had not obliterated the man of business. "I shall be happy to consider it," he said softly.

"Isabel's poor then. My mother tells me that she has but a few hundred dollars a year. I should like to make her rich."

"What do you mean by rich?"

"I call people rich when they're able to meet the requirements of their imagination. Isabel has a great deal of imagination."

"So have you, my son," said Mr Touchett, listening very attentively but a little confusedly.

"You tell me I shall have money enough for two. What I want is that you should kindly relieve me of my superfluity and make it over to Isabel. Divide my inheritance into two equal halves and give her the second."

"To do what she likes with?"

"Absolutely what she likes."

"And without an equivalent?"

"What equivalent could there be?"

"The one I've already mentioned."

"Her marrying – some one or other? It's just to do away with anything of that sort that I make my suggestion. If she has an easy income she'll never have to marry for a support. That's what I want cannily to prevent. She wishes to be free, and your bequest will make her free."

"Well, you seem to have thought it out," said Mr Touchett. "But I don't see why you appeal to me. The money will be yours, and you can easily give it to her yourself."

Ralph openly stared. "Ah, dear father, *I* can't offer Isabel money!"

The old man gave a groan. "Don't tell me you're not in love with her! Do you want *me* to have the credit of it?"

"Entirely. I should like it simply to be a clause in your will, without the slightest reference to me."

"Do you want me to make a new will then?"

"A few words will do it; you can attend to it the next time you feel a little lively."

"You must telegraph to Mr Hilary then. I'll do nothing without my solicitor."

"You shall see Mr Hilary to-morrow."

"He'll think we've quarrelled, you and I," said the old man.

"Very probably; I shall like him to think it," said Ralph, smiling; "and, to carry out the idea, I give you notice that I shall be very sharp, quite horrid and strange, with you."

The humour of this appeared to touch his father, who lay a little while taking it in. "I'll do anything you like," Mr Touchett said at last; "but I'm not sure it's right. You say you want to put wind in her sails; but aren't you afraid of putting too much?"

"I should like to see her going before the breeze!" Ralph answered.

"You speak as if it were for your mere amusement."

"So it is, a good deal."

"Well, I don't think I understand," said Mr Touchett with a sigh. "Young men are very different from what I was. When I cared for a girl – when I was young – I wanted to do more than look at her. You've scruples that I shouldn't have had, and you've ideas that I shouldn't have had either. You say Isabel wants to be free, and that her being rich will keep her from marrying for money. Do you think that she's a girl to do that?"

"By no means. But she has less money than she has ever had before. Her father then gave her everything, because he used to spend his capital. She has nothing but the crumbs of that feast to live on, and she doesn't really know how meagre they are – she has yet to learn it. My mother has told me all about it. Isabel will learn it when she's really thrown upon the world, and it would be very painful to me to think of her coming to the consciousness of a lot of wants she should be unable to satisfy."

"I've left her five thousand pounds. She can satisfy a good many wants with that."

"She can indeed. But she would probably spend it in two or three years."

"You think she'd be extravagant then?"

"Most certainly," said Ralph, smiling serenely.

Poor Mr Touchett's acuteness was rapidly giving place to pure confusion. "It would merely be a question of time then, her spending the larger sum?"

"No – though at first I think she'd plunge into that pretty freely: she'd probably make over a part of it to each of her sisters. But after that she'd come to her senses, remember she has still a lifetime before her, and live within her means."

"Well, you *have* worked it out," said the old man helplessly. "You do take an interest in her, certainly."

"You can't consistently say I go too far. You wished me to go further."

"Well, I don't know," Mr Touchett answered. "I don't think I enter into your spirit. It seems to me immoral."

"Immoral, dear daddy?"

"Well, I don't know that it's right to make everything so easy for a person."

"It surely depends upon the person. When the person's good, your making things easy is all to the credit of virtue. To facilitate the execution of good impulses, what can be a nobler act?"

This was a little difficult to follow, and Mr Touchett considered it for a while. At last he said: "Isabel's a sweet young thing; but do you think she's so good as that?"

"She's as good as her best opportunities," Ralph returned.

"Well," Mr Touchett declared, "she ought to get a great many opportunities for sixty thousand pounds."

"I've no doubt she will."

"Of course I'll do what you want," said the old man. "I only want to understand it a little."

"Well, dear daddy, don't you understand it now?" his son caressingly asked. "If you don't we won't take any more trouble about it. We'll leave it alone."

Mr Touchett lay a long time still. Ralph supposed he had given up the attempt to follow. But at last, quite lucidly, he began again. "Tell me this first. Doesn't it occur to you that a young lady with sixty thousand pounds may fall a victim to the fortune-hunters?"

"She'll hardly fall a victim to more than one."

"Well, one's too many."

"Decidedly. That's a risk, and it has entered into my calculation. I think it's appreciable, but I think it's small, and I'm prepared to take it."

Poor Mr Touchett's acuteness had passed into perplexity, and his perplexity now passed into admiration. "Well, you *have* gone into it!" he repeated. "But I don't see what good you're to get of it."

Ralph leaned over his father's pillows and gently smoothed them; he was aware their talk had been unduly prolonged. "I shall get just the good I said a few moments ago I wished to put into Isabel's reach – that of having met the requirements of my imagination. But it's scandalous, the way I've taken advantage of you!"

78

ALDOUS HUXLEY

Brave New World

Aldous Huxley's best-known work describes a future society ordered to eliminate human misery. Humans are created in artificial breeding units that produce different classes with different levels of intelligence. They are programmed to be happy in their different stations in life, and the mood-altering drug *soma* also helps to keep everyone content. John the Savage was brought up on an American Indian reservation, outside the influences of this brave new world. In this extract Bernard Marx has brought John to England, where they are taken to meet Mustapha Mond, the World Controller.

The room into which the three were ushered was the Controller's study.

"His fordship will be down in a moment." The Gamma butler left them to themselves.

Helmholtz laughed aloud.

"It's more like a caffeine-solution party than a trial," he said, and let himself fall into the most luxurious of the pneumatic arm-chairs. "Cheer up, Bernard," he added, catching sight of his friend's green unhappy face. But Bernard would not be cheered; without answering, without even looking at Helmholtz, he went and sat down on the most uncomfortable chair in the room, carefully chosen in the obscure hope of somehow deprecating the wrath of the higher powers.

The Savage meanwhile wandered restlessly round the room, peering with a vague superficial inquisitiveness at the books in the shelves, at the soundtrack rolls and the reading machine bobbins in their numbered pigeon-holes. On the table under the window lay a massive volume bound in limp black leather-surrogate, and stamped with large golden T's. He picked it up and opened it. MY LIFE AND WORK, BY OUR FORD. The book had been published at Detroit by the Society for the Propagation of Fordian Knowledge. Idly he turned the pages, read a sentence here, a paragraph there, and had just come to the conclusion that the book didn't interest him, when the door opened, and the Resident World Controller for Western Europe walked briskly into the room.

ALDOUS HUXLEY, pp. 260–5 and 285–8 from *Brave New World*. New York and London: Harper & Brothers Publishers, first published 1931. Reprinted by permission of HarperCollins Publishers Inc. and the Huxley Literary Estate.

Mustapha Mond shook hands with all three of them; but it was to the Savage that he addressed himself. "So you don't much like civilization, Mr Savage," he said.

The Savage looked at him. He had been prepared to lie, to bluster, to remain sullenly unresponsive; but, reassured by the good-humoured intelligence of the Controller's face, he decided to tell the truth, straightforwardly. "No." He shook his head.

Bernard started and looked horrified. What would the Controller think? To be labelled as the friend of a man who said that he didn't like civilization – said it openly and, of all people, to the Controller – it was terrible. "But, John," he began. A look from Mustapha Mond reduced him to an abject silence.

"Of course," the Savage went on to admit, "there are some very nice things. All that music in the air, for instance . . ."

"Sometimes a thousand twangling instruments will hum about my ears and sometimes voices."

The Savage's face lit up with a sudden pleasure. "Have you read it too?" he asked. "I thought nobody knew about that book here, in England."

"Almost nobody. I'm one of the very few. It's prohibited, you see. But as I make the laws here, I can also break them. With impunity, Mr Marx," he added, turning to Bernard. "Which I'm afraid you *can't* do."

Bernard sank into a yet more hopeless misery.

"But why is it prohibited?" asked the Savage. In the excitement of meeting a man who had read Shakespeare he had momentarily forgotten everything else.

The Controller shrugged his shoulders. "Because it's old; that's the chief reason. We haven't any use for old things here."

"Even when they're beautiful?"

"Particularly when they're beautiful. Beauty's attractive, and we don't want people to be attracted by old things. We want them to like the new ones."

"But the new ones are so stupid and horrible. Those plays, where there's nothing but helicopters flying about and you *feel* the people kissing." He made a grimace. "Goats and monkeys!" Only in Othello's words could he find an adequate vehicle for his contempt and hatred.

"Nice tame animals, anyhow," the Controller murmured parenthetically.

"Why don't you let them see *Othello* instead?"

"I've told you; it's old. Besides, they couldn't understand it."

Yes, that was true. He remembered how Helmholtz had laughed at *Romeo and Juliet*. "Well then," he said, after a pause, "something new that's like *Othello*, and that they could understand."

"That's what we've all been wanting to write," said Helmholtz, breaking a long silence.

"And it's what you never will write," said the Controller. "Because, if it were really like *Othello* nobody could understand it, however new it might be. And if it were new, it couldn't possibly be like *Othello*."

"Why not?"

"Yes, why not?" Helmholtz repeated. He too was forgetting the unpleasant realities of the situation. Green with anxiety and apprehension, only Bernard remembered them; the others ignored him. "Why not?"

"Because our world is not the same as Othello's world. You can't make flivvers without steel — and you can't make tragedies without social instability. The world's stable now. People are happy; they get what they want, and they never want what they can't get. They're well off; they're safe; they're never ill; they're not afraid of death; they're blissfully ignorant of passion and old age; they're plagued with no mothers or fathers; they've got no wives, or children, or lovers to feel strongly about; they're so conditioned that they practically can't help behaving as they ought to behave. And if anything should go wrong, there's *soma*. Which you go and chuck out of the window in the name of liberty, Mr Savage. *Liberty!*" He laughed. "Expecting Deltas to know what liberty is! And now expecting them to understand *Othello!* My good boy!"

The Savage was silent for a little. "All the same," he insisted obstinately, "*Othello's* good, *Othello's* better than those feelies."

"Of course it is," the Controller agreed. "But that's the price we have to pay for stability. You've got to choose between happiness and what people used to call high art. We've sacrificed the high art. We have the feelies and the scent organ instead."

"But they don't mean anything."

"They mean themselves; they mean a lot of agreeable sensations to the audience."

"But they're . . . they're told by an idiot."

The Controller laughed. "You're not being very polite to your friend, Mr Watson. One of our most distinguished Emotional Engineers . . ."

"But he's right," said Helmholtz gloomily. "Because it *is* idiotic. Writing when there's nothing to say . . ."

"Precisely. But that requires the most enormous ingenuity. You're making flivvers out of the absolute minimum of steel — works of art out of practically nothing but pure sensation."

The Savage shook his head. "It all seems to me quite horrible."

"Of course it does. Actual happiness always looks pretty squalid in comparison with the over-compensations for misery. And, of course, stability isn't nearly so spectacular as instability. And being contented has none of the glamour of a good fight against misfortune, none of the picturesqueness of a struggle with temptation, or a fatal overthrow by passion or doubt. Happiness is never grand. [. . .]

"In a properly organized society like ours, nobody has any opportunities for being noble or heroic. Conditions have got to be thoroughly unstable before the occasion can arise. Where there are wars, where there are divided allegiances, where there are temptations to be resisted, objects of love to be fought for or defended — there, obviously, nobility and heroism have some sense. But there aren't any wars nowadays. The greatest care is taken to prevent you from loving any one too much. There's no such thing as a divided allegiance; you're so conditioned that you can't help doing what you ought to do. And what you ought to do is on the whole so pleasant, so many of the natural impulses are allowed free play, that there really aren't any temptations to resist. And if ever, by some unlucky chance, anything unpleasant should somehow happen, why, there's always *soma* to give you a holiday from the facts. And there's always *soma* to calm your anger, to reconcile you to your enemies, to make you patient and long-suffering. In the past you could only accomplish these things by making a great effort and after years of hard moral training. Now, you swallow two or three half-gramme tablets, and there you are. Anybody can be virtuous now. You can carry at least half your morality about in a bottle. Christianity without tears – that's what *soma* is."

"But the tears are necessary. Don't you remember what Othello said? 'If after every tempest came such calms, may the winds blow till they have wakened death.' There's a story one of the old Indians used to tell us, about the Girl of Mátaski. The young men who wanted to marry her had to do a morning's hoeing in her garden. It seemed easy; but there were flies and mosquitoes, magic ones. Most of the young men simply couldn't stand the biting and stinging. But the one that could – he got the girl."

"Charming! But in civilized countries," said the Controller, "you can have girls without hoeing for them; and there aren't any flies or mosquitoes to sting you. We got rid of them all centuries ago."

The Savage nodded, frowning. "You got rid of them. Yes, that's just like you. Getting rid of everything unpleasant instead of learning to put up with it. Whether 'tis better in the mind to suffer the slings and arrows of outrageous fortune, or to take arms against a sea of troubles and by opposing end them . . . But you don't do either. Neither suffer nor oppose. You just abolish the slings and arrows. It's too easy." [. . .]

"What you need," the Savage went on, "is something *with* tears for a change. Nothing costs enough here." [. . .]

"Exposing what is mortal and unsure to all that fortune, death and danger dare, even for an eggshell. Isn't there something in that?" he asked, looking up at Mustapha Mond. "Quite apart from God – though of course God would be a reason for it. Isn't there something in living dangerously?"

"There's a great deal in it," the Controller replied. "Men and women must have their adrenals stimulated from time to time."

"What?" questioned the Savage, uncomprehending.

"It's one of the conditions of perfect health. That's why we've made the VPS treatments compulsory."

"VPS?"

"Violent Passion Surrogate. Regularly once a month. We flood the whole system with adrenin. It's the complete physiological equivalent of fear and rage. All the tonic effects of murdering Desdemona and being murdered by Othello, without any of the inconveniences."

"But I like the inconveniences."

"We don't," said the Controller. "We prefer to do things comfortably."

"But I don't want comfort. I want God, I want poetry, I want real danger, I want freedom, I want goodness. I want sin."

"In fact," said Mustapha Mond, "you're claiming the right to be unhappy."

"All right then," said the Savage defiantly, "I'm claiming the right to be unhappy."

"Not to mention the right to grow old and ugly and impotent; the right to have syphilis and cancer; the right to have too little to eat; the right to be lousy; the right to live in constant apprehension of what may happen to-morrow; the right to catch typhoid; the right to be tortured by unspeakable pains of every kind."

There was a long silence.

"I claim them all," said the Savage at last.

Mustapha Mond shrugged his shoulders. "You're welcome," he said.

79

HENRY JAMES

The Princess Casamassima

The Princess Casamassima revolves around a group of reformers and revolutionaries in early 1880s London. Hyacinth Robinson, a poor London bookbinder, becomes committed to an underground political movement. Among the people he meets through his political involvement are the charismatic revolutionary Paul Muniment, the torture survivor Hoffendahl, the beautiful Princess Casamassima, and Monsieur Eustache Poupin, who gives Hyacinth letters of introduction to revolutionaries on the continent. Traveling in France and Italy for the first time in his life, Hyacinth writes to the Princess.

Three weeks after this he found himself in Venice, whence he addressed to the Princess Casamassima a letter of which I reproduce the principal passages.

"This is probably the last time I shall write to you before I return to London. Of course you have been in this place, and you will easily understand why here, especially here, the spirit should move me. Dear Princess, what an enchanted city, what ineffable impressions, what a revelation of the exquisite! I have a room in a little *campo* opposite to a small old church, which has cracked marble slabs let into the front; and in the cracks grow little wild delicate flowers, of which I don't know the name. Over the door of the church hangs an old battered leather curtain, polished and tawny, as thick as a mattress, and with buttons in it, like a sofa; and it flops to and fro, laboriously, as women and girls, with shawls on their heads and their feet in little wooden shoes which have nothing but toes, pass in and out. In the middle of the campo is a fountain, which looks still older than the church; it has a primitive, barbaric air, and I have an idea it was put there by the first settlers – those who came to Venice from the mainland, from Aquileia. Observe how much historical information I have already absorbed; it won't surprise you, however, for you never wondered at anything after you discovered I knew something of Schopenhauer. I assure you, I don't think of that musty misogynist in the least to-day, for I bend a genial eye on the women and girls I just spoke of, as they glide, with a small clatter and with their old copper water-jars, to the fountain.

HENRY JAMES, from Chapter XXX in *The Princess Casamassima*, first published in 1886.

The Venetian girl-face is wonderfully sweet and the effect is charming when its pale, sad oval (they all look underfed), is framed in the old faded shawl. They also have very fascinating hair, which never has done curling, and they slip along together, in couples or threes, interlinked by the arms and never meeting one's eye (so that its geniality doesn't matter), dressed in thin, cheap cotton gowns, whose limp folds make the same delightful line that everything else in Italy makes. The weather is splendid and I roast – but I like it; apparently, I was made to be spitted and "done," and I discover that I have been cold all my life, even when I thought I was warm. I have seen none of the beautiful patricians who sat for the great painters – the gorgeous beings whose golden hair was intertwined with pearls; but I am studying Italian in order to talk with the shuffling, clicking maidens who work in the bead-factories – I am determined to make one or two of them look at me. When they have filled their old water-pots at the fountain it is jolly to see them perch them on their heads and patter away over the polished Venetian stones. It's a charm to be in a country where the women don't wear the hideous British bonnet. Even in my own class (excuse the expression – I remember it used to offend you), I have never known a young female, in London, to put her nose out of the door without it; and if you had frequented such young females as much as I have you would have learned of what degradation that dreary necessity is the source. The floor of my room is composed of little brick tiles, and to freshen the air, in this temperature, one sprinkles it, as you no doubt know, with water. Before long, if I keep on sprinkling, I shall be able to swim about; the green shutters are closed, and the place makes a very good tank. Through the chinks the hot light of the campo comes in. I smoke cigarettes, and in the pauses of this composition recline on a faded magenta divan in the corner. Convenient to my hand, in that attitude, are the works of Leopardi and a second-hand dictionary. I am very happy – happier than I have ever been in my life save at Medley – and I don't care for anything but the present hour. It won't last long, for I am spending all my money. When I have finished this I shall go forth and wander about in the splendid Venetian afternoon; and I shall spend the evening in that enchanted square of St Mark's, which resembles an immense open-air drawing-room, listening to music and feeling the sea-breeze blow in between those two strange old columns, in the piazzetta, which seem to make a portal for it. I can scarcely believe that it's of myself that I am telling these fine things; I say to myself a dozen times a day that Hyacinth Robinson is not in it – I pinch my leg to see if I'm not dreaming. But a short time hence, when I have resumed the exercise of my profession, in sweet Soho, I shall have proof enough that it has been my very self. I shall know that by the terrible grind I shall feel my work to be.

"That will mean, no doubt, that I'm deeply demoralised. It won't be for you, however, in this case, to cast the stone at me; for my demoralisation began from the moment I first approached you. Dear Princess, I may have done you good, but you haven't done me much. I trust you will understand what I mean by that speech, and not think it flippant or impertinent. I may have helped you to understand and enter into the misery of the people (though I protest I don't know much about it), but you have led my imagination into quite another train. However, I don't mean to pretend that it's all your fault if I have lost sight of the sacred cause almost altogether in my recent adventures. It is not that it has not been there to see, for that perhaps is the clearest result of extending one's horizon – the sense, increasing as we go, that want and toil and suffering are the constant lot of the immense majority of the human race. I have found them everywhere, but I haven't minded them. Excuse the cynical confession. What has struck me is the great achievements of which man has been capable in spite of them – the splendid accumulations of the happier few, to which, doubtless, the miserable many have also in their degree contributed. The face of Europe appears to be covered with them, and they have had much the greater part of my attention. They seem to me inestimably precious and beautiful, and I have become conscious, more than ever before, of how little I understand what, in the great rectification, you and Poupin propose to do with them. Dear Princess, there are things which I shall be sorry to see you touch, even you with your hands divine; and – shall I tell you *le fond de ma pensée*, as you used to say? – I feel myself capable of fighting for them. You can't call me a traitor, for you know the obligation that I recognise. The monuments and treasures of art, the great palaces and properties, the conquests of learning and taste, the general fabric of civilisation as we know it, based, if you will, upon all the despotisms, the cruelties, the exclusions, the monopolies and the rapacities of the past, but thanks to which, all the same, the world is less impracticable and life more tolerable – our friend Hoffendahl seems to me to hold them too cheap and to wish to substitute for them something in which I can't somehow believe as I do in things with which the aspirations and the tears of generations have been mixed. You know how extraordinary I think our Hoffendahl (to speak only of him); but if there is one thing that is more clear about him than another it is that he wouldn't have the least feeling for this incomparable, abominable old Venice. He would cut up the ceilings of the Veronese into strips, so that every one might have a little piece. I don't want every one to have a little piece of anything, and I have a great horror of that kind of invidious jealousy which is at the bottom of the idea of a redistribution. You will say that I talk of it at my ease, while, in a delicious capital, I smoke cigarettes on a magenta divan; and I give you leave to scoff at me if it turns out that, when I come back to London without a penny in my pocket, I don't hold the same language. I don't know what it comes from, but during the last three months there has crept over me a deep mistrust of that same grudging attitude – the intolerance of positions and fortunes that are higher and brighter than one's own; a fear, moreover, that I may, in the past, have been actuated by such motives, and a devout hope that if I am to pass away while I am yet young it may not be with that odious stain upon my soul."

ISSUES

1   Ralph Ellison, *Invisible Man*

For the nameless narrator of *Invisible Man*, the decisive question is whether to accept the inferior status allocated to him by whites in the segregated Southern culture in which he is growing up. In such an intimidating society, one in which "you've got to know your place at all times," he can scarcely be said to have an open future or a free choice. Nevertheless, through his grandfather he hears a different voice. His grandfather has taken one path of resistance, refusing to subordinate his view of the world to that of the racist white majority, but not showing open resistance. The narrator could follow a similar path, feigning his acceptance of white superiority and aiming only for the type of success open to him within the very definite limits set by the white majority. That would, with luck, be a moderately comfortable, safe existence, but one in which he would have to accept daily humiliation that violates his own sense of justice and dignity. The alternative path of open defiance, standing up for his own equality and that of all African Americans, may seem the right one, and the only possible vindication of his autonomy. But it is also likely to be dangerous, and – as it must have seemed during the long era of segregation – fruitless. Is it wrong to take the easy way out, if choosing any other course is going to mean that you get beaten into submission or even killed?

2   Kathy Lette and Gabrielle Carey, *Puberty Blues*

Subtle forms of coercion can constrain our decisions about our identity, and this is particularly the case with adolescents making choices about sex. The Australian girls portrayed in *Puberty Blues* make their choices under the tyranny of "cool." Barely teenagers, they consent to sex for which they feel no desire and from which they gain no pleasure. Unlike the narrator of *Invisible Man*, Deb will not be beaten or killed if she refuses to accept the rules of her culture. All that will happen is that her boyfriend will drop her, and she will lose her status as a member of the elite in-group. Can we think of them as really consenting to sex? And what kind of education or upbringing would have helped Deb make an informed decision?

The girls are, admittedly, exposed to different values. They live in a society that thinks girls their age should not be sexually active at all, and they know that their parents would strongly disapprove of their conduct. So it might be said that their decision to reject their parents' values in favor of those of the teenage group shows that they are able to choose their own values. Yet they can reject the conventional moral code only in favor of the group's standard, which requires them to provide sex as a service to the boys, irrespective of their own desire. Lacking a grandfather – or perhaps in this case, grandmother – with an independent view, Deb is less aware of her situation than the narrator of *Invisible Man*. They just accept that "that's the way it goes for girls." Would their situation have been different if feminist consciousness had become more widespread? In the absence of any feminist analysis of their situation, do they really have sufficient autonomy to challenge the supremacy of the boys?

Puberty Blues ends with Deb and Sue breaking all the codes of their clique by learning to surf themselves instead of just sitting on the beach watching their boyfriends. Does this show that all along they were capable of making their own choices?

3   James Baldwin, *Giovanni's Room*

After a sexual encounter with another boy, the narrator of *Giovanni's Room* rejects what he has done, fearing the loss of his manhood and considering his own desire "monstrous." Should David have followed his own inclinations and ignored the power of social convention and the pain his choice would have caused himself and others? That may seem the only authentic answer he could have given to the question "Who Am I?" But since David has so thoroughly internalized the values of the dominant heterosexual culture, it is not the answer he gives.

Those who hold homosexuality to be morally wrong would applaud David's choice. Even without taking that moral view, David might have concluded that in an era when homosexuals were considered "perverts" and it was impossible for them to be open about their sexuality, it was only by repressing his attraction for his own sex that he would be able to escape persecution.

What does David mean when he speaks of "lies I've told . . . lived, and believed"? In what way was he living a lie? Should we conclude that living, telling, and believing lies is a "false" life, and that the only possible moral life is one where you face, tell and live the truth about yourself and your world?

Today, when an openly homosexual man can become an Episcopalian bishop and there is growing support for recognizing same-sex marriage, would a young boy like David make the same decision?

4   Tom Wolfe, *The Bonfire of the Vanities*

Two hundred years ago the German philosopher Hegel wrote that "comfort" is "inexhaustible and illimitable" because "others can reveal to you that what you take to be comfort at any stage is discomfort, and these discoveries never come to an end." Remarkably, given the limited forms of advertising that existed in his time, Hegel added: "the need for greater comfort does not exactly arise within you directly; it is suggested to you by those who hope to make a profit from its creation."[1] Tom Wolfe might have written some passages of *The Bonfire of the Vanities* in order to illustrate the truth of Hegel's views.

Sherman McCoy moves in an elite group of the world's wealthiest people. He thinks of himself as one of the Masters of the Universe (which happens also to be the name of a popular toy at the time). He is well rewarded for selling billions of dollars of bonds for a few cents more in every hundred dollars than his Wall Street firm's cost price. But his needs expand with his income, and the money he earns brings no satisfaction. He is part of a social scene that requires his wife to wear a dress in which she cannot walk six blocks. He envies those who can afford to employ a chauffeur, own their own limousines, and, every few years, replace their wives with younger, even more beautiful women.

Socrates famously said that the unexamined life is not worth living. In a teenager like Deb in *Puberty Blues* we might excuse the failure to examine one's life – there is still time for that. McCoy, however, is an adult leading a highly privileged existence, and his failure to reflect on his life is less excusable. What really matters to him? Does he care about honesty, loyalty, or integrity, or about anyone other than himself?

If McCoy never thinks about whether there are better things he could do with his money, and more worthwhile causes he could take up, does this mean that he is not living an ethical life? (Note that characters who do take up such causes, such as Mrs Jellyby in Dickens' *Bleak House* and David Carr in Nick Hornby's *How to Be Good* are presented in other sections of this volume – where their conduct is subjected to different kinds of criticism.)

5 George Eliot, *Middlemarch*

Offered money that rightfully belonged to his mother, and which he could use to further the cause of social reform, Will Ladislaw turns it down because it is tainted. (His attitude to money makes a contrast to that of Sherman McCoy in *The Bonfire of the Vanities*.) Ladislaw wants to keep his honor unblemished, and is glad that his mother did not have what should have been hers. Then he would have had no choice about benefiting from it. Now, because it is offered to him after he became an adult, he is able to choose the kind of person he will be: "It ought to lie with a man's self," he says, "that he is a gentleman." In saying so, he not only chooses honor over wealth, he also defines himself as a person with a particular kind of moral view. A utilitarian would ask: what are the consequences of accepting this money, and are they better than the consequences of rejecting it? That calculation would very probably have led to the conclusion that Ladislaw could make better use of the money – better not only for himself, but for the prospects of social reform that would relieve the plight of the poor – than Bulstrode, the wealthy banker who offers it to him. Ladislaw, however, does not enter into such calculations. It is enough for him that he is a gentleman of honor, and a gentleman does not take tainted money, no matter how much good he could do with it.

Does the source of the money matter even if you can do good with it? Some Holocaust survivors have rejected compensation on the basis that what is being offered is "blood money" and taking it would be tantamount to accepting an apology and condoning what happened. They reject the idea that their suffering, and that of the others who died, is measurable in money terms. Another compensation scheme being mooted in the USA is to pay reparations to the descendants of former slaves for their ancestor's sufferings. Should those who are offered these forms of compensation accept the money? Is their situation different from that of Ladislaw?

Is there moral merit in Bulstrode's desire to make recompense if the only reason is his fear of being punished by God?

6　Arthur Miller, *The Crucible*

A crucible is a vessel in which metals are heated to extreme temperatures, melted down, and purified. *The Crucible* is based on real events but does not stick rigidly to the facts. It premiered when Senator McCarthy and the House Un-American Activities Committee's crusade against communism was at its peak. The newspapers were full of people being called before the Committee to testify and "name names." This was despite the fact that, as Miller notes in an interview, "the USA had the tiniest Communist party in the world." So the play's audiences were in no doubt about its contemporary relevance. Miller himself was called before the Committee in 1956.

Like Will Ladislaw in *Middlemarch*, but under far greater pressure, John Proctor must choose between what he considers honest and and what will bring about the best consequences. To avoid the gallows, should he confess to something he has not done? Proctor finds it difficult to lie, although he is unsure what is prompting him to refuse to do so. He knows that he is no saint, for he has been guilty of adultery, and deceived his wife about it. Is it just a pretense to try to be honest, when one's honesty is already "broke"? Nor does his religion require him to tell the truth, for the Reverend Hale advises him that life is God's most precious gift, and a man who throws it away may be damned more than one who lies to save it. In his desperate uncertainty, Proctor calls out: "God in Heaven, what is John Proctor, what is John Proctor?" Is it, as Proctor at one point suggests, only spite that has, up to this point, prevented him confessing, and thereby giving men he despises what they want? Is he guilty of pride in putting his honor above his life, and above his love for his wife?

Proctor is deeply concerned about how his actions will affect his wife and sons' view of him. He is reluctant to sign his name and cries, "How may I live without my name? I have given you my soul; leave me my name!" Can his concern for his own "self" and integrity be separated from his concern for his reputation and his concern for others? Loyalty to others means standing by your family and friends.

But in this case, if he stands by those he believes in, like Rebecca, and hangs with them, he will be deserting his family.

The intense confrontation between Proctor and Danforth is at the heart of this play. Danforth has his principles. Unlike Parris and Hale, he won't accept a lie, won't compromise. The choice for Proctor can be seen as one between integrity and compromise. Is this also the choice for Danforth? Are they both men of integrity? Do Parris and Hale lack integrity because they are ready to accept a lie?

It is clear that Proctor will not name others. He wants his confession to be a private, individual act. But is this possible in a situation when his confession can be seen to justify the actions of the court and the hanging of the others? Is it acceptable to lie to save yourself if you do not implicate others?

Proctor can be seen to represent the struggle of the individual against an unjust authority. It is in this crisis that Proctor believes that he finds his "good" self, his integrity. Does he eventually make the right choice?

7   William Shakespeare, *Macbeth*

Already a great nobleman, recently honored by Duncan, his king, Macbeth now has an opportunity to murder Duncan and seize his throne. But he knows that killing Duncan is wrong. It is murder, but made worse still because Duncan is Macbeth's kinsman, and Macbeth is Duncan's subject. He is also, on this occasion, Duncan's host, and hosts have a duty to protect their guests. Moreover, Duncan is no tyrant, but a man of virtue who has ruled well. At first glance, then, it seems that Shakespeare is presenting us with a man faced with a straightforward choice between doing what is right, and doing what is in his own interests. But on closer examination we see that Macbeth also understands that killing his king is likely to prove to be contrary not only to all moral principles, but even to his own interests. He recognizes that the "bloody instructions" offered by such an assassination will "return to plague the inventor" and he is not going to be able to enjoy a peaceful reign. With all these reasons against the deed, what is there on the other side? Ambition, Macbeth acknowledges, is his only spur. Yet he still goes ahead and kills Duncan. His ambition, urged on by his wife, proves stronger than morality and stronger than the rational understanding he has of what he himself is likely to suffer from his deed. Who is Macbeth? His choice determines that he is a man who will stop at nothing to reach the top, even while he suspects that reaching the top will not bring him what he wants.

For those who view adult humans as rational beings, such a choice may seem puzzling. In Plato's *Republic*, Socrates asserts that those who really know what is good will do it; doing what is wrong is a failure of knowledge. Macbeth, however, knows what is right and then does the opposite. Nor is he a rare example. Consider the real-life case of Ivan Boesky, the multi-millionaire arbitrageur whose career bears some resemblance to that of Gordon Gekko, played by Michael Douglas in Oliver Stone's film *Wall Street*. Boesky had, by shrewd investments, accumulated a personal fortune of over $100 million, and was widely acclaimed throughout the financial community as a skilful investor (a position that may be considered the modern equivalent of Macbeth's after he had won a great battle for Duncan, and new honors had been heaped upon him). Boesky did not kill his king, but he entered into a secret, illegal arrangement to gain inside information about pending takeovers. In doing so, he set in motion the chain of events that led to his financial ruin, his disgrace, and a prison sentence. Why did he do so? On what possible calculation of self-interest can it be worth risking everything in order to go from having $100 million to having, say, $200 million? In *Wall Street* Gordon Gekko says that he can never have enough money, because "It's a zero-sum game. Somebody wins, somebody loses." Perhaps that is Macbeth's assumption too – getting to the top is what really matters. Is this view irrational? Are people like Macbeth and Boesky mistaken in their priorities? If so, what priorities should they have?

8   Charlotte Perkins Gilman, "The Unnatural Mother"

Is it true that "No mother that was a mother would desert her child for anything on earth"? Or are there greater duties that can override a mother's obligation to put her own child first? (For other situations in which a parent is forced to choose between his duty, as he sees it, and the life of his child, see the readings in other sections from *Iphigeneia at Aulis* and from Genesis.)

When Charlotte Perkins Gilman wrote her story, few people thought that the theory of evolution had any relevance to human behavior. Does an understanding of evolution shed any light on the idea that it is natural for a mother to care more for her own child than for virtually anything else, including the lives of many other children? Would it have been just as "unnatural" for a father to have done what Esther Greenwood did? Would the older women have been equally critical of such a father?

9   Charles Dickens, *Bleak House*

Charles Dickens' celebrated portrait of Mrs Jellyby satirizes a mother who neglects her own children in order to work for the good of people in Africa. But Mrs Jellyby's schemes for Africa seem unlikely to do much good. Is Dickens saying that this is a necessary feature of "telescopic philanthropy," and a reason why we should look after those close to us, rather than concern ourselves with those far away? What would we think about Mrs Jellyby's lackadaisical standards of care for her children – who do after all seem generally healthy, and to whom she is always sweet-tempered – if her projects did lead to two hundred otherwise desperately poor and uneducated families "of Borrioboola-Gha, on the left bank of the Niger," getting an adequate income from growing coffee, and being able to educate their children?

As with the "The Unnatural Mother," we can ask: would the author have taken the same attitude to a father who behaves as Mrs Jellyby does? Do mothers have duties to their children that fathers do not have?

10 Joseph Kanon, *The Good German*

The character of Renate Naumann presents us with the mirror image of the question raised in "The Unnatural Mother." Where Gilman asks whether a mother may sacrifice her own child in order to do a great good, Renate Naumann says, "You can do anything for a child." To what extent does your duty to your child override other moral considerations? Perhaps she is the most "natural" of the three mothers who are at the center of the extracts about parents and children, but it would be more difficult to argue that she is also the one who acts most ethically.

Renate Naumann answers the question of how she could have done what she did by saying that there are two of her, one the monster she has become and the other the woman Jake knew before the war. Does the incredible pressure under which she was acting excuse what she did? Is it reasonable for those of us who have never been in her situation to condemn her?

11 Sophocles, *Antigone*

Brothers and sisters are part of the nuclear family, but on a more equal footing than parents and children. Antigone feels herself called on to do for her dead brother what no stranger would be asked to do. In her view, honoring her brother's corpse is an imperative that comes before her own safety and happiness, her love for her betrothed, and her duty to obey the law of the land. Ismene does not see her duty to her brother in the same way and refuses to support what she calls Antigone's "excessive gesture." Who is right? Should duty to a sibling come before the duty to obey the law?

The core issue of this play is the clash between the individual's views and the political imperatives of the state. Is Kreon a cruel tyrant, or a wise ruler exercising necessary firmness after a period of civil strife? (The French playwright Jean Anouilh wrote a version of Antigone that was staged in German-occupied France and understood as a rallying call to resist the Nazi regime; but it is not clear that Sophocles would have sympathized with this interpretation of his play.) Antigone knows that she will die and that her gesture is pointless. It will not reduce Kreon's power or bring a change to the law. Her brother will not remain buried. Is the fact that Antigone believes Kreon's decree to be wrong reason enough for her to sacrifice her life?

12 William Shakespeare, *Measure for Measure*

Like Antigone, Isabella is willing to lay down her life for her brother – or so she says. She is, however, in a different situation, and not only because her brother is alive. To save her brother, Isabella would have to sin. Assuming that doing as Angelo wants would be a sin if done from lust or for personal advantage, would it still be a sin if done to save a brother's life?

13   Zitkala-Ša, "The Soft-Hearted Sioux"

Zitkala-Ša presents a young man caught between two cultures – an increasingly common phenomenon in a multicultural world. The clash between the old and the new ways is also the clash between two conceptions of the family. The young Indian has joined the family of Christ, and is separated from his pagan parents and their tribe. Many young people convert to religions that cut them off from their parents. Zitkala-Ša forces us to ask whether religious belief should ever be allowed to override the duty of children to their parents.

In his efforts to obtain meat for his starving father, the young man commits a crime and then, without really knowing what he is doing, kills a man. What should he do when he can't fulfill both the dictates of his new God and his obligations to his father? What does he owe his father?

14   Ambrose Bierce, "A Horseman in the Sky"

Carter Druse must choose between killing his father and the dereliction of his duty as a soldier. There is no other option, for the Union forces are depending on the element of surprise to win the encounter. Druse makes his choice by framing it in terms of his father's injunction to him to do his duty. But his father never imagined such a circumstance. Can one's duty as a soldier require one to kill one's father? Would his father have supported his decision? And what if their situations were reversed? Would a father have been duty-bound to kill his son?

15   Alice Munro, "The Peace of Utrecht"

With women working and the proportion of elderly people in developed societies rising, the question of a child's obligations to sick and elderly parents has become increasingly common. Maddy and Helen have had to care for and meet their mother's needs since they were teenagers. The progressive disease she suffers from is never named but we know its symptoms. Does the fact that they wish to escape from the burden of caring for their sick mother mean that they are not doing what children owe their parents?

Their aunts disapprove of Maddy's refusal to bring her mother home from hospital, although she visited her there every day. The suggestion is that this refusal of Maddy's shortened her mother's life by many years. Maddy says, "I couldn't go on. . . . I wanted my life." What should Maddy have done? And what of Helen, who got married and stayed away? How should she have balanced her obligations to her own husband and children with the needs of her mother and sister?

Would the same expectations hold for a son in this situation?

16   Jane Austen, *Pride and Prejudice*

Lady Catherine seeks to dissuade Elizabeth from aspiring to a match with her nephew, Mr Darcy, whose station in life is far above that of Miss Bennet. But Lady Catherine and Elizabeth Bennet have very different conceptions of what kind of social differences debar marriage, and also of the extent to which those contemplating marriage should be influenced by the wishes of others. Jane Austen is clearly on Elizabeth's side, but is there a case for Lady Catherine's view? Is a difference in social position ever a reason against marriage?

In many traditional societies, parents arrange marriages and the young couple have little or no say in whom they will marry. Should young people today give any weight to the views of their elders before deciding on marriage?

17   William Shakespeare, *Romeo and Juliet*

Romeo risks death to catch sight of Juliet, and tells her he would give his life for her love. Yet earlier that evening he also risked his life by going to the Capulet ball to catch a glimpse of a different girl with whom he thought he was madly in love. What other duties should a young lover as impetuous as Romeo consider?

A generations-long feud exists between the Capulets and the Montagues. But Romeo and Juliet think only of "my true love's passion." Should they be more mindful of their obligations to their parents?

On the very day they meet, Romeo and Juliet are so sure of their love that they are already discussing marriage. But Juliet is not yet 14 and Romeo is just a little older. Can they really understand the significance of what they are doing? Since they will shortly meet tragic deaths, their passion has no time to cool, and Shakespeare does not have to concern himself with the future of the relationship. Romeo and Juliet at forty-something are difficult to conceive. One can only wonder what kind of a marriage they would have had.

18   Vikram Seth, *A Suitable Boy*

Lata has different feelings for each of the men she could choose for her husband, and with each of them she knows she would live a different kind of life. Her choice, therefore, is ultimately a choice about what kind of life she values most and what kind of person she wants to be. What kind of life does she most want?

Her friend Malati thinks she is making a terrible mistake in not marrying the man she loves most passionately. Probably most people in Western societies would agree with Malati. But since passion rarely lasts a lifetime, is Malati right?

19   Guy de Maupassant, "The Model"

In "The Model" the narrator puts the view that passion is not a good enough basis for a long-term relationship. He portrays a society in which there is a worldly acceptance of the fact that a man in the grip of passion will make promises to a woman that he later does not want to keep, while a woman will do everything she can to hold on to her man. (This story was written at a time when few avenues except marriage were open to women.) How much worth has a promise made in the heat of passion? Should a man keep his word when his feelings change? And is the upshot a form of just punishment for Jean Summer?

20   George Eliot, *Middlemarch*

Casaubon wants and expects Dorothea to promise to obey his wishes after his death, without even telling her what she would be commiting herself to. What "ideal" of marriage does Dorothea intend to act on when she eventually forces herself to give in to her husband's wish? Is it reasonable of Casaubon to ask this of his wife?

Casaubon has devoted his life to his scholarly project, the value of which Dorothea now doubts. Dorothea believes that the promise he wants her to make will involve her in continuing and completing this project. Should she say something about these doubts to her husband? Then, perhaps, he would have had a clearer idea why she was hesitating. But she could not bring herself to speak to him about her doubts. Should she then have refused his request outright? Or, since that would have caused him immense distress, and he would undoubtedly have become much more unpleasant to live with, should she have made the requested promise, while intending to break it after his death? (It is only when Casaubon's will is read after his death that the truth of what he really wanted of her is revealed.)

What difference does Casaubon's death make to what Dorothea should do? When he asks her to make this promise, she believes her husband may live for another fifteen years. Should she refuse "to do for him dead, what she was almost sure to do for him living"?

Even if Dorothea did not promise anything to Casaubon, do the wishes of the dead carry some weight? When we give people the kind of funeral they would have liked, and carry out their wills, we are respecting their wishes, even though they are no longer present to be pleased at what we are doing or upset at our failure to do it. So wouldn't it be wrong of Dorothea simply to throw out her husband's lifelong work? Does a spouse have a special duty arising from the marriage, to preserve and complete the project of her husband or wife? Assume that Dorothea is right in her view that the work is worthless. Is the work's intrinsic value the only factor that should bear on her decision?

21   Leo Tolstoy, *Anna Karenina*

"Happy families are all alike; every unhappy family is unhappy in its own way" is the famous first line of *Anna Karenina*. The Russian aristocracy of the period in which Tolstoy's classic is set had its own mode of dealing with sexual passion. Marriage was a lifelong union, but it was often based on family connections rather than love, and it was understood that married men and women might fall in love with someone else. What was wrong was not adultery, but causing a scandal. Extra-marital affairs were tolerated, as long as they were discreet. "Don't ask, don't tell – and above all, don't flaunt it" seemed to be the code. Such a code may preserve a marriage, and at least the appearance of family life, but it effectively involves consenting to being deceived. That is a troubling moral concept, but perhaps no more problematic than any other way of coping with the conflicts inherent in an ideal of monogamy that does not sit comfortably with the powerful realities of human sexuality.

Vronsky wishes to end the deception in which he and Anna are living. But doing so comes at an extraordinarily high cost for Anna. It will break up her marriage and bring disgrace to her family name. If she openly becomes Vronksy's mistress, she will be socially ostracized, and will have to give up her child. Is all this really better than continuing the deception? Or ending the relationship with Vronsky altogether? Is Anna in a position to decide where her best interests lie, or is she swayed so much by passion that she is not in a fit state to choose. If so, is it wrong of Vronsky to ask so much of her?

Passionate love, outside marriage and especially in a woman, is seen as a transgression. We can predict that if Anna and Vronsky openly live together, they will not live "happily ever after." Is the intense happiness Anna describes worth grabbing, and at what cost to others and yourself?

Many people condemn Anna not so much for leaving her husband but for abandoning her little boy. Was she wrong to do this? What were her options?

22   George Bernard Shaw, *Mrs Warren's Profession*

In his prologue Shaw argues that if he had made Mrs Warren a bookmaker, rather than the owner of a brothel, the play would have caused no controversy. Yet brothels do cater to real human needs that do not go away when brothels are suppressed, whereas for gambling there is, in Shaw's view, "absolutely nothing to be said." The same point holds true today. The parent who boasts about the well-paid job their son or daughter has in a casino would be appalled if she became a madam or he a pimp. Where prostitution is legal and well-regulated, does it do as much harm as gambling? Why is moral condemnation so often focused on sexual behavior?

Living off the earnings of prostitution is illegal in most countries and generally considered immoral. Yet millions of poor young women are employed in the sex industry world-wide. Does the prohibition of prostitution deny them the freedom to choose how to earn their living? Is Mrs Warren justified in being proud rather than ashamed of her achievements?

It seems that if Vivie was in the situation her mother had been in, Mrs Warren would advise her to become a prostitute rather than a servant. Does that make Mrs Warren an immoral mother?

23   John Cleland, *Memoirs of a Woman of Pleasure*

Just a few minutes before the events described in the extract, Fanny has said that she would have "spit" in the face of anyone who suggested she could be intimate with anyone but Charles, no matter how much money she was offered. Should Fanny be judged badly for her unfaithfulness to Charles, her true love? But later she says, "our virtues and our vices depend too much on our circumstances." Do you agree that "circumstance" is the cause of moral and immoral behavior, rather than having a good or bad character? Before you answer, you might like to consider some relevant research. Students at a theological seminary who were to give a talk in one building were first given a briefing in another building. At the end of the briefing, some were told that they were late, and needed to hurry; others were told that they had a few minutes before they needed to be there, and a third group were told to go over to the other building, without any indication about time. On the way to the next building, all students passed someone coughing and groaning, appearing to be having some kind of fit or attack. Of those students who were told that they were late, only 10 percent stopped to offer help, whereas of those who were told they had plenty of time, 63 percent stopped. This small difference in the circumstances made a more significant difference to how the students were likely to behave than other factors, including whether they saw religion as a means to an end, or as an end in itself, and whether they had recently been given to read the passage from the Bible about the parable of the Good Samaritan.[2]

The moral line between outright prostitution and other relationships in which sex is exchanged for financial support is not always clearcut. Unlike a prostitute, a "kept woman" has the advantage of having to be sexually available to only one man, but is that a significant ethical distinction? And is the woman who sets out to marry a millionaire so different from a kept woman?

Later in the novel, Fanny says of the behavior of Mr H. that his passion "had too little respected the condition I was in." Does she let him off too lightly? Should we consider him a rapist? If that charge is too severe, how should we view his conduct?

24   Daniel Defoe, *Moll Flanders*

In this novel Defoe questions many sexual taboos. This extract deals with a particularly powerful taboo – incest – that Betty (Moll Flanders) breaches inadvertently. Up to the moment Betty found out that her husband was her half-brother they were happy together. Would it have been just as wrong if she had never found out and they had continued as husband and wife?

Once Betty understands her situation, she has to struggle with her conscience, and with her own physical impulses, to decide what she should do. Her mother tells her to "bury the whole thing entirely" but Betty can't, though the consequences may have been better for all concerned if she had taken her mother's advice. Is this a situation in which it would have been better to remain ignorant than to discover the truth?

25 Maeve Binchy, "Shepherd's Bush"

In this story abortion is described as (almost) a normal event. May finds this odd because she has come from Ireland where she could not have an abortion. But for Helen and her friends, it is just another medical procedure. Not for them any anguished concern about taking a life. Is this a sign of a callous society, or one that has moved beyond the religiously based morality that believes in the sanctity of human life from conception?

May has made this decision on her own. Andy, the father of the child, does not even know that she is pregnant. Does he have a right to know and be involved in this decision? Or, given the kind of relationship that May and he are in, is it entirely hers to make?

We learn that Andy's morality condones cheating on his wife and having sex without taking responsibility for contraception, but he is opposed to abortion. What kind of ethical position is he likely to hold? What are May's alternatives to having an abortion?

26 Brian Clark, *Whose Life is it Anyway?*

In March 2002 the High Court of England decided a case very similar to that of Ken Harrison's as represented in *Whose Life is it Anyway?* A 44-year-old patient known only as Mrs B. was paralyzed from the neck down, and on a ventilator. She had repeatedly asked for the ventilator to be turned off, although she knew that without the ventilator she would die. The hospital refused. The court ruled that Mrs B. was competent, and entitled to end her life by refusing further life-support, which she then did. This decision marks the conclusion of a long struggle between the traditional paternalism of the medical profession, with its view that the physician's duty is always to preserve life, and patients seeking to assert their right to decide their own future. *Whose Life is it Anyway?* portrays this conflict. It reached a wide audience and was itself an influence on the shift towards greater respect for the rights of patients.

Nevertheless, the ability of people like Mrs B. and Ken Harrison to decide between life and death does not extend to all patients. Patients who do not require a ventilator or other form of life-support, but are physically unable to bring about their own death, cannot choose to die. It is illegal to assist such patients to die, except in a small number of jurisdictions, including the Netherlands, Belgium, Switzerland, and the state of Oregon. Is it right that a competent paralyzed patient like Ken Harrison should be allowed to decide to die? If so, is there any reason why such a patient should be able to make that choice if he requires a ventilator to continue to live, but not if he does not need any artificial means of life-support?

27   Kate Jennings, *Moral Hazard*

In the second extract, the doctors in the Emergency Room pay no heed to Cath's wishes and are not interested in seeing documents that Bailey signed expressing his wish not to be treated. Is it ethical for doctors to act in that way? When she is unable to get the doctors to act as Bailey would have wished, is Cath justified in taking more active steps to end her husband's life?

Before the onset of dementia, a person may think "I would not want to live like that." Yet the person with dementia may not be suffering, and is, in some sense, a different person. Should a decision to end life be based on what the person wanted when he or she was not demented or on how much the person with dementia is now suffering?

Cath says, "Truth be known, I was past questions of risk or morality...." We get a sense of the complexity of the motives propelling her to act as she does. She wants to escape the torture of watching helplessly what is happening to her husband, and she can see only one way out of this terrible problem. What would be the moral course of action for her to take? Does a spouse have special obligations in this situation? What other obligations does Cath have?

28   William Shakespeare, *Hamlet*

Hamlet's soliloquy is one of the most famous speeches in the English language. In it, a young prince, with his whole life ahead of him, asserts that, if it were not for the fear of what may happen after death, suicide would be a rational and attractive option. Is this a sign that he is mentally disturbed? If he did not believe in an afterlife, and therefore thought it right to end his life, would it be right for others to restrain him to prevent him doing so?

29   Arna Bontemps, "A Summer Tragedy"

This story shows the underside of growing old gracefully and portrays a couple who can no longer care for themselves, are in pain, and have no-one who cares about them. What are the ties that bind people to life? In making a decision to take your own life, are there considerations you should take into account apart from your own wishes? And what obligations does the community have to the poor and the elderly?

30   Elizabeth Gaskell, *North and South*

Thornton says that he knows what is best for his workers and doesn't need to explain his actions to them. He sees himself as like a benevolent father, and the "hands" as his children. Whatever is in his interest is, *ipso facto*, in their interest. Is there any substance in this view? What obligations, if any, do employers have to their workers?

Margaret Hale is shocked to find that if the men do not join the union they are ostracized, and no-one speaks to them. Higgins justifies pressurizing men to join the union. He argues that the bargaining power of labor depends on unity. This argument for the union principle of a "closed shop" is still used today. But isn't this view, that the union knows what's best for the worker, just as paternalistic as the view that the employers know best?

Employers today argue that they merely offer employment to workers, on specified terms, and the workers are free to accept or decline the offer. They see regulations setting minimum wages or conditions as interfering with freedom of choice. Unions too, if they operate a closed shop, are said to prevent the marketplace from operating freely. But do workers really have a choice? Can there be freedom of choice when power is so unequally distributed?

31   Edwin Seaver, *The Company*

There are people fortunate enough to have work they enjoy and know to be worthwhile. But most people work to earn money to be able to live. Aarons leaves a well-paid, secure job, doing work that comes easily to him. He has a wife and child to look after. Yet he appears to suggest that working for an advertising agency is akin to prostitution. Is that right? Is quitting his job the right decision?

"It seems to me a fellow owes something to the Company that's hiring him," says the narrator. The Company is seen as a collective more significant than the individual. What, if any, obligations does Aarons owe the Company?

Aarons' co-workers obviously consider a certain level of anti-Semitism acceptable: "we all liked him quite a lot even though he was a Jew," one of them says. How much of a problem is racial, ethnic, or religious prejudice in the workplace today?

32   Ruth L. Ozeki, *My Year of Meats*

Jane took the job of making *My American Wife* knowing that the series was to be made with the specific aim of selling American beef. The sponsor is understandably angry when, instead, Jane's program boosts the sales of Australian lamb. Isn't it Jane's professional duty to do the job she was hired, and is being paid, to do?

But that is not the only issue raised here. American culture promotes individualism, and applauds documentary film-makers who stand up for their professional independence. But Japanese culture sees loyalty to one's company as good, and to insist on one's individual views is seen as simply selfish. Is it possible to reconcile that difference?

Another issue raised here is that of the responsibility of the journalist, or in this case film-maker, to those interviewed for the programs. It is not unusual for television producers to conceal from those who will appear on the program some relevant information about the line that the program will take, or how the material will be edited and used. In some cases that may be the only way to obtain information that it is important for the public to have – for example, about whether a product is safe. But is it right to deceive in order to obtain that information?

When Jane learns that the product she is promoting could have serious health risks, Mr Ueno, her boss, dismisses her queries, telling her to stick to film-making and leave the safety of beef to the experts. Is Mr Ueno right? Should Jane restrict herself to her area of expertise?

33   Henrik Ibsen, *An Enemy of the People*

Unlike Jane Takagi-Little in *My Year of Meats*, Dr Thomas Stockmann is an expert. Yet his technical expertise is deemed insignificant when weighed against economic considerations. His brother, the Mayor, claims to be unconvinced by Dr Stockmann's evidence and argues that the issue is not just medical. How far should the opinion of the "expert" count in this case?

Dr Stockmann is surprised to learn that he will lose his job unless he does what his employer wants. There is obviously a difference in how he sees his role and duties as a professional and the way his employer sees him as an employee. What duties does he owe his employer, and what, if anything, overrides these obligations?

Dr Stockmann is under pressure to subordinate his values as a "man of science" to his brother's interests in covering up his mistakes regarding the construction of the baths, to the interests of his town, and to the welfare of his family. Should any of these considerations outweigh his responsibility as a "man of science"? His wife argues that Dr Stockmann's sacrifice of his own and his family's interests will be futile because "might" (power) will win out over "right" (truth). Should he persist even if he suspects he will fail and lose his livelihood, family, and reputation?

In *My Year of Meats* there is little emphasis on the potential loss of livelihoods for beef farmers or others who benefit from this industry. This is in contrast to the concerns for the employment prospects of the local community raised in *An Enemy of the People*. In considering the health of those who use the baths – and remember that at this time there was no treatment for typhus and it was often fatal – is it legitimate to take into account the harm done to the local community?

34   C. P. Snow, *The Search*

For Arthur Miles, in contrast to Dr Thomas Stockmann, the personal comes before the scientific. Arthur says it was an "instinctive drive" that made him burn the letter.

What does he mean by "instinct"? Should we make moral choices on the basis of our instincts? Arthur says he would have acted differently if the fraud had been committed by a stranger rather than a friend. Should this have influenced his decision?

Should Arthur Miles have sent the letter exposing Sheriff? Does his decision not to do so mean that he has become "an accessory after the fact" in allowing someone to get away with scientific fraud? In contrast to the situation in *An Enemy of the People*, in Sheriff's case there seems little likelihood of harm being caused to others. Should the consequences – good, bad, or neutral – be taken into account in such a decision?

35   Euripides, *Iphigeneia at Aulis*

Agamemnon finds himself in a situation that pushes patriotism to one's country to its limit. Clytemnestra is outraged by what her husband plans and is quick to point out that a lottery, or the sacrifice of Menelaos' daughter Hermione, would be a more just course of action. She argues that we should not obey gods who are devoid of sense. She warns, too, about the consequences of this act: that it will finally turn her against her husband (she and her lover Aegisthus murder Agamemnon when he returns from Troy ten years later), and that his other children, knowing that he is willing to kill them, will for ever after be unable to trust him. Should one's duty to one's country count for more than the life of one's child?

Clytemnestra asks: "do you think of nothing but waving scepters and leading armies?," suggesting that he cannot see what he owes to his own family. Do you think a mother could have made the decision that Agamemnon makes? Would the gods have asked such a thing of a mother?

In the end, despite her mother's arguments and implacable opposition, Iphigeneia comes to glory in her sacrifice, willingly going to her death for the sake of her country. Does this justify Agamemnon's action?

Agamemnon alleges that Iphigeneia must die or his wife and daughters will be killed anyway when the Trojans overrun Argos. Is this just a question of one's duty to make sacrifices in war-time? Note, though, that it is the Greeks who are readying to attack the Trojans rather than the other way round. Would Agamemnon's argument be valid if the Trojans were the aggressors, and there really was a danger that they would overrun Argos?

Notice the parallel here with the biblical story of Abraham and Isaac, which can be found in Section XI.

36   Geraldine Brooks, *Year of Wonders*

Colonel Bradford suggests that it is wrong to put ourselves and our family at risk in order to avoid the risk of harming strangers. Is he right? Do community leaders, like Colonel Bradford and the Minister, have greater obligations to the broader community? It is often claimed that human beings are inherently selfish – and sometimes that evolution makes it inevitable that we will never sacrifice our own interests, and those of our kin, to the interests of strangers. Is it possible to reconcile this view with the actions of the villagers in *Year of Wonders*? (Remember that the novel is based on fact. In Eyam, two-thirds of the villagers died, but the Plague did not spread further in Derbyshire. Thus the sacrifice of the villagers may have saved hundreds or even thousands of lives.)

There are similarities between the actions of the villagers in this novel, and that of Charlotte Perkins Gilman's "unnatural mother." Are the villagers "unnatural people" because they are prepared to sacrifice their own lives and those of their fellow-villagers for the lives of strangers?

37   Ian McEwan, *Enduring Love*

Regularly we read in the newspaper of someone who has rushed into a burning building to save people he or she doesn't know, or plunged into the surf to rescue a swimmer in trouble. Sometimes the hero comes out alive, sometimes both die. In *Enduring Love* five men respond to the child's cry. Joe Rose, the narrator of Ian McEwan's novel, must weigh risking his own life against trying to save a stranger's. There is hardly time to think, let alone to think about ethics, as he and the others run towards the hot-air balloon. But in looking back Rose analyzes the crucial moment when he decided that "Suddenly the sensible course was to look out for yourself. The child was not my child, and I was not going to die for it." What do we owe to others, those not related or close to us, and do these obligations extend to putting ourselves at risk? Does it make a difference that it is a child, not an adult, who is in danger?

All would have been well if the men had all hung onto the balloon's ropes. But as soon as one put his interest above that of the others, the delicate balance shifted. Note that the men couldn't have predicted who would hang on, or that the boy in the balloon would come down safely in the end. Is it true that altruism made no sense in this situation once one person let go? Why, then, did John Logan hang on?

The narrator sees the whole incident as an example of "morality's ancient, irresolvable dilemma: us, or me." This dilemma has been put in mathematically precise form in the shape of a well-known problem called "The Prisoner's Dilemma." Two prisoners are held in separate cells, unable to communicate with one another. The police make the same offer to each of them:

If you confess, and implicate the other prisoner, you'll be out of here tomorrow. If you hold out, and the other guy confesses, implicating you, you'll get twenty years. If you both confess, you'll both get five years. And if neither of you confesses, we can still hold you for six months for further interrogations. So think it through, and you'll find that whatever the other guy does, you'll be better off if you confess.

At the level of individual rationality – of "me" – the police are right. Each prisoner will be better off if he confesses than if he does not confess. By confessing, he'll either go free immediately (if the other prisoner does not confess) rather than be held for another six months, or he'll get five years (if the other prisoner does confess) rather than twenty. So if each prisoner thinks of himself, they will both confess and each will serve five years in prison. Yet if they had thought of "us" they would have seen that the best outcome for both of them would be not to confess, for then they would each have been free after six months.

In *Enduring Love* McEwan gives us an approximation to a multi-person prisoners' dilemma. If all of them hang on, they can achieve their joint objective of saving the child and themselves; but if one person lets go, it is in the interests of all to let go.

There are many situations in which individual rationality leads to collective irrationality. The commuter's dilemma is another example: we would all be better off if everyone took public transport, which could then be frequent, swift, and economical, but as things are, each of us is better off driving. Perhaps the biggest prisoner's dilemma of all, in many ways, is the problem of global warming. We would all be better off if everyone reduced the use of fuels that produce greenhouse gases, but it is in the interests of each of us individually to keep using them. Some argue that such situations show the need for a government or other form of authority that can take decisions and apply sanctions to those who do not obey. In *Enduring Love*, would things have turned out better if one person had somehow been able to take control?

38   Nick Hornby, *How to be Good*

David Carr believes we have an obligation to make the world a better place for others. But he has great trouble convincing his family to go along with his plans. The reactions of Katie – David's wife and the novel's narrator – his children, and his neighbors run the gamut of justifications that people use to do nothing in the face of the suffering and need of others around them. Some blame the homeless for their need, others say that it won't make a difference, or that it's the government's obligation to take care of the homeless, and that ordinary citizens should focus on looking after themselves and their families. The reader has to ask whether these are sound arguments, or rationalizations for selfishness.

If we do have an obligation to make the world a better place, on what basis can we decide what we owe to others? David says that he couldn't think of any arguments against the idea of taking in a homeless young person. The homeless strangers need help, there are people with empty rooms and so people should offer their rooms. But clearly it isn't that simple. It is difficult to change our way of thinking, and easy to find reasons against doing anything that would mean putting ourselves out or giving something up. So what part can logic and morality play in deciding this issue? Is Katie a "bad" person and David a "good" person?

39   Joyce Carol Oates, "The Undesirable Table"

Joyce Carol Oates presents us with a familiar occasion – a group of middle-class friends out for an evening's relaxation. Her tone suggests to the reader that these are not bad, unfeeling people – after all none of us like to be made to feel uncomfortable. How often has it happened to us that someone is in distress, but we don't help: we cross the road to avoid a miserable-looking beggar; we look away from a crying woman near us on the subway; we block our ears against the screams from next door; on our TV, we watch pictures of people who are starving, or without shelter or medical care after a natural disaster, but we do nothing. Haven't we earned our pleasures and the right to not have them spoilt by those less successful and fortunate? Since it is hard enough to cope with our own life-problems, don't we have a right to close our eyes and ears to the misery of others?

Katie Carr in *How to be Good* is embarrassed by her husband and his plans. The friends at "The Undesirable Table" are also concerned with behaving so as not to cause embarrassment, a form of discomfort. In fact the alleged heroism in this story is in not responding, not mentioning the unmentionable, so as not to spoil the talk of politics, religion, children. Even "undesirable" is a refined word, a euphemism carefully chosen instead of "awful" or "bad." The author shows us how words are used to deal with "unpleasantness," but never tells us what is beyond the plate glass. What is happening out there?

This story can also be read as a critique of armchair intellectuals, those who discuss issues passionately but do nothing about the real world beyond their pleasant middle-class lives. What does the narrator mean by "to *name* a problem is *to invest it with too much significance*"? The story concludes with the sentence: "It might be said we have no choice." Is that true?

40   Anthony Trollope, *Can You Forgive Her?*

Plantagenet Palliser must choose between his personal life and politics. This is a conflict often faced by those in political life with its demands to move to the capital and work long hours. Plantagenet must choose between the promise he made to his wife – and the future of his marriage to a woman he loves – and the prominent position for which he has been hoping and working. Moreover, he is told that his Party, and his country, need him. Is there a right decision in this situation? Does Palliser make it?

It is interesting to compare the actions of Glencora Palliser and Anna Karenina, who are both from upper-class milieus and in love with someone who is not their husband. In both cases their lovers pressure them to leave their husbands. Trollope writes that Lady Glencora, though sinful enough to think of it, was "neither bold enough nor wicked enough" to run away or kill herself. Does the difference in the actions of Anna and Lady Glencora lie in their character or in their circumstances?

41   Anonymous (Joe Klein), *Primary Colors*

Libby Holden insists that there is a moral difference between "busting dust" and "doing oppo." Does this distinction really hold?

The Stantons argue that if they don't make this information public the Republicans will do so after Fred Picker is nominated. Assuming that either of the leading Democrat candidates would make a better President of the United States than the Republican candidate, does this justify discrediting Picker, a "flawed but decent man"? Stanton has plenty of his own flaws. Would it be acceptable for Stanton to divulge the damaging facts he has on Picker if he revealed his own flaws at the same time?

Libby wanted the Stantons to reject the use of the material they gathered on Picker or, at least, to discuss the pros and cons, rights and wrongs. The Stantons fail "the Test." Are they worthy of Libby's loyalty?

Does the end justify the means? Can the use of "dirty tricks" in elections ever be justifiable? Are they an unavoidable part of political life? Is it possible that although in everyday life the end does not justify the means, it does in politics? Are those who use dirty tricks corrupted by the methods they've employed to get elected?

42   Anthony Trollope, *Phineas Finn*

Today it is unlikely that elected officials will show their anger at being kept in Parliament "beyond the time at which grouse should have been shot." In other respects, however, political life has changed less. Phineas Finn, a member of Prime Minister Mildmay's party, faces a crisis in deciding how to vote on the reform proposal put forward by the opposition party headed by Mr Turnbull. Finn knows that the cause of reform is just and right. But the Reform Bill will abolish Loughton, and thus threatens to end his brief political career. He votes against his conscience and with his party. For this he is rewarded with the paid junior cabinet position of Under-Secretary for the Colonies, and the promise that the party will find him another seat in Parliament. To what extent, if any, should Phineas have taken his own interest into consideration in deciding how to vote? And what is the extent of his obligations to the political party that got him elected?

43   Harriet Beecher Stowe, *Uncle Tom's Cabin*

Reading *Uncle Tom's Cabin* today it is hard to believe that only a little over a century ago it was considered justifiable to "own" another person, and acceptable to treat another human as a "thing." Although Mr Shelby is a kindly man, Stowe argues that there can be no good form of slavery. The real problem, Stowe argues, is that "the law considers all these human beings . . . only as so many *things* belonging to a master." Stowe thought that whether the owners are kind or cruel is not the issue – unless the institution based on owning human beings was abolished, the lives of the slaves would always depend on the whims of others. Are there parallels with aspects of modern society where we currently depend on people's kindliness or charity, but only changes in the laws and institutions can make a real difference?

Mr Haley uses the idea of the innate "difference" between blacks and whites to justify different treatment. He believes that a black mother feels less for her children than a white mother. No-one would use such an argument today in support of slavery, but it is sometimes still claimed that there are genetic differences between different races. Is it necessarily racist to make such a claim?

"I consider religion a valeyable thing in a nigger," says Mr Haley. Slavery has existed under the Greeks and Romans, and whether the prevailing religion was Islam, Judaism, Christianity, or Hinduism. How is it that belief in equality before God did not necessarily mean opposition to slavery?

Haley says he has "as much conscience as any man in business can afford to keep." Today those who raise animals for food say the same about humane methods of treating their animals, and industrialists make similar comments about the environmental impact of their manufacturing plants. Is it impossible for people in business to follow their conscience completely?

We see the limitations of Stowe's perceptions in her description of Harry: his clothes, his cavorting and contortions. Today this reads like a caricature, a ridiculous stereotype despite the fact that she was trying to present blacks in a positive way. Some people think that because of such stereotypes, and the use of derogatory words like "nigger," this book should not be read today. We believe, on the other hand, that it is important to understand how even the best-intentioned people saw African Americans during the era of slavery. Perhaps this will lead us to re-examine our own prejudices.

44   Lerone Bennett, Jr, "The Convert"

"The Convert" is set almost a hundred years after the abolition of slavery in the USA, yet the African Americans in Melina, Mississippi, are anything but free. Their safety and security depend on the whim of the white judge, sheriff, and banker. In Lerone Bennett, Jr's shocking story a man is beaten to death for going into the "whites-only" waiting room at the railway station. Why does this tiny act so infuriate the Sheriff and the other white men? Do these whites believe that the life of one black man counts for nothing? Are they responding in order to defend the power they have wielded for generations?

The main character's name is loaded with significance. Booker Taliaferro Washington (1856–1915) was an influential African American educator whose "accommodations philosophy" sought economic gains at the price of "not rocking the boat" over disenfranchisement and segregation. John Brown (1800–59), a white Abolitionist who favored armed resistance to free the slaves, was hanged in 1859.

It is clear that "separate but equal" did not work in the South of the United States nor in South Africa under apartheid. Can such a system ever be just?

In *Uncle Tom's Cabin*, Tom is a hero. Yet in this story, to "Tom" is to be a coward, to do what the white men want you to do. What is the significance of this change?

There is much in "The Convert" about "being a man." Aaron Lott is like Prometheus and Antigone in his heroic stand for principle no matter what the cost. The same could be said for Booker's evidence in court. The court will hear ten African Americans and twenty whites testify that Aaron Lott reached for Sheriff Sampson's gun. Is Booker's action therefore merely a pointless gesture, like Antigone's attempt to bury her brother? Is he right to do it nevertheless? Or is Booker more like John Proctor in *The Crucible*, standing up for the truth? Is it reasonable to stand up for the truth – even if you know that by doing so, you and your family will be worse off, and no-one else will be any better off?

45   William Shakespeare, *The Taming of the Shrew*

In some respects Katharina is in a similar situation to the slaves in *Uncle Tom's Cabin*. In the society in which she lives, marriage is a transaction between the father and the future husband. (Note the absence of a mother who might mediate on behalf of her daughters.) Bianca is a valuable chattel and so is sold off to the highest bidder, whereas Baptista Minola must pay to have the undesirable Katharina taken off his hands. Katharina's "shrewishness" can be seen as an expression of frustration at her position. But is Shakespeare then saying that the only way for her to achieve fulfullment and happiness is for her to accept her conventional role?

Shakespeare's comedies usually focus on the couple's courtship phase, whereas in *The Taming of the Shrew* we also see the early stage of Petruchio and Katharina's marriage. Once she is married, Katharina is completely at the mercy of her husband. The language is of "taming," domestication, and subjugation. It is even suggested that Petruchio's house could become a "taming school" for wives. Why is the "obedience" of their wives so important to these men? Do you consider Petruchio's behavior to be what we now call "spouse abuse"? Or is his "tough love" treatment necessary so that Katharina comes to see the error of her ways and finds true happiness?

Up to the end of the nineteenth century *The Taming of the Shew* was seen as a comedy with Petruchio's "taming" being played as innocent fun. With changing views about male–female relations and the status of women in society, Petruchio's behavior came to be seen as degradingly misogynist. George Bernard Shaw wrote in 1897 that he found the final scene of the play, our second extract, "altogether disgusting." Some more recent interpretations – where Petruchio is played as being as much of a misfit as Katharina – portray Katharina and Petruchio's wrangling and fighting as an erotic game played by two people who, eventually, come to recognize each other as kindred spirits.

Do you think that Katharina's submission at the end of the play is that of a genuinely happy married woman, or is she – like the grandfather in *Invisible Man* – mouthing these sentiments so that she can survive in a man's world? Or has Katharina's spirit and intelligence been extinguished by a sexist society that allows men to dominate women?

46   Henrik Ibsen, *The Doll's House*

This last act of this play reads like the late twentieth-century feminist denunciations of marriage as an institution that uses a woman's love of her husband and children to bind her to a lifetime of serving others, never discovering herself. Thorvald's response to the crisis reveals his self-centeredness and cracks open the façade of Nora's marriage. Nora recognizes for the first time that she has been kept in child-like ignorance. Nevertheless the end of the play sounds a note of hope.

Today there are many women in the world, perhaps the majority, who are still in Nora's situation. Is marriage a sexist institution? Can marriage be a real union of equals while women bear children and are primarily responsible for raising them?

When we look at society in general, we see that all over the world, on average, women earn far less than men. Even in the most progressive democracies, they are outnumbered by men in legislatures. With a few notable exceptions, women do not head governments or major corporations. Is this the result of sexism, or is it due to biological differences in the nature of women and men?

47　Leo Tolstoy, *War and Peace*

Prince Andrey Bolkonsky expresses, more and more heatedly, the lessons he has learned about the nature of war. He is especially angry at the way leaders "play" at war, which he considers to be "the vilest thing in life," only to be embarked on as a "fearful necessity." Because he sees this war as one of those rare wars that is a necessity – a war of self-defense – Prince Andrey would not take prisoners. In his view, those who attack his home are "all criminals." But many soldiers are conscripts or men with few other options for employment. If they have surrendered and no longer pose a threat, can it be right to kill them?

Prince Andrey also believes that in deciding on whether a war is just we should ask: is it worth dying for? He argues that there would be far fewer wars if we admitted we were going to kill and be killed. Is it still true that we take war too lightly, and go to war when there is no necessity for doing so?

Another issue addressed in this extract concerns the treatment of civilians, in this instance Russian and not "enemy" civilians. The previous Commander of the Russian forces, Barclay de Tolly, was strict about not allowing "pillaging and marauding," or taking from the peasants to supply his soldiers. Prince Andrey sneers that de Tolly would not "waste the country we were leaving for the enemy." Now Kutuzov has reversed this policy. How do you balance the need to defeat the enemy against the obligation not to take food from your own people, often leaving them to starve in the snow?

Tolstoy mocks the theoreticians of war, particularly the view that war is like a game of chess, for not understanding its chaotic and unpredictable reality. And yet how can we discuss the morality of behavior in war if everything is as completely unpredictable as Tolstoy says?

48　Pat Barker, *Regeneration*

Siegried Sassoon is not a pacifist. He is not opposed to all wars as a matter of principle. He believes that the prolongation of this particular war, the First World War, is unjust, and he objects to the continuing suffering and slaughter when peace could be negotiated. Sassoon blames those sitting at home in their comfortable armchairs, whom he says don't know or care about the suffering of the ordinary soldiers. But Sassoon's view is dismissed as that of a mere Second Lieutenant who can have no idea of the "big picture" of the operations of the war. Is it the duty of individual members of the armed forces to obey the orders of their government and their commanders without questioning the rights and wrongs of going to war? Sassoon says, "You can't just acquiesce." He believes that his duty is to protest, to defy the military authorities, rather than blindly obey.

Later in the novel Sassoon's friend and fellow-poet Graves, who agrees with Sassoon's views but not his actions, says, "The way I see it, when you put the uniform on, in effect you sign a contract. And you don't back out of a contract merely because you've changed your mind. You can speak up for your principles, you can argue against the ones you're being made to fight for, but in the end *you do the job.*" Is a soldier's duty to obey, or can he or she decide what to do on the basis of his or her own conscience? (This issue is also raised in the poem "S. I. W'", in the extract from "The Prisoner" and in the second extract from *Henry V.*)

Is Sassoon's protest pointless? How does it compare with Antigone's insistence on attempting to bury her brother, or Booker T. Brown's decision to tell the truth in court in "The Convert"?

Was Graves right to "rig" the Medical Board hearing? Sassoon agrees to co-operate because Graves convinces him that he will not be court-martialled as he hoped – giving him the opportunity to protest publicly – but will be committed to a lunatic asylum. Should Sassoon have nevertheless refused to co-operate in order to continue his protest? (Later Graves tells Rivers that although he swore on the Bible to Sassoon about the court-martial, it was a lie told so that his friend would not "destroy himself, for no reason.")

49 Wilfred Owen, "S. I. W."

Wifred Owen began this poem when he was at Craiglockart War Hospital with Siegfried Sassoon in 1917. "S. I. W." describes what happens to a young soldier after he has been proudly farewelled by his family and gone off to war. His real-war experience is contrasted with the ignorance of those who remain at home. The irony is that in trying to live up to his father's exhortation of "death sooner than dishonour," Tim takes his own life. Owen calls this "the reasoned crisis of his soul." Is Tim's response to trench warfare a reasoned one? Is suicide an honorable way out of an appalling situation? It is interesting to compare Tim's father's exhortation to the promise Carter Druse made to his father in Ambrose Bierce's 'A Horseman in the Sky" in Section II. Neither father predicts, nor could imagine, the circumstances in which his words would come back to haunt his son.

The army does not tell Tim's parents the truth about Tim's death. Is it right to keep the truth from them?

50   William Shakespeare, *King Henry V*
(Act III, Scene III)

At the outset of the play, Henry is deciding whether to go to war with France
in order to enforce his claim to the throne. The war is therefore not, from
the English perspective, a war of defense. In this scene Henry warns the French
governor of Harfleur that if the city does not surrender, he will not be able to
restrain his soldiers, who will rape the virgins and impale infants upon their pikes.
The guilt for this, he suggests, will be on the head of the governor for not
surrendering. Is this right? Shakespeare seems to think so, for Henry is, in his play,
a noble and just king. But since the war is not a war of self-defense, and since
Henry knows that war often brings with it rape and the murder of the innocent,
can Henry avoid the responsibility for whatever crimes the war brings about?

51   William Shakespeare, *King Henry V*
(Act IV, Scene I)

The exchange between King Henry, in disguise, and his two soldiers, Williams and
Bates, is a remarkably complex moral argument. The debate starts when Williams
states that the soldiers do not know if the king's cause is just, and Bates says that
it is enough that they know they are the king's subjects. The background assumption here is that killing in an unjust war is a crime, but, according to Bates, this
crime is wiped out for ordinary soldiers who are obeying their king. This part of
the conversation encapsulates the traditional "just war" line of thought on the issue
mentioned in the introduction to this section – whether it is up to individual
soldiers to judge whether their ruler's cause is just. As already noted, this is not a
defensive war. In these circumstances, the idea that soldiers are not responsible for
the justice of their ruler's cause was obviously a useful one for kings, who might
have more difficulty in getting troops to fight for them if the troops believed that
their salvation depended on the justice of the ruler's cause. The line that Shakespeare takes here is exactly that taken by the Spanish Catholic scholar Francisco
de Vitoria (1492–1546), sometimes considered the father of international law,
who argued that the state would fall into grave peril if subjects had to be satisfied
of the justice of the cause before enlisting in the army.

Williams then turns the focus to the king himself, who, if his cause is not just,
will be responsible for all the gory deaths of his soldiers in battle, and the hardships
their deaths cause for their wives and children. Henry's response is an appeal to
the doctrine of double effect, which we discussed in the introduction to Section IV,
in the context of doctors giving pain relief that they foresee will shorten the life of
the patient. Just as the supporters of this doctrine argue, in that context, that
doctors who intend to relieve the pain of their patients are not responsible for the
fact that the drug also shortens the patient's life, so here Henry argues, with
analogies, that the king does not intend or "purpose" the deaths of his soldiers
when he seeks their services in war. But is this a sound argument, given that, even

if Henry did not intend any of his soldiers to die, he must have foreseen, when he decided to go to war, that many of them would be killed?

You may like to compare Henry's argument here with the claims of modern leaders that they are not responsible for the deaths of civilians in wars that they initiate, since they strive to minimize civilian casualties. When George W. Bush launched the American attack on Iraq in 2003, he must have known that many innocent Iraqis would be killed by American bombs. By the most conservative estimates, at least 3,000 civilians died from the American bombardments. Does the fact that President Bush did not intend to kill Iraqi civilians absolve him of responsibility for those deaths?

In this speech from Shakespeare's play, Henry V goes on to consider not the mere deaths of the soldiers, but the fact that they may die in sin, and thus be damned for all eternity. Here he says that every soldier is responsible for the sins he has committed, and hence for the state of his own soul, before he goes into battle. Assuming the truth of the religious view of sin and damnation, as Henry does, is he justified in denying his responsibility for the damnation of those soldiers who die in a state of sin?

52 Alfred Tennyson, "The Charge of the Light Brigade"

The poem praises the courage of soldiers prepared to obey orders blindly and ride into almost certain death. The lines "Their's not to reason why, / Their's but to do and die" encapsulate what many see as a soldier's duty. But should soldiers be expected to obey orders that are going to lead to a military disaster and will benefit no-one? Is Tennyson glorifying as an act of courage what was really an act of madness or stupidity? Were the members of the Light Brigade brave heroes or, as we label others who undertake suicide missions, crazed fanatics?

53 S. Yizhar, "The Prisoner"

The narrator of "The Prisoner" is an Israeli soldier who wants to behave "decently." He tussles with his conscience. Should he obey orders, and go along with the army ethos, or choose the "simple, decent and human" thing to do? The narrator feels empathy for the Arab shepherd, but is empathy enough? He seems to have difficulty acting as "a human being at last the way you want to be." Is such vacillation characteristic of someone who thinks about these questions, neither blindly obeying orders, nor simply acting on instinct? Is it blameworthy, or is the pressure of being part of a team, in this case the army, too great for most people to resist?

The ostensible reason for capturing the shepherd is to learn about military activity in his village. The Israeli soldiers assume that every Arab is an enemy. Is such treatment of civilians justified? Would it be justified if the shepherd Hassan was a captured soldier? The narrator foresees the consequences of such treatment of civilians as a legacy of motherless children and growing bitterness and hostility in refugee camps. But how do you conduct war in conflicts involving guerrilla warfare where there is no clear separation between the army and civilians?

54   John Fowles, *The Magus*

War can be seen as a crucible for moral action. Colchis, the Mayor of Phraxos, is offered a fearful choice. Should he kill the two guerrillas to save the lives of eighty hostages? The villagers want him to kill the guerrillas. So why doesn't he? Colchis says, "I acted without reason." But is this true? Is "freedom" or "the refusal to cohere" a value greater than a human life or, in this case, eighty lives?

How significant is it that Colchis could have shot the two guerrillas but cannot club them to death? Is there a moral difference?

Is Colonel Wimmel innocent because he is mad? According to Colchis, "the real evil, the real monstrosity in the situation lay in the other Germans, those less-than-mad lieutenants and corporals and privates who stood silently there. . . ." Are those who acquiesce the guilty ones? Should they refuse to obey orders? Or are they, like the soldiers in the army of Henry V, ordinary people whose role it is to obey, rather than to think for themselves about whether what they are doing is right?

55   Desmond Stewart, "The Limits of Trooghaft"

The Troogs have developed a complex ideology and culture around their need for "protein." They lock up "capons" in terrible conditions to raise them for food; they allow some humans to live freely so that they can hunt them for sport during the season; they breed human pets with specific features; they develop gourmet dishes like pâté de foie gras; and try cooking methods like the ones sometimes recommended for use with live lobsters, supposedly to provide a more humane death. Even the lone Troog who questions the need for protein, and has come to believe that humans are sentient too, goes back to his human-eating ways. Tempted by his fellows, he justifies his return to eating humans by arguing that "at least now they live. . . . And while they live, they are healthy."

The arguments used by the Troogs for eating humans closely parallel the arguments many humans use for eating nonhuman animals. There are, therefore, three possibilities:

1   We are justified in eating animals, and if there were Troogs, they would be justified in eating us.
2   We are not justified in eating animals, and if there were Troogs, they would not be justifed in eating us.
3   There are morally significant differences between our situation regarding animals and the situation that Troogs would be in, if they existed, regarding us.

If we think that the third possibility is correct, then we have to specify what these differences are.

56   Richard Adams, *The Plague Dogs*

The instrumental view that we have of other species has provided the basis for large-scale experimentation, medical and other, on nonhuman animals. Tens of millions of animals are used each year in the United States alone, and around three million in the United Kingdom. The experiments Richard Adams describes in *The Plague Dogs* are closely based on actual experiments carried out initially on rats by C. P. Richter, a psychologist at Johns Hopkins University in Baltimore, Maryland. Subsequently, related experiments were carried out on dogs to study what psychologists call "variable reinforcement" and "learned helplessness." In the United Kingdom, the legal framework that provides "no general barrier to the use of animal experimentation" is the British Government's Littlewood Report, which Dr Boycott can quote by heart. Are these experiments justified for "the advancement of knowledge," as Dr Boycott claims? (There is no public scrutiny of what goes on in ARSE until the two dogs escape and become a possible threat to humans.)

In Tyson and Dr Boycott we are presented with two different kinds of workers, with different justifications for what they do. Dr Boycott, the scientist, is not dissimilar to Dr Frankenstein in Mary Shelley's book of that name (see the extract in Section XII). Both are blind to anything outside the pursuit of their own research. Tyson, on the other hand, does not see it as his role to question what those in charge are doing. His thinking should be compared to that of the soldiers in *Henry V*, in Section IX, and the narrator in *The Remains of the Day*, in Section XIV.

Richard Adams has written a crusading novel, calling forcefully for change. (He later served as President of the Royal Society for the Prevention of Cruelty to Animals.) Most people support animal experimentation as long as it is under strict constraints. This novel gives reasons for skepticism about whether such constraints can adequately protect animals, and raises the question of whether we should experiment on animals at all.

57   Douglas Adams, *The Restaurant at the End of the Universe*

The cow-like animal in this extract from Douglas Adams' *The Restaurant at the End of the Universe* wants to be eaten. In response to Earthman Arthur's horror, Zaphod asks the question for us: isn't it worse to eat an animal that doesn't want to be eaten than to eat one that does want to be eaten? Is Zaphod "heartless"? Given that the animal does want to be eaten – and will be very humane in killing itself – should Arthur eat the steak that has been served to him?

58   James Fenimore Cooper, *The Pioneers*

In the 1800s the American passenger pigeon existed in seemingly inexhaustible numbers. The ornithologist Alexander Wilson described a flock that "darkened the sky," being several miles wide, and taking hours to pass overhead. Uncontrolled

Issues

shooting, of the kind described in the extract from *The Pioneers*, and loss of habitat, ended that. The last known passenger pigeon died in the Cincinnati Zoo in 1914.

In Fenimore Cooper's story, progress and civilization have come to upstate New York. The farmers have cleared the forests. Now the pigeons eat the wheat the farmers planted. And the farmers kill the pigeons to protect their wheat. Leather-stocking, who seems to be speaking for the author, argues against the "wasteful and unsportsmanlike execution" of the birds. But if the object of the shooting is to eliminate the birds, which are pests because they damage crops, the charge of "wastefulness" hardly applies. Can Leather-stocking's objection to the shoot be sustained? Assuming that we regret the fact that passenger pigeons are now extinct, what should the farmers have done?

59   Aeschylus, *Prometheus Bound*

At the heart of *Prometheus Bound* is the conflict between the stubbornness of Prometheus and the power of Zeus. The king of the gods is pitted against the man who saved humanity with the gift of fire. If we accept the "divine command" theory, Prometheus should obey Zeus because everything that God commands is good. Is Prometheus wrong to disobey Zeus? Why does the reader, and presumably the author, side with Prometheus against his Zeus? (By the end of the trilogy, Aeschylus has Zeus becoming transformed into a more acceptable deity.)

60   Genesis 22

With no apparent hesitation, Abraham is willing to sacrifice his son Isaac to fulfill God's command. If God had not rescinded his command, would Abraham have been right to kill Isaac? More generally, should we do whatever God asks of us? What sort of a God would test the faith of a father in such a painful manner?

61   Fyodor Dostoyevsky, *The Brothers Karamazov*

This extract from *The Brothers Karamazov* opens with a report by Miusov that Ivan Karamazov put forward the proposition that there is no basis for morality except for the belief in God and immortality. If there is no God, he stated, then it is rational, "even honourable," to be egoistical because you know that you won't be punished for any wrongdoing. In saying this, Ivan is expressing a widely held view: that without religon there would be no ethics. Yet atheists and agnostics are often highly ethical. What reasons can they have for living ethical lives? Could they simply be compassionate and sympathetic people, who do not like to see others suffer? Or is it, as some philosophers have argued, that when we properly under-stand our interests, we will see that it really is in our interests to act ethically? Other philosophers have sought to defend morality independently of self-interest, as justifiable in terms of reason. And, of course, it is possible to take a skeptical view and hold that acting ethically is simply not rational at all. Ivan's question forces us to consider all of these possibilities.

62   Mary Shelley, *Frankenstein*

Mary Shelley's novel is narrated in hindsight by Victor Frankenstein, the scientist who is repelled and disgusted by the creature he creates. *Frankenstein* alludes to divine retribution in its subtitle, "The Modern Prometheus." And it is also heavy with biblical references pushing home the view that when humans take on God's role of creation, the results will be terrible. Today, whenever there is a scientific breakthrough in assisted reproduction, cloning, or genetic engineering, we will hear the accusation that scientists and doctors are "playing God." Is this a serious objection? Why is it "playing God" to use new medical techniques to bring human beings into existence, but not to use new medical techniques to save the lives of extremely premature infants? For those who do not believe in the existence of God, is there anything wrong in taking the role that religious believers may wish to see reserved for God?

Frankenstein, the scientist, is as much a monster as is his creation. Should the fact that his creation has not turned out as he wished absolve the scientist from any duty of care or affection? No wonder that Frankenstein has become the prototype for the mad professor. The reader feels the pain and unhappiness of the "monster," who is born fully grown and aware and is amazingly well educated. The "being" is never given a name – a name would endow him with an individual identity. In this novel, written long before Freud and before today's flood of articles about "damaged" children and abusing parents, the being blames Frankenstein's rejection of him for turning him into a murderous beast. The many descriptions of the creature as ugly and monstrous can be taken as showing how unlovable he is, but if a mother had given birth to this being, she would have been expected to care for it and love it anyway. Is there any reason why the same standards should not apply to scientists?

63   Karel Čapek, *The Makropulos Secret*

The Makropulos Secret argues the case for longevity and rejects it. But would we feel about it like Elina Makropulos? Don't we all want to live longer? And Čapek has ignored the aging issue altogether – Elina has never been old. In a culture where people pay large sums for cosmetic surgery and anti-aging drugs, a formula that prevented aging would be immensely popular – and lucrative for anyone who could patent it. Are people who strive to live longer and stay youthful making some kind of mistake?

At the outset everyone is fighting to get the formula, but in the end all reject it. Elina's experience, as a living example of this experiment, plays a large part in this decision. Dr Frankenstein had no previous model to warn him of the possible dangers of his experiment. Is it wrong to experiment with human lives without knowing what the outcome will be? If so, what does this tell us of the ethics of human reproductive cloning, or of genetic engineering? On the other hand, we now accept the use of *in vitro* fertilization to enable otherwise infertile couples to have children. Was this also, when it was first attempted, unethical human experimentation?

In discussing what should be done with the Makropulos formula, the different characters put forward various arguments about the ownership, use, and benefit of new technologies. To whom does the formula belong? Should it be made available to everyone or a select few? Should anyone profit from it?

64   E. Pauline Johnson, "The Sea-Serpent"

The personal accumulation of wealth and goods is, according to E. Pauline Johnson's story, contrary to the Native American ethic. This is in striking contrast to the "greed is good" ethic depicted in the corporate world of *The Bonfire of the Vanities*. It is significant that whereas Western myths about the origins of morality assume that humans are selfish and have to be given ethical standards in order to act well, in this story Native Americans appear to be naturally inclined to share, and were only made greedy by contact with Europeans. Which view of human nature is more plausible?

65   Daniel Defoe, *Robinson Crusoe*

After months of plotting how to attack and kill the "savages" he has witnessed killing and eating other human beings, Robinson Crusoe comes to a different view of the right course of conduct. He concludes that the cannibals are no more immoral than the Spanish and other European colonizers who killed the native populations they conquered, or Christian soldiers who kill prisoners taken in battle. Is Crusoe supporting the view that it is not wrong to act in accordance with the customs of one's culture? Is he voicing a form of ethical cultural relativism, and rejecting the idea of any objective standards of right and wrong that apply across different cultures?

Crusoe states that he would only have a duty to do something if he was first attacked by the cannibals. But doesn't he have a duty to save the lives of others? There are parallels here with arguments about international intervention to prevent governments from carrying out crimes against humanity. Do individuals and countries have duties to save others even when they are not under attack themselves?

Note Crusoe's comment: "They think it no more a Crime to kill a Captive taken in War, than we do to kill an Ox; nor to eat humane Flesh, than we do to eat Mutton." George Bernard Shaw, a vegetarian, once said that the diet of meat-eaters is "cannibalism with its most heroic dish omitted." If we continue to eat animals, are we in a position to condemn cannibalism?

66   Mark Twain, *The Adventures of Huckleberry Finn*

Huck Finn's conscience tells him that he is wrong to help the slave Jim to escape – he is depriving Miss Watson of her property. When Jim talks of trying to buy the freedom of his wife and children, and if the owner will not sell, of stealing them back, Huck thinks this is even worse. So he determines to tell some white men that Jim is a runaway slave. But in the end, moved by the trust Jim has placed in him, he cannot do it. He lies to protect Jim. Reflecting on his behavior, he "knows" that he has done wrong. He feels bad about that, but he also realizes that even if he had done what is right, and told the men that there was a runaway slave on his raft, he would still have felt bad. So he decides to give up on morality, and do "whichever comes handiest at the time."

Is conscience a reliable guide to right and wrong? Twain obviously thinks not – the conscience of someone brought up in a slave-owning society goes seriously astray. Huck ends up allowing his natural feelings of benevolence and friendship for Jim to override what he has been taught. So are our feelings, perhaps our "natural" instincts, a better guide than what we are taught? Has Huck really given up on morality when he decides to to do "whichever comes handiest at the time"? Or is that a better criterion of right and wrong than his conscience?

67   Graham Greene, *The Third Man*

In this scene from Graham Greene's *The Third Man*, Harry Lime expresses his contempt for ordinary people – "those dots," as he calls them. He doesn't care if his way of making money causes children to die. Is his claim that most people have such miserable lives that "they're happier dead" a justification for what he is doing? Or is he simply not interested in being an ethical person? Can you argue with someone who doesn't believe in morality, or should we just lock such people away where they can do no harm?

68   Tadeusz Borowski, "This Way for the Gas, Ladies and Gentlemen"

How is it possible for people calmly to oversee the murder of millions of men, women, and children? "This Way for the Gas, Ladies and Gentlemen" confronts us with the question of whether morality is just a luxury when we can afford it. Is there anything a person will not do when the circumstances are sufficiently extreme and his or her surivival is at stake? The only "charity" in the camp is not telling people on the transports that they are about to be murdered. Is that the right thing to do?

Borowski's story is narrated by a Polish political prisoner in Auschwitz. As a non-Jew, he has the privilege of obtaining food parcels from his family outside the camp. Why, then, does he still choose to join the "Kommando" that greets the new arrivals?

For the Germans, all "non-Aryans" are like the "dots" at the base of the Ferris wheel in *The Third Man*. They are seen as outside the moral universe, much as nonhuman animals are still seen today. So more or less anything goes. But even in this "hell" there are gradations of dehumanization, and choices to be made. Could you warn the Jews what is in store for them, and storm the guards? Or should you climb into the trucks with the Jews? In reading this story we cannot avoid asking ourselves how we would behave in such circumstances. "Are we good people?," the narrator asks Henri, and gets no answer.

69   Ursula K. Le Guin, "The Ones Who Walk Away from Omelas"

As we saw in the introduction to Section XIV, in Dostoevsky's *The Brothers Karamazov*, Ivan challenges Alyosha to consider whether it would be justifiable to create a society of "peace and rest" for humanity predicated on the "torture to death" of "only one tiny creature," such as a defenseless human baby. Ursula K. Le Guin's "Omelas" puts Ivan's question in the form of a short story. Are some things – like the torture of a child – always wrong, no matter what the circumstances? Or should we accept a society in which a single individual must be treated unjustly and made miserable if this is the only way in which all the rest can be safe, healthy, and happy?

Alyosha tells Ivan that he would not consent, and at least some of the inhabitants of Omelas seem to share his attitude. But others stay.

Suppose that the torture of the child was stopped and people in Omelas became more like normal human beings. Some did not earn enough to feed their children, or give them shelter from the cold. They did not receive assistance, and so the children starved or died of easily preventable diseases. Other people were brutal, and committed violent crimes, sometimes harming innocent children to satisfy their sadistic lusts. Would the decision to end the torture of the child have been the right one?

Are there any parallels between Omelas and the world we live in? Is our prosperity based on injustice, for example, to indigenous people, or to the poor in our own country, or in other countries? If so, should we walk away from it?

70   Fyodor Dostoyevsky, *Crime and Punishment*

We generally assume that it is always wrong to kill an innocent human being who wants to go on living. Raskolnikov, however, reasons that killing an old, spiteful, and rich woman, and doing something beneficial with her money, would be a good thing to do. Yet he has difficulty with his feeling that what he is planning to do is absurd, monstrous, and impossible. We sense that in pursuing his plan, he is going against his own nature. Should we therefore conclude that it is dangerous and wrong to reason about what we ought to do, rather than simply accept the customary moral rules? Or should we, instead, believe that his reasoning is correct, and he needs to get his feelings under control so that he can successfully carry out his plan?

71 Kazuo Ishiguro, *The Remains of the Day*

Traditionally, our station in life has determined our moral duties. The narrator of *The Remains of the Day* holds a traditional position: he is a servant to a lord, to be precise, he is his butler. He strives to do his duty with dignity, which involves, above all else, being loyal to his employer. According to Stevens, the duty of a servant, like that of a soldier, is to obey orders. When Miss Kenton objects to their employer's anti-Semitic action, Stevens says, "His lordship has made his decision and there is nothing for you and I to debate over." Stevens has his role and sticks to it, whereas Miss Kenton wants to leave rather than collude in this action. Are there values that override loyalty? (You may like to refer back to earlier sections where this issue was discussed in regard to soldiers, in *Henry V*, and the employee Tyson in *The Plague Dogs*.)

Behind Stevens' view of his role is his belief that "his lordship . . . is better placed to judge what is for the best." Today this understanding of the "bigger picture" is often ascribed to Presidents and Prime Ministers, company CEOs, and others in positions of power. Should Stevens have opposed his employer's decision? Or was he right to think that it is not his place to question what his lordship desires? In general, should we take our ethic from our role and place in life? Or should we each think through ethical issues for ourselves?

72 Anthony Trollope, *Dr Wortle's School*

Dr Wortle, the clergyman who is the central character of Trollope's novel, must make a decision which could threaten the existence of his school. Bigamy is illegal and remains a crime even today, and Trollope makes it clear what society and the church would have Dr Wortle do. But the Doctor finds that, in this case, his duty conflicts with "common humanity" and he can't "bring his conscience and inclination" together. Is the Peacockes' bigamy immoral, as well as illegal?

Trollope stresses that people should be judged on their "nature" or character as much as anything else – deciding right and wrong is not as simple as applying a rule. Mrs Wortle, initially, and Mr Puddicombe are of the view that the Peacockes should have parted as soon as they knew that Ferdinand Lefroy was still alive. Would that have been the right thing to do? Later, when Mrs Wortle wants to exonerate the Peacockes from wrongdoing, she states that Mrs Peacocke was acting morally in fulfilling her vows to obey her husband, that is, Mr Peacocke. Is that the best way of justifying Mrs Peacocke's decision to stay with Mr Peacocke?

73 Harper Lee, *To Kill a Mockingbird*

Bob Ewell was killed while trying to harm Atticus's children. Sheriff Tate knows who killed Ewell. But the Sheriff isn't even going to mention that Boo Radley was present when he died. Is it right for the Sheriff, the upholder and enforcer of the law, to lie so as to avoid dragging this shy, sensitive man into the limelight?

Atticus has brought up his children to do the right thing. In getting them to accept a lie, is he putting their moral character in jeopardy?

At first Atticus believes Jem has killed Bob Ewell, in self-defense, and thinks that the Sheriff is trying to cover this up in order to avoid causing problems for Jem. With that understanding, he rejects the idea of a cover-up. If this objection was based on an absolute moral rule or overriding moral principle, Atticus would presumably have continued to object even after he understood that the cover-up was to protect Boo Radley. What does this suggest about the nature of Atticus's objection to a cover-up?

74   William Shakespeare, Sonnet 138

In *To Kill a Mockingbird* we saw that there might be reasons that justify lying, even by an officer of the law. But Shakespeare's Sonnet 138 suggests that flattering lies between lovers are acceptable, even necessary. Here, however, there is no real need to lie. No-one will be seriously hurt by an insistence on the truth. Are there "white lies" that are not really wrong? Or is the rule against lying so weak that even quite minor concerns, for example about how old your lover will think you are, are sufficient to justify lying?

75   George Eliot, *Middlemarch*

Bulstrode makes a series of decisions that lead to Raffles' death. When does he cross over into wrongdoing? Once he remembered that he had forgotten to tell Mrs Abel when the doses of opium should cease, was he wrong not to go immediately to tell her? Or was the real wrong committed when she came to his room, and he still did not correct his mistake? Is his later act, in giving Mrs Abel the key to the wine-cooler, worse than his previous deliberate refraining from acting? Is Bulstrode morally responsible for Raffles' death? If it is true that Bulstrode wanted Raffles dead, and took steps that he knew would pose a serious risk to his life, is Bulstrode a murderer?

This extract also raises the issue of corruption, in particular the way connections and financial obligations can affect the behavior of a professional like Dr Lydgate. Would Lydgate have behaved differently on finding Raffles dead if he hadn't accepted the loan from Bulstrode? And if Lydgate had refused the money, would Bulstrode had made the decisions he did?

76   Daniel Defoe, *Robinson Crusoe*

Living alone on an island, Crusoe is forced to change his views about what really matters in life. In his circumstances, money and diamonds are useless. So is more of anything than he can use, whether it is corn, timber, grapes, or meat. He can, he says, satisfy all his wants – although he admits he would like some vegetable seeds, presumably to add variety to his diet, and a bottle of ink.

Is Crusoe right to say that we should not covet anything more than we need to satisfy our wants? Would the same be true if he were back in his own country? Does his experience show that, even when we do live in contact with others, we act wisely when we ensure that we have enough to meet our own needs, and seek to gain no more? What would Crusoe have said to Sherman McCoy, the bond trader in the extract from *The Bonfire of the Vanities* that is reprinted in Section I? Would McCoy have been able to defend his way of living?

77   Henry James, *The Portrait of a Lady*

Ralph Touchett asks his father to help Isabel Archer to be financially independent, saying "your bequest will make her free." Many people believe this about money. But being rich doesn't necessarily make you "independent" or free, as we saw in Tom Wolfe's *The Bonfire of the Vanities*. When the older Mr Touchett suggests that the money will make Isabel attractive to fortune-hunters, Ralph acknowledges the gamble. Unfortunately Mr Touchett's inheritance does makes Isabel attractive to the unscrupulous Gilbert Osmond. Ralph dies knowing that his gift had the opposite effect to that which he intended. Was he immoral to play with Isabel's future?

What is it that Ralph values? Is it the freedom that money brings, or is it the idea that a person of talent and fine taste should be free to indulge those traits without the constraint of having to think about money? Neither Ralph nor his father questions the justice of inherited wealth acquired through no efforts of your own. They do not consider any possible allocation of the money other than leaving it to Ralph or to Isabel. Why give £60,000 (a sizeable sum even today) to one person when you could do so much more good by spreading it further? Wouldn't it have been better for a thousand poor people to have received £60 – enough to have put many of them on their feet, financially, if they could use it wisely – than for one person to have received £60,000? Or the money could have been given to a hospital, or for schools for children who would otherwise not get an education. Are Ralph's ultimate values defensible?

78   Aldous Huxley, *Brave New World*

When first published, *Brave New World* was criticized by H. G. Wells, C. P. Snow, and others as being too negative about the benefits of scientific progress. People tend to read the book as prediction – about the misuse of drugs, indoctrination, cloning, advertising, and sex without love – and read into it whatever are their current dire prophecies about humanity. The world Huxley depicts is often called a dystopia: the opposite to a utopia.

Mustapha Mond argues that comfort, stability, and happiness are well worth the sacrifice of truth, beauty, and even science. How do we value happiness against the freedom to choose to be miserable? Is there any value in happiness if we have not consciously chosen it? And what weight do we give to the pleasure of reading Shakespeare, an elitist activity, if it makes people dissatisfied and unhappy?

79   Henry James, *The Princess Casamassima*

Awed by the beauties of Venice, Hyacinth Robinson has lost his belief in redistribution and equalizing. Elites, he writes, must be preserved so that they can continue to create these glories of art. Ironically, it is the Princess Casamassima who first introduced Hyacinth to opera, culture, and beauty and, inadvertently, changed his values.

If it is true that the existence of a wealthy elite is necessary for the creation of great works of art and architecture – and that claim could be challenged – does that justify inequality? Does it justify an economic system like that which prevailed in medieval Europe, in which the masses were desperately poor, while kings, popes, and a few wealthy merchants could afford to build palaces and commission great artists to paint for them? How can these very different values be compared?

When US troops occupied Baghdad in April 2003, there was an outcry over their failure to prevent the looting of the National Museum and the burning of a library containing priceless Islamic manuscripts. Was this outcry justified when less concern was voiced about the civilian casualties suffered by the Iraqi people, and the lack of medical supplies in Baghdad hospitals?

NOTES

1   G. W. F. Hegel, *The Philosophy of Right* (tr. T. M. Knox), Oxford: Oxford University Press, 1967, para. 191, Addition.
2   John Darley and Daniel Batson, "'From Jerusalem to Jericho': A Study of Situational and Dispositional Variables in Helping Behavior," *Journal of Personality and Social Psychology*, vol. 27 (1973), pp. 100–8.

NOTES ON AUTHORS

Douglas Adams (1952–2001) was born in Cambridge, England, and became a radio and TV writer and producer. *The Hitchhiker's Guide to the Galaxy* was first broadcast as a BBC radio series in 1978. Its success led Adams to turn it into the first of a series of novels. The adventures of Arthur Dent, who escapes from an earth about to be destroyed to make way for an interstellar bypass, continue in the other four books in the series.

Richard Adams was born in 1920 and worked in the British Civil Service for twenty-five years. His first book, the international best-seller *Watership Down*, was published when he was 52 years old. Among his other novels are *The Girl on a Swing* and *Shardik*.

Aeschylus (525 BCE–456 BCE) is known as the Father of Greek Tragedy. Although he is said to have written over ninety plays, only seven survive. *Prometheus Bound*, the third of these surviving plays, was written as part of a trilogy. Only fragments of the other two plays in the trilogy remain extant.

Jane Austen (1775–1817) wrote witty novels about the rituals of love and marriage in the genteel rural English society in which she lived. Her six complete novels are *Pride and Prejudice*, *Emma*, *Sense and Sensibility*, *Persuasion*, *Mansfield Park*, and *Northanger Abbey*.

American writer **James Baldwin** (1924–87) was born and grew up in New York City. Baldwin, an African American, wrote novels, plays, short stories, poetry, essays, and cultural criticism, many dealing with racial issues. He is probably best known for his first novel, the semi-autobiographical *Go Tell It on the Mountain*, published in 1953.

Pat Barker (1943–) was born and lives in the north of England. Her first novel, *Union Street*, was published in 1982. Best known for the *Regeneration* trilogy set in the First World War, she was awarded the Booker Prize for the final book in that trilogy, *The Ghost Road*.

Born in Mississippi in 1928, **Lerone Bennett, Jr.** is a social historian and writer of nine books about the lives and history of Black Americans. He began working at *Ebony* magazine in 1954 and has been Executive Editor since 1987. His best-known book is *Before the Mayflower: A History of Black America*, and his most recent is *Forced into Glory: Abraham Lincoln's White Dream*.

The American journalist and writer **Ambrose Bierce** (1842–1914?) is chiefly remembered for *The Devil's Dictionary*, and the mystery surrounding his disappearance and presumed death in Mexico. His Civil War stories draw on his own experiences fighting on the Union side.

Maeve Binchy (1940–) was born and lives in Dublin, Ireland. As well as novels, plays, and other works, she has published three collections of short stories. "Shepherd's Bush" appeared in *London Transport* in 1978. Among her many novels are *Light a Penny Candle*, *Circle of Friends* and *Tara Road*.

Arna Bontemps (1902–73) was one of the group of writers that became known as the Harlem Renaissance. He wrote twenty-five books of poetry, history, biography, and fiction, but he earned his living first as a high school teacher and later as a librarian. From 1943 to 1966 he was Head Librarian at Fisk University in Nashville, Tennessee.

Polish writer **Tadeusz Borowski** was born in the Ukraine in 1922. The publication of his first volume of poetry, *Wherever the Earth*, in Nazi-occupied Warsaw led to his arrest. He survived Auschwitz and Dachau and his post-war collection of short stories *Farewell to Maria* draws on his experience of those years. In July 1951 he used a gas oven to commit suicide.

Born in Sydney, Australia, **Geraldine Brooks** was a staff correspondent for *The Wall Street Journal* from 1983 to 1994. Her non-fiction includes the books *Nine Parts of Desire: The Hidden World of Islamic Women* (1995) and *Foreign Correspondence* (1999). *Year of Wonders* (2001) was her first novel.

Czech novelist, short-story writer, essayist, political thinker, and playwright, **Karel Čapek**, was born in Bohemia in 1890. His 1920 play *R.U.R.* (*Rossum's Universal Robots*) introduced into the English language the word *robot*, derived from the Czech word for "work." He died of pneumonia on Christmas Day, 1938.

Brian Clark (1932–) was born in Bournemouth, England. He is the founder of Amber Lane Press in Oxford, England, and has written many plays for television and the theater. *Whose Life is it Anyway?*, his most famous work, was first produced in 1972 as a teleplay, was revised and produced for the stage in 1978, and then made into a 1981 feature film with Richard Dreyfuss in the lead role.

John Cleland (1709/10–89) wrote *Memoirs of a Woman of Pleasure* (popularly known as *Fanny Hill*) in an English debtors' prison. His other works of erotic fiction were not as successful.

The American writer **James Fenimore Cooper** (1789–1851) wrote thirty-two novels, as well as a play, non-fiction works, and many pamphlets and articles. He wrote five Leatherstocking Tales, featuring Natty Bumppo, the independent frontiersman opposed to industrial society.

Novelist, pamphleteer, and journalist **Daniel Defoe** (c.1660–1731) was born Daniel Foe and changed his name in about 1700. He was nearly 60 years old when *Robinson Crusoe* was published. Considered the founder of the English novel, Defoe was one of the first to write stories about believable characters in realistic situations. He also wrote about 200 non-fiction works and 2,000 short essays in periodicals. At the age of 62 he published *Moll Flanders*, *A Journal of the Plague Year*, and *Colonel Jack*.

The great English novelist **Charles Dickens** (1812–70) wrote fifteen novels, as well as many short stories. He first achieved popular success with *The Pickwick Papers*, which came out in 1836–7.

Fyodor Dostoyevsky (1821–81) wrote emotionally charged novels that depict people struggling with issues of right and wrong. Some of his writings draw on the four years he spent in a penal settlement in Siberia, where he was sent after being arrested for political activities. Among his best-known novels are *Crime and Punishment*, *The Idiot*, *The Possessed*, and *The Brothers Karamazov*.

English writer and freethinker **George Eliot** (1819–80) was born Mary Ann Evans. As well as writing fiction, she worked as a translator and editor. *Middlemarch* was published in 1872. Among her other novels are *The Mill on the Floss* and *Daniel Deronda*.

Ralph Ellison (1914–94) was born in Oklahoma and trained as a musician at Tuskegee Institute. In 1936 he moved to New York and began writing fiction. *Invisible Man* was published in 1952 and won the National Book Award. *Juneteenth*, his only other novel, was published posthumously in 1999. Ellison also wrote short stories and essays. He taught at many colleges and was Albert Schweitzer Professor of Humanities at New York University from 1970 to 1980.

The Greek dramatist **Euripides** was born around 480 BCE and died in 406 BCE. He wrote the tragedies *Medea* and *The Trojan Women*. *Iphigeneia in Aulis* was first produced a year after his death.

English author **John Fowles** (1926–) first achieved success in 1962 with *The Collector*. *The French Lieutenant's Woman* was made into a film starring Meryl Streep and Jeremy Irons. Fowles writes poetry as well as non-fiction on various subjects, including conservation and natural history.

The English writer **Elizabeth Gaskell** (1810–65) is best known as the author of *Cranford* and *Wives and Daughters*, and as the first biographer of her friend Charlotte Brontë. Many of her novels take up pressing social and political problems of her day.

Charlotte Perkins Gilman (1860–1935) was an American writer of novels, stories, poems, and essays. Her most widely read story is "The Yellow Wallpaper." She also wrote a feminist utopian novel, *Herland*.

Graham Greene (1904–91) was born in Hertfordshire, England. He worked as a sub-editor for *The Times* in London until the successful publication of *The Man*

Within in 1927 allowed him to write full-time. Greene traveled extensively both for adventure and to gather material for his books. He published plays, novels, essays, screenplays, and travel books. He wrote what he called "entertainments" as well as "serious novels."

Nick Hornby was born in Maidenhead, England, in 1958. His first book, *Fever Pitch*, is a memoir of his obsession with football and his team, Arsenal. His novels include *High Fidelity*.

The critic, novelist, poet, essayist, and playwright **Aldous Huxley** was born in Surrey, England, in 1894 and died in Los Angeles, California, in 1963. *Crome Yellow*, his first novel, was published in 1921, and his most famous work, *Brave New World*, came out in 1931.

The playwright **Henrik Ibsen** (1828–1906) is Norway's most famous literary figure. His plays use a variety of styles, ranging from the realism of *Hedda Gabler* to the fantasy of *Peer Gynt*.

Kazuo Ishiguro was born in Nagasaki, Japan, in 1954 and moved to England in 1960. His novels present a reality filtered through the memory and perception of a narrator whom the reader gradually gets to know and distrust. Ishiguro's first novel, *A Pale View of Hills*, won the Winifred Holtby Prize of the Royal Society of Literature; his second, *An Artist of the Floating World*, won the Whitbread Prize; and in 1989 *The Remains of the Day* was awarded the Booker Prize.

American writer **Henry James** (1843–1916) was born in New York City, traveled in Europe, and then settled in England. He wrote twenty novels, 112 stories, and twelve plays, as well as literary criticism, travel books, and autobiographical works. Among his most famous novels are *The Bostonians*, *Portrait of a Lady*, *The Wings of the Dove*, and *The Ambassadors*.

Australian-born writer **Kate Jennings** has lived in New York City since 1979. Her other publications include *Snake*, a novel, and the short story collection *Women Falling Down in the Street*.

E. Pauline Johnson, the daughter of a Mohawk Chief, was born in Ontario, Canada, in 1861. She worked as a stage performer in the USA, Canada, and England. Her publications cover many genres, including poetry and stories for both adults and children. She died in Vancouver in 1913.

Joseph Kanon is the author of two previous novels, *Los Alamos* and *The Prodigal Spy*. Before becoming a full-time writer, he worked in book publishing in New York City.

Joe Klein admitted to being the author of the anonymously published *Primary Colors* less than a year after its publication in 1996. Klein, a political reporter, covered the 1992 Presidential campaign for *New York Magazine*. Since then, as well as publishing another novel, *The Running Mate*, he has worked for *Newsweek* and as the Washington Correspondent for *The New Yorker*. In 2003 Klein joined *Time Magazine*, where he contributes a regular political column.

Born in Monroeville, Alabama, in 1926, **Harper Lee** published her first and only novel in 1960. *To Kill a Mockingbird* was awarded the 1961 Pulitzer Prize. The novel is still widely read and many schools use it in their English courses.

American author **Ursula K. Le Guin** has published seventeen novels, eleven children's books, more than a hundred stories, two collections of essays, and five volumes of poetry. She is renowned for her science fiction and fantasy novels and stories. She has won several Hugo and Nebula Awards as well as the National Book Award for *The Farthest Shore*, which is one of the *Earthsea* series.

The authors of *Puberty Blues* were 18 years old when it was published in 1979. Both are still writing. **Kathy Lette** now lives in England and is the author of *Girls' Night Out*, *The Llama Parlour*, and *Altar Ego*. Gabrielle Carey's books include *In My Father's House* and *The Borrowed Girl*. She lives in Sydney, Australia.

Ian McEwan was born in Aldershot, England, in 1948. His 1998 novel *Amsterdam* was awarded the Booker Prize. As well as novels, he has written short stories, essays, children's books, and screenplays.

Although best known for his 300 short stories, the French author **Guy de Maupassant** (1850–93) also wrote six novels, three travel books, and one volume of verse.

Playwright **Arthur Miller** was born in New York City in 1915. His second play to appear on Broadway, *All My Sons*, won the 1947 Drama Critics' Circle Award. *Death of a Salesman* was awarded the Pulitzer Prize and the Drama Critics' Circle Award. *The Crucible* was produced on Broadway in 1953. Arthur Miller has written *Focus*, a novel, and *Timebends*, his autobiography, as well as essays, teleplays, and screenplays.

Canadian short story writer **Alice Munro** was born in 1931. She has published nine collections of short stories and one novel, *The Lives of Girls and Women*. Most of her stories are set in rural south-west Ontario. Her most recent book is *Hateship, Friendship, Courtship, Loveship, Marriage*.

Born in 1938 in upstate New York, **Joyce Carol Oates** has written more than seventy books: novels, plays, poetry, short story collections, essays, and literary criticism. She has received many honors and prizes, including the National Book Award for her novel *them*. Since 1978 she has been teaching at Princeton University.

The English poet **Wilfred Owen** (1893–1918) is remembered for his poems about the First World War. He enlisted in 1915 and was killed a week before the Armistice ended the conflict. Only five of his poems were published during his lifetime. Siegfried Sassoon, who encouraged Owen in his writing, arranged for the *Collected Poems* to be published in 1920.

Ruth L. Ozeki was born in the United States to an American father and Japanese mother. Like the heroine of her debut novel *My Year of Meats*, she is a documentary film maker and was once commissioned to make television programs for a Japanese audience by a meat lobby group. In 2003 she published her second novel, *All Over Creation*.

American writer **Edwin Seaver** was born in 1900. In the 1930s he contributed to many left-wing publications and in later years worked in the mainstream publishing industry. The best known of the works he edited is *Cross-Section 1947: A Collection of American Writing*. Among his many books is: *So Far, So Good: Recollections of a Life in Publishing*. He died in 1987.

Vikram Seth was born in Calcutta in 1952. He has written novels, children's books, poetry, travel books, and a libretto. He followed the success of *A Suitable Boy* with another novel, *An Equal Music*.

William Shakespeare (1564–1616) is without peer among writers of English. Among his greatest works are the tragedies *Macbeth*, *Hamlet*, and *King Lear*, and the comedies *A Midsummer Night's Dream* and *All's Well That Ends Well*. He also wrote 154 sonnets.

George Bernard Shaw (1856–1950) was born in Ireland. He used theater as a vehicle for promoting social change. The comic vitality of most of his plays ensures their regular revival to this day. Shaw also wrote political works, including *The Intelligent Woman's Guide to Socialism and Capitalism*.

English novelist **Mary Shelley** (1797–1851) was born to well-known parents: feminist writer Mary Wollstonecraft and philosopher William Godwin. At 16 she ran away with the already married poet Percy Bysshe Shelley, and married him in December 1816. Earlier that year in response to a suggestion of Byron's she had written *Frankenstein*. Among her other novels is *The Last Man*.

C. P. (Charles Percy) Snow (1905–80) was a British novelist, scientist, and public administrator. Noted for his efforts to bridge the gap between the disciplines of literature and science, Snow is best known for the series *Strangers and Brothers*, set between the years 1920 and 1950. His novels are very much concerned with the moral choices people face in the worlds of politics, academia, and science.

The Greek dramatist **Sophocles**, who lived from approximately 496 BCE to 406 BCE, wrote more than 120 plays, but only seven have survived intact. *Antigone* is probably the first of these seven to have been written, possibly in 442 BCE.

Desmond Stewart (1924–81) lived largely in the Middle East after 1948 and became a vegetarian in 1970. His novels include the trilogy *A Sequence of Roles*. Among his many works of non-fiction are *Theodor Herzl, Artist and Politician* and *T. E. Lawrence: A New Biography*.

American author and anti-slavery activist **Harriet Beecher Stowe** (1811–96) wrote poetry, travel books, biography, and children's book as well as novels for adults. Her most famous work, *Uncle Tom's Cabin*, initially appeared in serial form in the anti-slavery weekly *The National Era*. Published in book form in 1852, it sold 300,000 copies in the first year of publication, a record for its time.

Alfred Tennyson (1809–92) was appointed Poet Laureate of Great Britain in 1850 (after Wordsworth) and held that position until his death. He was created a baron in 1884. Among his most famous poems are "In Memoriam" ("'Tis better to have loved and lost/Than never to have loved at all"), "The Lady of Shalott," and "The Lotus Eaters".

The great Russian author Count **Leo Tolstoy** (1828–1910) published *Anna Karenina* in 1876. As well as his other very famous novel, *War and Peace*, Tolstoy wrote stories, novellas, and essays.

The prolific English writer **Anthony Trollope** (1815–82) wrote an astonishing number of excellent novels while holding down a demanding job in the Irish postal service. He first achieved success in 1852 with *The Warden*, the first of his Barsetshire series of novels focusing on religion, the church, and life in provincial England. As well as novels, Trollope published short stories, travel books, biography, and an autobiography.

Mark Twain (Samuel Langhorne Clemens) was born in Missouri in 1835. He worked as a printer, Mississippi river pilot, miner, journalist, and lecturer. The success of his second book, *The Innocents Abroad*, which sold over 100,000 copies in the three years after its publication in 1869, enabled him to write full-time. He wrote over forty books and pamphlets and died in 1910.

Tom Wolfe is a cultural critic and a leading figure in "new journalism," bringing the techniques of fiction into non-fiction. Among his non-fiction books are *The Electric Kool-Aid Acid Test* and *The Right Stuff*. *The Bonfire of the Vanities*, his first novel, was published in 1987. Born in 1931 in Richmond, Virginia, he has lived for many years in New York City.

S. Yizhar is the pen name of Israeli writer Yizhar Smilansky (1916–). He fought in the War of Independence and was a member of the Israeli Parliament for nineteen years. Winner of the Israel Prize in 1959, his best-known work is the novel *Yemei Tziklag* (*Tziklag Days*), published in 1958.

Zitkala-Ša (Red Bird) was born Gertrude Simmons on the Yankton Reservation in South Dakota in 1876. As well as writing memoirs, stories, and an opera, she was politically active in working for Indian rights, including being the founder and President of the National Council of American Indians. She died in 1938.

FURTHER READING
IN ETHICS

Part One Personal Moral Issues

I WHO AM I?

Jonathan Glover, *I, the Philosophy and Psychology of Personal Identity*. London: Penguin Press, 1988.

Onora O'Neill, "A Simplified Account of Kant's Ethics," in Tom Regan (ed.), *Matters of Life and Death*. New York: McGraw-Hill, 1986.

James Rachels, *The Elements of Moral Philosophy*. 4th edn, Boston: McGraw-Hill, 2003, Ch. 5, "Psychological Egoism."

Peter Singer, *How Are We to Live? Ethics in an Age of Self-Interest*. Amherst, NY: Prometheus, 1995.

Peter Singer, *Practical Ethics*. Cambridge: Cambridge University Press, 1993, Ch. 12, "Why Act Morally?"

II DUTIES TO KIN

Jane English, "What Do Grown Children Owe Their Parents?," in Onora O'Neill and William Ruddick (eds), *Having Children*. New York: Oxford University Press, 1979.

James Rachels, "Morality, Parents, and Children," in George Graham and Hugh LaFollette (eds), *Person to Person*. Philadelphia: Temple University Press, 1989.

Christina Hoff Sommers, "Filial Duty," *Journal of Philosophy*, vol. 83 (1986), pp. 439–56.

III LOVE, MARRIAGE, AND SEX

General

Linda LeMoncheck, *Loose Women, Lecherous Men: A Feminist Philosophy of Sex*. New York: Oxford University Press, 1997.

Martha Nussbaum, *Love's Knowledge*. New York: Oxford University Press, 1992.

Alan Soble (ed.), *The Philosophy of Sex: Contemporary Readings*. Totowa, NJ: Littlefield, Adams, 1980.

R. C. Solomon, *About Love: Reinventing Romance for Our Times*. New York: Rowman and Littlefield, 1994.

Marriage

Pedrag Cicovacki, "On Love and Fidelity in Marriage," *Journal of Social Philosophy*, vol. 24, no. 3 (Winter 1993), pp. 92–104.

Kathleen M. Higgins, "How Do I Love Thee? Let's Redefine a Term (A Response to Pedrag Cicovacki)," *Journal of Social Philosophy*, vol. 24, no. 3 (Winter 1993), pp. 105–11.

Mike W. Martin, "Adultery and Fidelity," *Journal of Social Philosophy*, vol. 25, no. 3 (1994), pp. 76–91.

Susan Muller Okin, *Justice, Gender and the Family*. New York: Basic Books, 1991, Ch. 7, "Vulnerability by Marriage."

Bertrand Russell, *Marriage and Morals*. London: Allen and Unwin, 1976 (first published 1929), especially the essays "Romantic Love," "The Place of Love in Human Life," "Marriage," and "Prostitution."

Prostitution

Lars O. Ericsson, "Charges Against Prostitution: An Attempt at a Philosophical Assessment," *Ethics*, vol. 90, no. 3 (Apr. 1980), pp. 335–66.

Carole Pateman, "Defending Prostitution: Charges Against Ericsson," *Ethics*, vol. 93, no. 3 (Apr. 1983), pp. 561–5.

Laurie Shrage, "Should Feminists Oppose Prostitution?," *Ethics*, vol. 99, no. 2 (Jan. 1989), pp. 347–61.

Homosexuality

Timothy F. Murphy, "Homosexuality and Nature," *Journal of Applied Philosophy*, vol. 4, no. 2 (1987), pp. 195–204.

IV ABORTION, EUTHANASIA, AND SUICIDE

Abortion

Jeff McMahan, *The Ethics of Killing: Killing at the Margins of Life*. Oxford: Oxford University Press, 2002, Ch. 4.

Donald Marquis, "Why Abortion is Immoral," *Journal of Philosophy*, vol. 68, no. 4 (1989), pp. 183–202.

Judith Jarvis Thomson, "A Defense of Abortion," *Philosophy and Public Affairs*, vol. 1 (1971), pp. 47–66.

Michael Tooley, "Abortion and Infanticide," *Philosophy and Public Affairs*, vol. 2 (1972), pp. 37–65.

Mary Ann Warren, "On the Moral and Legal Status of Abortion," *The Monist*, vol. 57, no. 1 (Jan. 1973), pp. 43–61.

Euthanasia

Robert M. Baird and Stuart E. Rosenbaum (eds), *Euthanasia: The Moral Issues*. Buffalo, NY: Prometheus, 1989.

Margaret Pabst Battin, *The Least Worst Death*. New York: Oxford University Press, 1994.

Ronald Dworkin, *Life's Dominion: An Argument about Abortion, Euthanasia, and Individual Freedom.* New York: Knopf, 1993, Chs. 7–8.

Stephen Holland, *Bioethics: A Philosophical Introduction.* Cambridge: Polity, 2003.

Helga Kuhse, *The Sanctity-of-Life Doctrine in Medicine.* Oxford: Clarendon Press, 1987.

Stephen G. Post, *The Moral Challenge of Alzheimer Disease: Ethical Issues from Diagnosis to Dying.* 2nd edn, Baltimore: Johns Hopkins University Press, 2000.

Suicide

Richard B. Brandt, "The Morality and Rationality of Suicide," in Seymour Perlin (ed.), *A Handbook for the Study of Suicide.* Oxford: Oxford University Press, 1975.

John Donnelly (ed.), *Suicide: Right or Wrong?* Buffalo, NY: Prometheus, 1990.

Part Two   The Community and Beyond

V   WORK

Tom L. Beauchamp and Norman E. Bowie (eds), *Ethical Theory and Business.* Englewood Cliffs, NJ: Prentice Hall, 1988.

Sissela Bok, *Secrets: On the Ethics of Concealment and Revelation.* New York: Pantheon Books, 1982.

Sissela Bok, "Whistleblowing and Professional Responsibility," *New York University Education Quarterly,* vol. 11 (1980), pp. 2–7.

William J. Broad and Nicholas Wade, *Betrayers of the Truth: Fraud and Deceit in the Halls of Science.* New York: Oxford University Press, 1985.

Albert Carr, "Is Business Bluffing Ethical?," *Harvard Business Review,* vol. 46 (1968), pp. 143–53.

Barbara Ehrenreich, *Nickel and Dimed: On (Not) Getting By in America.* New York: Metropolitan Books, 2001.

VI   WHAT DO WE OWE TO OUR COUNTRY, COMPATRIOTS, AND STRANGERS?

Will Aiken and Hugh LaFollette (eds), *World Hunger and Morality.* Englewood Cliffs, NJ: Prentice Hall, 1996.

Robert Axelrod, *The Evolution of Cooperation.* New York: Basic Books, 1984.

Robert McKim and Jeff McMahan (eds), *The Morality of Nationalism.* Oxford: Oxford University Press, 1997.

Martha Nussbaum et al., *For Love of Country: Debating the Limits of Patriotism,* ed. Joshua Cohen. Boston: Beacon Press, 1996.

Thomas Pogge, *World Poverty and Human Rights: Cosmopolitan Responsibilities and Reforms.* Oxford: Blackwell, 2002.

Peter Singer, *Practical Ethics.* 2nd edn, Cambridge: Cambridge University Press, 1993, Ch. 8.

Peter Singer, "The Singer Solution to World Poverty", *The New York Times Sunday Magazine,* September 5, 1999, pp. 60–3.

Peter Unger, *Living High and Letting Die.* Oxford: Oxford University Press, 1996.

VII ETHICS AND POLITICS

Amy Gutmann and Dennis Thompson (eds), *Ethics and Politics: Cases and Comments*. Chicago: Newson-Hall Publishers, 1984.

Thomas Nagel, "Ruthlessness in Public Life," in Stuart Hampshire (ed.), *Public and Private Morality*. Cambridge: Cambridge University Press, 1978.

Michael Walzer, "Political Action: The Problem of Dirty Hands," *Philosophy and Public Affairs*, vol. 2, no. 2 (Winter 1973), pp. 160–80.

Bernard Williams, "Politics and Moral Character," in Stuart Hampshire (ed.), *Public and Private Morality*. Cambridge: Cambridge University Press, 1978.

VIII RACISM AND SEXISM

General

Louis P. Pojman and Robert Westmoreland (eds), *Equality: Selected Readings*. New York: Oxford University Press, 1997.

Racism and slavery

Kwame Anthony Appiah, "Racisms," in David Theo Goldberg (ed.), *Anatomy of Racism*. Minneapolis: University of Minnesota Press, 1990.

Bernard Boxill (ed.), *Race and Racism*. Oxford: Oxford University Press, 2001.

Bernard B. Boxill, "Racism and Related Issues," in Lawrence C. Becker and Charlotte B. Becker (eds), *Encyclopedia of Ethics*, Vol. II. New York: Garland Publishing, Inc., 1992.

R. M. Hare, "What Is Wrong with Slavery," *Philosophy and Public Affairs*, vol. 8, no. 2 (1979), pp. 103–21.

Sexism

Allison Jaggar and Paula Rothenberg (eds), *Feminist Frameworks: Alternative Theoretical Accounts of the Relations between Women and Men*. 3rd edn, New York: McGraw-Hill, 1993.

Janet Radcliffe Richards, *The Sceptical Feminist: A Philosophical Enquiry*. Boston: Routledge & Kegan Paul, 1980.

Rosemarie Tong, "Feminist Ethics," *The Stanford Encyclopedia of Philosophy* (Winter 2003 edn), ed. Edward N. Zalta, http://plato.stanford.edu/archives/win2003/entries/feminism-ethics/.

IX WAR

General

Jonathan Glover, *Humanity: A Moral History of the 20th Century*. New Haven, CT: Yale University Press, 2001.

Brian Orend, "War," *The Stanford Encyclopedia of Philosophy* (Summer 2002 edn), ed. Edward N. Zalta, http://plato.stanford.edu/archives/sum2002/entries/war/.

David Rodin, *War and Self-Defense*. Oxford: Clarendon Press, 2002.

Michael Walzer, *Just and Unjust Wars: A Moral Argument with Historical Illustrations*. 2nd edn, New York: Basic Books, 1992.

Civilian casualties and the doctrine of double effect

G. E. M. Anscombe, "War and Murder," in P. A. Woodward (ed.), *The Doctrine of Double Effect*. Notre Dame, IN: University of Notre Dame Press, 2001.

Helga Kuhse, *The Sanctity-of-Life Doctrine in Medicine*. Oxford: Clarendon Press, 1987, Ch. 3, "The Intentional Termination of Life and the Principle of Double Effect."

Individual responsibility

Jonathan Glover, "It Makes No Difference Whether I Do it or Not," *Proceedings of the Aristotelian Society* suppl. vol. 49 (1975), pp. 171–90.

David Mapel, "Coerced Moral Agents? Individual Responsibility for Military Service," *The Journal of Political Philosophy*, vol. 6 (1998), pp. 171–89.

Bernard Williams, "A Critique of Utilitarianism," in J. J. C. Smart and Bernard Williams, *Utilitarianism For and Against*. Cambridge: Cambridge University Press, 1973.

X ANIMALS AND THE ENVIRONMENT

Animals

Susan Armstrong and Richard Botzler (eds), *The Animal Ethics Reader*. London: Routledge, 2003.

Peter Carruthers, *The Animals Issue*. Cambridge: Cambridge University Press, 1992.

Paola Cavalieri, *The Animal Question: Why Non-human Animals Deserve Human Rights* (tr. Catherine Woollard). New York: Oxford University Press, 2001.

David DeGrazia, *Taking Animals Seriously: Mental Life and Moral Status*. Cambridge: Cambridge University Press, 1996.

Tom Regan and Peter Singer, *Animal Rights and Human Obligations: An Anthology*. 2nd edn, Englewood Cliffs, NJ: Prentice Hall, 1989.

Peter Singer, *Animal Liberation*. 2nd edn, New York: Ecco, 2002.

Environmental ethics

Andrew Brennan and Lo Yeuk-Sze, "Environmental Ethics", *The Stanford Encyclopedia of Philosophy* (Summer 2002 edn), ed. Edward N. Zalta, http://plato.stanford.edu/archives/sum2002/entries/ethics-environmental/

Robert Elliot (ed.), *Environmental Ethics*. Oxford: Oxford University Press, 1995.

Peter Singer, *Practical Ethics*. 2nd edn, Cambridge: Cambridge University Press, 1993, Ch. 10.

XI DUTIES TO GOD

Kai Nielsen, *God and the Grounding of Morality*. Ottawa: University of Ottawa Press, 1991.

Gene Outka and John Reeder (eds), *Religion and Morality*. Garden City, NJ: Doubleday, 1973.

XII NEW LIFE FORMS

Allen Buchanan, Dan Brock, Norman Daniels, and Daniel Wikler, *From Chance to Choice: Genetics and Justice*. Cambridge: Cambridge University Press, 2000.

Jonathan Glover, *What Sort of People Should There Be?* Harmondsworth: Penguin, 1984.

Stephen Holland, *Bioethics: A Philosophical Introduction.* Cambridge: Polity, 2003.

Leon R. Kass and James Q. Wilson (eds), *The Ethics of Human Cloning.* Washington, DC: AEI Press, 1998.

Arlene Klotzko, *A Clone of Your Own?* Oxford: Oxford University Press, 2004.

Gregory Pence, *Who's Afraid of Human Cloning?* Lanham, MD: Rowman and Littlefield, 1998.

Lee Silver, *Remaking Eden: Cloning and Beyond in a Brave New World.* New York: Avon Books, 1997.

Gregory Stock, *Redesigning Humans: Our Inevitable Genetic Future.* New York: Houghton Mifflin, 2002.

Jon Turney, *Frankenstein's Footsteps: Science, Genetics and Popular Culture.* New Haven, CT: Yale University Press, 1998.

Bernard Williams, "The Makropulos Case: Reflections on the Tedium of Immortality," in Bernard Williams, *Problems of the Self.* Cambridge: Cambridge University Press, 1973.

Part Three   Reflecting on Ethics

XIII   THE NATURE OF ETHICS

Relativism, subjectivism, and the role of reason in ethics

R. M. Hare, *Moral Thinking: Its Levels, Method, and Point.* New York: Oxford University Press, 1981.

Gilbert Harman and J. J. Thomson, *Moral Relativism and Moral Objectivity.* Oxford: Blackwell, 1996.

J. L. Mackie, *Ethics: Inventing Right and Wrong.* Harmondsworth: Penguin, 1976.

James Rachels, *The Elements of Moral Philosophy.* 4th edn, Boston: McGraw-Hill, 2003, Ch. 2, "The Challenge of Cultural Relativism."

Conscience

Jonathan Bennett. "The Conscience of Huckleberry Finn," *Philosophy*, vol. 49, no. 188 (1974), pp. 123–34.

Ethics in concentration camps

Primo Levi, *If This is a Man* (tr. Stuart Woolf). London: Abacus, 1987.

Tzvetan Todorov, *Facing the Extreme: Moral Life in the Concentration Camps.* New York: Holt, 1997.

XIV   RULES, RIGHTS, DUTIES, AND THE GREATER GOOD

Absolute duties, rules, and consequences

John Finnis, *Natural Law and Natural Rights.* Oxford: Oxford University Press, 1980.

Brad Hooker, *Ideal Code, Real World*, Oxford: Clarendon Press, 2000.

David Nyberg, *The Varnished Truth: Truth Telling and Deceiving in Ordinary Life.* Chicago: University of Chicago Press, 1993.

J. J. C. Smart, "An Outline of a System of Utilitarian Ethics," in J. J. C. Smart and Bernard Williams, *Utilitarianism For and Against*. Cambridge: Cambridge University Press, 1973.

Loyalty and role ethics

R. E. Ewin, "Loyalty and Virtues," *The Philosophical Quarterly*, vol. 42, no. 169 (Oct. 1992), pp. 403–19.
Michael O. Hardimon, "Role Obligations," *The Journal of Philosophy*, vol. 91, no. 7 (July 1994), pp. 333–63.
Thomas E. Hill, "Servility and Self-Respect," *The Monist*, vol. 57, no. 1 (1974), pp. 87–104.

XV   ULTIMATE VALUES

Elizabeth S. Anderson, "What is the Point of Equality?," *Ethics*, vol. 109, no. 2 (Jan. 1999), pp. 287–337.
Peter Singer, *Ethics*. Oxford: Oxford University Press, 1994, Part II, Section A, "Ultimate Good" (Readings from Aristotle, Epicurus, Epictetus, Jesus, Jeremy Bentham, John Stuart Mill, William James, Henry Sidgwick, G. E. Moore, and others.)
Peter Singer, *How Are We to Live? Ethics in an Age of Self-Interest*. Amherst, NY: Prometheus, 1995.
Richard Taylor, *Good and Evil*. Rev. edn, Amherst, NY: Prometheus, 1999.

ACKNOWLEDGMENTS

The editor and publisher gratefully acknowledge the permission granted to reproduce the copyright material in this book:

1 **Ralph Ellison**, pp. 13–26 from *Invisible Man*. New York: Random House, 2002 (originally published 1947). © 1947, 1948, 1952 by Ralph Ellison; copyright renewed 1975, 1976, 1980 by Ralph Ellison. Used by permission of Random House, Inc.

2 **Kathy Lette and Gabrielle Carey**, pp. 25–7, 40–1, and 55–7 from *Puberty Blues*. Melbourne, Australia: McPhee Gribble Publishers, 1979. Reprinted by permission of Pan Macmillan and Ed Victor Ltd.

3 **James Baldwin**, extract from *Giovanni's Room*, pp. 223–6 in *James Baldwin: Early Novels and Stories* (Library of American edition), first published in 1956. © 1956 by James Baldwin. Used by permission of Doubleday, a division of Random House, Inc., and by arrangement with the James Baldwin Estate.

4 **Tom Wolfe**, pp. 67–72 and 343–8 from *The Bonfire of the Vanities*. New York: Bantam Books, 1988. © 1988 by Tom Wolfe. Reprinted by permission of Farrar, Straus and Giroux, LLC. First published by Farrar, Straus and Giroux in 1987.

5 **George Eliot**, from Book 7, Chapter LXI in *Middlemarch*, first published 1872.

6 **Arthur Miller**, extract from *The Crucible*, pp. 131–45 from the Viking Critical Library edition edited by Gerald Weales and published by Penguin Books. First published 1952. © 1952, 1953, 1954, renewed © 1980, 1981, 1982 by Arthur Miller. Used with permission of Viking Penguin, a division of Penguin Group (USA) Inc., and International Creative Management Inc.

7 **William Shakespeare**, from Act I, Scene VII in *Macbeth*, first published in 1623.

8 **Charlotte Perkins Gilman**, "The Unnatural Mother," pp. 281–5 from *The Forerunner*, a monthly journal on women's rights and related issues, edited (and mostly written) by Charlotte Perkins Gilman, which ran from November 1909 to December 1916. Currently available in Charlotte Perkins Gilman, *Herland, the Yellow Wall-Paper, and Selected Writings* (London: Penguin, 1999).

9 **Charles Dickens**, from Chapter 4 ("Telescopic Philanthropy") in *Bleak House*, first published 1852–3.

10 **Joseph Kanon**, pp. 243–7, 255–8, and 330–8 from *The Good German*. New York: Henry Holt and Co., 2001. © 2001 by Joseph Kanon. Reprinted by permission of Henry Holt and Company, LLC and by permission of the author c/o Rogers, Coleridge & White Ltd, 20 Powis Mews, London, W11 1JN, UK.

11 **Sophocles**, pp. 91–3 from *Antigone* in *The Thebans* (tr. Timberlake Wertenbaker). London: Faber & Faber, 1992. Reprinted by permission of Faber & Faber Ltd.

12 **William Shakespeare**, from Act III, Scene I in *Measure for Measure*, first published in 1623.

13 **Zitkala-Ša**, "The Soft-Hearted Sioux," pp. 505–8 from *Harper's* (March 1901). More recently reprinted in Karen L. Kilcup (ed.), *Native American Women's Writing* c.*1800–1924: An Anthology*. Oxford: Blackwell, 2000.

14 **Ambrose Bierce**, "A Horseman in the Sky," first published in his *Tales of Soldiers and Civilians*. San Francisco: E. L. G. Steele, 1891. More recently reprinted in Ambrose Bierce, *Civil War Stories*. New York: Dover Publications, 1994.

15 **Alice Munro**, from "The Peace of Utrecht," first published in *Dance of the Happy Shades: And Other Stories* (1968). Reproduced by the permission of McGraw-Hill Ryerson Ltd.

16 **Jane Austen**, from Chapter LVI in *Pride and Prejudice*, first published in 1813.

17 **William Shakespeare**, from Act II, Scene II in *Romeo and Juliet*, first published in 1597.

18 **Vikram Seth**, pp. 1285–99 (chapters 18.16–18.21) from *A Suitable Boy*. New York: HarperCollins, 1993. Copyright © 1993 by Vikram Seth. Reprinted by permission of HarperCollins Publishers, Inc.; Little, Brown and Company, Inc.; and Phoenix Books.

19 **Guy de Maupassant**, "The Model," pp. 96–103 from *Boule de Suif and Other Stories* (tr. H. N. P. Sloman). London: Penguin Books, 1946. Copyright in this translation by H. N. P. Sloman 1946.

20 **George Eliot**, from Book V, Chapter XLVIII in *Middlemarch*, first published in 1872.

21 **Leo Tolstoy**, from Part II, Chapters XXII and XXIII in *Anna Karenina* (tr. Constance Garnett), first published in 1876.

22 **George Bernard Shaw**, pp. 192–9 from *Mrs Warren's Profession*. London: Constable and Company, 1919. Reprinted by permission of The Society of Authors, on behalf of the Bernard Shaw Estate.

23 **John Cleland**, from *Memoirs of a Woman of Pleasure*. New York: G. P. Putnam's Sons, 1963 (originally published 1747).

24 **Daniel Defoe**, from Chapter XVII in *Moll Flanders*, first published in 1722.

25 **Maeve Binchy**, "Shepherd's Bush," from *London Transports*. London: Hutchinson, 1978. Now published by Century and reprinted by permission of the Random House Group Ltd.

26 **Brian Clark**, pp. 50–60, 79–83, and 130–44 from *Whose Life is it Anyway?* New York: Dodd, Mead & Company, 1978. Reprinted by permission of Judy Daish Associates Ltd.

27 **Kate Jennings**, pp. 42–6, 143–50, and 158–62 from *Moral Hazard*. London: Fourth Estate, 2002. Copyright © Kate Jennings, 2002. Reprinted by permission of HarperCollins Publishers Ltd and Pan Macmillan Australia.

28 **William Shakespeare**, from Act III, Scene I in *Hamlet, Prince of Denmark*, first published in 1623.

29 **Arna Bontemps**, "A Summer Tragedy," pp. 54–63 from John Henrik Clarke (ed.), *Black American Short Stories: A Century of the Best*. New York: Hill & Wang, 2000. The anthology first published 1966 by Hill & Wang as *American Negro Short Stories*; "A Summer Tragedy" originally published 1933. Reprinted with permission of the Arna Bontemps African American Museum and Cultural Arts Center, 1327 Third Street, Alexandria, Louisiana 71301, USA.

30 **Elizabeth Gaskell**, pp. 110–13 (Chapter XV), 214–16 (Chapter XXVIII), and 334–6 (Chapter XLII) from *North and South*, first published in 1854.

31 **Edwin Seaver**, pp. 145–52 from *The Company*. London: Macmillan, 1930.

32 **Ruth L. Ozeki**, pp. 35–6, 41, 163–7, 179–80, 182–4, and 211–13 from *My Year of Meats*. New York: Viking, 1998. Copyright © 1998 by Ruth Ozeki Lounsbury. Used by permission of Viking Penguin, a division of Penguin Group (USA) Inc.

33 **Henrik Ibsen**, pp. 174–85 from *An Enemy of the People* (tr. R. Farquharson Sharp). London: J. M. Dent, 1961. First published 1911.

34 **C. P. Snow**, pp. 334–43 from *The Search*. New York: Charles Scribner's Sons, 1934. Copyright 1934, 1958 by C. P. Snow. Reprinted by permission of Curtis Brown, Ltd.

35 **Euripides**, pp. 73–9 and 85–6 from *Iphigeneia at Aulis* (tr. W. S. Merwin and George E. Dimock, Jr). New York: Oxford University Press, 1978. Copyright © 1992 by W. S. Merwin and George E. Dimock, Jr. Used by permission of Oxford University Press, Inc.

36 **Geraldine Brooks**, "The Thunder of His Voice," "Venom in the Blood," and "Wide Green Prison," pp. 59–63 and 101–13 from *Year of Wonders*. London: Fourth Estate, 2001. Copyright © 2001 by Geraldine Brooks. Used by permission of Viking Penguin, a division of Penguin Group (USA) Inc. and HarperCollins Publishers Ltd.

37 **Ian McEwan**, pp. 1–3 and 7–16 from *Enduring Love*. London: Vintage, 1998. First published by Jonathan Cape, 1997. Copyright © 1997 by Ian McEwan. Used by permission of Doubleday, a division of Random House, Inc.; Random House Group Ltd; and Alfred A. Knopf Canada.

38 **Nick Hornby**, pp. 111–16 and 142–51 from *How to be Good*. London: Penguin, 2001. First published by Viking 2000. Copyright © 2001 by Nick Hornby. Used by permission of Riverhead Books, an imprint of Penguin Group (USA) and Penguin Books Ltd.

39 **Joyce Carol Oates**, "The Undesirable Table," pp. 213–18 from Joyce Carol Oates, *Will You Always Love Me? and Other Stories*. Princeton, NJ: E. P. Dutton, 1996. Copyright © 1996 by the Ontario Review, Inc. Reprinted by permission of Joyce Carol Oates.

40 **Anthony Trollope**, from Chapters LVIII and LIX in *Can You Forgive Her?*, first published in 1864–5.

41 **Anonymous** (Joe Klein), pp. 307–11 and 329–39 from *Primary Colors*. New York: Random House, 1996. Copyright © 1996 by Machiavelliana, Inc. Used by permission of Random House, Inc.

42 **Anthony Trollope**, from Chapter XLVII in *Phineas Finn*, first published in 1867–8.

43 **Harriet Beecher Stowe**, from Volume I, Chapter I in *Uncle Tom's Cabin*, first published in 1852.

44 **Lerone Bennett, Jr**, "The Convert," pp. 282–96 from John Henrik Clarke (ed.), *Black American Short Stories: A Century of the Best*. New York: Hill & Wang, 2000. This anthology first published 1966 by Hill & Wang as *American Negro Short Stories*. Copyright © 1963 by Lerone Bennett, Jr. Reprinted by permission of the author.

45 **William Shakespeare**, from Act II, Scene I and Act V, Scene II in *The Taming of the Shrew*, first published in 1623.

46 **Henrik Ibsen**, pp. 62–72 from *A Doll's House* (tr. R. Farquharson Sharp and Eleanor Marx-Aveling). London: Dent, 1985 (first published in 1911).

47 **Leo Tolstoy**, from Book X, Chapter XXV in *War and Peace* (tr. Constance Garnett), first published in 1865–9.

48 **Pat Barker**, extract from Chapters 1 and 2 in *Regeneration*. London: Viking 1991. Copyright © 1991 by Pat Barker. Used by permission of Dutton Signet, a division of Penguin Group (USA) Inc. and Penguin Books Ltd.

49 **Wilfred Owen**, "S. I. W.," from *Poems* (with an introduction by Siegfried Sassoon). London: Chatto & Windus, 1920.

50 **William Shakespeare**, from Act III, Scene III in *Henry V*, first published in 1598.

51 **William Shakespeare**, from Act IV, Scene I in *Henry V*, first published in 1598.

52 **Alfred Tennyson**, "The Charge of the Light Brigade," 1855.

53 **S. Yizhar** (Yizhar Smilansky), "The Prisoner" (tr. I. M. Lask), pp. 121–8 from Dalia Rabikovitz (ed.), *The New Israeli Writers: Short Stories of the First Generation*. New York: Sabra Brooks, Funk and Wagnalls, 1969. Copyright in the original Hebrew version by S. Yizhar and Zmora Bitan. Thanks to the assistance of the Institute for the Translation of Hebrew Literature.

54 **John Fowles**, pp. 429–35 from *The Magus: a Revised Version*. Boston: Little, Brown & Co., 1978. Copyright © 1965 by John Fowles Ltd. Reprinted by permission of Little, Brown and Company, Inc. and Anthony Sheil in association with Gillon Aitken Associates Limited.

55 **Desmond Stewart**, "The Limits of Trooghaft," from *Encounter*, London. February 1972. Reprinted by permission of Sheil Land Associates Ltd, London.

56 **Richard Adams**, pp. 3–6, 15–18, and 313–14 from *The Plague Dogs*. New York: Alfred A. Knopf, 1978. Copyright © 1978 by Richard Adams. Used by permission of Alfred A. Knopf, a division of Random House, Inc., and David Higham Associates, London.

57 **Douglas Adams**, pp. 115–17 from *The Restaurant at the End of the Universe*. London: Ballantine, 1996. Copyright © 1981 by Douglas Adams. Used by permission of Harmony Books, a division of Random House, Inc. and Pan Macmillan UK.

58 **James Fenimore Cooper**, from Chapter XXII in *The Pioneers*, first published in 1823.

59 **Aeschylus**, pp. 47–52 from *Prometheus Bound and Other Plays* (tr. Philip Vellacott). London: Penguin, 1961. Copyright © 1961 by Philip Vellacott.

60 **Genesis**, Chapter 22, p. 16 from *The New English Bible*, 1972. New English Bible © by Oxford University Press and Cambridge University Press, 1961, 1970. Reprinted by permission of Cambridge University Press.

61 **Fyodor Dostoyevsky**, extract from Part 1, Book 2, Chapter 6 in *The Brothers Karamazov* (tr. Constance Garnett), first published in 1879–80.

62 **Mary Shelley**, extracts from Chapters IV, V, X, XVII, and XX in *Frankenstein*, first published in 1818.

63 **Karel Čapek**, *The Makropulos Secret* (tr. Yveta Synek Graff and Robert T. Jones), pp. 167–77 from Peter Kussi (ed.), *Toward the Radical Center, A Karel Čapek Reader*. Highland Park, NJ: Catbird Press, 1990. Reprinted by permission of the publisher and the translators.

64 **E. Pauline Johnson**, "The Sea-Serpent," pp. 245–7 from Karen L. Kilcup (ed.), *Native American Women's Writing c.1800–1924: An Anthology*. Oxford: Blackwell, 2000.

65 **Daniel Defoe**, from Part V of *Robinson Crusoe*, first published in 1719.

66 **Mark Twain**, from Chapter XVI in *The Adventures of Huckleberry Finn*, first published in 1885.

67 **Graham Greene**, pp. 134–40 from *The Third Man*. London: Viking, 1950. Copyright 1949, 1950, renewed © 1976, 1977 by Graham Greene. Used by permission of Viking Penguin, a division of Penguin Putnam Inc., and David Higham Associates, London.

68 **Tadeusz Borowski**, "This Way for the Gas, Ladies and Gentlemen," pp. 29–49 from *This Way for the Gas, Ladies and Gentlemen* (tr. Barbara Vedder), New York: Penguin Books, 1976. First published in the USA by Viking Penguin, Inc., 1967. Copyright © 1967 by Penguin Books Ltd. Original text copyright © 1959 by Maria Borowski. Used by permission of Viking Penguin, a division of Penguin Group (USA).

69 **Ursula K. Le Guin**, "The Ones Who Walk Away from Omelas," from *New Dimensions* 3 (1973). Copyright © 1973, 2001 by Ursula K. Le Guin; reprinted by permission of the author and the author's agents, the Virginia Kidd Agency, Inc.

70 **Fyodor Dostoyevsky**, from Chapter VI in *Crime and Punishment*, first published in 1866.

71 **Kazuo Ishiguro**, pp. 145–54 from *The Remains of the Day*. London: Faber & Faber, 1989. Copyright © 1989 by Kazuo Ishiguro. Used by permission of Alfred A. Knopf, a division of Random House, Inc. and Faber & Faber Ltd.

72 **Anthony Trollope**, extracts from Chapters III, IX, and XIX in *Dr Wortle's School*, first published in 1880.

73 **Harper Lee**, pp. 262–79 from *To Kill a Mockingbird*. New York: Popular Library, 1962. Copyright © 1960 by Harper Lee. Copyright renewed © 1988 by Harper Lee. Reprinted by permission of HarperCollins Publishers Inc. and Random House Group Limited.

74 **William Shakespeare**, Sonnet 138, first published in 1609.

75 **George Eliot**, from Book VII, Chapters LXIX and LXX in *Middlemarch*, first published in 1872.

76 **Daniel Defoe**, from Part III of *Robinson Crusoe*, first published in 1719.

77 **Henry James**, from Chapter XVIII in *The Portrait of a Lady*, first published in 1881.

78 **Aldous Huxley**, pp. 260–5 and 285–8 from *Brave New World*. New York and London: Harper & Brothers Publishers, first published 1931. Reprinted by permission of HarperCollins Publishers Inc. and the Huxley Literary Estate.

79 **Henry James**, from Chapter XXX in *The Princess Casamassima*, first published in 1886.

Every effort has been made to trace copyright holders and to obtain their permission for the use of copyright material. The publisher apologizes for any errors or omissions in the above list and would be grateful if notified of any corrections that should be incorporated in future reprints or editions of this book.